International Economics Association
Series Standing Order ISBN 978–0–333–71242–9 (Hardback)
978–0–333–80330–1 (Paperback)

You can receive future titles in this series as they are published by placing a standing order. Please contact your bookseller or, in case of difficulty, write to us at the address below with your name and address, the title of the series and one of the ISBNs quoted above.

Customer Services Department, Macmillan Distribution Ltd, Houndmills, Basingstoke, Hampshire RG21 6XS, England

The Industrial Policy Revolution II

Africa in the 21st Century

Edited by

Joseph E. Stiglitz
University Professor, Columbia University, United States of America

Justin Lin Yifu
Honorary Dean, National School of Development, Peking University, China

and

Ebrahim Patel
Minister of Economic Development, South Africa

First published 2013 by
PALGRAVE MACMILLAN

Palgrave Macmillan in the UK is an imprint of Macmillan Publishers Limited, registered in England, company number 785998, of Houndmills, Basingstoke, Hampshire RG21 6XS.

Palgrave Macmillan in the US is a division of St Martin's Press LLC, 175 Fifth Avenue, New York, NY 10010.

Palgrave Macmillan is the global academic imprint of the above companies and has companies and representatives throughout the world.

Palgrave® and Macmillan® are registered trademarks in the United States, the United Kingdom, Europe and other countries.

ISBN 978–1–137–33522–7   hardback

ISBN 978–1–137–37450–9   paperback

This book is printed on paper suitable for recycling and made from fully managed and sustained forest sources. Logging, pulping and manufacturing processes are expected to conform to the environmental regulations of the country of origin.

A catalogue record for this book is available from the British Library.

A catalog record for this book is available from the Library of Congress.

Typeset by MPS Limited, Chennai, India.

Contents

List of Tables

List of Figures

List of Boxes

Notes on the Contributors

Editors

Joseph E. Stiglitz is University Professor at Columbia University. In 2001, he was awarded the Nobel Prize in economics for his analyses of markets with asymmetric information. He is currently the President of the International Economic Association (2011–14).

Justin Yifu Lin is honorary dean and professor of the National School of Development at Peking University. From 2008 to 2012, he served as Chief Economist and Senior Vice President of the World Bank. His many books include *Demystifying the Chinese Economy*, *The Quest for Prosperity*, and *The New Structural Economics*. He is a corresponding fellow of the British Academy and a fellow of the World Academy of Sciences for the Developing World.

Ebrahim Patel is Minister of Economic Development in South Africa. He is responsible, among other matters, for competition and trade policy, infrastructure coordination, industrial funding and small business development. He has published on economic and labor policy.

Contributors

Ludovico Alcorta is Director of UNIDO's Development Policy, Statistics and Strategic Research Branch. He has worked in academia, as a consultant for international organizations and in the private sector. He has published extensively in the areas of new technologies, innovation, industrialization and development, including in journals such as *World Development*, the *European Journal of Development Research*, *Research Policy*, *Industry and Innovation*, *Structural Change and Economic Dynamics* as well as in China's *Economic Research Journal*. He graduated in Economics at the Universidad del Pací fico, Lima, Peru and obtained his Master and PhD at the Institute of Development Studies, University of Sussex.

Yaw Ansu is the Chief Economist at the Africa Center for Economic Transformation (ACET) based in Accra, Ghana. Prior to joining ACET in 2010, he spent more than 26 years working at the World Bank in various capacities including Research Economist, Country Director, Director for Economic Policy, Head of the Economists Sector Board, and Regional Sector Director for Human Development for Africa. Yaw Ansu holds a BA in economics from Cornell University, and an MS and a Ph.D. in engineering-economic systems from Stanford University.

Vandana Chandra is a Senior Economist in the World Bank's Development Economics Prospects Group. She works on structural transformation, export diversification, and technological adaptation and innovation in developing countries. Her recent publications include *Light Manufacturing in Africa: Focused Policies to Enhance Private Investment and Create Jobs* (2012, co-authored), *Innovation and Growth: Chasing a Moving Frontier* (2010 and co-edited), and *Technology, Adaptation and Exports: How Some Developing Countries Did It* (2006 and co-edited). In each publication she explores how governments in developing countries can foster growth and job creation in specific industries.

C. P. Chandrasekhar is Professor at the Centre for Economic Studies and Planning, Jawaharlal Nehru University, New Delhi. His areas of interest include the role of finance and industry in development and the experience with fiscal, financial, and industrial policy reform in developing countries.

Ha-Joon Chang teaches economics at the University of Cambridge. In addition to numerous journal articles and book chapters, he has published 14 authored books (four co-authored) and ten edited books. His main books include *The Political Economy of Industrial Policy, Kicking Away the Ladder, Bad Samaritans,* and the best-selling *23 Things They Don't Tell You About Capitalism.* By the end of 2014, his writings will have been translated and published in 34 languages and 38 countries. He is the winner of the 2003 Gunnar Myrdal Prize and the 2005 Wassily Leontief Prize.

Mario Cimoli is the Director of the Division of Production, Productivity and Management at the UN Economic Commission for Latin America and the Caribbean (ECLAC). He obtained his Ph.D. at the SPRU (University of Sussex) and is Professor of Economics at the University of Venice (Ca' Foscari). In 2004 he was awarded the Philip Morris Chair of International Business at the Sant'Anna School of Advanced Studies (University of Pisa). He has been appointed as co-director (with Giovanni Dosi and Joseph Stiglitz) of two task-forces (Industrial Policy and Intellectual Property Rights Regimes for Development) of the Initiative for Policy Dialogue of the Columbia University (New York). He is co-chairing (with Justin Yifu, Dani Rodrik and Joseph Stiglitz) the Scientific Committee for Industrial Policy of the International Economic Association (IEA). He writes books and articles on innovation, technological change, and development, as well as science, technology and industrial issues, focusing on Latin America.

Klaus Deininger is a Lead Economist in the Development Economics Research Group in the World Bank, Washington DC, USA.

Calvin Djiofack is an Economist for the Economic Policy Unit of the Latin America and Caribbean Region of the World Bank. His recent publications have covered various topics, including trade in services, regional integration, migration, fiscal policy, natural resources, and CGE models.

Bruce Greenwald is a Professor at the Graduate School of Business, Columbia University.

Nobuya Haraguchi is an industrial research officer at the Development Policy, Statistics and Strategic Research Branch of UNIDO, conducting research on industrial structural change and drawing policy implications. He has published extensively in the areas of manufacturing development, industrial structural transformation, employment generation, and technological change. Before joining UNIDO, he taught macroeconomics at St John's University in the United States. He holds a Ph.D. degree in development economics from the University of London.

James Heintz is Research Professor at the Political Economy Research Institute of the University of Massachusetts, Amherst. His research has focused on macroeconomic and employment policies in a range of Sub-Saharan African countries, including Ghana, The Gambia, Kenya, Liberia, Madagascar, and South Africa. He has collaborated with numerous international institutions and agencies, including the International Labour Organization, the United Nations Development Program, UN-Women, the United Nations Industrial Development Organization, the Human Development Report Office, and the Economic Commission for Africa.

Jean Imbs is a professor at the Paris School of Economics (PSE), and Research Director at the Centre National de la Recherche Scientifique, which he joined in 2010. He has been a Research Fellow of the CEPR since 2006. Prior to joining PSE, he was a Professor at HEC Lausanne, and an Assistant Professor at the London Business School. He holds a Ph.D. in economics from New York University, and has taught at the University of Chicago, Princeton University, and New York University. Between 2003 and 2004, he was the Peter Kenen Fellow at Princeton University, and he has held visiting appointments at the International Monetary Fund, the World Bank, the Hong Kong Institute for Monetary Research, and the European Central Bank. His research centers around issues in international economics, and has been published in, among others, the *American Economic Review*, the *Quarterly Journal of Economics*, the *Journal of Financial Economics*, the *Journal of Monetary Economics*, and the *Journal of International Economics*.

Richard Joseph is John Evans Professor of International History and Politics, Northwestern University, and a non-resident Senior Fellow of The Brookings Institution. He has served as a Fellow for African Governance of The Carter Center. His publications include *Radical Nationalism in Cameroon* (1977) and *Democracy and Prebendal Politics in Nigeria* (1987). He is the editor of *State, Conflict and Democracy in Africa* (1999) and *Smart Aid for African Development*

(2009). He wrote the epilogue, "The Logic and Legacy of Prebendalism in Nigeria," for Wale Adebanwi and Ebenezer Obadare (eds), *Democracy and Prebendalism in Nigeria: Critical Interpretations* (2013).

Paul Jourdan is an African integrated development expert specializing in resource-based development strategies. He has wide experience working on economic growth and development in Mozambique, South Africa, Zimbabwe, the SADC, and West and East Africa. He spent 16 years in exile in Mozambique and Zimbabwe working as a geologist, geophysicist, and minerals economist, before returning to South Africa in 1991 to join the NUM. He is the past President of Mintek, the past Deputy Director-General in the DTI and the past ANC DEP Minerals & Energy Policy Coordinator. He is currently Chair of the Coega Development Corporation (CDC), on the board of the GGDA and its subsidiaries, advisor to the governments of South Africa and Mozambique on their SDI (Spatial Development Initiatives) programs and resource-based development, and was on the 2011 ANC SIMS (State Intervention in the Minerals Sector) research team. He has a BSc (in geology), a BA (in African government), a PGDip (in geophysics), an MSc (in mineral economics) and a Ph.D. (in politics).

Raphael Kaplinsky is Professor of International Development at the Open University. In recent years his research has concentrated on the related themes of China's global rise, processes of inclusion and exclusion in the global economy, the extension of global value chains, the commodities price boom, and the challenge of maximizing linkages from the resource sector to the industrial and service sectors. His future research focus will be on inclusive innovation.

Mushtaq H. Khan is Professor of Economics at SOAS, University of London. He was educated at Oxford and Cambridge and previously taught at Cambridge University. He has also been visiting professor at the universities of Chulalongkorn in Thailand and Dhaka in Bangladesh. He is currently a member of the Committee of Experts on Public Administration at the United Nations. His research interests are in the areas of institutional economics, industrial policy, governance, and political economy.

Julie Lohi joined the Bank as a consultant in July 2012 after graduating with a Ph.D. in economics from West Virginia University. Her main responsibilities include: drafting policy notes using data collected in TFF projects (for example, on transport observatory, Users Surveys, Time Release Studies (TRS)) to inform policy dialogue and for dissemination to wide audiences within and outside the Bank, particularly in TFF-eligible countries; undertaking research and policy analysis on a wide range of trade facilitation issues in countries, RECs, and along corridors covered by TFF activities. Her areas of expertise are international trade, monetary, economic development, and macroeconomics. She works with economics theories and empirical economics models, and manages databases to present econometric results and derive policy implications.

Célestin Monga is Senior Advisor at the World Bank where he has previously held various positions, including as Lead Economist in Europe and Central Asia, and as Manager of the Policy Review team in the Development Economics vice presidency. He also served on the Board of Directors of the Sloan School of Management's Fellows Program at the Massachusetts Institute of Technology (MIT) and taught at Boston University and the University of Bordeaux (France). Prior to joining the World Bank, he was Department Head and Manager in the Banque Nationale de Paris group. His books have been translated into several languages and used as teaching tools by academic institutions around the world. He holds degrees from MIT, Harvard, and the universities of Paris 1 Panthéon-Sorbonne, Bordeaux and Pau.

Streevarsen P. Narrainen was Assistant Professor in economics at the University of Manitoba and the University of Sherbrooke in Canada before joining the Ministry of Finance in Mauritius as economic adviser in 1990. He later served the senior economic adviser to the Prime Minister (1998 to 2000). He is currently senior economic adviser at the Ministry of Finance.

Dominique Njinkeu is Lead Trade Facilitation Expert and Program Coordinator of the Trade Facilitation Facility (TFF). He is a member of the Bank's Trade Practice Group of the African Region. He is also an active member of the African Economic Research Consortium (AERC), the Trade Policy Centre for Africa (TRAPCA), and the WTO Chairs Program. His work experience extends over over 25 years. He holds a MSc in Agribusiness Economics, a MSc in Statistics and Economics, and a Ph.D. in Economics from Southern Illinois University, Carbondale.

Akbar Noman is a Senior Fellow at the Initiative or Policy Dialogue (IPD) at Columbia University, where he has also been teaching at the School of International and Public Affairs. He came to IPD after several years at the World Bank. His other work experience includes being an economist at the IMF and Economic Adviser in Pakistan's Ministry of Finance.

Thia Jang Ping joined the Economics Division of the Ministry of Trade and Industry as part of the Singapore Government Economist Service in 2001. Since 2011, he has also been the Head of the Centre of Public Economics at the Civil Service College. He received his Ph.D. in Economics from the London School of Economics in 2008. His main professional interest is in International Economics. His secondary interests include economic geography and population issues. As the Director of the Economics Division, his key responsibility is to lead the division's efforts in economic surveillance, research, as well as economic policy analysis and evaluation. His key responsibility at the Centre of Public Economics is to advance the use of economics in the public sector.

Gabriel Porcile has been an Economic Affairs Officer at ECLAC since 2011. He obtained his Ph.D. at the London School of Economics (1995) and he is Professor of the Department of Economics of the Federal University of Paraná. He is also researcher at the Brasilian Conselho Nacional de Desenvolvimento Científico e Tecnológico (National Council for Scientific and Technological Development). He has written several articles in the fields, technology, and structural change.

Hamid Rashid is Senior Adviser for Macroeconomic Policy in the Department of Economic and Social Affairs (DESA) of the United Nations and leads a new UN-DESA initiative that provides development-centric macroeconomic policy advice to the member states to promote inclusive, equitable, and sustainable growth. Dr Rashid brings to DESA over twenty years of experience, working for the government of Bangladesh and also for UNDP. Dr Rashid earned his Ph.D. in Finance and Economics from Columbia University in New York, and his Bachelor of Science degree from the University of Texas. His research interest includes international finance, macroeconomic policies, financial market liberalization, and its impact on economic growth and development.

Gorazd Rezonja has been a consultant at UNIDO since 2009. During his assignment with the Development Policy, Statistics and Research Branch, he has been involved in conducting research and data analysis on industry structures, growth patterns, and market potentials in the manufacturing sectors in developed and developing countries. He graduated in Economics at the University of Maribor, Slovenia and obtained his Master degree in International Affairs at the Diplomatic Academy of Vienna, Austria.

Simon Roberts is Professor of Economics and Director of the Centre for Competition, Regulation and Economic Development at the University of Johannesburg. He held the position of Chief Economist and Manager of the Policy & Research Division at the Competition Commission of South Africa from 2006 to 2012. In addition, Simon has consulted extensively on competition matters over the past 15 years and has been an expert witness in a number of major cases. He has published widely on industrial development and competition policy.

Foreword

In 2012, the International Economic Association (IEA), the association of national economic associations/societies, convened a two-part series of roundtables on the theme of industrial policy. The first, "New Thinking on Industrial Policy," was hosted by the World Bank in Washington, D.C. on May 22–3, and the second, "New Thinking on Industrial Policy: Implications for Africa," was held in Pretoria, South Africa, on July 3–4, in partnership with the Economic Development Department of the South African government, and with the further financial support of UNIDO and the Department of Economic and Social Affairs of the United Nations. The two roundtables assembled an outstanding group of scholars to discuss the breadth of the topic of industrial policy, focusing in the second meeting on the African context. These scholars have all grappled with issues of development and growth over many years. The insights generated at the roundtable are critical in our policy debates, and are captured in this two-part IEA publication, which is the 151st volume of the International Economic Associations Proceedings of Roundtables and World Congresses. (The first part of the volume is titled "The Industrial Policy Revolution I. The Role of Government beyond Ideology.") Taken together, the two-part volume includes more than 30 papers selected from those presented at the Washington, D.C. and Pretoria roundtables, in addition to more than 20 commentaries on those papers, written by other roundtable participants. In many cases, the papers were revised after the conclusion of the roundtable to take into consideration discussions that took place at the event.

The roundtables were convened in recognition of the fact that industrial policy is a sort of lynchpin for the economics of development, that the countries that have been most successful in development have undertaken a wide variety of industrial policies, and that different countries can and should learn from these experiences.

Africa provides an especially clear example of why this refreshed emphasis on industrial policy is so important, and worthy of convening international experts on the scale achieved by the IEA in 2012. The continent has one billion people: potentially a great producer and consumer base for the development of strong, dynamic manufacturing industries. It has a large and growing workforce, with a youthful population. It has significant energy resources, from traditional feedstocks such as coal and oil to renewables in the form of rivers, sun and wind. It has enormous natural resources, with a host of minerals and swathes of rich agricultural land.

African growth rates have climbed in the past decade or more. Between 2000 and 2010, six of the world's ten fastest-growing economies were to be found on that continent. Yet that growth was largely fuelled by the export of raw materials to the production centers of Asia, Latin America, and Europe. The commodity price boom supported Africa's rapid growth. Oil made a significant contribution, as did higher prices for metals and agricultural products. But domestic manufacturing, which has been central to those countries which earlier achieved sustainable growth, lagged as a contributor of growth.

Yet the reality is that while Africa has many of the inputs and markets that would support the rise of a large manufacturing sector, the continent has a small industrial footprint and arguably saw a degree of deindustrialization in the commodity boom of the mid-2000s – a continuation of deindustrialization trends that have been in places since the structural adjustment programs.

According to UNCTAD data, for Africa as a whole, between 2000 and 2010 manufacturing fell from 13 percent of total value added to 10 percent. The decline was steepest in sub-Saharan Africa, where manufacturing dropped from 13 percent of value added in 2000 to 9 percent in 2010. In 2010, the share of manufacturing in value added in sub-Saharan Africa (excluding South Africa) was only just over half the global norm.

Meanwhile, between 2000 and 2010 raw materials climbed from 72 percent of all African exports to 78 percent, and manufactures dropped from 21 percent to 17 percent. In contrast, for the rest of the world in 2010, raw materials made up just 27 percent of exports and manufacturing some 67 percent.

Manufacturing matters, and especially so because Africa has to create millions of new jobs to meet the needs of its young people and the growing pressures of urbanization. And it has to create higher-quality jobs that can raise incomes on a large scale. Manufacturing is central to any sustainable job creation effort. It creates jobs directly, generally quality employment. It generates more jobs in supplier industries, from mineral processing to services. And its labor force supports still more jobs in agriculture, retail, production of consumer goods and infrastructure.

Manufacturing generally has a positive impact on foreign exchange earnings and the balance of payments, both increasing export earnings and reducing the import bill.

Recent economic history has shown that it is still possible for countries to achieve substantial growth in manufacturing, becoming successful in both manufacturing goods and product innovation. Many of these successes are found in Asia, from Japan's early lead, to Korea's development as an industrial economy and the present-day rise of China as the factory of the world. But successes can be found on a smaller scale for specific industries on the African continent, in countries as diverse as South Africa and Tunisia.

What these examples point to is the return of industrial policy as a valid focus of public policy. However, this resurgent industrial policy has learnt the lessons of both failure and successes elsewhere. It is smart industrial policy.

But modern industrial policy is not just concerned with expanding the industrial sector. It is predicated on the belief that government can play a constructive role in shaping the economy – indeed, there is no choice but for it to do so. That may entail encouraging the economy to move in more environmentally sustainable ways than it otherwise would; or to create more jobs. It might seek to create an economy with less inequality, or with a stronger research and development sector, or a more productive agriculture sector.

So how do societies industrialize and modernize successfully in a globalized world? And how do they maintain dynamic competitiveness?

This two-part volume seeks to lay the basis for a discussion that will look at lessons to take industrial policy beyond the provision of subsidies alone. Every successful industrializing economy used a wider toolbox of measures, one that drew on core state functions. These include:

- Shaping infrastructure and supply chain logistics to ensure that the output of emerging manufacturing industries can move cheaply and quickly between countries and from production centers to markets.
- Innovation and R&D as well as technology policies that deepen the local technological base especially by diffusing production and product innovations on a large scale. Critically, we must encourage the development and use of innovations that meet Africa's specific needs, including in rural areas, with technologies geared to the climate, biology, and logistics challenges facing the continent.
- Education, skills, and productivity policies that identify the best ways to empower millions of African workers and entrepreneurs.
- Competition policies that simultaneously improve market access and act against abuse of market power, not as aims in themselves but as tools to promote employment and industrial capacity.
- Trade policies that integrate markets, creating the critical mass and economies of scale, while maintaining space for new industries to emerge especially on a regional basis.
- Macro-policies that ensure stability and a competitive exchange rate.
- Financial policies that ensure access to finance at affordable terms, even by small and medium-sized enterprises.

Participants noted the long-standing challenge of the resource curse – that the very abundance of natural resources may inhibit the development of competitive downstream industries because entrepreneurs and governments can survive off the extraction of natural resources.

But the roundtables went further to reflect on the channels of competitiveness: what countries can do in developing skills and technology policies that spur industrialization. Crucially for policymakers, the participants looked at the role of institutions, drawing on the insights gained from the experience of fast-growing industrializing economies.

Washington, D.C. proved an ideal jumping-off point for the two-roundtable series. Pretoria, South Africa was a fertile and appropriate location for the Africa-focused companion roundtable. In total, the two roundtables drew 39 attendees, who participated in dozens of presentations and plenary discussions spread over different sessions, each focusing on a different aspect of industrial policy. This afforded a truly diverse and international range of perspectives, not always in agreement on the particulars, but with broadly shared common goals.

Part I of this volume, edited by Justin Yifu Lin and Joseph E. Stiglitz, encompasses the Washington, D.C. roundtable. Its chapters move from the broadly theoretical to the case-study specific, reflecting the organization of the meeting, which was divided into six sessions: (1) Conceptual Issues and Principles of Industrial Policy; (2) Special Issues for Developing Countries; (3) Instruments of Industrial Policy; (4) Regional Case Studies of Successful and Unsuccessful Industrial Policies; (5) Country Case Studies of Successful and Unsuccessful Industrial Policies; and (6) Industrial Policy Redux.

Part II of this volume, edited by Justin Yifu Lin, Ebrahim Patel, and Joseph E. Stiglitz, encompasses the Pretoria roundtable. The arc of the conference was similar to that in Washington, moving from the general to the particular, but focusing on how industrial policies could help transform Africa. After reviewing the results of the Washington meeting, and seeing how these and other broad perspectives that formed the foundations of the Revolution in Industrial Policy could provide general insights for policies in Africa, the discussion centered on certain key issues facing the region: Can the "Development State" work for Africa? How does the New Global Order affect prospects for African Reindustrialization? What are the most important things for African governments to do to create a good environment for industrialization? How can financial policies be used as an instrument of industrial policy? The conference then proceeded with papers analyzing the role of industrial policies in particular sectors, and by participants sharing experiences of industrial policies (with examples from Brazil, Mauritius, Singapore, South Africa, and Africa more generally). After an Open Discussion of the Role and Opportunities for Industrial Policy in Africa and Directions for Future Research, the Roundtable concluded with a panel for (and partly by practicing) policymakers.

The two volumes in this IEA Industrial Policy Roundtable series do not provide comprehensive records of all the papers that were presented at the roundtable, but hopefully they give a picture of the richness of the discussions and the potential for (and cautions in) the use of industrial policy. The editors have taken the liberty of rearranging the chapters. The whole program of the roundtables may be accessed by visiting the website of the IEA: http://www.iea-world.com/roundtables.php.

The convening of the conferences benefitted from the guidance of leading economists from across the world. In particular, the members of the Scientific Committee, Laura Alfaro, Mario Cimoli, Josh Lerner, Kaushik Basu, and K.Y. Amoako, deserve special mention for their work in formulating the agenda. Their wisdom, academic expertise and leadership, organizing competence and generous sharing of time made the roundtables enormously successful academic events. The IEA also owes a debt of gratitude to those who helped organize the roundtables on site in both Washington and Pretoria: Claudia Sepulveda, Julia Cunico, Nthato Minyuku and Pilar Palacios.

In addition, the hard work of the administrative staff and student assistants at the two roundtables ensured that the roundtables' operations ran smoothly, for which the IEA is also grateful. The IEA is grateful to Laurence Wilse-Samson for the invaluable assistance he provided as a rapporteur in Pretoria. We especially want to acknowledge the work of Eamon Kircher-Allen in both pulling the book together and in general editorial assistance.

The roundtable in Washington was financially supported by the World Bank, while the Pretoria roundtable was financially supported by the World Bank, the South African Economic Development Department (EDD), the United Nations Department of Economic and Social Affairs (UNDESA), and the United Nations Industrial Development Organization (UNIDO) The IEA would like to express deep gratitude to these donors for their generous support.

And finally, we are indebted to all the staff at the IEA Secretariat and Palgrave Macmillan for their great help in shepherding the volumes from conception to completion.

Joseph Stiglitz
IEA President

Acknowledgements

The publishers gratefully acknowledge the permission of The World Bank to reproduce material included in chapter 5.4 'The "Global" Rush for Land: Does it Provide Opportunities for African Countries' by Karl Deininger. © by International Bank for Reconstruction and Development/International Development Association and The World Bank.

The publishers gratefully acknowledge the permission of Penguin Books Ltd and Bloomsbury Publishing Plc to reproduce material from *23 Things They Don't Tell You About Capitalism* by Ha-Joon Chang (Penguin Books 2010, 2011). Copyright © Ha-Joon Chang, 2010.

Introduction: Industrial Policy in the African Context

Joseph Stiglitz, Justin Yifu Lin, Célestin Monga, Ebrahim Patel

In his celebrated memoirs, Nelson Mandela recounts the story of having to battle his political adversaries and friends alike to convince them of the necessity of launching an armed movement in their fight against the unbearable brutalities of apartheid. Even his closest allies and supporters resented the idea of resorting to such a controversial strategy, one that raised deep moral questions and required complex implementation capabilities. They opposed his views until he was able to explain that the battle for freedom and prosperity is never an elegant linear path, and that sometimes one has to take unexpected detours and rely on trial-and-error tactics. He finally got his way. And yet the most difficult challenge occurred after his recommendations were eventually validated by his peers, who then asked him to actually implement them. Mandela had no choice but to accept that responsibility. He quickly realized how testing it can be to move from impeccable theoretical reasoning to concrete action on the ground. He writes: "I, who had never been a soldier, who had never fought in battle, who had never fired a gun at an enemy, had been given the task of starting an army. It would be a daunting task for a veteran general, much less a military novice."[1]

Many economists who have long argued in favor of industrial policy – defined as a policy by which governments attempt to shape the sectoral allocation of the economy – now find themselves in a similar situation. After long suffering from benign neglect, if not outright contempt by some of their self-proclaimed "mainstream" colleagues who long dismissed it disdainfully, they are now listened to. Industrial policy is almost fashionable again. The global financial and economic crisis known as the Great Recession has forced researchers and policymakers to confront the reality that market forces alone generally do not lead to (constrained) Pareto-efficient outcomes.[2] Many important national and global policy objectives (equality of opportunity for all citizens, financial stability and inclusion, environmental protection and pollution control, and so on) are simply often not reflected in market prices and not achieved by markets on their own. In addition to traditional

1

justification for industrial policies – dealing externalities and coordination issues – economists and policymakers now acknowledge the need to foster learning at the level of each economic agent and throughout society, and the ultimate responsibility that the state must bear in that crucial process.

But converting the now widely accepted theoretical principles of industrial policy into practical frameworks for concrete government action is indeed a daunting task everywhere, and perhaps more so in the African context where the institutional underpinnings of effective government are often not as strong as one might have hoped. Just like Mandela, who found himself in the unviable position of having his controversial ideas recognized and being designated to make them work, proponents of industrial policy now have the responsibility of fleshing out an implementation framework that deliver results for policymakers in developing countries. In undertaking that overwhelming assignment, they could learn from Mandela's basic insights when he faced a comparable task: "I began in the only way I knew how, by reading and talking to experts, he writes. What I wanted to find out were the fundamental principles for starting a revolution. I discovered that there was a great deal of writing on this very subject, and I made my way through the available literature..."[3]

There is indeed a rich literature on industrial policy and several advanced and developing countries have successfully implemented industrial policies (though not always calling it by that name). Our understanding of industrial policy has been enriched through practice and constant learning. It is therefore almost a contribution to global public knowledge to review that literature. This book, the output from a conference held in Pretoria,[4] highlights its intellectual foundations and broad principles, outlines the contours of the policy agenda, reviews some interesting case studies of implementation, fleshes out the lessons learned, and identifies the issues for future research aims at doing just that. Its focus is on Africa, still the home to most of the "bottom billion" poor people in the world, but a continent on the move – the fastest-growing in the world.[5] Underlying all the papers collected here is the recognition that there has been substantial progress on the understanding and acceptance of industrial policy, and that Africa could benefit enormously from it, and from the unprecedented new opportunities brought to light by a multipolar world.

The acknowledgment of some self-evident truths

"To truth only a brief celebration of victory is allowed between the two long periods during it is condemned as paradoxical, or disparaged as trivial." (Schopenhauer 1958 [1818], p. xxv)

The idea of industrial policy has gone through these various stages. Once considered anathema among mainstream economics and in the public discourse, it has become a matter of almost common sense. Conservative and liberal leaders throughout the world are now promoting it as a vehicle for creating high-skilled jobs, building more equitable societies, and protecting the environment, and development institutions appear more inclined to acknowledge it as an essential tool to foster structural change in advanced and low-income nations.

There is now widespread recognition among researchers and policymakers of the many reasons countries should design and implement industrial policy: to correct market failures, situations where markets by themselves do not lead to efficient, or desirable, resource allocations, and in some cases, even to correct other government failures, where other, harder to alter, government policies "distort" resource allocations.

Such truths have been known and part of economic theory since at least Adam Smith, and the legitimacy of government intervention was well described by List et al. (1856). Following Marshall (1920), who pointed out the important role of externalities, and the work of Arrow and Debreu, which laid out the highly restrictive conditions under which markets resulted in (Pareto-)efficient outcomes, neoclassical theorists eventually acknowledged that markets often don't work as they are supposed to. But conservative economists continue to argue for a limited role for government intervention.

First, they argued that these market failures were limited in scope. In the wake of the environmental destruction and the financial collapses associated with unfettered markets, such views have little support today.

But even when conservatives acknowledged that there are extensive market failures, they had little confidence that government intervention would succeed in improving matters. They cited examples of government interventions to correct market failures that led to economic distortions. Against market failures they set what they argued were pervasive government failures, especially in developing countries. Some argued that these problems were especially severe in the area of industrial policies. Confronted with the implementation challenges associated with the task, many economists chose to dismiss entirely the notion of industrial policy.

Surprisingly, such bold claims were supported neither by theoretical or empirical/historical analyses. The latter made clear that there were many instances of successful government intervention. Around the world, there is a broad consensus that efforts to control environmental externalities have, by and large, worked, and have improved our wellbeing – by an amount that far exceeds any costs that may have been imposed. Cities where the air was unbreathable have become livable again; water that was badly polluted has become drinkable and swimmable.

Even in the area of industrial policy there have been notable successes. Indeed, the United States, for more than a hundred and fifty years, has benefited from such policies, from the development of the agricultural sector (the dominant sector in the economy in the mid-19th century), to the development of telecommunications (from the development of the first telegraph line in the first half of the 19th century to the development of the internet – one of the central areas of growth in the 21st century).

Arguably, the East Asia Miracle – the most remarkable episodes of growth in history—was based largely on government interventions into the market economy, including extensive use of industrial policies.[6]

These examples should make it clear that the "political economy" problems posed by critics of government intervention are neither inevitable nor universal. (These conservative critics of industrial policy provide no general theory that the political economy problems are severe, inevitable, and universal.)

This has led to a marked shift in the policy debate, to what are the circumstances under which industrial policies will work, and what forms of industrial policy are appropriate for countries in different stages of development and with different political and economic institutions.

For instance, some have made a distinction between economy-wide ("horizontal") policies, defined as consisting of general business environment policies that have only an indirect impact on any given sector or industry, and sector- or industry-specific types of industrial policy (often labeled as "vertical").

Thus, in the 1990s, it became the conventional wisdom that the former should be the foundation for policymaking – as they ensure a level playing field for market forces to determine successful industries – and the latter opposed – because governments could not be trusted to "pick winners." Even then, though, many, even in the international economic institutions, questioned this wisdom, questioning, for instance, the intellectual foundation for such a flawed distinction (Hoff and Stiglitz, 2001).

But it took the 2008 Great Recession to bring about a wider understanding of the deficiencies in the conventional wisdom and in the standard models upon which they rested. Those models failed, by all the most important tests of scientific theory. They did not predict that the financial crisis would happen; and when it did, they understated its effects. Monetary authorities allowed bubbles to grow and focused on keeping inflation low, partly because the standard models suggested that low inflation was necessary and almost sufficient for efficiency, growth and prosperity (Stiglitz, 2011). After the crisis broke, policymakers relying on the models floundered.

In the wake of the crisis, , macroeconomists from various ideological backgrounds are now re-examining some of the discipline's dogmas, questioning what was thought to be infallible certainties, and stressing the importance of new knowledge. Summing up the intellectual changes that are needed, Olivier Blanchard, the IMF Chief Economist, writes:

> We've entered a brave new world, a very different world in terms of macroeconomic policymaking. In the age-old discussion of the relative roles of markets and the state, the pendulum has swung – at least a bit – toward the state. There are many distortions relevant for macroeconomics, many

more than we thought was the case earlier. We had largely ignored them, thinking they were the province of the microeconomist. As we integrate finance into macroeconomics, we're discovering that distortions within finance are macro-relevant. Agency theory – about incentives and behaviour of entities or "agents" – is needed to explain how financial institutions work or do not work and how decisions are taken. Regulation and agency theory applied to regulators themselves is important. Behavioural economics and its cousin, behavioural finance, are central as well." (Blanchard, 2011)

Such candor and humility from a place known for its staunch defense of orthodoxy can only be welcome.

The crisis has made clear that these market failures are of first-order importance – they affected the overall performance of the economy. Macroeconomists have focused on how they affect economic volatility, and what public policies might stabililze the economy. Here we focus on *industrial policies,* policies directed at affecting the shape of the economy (including the sectoral allocation of resources and the choices of technology within any given sector). While discussions have traditionally focused on how such policies can affect the long-run rate of growth, the papers in this volume also discuss other social objectives to which such policies may be directed: improving the distribution of income, increasing employment, protecting the environment, ensuring sustainability.

The global financial and economic crisis has also brought to light the fact that market forces do not exist in a vacuum, and that they are all shaped by laws, rules, and regulations, each of which is never truly "neutral," as it explicitly or implicitly favors or discourages particular industries, sectors, firms, and social players. All governments really do have an industrial policy. The only difference is between those who construct their industrial policy consciously, and those who let it be shaped by others, typically by special interests, who vie with each other for hidden and open subsidies, for rules and regulations that favor them, usually at the expense of others.

In recent years, there has been an increasing understanding of the long list of "market" failures which government intervention should and could address. Many of the papers in this volume shed further light on them. For instance, it is now widely accepted that the government should try to do something about negative externalities (from pollution or from excessive risk taking in the financial sector). It has also become increasingly clear that government interventions are needed to ensure proper coordination of risky investment decisions that no single firm or private agent alone can pursue efficiently. So too, the government has played a constructive role in promoting industries and activities which give rise to *positive* externalities – most notably those associated with learning and research.

Thus, there is now an acceptance that governments should not limit themselves to engaging in just "horizontal" interventions. Those who reject industry-specific interventions must also confront the law of scarcity, especially in the context of developing countries. Identification of new industries and prioritization of government's limited resources (and more broadly, society's limited resources) to facilitate the development of those industries are both essential for successful growth strategies in Africa. Why? Because the infrastructure improvements required are often industry-specific. And markets cannot be relied upon to provide this infrastructure.

One simply has to look at the list of recent success stories in African countries to understand the role that industrial policies have already been playing: textiles in Mauritius, apparel in Lesotho, cotton in Burkina Faso, cut flowers in Ethiopia, mango in Mali, and gorilla tourism in Rwanda all required that governments provide *different* types of infrastructure. The refrigeration facilities needed at the airport and regular flights to ship Ethiopia's cut flowers to the auctions in Europe are obviously quite different from the improvements required at the port facilities for textile exports in Mauritius. Similarly, the type of infrastructure needed for the garment industry in Lesotho is distinct from the one needed for mango production and export in Mali or for attracting gorilla tourism in Rwanda. Because fiscal resources and implementation capacity are limited, the government in each of those countries had to prioritize and decide which particular infrastructure they should improve or where to optimally locate the public services to make those success stories happen.

Deng Xiaoping explained that pragmatic wisdom at the beginning of China's transition to a market economy when he advocated allowing a few regions and people to get rich first in order to achieve common prosperity for all people in the nation. The dynamic growth in those regions and industries would increase fiscal revenues, giving the government more resources to improve infrastructure (or education or technology) for other regions in the nation later.

Identification of new sectors or lines of business and the prioritization of infrastructure investment are also necessary because economies of scale may enhance the ability of a country (and the firms within the country) to be competitive in the globalized world. Without government coordination, firms may enter into too many different industries (all of which may be consistent with the country's long term or dynamic comparative advantage). As a result, most industries may not form clusters that are sufficiently large and will not be competitive in the domestic and international markets. A few clusters may emerge eventually after many failures. Such a "trial and error" process is likely to be long and costly, slowing down the country's economic development. It is therefore imperative for a "facilitating" state (or what is sometimes called a "developmental state"[7]) in a developing country to identify and select new industries that are consistent with comparative advantage, use its limited resources to improve infrastructure for a limited number of carefully selected industries, provide adequate incentives for first movers, and coordinate private firms' related investments in those industries so that clusters can be formed successfully and quickly.[8]

The extent to which governments perform the roles just described – how well they perform these roles – may be among the most important determinants of long-term economic success.

There is also wide acceptance of a new rationale for industrial policy. Economic development is the process of technological diffusion and industrial upgrading. It involves making knowledge available to the largest number possible of economic agents and fostering constant learning. Yet knowledge is different from conventional goods. It is, in a sense a *public good* (that is, the marginal cost for another person or firm enjoying the benefits of knowledge – beyond the cost of transmission – is zero). Moreover, usage is non-rivalrous. Markets (anywhere, whether in developed or developing countries) are not efficient in the production and distribution of public goods.

If economic development is essentially about the diffusion of knowledge among the broadest segments of society, then it is inevitable that there be, or there ought to be, a role for government intervention. It follows that industrial policy should also be about facilitating the generation and acquisition of new knowledge that empowers households and firms. In fact, formerly poor countries – those in East Asia – that have been able to converge toward the income levels of advanced economies have generally done so through learning. The mantra that governments should not be involved in "picking winners" is therefore beside the point: the objective of any government should be not only to correct negative externalities but also to promote positive externalities that arise from learning and sharing knowledge.

African opportunities and challenges[9]

Today, Africa is a continent facing unprecedented opportunities for and challenges to economic growth and development. The widely shared optimism was expressed by the *Economist* magazine:

> Never in the half-century since it won independence from the colonial powers has Africa been in such good shape. Its economy is flourishing. Most countries are at peace. Ever fewer children bear arms and record numbers go to school. Mobile phones are as ubiquitous as they are in India and, in the worst-affected countries, HIV infections have fallen by up to three-quarters. Life expectancy rose by a tenth in the past decade and foreign direct investment has tripled. Consumer spending will almost double in the next ten years; the number of countries with average incomes above $1,000 per person a year will grow from less than half of Africa's 55 states to three-quarters. (*Economist*, 2013)

But each statistic showing unprecedented success and new opportunities is matched by some highlighting the future difficulties the region faces.

Sub-Saharan Africa has averaged 5 percent growth or more over the past decade. There are also countries that have an average growth rate of over 7 percent. Many of the countries have demonstrated high levels of competency in macro-mangement, and even resolve in fighting corruption.

However, the average gross national income (GNI) per capita of about $1,200 in 2012 was less than Bolivia's ($1,810).[10] Moreover, the region's "most successful" economies are actually much poorer than the poorest countries in other regions of the world: Mozambique and Tanzania, which have been among the top-ten fastest-growing countries in the world over the past two decades, still have GNI per capita in the range of $400–500. Liberia and Sierra Leone, two countries often hailed as "turnaround successes," still rank very low at $160 and $340, respectively. The Democratic Republic of Congo, Africa's third largest country, comparable in size to Western Europe, and a place where wars have claimed roughly four million victims in the last five years alone (according to the United Nations), had a GNI of less than $200 – similar to Burundi's.

A static analysis using simply the mathematical rule of 72 indicates that at its current growth rate of 5 percent a year, it would take about a quarter-century for Sub-Saharan Africa to double its income per capita – and reach today's still low GNI per capita of Paraguay ($2,250). Even if one assumes a very optimistic elasticity of poverty with respect to income of 1.5, Sub-Saharan Africa's current rate of growth would translate into a reduction of only 3.3 percent per year of the region's high extreme poverty headcount index (1.7 points each year from the current 50 percent).[11] Other developing regions of the world have been able to do much better in recent decades.

Widespread poverty is not the only worry: there are concerns about the sustainability of economic growth, unemployment, and inequality. About a third of the continent's good growth performance is attributable to commodities, and many African countries are still discovering new oilfields and mineral deposits. But history shows that excessive reliance on raw natural resources is never a prudent development strategy. While today's prices are near record highs, commodity markets are known to often collapse abruptly. In addition, recent gains in agriculture may be undermined by climate change and environmental concerns. Already, savannahs are drying out, water tables are dropping, and rains either failing or becoming more irregular.

The dynamics of demographic growth makes things even more challenging: with average annual population growth projected to be 2.2 percent over the next 25 years, the African private sector faces the challenge of creating employment opportunities to absorb the youth bulge: about two-thirds of the Region's population is under the age of 24 and is underemployed – including those with college and university degrees. Most workers are trapped in very low-productivity activities in subsistence agriculture and the informal sector. Sub-Saharan Africa will have to generate between seven and ten million jobs annually in order to accommodate the high rate of population growth (World Bank 2013).

For a region facing such opportunities and challenges, industrial policy is not a speculative intellectual exercise for academic debates but rather a necessary economic tool to address the pervasive discrepancies between private gains and social returns, and to correct major sectoral or other misallocations. In the particular context of Africa, among the priorities are: (a) ensuring that resources (labor, capital, knowledge) are transferred from low- to high-productivity sectors and areas. This includes the migration of Africa's abundant unskilled rural labor to unskilled labor-intensive industries; and (b) increasing productivity, through learning and education.

Neither of these will occur on their own. Proactive action must be taken by policymakers. It is necessary, for instance, for the government to facilitate the growth of existing and emerging unskilled labor-intensive industries. Without such action, there is a risk that urban unemployment will increase even beyond the current high levels. On the supply side of the labor market, African governments must also provide basic education and training, to enhance the rural out-migrants' ability to adapt to the new working environment and requirements in the industrial sector.

African political leaders generally understand these responsibilities and should be – and often are – using all the tools at their disposal to meet their goals. In earlier periods, some in the international community discouraged them from using one important set of tools – industrial policies. This book is intended to "correct" this misguided advice – advice which arguably contributed to the deindustrialization of Sub-Saharan Africa (to the point where today, the industrial sector has a smaller share of GDP than in 1970[12]). (This deindustrialization is *one* of the factors that may have contributed to the decline in GDP per capita in Sub-Saharan Africa between 1976 and 1994.[13]) The question today is not whether African governments – like all governments in the world – *should* be engaged in industrial policy but whether they *are* doing it well, and how can they can do it better. The chapters in this book provide numerous insights that may help them to do so.

Realities and myths about Africa's capabilities

There has been persistent skepticism about the applicability of industrial policy to the particular context of Africa. Various factors – pathological politics, and pervasive corruption – are said to make industrial policy ineffective, or even counterproductive for the African countries. Skeptics also provide an impressive list of knowledge requirements about targeted industries that government officials would need to know in order to design a successful industrial policy. They question the capacity of governments in poor countries to meet those requirements.

Some of these arguments are deserving of serious attention. First, all countries at low-income level tend to lack high bureaucratic capacity by definition. But market failures also tend to be more pervasive, and there is often a shortage of private sector entrepreneurship. Hence, in many cases, state-led development (often employing marked mechanisms) has been shown to be the most effective development strategy. The point, as we have previously noted, is that these concerns should affect the form of industrial policy, not whether the government should undertake industrial policy.

On the other hand, the argument that the knowledge requirements for the effective design of industrial policies are beyond the capacities of developing countries is not very persuasive. Some of the so-called knowledge requirements identified for industrial policy are likely to be more relevant for more advanced industries in high-income countries. For industries with low technical content, the knowledge requirements are markedly more limited. Moreover, instead of analyzing the technical nature of various industries, government officials can rely on the advantage of backwardness and observe what the dynamically growing countries with similar endowment structures are already doing or have done in the past.

By the same token, broad-based measures, for example, encouraging the industrial sector broadly, do not necessitate the government making fine-tuned judgments. As Greenwald and Stiglitz argue, such policies are desirable so long as learning elasticities and knowledge spillovers are greater in those sectors. Industrial policies can "tilt" the playing field toward sectors or technologies with positive spillovers/externalities and away from those with negative spillovers/externalities.

Central to creating a modern economy is creating a *learning economy and society,* and government intervention can play an important role in doing this.

The difficulties of implementing *any* type of public policy anywhere in the world are well known. Critics point to the scope for rent seeking. Avoiding rent seeking is but one of the challenges facing the effective implementation of industrial policy. In some cases, governments have been tempted to ignore economic "rationality" and pursued more sophisticated sectors in their zeal to emulate advanced countries; sometimes they have extended even successful policies well beyond their effective timespan.

These concerns are legitimate but apply not only to whatever is labeled "industrial policy." The potential for abuse exists for any public policy: many governments around the world have misused monetary and financial regulatory policy, infrastructure policy, or education policy. But few would argue that, as a result, governments should eschew the use of monetary and financial regulatory policy, infrastructure policy, or education policy. The contrast between attitudes toward monetary and industrial policies is especially striking: While the fact that so many governments (including that of the USA) has mismanaged monetary policy is generally not viewed as grounds for abandoning monetary policy, the fact that industrial policies have *sometimes* been mismanaged has often been used as an argument against such policies. And there is ample evidence of "capture" of the US Federal Reserve by the financial market in the years before the crisis (and, some critics say, even afterward). Moreover, what some thought were mistaken industrial policies – such as those undertaken by Korea in the late 1960s and 1970s – proved enormously successful, propelling that country forward, to enable it to join the OECD, the club of the advanced industrial countries.

Pervasive governance issues are often offered as reasons not to engage in industrial policy. But the countries that successfully engaged in industrial policies in recent decades had, at the time they embarked on their development strategies, typically had far from perfect governance structures (and as the crisis illustrated, even the advanced countries have governance structures that are far from ideal).

While political economy problems need to be taken seriously, one should not let the best be the enemy of the good. To wait for the perfect African state to emerge before industrial policy can be implemented would imply never getting anything done. In the real world, successful countries are the ones that have managed to find "good enough" solutions to their political economy problems and implemented these sound policies. Deficiencies in governance should affect the type of industrial policies and the manner in which they are implemented, not the use of industrial policies themselves.

Moreover, the decades of success and failures in industrial policies have provided multiple lessons on how to design effect industrial policies. For instance Lin and Monga (2013) argue forcefully that the traditional type of industrial development strategies pursued by developing countries in the 1950s and 1960s often encouraged firms to enter industries that were inconsistent with their comparative advantage (even broadly defined to include "dynamic" comparative advantage). Firms in these industries were not viable in an open, competitive market. Their survival depended on heavy government protection, large subsidies, and direct resource allocations through measures such as monopoly rent, high tariffs, quota restrictions, and subsidized credits. The large rents embedded in those measures created many distortions and easily became the targets of political capture (Lin, 2012).

The success of East Asian economies in designing and implementing smart government interventions proves that it is possible to promote the development of industries that are consistent with the economy's latent comparative advantage. Firms are viable once the constraints to their entry and operation are removed. The incentives provided by the government to the first movers are to be temporary and small, solely for the purpose of compensating for their information externality. In that context, they have shown that the issues of pervasive rent-seeking and the persistence of government intervention beyond its initial timetable can be mitigated; indeed, their experiences provides insights into how this can be done. The likelihood of governance problems arising is much reduced when the government facilitates the development of new industries that are consistent with the country's changing comparative advantage determined by the change in its endowment structure (Lin and Monga 2012).

Other skeptical arguments against industrial policy in Africa are flawed and reminiscent of those made throughout history to dismiss industrialization attempts in other regions of the world.[14] Today's "structural" theories of "Afro-pessimism" are usually *ex post* justifications of the status quo, confusing the causes and the symptoms of underdevelopment. The notion of a capacity deficit in countries such as South Africa, Nigeria, Kenya, or Cameroon is simply a myth. In fact, it could be argued that these countries now have more capacity and potential access to financial resources from foreign savings with which to implement such policies than China had when it started its structural transformation process in the late 1970s. And in a world where labor has become a very mobile factor of production, even countries with much weaker human capital stocks and administrative capacity could easily attract foreign expertise to help design and implement these policies.

While the challenges of implementing industrial policy in *any* country need to be taken seriously, not only is this is a moment in which such policies are especially needed, this is a moment of real opportunity. They are needed in part because Africa is going through a major structural transformation, and markets by themselves manage such transformations poorly, for a variety of reasons that have been set forth elsewhere.[15] But there is, in addition, a major structural transformation going on globally: rising real wages and current appreciation in China will result in at least significant parts of its manufacturing base moving elsewhere. There is an opportunity for some of it, perhaps a substantial part, to move to Africa. If that were to happen, it would provide a significant boost to growth and employment. It would reverse the pattern of deindustrialization that began with the structural adjustment programs foisted on Africa in early decades. It would enhance the chances of creating the kind of learning society and economy that is often associated with the transition away from agriculture to manufacturing. But if this is to happen, active government policies will almost surely be needed. Many African countries have gotten the fundamentals right – they have achieved macro-stability and reduced corruption. But the inflow of foreign direct investment, apart from the natural resource sector, has been disappointing. There is at least some hope that, when combined with these other policies, there will be the kind of acceleration of growth that will be necessary if the region is to make the inroads into poverty for which it has so long strived.

Contents of this volume

The papers presented in this volume cover theoretical and policy issues of industrial policy, with a particular focus on the challenges and possibilities in the African context.

The book begins with a discussion of broad conceptual issues of industrial policy, and the respective roles of the state and the market in fostering inclusive economic growth and building equitable societies. Each subsequent section then takes up a particular aspect of Africa's industrialization challenge and debates what the scope should be and which policy instrument may be used to achieve sustained and inclusive growth. As we noted earlier, virtually every aspect of economic policy affects the structure of an economy – and can be viewed through the lens of industrial policy. Thus, we look not only at tradition "industrial policy" topics (trade, how to build industrial policies based on natural resource endowments), but non-traditional ones, such as macroeconomics and industrial structure, exchange rate policies, competition, entrepreneurship, financial markets, land outsourcing, and governance. Our discussions were grounded on country experiences, discussed extensively in several of the chapters.

The first section deals with new theoretical thinking on industrial policy and its transformational potential for Africa. In "Learning and Industrial Policy: Implications for Africa," Greenwald and Stiglitz open the section by arguing that pervasive market failures (and other distortions which result in private rewards being misaligned with social returns) provide a rationale for industrial policies. The chapter focuses on one particular set of market failures, those that arise in the process of learning: Learning is especially important for developing countries as they strive to close the gap between their incomes and those of the more developed countries. Disparities in incomes are as much related to gaps in knowledge as they are to gaps in resources. They argue that accordingly, a central focus of development policy should be, how to promote learning, how to create a "learning economy and society." Greenwald and Stiglitz note that much of the advice of the past, based on neoclassical models, not only gave short shrift to these concerns, but may actually have led to counterproductive policy prescriptions that were adverse to learning, and hence to long term increases in standards of living. For Africa, as it attempts to reindustrialize, to restructure its economies to become more integrated into the global economy and move away from excessive dependence on commodity exports, to raise standards of income, increase employment, reduce poverty and inequality, and protect a fragile environment, industrial policies are of especial importance.

Lin, in "From Flying Geese to Leading Dragons: New Opportunities and Strategies for Structural Transformation in Developing Countries," notes that economic development is a process of continuous industrial and technological upgrading in which any country, regardless of its level of development, can succeed if it develops industries that are consistent with its comparative advantage, determined by its endowment structure. The successful strategy for developing countries is to exploit the latecomer advantage by building up industries that are growing dynamically in more advanced, fast-growing countries that have endowment structures similar to theirs. By following carefully selected lead countries, latecomers can emulate the leader–follower, "flying-geese" pattern that has served catching-up economies well since the 18th century. Lin suggests that the successful large middle-income countries such as China, India, and Brazil will be new growth poles in the world; and their dynamic growth, their climbing of the industrial ladder, offer an unprecedented opportunity to all developing economies with income levels currently below theirs – including those in Sub-Saharan Africa.

The second section surveys lessons in structural transformation from economic history. In "Accumulation of Capabilities, Structural Change and Macro Prices: an Evolutionary and Structuralist Roadmap," Cimoli and Porcile present a brief theoretical background on learning, capabilities, and innovation, with the aim of building bridges between evolutionary micro-economics and the structuralist theories of economic development. They discuss the role that industrial policies play in reducing the technology gap and transforming the production structure within a developing context, giving special attention to the case of external shocks that affect the consolidation of technological capabilities. Chang, in "Industrial Policy: Can Africa Do It?," challenges the persistent skepticism about the applicability of industrial policy to Africa. He assesses the thesis that conditions in the region are so special that the continent can never use industrial policy productively. He critically reviews old arguments of "Afro-pessimism" on the bases of climate, geography, history, and culture, as well as new arguments on natural resource abundance, political economy, bureaucratic capabilities, and the changes in global economic rules. He suggests how constraints to the effective implementation industrial policy may be overcome through an appropriate mix of realism, reform, and investments.

The third section examines the new global order and its opportunities for African reindustrialization. Monga, in "Winning the Jackpot: Jobs Dividends in a Multipolar World," surveys some of the main strands of the theoretical literature on unemployment and employment, and stresses the fact that findings based on the experience of richer countries may not be transferable to low-income countries whose endowment and production structures are profoundly different from that of high-income economies. He then sheds light on the new economic opportunities that African countries may derive from the dynamics of globalization – especially the economic success of large emerging economies such as China and Brazil – and offers a simple analytical framework for identifying opportunities for labor arbitrage in global economy, with a practical policy framework for exploiting them.

In the next chapter, "Walking (Stumbling?) on Two Legs: Meeting Sub-Saharan Africa's Industrialization Challenge," Kaplinsky argues that Industrial development is currently framed by three major dynamics: the increase in the number of people living in absolute poverty despite high rates of growth; the emergence of China, India, and other southern economies as sources of efficient appropriate technologies; and the commodity price boom, which may not last. He suggests that these dynamics present both threat and opportunity to future industrial development, and justify government policy intervention.

Having laid down the rationale for industrial policy in Africa, the potential new benefits of globalization, and the potential role of industrial policies in helping African countries take advantage of these new opportunities, the book offers an operational agenda for the implementation of industrial policies. The fourth section is devoted to "enabling environment" for the vision to materialize, focusing on the macroeconomic and governance requirements. In "How Macroeconomic Policy Can Support Economic Development in Sub-Saharan African Countries," Heinz starts with the observation that because of institutional, ideological, and structural constraints, the scope for conducting macroeconomic policy to support industrial development in Africa has traditionally been rather limited. He recommends broadening macroeconomic policy to enable it to better serve as an "instrument" of industrial policy. To illustrate how this can be done, he focuses on management of the real exchange rate, monetary policy, and the mobilization of domestic fiscal resources.

Creating a good environment for industrial development also requires putting in place a level playing field that encourages growth, risk taking, and innovation, and that provides scope for new entry. In "Competition Policy, Industrial Policy and Corporate Conduct," Roberts examines the role of competition law in industrial development and the relationship between the work of competition authorities and industrial policy in South Africa. He notes that the South African competition authorities have been successful in uncovering cartel conduct and blocking anti-competitive mergers, but they have had little success in addressing the power of entrenched dominant firms whose decisions largely determine the development path of the economy. He suggests that altering the trajectory of industrial development will require a competition regime that reinforces industrial policy and curbs the power of dominant firms so that they can compete on the sole basis of dynamic capabilities.

The next paper, "Political Settlements and the Design of Technology Policy" by Khan, sets the governance conditions for effective industrial policy. Khan observes that policies designed to address specific problems of technology adoption also create rents that the beneficiaries of these policies can try to capture without necessarily delivering results. If the organizations benefiting from rents are powerful and can use rent-seeking strategies to block the implementation of necessary conditions for success, technology policies can have poor results. Defining the distribution of power across economic, political and bureaucratic organizations in a society as the prevailing "political settlement," Khan notes that the successful implementation of ambitious technology policies in East Asian developmental states happened in political settlements that enabled the imposition of difficult conditions on powerful organizations. While political settlements in most developing countries preclude many of these types of technology policy, there are usually several possible policy responses to any particular technology acquisition problem, with different conditions required for successful outcomes. Indeed, technology policies have worked in countries which did not have developmental states of the East Asian type when the required enforcement conditions were credible in their political settlements.

This raises the burning question: can the "development state" work for Africa's industrialization? Noman, in "Infant Capitalists, Infant Industries and Infant Economies Trade and Industrial Policies for Early Stages of Development in Africa and Elsewhere," points to the neglect of the institution of "capitalists/entrepreneurs" – of particular salience for countries at early stages of development. He suggests that there is an "infant capitalist" argument for protection, and lessons from successes and failures in trade and industrialization policies, including in institution building, can be used to establish well-designed systems of protection that help to divert rents to productive activities and learning.

Taking stock of intellectual progress and integrating some of the viewpoints expressed in this book, Joseph's chapter, "Industrial Policies and Contemporary Africa: Frontiers of Political Economy and Social Science," concludes this section, by providing a framework for multidisciplinary work on governance. He recommends that arguments, hypotheses, and models advanced by economists be more closely juxtaposed with the work of researchers in other social science disciplines.

Complementing the discussion of horizontal, cross-cutting problems of macroeconomics and governance, the fifth section tackles trade, finance, and sectoral issues. In "Does Financial Market Liberalization Promote Financial Development?," Rashid investigates whether the liberalization of financial markets did indeed promote financial development. His empirical analysis covers 13 Sub-Saharan economies and shows that financial market liberalization did not lead to financial development in these economies. He finds strong negative correlation between the level of financial market liberalization and domestic savings rate and credit to private sector and a strong positive correlation between financial liberalization with real interest rate and interest rate spread in these countries. While his results are robust across different model specifications and estimation methods, he also points to the need for further research to determine how various aspects of financial market liberalization – the abolition of credit targets and credit controls, the deregulation of interest rates, the removal of entry barriers, the privatization of the banking sector, and so on – affect various dimensions of financial development.

Chandrasekhar's chapter, "Financialization as an Obstacle to Industrialization," complements and reinforces Rashid's analysis. He notes that there is no monotonic, positive relationship between financial development and growth. Indeed, in certain circumstances, through a number of routes, excessive financialization constrains industrial growth. Moreover, it is not just the size of finance that matters, but also the structure of the financial system. Experience shows that late-industrializing countries need to shape the markets, institutions, and instruments that constitute their financial structures and regulate the financial system so to use finance as an instrument for industrial development. However, financial liberalization undermines such specially constructed systems and constrains industrial development, besides increasing financial fragility and precipitating crises.

The next chapter shifts the focus from the financial sector to natural resources – a subject of immense relevance to Africa, given the current dependence of so many of the countries in the region on resources. Jourdan, in "Towards a Resource-based African Industrialization Policy," takes a broad view of Africa's natural resource endowments, not only the hydrocarbons and minerals, but also its land and water, which support a wide range of industries, including agriculture, forestry, fisheries, and tourism. He shows how Africa's unique natural resource base could provide its peoples with an important lever to achieve industrialization and development objectives. But this will require moving away from the "free mining" mineral regimes inherited from colonialism, and taking advantage of, and developing, linkages – forward, backward, and horizontal. He shows in detail how industrial policies can play a pivotal role in ensuring that the resource rich countries move beyond simply a dependence on resources. He warns that the current polices risks leaving Africa with little more than ghost towns, or with exhausted soils and depleted fisheries, forests and other natural endowments.

A closely related and difficult issue is that of land tenure and land reform, which Deininger takes up in "The Global 'Rush' for Land: Does it Provide Opportunities for African Countries?" For countries dependent on agriculture, the recent wave of investor interest in farmland could, in principle, help set in motion a virtuous cycle for economic growth and poverty reduction. However, historical evidence suggests that these opportunities are often squandered, with negative long-term impacts. Deininger reviews past experience, quantifies country-level potential for area expansion vs intensification, and identifies the determinants of countries' attractiveness for investors in the initial stages of the "land rush." Noting that weak land governance seems to increase, rather than reduce, land demand, he argues that improving land and natural resource governance and enhancing the transparency and accountability of the process of land sales will be necessary if the benefits of these important assets are to be fully realized.

Njinkeu, Lohi, and Djiofack conclude this section with their chapter on "Trade Facilitation and African Industrialization: An Agenda for the Textile and Apparel Industry." As formal trade barriers have come down, in many instances, the increases in trade have proved disappointing. This has shifted attention to other barriers to trade, which include the absence of infrastructure, supply-side constraints (including the absence of finance),[16] and procedures and processes associated with the movement of goods across borders. The latter is referred to as trade facilitation. They show that even small improvements in trade facilitation could lead to substantial increases in exports and enhanced regional integration. Moreover, trade facilitation could offset the negative impacts of tariffs on African trade.

The last section of the book is devoted to analyses of cross-country experiences and case studies. In "Industrial Structural Change, Growth Patterns and Industrial Policy," Alcorta, Haraguchi, and Rezonja analyze industrial change through the examination of the relationship between growth patterns in value added, labor productivity and employment in a sample of relatively large countries. A key problem in the implementation of industrial policies noted earlier is the identification of sectors with potential for growth that should be receive support. They provide an empirical analysis and develop a methodology that may be helpful in doing so. They offer empirical evidence that while any industry can expand on the basis of rapid increases of labor resources, only those industries that improve productivity substantially survive in the long run. A threshold of about US$10,000 GDP per capita (2005 US$ PPP adjusted) is observed as a major turning point before labor-intensive industries start losing labor cost advantage and begin shedding labor. By contrast structural change beyond US$23,000 GDP per capita (2005 US$ PPP adjusted) involves the consolidation of industries that have continuously pursued technological upgrading, innovation and scale and capital intensity advantages.

Ansu, in "Industrial Policy and Economic Transformation in Africa: Strategies for Development and a Research Agenda," provides an overview of the evolution of economic development policy in Sub-Saharan Africa over the forty-year period from 1970 to 2010. He notes that whether the focus is on the state-led import-substitution subperiod (1970 to early 1980s) or the subperiod of Structural Adjustment Programs (mid-1980s to early 2000s), there has been very little progress on economic transformation. Drawing from the experiences in African and East Asian countries that have been successful in transforming their economies, he argues that successful transformations will be based on policies that will involve both the state and the private sector and proposes a framework to track and assess the emerging industrial policy regimes designed to bring about the necessary economic transformation.

In "The Premature De-Industrialization of South Africa," Imbs takes a closer look at the patterns of structural transformation in a country that represents about one-third of Sub-Saharan Africa's gross domestic product. He shows the South African economy has not only moved away from manufacturing, but displayed a sudden increased specialization of sectoral activity in the late 2000s, at a level of per capita GDP much lower than is customary in comparable economies. South Africa specialized in services, rather than extractive activities, whose share in the aggregate economy has trended downwards. The analysis of census data reveals that the country's specialization in services is homogeneous geographically. Regions that used to produce different goods now increasingly resemble each other, because services are increasingly produced everywhere. This is especially true of financial services, which were geographically concentrated prior to 2000, but subsequently developed across all the South African regions. Imbs argues this transition reflects the increasing international trade openness of South Africa.

Chandra studies industrial policy in Ethiopia, where the government wants to jumpstart structural transformation by fostering a light manufacturing sector. Ethiopia has the potential to compete with China and Vietnam, she argues, but its firms face too many constraints which its resource- and capacity-constrained government cannot resolve at once. A targeted industrial policy that selectively removes the most critical constraints in each industry to scale up production and exports can help, but government needs to first redress some market and policy-induced failures and increase competition. Sector-specific solutions include lowering input costs by liberalizing agricultural input, output and land markets, improving trade logistics, developing plug-and-play industrial parks, and fostering foreign direct investment to bring in managerial capital.

The book ends with two short case studies of successful industrial development. In "Industrialization: The Mauritian Model," Narrainen tells the story of the island country by weaving together the main elements, decisions, and policies that have underpinned economic growth. The model highlights the middle-of-the-road approach, sometimes combining a heterodox mix of policies, and the importance of timely shifting industrialization paradigms to adapt to changing global circumstances. In some ways, that strategy based on pragmatism is reminiscent of the one that Thia describes in "Sharing of Singapore's Industrial Policy Insights." Singapore's experience of industrial policy, which is accompanied by a strong educational sector, free trade, and good institutions, corroborates many of the elements of the new thinking presented in the conceptual chapters of the book – most notably the importance of learning and knowledge.

The collection of papers in this book reflects the revolution in thinking about industrial policy. They present the new understandings that see industrial policy as not just tinkering at the edges of correcting minor market failures, but as part of a country's core strategy for promoting development – for structural transformation and for creating the kind of "learning societies and economies" that have been the hallmark of those countries have succeeded.

Despite many areas of broad consensus on the objectives and principles, there are still disagreements on the use of some specific economic tools – this is reflected in the comments by discussants, which follow some of the papers.

But we believe that the large corpus of knowledge and experiences presented here provide a convincing case that the governments of Africa ought to make industrial policies an important pillar of their development strategy, and that they ought to think carefully about the impact of all their other policies – macroeconomic policies like exchange rate management, microeconomic policies like competition policy – on the structure of their economy. There is not a single policy that will work in all countries: one of the key messages of these chapters is that successful industrial policies have to be tailored to the circumstances of the country (including the "quality" of its governance and the capacities of both the public and the private sector). We believe that this book has shown the wide range of objectives that industrial policies in Africa should pursue, and the wide range of instruments by which those objectives can be achieved. Hopefully, this will enable the revolution in the theory of industrial policies to be translated into a revolution in the practice – a change which holds out the promise that the remarkable growth experienced in Africa over the past decade will be sustained, and that the development strategies will be even more successful in promoting inclusive growth, poverty reduction, and broad-based increases in living standards.

Notes

1. Mandela (1994: 325).
2. The case for rethinking and rehabilitating industrial policy in made in Lin and Stiglitz (forthcoming), the companion volume to this book.
3. Mandela, op. cit., idem.
4. The papers presented here were initially discussed at an International Economic Association roundtable conference on "New Thinking on Industrial Policy: Implications for Africa," held in Pretoria, July 3–4, 2012, and co-sponsored by the World Bank, UNIDO, and the South African Economic Development Department.
5. Over the past decade real income per person in Africa has increased by more than 30 percent, whereas in the previous 20 years it shrank by nearly 10 percent. Over the next decade its gross domestic product is expected to rise by an average of 6 percent a year.
6. See World Bank (1993) and Stiglitz (1996).
7. For a discussion, see Noman and Stiglitz (2012b).
8. Note that it may be more important to select *some* industry on which to focus attention than to select the *best* industry on which to focus.
9. For further discussions of these issues, see Stiglitz (2013) and Noman and Stiglitz (2012a and 2012b).
10. World Bank, *World Development Indicators*.
11. A back-of-the envelop calculation is as follows: 5 percent GDP growth a year with a projected 2.2 percent population growth for the next 25 years (according to United Nations projections) equals a GDP per capita of 2.2 percent a year. Multiplying that rate by a (generous) elasticity of poverty with respect to income

of 1.5 gives a reduction of poverty of 3.3 percent a year, which applied to the current headcount index of 50 percent is about 1.7 points.

12. The value added of industry as a proportion of GDP in Sub-Saharan Africa was 31.2 percent in 1970, increased to 37.8 percent in 1980, and is 30.4 percent today, after a 1998 low of 28.4 percent (World Bank World Development Indicators database).

13. GDP per capita in Sub-Saharan Africa increased fairly steadily from $416 in 1960 to $577 in 1977. At that point, it began an uneven decline (some intervening years marked increases) to $482 in 1994. It regained its 1977 level in 2006, and is now $640. (World Bank World Development Indicators database).

14. Chang (2008) reminds us that, not so long ago, it was not unusual to refer to "Lazy Japanese and Thieving Germans." People do differ in their tastes, norms, cultures, and behaviors (Basu, 2011). But social norms and customs are not hard-wired into genetic structure. There are fascinating studies which show how Japan, as recently as hundred years ago, was a very unpunctual society. There are studies showing that Koreans, barely, fifty or sixty years ago, lacked industry and drive. Given that Japan is today one of the world's most punctual countries and Koreans one of the most industrious people, this shows that norms which look ingrained are actually malleable. There is need for research to understand how good norms are formed and dysfunctional norms can be rooted out.

15. See Lin (2012).

16. These impediments to trade have given rise to the Aid for Trade movement. For a broader discussion of these issues, see Charlton and Stiglitz (2006, 2008, 2013).

References

Basu, K. (2011) *Beyond the Invisible Hand: Groundwork for a New Economics* (Princeton, NJ: Princeton University Press).

Blanchard, O. (2011). "The Future of Macroeconomic Policy: Nine Tentative Conclusions," *IMF Direct*, March 13. http://blog-imfdirect.imf.org/2011/03/13/future-of-macroeconomic-policy/

Chang, H.-J. (2008) *Bad Samaritans: The Myth of Free Trade and the Secret History of Capitalism* (New York: Bloomsbury Press).

Charlton, A. and Stiglitz, J.E. (2006) "Aid for Trade," *International Journal of Development Issues*, vol. 5, no. 2, pp. 1–41. (Reprint of paper prepared for Commonwealth Secretariat.)

Charlton, A. (2008) "Aid for Trade," Keynote Address, in F. Bourguignon and B. Pleskovic (eds), *Annual World Bank Conference on Development Economics 2007, Rethinking Infrastructure for Development* (Washington, DC: World Bank), pp. 29–46.

Charlton, A. (2013) "The Right to Trade," a Report for the Commonwealth Secretariat on Aid for Trade.

Delli Gatti, D., Gallegati, M., Greenwald, B.C., Russo, A., and Stiglitz, J.E. (2012a) "Mobility Constraints, Productivity Trends, and Extended Crises," *Journal of Economic Behavior & Organization*, vol. 83, no. 3, pp. 375–393.

Delli Gatti, D., Gallegati, M., Greenwald, B.C., Russo, A., and Stiglitz, J.E. (2012b) "Sectoral Imbalances and Long Run Crises," in F. Allen, M. Aoki, J.-P. Fitoussi, N. Kiyotaki, R. Gordon, and J.E. Stiglitz, (eds), *The Global Macro Economy and Finance*, IEA Conference, volume No. 150-III (Basingstoke and New York: Palgrave Macmillan), pp. 61–97.

Economist (2013) "Aspiring Africa," editorial, March 2.

Hoff, K. and Stiglitz, J.E. (2001) "Modern Economic Theory and Development," in G. Meier and J. Stiglitz (eds), *Frontiers of Development Economics* (New York: Oxford University Press), pp. 389–459.

Lin, J.Y. (2012) *The Quest for Prosperity: How Developing Economies Can Take Off* (Princeton, NJ: Princeton University Press).

Lin, J.Y. and Stiglitz, J.E. (eds), 2013. [*Volume from the Washington IEA-World Bank Roundtable*]

Lin, J.Y. and C. Monga (2013) "Comparative Advantage: The Silver Bullet of Industrial Policy," [*Volume from the Washington IEA-World Bank Roundtable*].

Lin, J. Y. and C. Monga (2012). "Solving the Mystery of African Governance," *New Political Economy*, volume 17, no. 5, pp. 659-666.

List, Friedrich, Matile, G.-A., Richelot, Henri, and Colwell Stephen (1856) *National system of political economy* (Philadelphia: J.B. Lippincott & Co.).

Mandela, N. (1995) *Long Walk to Freedom* (London: Abacus).

Marshall, A. (1920) *Principles of Economics* (London: Macmillan).

Noman, A. and Stiglitz, J.E. (2012a) "African Development Prospects and Possibilities," in E. Aryeetey et al. (eds), *The Oxford Companion to the Economics of Africa* (Oxford: Oxford University Press), pp. 33–40.

Noman, A. and Stiglitz, J.E. (2012b) "Strategies for African Development," in , A. Noman, K. Botchwey, H. Stein, and J.E. Stiglitz (eds), *Good Growth and Governance for Africa: Rethinking Development Strategies* (Oxford and New York: Oxford University Press), pp. 3–47.

Schopenhauer, A. (1958) [published in 1818]. *The World as Will and Representation*, Volume 1, English translation by E. F. J. Payne, Indian Hills, Colorado, Falcon's Wing Press.

Stiglitz, J.E. (1996) "Some Lessons from the East Asian Miracle," *World Bank Research Observer*, vol. 11, no. 2, pp. 151–177. (Reprinted as "Algunas ensenanzas del milagro del Este Asiatico (with English summary)," *Desarrollo Economico*, vol. 37, no. 147, pp. 323–349.)

Stiglitz, J.E. (2011) "Rethinking Macroeconomics: What Failed and How to Repair It," *Journal of the European Economic Association*, vol. 9, no. 4, pp. 591–645.

Stiglitz, J.E. (2013) "Introduction to TICAD African Symposium" [FULL CITATION TK BEFORE PUBLICATION.]

World Bank (1993) *The East Asian Miracle: A World Bank Policy Research Report* (Washington, DC: The World Bank).

World Bank (2013) *Youth Employment in Africa* (Washington, DC: World Bank).

Part I
New Thinking on Industrial Policy

1.1
Learning and Industrial Policy: Implications for Africa[1]

Bruce Greenwald and Joseph E. Stiglitz
Columbia University

Over the past thirty years, Africa has suffered from deindustrialization. The quarter century from the early 1980s was a period of declining per capita income and increasing poverty. Structural adjustment policies advocated by the IMF and the World Bank were predicated on the belief that by eliminating "distortions" in the economy, Africa would grow faster – by constructing an economy based on principles of free and unfettered markets, with the government restrained to ensuring macro-stability (which typically just meant price stability), economic performance would be increased and all would benefit.

It was recognized, of course, that eliminating trade protection would result in the loss of jobs, some in agriculture, many others in industry. The strongly held belief, however, was that these workers would quickly find jobs in new industries, consistent with the country's comparative advantage. Moving resources from inefficient protected sectors to more efficient competitive sectors would raise incomes. Little attention was paid to the distribution of income, perhaps because of an implicit belief in trickledown economics – somehow, if the economic pie grew, all would benefit.

Things didn't turn out as the advocates of these policies had hoped. Rather than growth there was decline. Job creation didn't always keep pace with job destruction, and so workers moved from low-productivity protected sectors to even lower-productivity unemployment, open or disguised. When there was growth, the benefits often went disproportionately to those at the top, and didn't trickle down to the rest of the economy.

When, growth resumed, in the first decade of the 21st century it was largely based on the boom in commodity prices. The share of global manufacturing value added in Africa in 2008 was 1.1 percent in 2008, down from 1.2 percent in 2000 (UNCTAD, 2011). Even countries that achieved macroeconomic stability and evidenced reasonably good governance seemed unable to attract much investment outside of the extractive sector.

It is imperative that this course of events be changed, particularly since the extractive sector typically does not give rise to many jobs, and certainly not enough jobs for the burgeoning labor force in many of the countries. (The African labor force is expected to grow – working-age Africans today comprise some 500m people; by 2040, that number will be 1.1 billion.[2])

A propitious time for Africa

Fortunately, there are a set of events that may be propitious for the subcontinent. First, increasing wages and an appreciation of exchange rate in East Asia may enhance Africa's comparative advantage in manufacturing. The high levels of productivity growth in manufacturing – exceeding the increases in demand – imply that global employment in manufacturing will be declining; but it may be possible for Africa to seize a larger share of these jobs.

Moreover, there are some spillovers from even imperfectly managed natural resources: higher incomes give rise to a demand for more consumption, and some of this will be locally produced and/or serviced. There is an increasingly large middle class. Indeed, by some estimates, only around a quarter to a third of the sub-continent's recent growth is directly attributable to natural resources.[3]

Moreover, with the weaknesses in Europe and the United States that began with the Great Recession of 2008 looking likely to extend for at least a decade, those with funds are looking elsewhere for places in which to invest their money. Africa is looking more attractive, with its share of global foreign direct investment projects increasing to 5.5 percent in 2011.[4]

But many African countries still face serious disadvantages. Deficiencies in infrastructure increase both the cost of production and also the costs of bringing goods to market and of obtaining necessary inputs. There are also important shortages of skilled personnel, even in an environment in which unskilled workers are in abundance.

This paper is predicated on the belief that these disadvantages can be overcome by appropriate government policies, but such policies necessitate moving further away from the structural adjustment/Washington Consensus (WC) policies, by embracing industrial policies – policies that were shunned under the WC programs. Industrial policies are what we call those policies that help shape the sectoral composition of an economy. The term is used more broadly than just those policies that encourage the industrial sector. Thus a policy that encourages agro-business, or even agriculture, is referred to as an industrial policy.

Such government policies can enhance the ability of African economies to seize an even larger share of global foreign direct investment, to create new domestic enterprises, and to expand existing enterprises. While many countries within Africa are benefitting from natural resources, most countries have not taken full advantage of those resources, to create new industries and to provide employment for more of their citizens.

Industrial policies and market failures

At the International Economic Association/World Bank meeting on industrial policy in Washington, in May, 2012,[5] there was a broad consensus on why countries should have such policies: to correct market failures, situations where markets by themselves do not lead to efficient, or desirable, resource allocations; and in some cases, even to correct other government failures, where other, harder to alter, government policies "distort" resource allocations.

Market failures arise whenever private rewards and social returns differ, and since the work of Greenwald and Stiglitz (1986) it has been recognized that such discrepancies are pervasive. Industrial policies are designed to correct major sectoral or other misallocations.

Objectives of industrial policies

For Africa, there are at least three objectives of such policies. With many countries facing high unemployment, there is an imperative to create more jobs. The labor market is not working the way it does in neoclassical models, where there is full employment. That means that the market price of labor is almost surely markedly higher than the "shadow price," the opportunity cost of labor. Government should encourage labor-intensive sectors and technologies. To the extent possible, government should be sensitive to the kinds of labor that are being demanded, using both industrial and educational policies to bring the demand and supply of, say, school-leavers and university graduates into better alignment.

Secondly, many African countries have been marked by large increases in inequality.[6] Industrial policies can affect the extent of inequality, by increasing the demand for lower-skilled workers, driving up their wages and lowering their level of unemployment. While policies focusing on distribution have traditionally been centered on tax and transfers, it has long been recognized that it may be better (more efficient) to have policies that change the before-tax- and -transfer distribution of income. Such policies reduce the burden imposed by distortionary redistributive policies (Stiglitz, 1998a).

Thirdly, it has increasingly been recognized that development requires the structural transformation of the economy (see Lin, 2012; Stiglitz, 1998c). Markets themselves are not very good at such structural transformations, partly because the sectors that are being displaced – resources that have to move from one sector to another – typically suffer large wealth and income losses, and are thus not well placed to make the investments required for redeployment. And well-understood capital market imperfections (based on information asymmetries) limit access to outside resources.[7]

Fourthly, it has long been recognized that what separates developed from developing countries is not just a gap in resources, but rather a gap in knowledge (Stiglitz, 1998b). More broadly, even in developed countries a large fraction of the increase in per capita income over the last two centuries is attributable to technological progress, to learning how to produce things more efficiently (see Solow, 1957). And the fact that some countries and firms have "learned how to learn" helps explain why the last two centuries have seen such remarkable increases in standards of living, in comparison to the millennia that preceded it, which were marked by stagnation (see Maddison, 2001).

If this is so, then it means that development strategies should be centered on promoting learning, and closing the knowledge gap between developing countries and less developed countries.

Market failures, learning, and industrial policies[8]

We suggested earlier that industrial policies are motivated (in part) by an attempt to correct market failures, by the failure of markets by themselves to yield socially desirable outcomes. There can be too much inequality, too high unemployment, too little growth. This paper centers around the failure of markets in learning.

Knowledge is different from ordinary products. Knowledge is essentially a public good, that is, its consumption is non-rivalrous (Stiglitz, 1987a, 1999). When one individual shares knowledge with someone else, it does not diminish the amount of knowledge that the first person has. Markets by themselves are never efficient in the production and utilization of public goods. The producer of the knowledge may restrict the usage of the knowledge (through secrecy or patents), in an attempt to appropriate returns, in which case there is underutilization. More generally, there will be underproduction, because – even with effectively enforced patents – there are important spillovers from learning. What one firm or industry learns enhances the productivity of others. When learning is a by-product of investment or of production, a corollary is that there will be underinvestment or under production (Arrow, 1962; Stiglitz, 2012a).

There are other market failures associated with learning: because learning is a fixed, sunk cost, sectors in which learning is important are likely to be imperfectly competitive.[9] Because investments in learning cannot be collateralized, imperfections of capital markets may restrain research expenditures, say, relative to real estate speculation. With learning-by-doing, optimal production may entail firms increasing production today, beyond the point where they are breaking even, in return for the benefit of lower production costs in the future, but with capital market imperfections, firms cannot finance the ensuing losses (Dasgupta and Stiglitz, 1988a). The fact that investments in learning are highly risky, and risk markets are absent (especially in developing countries), also discourages such investments.[10]

The general theory of learning and industrial policies is taken up in Greenwald and Stiglitz (2014a, 2014b). Here, we focus on several topics that illustrate the general themes discussed there and that are of particular relevance to Africa.

The inevitability of industrial policy

First, however, we want to reiterate an important point raised in our earlier paper: governments are inevitably involved in industrial policy, in shaping the economy, both by what they do and by what they do not do. If they don't manage well the macro-economy, then more cyclically sensitive industries will be discouraged. If they use interest rate adjustments to stabilize the economy, interest sensitive sectors will suffer. If they don't stabilize the exchange rate, then non-traded sectors are encouraged.

Some are wont to say, just let market forces shape the economy, but market forces don't exist in a vacuum. Every market is shaped by laws, rules, and regulations. A bankruptcy law that gives priority to derivatives encourages these financial products. A bankruptcy law that says that student loans can't be discharged, even in bankruptcy, encourages banks to make more student loans. A tax law that provides for deductibility of mortgage interest leads to more mortgages. A tax law that taxes capital gains at lower rates than ordinary income encourages land and financial market speculation.

Moreover, in almost all countries, governments play a central role in education, health, infrastructure, and technology, and policies and expenditures in each of these areas – and the balance of spending among these areas – also shapes the economy. In short, all governments really do have an industrial policy. The only difference is between those who construct their industrial policy consciously, and those who let it be shaped by others, typically by special interests, who vie with each other for hidden and open subsidies, and for rules and regulations that favor them, usually at the expense of others. Even the agenda of financial market liberalization was an industrial policy – one pushed by the banks and the financial sector, the effect of which in many countries was to lead to a bloated financial sector, rife with explicit and implicit subsidies (reaching record levels in the crisis of 2008–09), diverting resources from other uses that arguably would have led to high sustained growth. It was an industrial policy that led to more macroeconomic instability, which, as we explain below, was itself adverse to learning.

1.1.1 The Washington Consensus and learning

The Washington Consensus policies referred to earlier in this paper focused on static efficiency. They didn't even consider the consequences for innovation and learning. If there was learning and technological progress, it was assumed to be exogenous, outside the purview of policy, and certainly outside the purview of the economic policies on which they focused. That this was so was striking, given the observation, made earlier, that development was so much about learning and economic transformation.

Standard theory has long recognized that there could be a trade-off between learning, or dynamic efficiency, and static efficiency. The patent system creates a temporary monopoly and imposes restrictions on the usage of knowledge, but these significant static inefficiencies are justified on the basis of the increased innovation that results.

The success of the most successful countries in development – those in East Asia – is largely attributable to their recognition of the importance of learning. Korea, for instance, paid little attention to its static comparative advantage. Its static comparative advantage would have led that country to focus on rice farming. But it knew that even if it became the most productive rice-farming country in the world, its prospects would be limited. It could prosper only by focusing on sectors from which it could learn, and on the basis of which it could close the knowledge gap with more advanced countries. It developed complementary education and technology policies, and it succeeded, increasing its per capita income more than eight-fold in a span of less than four decades.

Had it followed the dictates of the Washington Consensus policies[11] it would have eschewed industrial policies, and it would have focused investments in education at the primary level – and it would have, at best, been a middle-income rice-growing country. Unfortunately, many countries in Africa have followed the dictates of the Washington Consensus policies, and through the structural adjustment programs they have taken a step backwards, as we have noted, becoming increasingly resource-dependent economies.

The Washington Consensus policies were predicated on the assumption that markets, by themselves, are efficient; and that therefore the major source of inefficiency or malperformance of the economy arises from government intervention. Hence, the first item in the reform agenda is to eliminate these interventions with the market. The only role of the government was to ensure price stability.

Even before these doctrines became fashionable, their intellectual underpinnings had been taken away. Greenwald and Stiglitz (1986) showed, for instance, that whenever information was imperfect (asymmetric) and risk markets incomplete (which is always the case, and especially so in developing countries) markets are not constrained Pareto-efficient (that is, taking into account the costs of obtaining and disseminating information or creating and maintaining markets).

But the financial crisis of 2008 reinforced the conclusion that markets, on their own, may be massively inefficient, and unstable. It showed also that maintaining price stability did not necessarily lead either to growth, stability, or efficiency.[12]

In short, the crisis has re-emphasized the importance of market failures. It is thus natural that there should not only be a rethinking of macroeconomic theory and policy, but also of microeconomic theory and policy, including the most important subject for Africa today, that of industrial policy, of how governments can help change the structure of the economy to promote learning – thereby increasing long-term sustainable growth.

1.1.1.1 Learning and "one-size-fits-all" policies

One critique of the Washington Consensus is that it has attempted to impose "one-size-fits all" policies. Such policies may be particularly inappropriate when it comes to creating a learning society.

A critical aspect of "learning" is that it takes place locally and must adapt to local differences in culture and economic practice. Thus "learning" prescriptions that apply in some environments will not apply in others. For example, in some economies what has been called (by outsiders) "crony capitalism" has a long and successful record. In others it does not.[13] Learning how to relate to government has value in most economies, but, in some, the skills required may concern those related to bidding processes, in others to interpersonal connections. American firms have had to learn to adapt to the Foreign Corrupt Practices Act.[14] Labor norms differ too among countries, and personnel policies have to accommodate such differences. Differences in consumer preferences and norms as well as in distributional channels necessitate different "learning" about marketing. Most importantly, and perhaps obviously, relative factor prices may differ, so that the returns to learning on how to save on the utilization of one factor versus another may differ.

These cross-country differences have numerous implications. They help explain why learning in a firm may spill over more easily to other firms in the same country than to firms in other countries. The learning in one country may simply be less relevant to production in the other country.

They help explain too why it is that in some economies public enterprises function well. In others they do not.[15]

They also help explain the limitations of globalization: local firms have a competitive advantage in having more knowledge about local circumstances.[16] Much financial information is chiefly available locally, and even when information is available, outsiders may have less of an understanding of the nuances of the country's distinctive institutional structure – as foreign investors have learned to their cost about US mortgages. Thus, effective capital deployment will often require local financial institutions.

Unfortunately, Washington Consensus policies which pushed capital and financial market liberalization did not take into account this local knowledge. Foreign banks succeeded in attracting depositors away from local banks, because they were perceived as safer (and, in some cases, may have been, because they had the implicit guarantee of governments with deeper pockets). But foreign banks were at an information disadvantage relative to local banks about small and medium-sized local firms, and it was thus natural that lending be diverted away toward loans to government, consumers, and large domestic firms (including local monopolies and oligopolies). But in doing so, local learning and entrepreneurship may have been undermined, and growth weakened. Rashid's paper in this volume (2014) provides data strongly supporting this conclusion.[17]

By the same token, WTO restrictions on industrial policies and domestic sourcing (and possibly other restrictions on financial markets) may impede the ability of developing countries to foster learning, and to garner for themselves the full learning benefits of foreign direct investment, or, as we shall see shortly, it may force them to employ second-best methods for promoting learning within their economies.

1.1.2   Macro-conditions for creating a learning society

Most of this paper is concerned with microeconomic policies, but in our earlier paper (Greenwald and Stiglitz, 2014), we argued that one of the objectives of industrial policies is to create an economic environment that is conducive to learning. For this, the macroeconomic environment is central. Economic stability appears to play an important role in creating a successful "learning" environment. Evidence for this comes from the experience of developed economies during recessions. Productivity growth is normally low during contractions and there is no offsetting gain during subsequent expansions.[18] The productivity loss during the dislocation associated with the recession appears to be permanent.[19]

There are several reasons why stability is important for learning. The first is that much information is embodied within existing institutions, in complex webs of interactions. Key institutions – firms – often die in the face of high levels of instability.

Moreover, managerial attention is limited. When firms are focusing on survival, they have less attention to devote to "learning," except learning how to survive.

Thirdly, high levels of macro-instability lead firms to act in a more risk-averse manner. When firms go into recessions, among the first things to be cut are investments in R&D, and this is even true among firms that are relatively dependent on innovation. Part of the reason is that learning is future-oriented. One has to make sacrifices today and undertake risks today, for future benefits. But in the presence of instability, there is a risk that there will be no future – and hence less reason to make the requisite investments today. Instability weakens future oriented incentives.

And fourthly, learning requires resources, including access to capital. Instability may make capital less accessible and more costly.[20] In downturns, capital is likely to be rationed, and investments in R&D are often sacrificed.[21]

This has important implications for policy: policies that *expose* countries to a high level of instability, or that increase the economy's instability (for example, by weakening automatic stabilizers) have an adverse effect on learning. Examples include financial and capital market liberalization and deregulation (Rashid, 2012; Stiglitz et al., 2006; Stiglitz, 2008), and tarrification (Dasgupta and Stiglitz, 1977).

By the same token, policies that focus on price stability, at the expense of *real* stability, may actually be counterproductive (see Stiglitz et al., 2006). Inflation targeting, with its focus on price stability attained by interest rate adjustments, may be "doubly" bad: Responding to inflation by increasing interest rates – even when the cause of the inflation is an exogenous supply shock – is an example of a pro-cyclical policy. And the increases in interest rates have a disproportionate effect on certain sectors, those that are most interest sensitive and which rely most on bank financing. Small businesses, in particular, bear the burden. Small firms that may be killed when interest rates are raised dramatically don't come back to life when they are subsequently lowered: there are important hysteresis effects. This is especially important in developing countries where there may be a dearth of entrepreneurship. If, as some claim, much of the learning and innovation in society occurs within small and young enterprises, then these policies increase the burden on these key "learning" sectors. But whether that is the case or not, these policies exacerbate the already adverse effects arising from the cyclical volatility in the "shadow" cost of capital.

1.1.3 Exchange rate policy

The exchange rate affects the competitiveness of the economy – the ability of exporters to export and of import-competing firms to compete with imports. The consequences of an appreciation of the currency (say as a result of the inflow of capital or foreign aid) can be severe: if the exchange rate increases by say 25 percent, there is no way that (in the short run) productivity can compensate, or for there to be offsetting adjustments of wages and the prices of other inputs. Moreover, there are, as we have noted, important hysteresis effects: a firm that dies because it can't compete is not brought back to life when the exchange rate subsequently falls. (Capital market imperfections imply that small and medium-sized firms will be especially unable to obtain the capital required to tide them over.)

By the same token, it is expensive for firms (especially small and medium-sized domestic firms) to manage exchange rate volatility, especially in emerging markets and in the least developed countries. In many of these countries, there may be no markets in which firms can hedge their exchange rate risks.

Thus, like it or not, exchange rate policy affects the industrial structure. A decision not to actively manage the exchange rate will result in a more volatile exchange rate and a smaller traded goods sector than would otherwise be the case. In the context of Africa, the decision of many resource rich countries to allow their exchange rate to appreciate has contributed to deindustrialization, and even the weakening of the agriculture sector.

There are several implications of this analysis. First, governments need to adopt policies that make exchange rates less volatile, for example, capital controls (or more generally, they have to adopt a portfolio of tools for capital account management).[22]

Secondly, governments need to keep exchange rates "low" so as to make domestic firms more competitive – to expand exports and import-competing sectors, which may also necessitate the build-up of reserves. This is especially true because low exchange rates help export sectors like manufacturing, which have higher learning elasticities and generate more learning externalities (see Greenwald and Stiglitz, 2006; 2014b).

But a concern about industrial policy means governments need to be attentive to *how* they intervene to stabilize and lower the exchange rate. If to prevent a large decline in the exchange rate they increase interest rates (as was the wont of the IMF), while they may thereby save large numbers of enterprises who have taken on foreign-denominated debts, at the same time they may kill other enterprises that were more prudent and took on only domestic debt. The effects may be particularly adverse to small and medium-sized enterprises (who typically do not take on foreign debt, because they do not have access to international markets) – as was evident in the East Asian crisis (Furman and Stiglitz, 1998).

There are alternative ways of stabilizing the exchange rates, and, even more so, keeping exchange rates low, which may be less costly – in particular, direct intervention, with the consequent build-up of reserves. Some have suggested that it is impossible to push the exchange rate down for more than a short period of time. But such arguments are based on a confusion: it is impossible to keep exchange rates above the "market" level through direct intervention, because to do so requires selling dollars (or other hard currency), and countries only have limited amounts of these in their reserves. But to push the exchange rate down requires selling one's own currency, and buying dollars (or other hard currencies), and this countries can easily do.

There are other instruments available for affecting especially the *level* of the exchange rate. Any regulation that affects the flow of money out of or into the country affects the exchange rate. Thus, making it easier for foreign companies to invest in the country leads to the appreciation of the currency; making it more difficult leads to the depreciation of the currency. In assessing foreign direct investment policy, one has to weigh the benefits of access to markets or technology or training with the costs to the rest of the economy from the exchange rate appreciation (including the adverse effects on learning). By the same token, loosening restrictions on citizens of the country investing their money abroad lowers the exchange rate. Since most countries have a broad array of regulations affecting inward and outward investment, there is, in a sense, no "free market" exchange rate. Through these regulations and through interest rates, as well as through direct interventions, governments "set" the exchange rate, either intentionally or not.

A lower exchange rate represents a broad-based mechanism for industrial policy – firms themselves decide whether they can compete at that lower exchange rate. The government has identified broadly that the export sector has more learning externalities, and therefore that sector should be encouraged relative to others; but it doesn't have to identify precisely which subsectors or firms should be encouraged. The market does that.

This has both an advantage and a disadvantage. More finely-tuned targeting may increase the overall (dynamic) efficiency of the economy; after all, each firm or sector takes no account of the extent of the benefits that accrue to others. A more targeted approach can offset the externality associated with research or learning in each sector. On the other hand, government attempts at fine-tuning may encounter more severe "political economy" problems. (See the discussion below.)

There are two questions about the use of each of the instruments. First, what really matters is the real exchange rate. The question is: can government affect, at least more than just briefly, the real exchange rate? Here, the critical question is the extent and speed of "pass through." For very open economies, importing and exporting a large fraction of their goods, lowering the nominal exchange rate leads to increases in nominal prices, which can undo the benefits, unless, say, monetary authorities take actions to dampen the potential inflation, but such actions themselves have costs (for example, higher unemployment). It is clear that many countries have managed to lower their *real* exchange rate for an extended period of time, and have done so at the same time that they have promoted growth.

Secondly, what are the costs of each of the interventions, and do the benefits exceed the costs? Some worry that the costs of preventing inflation from direct intervention are too high. The East Asian countries have managed to intervene in the exchange rate over long periods of time without facing either high inflation, or high costs of avoiding inflation. But, at least in China, there is another growing concern: to keep the value of their currency low, they have bought dollars, which yield a low return. Worse, dollars are depreciating relative to the RMB, implying that they are experiencing a (paper) capital loss.

Industrial policies can intervene in relative prices in ways that avoid these costs (and which can in fact be more targeted than lowering the real exchange rate), for example, by sectoral subsidies (including subsidized interest rates) or "infant industry" protection. But international trade agreements restrict the use of industrial policies. The only instrument left may be the exchange rate. Lowering the exchange rate simultaneously decreases the price of exports in foreign currency, leading to an increase in the demand for exports, and increases the price of imports (in domestic currency, relative to the price of non-traded goods). It thus encourages substitution away from imported consumption goods. Increased exports and reduced imports lead to a trade surplus.

In a two-period model, this means that the country consumes less than it could in the initial period, offset by increased consumption in the later period.[23] The static distortion (consuming less than what would normally maximize utility, based on the equality of the marginal rate of substitution and the interest rate) is justified by the dynamic benefits – producing more of the export good, say, leads to more learning, which generates a higher level of consumption in the second period than would otherwise be possible.

But if the learning effects are strong enough, even in an infinite period model, the benefits of expanding exports are sufficiently great that it may be possible that optimal policy requires the country to build up reserves forever, never to use them (essentially like throwing money away). The benefits of learning exceed the costs of the "forced saving" required to ensure that the exchange rate remains competitive. One can construct a model in which each period the world looks as it did the previous period, so that if it is desirable to have a surplus at time t, it is desirable to have a trade surplus at time $t + 1$.[24] (Of course, in a more general dynamic model, it may be desirable to have trade surpluses initially, to be spent at later dates.)

1.1.4 Investment policies

In some (but not all) of the successful countries, foreign direct investment (FDI) has played an important role.[25] For some countries with limited access to finance, FDI can be an important source of funds. But even in those countries with high savings rates, champions of FDI extoll its virtue in terms of the transfer of knowledge. But this doesn't happen automatically, and the learning spillovers are more important for some forms of FDI than others. Thus, there are two questions facing industrial policies: How can FDI, especially of the kind that might have more learning spillovers be promoted? And how can the amount of learning that results from any FDI that does occur be increased?

The theory of localized technological change (Atkinson and Stiglitz, 1969) explains that the spillovers from learning associated with one technology are more likely to be greater for "nearby" technologies. What matters is both the *relevance* of the knowledge associated with one technology for the improvement of another, and the *capacity* of those employing one technology to learn from another.

As Greenwald and Stiglitz (2014a) explain, spillovers may well be stronger across sectors for similar technologies than within the sector for markedly different technologies. Thus, just-in-time inventory practices have benefits for many sectors in which inventories play an important role.

Much of the knowledge that is embedded in, say, mining technologies is of limited relevance to most other sectors of the economy. Thus, the learning benefits of FDI associated with resource extraction are likely to be much more limited than those associated with, say, manufacturing, and this may help explain why so many resource-dependent economies remain "dual" economies, with few spillovers from the natural resource sector to the rest of the economy. If this is so, it means that FDI in this area – one that has dominated in Africa – is of much less benefit than FDI in other areas.

While it may be easiest to learn about adjacent technologies, the benefits of such learning may be more limited than those associated with making larger steps (sometimes referred to as leapfrogging). There is then a complicated optimization problem: Both the costs and benefits increase the larger the step. Moreover, one wants to move toward technologies from which one can learn the best going forward, and that may not always be easy to assess from one's current vantage point. Korea and Japan's industrial development was characterized by strategies that did involve moving some distance from the technologies that they were then employing.

The discussion so far has focused on "learning," but even more important is "learning to learn" (Stiglitz, 1987c). Industrial and trade policy can enhance an economy's learning capacities, its underlying "capabilities," and development strategies need to be focused on that, especially in an era with fast-changing technologies, where specific knowledge learned at one moment risks rapid obsolescence.

1.1.4.1 Government subsidies for FDI and other investment-related activities to promote learning

Government subsidies for FDI have typically been justified in terms of the government revenue and employment generated. But our analysis suggests another rationale: learning. But if this is so, then subsidies should be larger for those sectors and technologies that are likely to have large spillovers, and for firms that are willing to engage in practices that enhance the likelihood of such learning.

In many cases, entrepreneurial spillovers may be larger in the case of domestic enterprises than foreign, since domestic firms are likely to be more firmly embedded within the local community. Government policy should, accordingly, provide some preference for domestic firms relative to foreign firms, except when there are strong learning benefits that are specifically related to foreign firms, for example, because the foreign firm brings knowledge that is not locally available.

Government policies can affect factor prices, and therefore the level of investment, and thus the level of learning. The benefits of learning can more than offset the social costs of the distortion.

Compulsory employment/training programs and domestic procurement requirements (programs that compel firms to source locally) are more likely to lead to learning spillovers. The success of Malaysia's FDI was partially attributable to such requirements.

1.1.5   Making the most of one's natural resources

We noted earlier the large dependence of African economies on resource exports. In the previous section we argued that linkages between natural resource production and other sectors were typically weaker than, say, between manufacturing and the rest of the economy, helping to explain why there is typically such a large gap between the state of technology in the mining and natural resource sector and other sectors of African economies, and explaining in part why the abundance of natural resources has often not been accompanied by the hoped-for increases in standards of living.

The latter failure, which has become known as the "resource curse" or the "paradox of plenty" (Humphreys, Sachs, and Stiglitz, 2007; Karl, 1997), is partly explained by macroeconomic problems of high volatility and non-competitive exchange rates that mark resource-rich countries. We have explained why volatility and high exchange rates are especially bad for the creation of a learning economy, and thus for long-run increases in standards of living. But there are well-known effective policy responses, including stabilization and sovereign wealth funds and care in borrowing from abroad, especially in periods of commodity price booms.

But industrial policies have not played as important a role in addressing the problems of the resource curse as they should have done. This is partly because the issues on which we have focused in this paper (and this volume more generally) have not received the attention that they should.

Historically, African countries were thought of simply as a source of raw materials. In the development of the mines, little or no attention was given to how that development might affect the broader development of the economy (other than through the availability of resource rents). Transportation systems were designed to move the resources out of the country, not to promote the broader development of the country.

Trade policies in developed countries in the post-colonial era reinforced these colonial-era policies. Escalating tariffs, for instance, discouraged the development of value-added activities within the country. Neoclassical economics provided a rationale for reinforcing policies: because most present-day African countries do not have a static comparative advantage in these value-added activities, they have been discouraged from developing them. The only circumstances in which such activities might make sense (from that perspective) are when transportation costs offset these disadvantages – that is, it may make sense to do some processing if in doing so the costs of transportation are thereby reduced.

But from a learning–development perspective, matters look markedly different. One of the reasons that African countries may not have done as well as others is that the "natural" (market-driven) learning spillovers from mining and natural resource industries to the rest of the economy are less than those from, say, manufacturing. In this view, then, the high exchange rate and high volatility marking most natural resource-dependent countries has led to an economic structure that has discouraged activities with large learning spillovers. Better macro-policies (leading to less volatility and lower exchange rates) can go some way to correcting this distortion. But so can industrial policies, by leveraging off the countries' resource base (in which at least some countries have a degree of monopoly power).

This entails exploiting upstream, downstream, and horizontal linkages (Hirschman, 1958), and linkages that might be associated with processing and resource extracting itself. Some developing countries (like Malaysia) have actually succeeded in developing capabilities in resource extraction, by imposing employment and training conditions on foreign operators.

Even if much of resource extraction technology itself is not closely linked with other technologies that might provide the basis of broader growth and learning, many of the sub-activities entailed in the long and complex process of removing natural resources do. Buildings have to be built and people have to be hired. Workers have to be fed. There is a demand for people and vehicles for transportation and logistics. In short, for many African countries, the exploration and development of these linkages can be the basis of an effective industrial policy, one which enhances the capabilities of the people and firms within them. (For a more extensive discussion, see Jourdan, 2014.)

1.1.6 Distribution, employment, and environmental concerns

Standard industrial policy focused on changing the sectoral composition of GDP to enhance growth – in our case, to enhance learning. But it should be emphasized that the failure of markets to incorporate learning externalities is only one market failure, one instance in which private rewards and social returns are misaligned, and any misalignment provides a rationale for industrial policy.

Of particular relevance for many African countries are distribution, the environment, and employment. The market, by itself, seems to be creating too few jobs, is associated with socially unacceptable levels of inequality, and has adverse impacts on the environment. Industrial policy can and should be directed at each of these; and in some cases, policies directed at mitigating one problem may have benefits in addressing another.

More generally, what matters is not GDP, but the quality of life, "well-being" and the enhancement of individual and societal capabilities. What that entails – and how performance can be better measured,[26] and how better measured performance can be increased through industrial policy – should and can be a subject of rational inquiry.

For instance, environmental impacts are important for all countries, but especially for developing countries. The fact that natural resources and the environment are "underpriced" means that there are insufficient incentives to allocate resources (including those devoted to learning) toward the environment and natural resources – so more get expended on saving labor, even though labor is in surplus.

This highlights a difference between developed and developing countries, and a reason why it is important that developing countries have their own innovation policies. Much of innovation in advanced industrial economies has been directed toward saving labor. But in many developing countries, labor is in surplus, and unemployment is the problem. Labor-saving innovations exacerbate this key social problem.

Even when labor-saving innovation does not result in unemployment, it will have adverse distributional consequences, lowering wages. With inequality already so high in many African countries, this should be of concern.

But there are further reasons that we should be concerned about growing inequality. It can lead to increased political and social instability. There is, moreover, a growing understanding, even within the IMF, that inequality may lead to lower economic growth, more economic instability, and a weaker economy (Stiglitz, 2012b; Berg and Ostry, 2011). While there are many channels through which these adverse effects operate (for example, inequality diminishes the aggregate demand for domestic non-traded goods), one may be of particular importance in developing countries, where there is a need for heavy public investments in infrastructure, education, and technology.

In a society with very little inequality, the only role of the state is to provide collective goods and correct market failures. When there are large inequalities, interests differ. Distributive battles inevitably rage, and to prevent redistribution, wealthy elites often try to circumscribe the powers of government. But in circumscribing government, the ability to perform positive roles is also circumscribed. As we have argued here and elsewhere, government needs to play an important role in any economy, correcting pervasive market failures, but especially in the "creative economy."

Thus, our critique of non-inclusive growth goes beyond pointing out that it is a waste of a country's most valuable resource – its human talent – to fail to ensure that everyone lives up to his or her abilities. Non-inclusive growth can also lead to democracies that do not support high-growth strategies. There can be a vicious circle, with more inequality leading to a more circumscribed government, leading in turn to more inequality and slower growth.

The analysis of this section has several obvious but important implications: (i) Developing countries cannot just "borrow"/adapt technology from the North. There is a need for a new "model" of innovation. (ii) In particular, innovation needs to be directed (through industrial policies) at saving resources, protecting the environment, and improving the distribution of income. (iii) These objectives may be intertwined – industrial policies that promote more inclusiveness may promote more learning; better environmental policies may lead to a better distribution of income.

1.1.7 Political economy

One of the standard objections to industrial policies in the past has been political: the potential for misuse. The question is raised, can there be effective industrial policies in countries with significant deficiencies in governance? The argument has been put that even if such policies contributed greatly to the success of East Asia, elsewhere they were less successful, because they were abused. Critics suggest that industrial policies were largely to blame for Latin America's lost decade. The implication is that, while the ideal Government intervention might improve matters, in the "real world" interventions do not necessarily do so. Given the widely acknowledged deficiencies in governance in many African countries, they should shy away from such policies.

There are several responses to these objections. One is methodological: such political economy objections may be true – but the conclusion is based on political analysis, not economic analysis. And the political analysis is often more simplistic than economic analysis. The first question is not whether in some cases such interventions have failed, but whether in some instances they have succeeded, and the answer to that is unambiguously, yes. The second question is whether there are policies and institutions that can be adopted that are more likely to lead to success, that at least reduce the likelihood or extent of abuse.

Moreover, similar questions can be raised about every other aspect of policy. Many governments have not used monetary and financial regulatory policy well; in some cases, the misuse can be traced to problems of governance (some have argued that regulators and central banks in some advanced industrial countries were captured by special interests in the financial market, and this played an important role in the 2008 global economic crisis.)[27] But few would argue that as a result, governments should eschew the use of monetary and financial regulatory policy.[28]

1.1.7.1 Historical interpretation

We observed earlier that there is ample evidence that countries have successfully used industrial policies. Indeed, there are few successful economies in which the government has not successfully employed industrial policies, broadly understood.

Moreover, it is widely acknowledged that at the time that many of the East Asian countries began their industrial policies, not only was their economic development lower than some of the less developed countries today, but so too was their political development.

The conclusion that industrial policies were a failure in Latin America is, at best, contentious, at worst, simply wrong. Brazil, the most ardent adopter of such policies, had an impressive growth rate of almost 6 percent in the three quarters of a century before 1980. Industrial policies played an important role in that country's success in this period. The lost decade was a result of Latin American countries' excessive indebtedness in the 1970s, the period of the oil shock – understandable, perhaps, given the low, or even negative, real interest rates at which the petro-dollars were being recycled – followed by the unprecedented increase in interest rates, a result of the United States suddenly switching its monetary policy regime to monetarism. The lost decade of the 1980s was, in short, a result of a macroeconomic shock, rather than a failure of microeconomic policies. The subsequent adoption of the Washington Consensus policies, which eschewed industrial policies, prolonged the subsequent period of slow growth. The more recent revival of growth in Brazil, for example, has much to do with the government once again undertaking activist policies (Bértola and Ocampo, 2012).

In short, the historical experience shows that industrial policies can work. Even instances of failure need to be interpreted with caution. Good policies involve some risk – if every public or private investment succeeded, it would be indicative of insufficient risk taking. There are undoubtedly instances where industrial policy has failed because of abuses. But the relevant question is: are the problems inherent in political processes? The historical record suggests strongly that failure is not inevitable. The historical record does suggest caution, especially in countries with poor governance. And it suggests that countries do what they can to improve governance; there are institutional reforms in the political process that would reduce the risk of failure.

1.1.7.2   Implications of governance deficiencies for the design of industrial policies

But reforms to political processes are slow. The implication of deficiencies in governance is that one needs to tailor the design of the instruments of industrial policy around the capabilities and governance of the public sector.

This poses an important trade-off. Broad-based measures such as exchange rate interventions require only that the government ascertain that the sectors that would be encouraged by such interventions have more societal learning benefits than the sectors that would be discouraged – and there is ample evidence that that is the case (evidenced by the success of export-led growth strategies). Firms and sectors within the economy self-select, and the expansion of firms and sectors with greater learning enhances the dynamism of the economy. On the other hand, more targeted interventions can lead to even more learning and faster rates of growth.

Of course, no intervention completely "solves" the political economy problem: Sectors that benefit from exchange rate intervention may lobby for the maintenance of that intervention even in the absence of learning benefits.

Some countries have shown that they can manage the political economy problems of more targeted interventions. The East Asian countries did so by using rule-based systems in which interventions were linked to past export success.

The East Asian countries used the quest for "rents" in a positive way: competition for rents led to firms that learned more and became more competitive in the global marketplace. In other countries, though, rent seeking has diverted resources away from growth-inducing innovation. Firms have devoted their resources to learning how to circumvent regulations designed to make the economy more stable and to learning how to exploit consumers and their monopoly power better. Markets don't work well when private returns are not well aligned with social returns; and in those circumstances, incentives to innovate and learn are also distorted.

1.1.7.3   Liberalization and political economy

Finally, we note that liberalization is itself a political agenda. As we previously commented, markets do not exist in a vacuum. There are always going to be rules and regulations, even in a liberalized world. And the design of those rules and regulations will shape markets. The rules and regulations that were adopted in the process of "liberalizing" and deregulating financial markets in the United States and the United Kingdom led to bloated financial institutions backed by implicit guarantees from the monetary authority and ultimately the taxpayer – a perhaps unintentional industrial policy that distorted the economy.

1.1.8   Concluding comments

The central thesis of this paper is that pervasive market failures (and other distortions that result in private rewards being misaligned with social returns) provide a rationale for industrial policies – government interventions in sectoral allocations. We focused on one particular set of market failures, those that arise in the process of learning: Learning is especially important for developing countries as they strive to close the gap between their incomes and those of the more developed countries. A central focus of development policy should be how to promote learning and how to create a "learning economy and society." We noted that much of the advice of the past, based on neoclassical models, not only gave short shrift to these concerns, but may actually have led to counterproductive policy prescriptions that were adverse to learning, and hence to long-term increases in standards of living.

A focus on creating a learning society has broad implications for financial and capital market liberalization, the design of monetary policy and institutions, macroeconomic policies, intellectual property regimes, investment treaties, taxation, and expenditures on infrastructure, education, and technology, legal frameworks for corporate governance and bankruptcy – indeed for the entire economic regime. All need to be viewed through a learning perspective. Some have direct effects on learning, some have longer-term effects on learning capabilities or how they impact the acquisition of learning capabilities, while some have indirect effects, for example, as they create more macro-instability, which has adverse effects on investments in learning. Some have multiple effects.[29]

For Africa, as it attempts to reindustrialize, to restructure its economies to become more integrated into the global economy and move away from excessive dependence on commodity exports, to raise standards of income, increase employment, reduce poverty and inequality, and to protect a fragile environment, industrial policies are especially important. We have explained why the widely cited objections – that though industrial policy may have worked in East Asia, it is inappropriate for Africa because of deficiencies in governance – are unpersuasive. Governance issues are, of course, relevant in all countries, and are important in shaping the form that industrial policy takes and the instruments that are appropriately used.

The belated recognition of the potential of these policies comes at a fortunate time, for changes in the global economy may afford the countries of Africa a distinct opportunity to transform their economies in a way that will, at long last, narrow the gap that separates standards of living in the subcontinent from that of much of the rest of the world.

Notes

1. Paper presented to an International Economic Association roundtable conference on "New Thinking on Industrial Policy: Implications for Africa," Pretoria, July 3–4, 2012, co-sponsored by the World Bank, UNIDO, and the South African Economic Development Department. Research support from Laurence Wilse-Samson and the helpful comments of the other participants in the seminar is gratefully acknowledged. This paper is a companion to B. Greenwald and J.E. Stiglitz, "Industrial Policies, the Creation of a Learning Society, and Economic Development," presented to the International Economic Association/World Bank Industrial Policy Roundtable in Washington, DC, May 22–3, 2012 (Greenwald and Stiglitz, 2014a). Both papers are based on Greenwald and Stiglitz (2006) and Stiglitz (2014b, 2012a).
2. McKinsey, 2010.
3. See for example, McKinsey, 2010, Ibid. Exhibit 1 indicates that 24 percent of the growth between 2000 and 2008 in sub-Saharan Africa is attributable to resources (but a further 8 percent is derived from resource-financed government expenditure).
4. See Ernst & Young (2012).
5. Proceedings available as Lin and Stiglitz (2013) in accompanying volume.
6. It is difficult to track inequality due to data limitations. The Africa Progress Report (Africa Progress Panel 2012) states that 24 countries in Africa have Gini coefficients in excess of 42, the level in China. It also points out that in a number of cases, recent growth has not been matched by falling poverty – which they attribute to inequality (p.16), "In many countries, the pattern of economic growth is reinforcing these inequalities."

7. See Delli Gatti et al. (2012a, 2012b).
8. See Greenwald and Stiglitz (2014b), for a more extensive discussion of these market failures.
9. Moreover, potential competition is not an effective substitute for actual competition. See Dasgupta and Stiglitz (1988b); Stiglitz (1987b).
10. These failures (imperfections in capital markets) can themselves be explained by imperfections of information.
11. Broadly understood – not in the more restricted sense that the term was used by Williamson (1989).
12. For a discussion of the implications of the crisis for economic theory and policy, see Stiglitz (2011).
13. It is, perhaps, worth noting that what is viewed as corruption in one society may not be so viewed in that way by others. Many point to the American system of large campaign contributions and revolving doors, which seems to "buy" favorable legislation as a form of corruption, even if there isn't money stuffed into brown paper envelopes for the politicians themselves.
14. Dixit (2012) has argued that firms from developing countries may have a knowledge advantage in dealing with governments of other developing countries.
15. Herbert Simon emphasized that if there are differences in the performance of public and private enterprises, the differences could not be explained just by differences in incentives, since in both typically most individuals work for others, and have to be incentivized. See, for example, Simon (1991, 1995).
    "This examination of authority and organizational identification should help explain how organizations can be highly productive even though the relation between their goals and the material rewards received by employees, if it exists at all, is extremely indirect and tenuous. In particular, it helps explain why careful comparative studies have generally found it hard to identify systematic differences in productivity and efficiency between profit-making, nonprofit, and publicly controlled organizations" (Simon 1995: 288).
16. See Greenwald and Kahn (2005).
17. Greenwald and Stiglitz (2003) present the general theory.
18. There are exceptions, including the increase in productivity in the current US recession. While there are several explanations of this distinctive aspect of the downturn, one is that the increasingly shortsighted behavior of firms ignores the long run costs of firing or laying off trained workers. In that case, it will still be the case that there will be long-run adverse effects of the downturn on productivity. In the Great Depression productivity growth also appears to have been quite high in part due to important investments made by government (including in transportation) (Field, 2011).
19. This is, of course, consistent, with standard results on unit roots. See Dickey and Fuller (1981) and Phillips and Perron (1986).
20. This can be put slightly differently: With capital (debt and equity rationing) the shadow price of capital often increases dramatically. (See Greenwald, Stiglitz, and Weiss, 1984; Greenwald and Stiglitz, 2003).
21. Greenwald, Salinger, and Stiglitz (1990); Stiglitz (1994).
22. Moreover, as we noted above, learning benefits from having a stable environment.
23. See Stiglitz (2012a).
24. See Greenwald and Stiglitz, (2014b).
25. FDI did not play an important role in several of the countries of the East Asian miracle (Korea, Taiwan, and Japan).

26. See, in particular, Stiglitz, Sen, and Fitoussi (2010).
27. See, for example, Stiglitz (2010).
28. Though some conservatives do argue, on this basis, that there should be a return to the gold standard, and that there should be no role for discretionary monetary policy. However, since the failure of monetarism, these extreme positions have garnered little support among economists.
29. That is the case, for instance, for financial liberalization, which may lead to more macroeconomic volatility, and less access to finance by domestic small and medium sized firms, thus impeding the development of domestic entrepreneurship capabilities. See Rashid (2012, 2014) and Emran and Stiglitz (2009).

References

Africa Progress Panel (2012) "Jobs, Justice and Equity," *Africa Progress Report 2012*. Available online at http://www.africaprogresspanel.org/en/pressroom/press-kits/annual-report-2012/africa-progress-report-2012-documents/ (accessed November 2, 2012).

Arrow, K. (1962) "The Economic Implications of Learning by Doing," *Review of Economic Studies*, vol. 29, no. 3, pp. 155–173.

Atkinson, A.B., and Stiglitz, J.E. (1969) "A New View of Technological Change," *Economic Journal*, vol. 79, no. 315, pp. 573–578.

Berg, Andrew, and Ostry, Jonathan D. (2011) "Inequality and Unsustainable Growth: Two Sides of the Same Coin?," *IMF Staff Discussion Note* 11/08 (Washington: International Monetary Fund).

Bértola, Luis and Ocampo, José Antonio (2012) "Latin America's Debt Crisis and 'Lost Decade,'" presented at Institute for the Study of the Americas, "Learning from Latin America: Debt Crises, Debt Rescues and When and Why They Work," February 20, 2012. Available at http://americas.sas.ac.uk/events/videos-podcasts-and-papers/ (accessed September 26, 2012).

Dasgupta, P. and Stiglitz, J.E. (1977) "Tariffs Versus Quotas As Revenue Raising Devices Under Uncertainty," *American Economic Review*, vol. 67, no. 5, pp. 975–981.

Dasgupta, P. and Stiglitz, J.E. (1988a) "Learning by Doing, Market Structure, and Industrial and Trade Policies," *Oxford Economic Papers*, vol. 40, no. 2, pp. 246–268.

Dasgupta, P. and Stiglitz, J.E. (1988b) "Potential Competition, Actual Competition and Economic Welfare," *European Economic Review*, vol. 32, no. 2, pp. 569–577.

Delli Gatti, D., Gallegati, M., Greenwald, B., Russo, A., and Stiglitz, J.E. (2012a) "Mobility Constraints, Productivity Trends, and Extended Crises," *Journal of Economic Behavior and Organization*, forthcoming.

Delli Gatti, D., Gallegati, M., Greenwald, B., Russo, A., and Stiglitz, J.E. (2012b) "Sectoral Dislocations and Long Run Cycles," forthcoming in the Proceedings of the International Economic Association's 2011 Meetings.

Dickey, D.A., and Fuller, W. (1981) "Likelihood Ratio Statistics for Autoregresive Time Series with a Unit Root," *Econometrica*, vol. 49 pp. 1057–1072.

Dixit, A. (2012) "Governance, Development, and Foreign Direct Investment," Max Weber Lecture, European University Institute, Florence, Italy, January.

Emran, M.S. and Stiglitz, J.E. (2009) "Financial Liberalization, Financial Restraint and Entrepreneurial Development," working paper. Available at http://www.gwu.edu/~iiep/assets/docs/papers/Emran_IIEPWP20.pdf.

Ernst & Young (2012) "FDI into Africa accelerates as investor perceptions begin to shift," May 3. Available at http://www.ey.com/GL/en/

Newsroom/News-releases/FDI-into-Africa-accelerates-as-investor-perceptions-begin-to-shift (accessed November 2, 2012).

Field, A. (2011) *A Great Leap Forward: 1930s Depression and US Economic Growth* (New Haven, CT: Yale University Press).

Furman, J. and Stiglitz, J.E. (1998) "Economic Crises: Evidence and Insights from East Asia," *Brookings Papers on Economic Activity*, 1998(2), pp.1–114. (Presented at Brookings Panel on Economic Activity, Washington, September 3, 1998.)

Greenwald, Bruce C. and Stiglitz, J.E. (2014b) *Creating a Learning Society: A New Approach to Growth, Development and Social Progress (First Annual Lecture in Honor of Kenneth Arrow at Columbia University)* (New York: Columbia University Press).

Greenwald, B. and Kahn, J. (2005) *Golbalization: The Irrational Fear that Someone in China Will Take Your Job* (Hoboken, NJ: John Wiley & Sons).

Greenwald, B. and Stiglitz, J.E. (1986) "Externalities in Economies with Imperfect Information and Incomplete Markets," *Quarterly Journal of Economics*, vol. 101, no. 2, pp. 229–264. Reprinted in Nicholas Barr (ed.) (2000) *Economic Theory and the Welfare State*, Nicholas Barr (Cheltenham, UK: Edward Elgar).

Greenwald, B. and Stiglitz, J.E. (2003) *Towards a New Paradigm in Monetary Economics* (Cambridge: Cambridge University Press).

Greenwald, B. and Stiglitz, J.E. (2006) "Helping Infant Economies Grow: Foundations of Trade Policies for Developing Countries," *American Economic Review: AEA Papers and Proceedings*, vol. 96, no. 2, pp. 141–146.

Greenwald, B. and Stiglitz, J.E. (2014a) "Industrial Policies, the Creation of a Learning Society, and Economic Development," in Part I of this volume.

Greenwald, B., Salinger, M., and Stiglitz, J.E. (1990) "Imperfect Capital Markets and Productivity Growth," paper presented at NBER Conference in Vail, CO, April 1990, revised March 1991 and April 1992.

Greenwald, B., Stiglitz, J.E., and Weiss, A. (1984) "Informational Imperfections in the Capital Market and Macroeconomic Fluctuations," *American Economic Review*, vol. 74, no. 2, pp. 194–199.

Hirschman, A. (1958) *The Strategy of Economic Development* (New Haven, CT: Yale University Press).

Humphreys, M., Sachs, J., and Stiglitz, J.E. (eds) (2007) *Escaping the Resource Curse* (New York: Columbia University Press).

Jourdan, Paul (2014) "Towards a Resource-Based African Industrial Policy," in this volume.

Karl, Terry Lynn (1997) *The Paradox of Plenty* (Berkeley: University of California Press).

Lin, J.Y. (2012) *New Structural Economics: A Framework for Rethinking Development and Policy* (Washington, DC: The World Bank).

Lin, J.Y. and Stiglitz, (2014) The Industrial Policy Revolution I: The Role of Government Beyond Ideology, (New York and Houndmills, UK: Palgrave Macmillan.)

Maddison, A. (2001) *The World Economy: A Millennial Perspective*, Development Center of the Organization for Economic Co-Operation and Development (Paris: OECD).

Phillips, P.D.B., and Perron, P. (1986) "Testing for a Unit Root in Time Series Regression." Universite de Montreal. Centre de Recherche et Developpement en Economique 2186, Cahier, Canada.

Rashid, H. (2012) "Foreign Banks, Competition for Deposits and Terms and Availability of Credit in Developing Countries," working paper.

Rashid, H. (2014) "Does Financial Market Liberalization Promote Financial Development?," in this volume.

Simon, H.A. (1991) "Organizations and Markets," *Journal of Economic Perspectives*, vol. 5, no. 2, pp. 25–44.

Simon, H.A. (1995) "Organizations and Markets," *Journal of Public Administration Research and Theory*, vol. 5, no. 3, pp. 273–294.

Solow, R.M. (1957) "Technical Change and the Aggregate Production Function," *Review of Economics and Statistics*, vol. 39, no. 3, pp. 312–320.

Stiglitz, J.E. (1987a) "On the Microeconomics of Technical Progress," in Jorge M. Katz (ed.), *Technology Generation in Latin American Manufacturing Industries* (London: Macmillan Press), pp. 56–77. (Presented to IDB-CEPAL Meetings, Buenos Aires, November 1978.)

Stiglitz, J.E. (1987b) "Technological Change, Sunk Costs, and Competition," *Brookings Papers on Economic Activity*, vol. 3, pp. 883–947.

Stiglitz, J.E. (1987c) "Learning to Learn, Localized Learning and Technological Progress," in P.S. Dasgupta and P. Stoneman (eds), *Economic Policy and Technological Performance* (Cambridge, UK: Cambridge University Press), pp. 125–153.

Stiglitz, J.E. (1994) "Endogenous Growth and Cycles," in Y. Shionoya and M. Perlman (eds.), *Innovation in Technology, Industries, and Institutions* (Ann Arbor, MI:The University of Michigan Press), pp. 121–156.

Stiglitz, J.E. (1998a) "Pareto Efficient Taxation and Expenditure Policies, With Applications to the Taxation of Capital, Public Investment, and Externalities," presented at conference in honor of Agnar Sandmo, January 1998.

Stiglitz, J.E. (1998b) "Knowledge for Development: Economic Science, Economic Policy, and Economic Advice," in B. Pleskovic and J. Stiglitz (eds), *Annual World Bank Conference on Development Economics* (Washington, DC: World Bank), pp. 9–58.

Stiglitz, J.E. (1998c) "Towards a New Paradigm for Development: Strategies, Policies and Processes," 9th Raul Prebisch Lecture delivered at the Palais des Nations, Geneva, October 19, 1998, UNCTAD. Chapter 2 in Ha-Joon Chang (ed.) (2001), *The Rebel Within* (London: Wimbledon Publishing Company), pp. 57–93.

Stiglitz, J.E. (1999) "Knowledge as a Global Public Good," in Inge Kaul, Isabelle Grunberg, Marc A. Stern (eds), *Global Public Goods: International Cooperation in the 21st Century*, United Nations Development Programme (New York: Oxford University Press), pp. 308–325.

Stiglitz, J.E. (2008) "Capital Flows, Financial Market Stability, and Monetary Policy," in J. Carrera (ed.), *Monetary Policy under Uncertainty, Proceedings of the 2007 Banco Central de la República Argentina Money and Banking Seminar* (Buenos Aires: BCRA), pp. 123–134.

Stiglitz, J.E. (2010) *Freefall: America, Free Markets, and the Sinking of the World Economy* (New York: W.W. Norton).

Stiglitz, J.E. (2011) "Rethinking Macroeconomics: What Failed and How to Repair It," *Journal of the European Economic Association*, vol. 9, no. 4, pp. 591–645.

Stiglitz, J.E. (forthcoming) "Learning, Growth, and Development: A Lecture in Honor of Sir Partha Dasgupta," publication of the World Bank's Annual Bank Conference on Development Economics 2010: Development Challenges in a Post-Crisis World, forthcoming.

Stiglitz, J.E. (2012b) *The Price of Inequality: How Today's Divided Society Endangers Our Future* (New York: W.W. Norton).

Stiglitz, J.E. Ocampo, José Antonio, Spiegel, Shari, Ffrench-Davis, Ricardo, and Nayyar, Deepak (2006) *Stability with Growth: Macroeconomics, Liberalization, and Development*, with The Initiative for Policy Dialogue Series (Oxford: Oxford University Press).

Stiglitz, J.E., Sen, A., and Fitoussi, J.P. (2010) *Mismeasuring Our Lives: Why GDP Doesn't Add Up* (New York: The New Press).

UNCTAD (2011) "Economic Development in Africa: Fostering Industrial Development in Africa in the New Global Environment," United Nations Press. Available at http://unctad.org/en/docs/aldcafrica2011_en.pdf.

"What's Driving Africa's Growth?" Available at http://www.mckinseyquarterly.com/Whats_driving_Africas_growth_2601 (accessed September 5, 2012).

Williamson, John (1989) "What Washington Means by Policy Reform," in John Williamson (ed.), *Latin American Readjustment: How Much has Happened* (Washington, DC: Institute for International Economics).

1.2

From Flying Geese to Leading Dragons: New Opportunities and Strategies for Structural Transformation in Developing Countries[1]

Justin Yifu Lin
Peking University

1.2.1 Introduction

Before the 18th century, it took about 1,400 years for the western world to double its income level. In the 19th century, the same process took about 70 years, and in the 20th century only 35 years (Maddison, 1995). That dramatic acceleration in growth rates came about with the rapid technological innovation after the Industrial Revolution and the transformation of agrarian economies into modern industrialized societies, with agriculture's share of employment declining from more than 80 percent to less than 10 percent. This intriguing trend has led us to recognize that continuous structural change prompted by industrialization, technological innovation, and industrial upgrading and diversification are essential features of rapid, sustained growth.

But if the West took 300 years to innovate and industrialize, Japan less than 100, and the East Asian Tigers only 40 years to catch up, development economists must find the determining factors of successful catching-up strategies. More recently other emerging economies, such as China, Brazil, and India, also took off. And the list of low-income countries that are about to join the "club" keeps growing.[2] However, other lower-income countries, with more than one-sixth of humanity – the people counted as the "bottom billion," a term coined by Oxford economist Paul Collier – continue to be trapped in poverty. The mystery of diverging country performances, especially during the second half of the 20th century, persists.

This paper aims to shed some new light on the mystery and to understand how the government of a low-income country can accelerate structural change and sustainable income growth by facilitating the development of new industries that reflect the country's latent comparative advantage, and take advantage of new opportunities from the emergence of a multipolar-growth world. It is based on my work on the new structural economics (Lin, 2011a) and its implementation strategy, the Growth Identification and Facilitation framework or GIFF (Lin and Monga, 2011).[3]

The "flying geese–leading dragons" metaphor used in the title sums up the key message. Economic development is a process of continuous industrial and technological upgrading in which any country, regardless of its level of development, can succeed if it develops industries that are consistent with its comparative advantage, determined by its endowment structure. The successful strategy for developing countries is to exploit the latecomer advantage by building up industries that are growing dynamically in more advanced countries that have endowment structures similar to theirs. By following carefully selected any lead country that meets the criteria specified in the Growth Identification and Facilitation Framework (GIFF), latecomers can emulate the leader-follower, flying-geese pattern that has served well successfully catching-up economies since the 18th century.

The emergence of large middle-income countries such as China, India, and Brazil as new growth poles in the world, and their dynamic growth and climbing of the industrial ladder, offer an unprecedented opportunity to all developing economies with income levels currently below theirs – including those in Sub-Saharan Africa. Having itself been a "follower goose," China is on the verge of graduating from low-skilled manufacturing jobs and becoming a "leading dragon." That will free up nearly 100 million labor-intensive manufacturing jobs, enough to more than quadruple manufacturing employment in low-income countries. A similar trend is emerging in other middle-income growth poles. The lower-income countries that can formulate and implement a viable strategy to capture this new industrialization opportunity will set forth on a dynamic path of structural change that can lead to poverty reduction and prosperity.

The remainder of the paper is organized as follows: Section 1.2.2 discusses the mechanics and benefits of structural change, which characterizes the evolution of successful countries. Section 1.2.3 explores the reasons for success or failure to achieve successful structural transformation. Section 1.2.4 highlights the significance for low-income countries of the "graduation" of China's and other middle-income from low-skilled jobs. Section 1.2.5 offers some concluding thoughts.

1.2.2 The mechanics and benefits of structural change

While several researchers have documented the dynamics and benefits of structural change, policymakers in many developing countries – most notably in Africa – have not been able to foster that positive process.

1.2.2.1   Early insights on the leader–follower dynamics

Structural transformation, broadly defined as "the interrelated processes of structural change that accompany economic development" (Syrquin, 1988: 206), has been a subject of active research since the beginning of the modern growth period. Kuznets (1966 and 1971) took up the task of understanding and documenting long-run transformation through a series of stylized facts, though he was reluctant to offer a theory of development. His empirical studies identified four features of modern economic growth: First, there is a change in the sectoral composition of the economy as the share of the nonagricultural sectors increases and that of the agricultural sector decreases. Second, this sectoral shift is mirrored in the pattern of employment; that is, the proportion of the labor force employed in the nonagricultural sectors rises while that in the agricultural sector decreases. Third, there is a redistribution of the population between the rural and urban areas. And fourth, there is an increase in the relative size of the capital-labor ratio in the non-agricultural sectors of the economy.[4]

Industrialization, in particular, was recognized as one of the main engines of economic growth, especially in the early stages of development.[5] Its essential characteristics include an increase in the proportion of the national income derived from manufacturing activities and from secondary industry in general, except perhaps for cyclical interruptions; a rising trend in the proportion of the working population engaged in manufacturing; and an associated increase in the per capita income of the population (see Bagchi, 1990). Few countries have achieved the high-income status without industrializing. Only in circumstances such as an extraordinary abundance of natural resources or land have countries been able to do so (UNIDO, 2009). This is confirmed by the strong positive correlation that one can find in recent years (1993–2007) between the growth of value added in the manufacturing sector and the change in GDP per capita. As Figure 1.2.1 shows, the correlation is even stronger in Sub-Saharan Africa than in the rest of the world.

Looking at these facts, early development economists embarked on a search for a theory of structural change. A pertinent framework that also focused on structural transformation was that of Gerschenkron, who noted that prerequisites for growth can be substituted for. Analyzing the catching-up process among European countries after the Industrial Revolution, he observed that rapid industrialization started from different levels of "economic backwardness" and that capital accumulation was not a precondition for success. In fact, "the more backward a country's economy, the greater was the part played by special institutional factors [government agencies, banks] designed to increase the supply of capital to the nascent industries" (1962: 354).[6]

Akamatsu's work on Japan, a country starting from a much lower level of income than the western countries, was of great interest for developing countries. He observed what he called the "wild-geese-flying pattern" in economic development, noting that "wild geese fly in orderly ranks forming an inverse V,

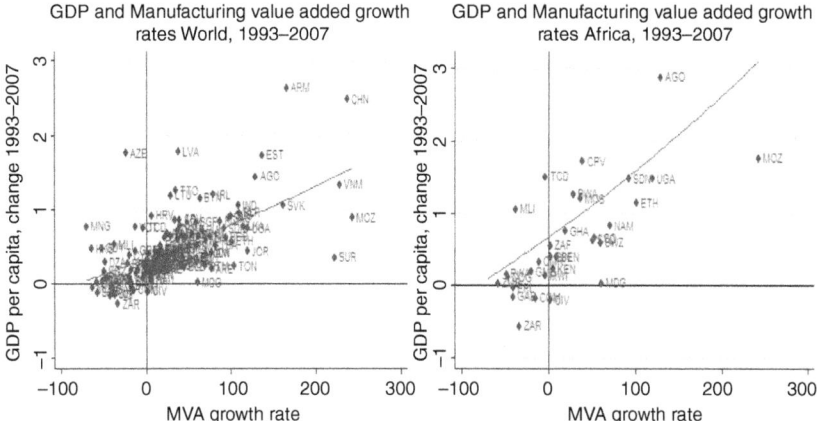

Figure 1.2.1 Industrialization as an engine of growth: manufacturing and income growth, 1993–2007

Source: Author's calculation using World Development Indicators, World Bank.

just as airplanes fly in formation" (1962: 11). In formulating his theory, Akamatsu outlined three different but interrelated stylized facts of industrial development in the dynamics of comparative advantage.

First, simply looking at statistical analyses of several pre-war Japanese industries, such as textiles, machine tools, and light machinery, over the period 1870–1939, he noted that product development within a particular developing country follows a typical pattern: its evolves over three time series curves, starting with imports, proceeding with production, and then ending with exports. The sequential trend curves of these activities resembled an inverted V-shaped flying formation of wild geese.

Second, he enriched that observation of intra-industry patterns with an analysis of inter-industry trends showing the sequential appearance and development of sectors: it appeared that industries were diversified and upgraded from consumer goods to capital goods and/or from simple to more sophisticated products. Such qualitative and structural transformations of goods and industries themselves were made possible by means of the "import-production-export" dynamics.

Third, he looked at the international positioning of Asian countries and noted a peculiar "alignment of nations along different stages of development": at a certain level of development, advanced economies had to relocate their old industries to developing countries, which allowed the latter to embark on their own industrial upgrading process, upgrade their comparative advantages from labor-intensive to gradually and increasingly more capital- and knowledge-intensive industries and achieve sustained economic growth.

While Akamatsu did not flesh out the causal relationships among these "flying-geese" patterns, research on the determinant of structural change (the factors and dynamics that drive poor countries from one rung to another up the ladder of economic development) has emphasized the importance of innovation in "leading-sector" (Ozawa, 2005, 2009, 2011) and changing comparative advantages across countries (Kojima, 2000), and provided a consistent an analytical framework for understanding the "Flying-geese" theory to economic development through the lenses of the 'new structural economics' (Lin, 2011a).[7]

1.2.2.2 Established stylized facts – and unexplained failures of transformation

The empirical literature on the catching-up process has gathered a lot of evidence on economic development as a process of structural change and on the patterns associated with that change.[8] It has established that in some fundamental ways low-income countries all look very similar. They have a large share of the population living in rural areas and employed in agriculture. And much of that agricultural activity is confined to subsistence agriculture. The basic starting point is therefore a transformation out of agricultural activities in rural areas.

A recent assessment by McMillan and Rodrik (2011), based on a decomposition of labor productivity growth into two components (sectoral productivity and structural change), is illustrative.[9] It shows that most of the difference between the recent growth in Asia and that in Latin America and Sub-Saharan Africa can be explained by the variation in the contribution of structural change to overall labor productivity (Table 1.2.1): it is actually the only region of the orld where the contribution of structural change has been positive during the period 1990–2005.

The situation of African economies is of particular interest because they constitute the core of the development challenge today. They exhibit many signs of limited structural transformation that corroborate the empirical analysis by McMillan and Rodrik and explain why progress has remained

Table 1.2.1 Contribution of structural change: decomposition of labor productivity growth, unweighted averages, 1990–2005

	Labor productivity growth	Component due to:	
		'Within'	'Structural Change'
Latin America & Caribbean	1.35%	2.24%	−0.88%
Africa	0.86%	2.13%	−1.27%
Asia	3.87%	3.31%	0.57%
High Income Countries	1.46%	1.54%	−0.09%

Source: McMillan and Rodrik (2011: Table 3).

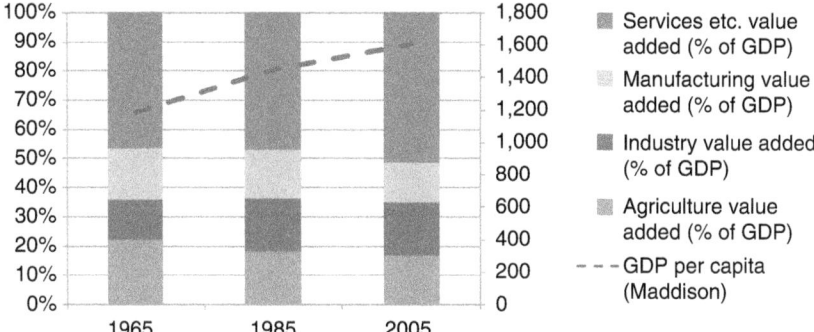

Figure 1.2.2 Limited structural transformation in Sub-Saharan Africa: sectoral contributions to GDP (left axis) and real GDP per capita (right axis), 1965–2005
Sources: For sectoral contributions to GDP, World Bank, *World Development Indicators* database; for GDP per capita, Maddison.

slow since independence. In 1965 agriculture contributed 22 percent of Sub-Saharan Africa's GDP, services 47 percent, and industry 31 percent (of which manufacturing contributed 17.5 percent). In 2005 it was estimated that agriculture still contributed 15 percent of GDP, while services contributed 52 percent and industry 33 percent (of which manufacturing declined to less than 15 percent; Figure 1.2.2).

Economic diversification has also been limited in Africa, as evidenced by the high degree of vulnerability of Sub-Saharan African countries to shocks and volatility of annual growth rates, much higher than in other developing regions. Many of these small economies rely primarily on exports. Yet exports have remained concentrated in a narrow band of primary commodities with volatile prices (see Monga, 2006) and in many cases have become more concentrated over time through the exploitation of mineral resources (see Gersovitz and Paxson, 1990; and Berthelemy and Soderling, 2001). Indeed, African countries have remained exporters of commodities or low-technology exports while Asian economies have been broadly successful in transforming their export sectors toward high-tech, higher value added goods (Figure 1.2.3).

The stagnation in export upgrading is not surprising: Sub-Saharan Africa's shares of world manufacturing production and exports have declined over the past three decades, from 0.4 and 0.3 percent, respectively, in 1980 to 0.3 and 0.2 percent, respectively, in 2008.

The limited number of employment opportunities created over recent decades in the formal sector should therefore be viewed as perhaps the most disturbing indicator of the lack of structural transformation in Sub-Saharan Africa. Figure 1.2.4, which presents only a small sample of countries because of data limitations, nevertheless tells a story that is typical of the region.

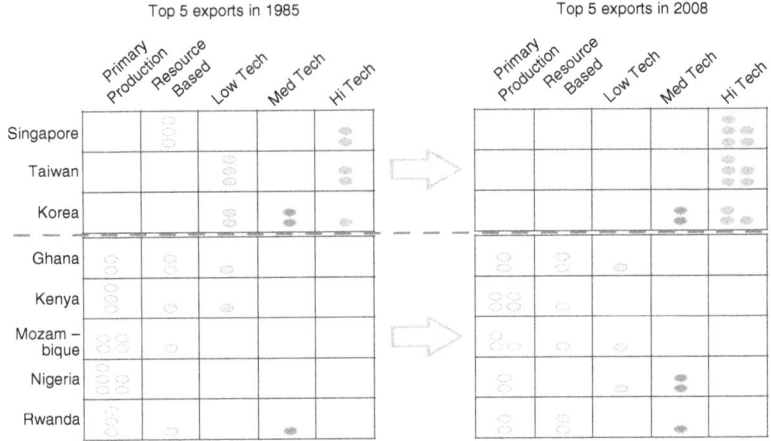

Figure 1.2.3   Diverging patterns in export composition in Asia and Sub-Saharan Africa
Source: Data from World Bank Institute and Amoako (2011).

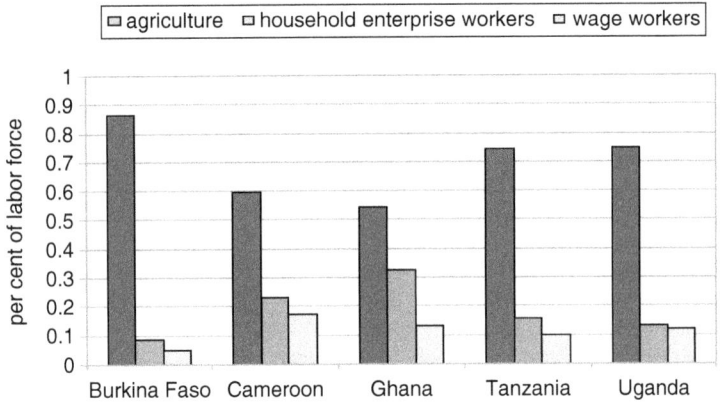

Figure 1.2.4   Composition of employment in a typical group of Sub-Saharan African countries
Source: Fox 2011.
Note: Data are for the most recent year available.

It shows that wage employment is very small and that agricultural workers constitute the bulk of the labor force.

Unlike other developing regions, especially Asia, Sub-Saharan Africa has gained only limited benefits from deindustrialization in high-income countries. The transition toward a service-dominated economic structure in the United States, the European Union, Japan, and other high-income OECD

Table 1.2.2 Global flows of foreign direct investment, 1990–2009 (current prices and exchange rates)

	1970	1980	1990	2000	2005	2009
Developing economies	28.9%	13.8%	16.9%	18.3%	33.5%	42.9%
Low income developing countries	6.5%	1.4%	3.7%	3.6%	11.7%	16.2%
Sub-Saharan Africa excluding South Africa	3.7%	0.5%	0.8%	0.4%	2.2%	3.4%
Southern Asia	0.7%	0.5%	0.1%	0.3%	1.5%	3.7%
Southern Asia excluding India	0.4%	0.4%	0.0%	0.1%	0.7%	0.6%
India	0.3%	0.1%	0.1%	0.3%	0.8%	3.1%
South-Eastern Asia	3.4%	4.9%	6.2%	1.7%	4.1%	3.3%
China		0.1%	1.7%	2.9%	7.3%	8.5%
World	100.0%	100.0%	100.0%	100.0%	100.0%	100.0%

Source: Author's calculations based on data from UNCTAD, *World Investment Report* (various years).

countries, often stimulated by innovation and technological upgrading, has involved a retreat of their industrial sector.

Globalization and the quest for competitiveness and profitability have led many firms in those countries to relocate their labor-intensive manufacturing production to middle- and low-income countries – as shown by the evolution of foreign direct investment flows in recent years (Table 1.2.2). So far Sub-Saharan African countries, excluding South Africa, have received only a small amount of those investment flows.

1.2.3 Intellectual lessons from failures and successes of structural transformation

The many insights of early development thinkers such as Akamatsu, Gerschenkron, and Kuznets certainly enriched the stock of development knowledge. However, they did not answer one of the most burning questions and issues facing policymakers in developing countries. How to facilitate the emergence of the "leading industries" that can be competitive in domestic and international market?

Despite the importance of this question, mainstream development economics in recent decades has paid only limited attention to industrialization and its role in structural transformation. This may be explained primarily by the failure of industrial policies in developing countries, and the theoretical argument that the state can do no better than the private sector in identifying new industries. The pervasive failures of government interventions – notably in Latin America, Africa, South Asia, and the countries of the former socialist planning economies – have led to the dominant view that policies aimed at "picking winners" are bound to create unsustainable and socially costly distortions.

But much of the literature on industrial policy fails to make an important distinction among country strategies: policies supporting new industries that are inconsistent with the comparative advantage of the economy or attempting to protect old industries that have lost comparative advantage generally fail, while policies facilitating the development of new industries that are consistent with the comparative advantage of the economy often succeed (see Lin and Monga, 2011).

The import-substitution strategy or heavy industries-oriented strategy advocated by the then mainstream structuralist development thinking and adopted by developing countries in the 1950s and 1960s was a comparative-advantage-defying strategy because it gave priority to capital-intensive industries even though capital in these economies was scarce. Firms in those prioritized industries were not viable in an open, competitive market – unless the government was willing and able to grant them strong protection through monopoly, large-scale subsidies or tax incentives (Lin, 2011a).

Examples of such strategies include Indonesia's launching a ship construction industry in the 1960s, when its GDP per capita was only 10 percent of that of its main competitor at the time, the Netherlands, or the attempt to build an automobile industry in Zaire (now the Democratic Republic of Congo) in the 1970s, when the country's GDP per capita was only 5 percent of the level in the industry leader. The common denominator of these strategies was that the government targeted industries in countries whose per capita income was far higher than its own country's. The capital cost is the main costs of investment and operation for a capital-intensive good. Consequently, with the scarcity in capital, the low-income country was unable to produce the capital-intensive goods at a cost advantage and therefore unable to compete in these industries with high-income countries.

The failure of the old structuralist policies prompted a shift in development thinking toward the free-market approach that became known as the Washington Consensus, which promoted economic liberalization, privatization, and the implementation of rigorous stabilization programs. In terms of growth and employment generation, however, the results of the policies presented as alternatives to the failed old structuralism were at best controversial (see Easterly, 2001, 2005; and World Bank, 2005a). The Washington Consensus also failed to foster structural transformation and sustained growth in low-income countries because it focused on the government failures without fully taking into consideration the crucial market failure issues of coordination and externalities inherent in the process of industrial upgrading and diversification (Lin, 2011a).

As policymakers in poor countries contemplate the difficult challenges facing their countries after decades or even centuries of mistaken strategic choices, they should learn from history and seize new opportunities. In an increasingly globalized world, where more and more countries have moved toward high-income status, there are indeed new possibilities for development.

1.2.4 A unique window of opportunity for Africa: the graduation of China (and other middle-income countries)

In the aftermath of the recent global recession, World Bank President Robert Zoellick (2010) observed that "We are now in a new, fast-evolving multipolar world economy – in which some developing countries are emerging as economic powers; others are moving towards becoming additional poles of growth; and some are struggling to attain their potential within this new system – where North and South, East and West, are now points on a compass, not economic destinies." Today's rapidly evolving world economy is indeed opening important opportunities for low-income countries. China's emergence as "the world's factory" for labor-intensive industries and its upcoming graduation from such economic activities deserve particular attention.

1.2.4.1 Multipolarity and its potential dividends

During the first decade of this century a burst of convergence occurred as developing countries grew substantially faster than high-income countries. In the 1980s and 1990s, among the top five contributors to global growth, all except China were G7 industrialized countries. But in 2000–09 all except the United States were emerging economies – with China having become the top contributor (Figure 1.2.5). The trend is being reinforced in the aftermath of the current global crisis: the recovery is characterized by a two-speed pattern, with developing countries as a group growing more than twice as fast as high-income countries.

That shift in economic weight is likely to produce major benefits for the world economy, with positive effects for both high-income and developing

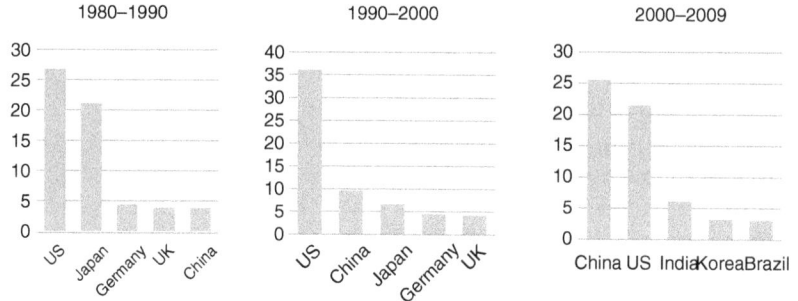

Figure 1.2.5 Top five contributors to global economic growth by decade (percentage)
Source: Author's calculations based on data from World Bank, World Development Indicators database.

countries. For high-income countries the growth of emerging economies will expand markets for their exports of capital goods and intermediate goods. For many developing countries that are still major producers of agricultural and natural resource commodities, higher consumption and production levels in the new growth poles will continue to support adequate prices for their commodity exports. In addition, firms and governments in emerging economies will provide funds for infrastructure and natural resource investment in developing countries.

These benefits are already happening – and are likely to continue into the future. Propelled by domestic demand for raw materials, Brazil has rapidly expanded investment and trade with Africa, with imports from the continent rising from $3 billion in 2000 to $18.5 billion in 2008.[10] Similarly, bilateral trade between China and Africa increased from $10 billion in 2000 to $91 billion in 2009 and China's investment in Africa jumped from $490 million in 2003 to $9.33 billion in 2009 (China, Information Office of State Council, 2010). Indeed, Chinese finance has a growing role in Africa, the developing region facing the greatest constraints on access to finance (Wang, 2009). Meanwhile, the government of India – observing that 5 of the world's 12 fastest-growing economies are in Sub-Saharan Africa, a continent richly endowed with natural resources – has announced plans to invest in infrastructure development in Africa in the next decade.[11]

More important than these beneficial trade and financial flows, the dynamic growth of the new poles will provide golden opportunities for industrialization in lower-income countries. China, because of its size and income level, should be of particular interest. After a long period of sustained growth (at 9.9 percent annually in real terms for 30 years), the Chinese economy is now at an important crossroad, with wages rising rapidly and surplus labor disappearing. All countries experiencing economic success over such a long period eventually face such challenges, and China will need to upgrade its industrial structure and enter new industries in order to maintain its dynamic growth. As China moves into more sophisticated product markets, it will leave market space for other developing countries to enter the more labor-intensive industries.

1.2.4.2   A tectonic shift ahead – with opportunities

The early 1980s marked the beginning of a new era of economic development in which China has emerged as a powerhouse (Lin, 2011c and2011d). It is hard to remember that only 30 years ago, in 1980, China was much poorer than most countries in Sub-Saharan Africa; its GDP per capita, at $195, was lower than that of Ethiopia or Mozambique. In 1990 China was still a low-income country, with a per capita income (measured in purchasing power parity) 30 percent lower than the Sub-Saharan African average. Today China is an upper middle-income country, with a per capita income three times the Sub-Saharan African average, at nearly $4,500. Its share of world

Table 1.2.3 The dragon in the global marketplace for low-tech products: China's percentage share of labor-intensive exports, 1976–2009

SITC CODE	PRODUCT	1976	1980	1990	2000	2005	2009
83	Travel goods, handbags	1.6	2.8	5.6	31.7	38.2	47.5
75	Office machines and automatic data processing equipment	0.0	0.0	0.3	5.2	25.1	40.4
85	Footwear	1.4	1.7	7.4	25.9	32.8	39.0
84	Articles of apparel and clothing accessories	2.1	4.2	9.3	18.5	27.0	35.9

Source: UN COMTRADE (SITC two-digit level).

GDP is nearing 9 percent, and its economy ranks as the world's second largest, next only to the United States. Without oil, cocoa, coffee, cotton, timber, diamonds, or uranium to export, China, a country of 1.3 billion people, has achieved spectacular progress.

China is unquestionably the dragon in the global marketplace for low-tech products today. In the four product categories in which it has the highest global market concentration, China's share of global exports exceeds 35 percent – and in travel goods and handbags is close to 50 percent (Table 1.2.3). Most impressive is the rate at which its share has grown. For travel goods and handbags, for example, its share in 1976 was only 1.6 percent.

An important consequence of China's rapid rise to dominance as a global exporter of labor-intensive products has been the absorption of its vast reserves of unskilled labor, especially from rural areas. Some labor economists still predict that China will remain a "labor surplus" country until 2014. But the growing demand for service sector employees as well as the reluctance of some workers to leave rural areas will gradually stretch China's job market, particularly at the low end (McMillan, 2011). So will China's shift, following the "flying-geese" pattern of development, from labor-intensive industries toward a more advanced industrial structure, with machinery increasingly dominant in manufactured exports. Labor productivity is indeed a key driver of wage dynamics. As the economy continues the process of industrial upgrading against the backdrop of burgeoning global demand for labor-intensive products, wage rates will rise and erode China's competitive edge in such products.

Indeed, China has already seen rapid growth in wages. Unskilled workers' wages rose from just over $150 a month in 2005 to around $350 in 2010 (about $4,200 a year).[12] As a consequence, the wage gap between China and some upper-middle-income countries is closing, and this trend is almost certain to continue over the coming decade. China's 12th Five-Year Plan projects that the economy will grow at 7 percent a year on average during 2011–15 – and, for the first time in the country's history, proposes that real wages will grow at least as fast as GDP. Both growth rates are likely to be achieved. That would imply a doubling of real monthly wages over the next decade, to around $700 a month. If the likely continued currency appreciation is added up, China's real wages could approach $1,000 a month within a decade, the level in such upper-middle-income countries as Brazil and Turkey today – and $2,000 a month by 2030, the level in Korea and Taiwan, China today.

China is at a stage like that reached by Japan in the 1960s and Hong Kong SAR, China; Korea; Singapore; and Taiwan, China, in the 1980s. To continue growing dynamically against the background of declining wage competitiveness, China will have to follow the path of the earlier Asian "geese" and start to relocate its labor-intensive industries to low-income countries.[13] Indeed, this is already happening. A large share of China's outward foreign direct investment in Africa, which had reached $9.33 billion in 2009, has gone to manufacturing (22 percent), second only to the share in mining (29 percent). And China is building six economic and trade cooperation zones in the Arab Republic of Egypt, Ethiopia, Mauritius, Nigeria, and Zambia (China, Information Office of State Council, 2010). More such initiatives are likely to happen.

1.2.4.3   How big might the benefits be?

As China moves forward, there will be a major difference with earlier patterns of industrial upgrading: its economy is significantly larger than those of the geese that led the first round of structural transformation in Asia (Table 1.2.4). China has an estimated 85 million workers in manufacturing, most of them in labor-intensive sectors. The reallocation of these workers to higher value-added, more sophisticated products and tasks will open up great opportunities for labor-abundant, lower-income countries to step in and produce the labor-intensive manufacturing goods that China leaves

Table 1.2.4 Comparing manufacturing in China with that in earlier geese at similar levels of development

Country	Year	GDP per capita (constant US$)		Manufacturing		
		2000 US$	2005 US$ (PPP)	Share of value added (%)	Share of labor (%)	Employment (millions)
China	2009	2,206	6,200	43	17.7	85
Japan	1960	5,493	6,976	35	20.0	9.7
Korea, Rep.	1982	3,709	6,123	25	14.6	2.3

Sources: World Bank, World Development Indicators database; International Labour Organization, LABORSTA; China, National Bureau of Statistics (2010).

behind. As a result, China will not be a *goose* in the traditional leader–follower pattern of industrialization for a few lower-income countries but a *dragon*.

In 2009 alone, China exported $107 billion of apparel to the world, compared with Sub-Saharan Africa's total apparel exports of $2 billion (2 percent of Chinese apparel exports). Let's assume that as a result of rising wages, 1 percent of China's production of apparel is shifted to lower-wage African countries. All things equal, that alone would boost African production and exports of apparel by 47 percent.

In the absence of detailed data on manufacturing employment in all African countries, one can only conjecture about the size of the potential gains for the region. Still, even back-of-the-envelope calculations suggest that the benefits would be enormous. Africa's population (north and south of the Sahara) is 1 billion, slightly less than India's 1.15 billion. In 2009 manufacturing value added was 16 percent of GDP in India, 13 percent in Sub-Saharan African countries, and 16 percent in North African countries such as Egypt, Morocco, and Tunisia.[14] India's employment in manufacturing was 8.7 million in 2009. So it is reasonable to assume that total manufacturing employment in Africa is at most 10 million. This suggests that the relocation of even a small share of China's 85 million labor-intensive manufacturing jobs would go a long way toward creating new opportunities for employment and sustained growth in Africa.[15] Clearly, the potential opportunities for Africa's labor-intensive economies, which today are exporting mostly minerals, are enormous.

The story for low-income countries elsewhere in the world is similar. In 2009, with a total population of 846 million and 13 percent of their GDP coming from manufacturing, their employment in the sector likely amounted to no more than 10 million. Thus, as in the case of African countries, China's industrial upgrading would provide them a golden opportunity for dynamic manufacturing-led growth. But for developing countries everywhere, the ability to benefit from the opportunities depends on their quickly formulating and implementing credible economic development strategies that are consistent with their comparative advantage and the flying-geese paradigm.

1.2.4.4 A roadmap for seizing the moment: the Growth Identification and Facilitation Framework

The coming graduation of China and other middle-income growth poles from low-skilled manufacturing jobs is a golden opportunity for low-income countries in the world – especially those in Africa. Despite the region's grim long-run performance and the potentially heavy economic and human cost of the recent global crisis, there is renewed optimism about its economic prospects: since the mid-1990s Africa has embarked on a new and higher growth trajectory. The main challenge facing African leaders is to avoid the policy mistakes of the past and instead implement the winning strategy.

Africa may be on the verge of an economic take-off, recent empirical work suggests (Young 2010; Pinkovskiy and Sala-i-Martin 2010; Radelet 2010). While the region's collective GDP is still roughly equal to that of a single emerging economy such as Brazil (about $1.6 trillion in 2008), its recent economic progress cannot be underestimated. Since 1990 Sub-Saharan Africa has almost tripled its exports and diversified its trade partners.[16] Natural resources will clearly continue to be the region's main source of export revenue as global demand grows. But with continued reforms and increasing foreign direct investment going to industries with overt or latent comparative advantages, African economies are likely to become more diversified in the future, with the global demand for nontraditional exports also growing.

Still, per capita growth rates in the range of 2–3 percent a year may not be enough to combat poverty and generate prosperity. So far, Africa's economic development has been driven primarily by higher consumption – supported in part by an inflow of remittances – and the growing contribution of natural resources to GDP. For growth to be sustainable and to create jobs, it also needs to be supported by structural change based on manufacturing-driven industrialization.

It is therefore imperative that African countries follow the "flying-geese" pattern to seize the golden opportunity provided by the industrial upgrading of China and other leading dragons. The key challenge is to find a way to sustain the momentum and foster structural transformation in Sub-Saharan Africa so as to achieve annual growth rates of 8 percent or more. This is feasible if policy makers help their economies develop industries according to their comparative advantage and tap the potential of the advantage of backwardness.

Policymakers in any developing country can do so through the Growth Identification and Facilitation framework proposed by Lin and Monga (2011) as an implementation tool for the new structural economics. That framework is built on two main ideas: first, the acknowledgment that the market is an important resource allocation mechanism at any given level of development. Economic growth occurs when firms are given the incentive system to take advantage of existing opportunities determined by the country's endowment structure. They can also create potential new business niches by identifying and exploiting the economy's latent comparative advantage. They spontaneously enter industries and choose technologies consistent with the economy's comparative advantage only when the price system reflects the relative scarcity of factors in the country's endowment. Therefore, a competitive market system should be the economy's fundamental mechanism for resource allocation at each stage of its development.

Second, the framework also conceptualizes economic development as a dynamic process that requires industrial upgrading and corresponding improvements in "hard" (tangible) and "soft" (intangible) infrastructure at each stage. Such upgrading requires coordination and entails large externalities to firms' transaction costs and returns to capital investment. Thus, in addition to an effective market mechanism, the government should play an active role in facilitating industrial upgrading and infrastructure improvements. This can be done through a six-step process:

(i)   Developing country governments can identify the list of tradable goods and services that have been produced for about 20 years in dynamically growing countries with similar endowment structures and a per capita income that is about 100 percent higher than their own;

(ii) Among the industries in that list, the government may give priority to those in which some domestic private firms have already entered spontaneously, and try to identify and help remove the obstacles to their development;

(iii) Some of those industries in the list may be completely new to domestic firms; in such cases, the government could adopt specific measures to attract firms in the higher-income countries identified in the first step to invest in these industries;

(iv) Developing country governments should pay close attention to private enterprises' successful self-discoveries of industries that are not included in the list identified in step i and provide support to scale up those industries;

(v)   In developing countries with poor infrastructure and an unfriendly business environment, the government can invest in industrial parks or export processing zones and make the necessary improvements to attract domestic private firms and/or foreign firms to invest in the targeted industries; and

(vi) Limited incentives may also be provided to domestic pioneer firms or foreign investors that work within the list of industries identified in step i in order to compensate for the non-rival, public knowledge created by their investments.

1.2.5   Conclusion

Only a small group of countries in Europe, Asia, Latin America, and Africa have been able to engineer sustained dynamic growth and structural transformation and achieve convergence with high-income countries. They have generally done so by using market mechanisms and government facilitation to replicate, in different contexts, the same types of development paths that allowed previously successful countries to ignite what Kuznets called the period of "modern economic growth."

The lessons from their success and from economic theory are now clear: regardless of size, location, or natural resources, all developing countries can achieve annual growth rates of 8 percent or more for decades and embark on the path of prosperity, provided that they carefully follow their comparative advantage, tap the potential of the latecomer advantage, and engage in activities that will dynamically transform their economic structure. This paper has suggested a framework for doing just that. Drawing from previous work on the new structural economics, it has provided a consistent analysis of economic success and failure – and explained how lower-income countries today may benefit from the opportunity arising from the dynamic industrial upgrading of leading dragons such as China and other large emerging economies.

For low-income countries in Africa and elsewhere, the news is good: in an increasingly globalized world, opportunities for economic transformation abound. Far from being a curse, the emergence of a multipolar-growth world is in fact a blessing for even the most backward economies – because it provides them the opportunity to enter a new age of rapid industrialization and structural transformation. In the next decade China, with some 85 million labor-intensive manufacturing jobs today, will have to move up the industrial ladder and therefore graduate from low-skilled sectors. This will free up a gigantic reservoir of employment possibilities that African and other low-income countries can tap. The dynamic growth of other middle-income economies – such as Brazil, India, and Indonesia – will provide a similar opportunity. But to fully benefit from those opportunities, policymakers in low-income countries must quickly plan for it and implement economically viable growth strategies, those that rely on the benefits of their comparative advantage at any given level of development.

Notes

1. The article is a shortened version of the 15th UN–WIDER Lecture delivered at Maputo, Mozambique on May 4, 2011. It is published in *Global Policy*, vol. 3, issue 4, November 2012, pp. 397–409. I would like to thank Finn Tarp, director of WIDER, for the invitation to give this prestigious lecture, and Célestin Monga, Vandana Chandra, David Rosenblatt, Volker Treichel, and Doerte Doemeland for excellent support in preparing this lecture. Comments from two anonymous reviewers on a previous draft are gratefully acknowledged.
2. According to the 2008 *Growth Report* by the Commission on Growth and Development, led by Nobel Laureate Michael Spence, 13 economies achieved an average annual growth rate of 7 percent or above for 25 years since the end of World War II. In 2000–08, 29 economies achieved that average annual growth rate, and 11 of them were in Sub-Saharan Africa (Lin, 2011b).
3. The new structural economics proposes to apply a neoclassical approach to study the determination of economic structure and the mechanism of its evolution in an economy. It is called new structural economics rather than structural economics to distinguish it from the structuralism that prevailed in the early years of development economics. See Lin (2011a).
4. The transformational pattern from agriculture to manufacturing and services has been widely observed throughout the history of economic growth and is often

referred to in the literature as the "Petty-Clark's law." See Sundaram (2005) for a discussion.

5. Earlier analyses of the process, dating back to the 1950s and 1960s, found that manufacturing in particular tends to play a larger role in total output in richer countries and that higher incomes are associated with a substantially bigger role of transport and machinery sectors. See Datta (1952); and Kuznets (1966).

6. From the point of view of the new structural economics, the targeted industries for catching up should be consistent with a latecomer country's latent comparative advantage so that the state's role is limited to facilitating the private sector's entry into the new industry by overcoming the coordination and externality issues, which are beset with market failures. The most advanced country's industries will not be a catching-up country's latent comparative advantage if the gap between the two countries' levels of development is too large. Private firms in those industries will not be viable in open, competitive markets. Their initial investments will depend on the government's large capital mobilization, and their continual operations will require the government's continual subsidies and protections. As I will discussed in section 1.2.3, the attempt to develop industries too far ahead of a country's level of development is the root cause of the failure of many governments' interventions in their country's industrial development.

7. The new structural economics approach to development considers structural differences between developed and developing countries to be in large part endogenous to their endowment structures and determined by market forces, rather than resulting from the distribution of power or other exogenously determined rigidities as assumed by the old structural approach. It therefore argues that acknowledging the importance of structures in economic development and understanding the market as the fundamental institution for resource allocation and the role of the state as a strategic facilitator are the determinants of economic success everywhere. It also offers an analytically consistent explanation to the stories of success and failure in a developing country's catching-up process: developing countries throughout history, which have relied on their comparative advantage to guide its choice of industry and technology, become competitive in domestic and international markets, produced the largest possible economic surplus, accumulated the largest possible capital, and upgraded their human capital, technology and industry in the fastest possible way. By contrast, developing countries that have attempted to violate their comparative advantage have encountered stagnation and various crises.

8. See, for example, Syrquin (1986); Syrquin and Chenery (1986); Fei and Ranis (1964); and Haraguchi and Rezonja (2009, 2010).

9. McMillan and Rodrik (2011) construct a simple index based on the idea that productivity differentials exist both between broad sectors of the economy and within modern manufacturing activities. These gaps are indicative of the allocative inefficiencies that reduce overall labor productivity. But they can potentially be an important engine of growth. When labor and other resources move from less productive to more productive activities, the economy grows even if there is no productivity growth *within* sectors. This kind of structural change can be an important contributor to overall economic growth.

10. See Lapper (2010). In Mozambique, for example, Brazilian companies are working to develop coal reserves, build a power station, and construct rail and port infrastructure to bring the coal to export markets. In Angola a Brazilian firm has

become the largest private sector employer, with activities including food and ethanol production, offices, factories, and supermarkets.

11. Statement by Indian Minister of Commerce and Industry Anand Sharma reported by *Leadership* (Abuja, Nigeria), January 15, 2010.

12. Data from Oxford Analytica, March 28, 2011.

13. Based on the estimation by Maddison (2010), China's per capita income (measured in purchasing power parity) was 6,725 international dollars in 2008, the same level as in Japan in 1966, Korea in 1986, and Taiwan, China, in 1983. These economies started to relocate their labor-intensive manufacturing industries at that income level, Japan to the East Asian Tigers and Korea and Taiwan, China, to mainland China.

14. Data from the World Bank, *World Development Indicators* database.

15. The creation of manufacturing jobs, especially through foreign direct investment, generally leads to the creation of jobs in other sectors through backward and forward linkages (see UNCTAD, *World Investment Report 2006*) and through multiplier effects as additional employment raises income levels. Backward linkages tend to be weaker in developing countries because it is often difficult to source local products. But forward linkages can have a substantial effect on employment. In Lesotho, for example, computable general equilibrium model simulations indicate that the employment of 56,000 workers in the garment sector, sustained by foreign direct investment flows, could have led to the creation of 77,000 additional non-manufacturing jobs (see World Bank 2005b). In India it is estimated that creating 2.5 million jobs in the information technology sector could lead to 8.3 million additional jobs (NASSCOM, 2011).

16. Okonjo-Iweala (2010) notes that the share of Sub-Saharan Africa's exports going to the European Union and the United States fell from 73 percent in 1990 to 49 percent (2008). During this time the region's exports to China increased from $64 million to more than $13 billion.

References

Akamatsu, K. (1962) "A Historical Pattern of Economic Growth in Developing Countries." *The Developing Economies* (Tokyo), supplement issue no. 1: 3–25.

Amoako, K.Y. (2011) "The Africa Transformation Report," Powerpoint presented at the African Center for Economic Transformation Workshop on Growth and Transformation in Africa, Bellagio, Italy, April, 2011.

Bagchi, A.K. (1990) "Industrialization," in *The New Palgrave: Economic Development*, edited by John Eatwell, Murray Milgate, and Peter Newman (New York: W.W. Norton & Co.), pp. 160–73.

Berthelemy, J.-C., and Soderling, L. (2001) "The Role of Capital Accumulation, Adjustment and Structural Change for Economic Take-Off: Empirical Evidence from African Growth Episodes," *World Development*, vol. 29, no. 2, pp. 323–343.

China, Information Office of State Council (2010) "White Paper on China–Africa Economic and Trade Cooperation," September 23. Available online at http://news.xinhuanet.com/english2010/china/2010-12/23/c_13661632.htm.

Datta, B. (1952) *Economics of Industrialization* (Calcutta: World Press).

Datta, B. (2001) "The Lost Decades: Explaining Developing Countries' Stagnation in Spite of Policy Reform 1980–1998," *Journal of Economic Growth*, vol. 6, no. 2, pp. 135–157.

Easterly, W. (2005) "What Did Structural Adjustment Adjust? The Association of Policies and Growth with Repeated IMF and World Bank Adjustment Loans," *Journal of Development Economics*, 76 (February), pp. 1–22.

Fei, J.C.H. and Ranis, G. (1964) *Development of the Labor Surplus Economy* (Homewood, IL: Irwin).

Fox, L. (2011) "Why Is the Informal Normal in Low-Income Sub-Saharan Africa?" Paper presented at World Bank, Washington, DC, March 2011.

Gerschenkron, A. (1962) *Economic Backwardness in Historical Perspective: A Book of Essays* (Cambridge, MA: Belknap Press of Harvard University Press).

Gersovitz, M., and Paxson, C. (1990) "The Economies of Africa and the Prices of Their Exports," Princeton Studies in International Finance, no. 68, International Finance Section, Department of Economics, Princeton University, Princeton, NJ.

Haraguchi, N. and Rezonja, G. (2009) "Patterns of Manufacturing Development Revisited," Working Paper 22/2009 (Vienna: United Nations Industrial Development Organization (UNIDO)).

Haraguchi, N. and Rezonja, G. (2010) "In Search of General Patterns of Manufacturing Development," Working Paper 02/2010 (Vienna: UNIDO).

Kojima, K. (2000) "The 'Flying Geese' Model of Asian Economic Development: Origin, Theoretical Extensions, and Regional Policy Implications," *Journal of Asian Economics*, vol. 11, pp. 375–401.

Kuznets, S. (1966) *Modern Economic Growth* (New Haven, CT: Yale University Press).

Kuznets, S. (1971) *Economic Growth of Nations: Total Output and Production Structure* (Cambridge, MA: Harvard University Press).

Lapper, R. (2010) "Brazil Accelerates Investment in Africa." *Financial Times*, February 9.

Lin, J.Y. (2009) *Economic Development and Transition: Thought, Strategy and Viability* (Marshall Lectures). Cambridge: Cambridge University Press.

Lin, J.Y. (2011a) "New Structural Economics: A Framework for Rethinking Development," *World Bank Research Observer*, no. 2, vol. 26 (September 2011), pp. 193–221.

Lin, J.Y. (2011b) "A Global Economy with Multiple Growth Poles," in Shahrokh Fardoust, Yongbeom Kim, and Claudia Sepulveda (eds), *Postcrisis Growth and Development: A Development Agenda for G-20* (Washington, DC: World Bank Press), pp. 77–105.

Lin, J.Y. (2011c) *Demystifying the Chinese Economy* (Cambridge: Cambridge University Press).

Lin, J.Y. (2011d) "China and the Global Economy," *China Economic Journal*, vol. 4, no. 1, pp. 1–14.

Lin, J.Y. and Monga, C. (2011) "Growth Identification and Facilitation: The Role of the State in the Dynamics of Structural Change," *Development Policy Review*, vol. 29, no. 3, pp. 264–290.

Maddison, A. (1995) *Monitoring the World Economy, 1820–1992* (Paris: OECD).

Maddison, A. (2010) Historical Statistics of the World Economy: 1-2008 AD (www.ggdc.net/maddison/Historical_Statistics/vertical-file_02-2010.xls).

McMillan, A.F. (2011) "China's Role as 'World's Factory' Coming to an End," *CNBC.com*, February 6.

McMillan, M., and Rodrik, D. (2011) "Globalization, Structural Change and Productivity Growth." Paper prepared for a joint ILO–WTO volume, http://www.hks.harvard.edu/fs/drodrik/Research%20papers/Globalization,%20Structural%20Change,%20and%20Productivity%20Growth.pdf.

Monga, C. (2006) "Commodities, Mercedes-Benz, and Adjustment: An Episode in West African History," in E. K. Akyeampong (ed.), *Themes in West Africa's History* (Oxford: James Currey), pp. 227–264.

NASSCOM (2011) *The IT BPO Sector in India: Strategic Review 2011* (New Delhi, India: International Youth Centre).

Okonjo-Iweala, N. (2010) "Fulfilling the Promise of Sub-Saharan Africa." *McKinsey Quarterly* (June). Available at: https://www.mckinseyquarterly.com/PDFDownload. aspx?ar=2603.

Ozawa, T. (2005) *Institutions, Industrial Upgrading, and Economic Performance in Japan: The 'Flying-Geese' Paradigm of Catch-Up Growth* (Cheltenham: Edward Elgar).

Ozawa, T. (2009) *The Rise of Asia: The 'Flying-Geese' Theory of Tandem Growth and Regional Agglomeration* (Cheltenham: Edward Elgar).

Ozawa, T. (2011) "The (Japan-Born) 'Flying-Geese' Theory of Economic Development Revisited-and Reformulated from a Structuralist Perspective," *Global Policy*, vol. 2, no. 3. pp. 272–285.

Pinkovskiy, M. and Sala-i-Martin, X. (2010) "African Poverty Is Falling... Much Faster Than You Think!," Massachusetts Institute of Technology and Columbia University. Available at http://www.columbia.edu/~xs23/papers/pdfs/Africa_Paper_VX3.2.pdf.

Radelet, R. (2010) *Emerging Africa: How 17 Countries Are Leading the Way* (Washington, DC: Center for Global Development).

Sundaram, J.K. (2005) *The Pioneers of Development Economics: Great Economists on Development* (London and Delhi: Zed Books and Tulika).

Syrquin, M. (1986) "Sector Proportions and Economic Development: The Evidence since 1950." Paper presented at the 8th World Congress of the International Economic Association, New Delhi, India.

Syrquin, M. (1988) "Patterns of Structural Change," in H. Chenery and T.N. Srinivasan (eds), *Handbook of Development Economics*, vol. 1 (Amsterdam: Elsevier Science).

Syrquin, M., and Chenery, H.B. (1986) *Patterns of Development: 1950 to 1983* (Washington, DC: World Bank).

UNCTAD (United Nations Conference on Trade and Development) (various years) *World Investment Report* (Geneva: UNCTAD).

UNIDO (United Nations Industrial Development Organization) (2009) *Industrial Development Report 2009: Breaking In and Moving Up – New Industrial Challenges for the Bottom Billion and the Middle-Income Countries* (New York: United Nations).

Wang, Y. (2009) "Development Partnerships for Growth and Poverty Reduction: A Synthesis of the First Event Organized by the China–DAC Study Group" (Beijing: International Poverty Reduction Center in China), October 28–9.

World Bank (2005a) *Economic Growth in the 1990s: Learning from a Decade of Reform* (Washington, DC: World Bank).

World Bank (2005b) "Lesotho: Growth and Employment Option Study," Country Economic Memorandum (Washington, DC: World Bank).

Young, A. (2010) "The African Growth Miracle," Department of Economics, London School of Economics. Available at http://federation.ens.fr/ydepot/semin/texte0910/ YOU2010AFR.pdf.

Zoellick, R.B. (2010) "The End of the Third World? Modernizing Multilateralism for a Multipolar World," Speech at the World Bank–International Monetary Fund Spring Meetings, Washington, DC, April 14.

Part II
Structural Transformation: Lessons from History

2.1

Accumulation of Capabilities, Structural Change, and Macro Prices: an Evolutionary and Structuralist Roadmap*

Mario Cimoli and Gabriel Porcile
ECLAC

Introduction

Both economic history and economic theory generally acknowledge a deep relationship between technical change and economic development. It is quite intuitive that improvements in the efficiency of production techniques or in product performances may be a determinant or at least a condition for growth in productivity and industrialization. The opening of the technological black box has often gone hand in hand with important insights on how learning and technological capabilities develop in less developed economies. Studies on the sources, mechanisms, and patterns of learning and its microeconomic impact on productivity growth have flourished over the last four decades.

Structuralist and evolutionary theories agree on the fact that one of the main challenges of development is diffusing technological progress so as to change the pattern of specialization by incorporating new sectors and reducing intersectoral disparities, raising productivity levels and improving income distribution. Since its beginning in the 1950s, the Structuralist school has focused on the relationship between structural change and economic development, investigating how the participation of industry in total value-added would generate spillover effects, backward and forward

*A first version of the first part of this paper has been published in *Economics of Innovation and New Technologies*, vol. 18, no. 7, pp. 675–694, with the title "Sources of Learning Paths and Technological Capabilities: An Introductory Roadmap of Development Processes". A version of the second part is forthcoming within the volume *The Triple Challenge of Development: Changing the Rules in a Global World,* with the title "Still blowin' in the wind: industrial policy and distorted prices for structural transformation" (co-author. Elisa Calza) linkages, technological externalities, which in turn accelerate capital accumulation, a continual upgrade towards new industries and more dynamic sectors with higher rates of demand growth and higher opportunities for technical change. Technological capabilities are the engine at the root of these transformations: they are the basis for the expansion of production and employment at the firm, sector and industrial levels, and the building of capabilities requires a continuous process of learning.

Building and accumulating technological capabilities would require a continuous process of learning, time and resources. Analyzing this process is not an easy task, and one of the main contributions of the Evolutionary school is precisely having looked into the "black box" of these dynamics at the micro level. Since at least the beginning of the 1970s, it has been recognized that in developing economies productivity growth relies on borrowing, imitating, mastering, and improving on the advanced technology used by countries that had reached the technological frontier. Significant factors favouring such a process include the literacy and skill level of the workforce, the skills and technical competence of engineers and designers in the mechanical artefacts and (increasingly) the existence of managers capable of efficiently running complex organizations.

This paper aims at building bridges between evolutionary microeconomics and the structuralist theory of economic development. In doing so, some key aspects of development which usually receive less attention in the literature come to the forefront.

Firstly, the scope of the analysis of technical change broadens, from focusing on a framework which describes only the evolution of productivity, to including also the evolution of aggregate income and employment levels in the economy. This helps to illuminate in which cases technical change translates into higher rates of economic growth and in which cases it basically gives rise to underemployment and heterogeneity in the labor market. With this objective it is offered a new representation of the process of technical change (in the productivity–aggregate income space) which differs from the traditional representation, which focuses on the efficient utilization of production factors.

Thus, a complementary view on learning and technological capabilities that incorporates a micro-macro perspective is suggested. In the early 1980s the literature highlighted and gave a full description of the supply-side efforts required to adapt imported technologies to local conditions and improve their efficiency and design. A more complete picture emerges when these findings are integrated within demand-led growth models. When supply efforts and demand-led growth mechanisms are integrated, the analysis produces a more comprehensive understanding of how the innovation system works and how this affects economic growth.

Secondly, the paper highlights the need to consider at all times the dynamics of learning and structural change, in particular why some countries *traverse* to a path where learning, production capabilities and institutions interact virtuously, while others remain in a *hysteresis* state (Cimoli and Porcile, 2008, 2009). There is a great deal we can learn from the microeconomics of learning that could explain why these low-growth traps emerge and why they are so persistent and hard to overcome.

In this sense, the case of shocks negatively affecting the consolidation and accumulation of technological capabilities is particularly considered and analysed. For example, the behavior of macro prices: a decrease (appreciaction) of the real exchange rate (RER) may induce a destruction of existing technological capabilities, when the appreciation is so strong or its volatility so high so as to affect negatively the development of strategic technological sectors by limiting their export performance and thus their expansion.

Moreover, if the macroeconomic shocks are repeated and/or fluctuations are recurrent, this could even lead to a state of *hysteresis*, locking the economy into a self-reinforcing path of capabilities destruction, a lack of structural change, and low (and even decreasing) productivity. The effects of a shock can become particularly persistent because technological capabilities are sticky, non-reversible and fragile. Stickiness in capabilities and technologies is a feature that characterizes the real economy, and it helps explain why the process of re-composition and re-adaptation of the microeconomic structure cannot be smooth and fast and why the technological and production systems cannot respond in a flexible way to changes in market signals. These properties suggest that the effects of macro shocks on the production structure are difficult to be reversed. They may leave, long-lasting marks in productivity growth and in the production structure if they affect the learning paths of capabilities accumulation (Cimoli and Porcile, 2008, 2011b).

Given its peculiarities and its importance for long-term economic growth, the generation of technological capabilities and the transformation of the production structure in developing economies should not be left at the mercy of market forces and at the volatility of market signals (Cimoli, Dosi, and Stiglitz, 2009). Although the idea that successful catching up requires active industrial policies[1] has only gradually reached mainstream economics, this is an old, well-established point in the tradition of economic history and heterodox growth theory,[2] where industrial policies are seen as fundamental tools for reducing the technology gap and increasing international competitiveness. Furthermore, a certain degree of coordination across economic policies also has to be pursued and macroeconomic priorities should be set consistently with innovation and industrial targets; on the contrary obsessively pursuing what are believed to be the "right" macroeconomic prices could nullify the efforts of even the strongest industrial policy.

However, once applied to the actual international situation, the structural "recipe" of active policies for structural change and development may turn out to be just a naïve theoretical exercise, in practice unable to attain its final goals in industrializing countries affected by a widening technology gap. In fact, active industrial policies and consistent macroeconomic policies are a necessary condition for reducing technological asymmetries and boosting structural change, but they are far from being enough in the current global economic scenario.

In order to carry on with the process of structural change, the industrializing and catching-up countries have to expand their effective demand and to import from abroad the technological and capital goods that they need to upgrade the technological contents of their productions and to grow. In this way, they activate what has been defined by the Structuralist school as "the principle of implicit (or automatic) reciprocity," which states that the industrializing countries will spend in imports every dollar of foreign exchange they obtain from exports. There is reciprocity in the sense that they will use export revenues to buy capital goods from abroad, implicitly sustaining the expansion of effective demand and growth in advances countries.

The shortcoming of the implicit reciprocity is its sustainability in the long run. In fact, given the import of technological goods, the industrializing and catching-up countries will end up facing serious disequilibria of the balance of trade in the long run, thus constraining their growth potentials. This situation can be warded off only by a parallel expansion of export, which will help ease the external constraint on growth and will make it possible to maintain the inflow of foreign exchange.

However, sustaining an actual increase of the export does not depend solely on industrializing countries, but it requires global political cooperation. A corollary of the principle of implicit reciprocity argues that technologically advanced countries should open their markets and implement parallel expansionary policies to sustain the rise of industrializing countries' exports. This will not only facilitate structural change in industrializing countries, but will also represent a win–win solution of mutual growth for both groups of countries. On the contrary, if advanced countries do not offer space to sustain this expansion, protectionism and barriers to trade represent the only viable solution for industrializing countries to transform the production and employment structure and to generate the technological capabilities without incurring in unsustainable trade unbalances (Cimoli and Porcile, 2011a).

Hence, the corollary of the principle of implicit reciprocity suggests that a Keynes plus Schumpeter policy-mix contains the ingredients required for both catching up and a positive-sum game in the international system. This approach sharply contrasts with the combination of orthodox monetary and fiscal policies plus a static Ricardian approach to trade which has been so frequent in Latin America since the 1990s, and that now, in the aftermath of the economic crisis, is starting to be applied in many developing economies with the aim of restrictive fiscal adjustments. Reducing the lack of structural change and technological asymmetries at the global level requires a consensus about new international rules for political cooperation. The time has come to rethink rules in a global world and to suggest solutions in which concerns with growth and distribution at global level are paramount. The principle of implicit (or automatic) reciprocity and its corollary propose a "win–win" scenario of growth based on coordinated expansionary policies, and it represents a new pillar for renewed global governance based on international coordination.

This paper is structured as follows. The first section briefly presents the background theoretical context on learning, technological capabilities, and innovation. In section 2.1.2 different approaches – supply *versus* demand driven – on learning and technological capabilities are analysed and integrated in a broad picture that describes alternative paths in the catch-up process. Section 2.1.3 incorporates the tools provided by the literature on innovation systems, which expands the understanding of the role of institutions on learning paths and catching up. Section 2.1.4 describes the impact and opportunities that developing countries face when new paradigms appear. Section 2.1.5 describes how the learning paths can lead to either a virtuous pattern or a *hysteresis* state. Section 2.1.6 and 2.1.7 give a deeper insight about the phenomenon of *hysteresis*, analysing the effect of shocks on macro prices – such as the real exchange rate (RER) – on technological capabilities and the diversification of the production structure. Section 2.1.8 presents the principle of implicit reciprocity and its policy implications. The last section concludes.

2.1.1 Learning and technological capabilities: supply-side efforts

The dependence theory of the 1960s and 1970s argued that technological capabilities cannot be fully developed in developing countries (Cardoso and Faletto, 1969; Cardoso, 1973). According to this literature, technological dependency is associated with the export of primary goods in order to obtain the financial resources required to import capital goods and industrial products. As a result developing countries were unable to build up their own industrial sectors, technological skills and organisation, which form the basis for developing technological capabilities.

At the beginning of the 1970s, Schumpeterian ideas increasingly began to permeate the empirical and theoretical analysis of technical change in developing economies. Analysts recognised that some developing countries succeeded in promoting structural change and absorbing technology. This modified the prevalent view of the 1960s regarding the impossibility of endogenously developing technological capabilities. The process of development and industrialization was strictly linked to the inter- and intranational diffusion of "superior" techniques (Fransman and King, 1984). At any point in time, there are likely to be, at most, a very few best-practice techniques of production, which correspond to the technological frontier. The process of creating technological capabilities is thus closely linked with the borrowing, imitation, mastering, and adaptation of advanced technology from countries on the technological frontier.

This view predicts persistent asymmetries among countries in terms of mastering production processes and introducing innovations. Wide differences apply to the capabilities for developing new products and the different time lags in producing them after their introduction into the world economy. Indeed, the international distribution of innovative capabilities for new products is at least as uneven as that for production processes (Posner, 1961; Freeman, 1963; Hirsch, 1965; Hufbauer, 1966; Vernon, 1966). Technological asymmetries are thus associated with the different phases in the evolution of technology and a specific international distribution of innovation capacity in the production of new goods. In the initial phase, innovative advantage is the main factor driving the production of new goods in the advanced countries. Over time, the technology evolves into a mature phase characterized by the standardization of products and processes. International competition is then based on transfers of technology, productivity improvements and production cost advantages.

Technological change progressively incorporates visions of how to do things and how to improve them, often shared by the community of practitioners in each particular activity within firms (Fransman and King, 1984; Katz, 1984; Lall, 1982; Teitel, 1984, 1987; Teubal, 1984). The empirical studies on technical change in developing countries show that the diffusion of technology in these countries implied a stream of minor adaptations and innovations, thereby reviving the broader definition of innovation set forth by Schumpeter:

> By changes in the methods of supplying commodities we mean a range of events much broader than the phrase covers in its literal acceptance. We include the introduction of new commodities which may even serve as the standard case. Technological change in the production of commodities already in use, the opening up of new markets or of new sources of supply, Taylorisation of work, improved handling of material, the setting up of new business organisations such as department stores – in short, any "doing things differently" in the realm of economic life – all these are instances of what we shall refer to by the term Innovation. (Schumpeter, 1939: 84)

The path of technological learning was thus related to the capacity to acquire technologies (capital goods, know-how, and so forth) and adapt them to local conditions. A number of empirical studies describe the increased technological capabilities that matured in some developing countries from the 1950s to the early 1980s; in fact, some of these countries even became technology exporters. In this respect, considerable microeconomic technological evidence now highlights the mechanisms that stimulate and limit endogenous learning in developing countries.

Since the mid-1980s, the Schumpeterian evolutionary literature has steadily developed new microeconomic tools for analyzing learning in catching up economies.[3] The opening of the technological "black box" by the Schumpeterian literature has produced new insights on how learning and technological capabilities coevolve and why technology gaps rise or fall across nations and time (Cimoli and Dosi, 1995). Technological learning features a set of inter-related regularities that can be briefly summarized as follows:

(i) Requires real time;
(ii) It is subject to path-dependency, i.e. the evolution of capabilities depends on previous experience and directions of past learning;
(iii) There exists complementary between sectors and capabilities, in such a way that externalities and increasing returns are crucial at both the industrial and economy levels;
(iv) There is irreversibility in the building of certain (physical and technological) assets, which cannot be just abandoned or replaced;
(v) It has a critical tacit component that could not be obtained from importing capital goods nor from reading manual and other forms of codified information;
(vi) Countries and firms that are closer to the technological frontier have an advantage in innovation and will tend to increase their distance with respect to the laggards. There exists cumulative processes leading to vicious or virtuous cycles that contribute to explain why some countries traverse to a path where learning, production capabilities and institutions interact virtuously, while others remain in a hysteresis state within a low-growth (divergence) trap.

These properties suggest that there is no reason for naïve optimism about convergence, since phenomena such as path-dependency and cumulativeness lead to strong inertia in the patterns of learning and specialization. Reducing the technology gap requires further forms of supply efforts in adapting and improving the use of capital equipment and the sequential development of various forms of tacit and incremental learning, related to the transfer and acquisition of foreign technology.[4] This mainly refers to microeconomic learning activities such as the use of equipment, the development of engineering skills in machine transformation and the adaptation of existing machines and final products to specific environmental conditions. Significant factors favoring this process include the literacy and skill level of the workforce, the skills and technical competence of engineers and designers in the mechanical artefacts, and (increasingly) the existence of managers capable of efficiently running complex organizations.[5]

The organization of production processes progressively incorporated and diffused Taylorist and Fordist methods in most manufacturing sectors. This process required time and progressive learning in organizations. Initial efforts concentrated on product design activities (most likely as a result of past incentives provided by import substitution policies) and, increasingly, on quality improvements and product differentiation. Attention was later directed toward engineering, the organization of production and mechanized production processes. The organization sometimes developed managerial organization, such as the scientific design of production processes, the search for a higher division of labor (deskilling jobs and separating mental and manual labor), the organization of fixed product lines and the implementation of vertical integration to improve learning.

Bell and Pavitt (1993) capture the complementarities between learning in production processes and learning in organization, emphasizing the distinction (which indeed bears some Listian flavor) between the development of technological capabilities and production capacity. Technological capabilities rest on the knowledge and resources required for generating and managing technical change. Production capacity concerns the stocks of resources, the nature of capital-embodied technologies, labor skills, product and input specification and the organizational routines in use. There seem to be some patterns, albeit rather loose, in the development of national production capacity. For example, practically every country starts with clothing and textile manufacturing and perhaps with the processing of natural resource, and it then moves on – if it does – to more complex and knowledge-intensive activities.

This process of technological learning, redefining production capabilities, also has a demand side that cannot be ignored. Both learning and demand growth should go hand in hand in the process of development to avoid unemployment. Figure 2.1.1 illustrates this point by putting together the evolution of labour productivity (π) and the evolution of aggregate demand/production (Y). In the space of π-Y, the points a and c indicate the prevailing levels of productivity and income in developing and developed countries, respectively. Naturally, these levels are higher in the developed countries.[6] In turn, N_a and N_c indicate levels of employment, which are also higher in the developed economy. The ratios 1/Na and 1Nc correspond to the declivity of the lines drawn from the origin to points a and c. These ratios multiplied by the productivity level give the total product and total aggregate demand. It is important to stress that these lines are hypothetical and do not represent actual paths: what counts for the argument are the different combinations of productivity and aggregate demand, and the various forms that each country traverses between two or more points.

The differences between the developed and the developing economies stem from a stronger process of industrialization in the former which stimulated demand along with productivity growth. On the other hand, in the developing country this virtuous interaction between productivity and demand growth did not happen. Consider for instance a supply-side effort to learn and improve technological capabilities in the developing economy,

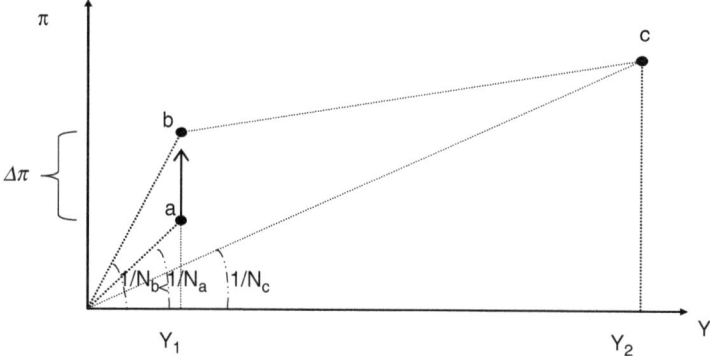

Figure 2.1.1 Supply efforts and learning
Source: Cimoli and Porcile, (2009).

from *a* to *b* in Figure 2.1.1. Although the increase in productivity $\Delta\pi$ implies a reduction of the technology gap, there is also a reduction of employment, which decreases from N_a to N_b.

Thus, this illustration aims to capture the missing link between supply-side efforts and the aggregate demand mechanisms provided by the expansion of the industry. In other words, in developed economies the expansion of employment along with labor productivity is related to the diversification of the economy, the expansion of high-tech activities and exports and the consequent dynamism of domestic and international demand. In developing economies, on the contrary technical change is highly localized in few export activities (both in the agricultural and industrial sector) with feeble effects on total demand and structural change. As a result, productivity tends to grow at higher rates than demand, implying that unemployment and underemployment persist. This is what the structuralist literature denominates "structural heterogeneity": labor productivity varies enormously across and within sectors, with a large part of total employment allocated to subsistence sectors (Pinto, 1970, 1976; Sunkel, 1978).

These results pertain to specific historical and analytical circumstances, corresponding to a period of commercial protection and active industrial policies. From the 1950s to the 1970s, such protection often served to build up the minimum capabilities at the plant level for developing the skills and organisation needed to industrialise. In Figure 1, the starting point *a*, is clearly inefficient compared with *b*. To cover the gap in productivity, the industry (or production plant) has to pass through different stages of learning to accumulate technological capabilities (Bell, 2006).

Assuming a simple mark-up equation and equal wages (*w*), prices can be written as follows: $p_a = mw/\pi_a$, and $p_b = m^*w/\pi_b$. Assuming constant and equal mark-ups in the two countries, the gap between the points *a* and *b* is reflected in the unit prices, $p_a > p_b$. To maintain an inefficient industry (or plant) in the market, some sort of "learning protection" must be introduced (Lall, 1982); alternatively, wages have to be reduced in developing countries, or the exchange rate devaluated. The debate on free trade and protection was approached pragmatically in the literature of the 1980s. In an initial stage, a combination of import substitution and export orientation was considered the most appropriate regime for learning and building up the minimum capabilities required in the development process (Fransman and King, 1984).

2.1.2 Assembling supply efforts and demand-led mechanisms

Thus far we have mainly described the learning capabilities from supply-side efforts at a microeconomic level. Demand growth increases productivity and employment through the diffusion of dynamic increasing returns in the industry, which, in turn, increases its production capacity and output. From the Smith–Young–Kaldor perspective, output growth triggers increases in the division of labour of production processes and also improves learning in each of the complementary activities and skills required in the use of equipment, the adaptation and transformation of machines tools and the management of complex organizations. These increases in productivity and per capita income then induce a recursive process that further reinforces the increase in production capacity, output and employment.[7]

The expansion of productivity, employment, and output also involves the transformation of the production structure. The relationship between structural change and economic development was first explored by the pioneers of development theory.[8] Development required the reallocation of production factors from low-productivity sectors to high-productivity areas in which increasing returns prevailed. Industrialization was thus seen as the way out of the "backward" condition. The manufacturing sector would provide increasing returns and allow the development of technological learning. The increasing participation of industry in total value added would generate spillover effects, backward and forward linkages and technological externalities, which in turn would accelerate capital accumulation and growth.[9] This process would be reinforced by the continual development of new industries and new knowledge if demand and investment in new products were sustained (Metcalfe, 2001).

Furthermore, one might still be able to identify some differences in the predominant modes of sectoral technological learning. In this respect, the taxonomy of the sectoral patterns of the acquisition of innovative knowledge suggested by Pavitt (1984) was largely adopted to describe the differences across sectors. Pavitt distinguishes four groups of industrial sectors: (i) supplier-dominated sectors, where innovations mainly enter as exogenously generated changes in capital and intermediate goods and where learning is primarily associated with adoption and production skills; (ii) specialized suppliers, which provide equipment and instruments to the industrial system and rely on their innovative activities on both formal (more or less scientific) knowledge and more tacit one based also on the user-producer relationships; (iii) scale-intensive sectors, whose innovative abilities draw on the adoption of innovative equipment, the design of complex products, the exploitation of scale economies and the ability to master complex organizations; and (iv) science-based sectors, whose innovative opportunities are more directly linked with advances in basic research.

In this paper we are particularly interested in whether one may use that taxonomy to identify specific patterns in the development process. The emergence of a manufacturing sector is generally characterized by an initial stage in which supplier-dominated sectors prevail, accompanied by the emergence of specialized suppliers. The process of technical change in these sectors is characterized by a sequential development of various forms of tacit and incremental learning related to the transfer and acquisition of foreign technology (Cantwell, 1991). These learning activities are mainly related to the use of equipment, the development of engineering skills in machine transformation, and the adaptation of existing machines and final products to specific environmental conditions. The emergence of scale-intensive industries entails other forms of learning related to the development and use of capital equipment. Unlike supplier-dominated sectors, scale-intensive industries focus their technological efforts on (i) the development of technological synergies between production and use of innovations, often internalized via horizontal and vertical integration; (ii) the exploitation of static and dynamic economies of scale; and (iii) the establishment of formal institutions undertaking research (typically, corporate R&D laboratories), which is complementary to informal learning and the diffusion of technological knowledge.

In fact, sectors are different in terms of their potentials of generating and accumulating technological capabilities: some of them boost externalities, complementarities, innovation and technological innovation and diffusion, while others do not. Thus, the diversification of production leads to the creation of higher-productivity strata and various forms of increasing returns, stemming from new skills, capabilities and knowledge spillovers that a more complex economic structure makes possible. Moreover, there is a clear association between technological capabilities and the ability to compete in sectors whose demand grows faster – thus, facilitating to overcome the balance-of-payment constrain on growth.

At the same time, innovation and diffusion occur unevenly: technology gaps and technological asymmetries between groups of countries emerge precisely because the most dynamic activities of the continuum of (heterogeneous) activities concentrate in a few areas, while lower-end activities prevail in the rest of the world – thus, such as in catching up countries. This is why heterogeneity is the inevitable result of Schumpeterian competition.

This historical experience revealed how the manufacturing sector holds a special role in the process of structural change. In fact, the increasing returns provided by the manufacturing sector make it a privileged *locus* for the development of technological learning, accumulation of technological capabilities and diffusion of technology to the whole economic system. Manufacturing does not monopolize learning, but it tracks well the learning process in a developing economy. While other sectors play an important role in development and production of externalities, a rising share of technology-intensive activities in manufacturing is a good proxy for the process of learning in the whole economy. In addition, manufacturing responds for a significant share of total employment, along with construction and services. What happens to employment in manufacturing has significant repercussions for employment and productivity in the rest of the economy.

The process of development consists precisely in moving labor from low-productivity strata to high-productivity strata; hence, catching up and industrializing countries need to accumulate technological capabilities and grow at very high rates to be able to transfer the labor force underemployed in low-productivity sectors toward higher-productivity sectors. This is the only form of overcoming heterogeneity in labor productivity. The direct implication of this is that the only engine that could drain labor out of the subsistence sector is structural change: it will not be possible to move workers to better jobs if there is no creation of new sectors and technological upgrading, and in order to create these higher-productivity strata it is necessary to transform the production structure. In less technologically advanced countries, job creation and the reduction of underemployment critically depends on the diversification of the production and export structures.

The ensemble of supply efforts and demand-led inducement to learning can be viewed as an adaptive process, which incorporates the bottom-up and the aggregate-down mechanisms for development (Setterfield and Cornwall, 2002; Ocampo, 2005, Metcalfe, Foster and Ramlogan, 2006). On the one hand, learning and innovation underlie the transformation of industrial structures in sectors with greater investment opportunities and higher productivity. On the other, the top-down mechanism captures the virtuous impact of demand on productivity and industrial production capacity. Moreover, some technologies have very wide domains of application, and they play a crucial role in the process of learning and industrialization. These core technologies often also imply basic infrastructures and networks common to a broad range of activities (such as the electricity grid, the road system, telecommunications and the information network). Many pieces of empirical evidence strongly convey the idea that establishing dynamic technological processes in developing countries is impossible without major structural changes and the sequential construction of a growing manufacturing sector based on indigenous skills in a set of core technologies (Rosenberg, 1976; Chudnovsky, Nagao and Jacobson, 1984; Fransman, 1986).

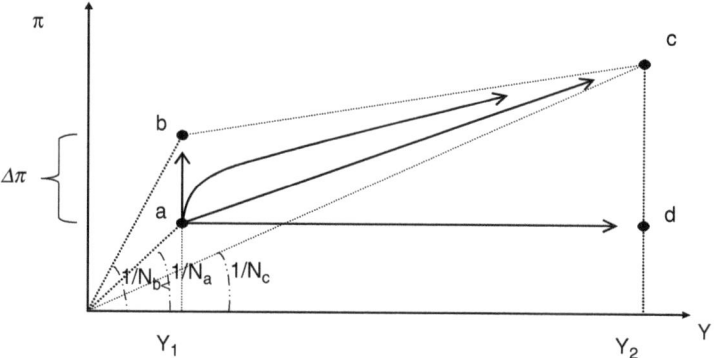

Figure 2.1.2 Assembling supply efforts and demand-led mechanism
Source: Cimoli and Porcile, (2009).

In Figure 2.1.2 different paths can be observed that lead from point *a* to point *c*, each of which is characterized by different combination of supply efforts and demand-driven mechanisms for growth and learning (domestic demand and exports). There is both an income gap (Y_2 and Y_1) and a productivity gap ($\Delta\pi$) between the developed and the developing economies. Two extreme cases emerge from the figure: a purely supply-side path traced from *a* to *b*, where higher levels of productivity are reached with no increase in output and employment; and a pure demand-side path from *a* to *d*, where demand growth boosts employment with no increase in productivity. Between these two extremes there are many paths stemming from the interaction between supply efforts and demand-led mechanisms. One of them relies initially on stronger learning efforts that elicit in the sequence a demand response. In the other case the starter of the virtuous circle is the dynamism of demand (for instance, by exporting to worldwide markets based on cheap labor or other abundant factor), which is then used to speed up learning and structural change.

The alternative paths represent different ways of reducing the income and productivity gap. Demand growth allows for the expansion of production capacity and affects the share of the industrial sectors in total value added, which may generate spillover effects, backward and forward linkages and technological externalities. At point *c* the industrial sector has expanded and the employment increased from N_a to N_c. This path combines simultaneous efforts of learning within plants – and firms – and the impact of demand on productive resources, improving skills and competences in the workforce and use of capital goods. These are the sources of increasing returns, which are captured in the aggregate by growing productivity, industrialization and output.

The demand for exports is a critical component of aggregate demand, as suggested by the Structuralist and Keynesian theory of the external constraint on growth. Exports therefore play a central role in explaining the accumulation of capabilities. This is mostly true in open economies, where products, production processes, and sectors emerge and disappear rapidly in the international economy. The approach that integrates the Schumpeterian perspective with the Keynesian balance-of-payments-constrained growth models, which highlight the role of demand for exports, individuate the prevalent trade-offs in the process of structural transformation and specialization (Cimoli, 1988; Metcalfe, 1989; Dosi, Pavitt and Soete, 1990; Cimoli and Soete, 1992).

The specialization pattern is embedded in the income elasticities of demand for exports and imports (Rodríguez, 1976; Thirlwall, 1979; McCombie and Thirlwall, 1994), thus being the link between specialization patterns and demand implicitly present in these models. They permit to look at elasticities as the outcome of a process of structural change and define the relative rates of innovation and technology diffusion in the international economy. It is generally recognized that the income elasticity of demand is lower for most primary commodities than it is for manufactured products which are knowledge-intensive. The lower income elasticity of demand for primary commodities means that, for a given increment in world income, the balance of payments of the commodity-producing developing country will automatically deteriorate. And thus aggregate demand has to be reduced, affecting negatively the expansion of aggregate output and the learning process associated with this expansion. Conversely, if the economy specializes in goods that increasingly incorporate learning and produce positive externalities, then the elasticity of exports rises and the virtuous path of learning is sustained in the long term.

In sum, countries far from the technological frontier may exhibit patterns of factor allocation which are "efficient" in terms of relative prices, for a given distribution of technological capabilities. Yet this allocation efficiency may well entail negative long-run implications for growth as it would be associated with a lower income elasticity of the demand for the goods that the country can competitively produce (compromising the "growth efficiency") and with a lesser innovative potential (compromising the "innovative efficiency"). Whenever trade-offs between different notions of efficiency arise, "suboptimal" or "perverse" macroeconomic outcomes may emerge. Since the *future* pattern of technological advantages/disadvantages is also related to the *present* allocative patterns, we can see at work here dynamic processes which Kaldor called of "circular causation": economic signal related to intersectoral profitabilities – which lead in a straightforward manner to "comparative advantages" and relative specializations – certainly control and check the allocative efficiency of the various productive employments, but may also play a more ambiguous or even perverse role in relation to long-term macroeconomic trends.

2.1.3   Spaces and complementarities between market and non-market institutions

Learning activities hold a special status in the construction of the institutional system. Sound theoretical arguments and growing empirical evidence indicate that the observed patterns of industrial structures are the outcome of the interaction of specific modes of learning and institutions supporting technical change. Nations are characterized by particular modes of institutional governance, which to a certain extent make them diverse auto-reproducing entities. There is also an element of nationality stemming from the shared language and culture, as well as from the national focus of other policies, laws, and regulations that constrain or stimulate the innovative environment. These factors contribute to the organizational and technological context within which each economic activity takes place. In a sense, they set the opportunities and constraints facing each individual process of production and innovation, including the availability of complementary skills, information on intermediate inputs and capital goods and demand stimuli to improve particular products.

A significant body of literature outlines the importance of institutions and their role in learning and technological capabilities (Freeman and Perez, 1988; De Bresson and Amesse, 1991; Cimoli et al., 2006). This literature provides examples of the functioning of national innovation systems (NIS).[10] A variety of overlapping definitions of national innovation systems have been introduced, with differing emphasis on firms and on the meso- and macro-economic levels (Freeman, 1987; Nelson, 1993). Metcalfe (1995) provides a policy-oriented definition of a NIS as a "set of institutions which jointly and individually contribute to the development and diffusion of new technologies and which provides the framework within which governments form and implement policies to influence the innovation process." He argues that the nature of each NIS is fundamentally shaped by both the division of labor and the peculiarities of information, which cause a predominance of coordination by non-market means. The institutions that compose these systems (including private firms, universities, and other educational institutions, public research labs, private consultancies, professional societies, and industrial research associations) "make complementary contributions, but they differ significantly with respect to motivation and to a commitment to dissemination of the knowledge they create."

The empirical findings on NIS reveal other elements and linkages that affect the learning process and the generation of technological capabilities. In particular, firms themselves are nested in networks of linkages with other firms and also with other non-profit organizations (such as public agencies). These networks, or lack thereof, enhance or limit the opportunities for each firm to improve its problem-solving capabilities. The general point here is that competition and efficiency are not made by single firms, but by networks of dissimilar organisations, both public and private. Firms must adapt to rapidly changing market conditions or take the lead by innovating their products and production processes in a world where technological developments are occurring at an ever-increasing speed and where the rate of specialization (through division of labour) is also rising. It is becoming increasingly difficult for individual firms to produce all the relevant knowledge themselves and to translate this knowledge into innovative products or production process (Teece, 1998; Teece, Pisano and Shuen, 1990).

Learning patterns are clearly nested into the broader ("macro") conditions of the institutional system (Teitel, 2004; Kanatsu, 2006). For example, the literacy and skill level of the workforce, the skills and technical competence of engineers and designers in the mechanical and (increasingly) electronics fields, the existence of managers capable of efficiently running complex organizations and the quality of higher education and research capabilities are all clearly relevant. Moreover, sectoral learning patterns and overall national capabilities are dynamically coupled via input–output flows, knowledge spillovers, complementarities, and context-specific externalities.

Can we measure the "goodness" or "badness" of a specific NIS? Recall that the path from *a* to *c* involves the interaction between the supply efforts, demand-led mechanisms, and the virtuous impacts of institutions that promote technical progress. In Figure 2.1.3, the triangle where productivity and employment increase ($+\Delta\pi$ and $+\Delta N$, represented by the set of points to the left of the *au* line segment) indicates the area in which the virtuous paths of productivity, output, and employment take place under the stimulus of non-market institutions. This area defines the industrializing path of those countries that have reached the technological frontier in the last thirty years. Evidence from the industrialized countries (such as USA, Germany, the Scandinavian countries, Japan, etc.) show that they not only learned and accumulated technological capabilities but also expanded industry and

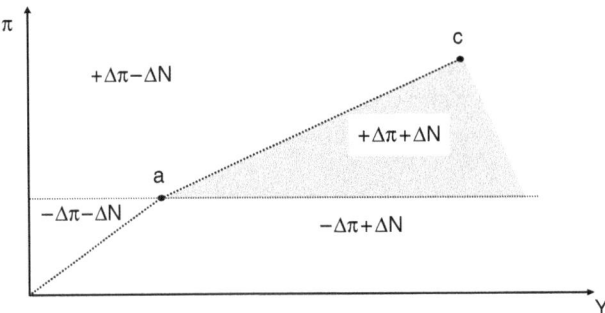

Figure 2.1.3   Institutional space for learning and industrialization
Source: Cimoli and Porcile, (2009).

employment. These paths also characterize the economies that are industrializing (Korea and China), which have successfully assembled both the supply efforts, demand-led mechanism, and non-market institutions.

Given the microfoundations of learning introduced above, it may be possible to explain why technological gaps rise or fall across different nations over time. Such gaps may open up because individual responses produce different (sometimes suboptimal) collective outcomes. The existence of diverse institutions and organizations, with specific modes of interaction, determines unique national innovation systems which, over time, exhibit certain invariant characteristics. These invariances account for phases of relative technological success and failure. Well-organized innovation systems thus serve as a powerful motor of progress, whereas poorly organized systems can seriously inhibit the whole process (Nelson, 1993; Cimoli and Dosi, 1995; Katz, 1997; Kim, 1997; Lall, 1997; Cimoli, 2000).

Far from reviewing the immense evidence on these issues, we draw on selected examples from developed countries and, in particular, a somewhat archetypical comparison between the experiences of East Asia and Latin America. In the case of the newly industrialized economies of the Pacific Rim, the process underscores the message that learning does not proceed in isolation. Firms were integrated into and interacted within a network with other firms and institutions (public and private). The resulting system was capable of expanding the education system to provide a high degree of engineering studies, increasing scientific activities within firms and the public sector, developing technological infrastructure, diffusing linkages between public and private institutions, generating financial incentives in innovative activities and improving and diversifying learning activities. Moreover, the success of institutions in some newly industrialized economies (namely, South Korea and Taiwan) has to be understood in terms of the capacity of establishing and applying performance criteria, so that, for example, credit allocation by the state was tightly bound with export performance; in this way, international competition was used to foster internal learning (Amsden, 1989; Wade, 1990).

All this contrasts sharply with the experience of Latin America, where the arrangement between the state and the private sector has often been more indulgent as regards inefficiencies and rent accumulation and less attentive to the accumulation of socially diffused technological capabilities and skills (Fajnzylber, 1990). Furthermore, the changes in technology policies and in the corresponding institutional infrastructure engendered a radical shift in science and technology priorities from learning dynamics to the accessibility of information. Innovation-related institutions came to be regarded as "markets" for trading or exchanging information rather than as part of an articulated and flexible system for transferring know-how and codified and non-codified knowledge embodied in routines, production processes or research results. Latin American integration with global trade is thus occurring asymmetrically. Domestic agents participate in international production processes, but they are marginal actors in the globalisation of scientific, technological and economic activities.

2.1.4   Paradigms and their radical impacts on learning

Paradigms generally define basic models of artefacts and systems, which are progressively modified and improved over time.[11] These basic artefacts can also be described in terms of some fundamental technological and economic characteristics. For example, the basic attributes of an airplane can be described not only in terms of inputs and production costs, but also on the basis of some salient technological features such as wing load, take-off weight, speed, the distance it can cover, and so forth. Technical progress seems to display patterns and invariances in terms of these product characteristics. Similar examples of technological invariances can be found in automobiles, agricultural equipment and a few other microeconomic technological studies. Paradigms also evolve with specific forms of production organization. In the mechanical and electrical paradigms, learning and technological capabilities were developed under the Taylor and Ford methods of production. In the case of information and communications technologies (ICT) and biotechnologies, the pattern of learning evolves with different forms of organization in production process.

Even if microeconomic paradigms present considerable invariances across countries, the ways that various paradigms interact with each national innovation system – shaped by country-specific institutions and policies – highlight a considerable variety of outcomes. The diffusion of ICT and biotechnologies paradigms is not the exception. It has radical effects on learning patterns and technological capabilities, increasing the role of science-based activities and non-market institutions (Perez, 1985; Freeman, 2001; Miozzo and Walsh, 2006; Rothaermel and Thursby, 2007).

Countries that have experienced successful structural change showed, simultaneously and not surprisingly, an adaptive pattern of learning that favored science-based activities in the public sector and firms, networking and complementarities between firms and the public sector, a Taylorist organization of R&D activities (basic and applied), human capital incorporating tacit knowledge and expertise in specialized areas of science, intellectual property governing the market for knowledge and the intangibility of results, potential products and production processes. This is the typical case of Southeast Asian countries. In the last thirty years, these countries have experienced changes in the composition of the production structure, while the rise in their R&D expenditure generally stemmed from the application of a set of long-term coordinated policies directed at the accumulation of technological capabilities. Industrial and trade polices in Korea promoted a gradual upgrading of domestic technological capabilities and subsidies to public science- and technology-intensive activities.

This is also the case with ICT, where the asymmetries in the absorption and diffusion of these technologies are now clear. Southeast Asian countries developed learning and technological capabilities in the production and use of ICT, whereas Latin America countries have not transformed their production structures and learning patterns toward sectors that produce tangible and intangible components (such as semiconductors, hardware and software). The main impact has been on activities that use and diffuse these technologies.

The pervasiveness of ICT has affected production processes by increasing the share of capital and the incorporated technologies, particularly in sectors with high export shares and services. Their impacts are also displayed in other essential activities, such as design, production, marketing and transport. Table 2.1.1 summarizes the impact of ICT in Latin America.

The natural resource sector increasingly uses ICT. Natural-resource-processing industries producing commodities for highly competitive world markets are now highly capital intensive, with incorporated technologies that are mainly imported. These industries have largely managed to improve their relative labor productivity. They are highly automated, with a large ICT component incorporated in their capital goods and production processes. It is in this sector, as well as in non-tradables sectors such as telecommunications or energy and transport services, that Latin American countries have partially closed the relative productivity gap with more mature industrial economies. In contrast, activities intensive in R&D and engineering (such

Table 2.1.1 ICT impact

	ICT impact	
Learning	**Production and adoption**	**Use and diffusion**
Opportunities	Modernisation (incorporated in capital goods and production processes) and reduction of transaction costs	Employed by natural-resource-processing and low-skill industries and services
	Enhanced linkages and efficiency with world centres of technology and multinational corporations	Increased efficiency and reduction of transaction costs in approaching input market for developed and industrialising economies
Constraints	Structural inertia and sticky diversification pattern	Reduced capabilities in R&D and engineering-intensive industries
	Polarised production systems and scant density of domestic linkages	Persistence of informal activities and income distribution

Source: Cimoli and Porcile, (2009).

as the production of pharmaceutical raw materials and capital goods) and unskilled-labor-intensive industries (such as the manufacture of shoes, garments or furniture for the domestic markets) have done worse, rapidly losing ground vis-à-vis the evolving international efficiency frontier. ICT also has important consequences for these industries.[12]

The effects of ICT reflect the fact that most of the knowledge-production centers are localized in advanced economies, including research on new material, basic science research and product design. Under this scenario, ICT clearly facilitates and speeds the exchange of information, which does not necessarily support the relocation of the above activities to Latin American economies. On the contrary, this technology promotes communication and the exchange of information, but not the local creation and diffusion of knowledge. For example, the automobile industry evaluates quality control and certification online, based on the exchange of information from one part of the world to the other.

Subsidiaries of multinational corporations and large domestic firms tend to operate in real time, planning their production activities online with their external licensors and technological services. Controlling companies, which are mainly located in advanced economies, benefit from comparative advantages in technology and innovation and the exchange of information in real time to operate production and R&D activities. Multinational companies concentrate the bulk of their research and development activities in their countries of origin or, as recent trends suggest, in strongly dynamic economies that specialize in highly technology-intensive industries and that represent huge potential markets for technological products, like China, Korea and Malaysia.

Since the 1970s, the emergence of the biotechnology paradigm has also affected the sources and paths of learning. The technologies of genetic, protein and cell and tissue engineering have an impact on human and veterinarian health and on a range of industrial and agricultural activities.[13] Opportunities to develop new products and processes can still effectively emerge almost anywhere (Ebers and Powell, 2007). In fact, science activities, production and business opportunities are in a continuous process of transformation. However, some stylised learning patterns and their implication for development can be identified. The public science sector plays an important role and has the potential to revolutionise the pharmaceutical, chemical and agricultural industries. At the same time, the ability of firms to evaluate and absorb external knowledge explains a large part of the learning and innovation process (McMillan, Narin and Deeds, 1999). The networks between public institutions, large companies and small and specialised firms are at centre of the organisation of production patterns.

Thus, as occurred with ICT, learning patterns can change radically with the diffusion of biotechnologies. Science and R&D are increasingly the main activities in learning and the creation of technological capabilities (Chataway, Tait and Wield, 2004). Networks and alliances among firms and between public and private institutions seem to offer opportunities to complement the specialization in research activates and exploration of new frontiers. Again, Southeast Asian countries are increasing their resources in those activities and transforming the institutional setting to integrate public and private actors. The ability of these countries to catch up in mechanical-electronics technologies and diffuse ICT in their production systems gives them the learning and technological capabilities to experiment with and absorb the biotech paradigm. In contrast, Latin American countries have remained anchored to their learning pattern in adopting and mastering technologies in more mature sectors. In the case of the agribusiness and food sectors, the diffusion of science activities among public and private agents seems too incipient to foster the adoption and diffusion biotechnologies.

2.1.5 Dynamics of learning paths: traverse and hysteresis

The achievement of learning and technological capabilities implies that developing countries have to move to a virtuous path characterized by increasing productivity, the generation of new products and an institutional system that supports and diffuses these capabilities. This transition from one path to another, which is termed traverse, may or may not be possible, depending on the sequence of change and adjustment at a microeconomic level, as describe above, and on structural changes in production capacity and innovation systems (Setterfield and Cornwall, 2002; Setterfield 2002). Examples from developed countries and, in particular, East Asia illustrate the successful transition to a virtuous path in learning and technological capabilities. In Figure 2.1.4, the path that moves from a to the area characterized by $+\Delta\pi$ and $+\Delta N$ captures this process.

The ability to promote structural change in order to profit from new technological paradigms and demand growth is a critical determinant of a country's relative economic performance in the international arena. This is especially true in open economies, where products, production processes and sectors quickly emerge and disappear at the international level. This idea is directly related to theories of production that allow for dynamic increasing returns, from Young and Kaldor to the recent and more rigorous formalisations of path-dependent models of innovation diffusion, whereby the interaction between microeconomic decisions and some form of learning or externalities produces irreversible technological paths and lock-in effects with respect to technologies that may well be inferior, on any welfare measure, to other notional ones, but still happen to be dominant (loosely speaking) because of the weight of their history (David, 1985; Arthur, 1989). However, paradigms are generally embodied in larger technological systems and in even bigger economy-wide systems of production and innovation.

The path of learning and technological capabilities can be affected by macroeconomic shocks and new paradigms. After a negative shock, for

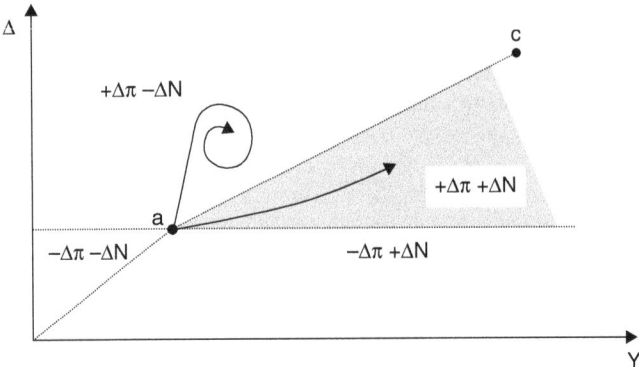

Figure 2.1.4   Traverse in development process and *hysteresis*
Source: Cimoli and Porcile (2009).

example, an economy cannot return to its previous path and, at the same time, does not invoke a virtuous path in the accumulation of learning and technological capabilities. The impact of an exogenous shock persists in the system even after the shock ceases; this is the case of a hysteresis state.[14] This case is sketched in Figure 2.1.4, which summarizes the development stage of Latin American countries and their difficulties in reaching the area defined by $+\Delta\pi$ and $+\Delta N$. Learning and technological capabilities do not traverse to a path where the supply efforts, the demand-driven mechanisms and NIS interact virtuously (Cimoli and Correa, 2005). Moreover, the lack of all these factors does not favour the ability to absorb established new paradigms. The learning path does not develop the potential to achieve point *c*, and the country remains in a hysteresis state in an area with a lower combination π–Y relative to the industrializing countries and the technological frontier.

In the long term, the learning paths should be developed through different stages that incorporate supply efforts in production, demand-driven mechanisms and innovation systems that increasingly incorporate science and R&D activities. Each of these components interacts with the others and further increases learning opportunities and capabilities.

Latin American countries have undergone economic reforms that affected the sources of learning and technological capabilities. These reforms include the new set of rules established under a different trade regime (determined by the elimination of many of the trade barriers adopted in the previous decades), the privatization of large domestic firms (particularly in the service sector) and the deregulation of labor and financial markets. This "shock" provides an effective way to retool economic activities, by combining a new environment in terms of relative prices with new incentives that affect learning and technological capabilities. Since the beginning of this liberalization period, most countries have experienced an increasing internationalization process. The specialization pattern in Latin America can be mapped out on the basis of comparative advantages and access to abundant factors of production, namely, natural resource endowments or cheap labor. Geographically, two separate patterns have emerged: the South American countries have intensified their specialisation in natural resources and standardized commodities, while Mexico and the Central American countries have globalized their manufacturing and assembly activities on the back of relatively abundant cheap labor (Mortimore and Peres, 2001).

Trade liberalization and the massive inflow of imports have modified the pattern of learning in many production activities. Technology-intensive fields, in particular, have rapidly proceeded toward vertical production organization technologies, substituting domestically produced intermediate inputs with cheaper (and sometimes better) imported inputs and reorganizing themselves as assembly-type operations based on a much higher unit-import content. The share of large firms (either local subsidiaries of transnational corporations or domestically owned conglomerates) in gross domestic product (GDP) has significantly increased during the adjustment process. Most of the empirical evidence further indicates that the sources of learning have changed dramatically.

The learning path remains anchored in activities that modernize production processes and reduce costs in export sectors. Imported capital goods and learning in process improve productivity in selected sectors, while plants and production units absorb technology according to their segment in the international production networks. Learning activities are enforced in the Taylorist and Fordist organization of production, with only a few cases in which new products are created and adapted. Supply efforts and demand-led mechanisms are circumscribed to some sectors. The national innovation system and public policies have not been capable of diffusing networking activities and enforcing science-based activities in the public sector.

2.1.6   RER and structural change

In conventional trade theory, the pattern of specialization depends on endowments, which define the relative cost of producing goods with different factor intensities. This theory is at the very least insufficient: also technology contributes to define competitive advantages in international trade, and technological leads and lags play a dominant role in trade of goods with medium and high technological intensity. At the same time, trade can be a valuable handmaiden in fostering structural change. However, various variables affecting trade may have a more prominent and interesting part in influencing the direction and intensity of the diversification process; among others, the role of the real exchange rate (RER) will be discussed in this section.[15]

In recent years the literature has investigated the importance of the RER in structural change and growth.[16] Since the real exchange rate (RER) is a significant policy variable affecting trade, its movements affect the pattern of specialization, leading to the reallocation of resources across sectors. Such a reallocation, however, does not just represent a quantitative variation: it means more than just producing different quantities of the same goods produced before, and it frequently implies beginning new activities and/or closing those that cease to be competitive. Thus, behind reallocation there is a story of structural change that may either strengthen or dampen sectors intensive in technology and knowledge, reflecting the behavior of firms that are creating capabilities. As a result, managing the RER may have significant implications for the subsequent trajectory of technological learning.

A simple form of directly linking RER and technology to the production structure is provided by a Ricardian model, as the one show in Figure 2.1.5. Figure 2.1.5 presents a two-axis diagram, where the level of the RER lies on the vertical axis and the groups of goods produced are on the horizontal axis, monotonically ordered from higher to lower relative productivity sectors. The curve that represents the relative productivity of industrializing and catching-up countries (in the model, the South) with respect to technologically advances countries (in the model, the North) has a positive slope (North–South productivity gap), and its interception with the RER line will give the degree of diversification of the production structure.

Two main features of the model can be highlighted. First, a depreciation (rise) of the RER favors the diversification of exports: if the RER increases from q_1 to q_2, the Southern economy diversifies from z_1 to z_2 (increase in z). Secondly, a rise in RER is not neutral across sectors: the move from z_1 to z_2 implies moving toward activities that are more technology-intensive than

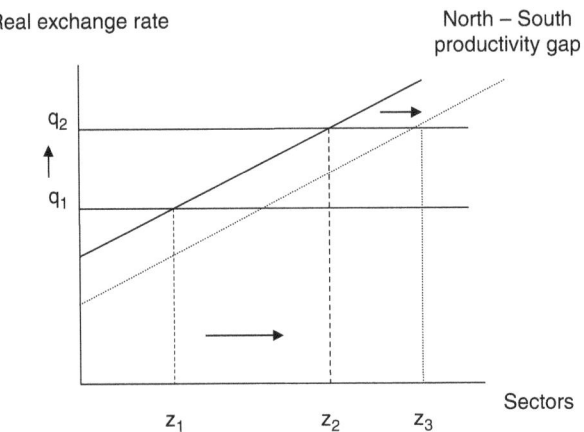

Figure 2.1.5   RER and specialization
Source: Cimoli, Calza and Porcile (2013).

before – thus, it is assumed that an increase in z implies an increase in the technological intensity of the goods produced in the South.

Furthermore, the adjustment process does not end at point z_2: given the existence of increasing returns and of cumulativeness in learning processes and productivity growth (the mechanisms of the Kaldor–Verdoorn Law) that accompanies structural change, now a lower productivity gap is associated to every level of z and the productivity gap curve shifts to the right. Thus, the learning process that accompanies structural change prompts further diversification in the South until the good denoted by z_3. The economy emerges from the adjustment process with new technological capabilities and skills (Cimoli, Fleitas and Porcile, 2012).

However, the final degree of diversification (and hence the positioning of z_3) depends also on another factor: the adoption of industrial and technological policies in compensating for the effects of the RER on the composition of production structure. Although a depreciation (rise) of the RER may serve as a starter for a surge in exports and a consequent (via increasing returns) upgrading of the export structure, it should be combined with active industrial and technological policies further boosting both, the learning coefficients of the Kaldor–Verdoorn Law and the implantation of new sectors not related to current comparative advantages. In the opposite case, in absence of industrial and technological policies, an appreciation (decrease) of the RER could affect the pattern of specialization in the long run by reducing the diversification and the intensity of technological capabilities in the economy.

This last case resembles the experience of several economies in Latin America, that in past decades have gone through periods of currency appreciation with subsequent external crises, as a result either of cyclical improvements in the terms of trade (for example, the case of a rising commodity demand) or of cycles of high liquidity in the international financial markets. In both cases, the negative shocks of the RER (appreciation) affect the productive structure of industrializing countries in the long run.

In sum, the role of the RER on the transformation of the pattern of specialization is a key issue in economic development and long run growth. When a RER appreciation discourages the production of tradable goods, particularly those of medium and high technological content, it may lead to a slowdown of structural change (if these goods cannot be absorbed by a rising internal demand). Only strong and active policy measures can compensate for an uncompetitive (appreciated) RER and can overcome the constraints on by altering the parameters governing structural change.

2.1.7 Macro shocks and hysteresis

This section aims to understand what happens to the microeconomics of learning when an unexpected macroeconomic shock hits the economy. The characteristics of technological capabilities and its relation with economic growth have to be kept in mind.

Stickiness in capabilities implies that the technological and production systems cannot respond in a flexible way to fluctuations and changes in market signals. If macro shocks (such as speculative shocks, or price volatility in commodities and in the RER) are recurrent, they may produce a process of a gradual, but continuous weakening of capabilities and of productivity. Their consequences may seem less dramatic than those produced by a financial crisis, but they may not be less costly in the long run, given their lasting marks in terms of loss of productivity and of potential growth: the more the shocks affects the microeconomics of learning and the process of accumulation of technological capabilities, the deeper and more persistent will be the impact on the whole economic structure (Cimoli and Porcile, 2008, 2011a).

Figure 2.1.6 summarizes this interrelation between loss of capabilities, productivity, and systemic effects during a period of recurrent shocks. An abrupt shock (in price or/and GDP) obliges the firm to readapt and reorganize the production process and, consequently, to redefine the needed capabilities. These changes require time and resources and, despite the fact that the velocity with which the firm responds is crucial to remain competitive in the market, the effects of readaptation on productivity will not be immediate; it takes time, and during this time there will necessarily be a slowdown in productivity growth. According to the Smith–Young–Kaldor perspective, output growth triggers increases in the division of labor and improves learning in each of the complementary activities, as well as the skills required in the use of equipment; conversely, productivity growth

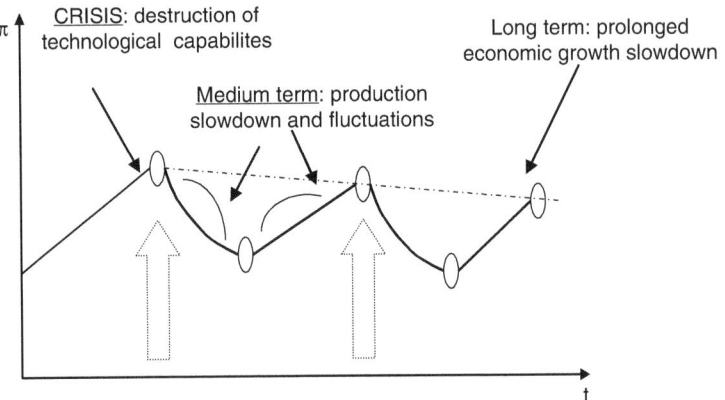

Figure 2.1.6   Productivity slowdown and destruction of technological capabilities
Source: Cimoli et al. (2011).

falls when the expansion of production falls, and increasing returns are lost. In Figure 2.1.6, this is represented by the first segment of the productivity curve with negative slope.

After this initial after-shock slowdown (or even a transitory fall) in productivity, this variable will grow again at the same or at higher rates than at the moment of the shock. But if shocks are recurrent and/or uncertainty persists, the firm would have to be constantly readapting its processes and the product mix, or will have to adjust at a slower pace (as it is represented in Figure 2.1.6), at least until the emerging structure of relative prices becomes more transparent. At the end of the day, the evolution of the firm productivity with successive shocks and uncertainty will look like as if productivity were stagnant (or even constantly declining), while it indeed fluctuates; adding up the productivity slowdown across firms, it gives a lower rate of productivity growth in the aggregate.

Short-term fluctuations in productivity may represent more than a temporary loss in the quantities produced: if fluctuations are recurrent, they also represent a loss of capabilities and therefore a loss of future potential growth. In fact, if technological capabilities and complementary assets are weak and/or have previously been destroyed, after the shock the productivity growth will slow down for a period of time eventually longer than the adjustment process alone; in this way, when the shock ends, the economy will be less able to respond to new challenges, or to increase productivity at the same rate as before. Hence, when the destruction of knowledge has occurred, each shock may depress the rate of productivity growth, even after the adjustment, for an indefinite time span. The countries will be running at a slower pace than the rest of the world, being unable to advance and thus keep in the same place – a phenomenon that has been defined as "the Red Queen effect" (Cimoli and Porcile, 2008).

This progressive destruction of technological capabilities represents one of the main threats to the process of structural change of industrializing and catching-up countries, since they are precisely creating and consolidating their (still frail) endogenous capabilities. This point holds, in particular, for commodity-rich countries. In fact, specializing in primary commodities does not seem to represent the best option in the attempt to upgrade technological capabilities: when rising commodity prices favor the development of sectors that are less technology-intensive and whose stimulus to human capital formation is weak, this may inhibit the surge of knowledge-intensive sectors and the economic structure that emerges will have less technological capabilities and less diversification (fewer sectors), implying a reduction of systemic learning and economic returns. Both effects combine and reinforce each other, giving rise to vicious circles that will hamper economic growth in the long run. Thus, commodities may provide early industrialization opportunities, but they limit the possibilities of maintaining rapid development through deepening and diversification in the primary sector.

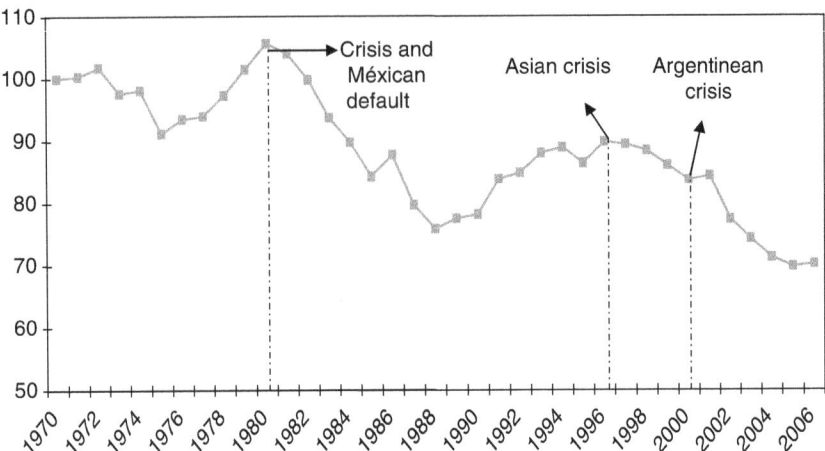

Figure 2.1.7   Productivity gap between Latin America and the United States
Source: Cimoli and Porcile (2011b).

Countries rich in natural resources can delay industrialization, but in general they cannot reach a sustained growth without a strong industrial base that permit to minimize the risks of price fluctuations (ECLAC, 2008, 2010).

Most of the discussed features of the effects of shocks on production structure and productivity can be identified in the historical experience of many Latin American economies. By comparing the productivity levels in the region with that of the USA (considered here as the technological frontier), Figure 2.1.7 shows how relative productivity (of labor) has moved very slowly over time in Latin America. Since the 1980s, the index of relative productivity between Latin America and the USA decreased (meaning that the productivity gap increased) and this fall was especially intense in the latter part of the decade. Despite a sustained economic growth between 2003 and 2008, the performance of the region in terms of relative productivity was the worst of the last 36 years – with the only exception of the eighties (the lost decade).

The effects of the shocks on Latin America are clearly visible in Figure 2.1.7 (and they remind the shape of productivity line in Figure 2.1.6). The three main breaks in the curve represent: a dramatic fall during the Latin American debt crisis of the 1980s, followed by a moderate improvement in the early 1990s; a new fall after the Asian crisis in the second half of the 1990s; and another in early 2000s, in the aftermath of the Argentinean crisis. These breaks are preceded by periods of slow increases in relative productivity, interrupted by negative shocks that reduce productivity, employment, and output and that destroy the existing technological capabilities in sectors with medium or high technological intensity, without the symmetric construction of new ones. Thus, the region seems still unable to break out this vicious circle and unable to "close the gap" with the developed world (Cimoli and Porcile, 2011b).

Summarizing, in general every shock (in prices and/or GDP) will induce a productivity slowdown during the adjustment process. When the shock has an impact on the economic structure, and some sectors and capabilities are destroyed (R&D departments are closed, producer–user interactions ceased, public research agencies underfinanced, human capital lost and so on and so forth), productivity growth may fall after the adjustment. Given the destruction of technological capabilities, the efforts of the firms to adjust to new shocks will become increasingly less effective, and the ability to learn and restore productivity growth undermined. This will be particularly the case if shocks are frequent.

2.1.8 Implicit reciprocity and its corollary

In the aftermath of international financial crisis, which global rules should be implemented to foster sustained and long term global growth? So far the focus has been placed on the need of devising new rules for the international financial system, which is probably the most urgent challenge to be addressed in the next years. However, other dimensions of the global growth equation have not been yet adequately considered, despite their important implications in the long run - first of them, structural change. In this sense, a structuralist perspective on international trade and development could be a useful starting point for discussing a new set of policies in which concerns with structural change, distribution and global growth are paramount.

In order to undertake a process of structural change – and thus overcoming heterogeneity in labor productivity and transferring the labor force underemployed in low-productivity sectors towards higher-productivity sectors, industrializing countries need to accumulate technological capabilities and grow at very high rates. This implies that will require importing from abroad (in practice, from more technologically advanced countries) the technological and capital goods that they need to upgrade the contents of their productions. However, in this way their process of structural change and growth will be constrained by the availability of foreign exchange.

The need of industrializing countries to speed up growth and absorb the underemployed is expressed in a key tenet of the Structuralist school: the principle of implicit (or automatic) reciprocity (Prebisch, 1950, 1976). Based on structuralist ideas on trade and growth (Prebisch, 1959), the principle states that the industrializing countries offer implicit (or automatic) reciprocity to the industrialized ones because they convert in imports of technology-intensive goods all the foreign exchange obtained from exports. In other words, the industrializing countries will not accumulate reserves, but convert every additional unit of foreign exchange into global growth – by purchasing additional imports of capital and high-tech goods from the advanced countries.

However, external disequilibria set a limit to the intensity of implicit reciprocity. Implicit reciprocity ensures that fiscal policy in industrializing countries is managed with a view to filling in any gap between actual growth and the balance-of-payment-constrained growth: in case of an alleviation of the external constraint, this will stimulate the government to pursue a more active fiscal policy aimed at reducing unemployment and underemployment; inversely, if fiscal policy is used as the only instrument to sustain demand without diversifying and expanding exports and improving international competitiveness, then growth will be hampered by external disequilibrium.

These external unbalances can be avoided only with a sustained expansion of exports, which will help ease the external constraint on structural change and growth.[17] A corollary of the principle of implicit reciprocity argues that the participation of industrializing countries in international trade is, to a large extent, a function of its own capacity to export. Hence, according this corollary, technologically advanced countries should open their markets to sustain the rise of industrializing countries' exports), thus calling for international cooperation in reducing the lack of structural change at global level. On the contrary, if advanced countries do not offer space to sustain this expansion, protectionism and trade barriers represent the only viable solution for industrializing countries to transform the production and employment structure and to generate the technological capabilities required to foster long-term economic growth, without incurring in unsustainable trade unbalances.

The lesson of the implicit reciprocity and its corollary holds even when applied to macroeconomic policies. When both groups of countries coordinate expansive policies, industrializing ones can sustain the process of expansion of effective demand and of diversification of production structures, combining consistently macro and industrial policies; inversely, if the implementation of Keynesian expansive policies adopted by industrializing countries will not come along with similar policies in technologically advanced countries, which instead pursue austerity and fiscal consolidation policies, the efforts toward structural change in catching up regions will be nullified and global growth will slow down. Thus, there is a real threat that the technological asymmetries that characterized these blocks of countries at different stages of structural change will turn into irreconcilable political asymmetries. This picture resembles the contraposition that is taking shape in the actual international scenario between the fiscal austerity policies adopted by advanced countries and the expansionary and diversification-led policies undertaken by some industrializing and catching up countries.

In an interdependent international economy with significant technological and productive asymmetries, a purely market-led approach to international relations will fail to explore all the potential of trade for global growth. For industrializing countries, a purely pro-competitiveness policy and a purely activist fiscal policy will be both, at the end of the day, self-defeated: a "pure" structural change approach may produce a mercantilist drive in trade policy, while a "pure" fiscal policy approach will meet the barrier of the external constraint. Furthermore, for a sustainable global growth, not just industrializing countries, but also advanced ones should support a combination of policies stimulating structural change along with traditional Keynesian macroeconomic policies. Thus, the corollary of implicit reciprocity suggests that a Keynes plus Schumpeter policy-mix contains the ingredients required for both catching up and a positive-sum game in the international system (Cimoli and Porcile, 2011a).

In sum, the principle of implicit (or automatic) reciprocity and its corollary propose a win–win solution of mutual growth for both industrializing and advanced countries. Advanced countries should stimulate the export of industrializing countries, as this would not compromise its own growth objectives; in turn, industrializing countries should combine fiscal and industrial policies in order to keep the rule of automatic reciprocity working. This offers a rationale for international coordination across blocks or groups of countries which are at different developmental and technological stages. For this reason, the implicit reciprocity could represent a new pillar for renewed global governance based on international coordination.

2.1.9 Conclusions

This paper discussed the need to combine evolutionary microeconomics with the structuralist and Keynesian focus on structural change and demand growth. In the 1950s to the 1970s, the structuralist tradition lacked the microeconomic foundations that could sustain its approach to growth and trade. Such bases would only be developed by evolutionary theory since the beginning of the 1980s. Patterns of learning and the accumulation of technological capabilities change over time. From the 1940s to the 1970s, the dominant learning path was based on the ability to acquire technologies (including capital goods, know-how and so forth), absorb these technologies and adapt them to local conditions. The sequential stages include product design activities, quality improvement, process engineering and economies of scale. Production processes also evolve with the improvement of managerial capabilities. To fully develop these supply efforts, demand-led mechanisms should operate, increasing production capacity and diffusing the industrial sector in the economy. Countries that combine supply efforts and demand mechanisms have industrialised and increased employment in manufacturing activities.

With the new paradigms, the learning pattern develops in a new institutional setting and NIS configuration. Learning and capabilities are now based mainly on the interaction between science-based activities in the public sector and firms, Taylorist organization of R&D activities and human capital in scientific areas. This does not mean that the previous pattern disappears. Rather, they interact and coevolve. The new technologies define the opportunities to produce new goods and processes, however, and they thus introduce novelty into the economy. Countries that have developed these patterns and transformed their production structures to incorporate R&D activities have captured the opportunities of new paradigms. They have traversed from the previous path to this new one, closer to the technological frontier. In contrast, countries that remain anchored only to their supply efforts have not benefited from the demand-led mechanisms, and their industrial sector remains truncated. The impact of trade liberalization, the inertia in industrial structures, and the lack of a national innovation system capable of creating incentives for science and R&D activities put these countries in a state of hysteresis in their learning pattern, technological capabilities, and, hence, development process. There is no endogenous mechanism that could spontaneously move the economy away from the state of hysteresis. To devise new institutions capable of placing the economy in a new growth trajectory (in which productivity growth advances *pari passu* with aggregate demand growth) is the key challenge that policymakers will have to address in the following years.

From the combination of both approaches can be derived a research agenda which differs from the mainstream growth theory and seems particularly adequate for analyzing the process of economic development. Some aspects are worthwhile stressing in this respect. As mentioned, patterns of learning vary across sectors and not all sectors display the same technological opportunities nor generate the same externalities. The traverse from a structure in which technology-intensive sectors are poorly represented toward a structure in which they respond for a higher share of total output is a critical research field, particularly in a period in which technological paradigms are rapidly changing. More research on the links between productivity growth and patterns of structural change in developing countries are required.

Secondly, it is necessary to look more closely at how learning, demand, and productivity growth interact so as to avoid the emergence of unemployment and underemployment (and, as a consequence, of heterogeneity in production and labor market). Very high rates of productivity growth do not imply higher welfare levels if unemployment is rising. Moreover, to the extent that demand growth feeds productivity growth in a virtuous spiral, the latter would be compromised if there is no parallel increase in aggregate demand. Researchers should look at the evolution of aggregated demand (particularly exports) as carefully as they look at the process of technological innovation and diffusion.

Last but not least, the research agenda should give a role to the interactions between macroeconomic policies, relative prices and economic growth. In the past, policies of rapid trade liberalization combined with real currency appreciation led to severe debt crises, as in 1982 and 1999–2000. These crises in turn elicited a sharp contraction in aggregate demand and investment. Both deeply affected learning and productivity growth, producing a vicious circle of loss of competitiveness and capabilities. More recently, higher prices for commodity exports have reinforced the prevailing pattern of specialization in natural resources in several developing countries. To the extent that this pattern is less dynamic from the point of view of aggregate demand growth and technological learning, the impact of recent changes in relative prices may have negative long run implications.

Capabilities embodied in people and firms engaged in production are destroyed when they run out of business because of sharp fluctuations in the real exchange rate. In this sense, a special attention has been given to understanding the process of destruction of technological capabilities and of the loss of diversification that can follow a macroeconomic shock such as an appreciation (decrease) of the RER. Such capabilities would be difficult to rebuild thereafter, as new paradigms are emerging and increasingly more sophisticated capabilities required.

This paper also aims at proposing feasible policy solutions to address the lack of structural change through new global governance rules. In fact, the shortcomings of current international economic regulations have become evident after the outbreak of the financial crisis. The increasing asymmetries and the uncertainty that characterizes the post-crisis scenario have been generating a debate on the urgency of rethinking forms of governance and changing rules for a renewed development model.

Structural change requires the adoption of adequate industrial and technological policies. In newly industrializing countries, the role of industrial policy is to reduce the technology gap, increase international competitiveness, and allow for an expansion of exports in global markets, thereby alleviating the external constraint on growth. Moreover, for industrial and technological policies to be effective, the existence of a strong consistency between macroeconomic priorities and industrial and technological policy targets has to be pursued. On the contrary, focusing on the "right" macroeconomic fundamentals without taking into account their impact on the production structure could nullify the effects of even the strongest industrial policy. In this sense, the experience of countries that succeeded in catching up – like Korea and, more recently, China – shows a macro policy committed to competitiveness and comprehensive industrial and technological policies.

However, reducing the lack of structural change and technological asymmetries at the global level needs more than the adoption of adequate policies in industrializing countries; it requires a consensus about new international rules for political cooperation. In the actual interdependent global economy, the time has come to propose solutions in which concerns with global growth and distribution are paramount.

Notes

1. Industrial policy is defined in the paper in a very broad sense, including all measures that create incentives in favor of and/or directly allocate resources to industrial growth and technological change.
2. Amsden (1989), Bell (2006), Cimoli and Porcile (2009; 2011b).
3. See among other s Bell and Pavitt (1983), Lall (1982), Fransman and King (1984), Katz (1984), Teitel (1984, 1987), Teubal (1984) and Bell (2006).
4. The same view is prevalent in the literature on technology and industrialization in developed economies, which explicitly emphasizes that the means, methods, and know-how through which agents "do things" define the concept of technology. It concerns problem-solving activities involving – to varying degrees – tacit forms of knowledge embodied in individuals and organizational procedures, as well as the means and interfaces through which knowledge is produced, codified, or transformed in transferable artefacts (Dosi, 1982, 1988; Pavitt, 1987; Rosenberg, 1976, 1982; Freeman, 1982, 1994).
5. This explicitly corroborates the view that technologies are, to a fair extent, incorporated in particular organizations (namely, the firms) whose learning capabilities are fundamental in shaping the rates and directions of technological advance (Atkinson and Stiglitz, 1969; Antonelli, 1995; Metcalfe, 1995). This learning, in turn, is local, in that the exploration and development of new techniques is likely to occur in the neighborhood of the techniques already in use, and cumulative, in that current technological development – at least at the level of individual business units – often builds on past experiences of production and innovation, and it proceeds via sequences of specific problem-solving junctures.
6. After all, not much prove of this is needed: informed tourists recognize that most countries can be unequivocally ranked in terms of average productivity and income gaps.
7. This literature suggests that optimizing choice among technical alternatives commonly shared by all agents has little to do with all this, and that one should rather look for an explanation of the accumulation of technological learning and capabilities. The contrast between (imperfect) learning and optimal resource allocation as the fundamental engine of development is emphasized by Kaldor, Pasinetti, and Schumpeter, among others.
8. Hirschman, Prebisch, Rosenstein-Rodan, Gerschenkron, Chenery, and Sirkin are among the classical authors in development theory.
9. Diversification of production structures and increasing returns in R&D-intensive sectors explain sustained per capita income growth in the long term, and structural change depends on the creation of new capital assets, increasing labor division and improvements in the quality of industrial products. At the same time, the innovation pace of the R&D-intensive sectors sustains production structure diversification and increasing returns.
10. Most of these approaches point out that learning is not automatic. Learning needs a "social capability" which can be viewed as a "rubric that covers countries' levels of general education and technical competence, the commercial, industrial and financial institutions that bear on their ability to finance and operate modern, large-scale business, and the political and social characteristics that influence the risks, the incentives and the personal rewards of economic activity, including those rewards in social esteem that go beyond money and wealth" (Abramovitz, 1989).
11. A variety of concepts have recently been put forward to define the nature of radical changes in technology: paradigms, technological regimes, trajectories, salients,

guideposts, dominant designs, and so on. These concepts overlap in that they try to capture a few common features of the procedures and direction of technical change and how change occurs when a new paradigm appears (Dosi, 1988).

12. In the extreme case of *maquila* industries, which are intensive users of low-skilled labour, ICTs are abundantly incorporated in capitals goods and production processes (Capdevielle, 2005). On the one hand, firms and plants reach the efficiency of those on the technological frontier. On the other, these industries have neither increased their productivity nor displayed strong linkages with the rest of the economy; in fact, increasing integration with international markets does not imply increasing dynamism in all domestic technological activities. In particular, regional technological capabilities in hardware and artefacts that can be associated with ICT are mainly explained by policies that promote foreign direct investment, as in the case of *maquila* industries, Mexico's Temporary Import Program for Exporters (PITEX), and free trade zones. Most of the "locally installed" regional production capacity is accounted for by subsidiaries of multinational corporations, which are leaders in electronics, semiconductors, printed circuit, microprocessors, mobile phones, televisions (LCD and plasma), and personal computers. It is not surprising that these corporations are from regions and countries – such as Europe, Japan, Korea, Singapore and the United States – that have radically transformed their industrial structures to promote the expansion of firms and sectors associated with the ICT paradigms.

13. Nevertheless, the biotechnology industries have not met performance expectations. After four decades, the industry has not achieved expected profits, and it has suffered from the tension between the requirements of science and those of business (Pisano, 2006; Silverthorne, 2006).

14. Derived from the Greek *hysterein*, meaning to be late or to fall short, hysteresis is one of many economic concepts drawn from physics, where it was originally used to refer to the process by which a magnetized ferric metal does not immediately return to its unmagnetized state after the magnetic force is removed from it. In economics, it has come to mean that the impact of an exogenous shock persists in the system in some way, even after the shock ceases.

15. The RER is defined as the price of the foreign goods in terms of the domestic good. A higher RER implies a depreciation (devaluation) of the domestic currency and an increase in international price-competitiveness. On this see also Cimoli (1992), Bertola and Porcile (2006).

16. The literature is extensive; see, for instance, Frenkel (2004), Pacheco-Lopez and Thirlwall (2006), Bresser-Pereira (2008), Eichengreen (2008), Freund and Pinerola (2008), Rodrik (2008) and Razmi et al. (2009), Rapetti (2011). Early contributions are Baldwin (1988), and Baldwin and Krugman (1989).

17. For a discussion of the external constraint on growth from the perspective of the Latin American structuralism, see Rodriguez (2007). Recent revisions and extensions are Blecker (2010), Cimoli and Porcile (2011), Setterfield (2009) and Thirlwall (2011).

References

Abramovitz, M. (1989) *Thinking about Growth* (Cambridge: Cambridge University Press).

Amsden, A. (1989) *Asia's Next Giant: South Korea and Late Industrialization* (New York: Oxford University Press).

Antonelli, C. (1995) *The Economics of Localized Technological Change and Industrial Dynamics*. (London: Kluwer Academic Publishers).

Arthur, W.B. (1989) "Competing Technologies, Increasing Returns and Lock-In by Historical Events," *Economic Journal*, vol. 99, no. 1, pp. 116–131.

Atkinson, A. and Stiglitz, J. (1969) "A New View of Technological Change," *Economic Journal*, vol. 79, no. 315, pp. 573–578.

Baldwin, R, and Krugman P.R. (1989) "Persistent Trade Effects of Large Exchange Rate Shocks," *Quarterly Journal of Economics*, vol. 104, pp. 635–654.

Baldwin, R. (1988) "Hysteresis in Import Prices: The Beachhead Effect," *American Economic Review*, vol. 78, pp. 773–785.

Bell, M. (2006) "Time and Technological Learning in Industrialising Countries: How Long Does it Take? How Fast is it Moving (if at all)?," *International Journal of Technology Management*, vol. 36, nos 1–3, pp. 25–39.

Bell, M. and Pavitt, K. (1993) "Technological Accumulation and Industrial Growth: Contrasts Between Developed and Developing Countries," *Industrial and Corporate Change*, vol. 2, no. 1, pp. 157–210.

Bértola, L. and Porcile, G. (2006) "Convergence, Trade and Industrial Policy: Argentina, Brazil and Uruguay in the International Economy, 1900–1980," *Revista de Historia Económica – Journal of Iberian and Latin American Economic History*, vol. XXIV, pp. 120–150.

Blecker, R. (2009) "Long-Run Growth in Open Economies: Export-Led Cumulative Causation or a Balance-of-Payments Constraint?," Paper prepared for presentation at the 2nd Summer School on "Keynesian Macroeconomics and European Economic Policies," Research Network Macroeconomics and Macroeconomic Policies, Berlin, Germany, August 2–9.

Bresser-Pereira, L.C. (2008) "Dutch Disease and Its Neutralization: a Ricardian Approach," *Brazilian Journal of Political Economy*, vol. 28, no. 1, pp. 47–71.

Cantwell, A.J. (1991) "The Theory of Technological Competence and Its Application to International Production," in D.G. McFetridge (ed.), *Foreign Investment, Technology and Growth* (Calgary: University of Calgary Press).

Capdevielle, M. (2005) "Globalización, Especialización y Cambio Estructural en América Latina," in M. Cimoli (ed.), *Heterogeneidad Estructural, asimetrías Tecnológicas y Crecimiento en América Latina* (Santiago: BID-CEPAL).

Cardoso, F. (1973) *Problemas del subdesarrollo latinoamericano* (Mexico City: Nuestro Tiempo).

Cardoso, F. and Faletto, E. (1969) *Dependencia y desarrollo en América Latina* (Mexico City: Siglo XXI).

Chang, Ha-Joon (2001) "Infant Industry Promotion in Historical Perspective. A Rope to Hang Oneself or a Ladder to Climb With?," document prepared for the conference "Development Theory at the Threshold of the Twenty-first Century," Economic Commission for Latin America and the Caribbean (ECLAC), August.

Chang, Ha-Joon (1994) *The Political Economy of Industrial Policy* (London: Macmillan/St. Martin's Press).

Chataway, J., Tait J., and Wield, D. (2004), "Understanding Company R&D Strategies in Agro-biotechnology: Trajectories and Blind Spots," *Research Policy*, vol. 33, nos 6–7, pp. 1041–1057.

Chudnovsky, D. Nagao, M., and Jacobson, S. (1984) *Capital Goods Production in the Third World: An Economic Study of Technical Acquisition* (London: Francis Pinter).

Cimoli, M. (1988) "Technological Gaps and Institutional Asymmetries in a North–South Model with a Continuum of Goods," *Metroeconomica*, vol. 39, no. 3, pp. 245–274.

Cimoli, M. (1992) "Exchange Rate and Productive Structure in a Technological Gap Model," *Economic Notes*, vol. 21, no. 3, pp. 490–510.

Cimoli, M. (ed.) (2000) "Developing Innovation Systems: Mexico in the Global Context", in Pinter Series: Science, Technology and International Political Economy, London and New York.

Cimoli, M. and Dosi, G. (1995) "Technological Paradigms, Pattern of Learning and Development: an Introductory Roadmap," *Journal of Evolutionary Economics*, vol. 5, no. 3, pp. 243–268.

Cimoli, M. and Correa, N. (2005) "Trade Openness and Technological Gaps in Latin America: a Low Growth Trap," in J.A. Ocampo (ed.), *Beyond Reforms: Structural Dynamics and Macroeconomic Vulnerability* (Stanford, CA: Stanford University Press).

Cimoli, M. and Porcile, G. (2008) "Volatility and Crisis in Catching-up Economies: Industrial Path-Through Under the Stickiness of Technological Capabilities and 'The Red Queen Effect'," Paper presented at the Mount Holyoke College Development Conference, Mount Holyoke College, Springfield, Massachusetts, November 14–16.

Cimoli, M. and Porcile, G. (2009) "Sources of Learning Paths and Technological Capabilities: An Introductory Roadmap of Development Processes," *Economics of Innovation and New Technology*, vol. 18, issue 7, pages 675–694.

Cimoli, M. and Porcile, G. (2011a) "Global Growth and Implicit Reciprocity: A Structuralist Perspective," *Cambridge Journal of Economics*, vol. 35, no. 2, pp. 383–400.

Cimoli, M. and Porcile, G. (2011b) "Learning, Technological Capabilities and Structural Dynamics," in J.A. Ocampo and J. Ros (eds), *The Oxford Handbook of Latin American Economies* (New York and Oxford: Oxford University Press), pp. 546–567.

Cimoli, M. and Soete, L. (1992) "A Generalized Technology Gap Trade Model," *Economie Appliquée*, vol. 45, no. 3, pp. 33–54.

Cimoli, M., osi, G., and Stiglitz, J. (eds) (2009) *Industrial Policy and Development, The Political Economy of Capabilities Accumulation* (Oxford: Oxford University Press).

Cimoli, M., G. Dosi, R. R. Nelson and J. Stiglitz (2006), "Institutions and policies shaping industrial development: an introductory note", LEM Working Paper, No. 2006/02, Pisa, Italy, Laboratory of Economics and Management.

Cimoli, M.; Porcile, G. Rovira, S. (2010) "Structural Convergence and the Balance-of-Payments Constraint: Why Did Latin America Fail to Converge?," *Cambridge Journal of Economics*, vol. 34, no. 2, pp. 389–411.

Cimoli, M.; Fleitas, S., and Porcile, G. (2012) "Real Exchange Rate and the Structure of Exports," mimeo.

Cimoli, M.; Calza, E., and Porcile, G. (2013) "Still Blowin' in the Wind: Industrial Policy and Distorted Prices for Structural Transformation", in Eve Paus (ed.), *The Triple Challenge of Development: Changing the Rules in a Global World*, forthcoming.

David, P.A. (1985) "Clio and the Economics of QWERTY," *American Economic Review*, vol. 75, no. 2, pp. 332–337.

De Bresson, C. and Amesse, F. (1991) "Networks of Innovation: a Review and Introduction to the Issues," *Research Policy*, vol. 20, no. 5, pp. 363–381.

Dosi, G. (1982) "Technological Paradigms and Technological Trajectories: a Suggested Interpretation of the Determinant and Direction of Technological Change," *Research Policy*, vol. 11, no. 3, pp. 147–162.

Dosi, G. (1988) "Sources, Procedures and Microeconomic Effects of Innovation," *Journal of Economic Literature*, vol. 26, no. 3, pp. 1120–1171.

Dosi, G., K. Pavitt and L. Soete (1990), *The Economic of Technical Change and International Trade* (London and New York: Harvester Wheatsheaf Press/New York University Press).

Ebers, M. and Powell, W.W. (2007) "Biotechnology: Its Origins, Organization, and Outputs," *Research Policy*, vol. 36, no. 4, pp. 433–437.

ECLAC (2007) "Progreso Técnico y Cambio Estructural en América Latina," División de Desarrollo Productivo, CEPAL, October (Santiago de Chile: CEPAL).

ECLAC, (2008) "Structural Change and Productivity Growth, 20 Years Later Old problems, new opportunities," (LG/G.2367(SES.32/3)), Chile. United Nations publication.

ECLAC (2010) La hora de la igualdad. Brechas por cerrar, caminos por abrir, ECLAC, LC/G.2432 (SES.33/3). Santiago de Chile, May.

Eichengreen, B. (2008) "The Real Exchange Rate and Growth," Working Paper no. 4, Commission on Growth and Development.

Fajnzylber, F. (1990) *De la Caja Negra al Casillero Vacío* (Santiago de Chile: CEPAL).

Fransman, M. (1986) *Technology and Economic Development* (Brighton: Wheatsheaf).

Fransman, M. and King, K. (1984) *Technological Capability in the Third World* (London: Macmillan).

Freeman, C. (1994) "Technological Revolutions and Catching-up: ICT and the NICs," in J. Fagerberg, N. von Tunzelman, and B. Verspagen (eds), *The Dynamics of Technology, Trade and Growth* (London, Edward Elgar).

Freeman, C. (1963), "The Plastic Industry: a Comparative Study of Research and Innovation," *National Institute Economic Review*, no. 26, pp. 22–62.

Freeman, C. (1982) *The Economics of Industrial Innovation* (London: Francis Pinter).

Freeman, C. (1987) *Technology Policy and Economic Performance: Lessons from Japan* (London: Francis Pinter).

Freeman, C. (2001) "A Hard Landing for the 'New Economy'? Information Technology and the United States National System of Innovation," *Structural Change and Economic Dynamics*, vol. 12, no. 2, pp. 115–139.

Freeman, C. and Pérez, C. (1988) "Structural Crises of Adjustment, Business Cycles and Investment Behaviour," in G. Dosi and others (eds), *Technical Change and Economic Theory* (London: Pinter Publishers).

Frenkel, R. (2004) "From the Boom in Capital Inflows to Financial Traps," ECLAC research project on Management of Volatility, Financial Globalization and Growth in EEs, supported by the Ford Foundation, to be published in IPD Capital Account Liberalization volume.

Freund, C. and Pinerola, M.D. (2008) "Export Surges: The Power of a Competitive Currency," World Bank Policy Research Working Paper 4750, October.

Hirsch, S. (1965) "The US Electronics Industry in International Trade," *National Institute Economic Review*, vol. 34, pp. 92–107.

Hufbauer, G. (1966) *Synthetic Materials and the Theory of International Trade* (London: Duckworth).

Kanatsu, T. (2006), "Why Toyota Does Not Fly While Bandeirante Does: Comparative Study of the Japanese and the Brazilian Aircraft Industry," Hofstra University, Department of Political Science.

Katz, J. (1984) "Domestic Technological Innovations and Dynamic Comparative Advantage," *Journal of Development Economics*, vol. 16, pp. 13–38.

Katz, J. (1997) "Structural Reforms, the Sources and Nature of Technical Change and the Functioning of the National Systems of Innovation: the Case of Latin America," paper presented at the STEPI International Symposium on Innovation and Competitiveness in NIEs" Seoul, Korea, May.

Khan, M. and Blankenburg, S. (2009) "The Political Economy of Industrial Policy in Asia and Latin America," in M. Cimoli, G. Dosi, and J.E. Stiglitz (eds), *The Political Economy of Capabilities Accumulation: the Past and Future of Policies for Industrial Development* (Oxford: Oxford University Press).

Kim, L. (1997) "Korea's National Innovation System in Transition," paper presented at the STEPI International Symposium on Innovation and Competitiveness in NIEs, Seoul, Korea, May.

Lall, S. (1997) "Technological Change and Industrialisation in the Asian NIEs: Achievements and Challenges," paper presented at the STEPI International Symposium on Innovation and Competitiveness in NIEs, Seoul, Korea, May.

Lall, S. (1982) *Developing Countries as Exporters of Technology: A First Look at the Indian Experience* (London: Macmillan).

McCombie, J.S and Thirlwall A. (1994) *Economic Growth and the Balance of Payments Constraint* (New York: St. Martins Press).

McMillan, G.S., Narin, F., and Deeds, D. (1999) "An Analysis of the Critical Role of Public Science in Innovation: the Case of Biotechnology," *Research Policy*, vol. 29, no. 1, pp. 1–8.

Metcalfe, J.S. (1989) "Evolution and Economic Change," in A. Silberston (ed.), *Technology and Economic Progress* (Basingstoke: Macmillan).

Metcalfe, J.S. (1995) "The Economic Foundations of Technology Policy," in P. Stoneman (ed.), *Handbook of the Economics of Innovation and Technical Change* (Oxford: Blackwell).

Metcalfe, J.S. (2001) "Institutions and Progress," *Industrial and Corporate Change*, vol. 10, no. 3, pp. 561–586.

Metcalfe, J.S., Foster, J., and Ramlogan, R. (2006) "Adaptive Economic Growth," *Cambridge Journal of Economics*, vol. 30, no. 1, pp. 7–32.

Miozzo, M. and Walsh, V. (2006), *International Competitiveness and Technological Change* (Oxford: Oxford University Press).

Mortimore, M. and Peres, W. (2001) "Competitividad empresarial en América Latina y el Caribe," *Revista de la CEPAL*, no. 74, pp. 37–59.

Nelson, R. (ed.) (1993) *National Systems of Innovation* (Oxford: Oxford University Press).

Ocampo, J.A. (2005) "The Quest for Dynamic Efficiency: Structural Dynamics and Economic Growth in Developing Countries," in J.A. Ocampo (ed.), *Beyond Reforms: Structural Dynamics and Macroeconomic Vulnerability* (Stanford, CA: Stanford University Press).

OECD (2012) Economic Policy Reforms: Going for Growth 2012, OECD Publishing. http://dh.doi.org/10.1787/growth-12-en.

Pacheco-Lopez, P. and Thirlwall, A.P. (2006) "Trade Liberalization, the Income Elasticity of Demand for Imports and Economic Growth in Latin America," *Journal of Post-Keynesian Economics*, vol. 29, no. 1, pp. 41–61.

Pavitt, K. (1984) "Sectoral Patterns of Technological Change: Towards a Taxonomy and a Theory," *Research Policy*, vol. 13, no. 6, pp. 343–375.

Pavitt, K. (1987) "The Objectives of Technology Policy," *Science and Public Policy*, vol. 14, no. 4, pp. 182–188.

Pérez, C. (1985) "Micro-electronics, Long Waves and World Structural Change: New Perspectives for Developing Countries," *World Development*, vol. 13, no. 3, pp. 441–463.

Pinto, A. (1970) *Heterogeneidad estructural y modelo de desarrollo reciente de la América Latina" en Inflación: raíces estructurales* (México, D.F.: Fondo de Cultura Económica).

Pinto, A. (1976) "Naturaleza e implicaciones de la heterogeneidad estructural de la América Latina," *El Trimestre Económico*, vol. 37, no. 1.

Pisano, G. (2006) "Can Science Be a Business? Lessons from Biotech," *Harvard Business Review*, vol. 84, no. 10, pp. 114–125.

Posner, M.V. (1961) "International Trade and Technological Change," *Oxford Economic Papers*, vol. 13, no. 3, pp. 323–341.

Prebisch, R. (1950) *The Economic Development of Latin America and Its Principal Problems* (New York: United Nations).

Prebisch, R. (1959) "Commercial Policy in the Underdeveloped Countries," *American Economic Review*, vol. 49, no. 2, pp. 251–273.

Prebisch, R. (1976) "A Critique of Peripheral Capitalism," *CEPAL Review*, no. 1, pp. 9–76.

Prebisch, R. (1981) *Capitalismo periférico: crisis y transformación* (Mexico: Fondo de Cultura Económica).

Rapetti, M. (2011) "Macroeconomic Policy Coordination in a Competitive Real Exchange Rate Strategy for Development," Working Paper, Department of Economics, University of Massachusetts, Amherst, 2011-9.

Razmi, A., Rapetti, M. and Skott, P. (2009) "The Real Exchange Rate as an Instrument of Developing Policy," Working Paper, Department of Economics, University of Massachusetts, Amherst, 2009-07.

Rodríguez, O. (1976) "Sobre la Concepción del Sistema centro-Periferia," *Revista de la CEPAL*, First Semester.

Rodríguez, O. (2007) *El Estructuralismo Latinoamericano* (Mexico: Siglo XXI).

Rodrik, D. (2008): "The Real Exchange Rate and Economic Growth," Brookings Papers on Economic Activity, 2008:2.

Rosenberg, N. (1976) *Perspectives on Technology* (Cambridge: Cambridge University Press).

Rosenberg, N. (1982) *Inside the Black Box* (Cambridge: Cambridge University Press).

Rothaermel, F. and M. Thursby (2007) "The Nanotech Versus the Biotech Revolution: Sources of Productivity in Incumbent Firm Research," *Research Policy*, vol. 36, no. 6, pp. 832–849.

Schumpeter, J.A. (1939) *Business Cycles* (New York: McGraw-Hill).

Setterfield, M. (2002), "A Model of Kaldorian Traverse: Cumulative Causation Structural Change and Evolutionary Hysteresis," in M. Setterfield (ed.), *The Economics of Demand-Led Growth* (Cheltenham, UK, Edward Elgar).

Setterfield, M. (2009) "Neoclassical Growth Theory and Heterodox Growth Theory: Opportunities For and Obstacles To Greater Engagement," Trinity College Department of Economics, Working Paper 09-1, December.

Setterfield, M. and J. Cornwall (2002) "A Neo-Kaldorian Perspective on the Rise and Decline of the Golden Age," in M. Setterfield (ed.), *The Economics of Demand-Led Growth* (Cheltenham, UK: Edward Elgar).

Silverthorne, S. (2006) "Science Business: What Happened to Biotech?," HBS Working Knowledge, November 13.

Stalling, B. and Peres, W. (2000) *Growth, Employment and Equity: The Impact of Economic Reforms in Latin America and the Caribbean* (Washington, DC: Brookings Institution Press).

Sunkel O. (1978) "La dependencia y la heterogeneidad estructural," *Trimestre Económico*, vol. 45, no. 1, pp. 3–20.

Teece D. (1998) *Strategy, Technology and Public Policy: The Selected Papers of David Teece*, vol. 2 (London: Edward Elgar).

Teece, D.J., Pisano, G., and Shuen, A. (1990) "Firm Capabilities, Resources, and the Concept of Strategy," Working Paper, University of California at Berkeley.

Teitel, S. (1984) "Technology Creation in Semi-industrial Economies," *Journal of Development Economics*, vol. 16, nos 1–2, pp. 39–61.

Teitel, S. (1987) "Science and Technology Indicators, Country Size and Economic Development: an International Comparison," *World Development*, vol. 15, no. 9, pp. 1225–1235.

Teitel, S. (1987) "Towards Conceptualisation of Technological Development as an Evolutionary Process," in J. Dunning and U. Mikoto (eds), *Structural Change, Economic Interdependence and World Development* (London: Macmillan).

Teitel, S. (2004) "On Semi-industrialized Countries and the Acquisition of Technological Capabilities," ICER Working Paper, No. 19-2004 (Turin: International Centre for Economic Research).

Teubal, M. (1984) "The Role of Technological Learning in the Exports of Manufactured Goods: the Case of Selected Capital Goods in Brazil," *World Development*, vol. 12, no. 8, pp. 849–65.

Thirlwall, A.P. (1979) "The Balance of Payments Constraint as an Explanation of International growth rates Differences," *Banca Nazionale del Lavoro Quarterly Review*, September.

Thirlwall, A. (2011) "Balance of Payments Constrained Growth Models: History and Overview," University of Kent, School of Economics Discussion Paper 1111, May.

Vernon, R. (1966) "International Investment and International Trade in the Product Cycle," *Quarterly Journal of Economics*, vol. 80, no. 2, pp. 190–207.

Wade, R. (1990), *Governing the Market: Economic Theory and the Role of Government in East Asian Industrialisation.* (Princeton, NJ: Princeton University Press).

2.2
Industrial Policy: Can Africa Do It?[1]

Ha-Joon Chang[2]
University of Cambridge

2.2.1 Introduction

After over three decades of ideological grandstanding, the debate on (selective) industrial policy is finally inching toward more pragmatic discussions on how to design and implement it – this and other conferences organized by the IEA this year being the best examples of such discussions (for a review of the industrial policy debate since the 1980s, see Chang, 2011).

Gone is the dominance of the view that markets work more or less well and that therefore there are very few justifications for industrial policy. In the last decade or so, there has been a revival of the infant industry argument in various guises (Chang, 2002; Shaffaedin, 2005; Greenwald and Stiglitz, 2006; Dosi et al. (eds), 2009). Even among the more orthodox economists, there is an increasing acceptance that there are many types of market failures that need to be addressed through industrial policy – not just the more conventional 'externalities' problem but also economies of agglomeration and coordination failures (Lin's interventions in Lin and Chang, 2009; Lin and Monga, 2012).

There has also been a significant change in the reading of the evidence on industrial policy. There is a growing recognition that industrial policy is not some highly idiosyncratic practice found only in East Asian 'miracle' economies (Japan, South Korea, Taiwan, and Singapore). Now it is increasingly accepted that most of today's rich countries used at least some industrial policy, especially trade protectionism, when they were catch-up economies themselves (Bairoch, 1993; Chang, 2002 and 2007; Reinert, 2007). Some econometric studies have even identified a positive correlation between protectionism and economic growth in the late 19th and the early 20th century (O'Rourke, 2000; Vamvakidis, 2002; Clemens and Williamson, 2001; Irwin, 2002, provides a criticism of these studies, which is then countered by Lehmann and O'Rourke, 2008). In particular, the exposure of Britain and the USA – conventionally considered the home of free market and free trade policies – as the pioneers of infant-industry promotion through protectionism and other forms of industrial policy has added a whole new complexion to the history of capitalist development. The practice of infant industry promotion was first systematically applied by Robert Walpole, the British Prime Minister of 1721–42, and the theory was invented by Alexander Hamilton, the first US Treasury Secretary, in his report to the US Congress in 1791 (see Chang, 2002, for further details; Hamilton's original report is Hamilton, 1791).

There is also a more nuanced interpretation of the industrial policy experiences of non-East-Asian developing countries during the import-substitutiin industrialization (ISI) period. The role of industrial policy in the significant economic progress made by many Latin American countries between the 1930s and the 1980s is increasingly recognised, as well as the success of earlier protectionism in the continent in the late 19th and the early 20th century (on the latter, see Clemens and Williams, 2004). Even the depiction of industrial policy in Africa, especially Sub-Saharan Africa, in the 1960s and the 1970s as an unmitigated disaster is being subject to criticisms (Jerven, 2011).

On top of all this, the 2008 global financial crisis has enhanced the legitimacy of industrial policy in a number of ways. First, the crisis prompted some major industrial policy actions – both defensive and proactive – by the rich countries that used to preach against industrial policy. The bailout of US automakers is the best example of defensive industrial policy and the 'green' subsidies to the auto industry in the USA and other countries are the best examples of proactive industrial policy. Second, having originated from overdevelopment of the financial sector, the crisis has restored the legitimacy of industrial policy even in countries like the USA and the UK, where it had been a taboo. Third, the continued rise of China and the solid performance of Germany, both of which have never been shy about using and talking about industrial policy, throughout the crisis period have also made people re-assess the importance of industrial policy.

Despite all of this, however, there is a persistent skepticism about the applicability of industrial policy to the African countries. However well the policy may have worked in countries like Japan and Korea in the past, it is argued, it simply won't work in most developing countries, especially those in Africa. The reasons cited are varied – ranging from excessive natural resource endowments (the so-called 'resource curse' thesis), pathological politics, the lack of bureaucratic capabilities, and the changes in the global economic rules – but the implication is that the African countries would be better off sticking to their natural resource advantages, rather than trying to develop manufacturing industries through industrial policy.

2.2.2 Structural impediments to Africa's growth – climate, geography, culture, and history

Before we consider factors that are more specifically related to the industrial policy, we need to address a more general argument that Africa's climate, geography, culture, and history structurally condemn it to underdevelopment – an argument known as 'Afro-pessimism' (the most prominent examples include Easterly and Levine, 1997; Bloom and Sachs, 1998; Collier and Gunning, 1999; Sachs and Warner, 2001; Acemoglu et al., 2001).

Of course, in discussing all of this, we should be careful not to lump together all African countries. After all, it is a continent of nearly 60 countries (the exact number depending on your attitude toward entities like Western Sahara) with very varied natural and human conditions. Many African economies share common features not because they are in the same continent but mainly because all economies – African or otherwise – at low levels of development look rather similar to each other, due to lack of specialization and diversification in the production structure and consequently in their occupational structures, social organizations, and lifestyles. Bearing this important point in mind, let us see how those arguments that emphasize (at least nearly) immutable conditions, like climate, geography, culture, and history.

2.2.2.1   The arguments

The climate argument says that, being too close to the equator, the African countries suffer from tropical diseases, such as malaria, which reduce worker productivity and raise healthcare costs.

Being landlocked, the geography argument points out, many African countries find it difficult to integrate into the global economy. The African countries are also in 'bad neighbourhoods' in the sense that they are surrounded by other poor countries that have small markets (which restrict their trading opportunities) and, frequently, violent conflicts (which often spill over into neighbouring countries).

The history argument highlights two things – ethnic diversity and colonialism. African nations are ethnically too diverse, it is argued, which makes people distrustful of each other and thus makes market transactions costly. It is argued that ethnic diversity may encourage violent conflicts, especially if there are a few equally strong groups (rather than many small groups, which are more difficult to organize). The history of colonialism is thought to have produced low-quality institutions in most African countries, as the colonizers did not want to settle in countries with too many tropical diseases (so there is an interaction between climate and institutions) and thus only installed the minimal institutions that were needed for resource extraction ('extractive institutions' of Acemoglu et al., 2001), rather than bringing in institutions that are necessary for the development of the local economy.

Although it is frequently presented in a convoluted way to avoid the accusation of racism, the cultural argument is essentially that African culture is bad for economic development – Africans do not work hard, do not plan for the future, and cannot cooperate with each other. In explaining the economic divergence between South Korea and Ghana, two countries that were at similar levels of economic development in the 1960s, Samuel

Huntington of *The Clash of Civilizations* fame argues: "Undoubtedly, many factors played a role, but ... culture had to be a large part of the explanation. South Koreans valued thrift, investment, hard work, education, organisation, and discipline. Ghanaians had different values. In short, cultures count" (Huntington, 2000: xi).[3]

2.2.2.2 The criticisms

Many of the above arguments contain germs of truths. However, there are many different ways in which those structural factors can play out. The fact that a factor is structural (that is, it is given by nature or history) does not mean that the outcome is predetermined. Indeed, the fact that all those structural handicaps are not insurmountable is proven by the fact that most of today's rich countries have also suffered from similar handicaps (Chang, 2009a and 2009b).

Climate

First of all, it should be pointed out that many of today's rich countries used to have malaria and other tropical diseases, at least during the summer – not just Singapore, which is bang in the middle of the tropics, but also Southern Italy, the Southern USA, South Korea, and Japan. These diseases are no longer very important only because these countries have better sanitation (which has vastly reduced their incidences) and better medical facilities, thanks to economic development.

A more serious criticism is that frigid and arctic climates, which affect a number of rich countries, such as Finland, Sweden, Norway, Canada, and parts of the USA, impose burdens as economically costly as tropical ones – machines seize up, fuel costs skyrocket, and transportation is blocked by snow and ice. The Scandinavian countries used to be effectively landlocked for half of the year, until they developed the ice-breaking ship in the late-19th century. Once again, cold climate does not hold the rich countries back because they have acquired the money and the technologies to deal with it (the same as in the case of Singapore's tropical climate).

Also, there is no *a priori* reason to believe that a cold climate is better than a hot climate for economic development. Indeed, in *Politics* (Book VII, chapter 7), Aristotle argued that the European societies are not very developed because their climate is too cold, which makes their people, well, stupid. He said:

> Those who live in a cold climate and in Europe are full of spirit, but wanting in intelligence and skill; and therefore they retain comparative freedom, but have no political organization, and are incapable of ruling over others. Whereas the natives of Asia are intelligent and inventive, but they are wanting in spirit, and therefore they are always in a state of subjugation and slavery. But the Hellenic race, which is situated between

them, is likewise intermediate in character, being high-spirited and also intelligent. Hence it continues free, and is the best governed of any nation, and if it could be formed into one state, would be able to rule the world. (Aristotle, 2001: 1286)

So blaming Africa's underdevelopment on climate is confusing the cause of underdevelopment with its symptoms – poor climate does not cause under-development; a country's inability to overcome the constraints imposed by its poor climate is a symptom of underdevelopment.

Geography

In terms of geography, much has been made out of the landlocked status of many African countries. It is difficult to deny the handicap being brought on by landlockedness, but then what about Switzerland and Austria? These are two of the richest economies in the world, but they are both landlocked. Some people would respond to this point by saying that those countries could develop because they had good river transport, but many landlocked African countries are *potentially* in the same position; for example, Burkina Faso (the Volta), Mali and Niger (the Niger), Zimbabwe (the Limpopo), and Zambia (the Zambezi). So, once again, there is a confusion between the cause and the symptom – it is the lack of investment in the river transport system, rather than the geography itself, that is the problem.

A 'bad neighborhood' effect may exist, but it need not be binding – look at the recent rapid growth of India, which is located in the poorest region in the world (poorer than Sub-Saharan Africa), which has its share of con-flicts (the long history of military conflicts between India and Pakistan, the Maoist Naxalite guerillas in India, Hindu–Muslim violence in India, the Tamil–Sinhalese ethnic war in Sri Lanka, and so on).

History

Ethnic divisions can hamper growth in various ways, but their influence should not be exaggerated. Ethnic diversity is the norm elsewhere too. Even ignoring ethnic diversities in immigration-based societies like the USA, Canada, and Australia, many of today's rich countries in Europe have suf-fered from linguistic, religious, and ideological divides – especially of the 'medium-degree' (that is, a few, rather than numerous, groups) that is sup-posed to be most conducive to violent conflicts. Belgium has two (and a bit, if you count the tiny German-speaking minority) ethnic groups. Switzerland has four languages and two religions, and has experienced a number of mainly-religion-based civil wars. Spain has serious minority problems with the Catalans and the Basques, which have even involved terrorism. Due to its 560-year rule over Finland (1249 to 1809, when it was ceded to Russia), Sweden has a significant Finnish minority (around 5 percent of the popula-tion) and Finland a Swedish one of similar scale. And so on.

Even the East Asian countries, which are supposed to have particularly benefited from their ethnic homogeneity, have serious problems with internal divisions. You may think Taiwan is ethnically homogeneous, as its citizens are all 'Chinese,' but the population consists of two (or four, if you divide them up more finely) linguistic groups (the 'mainlanders' vs the Taiwanese) who are hostile to one another. Similarly, Japan has serious minority problems with the Koreans, the Okinawans, the Ainus, and the Burakumins. South Korea may be one of the most ethno-linguistically homogeneous countries in the world, but that has not prevented my fellow countrymen from hating each other. For example, there are two regions in South Korea that particularly hate each other (Southeast and Southwest), so much so that some people from those regions would not allow their children to get married to anyone from 'the other place.' Very interestingly, Rwanda is nearly as homogeneous in ethno-linguistic terms as Korea, but that did not prevent the ethnic cleansing of the formerly dominant minority Tutsis by the majority Hutus – an example that proves that ethnicity is a political, rather than a natural, construction.

Thus seen, rich countries do not suffer from ethnic heterogeneity not because they do not have it but because they have succeeded in nation building (which, we should note, was often an unpleasant and even violent process).

As for the view that bad institutions are holding back Africa (and often they are), when the rich countries were at similar levels of material development to those we find in Africa currently, their institutions were in a far worse state (Chang, 2002: ch. 3). Despite that, they continued to develop. They built the good institutions largely after, or at least in tandem with, their economic development. This shows that institutional quality is as much an outcome as the causal factor of economic development. Given this, bad institutions cannot be a main structural impediment to economic development in Africa.

Culture

People talk about 'bad' cultures in Africa, but most of today's rich countries had once been argued to have comparably bad cultures (Chang, 2007: ch. 9).

Until the mid-19th century, the British would go to Germany and say that the Germans were too stupid, too individualistic, too emotional to develop their economies (Germany was not unified then) – the exact opposite of the present-day stereotypical image of the German and exactly the sort of comments that people make about the Africans. For example, John Russell, an early-19th-century British traveler in Germany, remarked: "The Germans are a plodding, easily contented people... endowed neither with great acuteness of perception nor quickness of feeling... It is long before [a German] can be brought to comprehend the bearings of what is new to him, and it is difficult to rouse him to ardour in its pursuit" (Russell, 1828: 394).

Until the early 20th century, Australians and Americans visitors to Japan would remark on the laziness of the people. Having toured many factories in Japan, an Australian engineer remarked in 1915: "My impression as to your cheap labour was soon disillusioned when I saw your people at work. No doubt they are lowly paid, but the return is equally so; to see your men at work made me feel that you are a very satisfied easy-going race who reckon time is no object. When I spoke to some managers they informed me that it was impossible to change the habits of national heritage" (*Japan Times*, August 18, 1915).

The Koreans were considered even worse. In 1912, they were condemned as "12 millions of dirty, degraded, sullen, lazy and religionless savages who slouch about in dirty white garments of the most inept kind and who live in filthy mudhuts" – the remark came from a leading female socialist intellectual at the time, that is, Beatrice Webb of the Fabian movement (Webb and Webb, 1978: 375), so one can imagine what a regular European male conservative would have said about the Koreans, had he visited the country.

All these 'bad' cultures of the Germans, the Japanese, and the Koreans have been eventually transformed thanks to economic development, as the demands of a highly organized industrial society made people behave in more disciplined, calculating, and cooperative ways. In that sense, culture is more of an outcome than a cause, of economic development. It is wrong to blame the underdevelopment of Africa (or indeed any region or country) on its culture.

2.2.3   Natural resources and industrial policy

In the discussion of industrial policy in the African context, natural resources play an important role in two ways. First, it is argued that, given their natural resource abundance, the African countries should not try to industrialize, as that would be defying their comparative advantages. This makes industrial policy redundant. Second, natural resource abundance is argued to generate perverse politics in the forms of corruption and violent conflict (a form of 'resource curse'), so trying to graft industrial policy on to that political economy, even if it worked elsewhere, will mean that the policy measures are only abused.

2.2.3.1   Does Natural Resource Abundance Make Industrial Policy Unnecessary for Africa?

Before we ask whether abundant natural resource endowments make industrialization – and industrial policy – unnecessary for the African countries, we first need to ask whether the African countries actually *are* well endowed with natural resources.

The conventional wisdom is that they are, but in fact this is only the case for a few countries (see Chang, 2006, for further details). Fewer than a dozen African countries have any significant mineral deposits. Only South Africa and the Democratic Republic of Congo (DRC) are exceptionally well endowed, each with more than one mineral resources. Most African countries may have low population density, but only a handful of them (Niger, Liberia, DRC, Chad, Senegal, Sierra Leone, and the Central African Republic) are exceptionally well endowed with arable land. In other words, most African countries look abundantly endowed with natural resources only because they have so few man-made resources, such as machines, infrastructure, and skilled labor.

Even in the case of countries that have exceptional natural resource endowments, it is questionable whether exploiting them without any clear long-term industrial policy will allow them to develop their economies sufficiently.

No country – not even the USA, Australia, or Canada, the three countries that are best endowed in the world with natural resources – has been blessed by nature to such an extent that it could become rich only by doing things that came 'naturally.' All the resource-rich advanced economies have highly developed manufacturing industries. Among the rich countries Australia has the smallest manufacturing sector (in per capita terms) by far (it is one-third smaller than the next smallest ones) owing to its abundant natural resource endowments. However, even it produces, at $2,422, manufacturing value added (MVA) per capita that is 35 times greater than relatively more industrialized Senegal ($69) and 220 times greater than the least industrialized Niger ($11) (all figures are as of 2005, in 2000 dollars; UNIDO, 2009: p. 129, Table 1). Given that Sengal and Niger have natural resource endowments that are not even remotely as abundant as those of Australia, they will have to industrialize to a much greater extent than Australia has done, if they are to have living standards that are comparable with those of present-day Australia.

Moreover, it is not even as if all 'natural' products are really natural. Many of them are products of colonialism. For example, many African countries export cocoa and tea, which were brought from, respectively, Central America and China to Africa by the colonizers. Especially when it comes to high-productivity activities whose existence determines whether a country is economically developed or not, countries become good at something only because they deliberately decide to become so – there is really no "natural" reason for the Japanese to be good at building cars, the Finns at making mobile phones, or the Korean at making steel.

High-productivity industries simply will not get established in developing countries, if we lave things to the market, as there are already superior producers from the more advanced countries. This means that developing country governments need to protect and nurture those 'infant industries' through tariffs, subsidies, and other means of industrial policy. This is, in a nutshell, the logic of infant industry promotion, which has formed the foundation of all successful catch-up attempts, starting with 18th-century Britain, through 19th-century USA, Germany, and Sweden, down to 20th- and 21st-century East Asian countries.

Thus seen, if they are to develop their economies, the African countries need an industrial policy that will eventually make their 'natural advantage' industries unimportant by developing higher-productivity activities.

This is not to say that it should ignore its natural-resource-based industries. First of all, it takes a lot of time to develop new industries. For example, it took 40 years for the Japanese carmakers (established in the early 1930s) to break into the world market, while it took 17 years for Nokia electronics (founded in 1960) to make any profit. So, before the new industries develop fully, the natural-resource-based sectors need to provide the output, jobs, and, above all, export earnings that will finance the imports of machinery and technologies for the new industries. Second, the scopes for upgrading in natural-resource-based industries are not to be under-estimated (on how to upgrade out of the natural resources sectors, see discussions in Chang, 2008, Section III). For a dramatic example, the Netherlands is the third largest agricultural exporter in the world, despite having very little land (the fifth-highest population density in the world, excluding island- and city-states).

However, in the long run, without substantial industrial upgrading, it is not possible to attain high living standards. Even the natural-resource-based industries require successful industrialization, if they are to attain high productivity. The Netherlands has a high-productivity agricultural sector only because it has 'industrialized' the sector, using its strengths in industries like electronics (for example, computer-controlled feeding) and chemicals (for example, fertilizers, pesticides). In the end, the African countries will have to get into many industries that today no one – and I repeat, no one – would think they can succeed in, if they are going to become economically developed. And, as we argued above, that requires systematic industrial policy.

2.2.3.2   Does natural resource abundance make industrial policy counterproductive for Africa?

As for the argument that, given their perverse political economy created by natural resource abundance, industrial policy will be counterproductive for the African countries, we first need to point out that, even if it were true, it would apply to only a handful of African countries, as most of African countries are not that particularly well endowed with natural resources in the first place, as I have pointed out above.

Second, there is no inevitable relationship between a country's natural resource endowments and the form of politics. If natural resource abundance inevitably led to perverse politics, we cannot explain how many countries – not just super-well-endowed USA, Canada, and Australia, but also the Scandinavian countries – have not developed perverse political economy and have developed their economies despite (or in many cases rather because of) their abundant natural resource endowments (Wright and Czelusta, 2004 and 2007, on the role of natural resources in the economic development). Moreover, in the late 19th and early 20th century, the fastest-growing regions of the world were resource-rich areas like North America, Latin America, and Scandinavia, suggesting that the 'resource curse' is not inescapable.

2.2.4 Political economy: political leadership, state coherence, and the state–society relationship

Natural resource abundance aside, there is a general concern that the political economy of most African countries will make effective implementation of industrial policy impossible. Many people characterize the African countries as suffering from 'neopatrimonial' politics, which undermines economic rationality in favor of 'Big Man' politics (for a comprehensive critique of this literature in general, see Mkandawire, 2012). Given this political economy, it is argued, any attempt to suspend market discipline will be hijacked and abused. Even industrial policy measures that may have worked in East Asia or Europe simply wouldn't work in Africa, it is argued.

Indeed, the long-running debate on industrial policy has revealed that a key difference between industrial-policy success stories and failure stories lies in the differences in their political economy (Toye, 1987; Amsden, 1989; Chang, 1994; Evans, 1995). This is at least at three levels.

First, the nature of political leadership is an important determininant of the nature of industrial policy. Even if we ignore some extreme cases in which the leaders are interested only in personal wealth and aggrandisement, the leaders may have a "wrong" vision. They may be looking backward, rather than forward, as Thomas Jefferson did when he opposed Hamilton's infant industry protection – his ideal society was one made up of respected landlords and yeoman farmers (plus the slaves). Or they may be hostile to private sector development, as many African country leaders were in the 1960s and the 1970s. Or, as many liberal politicians did in the 19th century, they may think that doing nothing, apart from protecting private property, is really the best industrial policy.

Second, even if the political leaders are interested in promoting economic development through industrial policy, they need to impose that vision on the rest of the state apparatus. While in theory the state is a hierarchical organization, in practice the wish at the top does not always permeate through the hierarchy. There will be some degree of self-seeking by government bureaucrats, although not as much as it is assumed in the public choice theory. There will also be problems arising from clashing visions (for example, the bureaucrats may be more conservative than the political leaders), turf wars within the bureaucracy, 'tunnel vision' that specialized organizations are wont to develop, internal coordination failures (coming from poor organizational design or the emergence of new issues that cut across the existing organizational structure), and many other reasons.

Third, even if the leadership has the right vision and even if there is an internal coherence within the state, the state still has to be able to impose its will on other agents in the society. In some extreme cases, the state may not even have full control of its claimed territories. In some countries, the state cannot implement policies effectively due to manpower and resource shortages. Even when the state has enough enforcement capabilities, there will be attempts by some private sector agents to neutralize or even pervert policies through lobbying and bribing.

Although it is typically assumed that these political economy problems are uniquely serious in the African countries, this assumption lacks empirical foundations (Mkandawire, 2012). Moreover, in the past all the advanced economies suffered from these problems. Indeed, when they were at levels of economic development comparable to today's African countries, today's developed countries were actually much worse in terms of suppression of democracy, corruption, state capture, incoherence of the state machinery, nepotism, and other 'pathological' forms of politics (Chang, 2002: ch. 3).

More importantly, we should not let the best be the enemy of the good. The existence of numerous political economy problems should not make us believe that therefore we have to wait for a perfect state to emerge before doing anything. In the real world, the successful countries are those that have managed to find 'good enough' solutions to their political economy problems and gone on to implement industrial (and other) policies, rather than sitting around bemoaning the imperfect nature of their political system.

Indeed, quite a few of the successful 'industrial policy states' themselves overcame their political obstacles to effective statecraft in situations that did not instil much hope. For example, between the fall of Napoleon and the end of the World War II, the French state was notoriously *laissez-faire*, ineffectual, and conservative. However, this was completely changed after the War, with the rise of *Gaullisme*, the establishment of the planning commission, and the foundation of the ENA (Ecole Nationale d'Administration), the famous school for elite bureaucrats (Cohen, 1977; Kuisel, 1981). For another example, the Kuomintang (Nationalist Party) bureaucracy was arguably one of the most corrupt and inefficient in modern history when it ruled mainland China. But after being forced to migrate to Taiwan, following the defeat by the Communists in 1949, it was transformed into a highly efficient and relatively clean one. This was done through a gradual but deliberate process of building 'islands of competence' and then giving them greater responsibilities as they succeeded and increased their legitimacy and status within the bureaucracy, finally replacing much of the old bureaucracy with the new one (Wade, 1990).

2.2.5   Bureaucratic capabilities: "Do Not Try This At Home"?

However willing, coherent, and strong the state may be and however 'correct' its vision may be, policies are likely to fail if the government officials implementing them are not capable. Difficult decisions have to be made with limited information and fundamental uncertainty, often under political pressure from inside and outside the country. Dealing with all this requires decision-makers with intelligence and adequate knowledge. On this ground, people have argued that 'difficult' policies such as (selective) industrial policy should not be tried by countries with limited bureaucratic capabilities, especially the African countries (World Bank, 1993, is the best example).

The argument is the policy-world equivalent of "do not try this at home" (DNTTAH) warning that accompanies the demonstration of difficult and dangerous stunt acts in TV shows. However, there are numerous problems with this argument.

First, the assumption behind the DNTTAH that industrial policy is exceptionally difficult is made without any theoretical reasoning or empirical evidence. For example, World Bank (1993) assumes that policies getting the 'fundamentals' – such as human capital, agriculture, and macroeconomic stability – right are easier than industrial policy, but there can be no such presumption. First, different governments have competences in different areas – the Japanese government was good at industrial policy but really messed up its macroeconomic policies in the 1990s. Second, the ease of a policy will also partly depend on its scale. For example, promoting a few industries may be a lot easier than organizing a mass education programme. Third, it will also depend on the number of agents involved in the policy. Trying to coordinate investments among a few large firms may be easier than organising a country-wide distribution of subsidised fertilizer that involve millions of small farmers who are not organised into co-operatives and scattered all over the country.

Second, another implicit assumption behind the DNTTAH argument is that industrial policy requires sophisticated knowledge of economics, as exemplified by the following comment by Alan Winters, the former head of Research Department at the Bank and the former chief economist of the UK government's DfID (Department for International Development) – "the application of second-best economics needs first-best economists, not its usual complement of third- and fourth-raters" (Winters 2003: 66). But is this true? An especially interesting fact in this regard is that, while the East Asian bureaucracies were staffed by smart people, they were certainly *not* 'first best economists.' Indeed, most of them were not even economists. The Japanese economic officials that engineered the country's 'miracle' were mostly lawyers by training. Until the 1980s, what little economics they knew were mostly of the 'wrong' kind – the economics of Karl Marx and Friedrich List, rather than neoclassical economics. In Taiwan, most key economic bureaucrats were engineers and scientists, as is the case in China today. Korea also had a high proportion of lawyers in its economic bureaucracy until the 1970s, while the brains behind the Korean Heavy and Chemical Industrialization (HCI) program in the 1970s, Oh Won-Chul, was an engineer by training. Both Taiwan and Korea had rather strong, albeit officially unacknowledged, communist influence in their economic thinking until the 1970s.[4]

Third, many people who advance the DNTTAH argument believe that high-quality bureaucracies are very difficult to build and that the East Asian countries were exceptionally lucky to have inherited them from history. However, a high-quality bureaucracy can be built pretty quickly, as shown by the examples of Korea and Taiwan themselves. Contrary to the popular myth, Korea and Taiwan did *not* start their economic 'miracles' with high-quality bureaucracies. For example, until the late 1960s, Korea used to send its bureaucrats for extra training to – of all places – Pakistan and the Philippines. Taiwan also had a similar problem of generally low bureaucratic capabilities in the 1950s and most of the 1960s (see above). These countries could construct a high-quality bureaucracy only because they invested in training, organizational reform, and improvement in incentive systems. In addition, there was also a lot of "learning-by-doing." By trying out industrial policy from early on, the East Asian bureaucrats could more quickly pick up and improve the capabilities they needed in effectively running industrial policy. In other words, there has to be *some* 'trying at home,' if you aspire to become good enough to appear on TV with your own stunt act.

Last but not least, the fact that something is 'difficult' cannot be a reason for not recommending it. When it comes to personal advancement, we actually go to the other extreme and encourage our youngsters to aspire to become the best of the best, when most of them are going to end up as production-line workers or shop assistants, rather than prime ministers or business tycoons. Even when it comes to countries, developing countries are routinely told to adopt the 'best practice' or 'global standard' institutions used by the richest countries, when many of them clearly do not have the capabilities to effectively run the American patent law, the British accounting system, or the Scandinavian welfare system. But when it comes to industrial policy, countries are told to aim low and not to try at all, or at best try to learn from the Southeast Asian countries, which used more market-conforming (and therefore presumably easier) industrial policy than did the East Asian countries (this is the position taken by World Bank, 1993). I am all for people warning against the risks involved in 'aiming too high,' but why should countries aim low only when it comes to industrial policy?

The difficulties arising from the poverty of bureaucratic capabilities in the implementation of industrial policy are real in most African countries. However, they should not be exaggerated. They are not unique to industrial policy, nor are they unique to Africa. And there can be no presumption that industrial policy is necessarily more demanding in bureaucratic capabilities than other policies are. Even more importantly, in the longer run, bureaucratic capabilities may be enhanced (and quite quickly at that) with appropriate investments and 'learning-by-doing,' so its poverty at this moment cannot be an excuse for not using industrial policy ever.

2.2.6 Changes in the rules of the global economy

Thanks to the changes in global rules of trade and investment since the 1990s, the use of many of the classic tools of industrial policy are now either banned or significantly circumscribed by the WTO (World Trade Organization), various bilateral and regional FTAs (Free Trade Agreements), and BITs (Bilateral Investment Treaties). Given this, it is frequently argued, industrial policy is not relevant any more, if it ever was. Developing countries, including the ones in Africa, the recommendation goes, should not waste their time thinking about policies that cannot be used anyway.

The most important changes have been brought about by the Uruguay Round of the GATT (General Agreement on Trade and Tariffs) talks (1986–94) and the resulting launch of the WTO in 1995. Quantitative restrictions (for example, quotas) have been banned altogether. Tariffs have been reduced and 'bound,' that is, tariff ceilings have been set. Export subsidies are now banned. Most other subsidies (except those frequently used by the rich countries, such as those for agriculture, R&D, and regional equalization) have become open to countervailing duties and other retaliatory measures. New issues, like regulations on FDI (foreign direct investment) and intellectual property rights, have been brought under the jurisdiction of the WTO, making it difficult for countries to 'borrow' foreign technologies for free by violating intellectual property rights or put performance requirements on the TNCs (transnational corporations) that make FDI.

The WTO has certainly made industrial policy more difficult to implement. However, the constraints should not be exaggerated.

First, even on paper, the WTO by no means obliges countries to abolish all tariffs – only to bind them. Although the middle-income developing countries were forced to bind most of their tariffs, the least developed countries (LDCs), including most countries in Africa, were exempt from tariff-binding. Even though some low-income countries chose to bind some tariffs, the extent of such binding is small and the ceilings quite high. So, the 'policy space' for using tariffs is still considerable for the LDCs.[5]

Second, there are still provisions for emergency tariff increases ('import surcharges') on two grounds. The first is a sudden surge in sectoral imports, which has already been used by a number of countries. The second is the overall balance of payments (BOP) problem, for which almost all developing countries, including those in Africa, would qualify and which quite a few countries have also used. Since countries have discretion over the coverage and the levels of emergency tariffs that are meant to lessen the BOP problem, there is still room for the targeting of particular industries.

Third, not all subsidies are 'illegal' for everyone. For example, the LDCs, many of them African countries, are allowed to use export subsidies. Given the enormous benefits that exports generate for developing countries – by enabling them to import better technologies, by exposing them to international quality standards, and by making it easier for them to measure performance of the recipients of industrial policy supports – this is a very valuable policy tool that many African countries can utilize. In addition, subsidies for agriculture, regional development, basic R&D, environment-related technology upgrading are *de facto* allowed.[6] Even though some of these subsidies are not relevant for most African economies (for example, R&D subsidies), others (for insrance, agricultural subsidies) are, so they should use them proactively. Moreover, the subsidy restrictions only cover 'trade-related' ones, which means that 'domestic' subsidies can be used more actively (including subsidies on equipment investments and subsidies for investment in particular skills).

Fourth, the TRIPS (trade-related intellectual property rights) agreement has certainly made technology absorption more expensive for developing countries (Chang, 2001). However, this mainly affects the middle-income countries. The technologies that most African countries need are often the ones that are too old to have patents.

Last, as for the TRIMS (trade-related investment measures) agreement, it bans measures like local contents requirements and trade balancing requirements, which had been successfully used by both the developed and the developing countries in the past (Kumar, 2005). However, countries can still impose conditions on TNCs regarding the hiring of local labour (a good way to create technological spillover effects), technology transfer, and the conduct of R&D in the host country. They can also provided targeted subsidies, directed credits, and tailor-made infrastructure (measures that Singapore and Ireland have used, to attract FDI into targeted industries; Chang, 2004), provided that these do not violate the MFN (most-favoured nation) provision (Thrasher and Gallagher, 2008). Many of these measures are relevant for the African countries.

Of course, even though the WTO rules allow quite a lot of industrial policy measures, especially for the LDCs and other poor economies, many of which are in Africa, this policy space is in practice highly constrained by other international factors. First, the conditions attached to bilateral and multilateral aids and loans, on which they are quite dependent, significantly constrain their industrial policy space. Second, many developing countries are also parties to bilateral and regional trade and investment agreements, which tend to be even more restrictive than the WTO agreements (Thrasher and Gallagher 2008).

So, all in all, the range of industrial policy measures that developing countries can use has become considerably smaller, compared to the 1960s and the 1970s, because of the changes in global rules of trade and investment. However, there is still room for manoeuvre for countries that are clever and determined enough, especially for the poorest economies, many of which are African, that are subject to less systemic restrictions (especially in relation to tariffs and subsidies).

Moreover, it is not as if the new global rules of trade and investment are some unalterable laws of nature. They can be, and should be, changed, if they are found wanting. The modification of the TRIPS agreement in relation to the HIV/AIDS drugs is a good, if a relatively small, example.

2.2.7 Conclusion

Despite the increasing acceptance of the potential benefits of industrial policy, the skepticism about its applicability to the poorer developing countries, especially the African countries, has persisted.

This paper has critically examined various arguments behind this skepticism in relation to the African countries. After critically scrutinizing the more general arguments espousing 'Afro-pessimism' on the bases of climate, geography, history, and culture, the paper examined four different types of arguments expressing skepticism of the applicability of industrial policy to the African context – natural resource abundance, political economy, bureaucratic capabilities, and the changes in the global economic rules. The paper has shown that, while all these arguments contain some germs of truths (some more than others), they are all highly biased and partial.

Given that all African countries – even the exceptionally well-endowed and the most industrialized South Africa – need huge amounts of industrial development and that such developments would require substantial degrees of industrial policy, getting industrial policy right and getting the conditions for its successful implementation right are not matters of choice but imperatives for the African countries. The paper has tried to show how the existing possibilities may be exploited and the constraints overcome in all sorts of areas – ranging from landlockedness to bureaucratic capabilities – through an appropriate mix of realism, reform, and investments.

Notes

1. Section 2.2.2 of this paper draws on Chang (2010), Thing 10, while sections 2.2.4–2.2.6 draw on Chang (2011).
2. I thank for their helpful comments made by the participants at the conference, especially, in alphabetical order, Mario Cimoli, Akbar Noman, Simon Roberts, and Joseph Stiglitz.
3. Daniel Etounga-Manguelle (2000), a Cameroonian engineer and writer, writes: "The African, anchored in his ancestral culture, is so convinced that the past can only repeat itself that he worries only superficially about the future. However, without a dynamic perception of the future, there is no planning, no foresight, no scenario building; in other words, no policy to affect the course of events" (p. 69).

And then he goes on to say that "African societies are like a football team in which, as a result of personal rivalries and a lack of team spirit, one player will not pass the ball to another out of fear that the latter might score a goal" (p. 75).

4. The Nationalist Party's constitution was a copy of the Soviet Communist Party constitution. Taiwan's second president, Chiang Ching-Kuo, who succeeded his father Chiang Kai-Shek, was a communist as a young man and studied in the Soviet Communist Party school in Moscow with future leaders of the Chinese Communist Party, including Deng Xiao-ping. Korea also had its share of communist influence. General Park Chung-Hee, who masterminded the Korean economic miracle, was a communist in his younger days. He was sentenced to death in 1949 for his involvement in a communist mutiny in the South Korean army but earned an amnesty by publicly denouncing communism. Many of his lieutenants were also communist in their younger days.

5. Of course, if the rich countries have their ways in the current NAMA (non-agricultural market access) negotiations of the Doha Round in the WTO, industrial tariffs in the developing countries are, at 5–10 percent, likely to fall to the lowest level since the days of colonialism and unequal treaties (Chang, 2005: 4). However, this is yet to happen.

6. These subsidies were explicitly allowed ('non-actionable' in WTO parlance) until 1999. Even though the first three have become 'actionable' since 2000, not a single case has been brought to the dispute settlement mechanism since then, suggesting that there is an implicit agreement that they are still acceptable.

References

Acemoglu, D., Johnson, S. and Robinson, J. (2001) "The Colonial Origins of Comparative Development: an Empirical Investigation," *American Economic Review*, vol. 91, no. 5, pp. 1369–1401.

Amsden, A. 1989. *Asia's Next Giant* (New York: Oxford University Press).

Amsden, A. 2005. "Promoting Industry under the WTO Law" in K. Gallagher (ed.), *Putting Development First*, Zed Books, London.

Aristotle (2001) *The Basic Works of Aristotle*, edited by Richard McKeon (New York: Random House).

Bairoch, P. (1993) *Economics and World History – Myths and Paradoxes* (Brighton: Wheatsheaf).

Bloom, D. and Sachs, J. (1998) "Geography, Demography and Economic Growth in Africa," *Brookings Papers on Economic Activity*, vol. 2, no. 2, pp. 207–273.

Chang, H.-J. (1994) *The Political Economy of Industrial Policy* (London and Basingstoke: Macmillan).

Chang, H.-J. (2001) "Intellectual Property Rights and Economic Development – Historical Lessons and Emerging Issues," *Journal of Human Development*, vol. 2, no. 2, pp. 287–309.

Chang, H-J. (2002) *Kicking Away the Ladder: Development Strategy in Historical Perspective* (London: Anthem Press).

Chang, H.-J. (2004) "Regulation of Foreign Investment in Historical Perspective," *European Journal of Development Research*, vol. 16, no. 3, pp. 447–464.

Chang, H.-J. (2005) *Why Developing Countries Need Tariffs – How WTO NAMA Negotiations Could Deny Developing Countries' Right to a Future* (Oxford: Oxfam International and Geneva: South Centre).

Chang, H.-J. (2006) "How Important were the 'Initial Conditions' for Economic Development – East Asia vs. Sub-Saharan Africa," in H.-J. Chang, *The East Asian Development Experience: The Miracle, the Crisis, and the Future* (London: Zed Press).

Chang, H.-J. (2007) *Bad Samaritans* (London: Random House and New York: Bloomsbury USA).

Chang, H.-J. (2008) "State-owned Enterprise Reform," in UNDESA (United Nations Department of Economic and Social Affairs) (ed.), *National Development Strategies – Policy Notes* (New York: United Nations).

Chang, H.-J. (2009a) "Under-explored Treasure Troves of Development Lessons – Lessons from the Histories of Small Rich European Countries (SRECs)," in M. Kremer, P. van Lieshout, and R. Went (eds), *Doing Good or Doing Better – Development Policies in a Globalising World* (Amsterdam: Amsterdam University Press).

Chang, H.-J. (2009b) "Economic History of the Developed World: Lessons for Africa," in S. Tapsoba and G. Oluremi Archer-Davies (eds), *Eminent Speakers Series Volume II – Sharing Visions of Africa's Development*. (Tunis: African Development Bank) (can be downloaded from: http://www.econ.cam.ac.uk/faculty/chang/pubs/ChangAfDBlecturetext.pdf).

Chang, H.-J. (2010) *23 Things They Don't Tell You About Capitalism* (London: Allen Lane).

Chang, H.-J. (2011) "Industrial Policy: Can We Go Beyond an Unproductive Confrontation?," in J. Lin and B. Pleskovic, (eds), *Annual World Bank Conference on Development Economics 2010, Global: Lessons from East Asia and the Global Financial Crisis* (Washington, DC: World Bank).

Clemens, M. and Williamson, J. (2001) "A Tariff–Growth Paradox? – Protection's Impact on the World Around 1875–1997," NBER working paper, no. 8459. (Cambridge, MA: National Bureau of Economic Research).

Clemens, M. and Williamson, J. (2004) "Closed Jaguar, Open Dragon: Comparing Tariffs in Latin America and Asia," NBER Working Paper no. 9401 (Cambridge, MA: National Bureau of Economic Research).

Cohen, S. (1977) *Modern Capitalist Planning: The French Model*, 2nd edn (Berkeley, CA: University of California Press).

Collier, P. nd Gunning, W. (1999) "Why Has Africa Grown Slowly?," *Journal of Economic Perspectives*, vol. 13, no. 3, pp. 3–22.

Dosi, G., Cimoli, M., and Stiglitz, J. (eds) (2009) *Industrial Policy and Development: The Political Economy of Capabilities Accumulation* (Oxford: Oxford University Press).

Easterly, W. and Levine, R. (1997) "Africa's Growth Tragedy: Policies and Ethnic Divisions," *Quarterly Journal of Economics*, vol. 112, no. 4, pp. 1203–1250.

Etounga-Manguelle, D. (2000) "Does Africa Need a Cultural Adjustment Program?," in L. Harrison and S. Huntington (eds), *Culture Matters – How Values Shape Human Progress* (New York: Basic Books).

Evans, P. (1995) *Embedded Autonomy* (Princeton, NJ: Princeton University Press).

Greenwald, B. & Stiglitz, J. 2006. "Helping Infant Economies Grow: Foundations of Trade Policies for Developing Countries," *American Economic Review*, vol. 96, no. 2, pp. 141–146.

Hamilton, A. (1791 [2001]) *Report on the Subject of Manufactures, 5 December 1791*, as reprinted in *Alexander Hamilton – Writings* (New York, The Library Classics of the United States, Inc.).

Huntington, S. (2000) "Foreword: Cultures Count," in L. Harrison and S. Huntington (eds), *Culture Matters – How Values Shape Human Progress* (New York: Basic Books).

Irwin, D. (2002) "Interpreting the Tariff-Growth Correlation of the Late 19th Century," *American Economic Review*, vol. 92, no. 2, pp. 165–169.

Jerven, M. (2011) "The Quest for the African Dummy: Explaining African Post-colonial Economic Performance Revisited," *Journal of International Development*, vol. 23, no. 2.

Kuisel, R. (1981) *Capitalism and the State in Modern France* (Cambridge: Cambridge University Press).

Kumar, N. (2005) "Performance Requirements as Tools of Development Policy: Lessons from Developed and Developing Countries," in K. Gallagher (ed.), *Putting Development First* (London: Zed Books).

Lehmann, S. and O'Rourke, K. (2008) "The Structure of Protection and Growth in the Late 19th Century," NBER Working Paper no. 14493 (Cambridge. MA: National Bureau of Economic Research).

Lin, J. and Chang, H.-J. (2009) "Should Industrial Policy in Developing Countries Conform to Comparative Advantage or Defy It? – A Debate between Justin Lin and Ha-Joon Chang," *Development Policy Review*, vol. 27, no. 5, pp. 483–502.

Lin, J. and Monga, C. (2012) "Comparative Advantage – The Silver Bullet of Industrial Policy," a paper presented at the Roundtable on New Thinking on Industrial Policy, organized by the International Economic Association (IEA) and the World Bank, Washington, DC, May 22–3.

Mkandawire, T. (2012) "Neopatrimonialism and the Political Economy of Economic Performance in Africa: Critical Reflections," mimeo., London School of Economics.

O'Rourke, K. (2000) "Tariffs and Growth in the Late 19th Century," *Economic Journal*, vol. 110, no. 4, pp. 456-483.

Reinert, E. (2007) *How Rich Countries Got Rich and Why Poor Countries Stay Poor* (London: Constable).

Russell, J. (1828) *A Tour in Germany*, vol. 1 (Edinburgh: Archibald Constable & Co.).

Sachs, J. and Warner, A. (2001) "The Curse of Natural Resources," *European Economic Review*, vol. 45, nos 4–6, pp. 827–838.

Shaffaedin, M. (2005) *Trade Policy at Crossroads – The Recent Experiences of Developing Countries* (Basingstoke: Palgrave Macmillan).

Thrasher, R. and Gallagher, K. (2008) "21st Century Trade Agreements: Implications for Long-Run Development Policy," The Pardee Papers, no. 2 (Boston, MA: Frederick S. Pardee Center for the Study of the Longer-range Future, Boston University).

Toye, J. (1987) *Dilemmas of Development* (Oxford: Blackwell).

UNIDO (2009) *Industrial Development Report 2009* (Vienna: United Nations Industrial Development Organization).

Vamvakidis, A. (2002) "How Robust is the Growth–Openness Connection? – Historical Evidence," *Journal of Economic Growth*, vol. 7, no. 1, pp. 57–80.

Wade, R. (1990) *Governing the Market* (Princeton, NJ: Princeton University Press).

Webb, S. and Webb, B. (1978) *The Letters of Sidney and Beatrice Webb*, edited by N. MacKenzie and J. MacKenzie (Cambridge: Cambridge University Press).

Winters, A. (2003) "Trade Policy as Development Policy," in J. Toye (ed.), *Trade and Development – Directions for the Twenty-first Century* (Cheltenham: Edward Elgar).

Wright, G. and Czelusta, J. (2004) "The Myth of the Resource Curse," *Challenge*, March/April.

Wright, G. and Czelusta, J. (2007) "Resource-based Growth, Past and Present," in D. Lederman and F. Maloney (eds), *Natural Resources: Neither Curse nor Destiny* (Stanford, CA: Stanford University Press).

World Bank (1993) *The East Asian Miracle* (New York: Oxford University Press).

Part III
New Global Order and African Reindustrialization

3.1
Winning the Jackpot: Jobs Dividends in a Multipolar World*

Célestin Monga
World Bank

3.1.1 Introduction

In an intriguing book on the methodology and dynamics of knowledge creation, Firestein (2012) makes the point that the most promising and fruitful approaches in hard sciences are generally not those that try to build on the existing body of truths but rather those that focus on things that are still unknown. As a neuroscientist, he draws on his own experience to advocate tolerance for radically different pursuits, "the pleasures of scientific mystery, and the cultivation of doubt." He writes: "When I sit down with colleagues over a beer at a meeting, we don't go over facts. We don't talk about what's known. We talk about what we'd like to figure out, about what needs to be done." The celebration of uncertainty has led him to rehabilitate ignorance, seen as a particular condition of knowledge and the most critical part of the scientific enterprise.

While economics is still not yet a hard science, Firestein's basic recommendation applies there, especially with regard to the issue of job creation, which has now become the single most important economic question of our time. It is perplexing indeed, that the economics profession has devoted a lot of resources to the painstaking study of employment, unemployment, and labor market issues in general without focusing on the unknown – that is, trying to understand the strategies and policies that have allowed some densely populated countries to create enough full-time jobs to achieve sustainable and inclusive growth while maintaining social stability. Most East Asian countries in particular – starting with China, the most populous country in the world – have so far managed to meet that goal. Yet very few articles appear in top economic journals on employment creation strategies and policies in these countries.

---

*The author wishes to thank Joe Stiglitz, Alan Krueger, and Justin Yifu Lin for comments and for many insightful discussions of the arguments in this paper.

If one is to take ignorance seriously, one must examine the various ways in which jobs have historically been created in successful countries, and explore the potential lessons for African countries, especially in the current context of a new phase of globalization. This paper attempts to do just that. Without succumbing to the risk of teleological reasoning and assuming a linear course of human history (that is, the notion that past economic developments will repeat themselves in the future), it explains why existing theories of unemployment have yielded few useful policy insights for low-income countries. It then suggests that a shift of focus from abstract theorizing of labor markets to gaps in existing knowledge can yield big intellectual and policy payoffs. This is particularly true in the current context of an increasingly interdependent world economy where the ascendancy of new players could bring new benefits to low-income countries, especially those in Africa.

The economic success of large emerging countries such as China or Brazil reflects their evolving endowment structures and changing comparative advantage. It also ignites new dynamics in the distribution of responsibilities in the global production system: these newcomers are now well positioned to increasingly produce many of the high-value-added goods that used to be the exclusive prerogative of advanced economies. In order to remain successful, they must continue climbing the industrial and technological ladder and get more involved in capital-intensive industries. At the same time, they will have to free up much of their current manufacturing space to low-income countries that could be more competitive in labor-intensive industries. The necessary relocation of large parts of their supply chains in lower production cost countries will affect the price of goods, job patterns, and wages everywhere (Spence, 2011).

Labor arbitrage, which consists of exploiting lower-wage opportunities in various places around the world – mainly in low-income countries – has never been the only motivation for firms to locate their activities abroad. Other transaction costs are also important determinants for such decisions. But in a world where governments are increasingly offering geographic enclaves such as industrial parks with excellent infrastructure good business conditions and decent governance, labor costs once again become important. As emerging economies are booming, wages there are rising fast,[1] forcing firms to look for labor arbitrage opportunities elsewhere – including in Africa.

The remainder of the paper is organized as follows: section 3.1.2   surveys of some of the main strands of the theoretical literature on unemployment and employment, and stresses the fact that their interesting frameworks may not be transferable to low-income countries whose endowment and production structures are profoundly different from that of high-income economies. Section 3.1.3   tries to tackle the knowledge deficit on employment creation in Africa by shedding light on the new economic opportunities that African countries may derive from the dynamics of globalization. It then offers a simple analytical framework for identifying opportunities for labor arbitrage in global economy, and suggests a practical policy framework for exploiting them. Section 3.1.4   provides concluding remarks.

3.1.2   The limits of existing theoretical frameworks

This section outlines some of the basic conceptual issues that have not yet been addressed satisfactorily by theories of unemployment. It also examines some of the most promising approaches such as the search for an aggregate matching function, and discusses whether the dominant frameworks in the existing literature apply to developing countries.

3.1.2.1   Basic conceptual issues and Manichean approaches

Economists have long struggled to make sense of involuntary unemployment and to come up with convincing theories that explain a phenomenon that is still conceptually hard to grasp. The basic intellectual obstacle they have not been able to overcome satisfactorily is to reconcile the popular, intuitive conception of unemployment, with the official definitions commonly used by government statistical agencies and the ILO.[2] That intellectual gap, which has never been filled adequately, has always been the source of theoretical confusion and frustration.

Most people would probably define involuntary unemployment as situations where workers are unsuccessfully looking for jobs at the prevailing wages when they are as qualified as those holding these jobs, or where workers are willing to work at less than the prevailing wages for jobs which they could usefully fulfill, but are unable to find such jobs. Such situations (let's call them Type A) raise issues of economic inefficiency and social injustice: large segments of population, often with useful skills, are kept out of the productive economy, which obviously makes the process of national wealth creation sub-optimal. This is true even if the unemployed are less productive than those who hold employment. Furthermore, the people left outside the economic system are often a burden to those who are employed and feel disenfranchised, which makes them a potential source of social instability and constant threat to social peace.

Government agencies and international organizations usually treat unemployment differently, in terms of both their definition and the way in which they count it. Broadly speaking, they focus only on people of "working age" (whatever they choose it to be), who are out of work (whatever is considered "work") and capable of submitting evidence (whatever is deemed acceptable) of having looked for work in the recent past. Clearly, it is possible for a person to qualify for these Type B situations and not qualify for Type A; for example, it is possible for a skilled worker who has been laid off and is looking for a job not to qualify for inclusion in unemployment statistics because he/she is temporarily helping in a family business (and therefore technically not out of work), or has not been able to produce "acceptable evidence" of having looked for a job. And vice versa: it is possible for a young college graduate while officially included in unemployment statistics to seek work at real wages in excess of his/her potential contribution to society.

Such plausible scenarios raise several questions which economic theories of unemployment have attempted to answer over the decades, generally with little success: why are market economies often unable to provide all the jobs that people are looking for? Why are certain economic systems unable to attract workers who would be willing to demand real wages that fall short of their potential contribution to society? Why are firms unwilling or unable to capture the economic opportunities that are associated with the existence of a large pool of unemployed workers? Why are involuntary unemployed workers unwilling or unable to employ themselves (and others) by starting new firms or to underbid their employed counterparts? Etc.

Unemployment theorists have so far been unable to design rigorous analytical tools to provide convincing answers to these questions. Defining unemployment requires that one implicitly assigns value to various types of work, occupation patterns, and sources of income. This supposes that one also makes subtle value judgments about topics that are actually outside the typical boundaries of economics, as it implies dealing with issues of interpersonal comparisons of wellbeing: what is to be considered "work"? Who defines it, and for whom? When does any activity rise to that qualification? Do subjective perceptions have a role in the definition of work? Should a worker who thinks of him-/herself as unemployed but occupies part of his/her days in temporary, unfulfilling pastime activities (say, to "stay away from trouble") be truly considered an active member of the labor force? Does any occupation necessarily allow the person who holds it develop useful "soft skills" that may be of use over the course of their lifetime? Such questions fall far beyond the realm of the economic discipline and answering them adequately would require that researchers be willing to venture into new territories and engage deep philosophical questions. While that may be the right approach to economic research and policy, mainstream economics has so far stayed away from methodological adjustment that imply embracing cross-disciplinary complexity (Monga, 2011).

As a consequence of such unwillingness, normative theories of unemployment have long been confined to a dichotomy between various iterations of the Keynesian tradition on one side, and free-market explanations on the other. Keynes originally explained unemployment as resulting from an insufficient demand for goods. Its persistence was attributed to unemployment itself – firms hired fewer workers because their customers purchased too few goods, precisely because of a limited purchasing power mainly due to... unemployment. Government demand-management policies (fiscal, monetary) were thus presented as the right strategy to break such a vicious cycle. Using microeconomic theory, classical economists argued that economic agents buy and sell all that they wish at the prevailing wages and prices so that markets clear and full employment prevails.[3] Moreover, empirical evidence showed that fluctuations in aggregate demand did not consistently push inflation and unemployment in opposite directions. Contrary to Keynesians, they concluded that unemployment was most likely the outcome of misguided government regulations or errors in people's price expectations. This suggested a (simplistic) solution to involuntary unemployment: the elimination of harmful government interventions.

Arguments on both sides were subsequently refined by several generations of researchers. Still, even with sophisticated improvements in the theoretical foundations of the models, they eventually led to a standoff, with each camp holding firm its position: reappraisers of Keynes still reject the New Classical approach, on three grounds: they observe that the big assumption of clearing markets was illusory; they object to the idea that errors in wage-price expectations are large enough to account for the magnitude and length of fluctuations in unemployment; they also wonder why rational economic agents do not acquire the information needed to avoid expectations errors – through newspapers, think-tanks, statistics agencies, and so on. As a result, they have developed some microeconomic foundations for their unemployment theory and concluded that involuntary unemployment persists because wages or prices are not always responsive to market conditions, and that, under such rigid conditions, firms may have no incentive to recruit unemployed workers who would them produce goods with insufficient demand.

Meanwhile, new classical economists have continued to oppose Keynesian-like macroeconomic theories that cover quantities determination but not price determination – even though quantities of labor demanded and supplied do, in their view, depend on wages. They still argue that when markets fail to clear, agents face unexploited gains from the exchange: by changing prices (wages) and quantities (labor, time) at which they trade, some rational agents could be made better off without any others being made worse off. On the basis of that rationale, new classical economists tend to build models in which expectations errors cause swings in the unemployment rate. That is the basis of their the "natural rate hypothesis," which posits that all deviations of unemployment from its natural rate are related to errors in wage-price expectations.

While recent studies of unemployment dynamics have attempted to break these Manichean views and recognize the existence of both imperfect information and price-setting behavior, the problem of unemployment – especially in developing countries – has not yet been fully understood by economic theorists. A number of enlightening analyses have certainly emerged from these intellectual battles, most notably the so-called increasing returns approach, the efficiency wage theories, and the insider–outsider theories; the first is of particular interest to developing countries, as it is concerned primarily with the reasons why opportunities for self-employment are often limited; the second and third try to explain why the unemployed and laid-off workers do not underbid.[4] But despite their useful insights on some microeconomic issues, they provide little guidance to policymakers who need a consistent framework for macroeconomic development strategies. And they would be of little use to the political leaders in Africa and elsewhere who are confronted with the challenge of putting large segments of their labor force to work in the formal sector.

In fine, and whether they are inspired by Keynesianism of by new classical economics, conventional theories typically explain labor market issues as resulting from one of two (extreme) scenarios: on the one hand, there are the so-called frictionless equilibrium situations when the labor market adjust rapidly to shocks (such as oil crises, interest rates hikes, rapid devaluation of a currency, or sudden productivity changes)[5] and when the unemployment rate simply reflects a long-term equilibrium in which none of the major stakeholders (employers, workers, unions) has any incentive to change their behavior if other exogenous variable do not change.

On the other hand, there are situations where the labor market is slow to respond to shocks because of their high cost or because of the difficulty of adjusting to them. Proponents of that thesis tend to stress the importance of lags the way labor markets adjust to shocks. In such situations, unemployment may not reflect the long-term equilibrium rate. These ideas have generated a mainstream consensus according to which labor markets everywhere never reflect either one of these theories exclusively but include elements of both.[6] Still, their main shortcoming is their focus on micro issues, which may yield useful knowledge only for industrial economies where the labor force is relatively homogenous and market institutions well developed. They do not address the fundamental "big-picture" question that policymakers struggle with – namely, how to create enough decent jobs for large segments of the mainly low-skilled labor force of developing countries.

3.1.2.2   The quest for an aggregate matching function

One of the most promising analytical frameworks for thinking about the dynamics of hiring and employment is the observation that labor markets experience a constant churning of workers and jobs, and that the matching process should take center stage. This has led to the idea of an aggregate matching function, which provides a good understanding of economies characterized by large flows and the constant reallocation of workers across jobs (Blanchard and Diamond, 1990).[7] The model, which posits that, at any point in time, many firms are looking for workers, and many workers are looking for jobs, has two main ingredients: the first is that it takes time to reallocate, to match workers to jobs; the second is that there is perpetual job destruction, continual layoffs, job creation, and posting of vacancies. A strong assumption is made about wages, which have no allocation role in the short run and therefore no tight connection with employment.

The labor market is then seen as a place where each worker and firm is engaged in a time consuming and stochastic process of looking for and waiting for an appropriate match. The formalization of that process by an aggregate function shows new hires, *h*, as a function of unemployment and vacancies

$$h = \propto m(U,V),$$ (1)

where $\propto$ is a scale parameter, and m_u, $m_u \geq 0$, $m(0,V)=m(U,0)=0$.

Changes in skills or geographic distributions of workers and jobs (mismatch) and differences in search and match acceptance decisions are captured by the parameter $\propto$. New hires are constructed as the sum of flows into employment from unemployment and from out of the labor force. The basic specification of the aggregate matching function gives new hires as a Cobb-Douglas function of vacancies and unemployment of the form

$$\ln(H_t) = a + btime + c\ln(V_{t-1}) + d\ln(U_{t-1}) + \varepsilon_t,$$ (2)

where all the variables are defined as above.

The model offers predictions about how different shocks affect unemployment, vacancies, and wages. Applying it to the United States, Blanchard and Diamond find that contractions in aggregate activity increase unemployment and decrease vacancies, both putting downward pressure on wages. In contrast, periods of intense reallocation increase both vacancies and unemployment, but may be associated with little or even no pressure on wages. They conclude that in the post-war United States, major movements in unemployment have been mostly the result of changes in aggregate activity, rather than changes in the intensity or the effectiveness of the reallocation process.

Besides the heavy data requirements necessary to estimate such a model, which would be unavailable for most developing countries, at least two types of objections can be made: first, the analytical usefulness of the notion of vacancies is questionable. Because of its vagueness (at least as compared to unemployed), the concept of vacancy may not be a sound empirical tool. Moreover, no country in the world – not even the USA – holds comprehensive vacancy series that are as reliable or meaningful as the unemployment series. Also, vacancies are only intermediary variables, which may not yield much information on how they evolve over time and how the job matching process is eventually settled. Blanchard and Diamond acknowledge that "it is indeed true that the matching function is only part of the story; any complete story must account for job creation and job destruction and their determinants." (1990, p. 163)

3.1.2.3 Multiple production functions and asymmetries

Even if one could satisfactorily specify and estimate aggregate matching functions for a low-income country, there would still be the conceptual issues of asymmetries of production and organization that characterize many developing economies and which are not easily dealt with. In order to capture their particular features that are relevant for analysis, and enable a more accurate understanding of labor market developments and policies, one would need to build dual-economy models that go well beyond the two usual sectors (traditional and modern) and their production asymmetry, and display other types of asymmetries.[8]

For instance, in much of Africa's agricultural sector which is dominated by family farms, production decisions are often made according to family ties, social networks, and the prevailing conventional norms. By contrast, in sub-sectors where that are dominated by landlords and in the manufacturing sector, production decisions are made with the objective of maximizing profits. That production asymmetry leads to inefficiency, at least from the perspective of static analysis. Maximization of national output and employment would require that the marginal product of each factor (labor, capital, land) be equalized across the traditional and modern sectors. Capital is barely used at all in the agricultural sector, while land too is insufficiently used in industry.

An important stylized fact of African labor markets – also observed in many developing economies – is the persistence of rural to urban migration despite high unemployment and underemployment in big cities. The explanation is the expectation of better income in urban areas, even for workers who give up some secure (and generally much lower) income in rural areas. The so-called replacement of the equality of wages by the equality of expected wages as the basic condition in a segmented, but homogeneous labor market has been at the core of labor market theories for developing economies. Often referred to as the Harris–Todaro hypothesis, it formalizes the motivation of the migrant worker from the countryside who leaves behind his/her secure rural wage W_r to pursue a higher expected urban wage W_u^e despite the probability of unemployment. That expected urban wage is expressed as

$$W_u^e = W_u \left(\frac{E_u}{E_u + U} \right) + 0 \left(\frac{U}{E_u + U} \right) \tag{3}$$

$$W_u^e = W_u (1 / (1 + U / E_u)) = W_u \left(\frac{1}{1 + \lambda} \right) \tag{4}$$

where W_u is the urban wage, E_u is the number of employed urban workers, U is the number of urban unemployed, and λ is rate of urban unemployment. The Harris–Todaro hypothesis is therefore expressed as the equilibrium condition

$$W_r = W_u^e \Leftrightarrow W_u = W_r(1 + \lambda). \tag{5}$$

which is often embedded in two-sector, general equilibrium models. While that approach seems straightforward and certainly more likely to yield interesting analytical results about segmented African labor markets, it also introduces a new requirement, namely the equilibrium rate of unemployment. This in turn presupposes a theory of urban wage determination. Researchers have proposed various ways of dealing with the issue, from assuming urban wages to be an exogenously given constant to modeling wage determination as an endogenous process.[9] In the end, the actual use of the model appears to be much less complex than it appears. Unfortunately, despite its realism, the model has not been successfully applied to developing countries where unemployment stories are usually not just about the demand but also about the limited supply of jobs.

3.1.2.3   Unemployment in developing countries: the failure of theories

The main assumption underlying conventional theories of unemployment is the notion that the economy tends to move toward its frictionless equilibrium rate, a non-accelerating inflation rate of unemployment (NAIRU) which is established in the medium term. The economy responds to shocks by adjusting more or less slowly toward equilibrium, with the pace of adjustment depending on the real wage and the existing institutions (Layard et al., 1991). The dynamics of the process itself is often assumed to have little or no effect at all on the NAIRU. A rise in unemployment is therefore a reflection of changes in structural factors that affect the NAIRU, most notably the level of social security benefits, taxation, employment protection, the degree of influence of trade unions in wage bargaining, the pace of geographic and occupational mobility in the job market, the quality of human capital (labor force education), the nature of active labor market policies, and so on. Interestingly, that list of fundamental variables usually does not include the quantity and quality of jobs created by the economy (the supply side of the labor market), which is implicitly assumed to be exogenous to the theoretical analysis of unemployment.

There are many unresolved conceptual issues with that dominant theory of unemployment, including whether they could be applied to developing countries where economies tend to have a distinctly different structure. The ambiguities of defining unemployment and comparing it across countries have also been a source of difficulty. Official definitions of unemployment and underemployment are widely accepted but their operational significance and true meaning is still the subject of debate. The ILO defines an *unemployed* as a member of the labor force who meets the following criteria: not employed during the past seven days, even for one hour; looking for work; and available for work. The *underemployed* are the unemployed plus those who are employed part time (less than 30 hours per week) and want to work full time.

Survey results of the percentage of the workforce unemployed in 129 countries conducted by Gallup World Poll show that Africa's performance is generally a little worse than the world average of 7 percent, but many countries there appear to perform rather well, or at least in the same bracket as Canada, Australia, Finland, Denmark, Belgium, Israel, Brazil, Argentina, Poland, India, Russia, and many other better performing countries.[10] One realizes that something is wrong with the official numbers when countries such as Nigeria,

Cameroon, Kenya, Zambia, or the Central African Republic, score much better on that criterion than the United States, France, Italy, Spain, or South Africa. The story changes when the coin is flipped and one measures the portion of the labor force employed full time for an employer (those working for an employer at least 30 hours per week): Africa's general performance is suboptimal.

The switch from unemployment to employment is important in general and particularly in the African context. First, the global picture of unemployment generally shows a weak relationship with GDP per capita, and the year-over-year change in the unemployment rate has a weak relationship with GDP growth across countries (Figure 3.1.1).[11] By contrast, employment appears to be strongly correlated to with GDP growth.

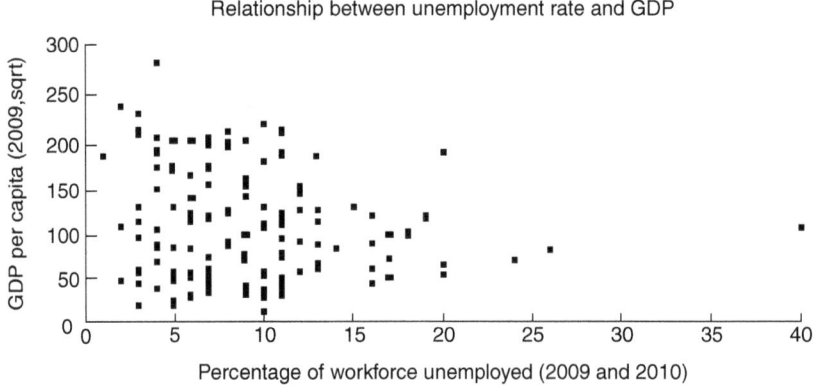

Spearman's rho = −.16 (N=127)

Spearman's rho = −.85 (p<.001;N=127)

Figure 3.1.1 Unemployment, employment, and economic performance: a global picture
Source: Krueger (2011).

If the relationship between unemployment and economic performance is not easily tractable, at least in the short term, unemployment statistics and theories may be less meaningful in the African context than often thought, and the analytical focus should be on tracking information on employment and wages. Employment appears to be less complicated to measure, especially in the high-under-unemployment environment of the developing world. Another reason for focusing on employment is its strong conceptual and economic appeal: analyzing job creation instead of experience with unemployment offers better insights to policies that may be necessary to sustain employment growth. Unemployment statistics shed little light on the anatomy of African labor markets (types of jobs available, fastest/slowest job-creating industries, relative shares of full-time and part-time workers, formal/informal sectors, wage earners and self-employed, social groups and gender balance in the labor force, and so on) and their dynamics over time. An understanding of these factors allows for an assessment of whether structural change – perhaps the single most important indicator of sustained, inclusive growth – is actually taking place or not.

Official definitions of unemployment and employment allow for comparative analysis. However, these concepts do not reflect labor market realities of low-income countries that often exhibit dual economies, and are not operationally useful to policymakers there.[12] In Sub-Saharan Africa, 70–90 percent of the labor force is engaged in non-wage employment. About 80 percent of these non-wage jobs are in agriculture, 10 to 30 percent are in household or microenterprises (this primary employment only). About one-third of those outside the wage and salary sector typically report multiple economic activities over the year – combining agriculture and non-agricultural enterprises. Almost all of the labor force participants in low income households are engaged in household-based activities – family farming, and very small non-farm enterprises, commonly called "informal enterprises" (Figure 3.1.2).

The still under-studied household enterprise sector generates the majority of new non-farm jobs in most African countries, even during times of high economic growth (Fox and Gaal, 2008). Household survey data show that, for the past decades, the informal sector (non-farm) has been a growing source of employment for a large fraction of the African youth, but also for older workers trying to seize entrepreneurial opportunities. Its contribution to GDP and poverty reduction has been substantial, and it has become a major point of entry into the labor market for many. For youth in large cities such as Addis Ababa, Lagos, Kinshasa, Abidjan, Douala, Nairobi, or Dar-es-Salaam, the informal sector is indeed the only viable option for making a modest living, even for those with secondary, vocational, and tertiary education, as the number of employers in the formal sector is limited and there is evidence of skills mismatch in the labor market.

Figures 3.1.2 and 3.1.3 reveal the fundamental difference in structure between high-income and low-income labor markets. They also explain why

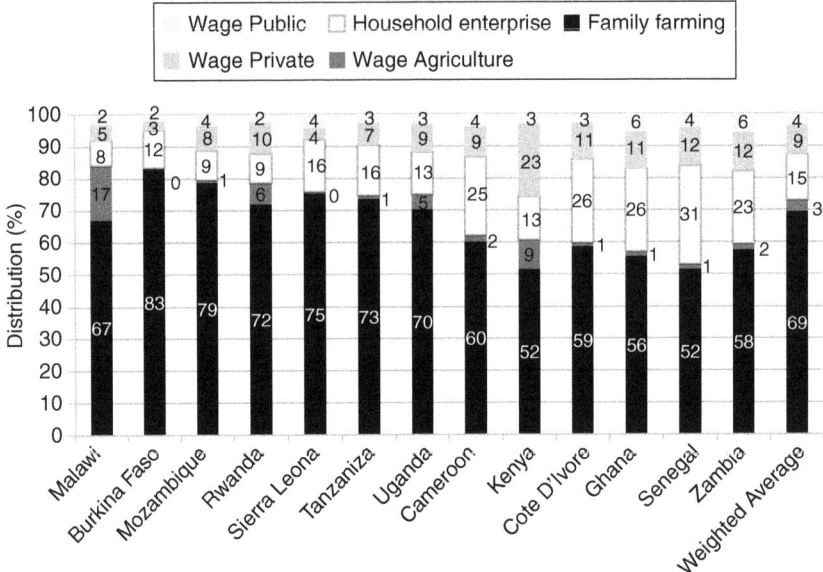

Figure 3.1.2   Distribution of primary employment in Sub-Saharan Africa (percentage)
Source: Fox and Sohnesen (2012).

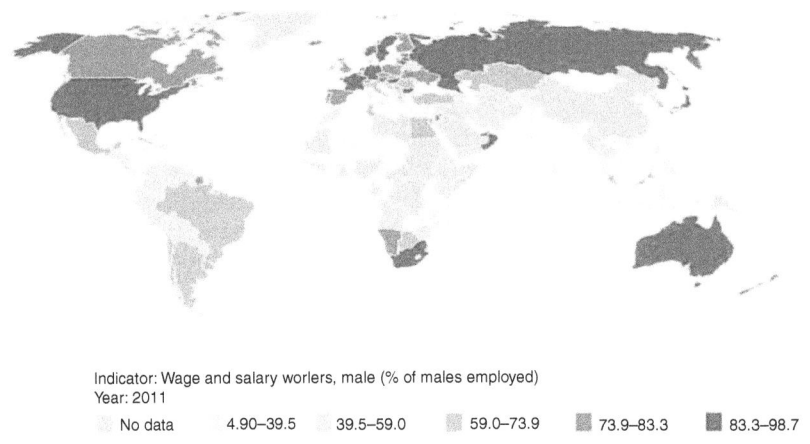

Figure 3.1.3   Wage and salary workers

the basic concepts of unemployment/employment and traditional theories
have proved ineffective in helping policymakers in Sub-Saharan Africa.

Summing up, it can therefore be said that despite their increasing levels
of sophistication, economic theories of unemployment and employment

have so far yielded little useful policy guidance for developing countries. While they have provided important insights on specific and often limited micro issues, they have generally fallen short of proposing a framework that governments in poor countries could follow to create employment for the large, often underutilized segments of their labor force. From a policy perspective, it is important to shift the focus to concrete opportunities for creation formal sector employment in African and low-income countries where production costs remain potentially competitive and can provide opportunities for labor arbitrage.

3.1.3   Labor arbitrage: new ways of creating employment

Because the search for solutions to unemployment and underemployment has too long focused on the wrong questions, traditional, mainstream remedies have failed to provide useful answers to developing country policymakers. Learning from ignorance would require drawing lessons from economic history and the experience of other countries where structural change has involved a variety of industrial processes. The transformation of the world economy and the emergence of large developing countries open up new possibilities for latecomers. African countries accelerate the shift of labor from low productivity jobs in agriculture and the informal sector to higher productivity jobs in agro-industry, manufacturing or tradable services and achieve sustained growth and poverty reduction. But in order to do so, new and more strategic forms of industrial policies that avoid the pitfalls of the past must be designed and implemented.

3.1.3.1   Tackling the deficit of knowledge: beyond traditional remedies

Motivated by the need to preserve sociopolitical stability, many African governments have used public sector employment as a tool for social redistribution. Civil servants are thus often recruited on the basis of education credentials – not on the basis of the country's economic needs. Wages in the civil administration are often been based on seniority (rather than individual productivity or market conditions). Public policies tend to reward education degrees rather than productivity, and labor laws are often adopted to extend these rules to the formal private sector. These policies are misguided attempts to provide employment in countries where it is seen as the main determinant of poverty reduction. They reflect the shortage of good jobs and the unpleasant facts of the African labor markets described in the previous section. But they are usually analyzed in the mainstream economic literature as evidence of distortion in the monetary signals that guide investment in human capital across the continent.

Not surprisingly, the proposed solutions to unemployment from conventional economic analysis tend to focus on the removal of distortions in the business environment, and typically include a list of reforms to make the labor market more flexible:

- Changes in hiring and firing practices to reduce transaction costs for firms and give them more leeway – it is assumed that strong employment protection tends to make employers more reluctant to hire workers because it is then more difficult to let them go when business conditions change;
- Changes in the benefit system (level of benefits, duration, coverage, and tightness of the implementation criteria), which are viewed as important factors affecting the reservation wage;
- Reduction of the tax wedge (tax-related difference between the cost to employ a worker and the worker's take-home pay) to improve the supply and demand for labor;
- Changes in the wage bargaining institutions – the coverage and strength of trade unions and their ability to bargain for higher wages or to organize strikes are seen as determinants of unemployment; and
- The implementation of active labor market policies (training, employment subsidies, help with job matching and job applications, and so on) to increase the chances of the unemployed finding employment.

That reform agenda is generally appropriate in OECD countries where the levels of full-time employment are high and where labor has become an expensive factor of production, though the empirical evidence on their effectiveness is often ambiguous. In developing countries where full-time employment is low and where there are still labor surpluses, those policy measures rarely deliver the expected results.

Moreover, the implementation of policy recommendations derived from traditional theoretical models of employment has often proven to be particularly difficult in the African context, for several reasons: they leave little room for strategic selectivity. Yet, because of limited financial resources and administrative capacity, not everything can be done at once. Limited financial resources also make the implementation of various active labor market policies (ALMP) – especially their sectoral and geographical targeting – either random or politically motivated. Also, because of vested interests, some binding constraints are politically too costly to remove all at once, or require large amounts of funding when envisaged at the level of the whole country (infrastructure).

It is therefore not surprising that job creation policies have led to disappointing results: most Sub-Saharan African countries started liberalizing their economies in the 1970s and 1980s and have implemented serious market reforms for several decades. Labor market regulations were substantially relaxed to make firing decisions by firms easier. While labor productivity (measured as the percentage growth of GDP per person employed) is reported to have increased from –5.3 in 1990–92 to 4.4 in 2005–08, the employment to population ratios showed little change: in 2008, it was still averaging 64 percent for the entire population (15 years and older), the same level observed in 1991. For youths (ages 15–24), it has declined slightly in that twenty-year period, from 50 to 49 percent.[13] Clearly, the labor market reforms have not led to the creation of new formal sector employment opportunities.

The dynamics of population growth makes things even more challenging (Figure 3.1.4). With annual population growth projected to be 2.2 percent in the next 25 years and about 2–3 million young people entering the labor force every year, Africa's workforce will grow by 11-14 million a year

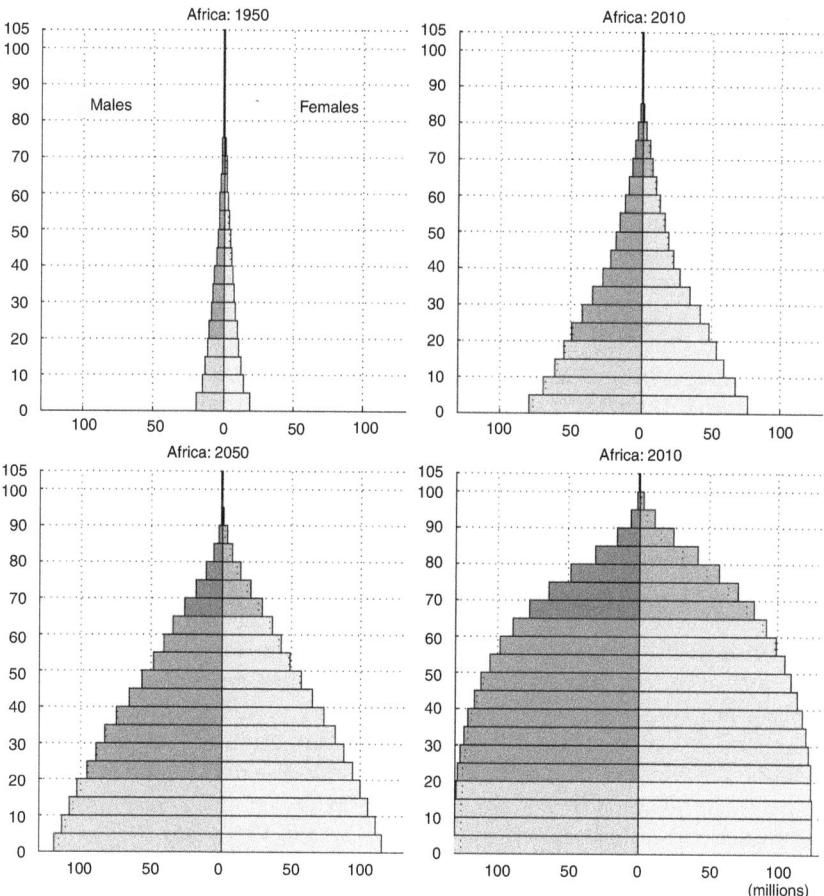

Figure 3.1.4 Population by age groups and sex (absolute numbers)
Source: Data from the United Nations.

for the next couple of decades. The African private sector faces the challenge of creating employment opportunities to absorb the youth bulge: about two-thirds of the region's population is under the age of 24 and is underemployed – including those with college and university degrees. Most workers are trapped in very low productivity activities in subsistence agriculture and the informal sector. Sub-Saharan Africa will have to generate large employment opportunities annually in order to accommodate the high rate of population growth.

Economic development should not be left to chance or to generic reform prescriptions. The ultimate goal of development strategies in Sub-Saharan Africa should be to achieve structural transformation and to lift the 80–90 percent of the people currently in low-productivity (subsistence) activities that are too often only disguised unemployment into industries and sectors where there is potential for gradual shift towards higher-productivity and higher-value industries. Lessons from history suggest that manufacturing is the most reliable route towards that goal.

3.1.3.2   The economic magic of manufacturing

What explains Asia's good performance in creating full-time jobs in both resource-poor and resource-rich countries? The economic literature has provided a wide variety of answers, which can be grouped into three categories: first, the suggestion that Asian countries, especially those in East Asia, were better endowed with experienced entrepreneurs and educated labor forces than other developing countries (Perkins and Roemer, 1994); second, the assertion that in the 1960s many Asian countries went through political changes that brought "more competent, developmentally focused regimes, a revolution that has touched only a few African countries" (Roemer 1994 234–5); and third, the related argument that Asian countries had more human and administrative capacity to design and implement good policies than African countries.

None of these theses appears to be supported by empirical evidence. Researchers from a wide range of academic disciplines have long documented the millennial experience of private business people throughout the continent of Africa (Iliffe, 1983; Kennedy, 1988; Cissé, 1988; Taylor, 2012). Likewise, the prevailing view of competent and development-focused governments in Asia is not consistent with the political history of countries such as China, Vietnam, or Cambodia, where authoritarianism, political turmoil, and even terrible genocides were as prevalent as anywhere else in the developing world. Finally, the suggestion that the problem was the comparatively lower levels of capacity in Africa neglects the facts that in the 1960s and 1970s countries such as Ghana, Cameroon, Senegal, or Kenya, had better administrative capital and human capital than most Asian countries. Moreover, in a world where skilled labor is highly mobile, capacity can be built or attracted from abroad, and retained and used as necessary – as shown by the large number of foreign expertise in many government ministries and agencies in good-performing Asian countries such as Qatar, Laos, or Malaysia.

The main reason why some countries that have managed to achieve sustained, inclusive growth over long periods of time, create enough full-time jobs to keep large fractions of their labor force employed, and move from low- to middle- and even high-income status, is that they were able to ignite and sustain rapid industrialization (Lin and Monga, 2011). Their development strategy was based on the acknowledgment that economic growth is a process of continuous industrial and technological upgrading that also affects the dynamics of institutional change.

Industrialization has always played a key role in growth acceleration processes that are sustained over time and eventually transform economies from "poor" to "rich." In the early phases of modern economic growth, which began with the Industrial Revolution, manufacturing in particular played a larger role in the total output of successful countries and their higher incomes were associated with a substantially bigger role of transport and machinery sectors. Throughout the 19th and 20th centuries, countries in North America, Western Europe, and Asia were able to transform their economies from agrarian to industrial powers, which included a rapidly growing services sector fuelled in large part by the multiplier effect of manufacturing. As a result, they built prosperous middle classes and raised their standards of living. Recent empirical studies show that manufacturing has been a key factor to the prosperity of nations, with over 70 percent of the income variations of 128 nations explained by differences in manufactured product export data alone (Hausman et al., 2011). In fact, few countries have achieved high-income status without industrializing. Only in circumstances such as an extraordinary abundance of natural resources or land have countries been able to do so (UNIDO, 2009).

Manufacturing has evolved and changed the dynamics of the world economy. Profound changes in geopolitical relations among world nations, the widespread growth of digital information, the decline of transportation costs and the development of physical and financial infrastructure, computerized manufacturing technologies, and the proliferation of bilateral and multilateral trade agreements have contributed to the globalization of manufacturing. These developments have permitted the decentralization of supply chains into independent but coherent global networks that allow transnational firms to locate various parts of their businesses in different places around the world. The creative design of products, the sourcing of materials and components, and the manufacturing of products can now be done more cheaply and more efficiently from virtually any region of the planet while final goods and services are customized and packaged to satisfy the needs of customers in faraway markets.

The globalization of manufacturing has thus allowed developed economies to benefit from lower-cost products driven by the lower wages used for production in developing countries such as China, India, Bangladesh, Costa Rica, Mexico, or Brazil while creating job and learning opportunities in these formally poor nations. The intensity of these exchanges has led to new forms of competition and co-dependency.

3.1.3.3 The myth of the dying golden goose

In recent decades, innovation, technological developments and new sources of economic growth have led some economists to question whether "manufacturing still matters." Manufacturing's share of global value added has declined steadily over the past nearly 30 years as the global value added of services has grown. In 1985, manufacturing's share of global value added was 35 percent. By the late 2000s, it had declined to 27 percent. Services grew from 59 percent to 70 percent over the same period (UNIDO, 2009). However, these trends are mainly observed in high-income countries. They can be explained by several factors: productivity increases and rising standards of living in advanced economies, which have pushed up wages and forced many industries to delocalize their production in lower-costs nations; the decrease in relative prices of consumption goods due to higher levels of efficiency in the world economy and the simultaneous growth of the demand for services such as healthcare, security, or transportation; and, perhaps even more important, the multiplier effect of manufacturing on services jobs – the development of industries everywhere automatically generates a wide variety of new economic activities, from transportation to housing, from restaurant to entertainment.[14]

Concerns about the future of manufacturing as a viable source of economic growth have been investigated empirically by Hausmann, Hidalgo, et al. (2011) with a measure of the sophistication of an economy based on how many products a country exports successfully and how many other countries also export those products. Looking at the composition and quantity of a nation's manufacturing, they observe that sophisticated economies export a large variety of "exclusive" goods that only a few other countries can produce. To do this, these economies have typically accumulated productive knowledge and developed manufacturing capabilities that others do not have. It therefore appears that national income and economic sophistication ("economic complexity") tend to rise in tandem, and the linkage between manufacturing, economic complexity, and prosperity is highly predictive, with economic complexity being much better at explaining the variation in incomes across nations compared to any other leading indicators. In other words, even basic manufacturing expertise and capabilities can gradually breed new knowledge and capabilities and thus new, more advanced products, provided that the right strategic and business decisions are made on industrial and technological upgrading. In the words of Hausmann and Hidalgo, economic development is "a social learning process, but one that is rife with pitfalls and dangers. Countries accumulate productive knowledge by developing the capacity to make a larger variety of products of increasing complexity. This process involves trial and error. It is a risky journey in search of the possible. Entrepreneurs, investors and policy-makers play a fundamental role in this economic exploration. Manufacturing, however, provides a ladder in which the rungs are more conveniently placed, making progress potentially easier" (2012: 13).

Still, some very valid questions remain about whether or not manufacturing as a long-term source of economic growth is a dying golden goose, especially for low-income countries that may not be well prepared to reap the economic advantages of globalization. Several arguments can be made indeed to question the viability of labor-intensive industries as a means of catching up in a world economy that is increasingly dominated by high-tech and sophisticated industries and innovative services. While it is true that technological developments and the logic of mass -production make it likely for an increasing share of goods to be produced more efficiently by machines, it is also certain that hand-made labels will remain highly valuable features to customers of tradable goods around the world – just like the global rise of genetically modified food has not suppressed the large market for organic food. In addition, some industries will remain labor-intensive by their very nature (most notably tourism) despite technological progress.

Another concern about the size of the potential benefits of manufacturing in developing countries has resurfaced recently in the economic literature in the form of export pessimism. This is based on the view that policies aiming to expand exports by developing countries will lead to a decline in their terms of trade because of an inability (due to weak demand created by the global recession) or an unwillingness (expressed via new forms of protectionism) on the part of developed countries to absorb these exports. Two reasons are often given to justify skepticism to the idea that today's poor economies can follow instead the export-led model that allowed many Asian countries to transform their economies: first, it is assumed that over the next decade the major international macroeconomic adjustment will consist of the reduction in excess demand by a few countries, notably the USA, and a concomitant increase in domestic absorption of GDP in a number of surplus countries, mainly in Asia. The argument here is twofold: it will be difficult for low-income countries to attract a substantial share of US imports, which are projected to decline if rebalancing is to take place; and it has never been easy for poor countries to penetrate the Chinese and other Asian markets where the main policy priority is to increase domestic consumption. Second, it is often said, the existence of very large and powerful industrial complexes benefitting from agglomeration economies, particularly in China, makes it difficult for new entrants to compete.

These arguments may not hold close scrutiny. Even if the reduction of excess demand in large economies like the USA occurs, it is likely to be more than compensated by the increase in excess demand in other industrialized and emerging economies where rising income almost always changes saving and spending habits. Moreover, the narratives of global imbalances may be less of a threat to the world economy as often thought (Monga, 2012b) and they have been changing constantly. For much of the past few years, China was criticized for its contribution to global imbalances and a corresponding shortfall in global aggregate demand. It now appears that the surpluses of oil-exporting countries may actually bear the main responsibility for these imbalances.[15] But there is no reason to assume that oil exporters will necessarily save most of their petrodollars, which would indeed reflect a permanent transfer of income from oil consumers to oil producers, with depressing implications for global demand.[16]

While it seems quite likely that the rates of export growth that prevailed during the period 1960–2005 may not be sustained in the post-Great Recession era, it is highly unlikely that there will be a decline in global trade volumes, which have increased constantly for more than half a century. Despite recurrent threats of protectionism, it is very likely that globalization will continue to shift an increasing proportion of manufacturing capacity from developed to emerging and even low-income countries and substantial new markets will appear in the world economy – not least because large new players such as China, India, Brazil, and others, will find themselves on the receiving ends of low-skilled manufacturing products that made them successful. For low-income countries, including those in Sub-Saharan Africa, it will always be possible to find a niche in which a country may achieve low costs and thus penetrate advanced markets. The challenge will be to identify the niche, and design pragmatic and targeted policies to exploit these opportunities (Page, 2012).[17]

The other pessimistic suggestion that the mere existence of strong industrial complexes in Asia or elsewhere makes it difficult for new entrants to compete is both true and inconsistent with lessons from economic history. That same argument could have been made with regard to Japan in the 1950s and 1960s, or to dismiss industrialization attempts by other Asian countries in the 1970s and 1980s. They would have proven erroneous because the great adventure of economic development has always been the story of the rise and fall of manufacturing powerhouses once considered unshakable yet eventually overtaken by new competition, and a chronicle of creative destruction. The fact that mass production and close business links have already been established in most competitive and profitable industries simply makes it necessary for latecomers to find ways to integrate such networks. The wage-productivity dynamics makes it difficult, if not impossible for the successful Asian economies to permanently hold on to their comparative advantage in labor-intensive, low-skill manufacturing industries. That also opens up new manufacturing opportunities for lower-wage countries around the world.

The incessant improvement of transportation and telecommunication services will continue to facilitate the distribution of production chains – even in the same industries – in various locations around the world. This will open up an infinite number of manufacturing opportunities for low-income countries, because locations need to have fewer "personbytes" in place than in the past. The various elements of the value chain (design, procurement, marketing, distribution, and manufacturing) need not occur in the same place, meaning that places with few "personbytes" can more easily get their foot through the door and then add functions more gradually (Hausmann and Hidalgo, 2012). Such changes will make the manufacturing space accessible to more countries, with the concomitant reduction of manufacturing jobs in the advanced countries. Manufacturing will therefore provide more long-term economic benefits to African economies than other activities: it still generates economies of scale, sparks industrial and technological upgrading, fosters innovation, and has big multiplier effects.

3.1.3.4   The hidden treasures of a multipolar world

Human history is certainly not a linear or a teleological process but one can conjecture with some level of confidence that today's low-income countries could still benefit enormously from the new job opportunities made possible by the economic progress observed in many large emerging economies over the past three decades. The world economy has changed dramatically in the period 1980–2010. Emerging and developing economies now represent about half of global GDP (measured in PPP terms), as shown in Figure 3.1.5.

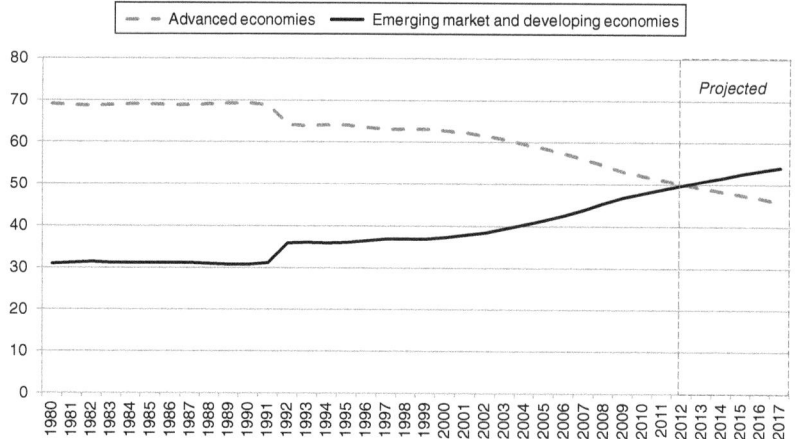

Figure 3.1.5   GDP based on PPP, share of world (percentage of world)
Source: IMF Data Mapper, October 2012.

The upcoming economic "graduation" of large emerging countries such as China, Brazil, or India from low-wage, labor intensive industries opens up enormous growth and job-creation opportunities (an estimated 119 million manufacturing sector jobs will have to be relocated to low-income countries as estimated in Lin's contribution in this volume) to low-income countries – provided that they can organize themselves to attract these jobs with more competitive wages and lower transaction costs. The average wage per worker in the manufacturing sector is about 25 percent of that of China's and 70 percent of that of Indian workers, and it compares favorably with Vietnam (see Table 3.1.1).

For Sub-Saharan Africa, the advent of a multipolar world may convert the demographic challenges outlined above into new possibilities. Africa's "youth bulge" represents an unprecedented opportunity to generate inclusive growth and reduce poverty (opportunities): with the rest of the world, especially the developed world, ageing, Africa can be the main supplier of the world's workforce. At the macroeconomic level, all these unemployed and underemployed young people not only need jobs, but they can potentially create jobs and foster economic growth. Also, increasing population density can be an asset to development (World Bank, 2008).

At the sectoral level, Sub-Saharan Africa can take advantage of rising manufacturing wages in China, India, Brazil, and other large, successful middle-income countries by attracting most of the estimated 119 million jobs that will

Table 3.1.1   Average monthly wage including benefits, by industry (US dollars)

Sector	Tanzania All workers	Ethiopia Unskilled-skilled	Nigeria Unskilled-skilled	Vietnam Unskilled-skilled	China Unskilled-skilled
Food	84	26–141	87–135	78–363	192–442
Garments	80	26–185	54–85	79–181	237–370
Textiles	61		71–120		
Machinery & Equipment	60–151		125–163		
Wood, wood products	67	37–119	67–102	85–259	206–442
Metal and Metal products	124	89–181	82–107	117–233	192–369
Other manufacturing	168	67–154	87–130		
Average manufacturing	181				

Note: Since Tanzania Survey does not distinguish unskilled or skilled workers, wages for both unskilled and skilled workers are used for other countries.

Source: For Tanzania, Annual Survey of Industrial Production and Performance, 2008; for Nigeria, Lin (2012a). Other statistics are from Dinh et al. (2011: vol. II).

be relocated – provided that it can out-compete other low-income regions of the world by quickly and effectively implementing key strategic reforms that are required to accommodate domestic and foreign investors. Employment in Africa's manufacturing sector is still at very low levels. There are already many signs of outsourcing in the services sector, as call centers and financial services emerge in countries such as Kenya or Nigeria. In the agriculture sector, changes in global food markets – most notably increased demand and prices – are also likely to bring new opportunities for job creation to Africa.

In addition to light manufacturing potential, many African countries are endowed with vast amounts of arable land (often with a cultivation rate of less than 10 percent) and rich minerals (including oil, copper, gold, diamonds, coal, iron, uranium, nickel, chrome, tin, platinum, and so on). The challenge is how best to turn the untapped natural resources into productive assets in diversified economies that generates jobs and income.[18] Lessons from other countries that have successfully exploited similar opportunities to diversify and industrialize their economies can inform policy design and implementation.

3.1.3.5   A simple analytical framework for labor arbitrage

Why have African economies not been able so far to attract substantial manufacturing industries in search for competitive platforms of production? The question can be answered using a simple Ricardian model based on international comparisons of unit labor costs to assess international competitiveness.[19] At a disaggregated level, that framework provides a coherent basic tool for understanding the main macro- and microeconomic determinants of trade flows. Applications of various versions of the model to the African context have almost always assumed that labor costs there are the central point of contention. The relative unit labor cost (comparative measure of the ratio of wages to productivity) is indeed an essential relative price in the Ricardian model of trade. Edwards and Golub even make the point that "in a world where capital is mobile and production is footloose between countries, it is the relative price of nontradable *inputs*, notably labor, rather than *outputs* that matters" (2004: 1326).

It is useful to start with the traditional framework before explaining why a modification is needed. The typical approach, as in Ceglowski and Golub (2011), focuses on a_i as the unit labor requirement (or the inverse productivity) for a given sector or industry, i. It can be said that

$$a_i = \frac{L_i}{Q_i} \qquad (6)$$

with L representing labor employment and Q the value added. Marginal productivity and hence are a_i assumed to be constant with respect to variations in a_i. The symbols w and e are then use to denote the average labor compensation per worker and the exchange rate (domestic currency per unit of foreign currency), respectively. Then the big assumption is made that labor is the only factor of production (or that other factor costs do not differ across countries). The logical next step from such a big assumption is that average costs of productions are equal to unit labor costs (ULC), $a_i w_i$. Therefore, international competitiveness in sector i depends on relative unit labor costs (RULC),

$$RULC_i = \frac{a_i w_i}{a_i^* w_i^* e} \tag{7}$$

It follows that the home country would have competitive advantage in sector i when its unit labor costs are below those of its trading partners, meaning that $RULC_i < 1$. A rewriting of equation (7) provides a decomposition of relative unit labor costs into components that sheds light into policymaking:

$$RULC_i = \frac{a_i w_i}{a_i^* w_i^* e} = \left(\frac{a_i}{a_i^*}\right)\left(\frac{w_i}{w_i^* e}\right) = \left(\frac{a_i}{a_i^*}\right)\left(\frac{w_i}{w_i^* e_i^{PPP}}\right)\left(\frac{e_i^{PPP}}{e}\right) \tag{8}$$

Where e_i^{PPP} represents the purchasing power parity exchange rate for sector i defined as the ratio of domestic to foreign price levels. A further substitution of the definition of e_i^{PPP} as $\frac{pi}{p_i^*}$ into equation (8) highlights the decomposition of relative unit labor costs into relative productivity and relative wages (measured in a common currency). Lindauer and Velenchik (1994) followed a similar approach but they too limit their analysis of labor costs, which are in reality only one aspect of labor arbitrage.

There are obvious advantages in using such a formulation: a country's competitiveness (gains or losses) vis-à-vis others is seen to depend on one or several of the following three elements: (i) its labor productivity relative to others; (ii) its real wages relative to others or, equivalently, its relative nominal wages evaluated at e_i^{PPP}; and (iii), the level of its domestic currency exchange rate relative to its purchasing power parity level.

The main problem, however, is that the relative unit labor cost framework is a very aggregate concept. It focuses on labor costs and labor productivity, and neglects other costs of doing business such as infrastructure (transportation, electricity, water, telecommunications, access to capital, availability of human capital, rent-seeking and state capture, and so on), which are assumed to be embodied into the production function. The rationale often given for excluding such important costs is that the limitation is mitigated insofar as the availability and costs of infrastructure, human capital, and other services, influences labor productivity and consequently are reflected in relative unit labor costs. It is also assumed that the relative costs of non-tradable inputs, especially labor, matter more for export competitiveness than the costs of tradable inputs such as capital and energy, which are viewed as equalized internationally.

These assumptions can be misleading. If things were so simple, lower-wage, labor-intensive African economies such as the Democratic Republic of Congo, Ethiopia, or Tanzania, would be attracting manufacturing firms from China, Brazil, and other emerging economies – and in large proportions. Moreover, in today's world, it is not just capital that is mobile: all factors of production are much more mobile than several decades ago. This includes skilled labor, which poor economies do not have in adequate supply. Therefore, engineers, talented managers, equipment repair technicians, and so on, should be moving across boundaries to settle in poor African countries where their specialized skills are needed – as they do in many countries in the Middle East. Clearly, there is more to the story of the determinants of delocalization decisions in global manufacturing than relative unit labor costs.

A more explicit and policy-relevant organizing framework would therefore go beyond unit labor costs to stipulate transaction costs, defined to include other important costs of doing business. Theoretically, it should be possible to compare unit production costs (UPCs) across countries, at least for homogenous outputs, with lower UPCs predicting better performance in the sale of manufactured goods, or higher level of attractiveness for firms in need of relocalization of specific components of their supply chains. Unit production cost is defined as

$$UPC = \left[\left(\frac{w_m L}{Q} \right) + \left(\frac{Z}{Q} \right) \right] \left(\frac{1}{e} \right) \qquad (9)$$

where w_m is more specifically the manufacturing sector wage, Q a physical measure of output, and Z a vector capturing all other transaction costs needed for production and doing business in the country.

Equation (4) can be reformulated with a focus not on an aggregate Q but on the average product of labor, AP_L:

$$UPC = \left[\left(\frac{W}{AP_L} \right) + \left(\frac{Z}{AP_L} \right) \right] \left(\frac{1}{e} \right) \qquad (10)$$

That formulation highlights three major factors influencing competitiveness, and, therefore, determining the potential for any low-wage economy to attract industries that must be delocalized from successful emerging countries: the ratio of wages to productivity (the first term in the right side), the level of transaction costs per worker, and the exchange rate whose importance has too often been overlooked in the economic discourse on Africa.[20] The UPC formulation provides a broader picture of the conditions under which labor arbitrage can occur. It also lays out the policy framework that low-income countries should follow in order to reap the new benefits of globalization. The first term in equation (10) simply states that the ratio of wages to productivity is the main driving force behind unit labor costs, which are only part of unit production costs. Therefore, countries can be internationally competitive regardless of whether they are high-wage/high-productivity or low-wage/low-productivity – provided that they can keep their unit labor costs low. The second term in equation (10) indicates that the important factor that complements decisions about labor arbitrage and relocation of industries from high- to low-wage countries is the relative level of transaction costs per worker. The third term stresses the importance of the exchange rate, which should not be overvalued in low-income countries.

For African countries trying to attract these manufacturing employment opportunities that will have to be outsourced from China, Brazil, and other emerging economies because of the steeply rising wages there, the policy prescriptions are relatively straightforward: in addition to exploiting their lower wage advantages, they should credibly ensure that the cost of doing business and exchange rate remain competitive. The question is how to do that in economies that have long suffered multiple and compounded distortions – sometimes over centuries. The next section offers a practical policy framework for job creation.

3.1.3.6   Winning the globalization jackpot: a policy framework for job creation

For policymakers in Sub-Saharan Africa, the big question then is: How to attract the jobs bonanza created by rising wages in successful large middle-income countries, foster manufacturing, and stimulate structural transformation? The answer boils down to two main obstacles that must be overcome: high factor costs (often due to distortive regulations and rigidities in land policy) and high transaction costs (often due to weak infrastructure and poor governance). In order to bring large fractions of the unemployed or underemployed labor force into the formal job market, lift millions out of poverty, and achieve social stability and prosperity, policymakers must recognize that their meager government budgets and administrative capacity must be allocated not to generic, broad-based reforms or to "priority sectors" vaguely defined as "agriculture," "education," "infrastructure," or "private sector development," but to a small number of strategically targeted programs, reforms, and industries in which private firms can emerge and become competitive domestically and internationally.

The diverse set of country experiences where industrialization has been successful in creating a critical mass of full-time employment shows that active labor market policies (ALMPs) only deliver results within a sensible framework for identifying competitive industries and facilitating public–private partnerships. These policy packages include various measures aiming at increasing the quality of the labor supply through activities such as launching programs for direct job creation, retraining, and providing assistance for job search to improve job matching. Their main goal is generally to increase the probability that the unemployed will find jobs and that the underemployed will improve their marketability, productivity, and earnings – a dynamics seen as conducive to higher participation rates and better social inclusion. But their effectiveness and sustainability are contingent to a broader industrialization strategy.[21]

Lin and Monga (2011) suggest a practical six-step growth identification and facilitation (GIF) framework to help policymakers in Sub-Saharan Africa and in other developing regions identify reliable growth paths and facilitate the emergence of employment-generating industries: First, identify those tradable goods and services that have existed for a period of about 20 years in dynamically growing countries that have similar endowment structures but with a per capita income that is about double their own. The focus should be not on natural resources which do not directly create many employment opportunities, but on labor-intensive industries that can be relocated across borders. Simply looking at Sub-Saharan Africa's GDP per capita of $1,200 in 2011,[22] it appears that a relatively large group of upper-middle-income countries such as Peru, Brazil, Chile, China, Malaysia, or Thailand could be good targets/anchors for its job creation strategy.

In a globalized world where the private firms that are competitive in international markets must cluster in sectors consistent with their country's comparative advantage (in order to lower both production costs and transaction costs), certain specific sectors must be given priority. Government capacity must be devoted to the facilitation of these carefully selected industries – and to a small number of localized reforms that are realistic in any given sociopolitical context. By facilitating the emergence and clustering of competitive private firms in some geographic locations with excellent logistics (without using the distortive instruments of old industrial policies such as tariffs or other forms of heavy protection), governments can foster the backward and forward linkages that brings capital and knowledge to national economies. Ultra-selectivity in the choice of potentially competitive industries and reforms therefore requires both realism and boldness in public policies: focusing on a limited number of initial sectors with high likelihood of success (because they are consistent with a country's comparative advantage) is the most sustainable strategy for economic development (Lin, 2012a, 2012b).

Second, among the industries on that list, identify those that have already attracted domestic private firms and generated employment, and try to pinpoint: (i) any obstacles that may be preventing them from upgrading the quality of their products, or (ii) any barriers that may be discouraging other private firms (both formal and informal) from entering. This could be done using value chain analysis or the Growth Diagnostics framework suggested by Hausmann, Rodrik, and Velasco (2008). The government can then implement policies to remove the constraints at home, and carry out randomized controlled experiments to test their effectiveness of eliminating the constraints before scaling those policies up to the national level.

Third, some of the identified industries may be completely new to domestic firms. African governments could encourage firms in the higher-income countries identified in the first step to invest in these industries, since those firms have the incentives of lower labor costs to relocate some of their low-skill activities in lower-income countries. Governments could also set up incubation programs to induce the entry of private domestic firms into these industries. China, whose GDP per capita is currently about twice that of many leading African countries, is a particularly interesting potential target. As noted by Lin (2011), after thirty years of double-digit growth, it is now facing the challenge of rising wages. In order to successfully pursue its economic development process, it must press on with the process of continuous industrial and technological upgrading, and shift its manufacturing base from low- to higher-skilled jobs. This will free up a large proportion of the country's current 85 million manufacturing jobs. Other countries such as Brazil are facing the same challenge.

Fourth, unexpected opportunities for many African economies may arise from technological breakthroughs around the world. The authorities should therefore pay close attention to successful discoveries and engagement in new business niches by private domestic enterprises and provide support to scale up those industries, especially those that create job opportunities.

Fifth, Africa is still a region with relatively poor infrastructure and unfriendly business environments (Figure 3.1.6). It would be unrealistic to expect that such problems can be addressed quickly. But well-located, well-equipped special economic zones or industrial parks could help overcome barriers to firm

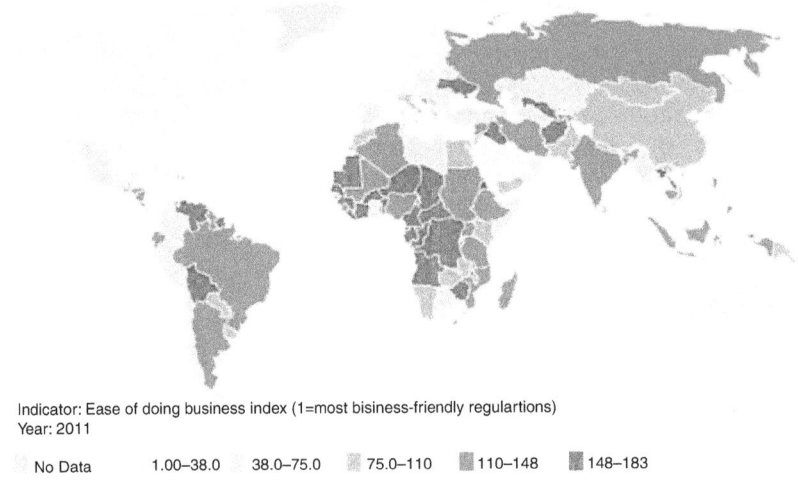

Indicator: Ease of doing business index (1=most bisiness-friendly regulartions)
Year: 2011

No Data   1.00–38.0   38.0–75.0   75.0–110   110–148   148–183

Figure 3.1.6   Ease of Doing Business Index, 2011

entry and foreign investment. These can create "islands" of well-functioning environments in places where budget and capacity constraints make it difficult to implement economy-wide reforms in a reasonable timeframe.

Sixth, African governments can compensate pioneer firms that take the risk to enter competitive new industries and create jobs through time-limited tax incentives, co-financing of investments, or access to foreign exchange. Tax incentives or credit guarantees granted to viable labor-intensive small and medium-sized enterprises seem to have worked well in many emerging markets and transition economies during recent the global financial crisis. To avoid rent seeking and the risk of political capture, these incentives should be limited both in time and in financial cost, and should not be in the form of monopoly rent, high tariffs, or other distortions.

3.1.7 Making ALMP work: a menu of possibilities

Empirical analyses of the effectiveness of ALMPs as remedies to unemployment or recipes for job creation rarely yield conclusive results (Betcherman et al., 2004). The job creation approach suggested in this paper provides a context in which ALMPs would have the highest likelihood of success. By highlighting the prime importance of the identification of potentially competitive industries and ensuring that reforms and resources are targeted to activities, programs, and projects that are economically viable, the GIF approach offers a policy framework where macroeconomic and ALMPs are specifically not implemented generically and randomly but geared towards enhancing an already competitive growth.

Macroeconomic stability is certainly of crucial importance in African countries and elsewhere. However, the role of demand policies in the fight against unemployment should not be neglected, especially in developing countries with relatively good fundamentals. Output growth is the most important determinant of employment growth. Using fiscal and monetary policies whenever possible to support the economic recovery and sustain growth can help reduce uncertainty. It would also make firms more inclined to invest and recruit.

There is generally little room for monetary policy, especially in countries where interest rates are already relatively low. But when the threat of inflation is not too severe, central banks can resort to unconventional monetary policy tools to provide an enabling environment for business development. Monetary policy can also have large and long lasting effects on real interest rates, and, by implication, on output or unemployment. Furthermore, a sustained increase in real interest rates induced by monetary policy can affect not only the actual rate of unemployment but also the natural rate: unemployment puts pressure on wages, even when bargaining is only between employed workers and firms.

Many unemployed college graduates throughout Africa eventually give up search or lose their skills, which imply that sustained high unemployment will lead to an increase the natural rate itself. When monetary policy is able to affect real interest rates for a long period of time, it can also affect the natural rate of unemployment through capital accumulation. Real interest rates affect the cost of capital; the cost of capital affects capital accumulation; the capital stock affects the demand for labor; and the demand for labor affects unemployment.

In some countries, there may be some room for well-targeted fiscal measures that can increase economic output and job possibilities. Direct employment creation – that is, temporary jobs through public works – for example, would have a stabilizing effect in a climate of heightened sociopolitical tensions. But the public finance situation in many countries across the continent may not be able to accommodate such a measure. When the fiscal space becomes available to do so, governments should refrain from hiring the unemployed directly, but contract instead with private firms or non-profit organizations to provide jobs. Vulnerable groups and people in the poorest regions and industries should be the targets of such measures.

In addition to providing much-needed income to people who are typically among the urban poor, well-targeted public works in infrastructure (new investment, repair, or maintenance) could remove bottlenecks to growth and create the conditions for increased productivity. Accelerating the implementation of shovel-ready labor-intensive, productive infrastructure projects should be a priority. Spending on productive infrastructure that remove bottlenecks on growth (with good rates of returns) and operations and maintenance spending can both boost demand and generate sources of growth in the longer run. Evidence from empirical work on Latin American and Caribbean countries suggests that infrastructure investment can have a sizable impact on employment generation (Calderon and Servén, 2010). It is true that they may crowd out some private sector jobs, especially if the targeting is ineffective. Salary levels should therefore be set carefully so that these programs are cost-effective.

Wage subsidies could also be considered for industries that are clearly competitive but facing temporary shocks. They would encourage employers to keep employees on their payroll that they would have otherwise laid off for economic reasons, and also to hire young workers or women by paying part of the salary for a given period of time. Wage subsidies often allow such workers to acquire or develop important skills that eventually give them the opportunity for long-term employment. It also helps them maintain contact with the labor market. However, because some employers may view subsidies simply as a temporary source of cheap labor, the risk of deadweight losses should also be considered. Governments should therefore be prudent and even conservative in determining the level and duration of the subsidies.

More fundamentally, an extensive reliance on public sector employment as a source of jobs and income often produces deep social and cultural consequences, and even hysteresis: some regions can be caught in equilibrium of dependency in which public sector jobs become the only source of income and opportunities for private sector development do not material-ize; this creates a vicious, self-fulfilling circle whereby entrepreneurship is discouraged while dependency on government for livelihood is enhanced. The end-result is often the creation of powerful political constituencies of public sector employees and unions who oppose labor market reforms. Not surprisingly, increasing public employment is much easier than reducing it, even in difficult times. The question is whether public sector employment can be used successfully as a sociopolitical tool, and for how long. Figure 3.1.7 offers a broad picture of the relationship between public wage bills and GDP in a sample of countries. It shows that African countries tend to pay more for public sector wage bills than the rest of the world.

Support to small and medium-sized enterprises should be envisaged as a potential tool for overcoming market failures in the financial sector. One possible instrument could be the provision of special lines of credit funded by multilateral banks and new institutions such as the African Investment Bank[23] and from which banks could lend to small businesses. If designed to support the development of industries that are consistent with the country's comparative advantage, these instruments could help both on the supply and on the demand side of Africa's labor market.

Training programs to help new workers and those laid off in recent years accumulate of regain skills could contribute to the increase in productivity if

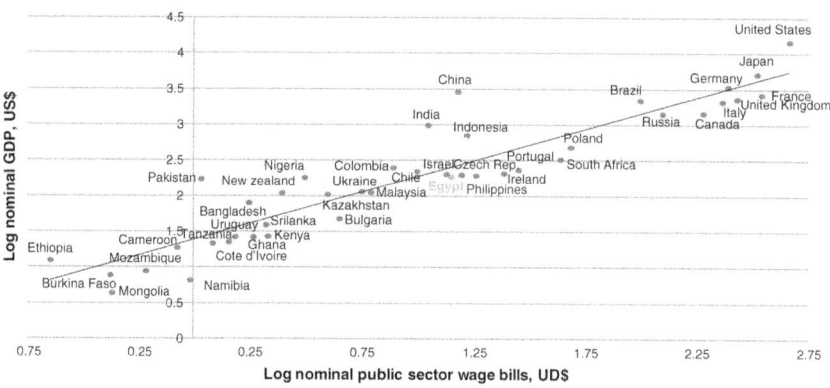

Figure 3.1.7 Public sector wage bill and economic development in a sample of countries

Source: IMF, International Financial Statistics and countryreports; World Bank, World Development Indicators and staff reports.

Note: Most recent data used. 2010: Brazil, Bulgaria, Chile, Czech Republic, Egypt (estimate), France, Germany, Indonesia, Ireland, Italy, Pakistan, Philippines, Poland, Portugal, United Kingdom, United States; 2009: Canada, Colombia, Ghana, Israel, Japan, Kazakhstan, South Africa, Tanzania, Ukraine; 2008: Bangladesh, Kenya, Mongolia, Nigeria, Russia, Sri Lanka; 2007: Burkina Faso, Côte d'Ivoire, Mozambique, Uruguay; 2006: Cameroon, China, India; 2005: Ethiopia, New Zealand; 2004: Namibia; 2003: Malaysia.

such programs are targeted at the neediest groups (the youth, the disadvantaged, or women). Youth-oriented programs designed with private firms to assess demand for skills and to provide corresponding tailored training programs for young people (following the German model) seem to yield good results in some African countries. It must be acknowledged, however, that such programs are often costly, and may not yield tangible results if the rate of economic growth does not accelerate. To ensure the maximum chance of success, they should be designed and implemented in close partnership with the private sector and tailored to suit the business needs of the potentially competitive industries in each country.

Finally, job search assistance and employment services currently favored by many African governments can indeed help match jobs and job seekers. They are usually inexpensive and often help reduce the length of unemployment. But they typically benefit only a small number of active jobseekers. Promoting access to the information and communications technologies (ICT) sector could help remove supply- and demand-side constraints in the labor market. Recent sociopolitical developments across the Arab world have demonstrated that the youth are the biggest consumers of technology, which they use to enhance their skills, seize opportunities, and connect to a global audience. Well-targeted policy measures to provide disadvantaged groups with access to ICT (IT alphabetization, investments to create ICT communal areas for rural youth and women, and so on) could foster the emergence of new economic activities and generate employment.

3.1.4 Conclusion

The multidimensional benefits of employment for all human societies have always been well understood by researchers and policymakers and are now empirically documented (World Bank, 2012). Economists have long attempted to design theoretical and policy frameworks aimed at optimal labor market conditions. But too often these intellectual ventures have focused on unemployment – a poor predictor of growth and economic performance – and have been tailored to suit the structure of advanced economies. While there has been a rich and vibrant economic literature on unemployment in developing countries, especially since the 1970s and 1980s, the models derived from it have not resulted in actionable policy recommendations that yield satisfactory results. Often designed for high-income countries where the labor market is relatively homogeneous, they have tended to focus on generic business environment issues and labor market institutions while strategies and policies to raise the demand for workers in competitive industries were neglected on the rationale that they would imply activist and inefficient industrial policies. Yet almost all economies that have succeeded in moving from low to high-income countries – especially the East Asian countries – have also proactively addressed the issue of employment creation by competitive private firms.

Following Firestein (2012)'s knowledge generation strategy of not simply looking to improve on what appears to be already understood but focusing instead on what is missing, this paper has attempted to shift the focus from theories of unemployment to practical policies that would allow generate employment in low-income countries. It has argued that the economic success of large emerging countries opens up unprecedented new opportunities for lower-income countries to exert labor arbitrage and reap the new dividends of globalization. With ample labor available in labor-intensive and low-skilled industries throughout the tradable sector globally and rising wages in China or Brazil, it is inevitable that private firms will have strong incentives to relocate some segments of their supply chains to places where strategic government policies can provide the most competitive factor and transaction costs. These structural trends in the global economy are stimulated by technological developments that allow for and lower transportation costs while ensuring just-in-time deliveries and customization.

Like many regions of the world, Africa is currently undergoing a deep sociopolitical transformation, which reflects and stimulates the need and desire for profound economic change. The mostly underemployed young people who are taking to the streets across the continent and often toppling well-entrenched authoritarian regimes in just a matter of days have many requests on their agenda, among which are the need for good, decent jobs that could help them escape poverty and live with dignity. The issue of youth employment is indeed crucial to inclusive development and sociopolitical stability in the region, which has the world's youngest population together with the highest underemployment rate. It is also of crucial importance for global stability, peace, and security. In addition to its enormous economic benefits and positive externalities, it is also today's most valuable political currency.

Despite the many economic and political challenges they currently face, developing countries can seize that opportunity – and win the jackpot – by identifying small numbers of well-targeted industries in which they have comparative advantage, and build industrial parks in which they can deliver low factor and transaction costs through high-quality infrastructure, excellent governance, and backwards and forward linkages that spark employment creation in the formal sector. Winning the battle for employment in Africa would bring infinite rewards to the continent and to the world.

Notes

1. It is estimated, for instance, that pay for factory workers in China soared by nearly 70 percent in just five years (2005–10). Source: *The Economist* (2011: 79).

2. According to ILO's standard definition from the 1982 Thirteenth International Conference of Labour Statisticians, the "unemployed" comprise all persons above a specified age who during a reference period were: (a) "without work", that is, were not in paid employment or self-employment; (b) "currently available for work", that is, were available for paid employment or self-employment during the reference period; and (c), "seeking work", that is, had taken specific steps in a specified reference period to seek paid employment or self-employment. The specific steps may include registration at a public or private employment exchange; application to employers; checking at worksites, farms, factory gates, market or other assembly places; placing or answering newspaper advertisements; seeking assistance of friends or relatives; looking for land, building, machinery or equipment to establish own enterprise; arranging for financial resources; applying for permits and licenses, etc. The national definitions used vary from one country to another as regards inter alia age limits, reference periods, criteria for seeking work, treatment of persons temporarily laid off and of persons seeking work for the first time.
3. See Azam (1994) for a detailed discussion of these debates on labor markets and the macroeconomy in developed countries, and some inference of their relevance to developing countries.
4. See Lindbeck and Snower (1985) for a detailed discussion of the pros and cons of these analyses.
5. Shocks typically refer to unexpected events due to exogenous factors that affect endogenous economic variables. Political events, natural disasters, accidents, or even brutal changes in policies can create positive or negative shocks. When due to constrained supply or demand, they usually lead to big changes in prices. Technological shocks can affect productivity.
6. Persistent unemployment in Europe for instance has often been viewed as the result of labor market shocks, inappropriate institutions that slow down the adjustment process to these shocks, and the interaction between shocks and institutions (Blanchard and Wolfers, 2000; Karnassou et al., 2002).
7. Estimation of an aggregate matching function can "shed light on the role of different classes of workers (for example, short term-long term, skilled-unskilled, in and out of the labor force) in the matching process. Micro-studies are no substitute for that information. For example, cross-section results on the importance of unemployment compensation for the likelihood of finding a job do not translate directly into implications for aggregate unemployment because less availability by some workers will raise the probability of job finding by others." (Blanchard and Diamond, 1990: 162–3).
8. The determination of the returns to factors should not be the only asymmetry. African farmers or industrialists do not necessarily have the typical, economics textbook-like, objective function (Ela, 1980, 1990). The different objectives often observed in the behavior of farmers in the African traditional modern sectors also suggest an organizational asymmetry. Furthermore, some product markets are largely competitive, while others are mostly oligopolistic. The non-clearing product market for one of the sectors is therefore another important source of dualism (see Taylor, 1983).
9. The exogenous approach was proposed by Harris and Todaro themselves (1970). Theories of endogenous urban wage determination can be found in Stiglitz (1974) or Calvo (1978).
10. Unemployment rates in low-income Africa are about 5–7 percent, with rate of youth unemployment slightly higher. The situation in South Africa and in some

other middle-income mineral-exporting countries such as Angola, Botswana and Namibia is almost the inverse of that of low-income countries, with unemployment rates ranging from 25 to 40 percent, with youth unemployment also higher. Source: World Bank data.

11. The Sqrt (square root) of GDP is used on the y-axis, though a logarithmic scale would have been probably more revealing. The Spearman Rho correlation shows the magnitude (strength of the correlation) and direction of the association between the two variables. The closer the correlation is to either +1 or –1, the stronger the correlation. If the correlation is 0 or very close to 0, there is no association between the two variables. Here, we have a weak correlation ($r = -.16$).

12. The conceptual challenge here also hinges on issues of interpersonal welfare: who is to decide what is really an acceptable employment opportunity? Large segments of the labor force in developing countries tend to define themselves as unemployed even though they hold some type of provisional employment, which they sometimes hold purely for psychological reasons – to keep their mind busy – and not even for subsistence. While it still makes analytical sense to classify such people as "employed", the reality is that they still perceive themselves as "unemployed" and would often behave as if they were completely. Many of them are young and educated, often with college degrees, and are at the forefront of sociopolitical uprising for jobs.

13. Source: World Development Indicators.

14. A study by the US Department of Commerce, Bureau of Economic Analysis, shows that manufacturing has a higher multiplier effect on the American economy than any other sector with US$1.40 in additional value added in other sectors for every US$1.00 in manufacturing value added. Source: World Economic Forum (2012).

15. The largest counterpart to the US current-account deficit is the combined surplus of oil-exporting economies, which have experienced big windfalls from high oil prices. The IMF projects them to run a record surplus of $740 billion in 2012, most of which will come from the Middle East. That would dwarf China's expected surplus of $180 billion. Since 2000 the cumulative surpluses of oil exporters have come to over $4 trillion, twice as much as that of China.

16. It is estimated that after the oil-price shocks in the 1970s, about 70 percent of the increase in export revenues was spent on imports of goods and services (*Economist*, 2012).

17. Lin and Monga (2011) offer a menu of policy options that all low-income countries could choose from to exploit the benefits of backwardness, including those countries with low physical and human capital and technology.

18. Throughout the world, it is estimated that 445 million hectares of land are uncultivated and available for farming. About 201 million hectares are in Sub-Saharan Africa, 123 million in Latin America, and 52 million in Eastern Europe. See Deininger et al. (2011).

19. See Dornbusch et al. (1977) for the general formulation.

20. This is true in particular for the 14 African countries whose national currencies have been pegged at a fixed exchange rate to the French Franc and the Euro, with mostly devastating consequences on competitiveness. See Monga (1997) and Devarajan and de Melo (1991).

21. For a critical review, see Betcherman et al. (2001). The debate over ALMP is often framed in terms of their supposed superior benefits when compared to *passive* labor market policies such as social transfers or unemployment insurance, which are typically designed to mitigate the pain of unemployment and provide

financial support to the unemployed – without directly improving their skills and marketability.
22. Source: World Development Indicators.
23. For a discussion of the rationale for an African Investment bank (in addition of the existing African Development Bank), see Monga (2012a).

References

Azam, J.-P. (1994) "Recent Developments in the Developed-Country Literature on Labor Markets and the Implications for Developing Countries," in S. Horton, R. Kanbur, and D. Mazumdar (eds), *Labor Markets in an Era of Adjustment, vol. 1, Issues Papers* (Washington, DC: World Bank), pp. 61–103.

Betcherman, G., Dar, A., Luinstra, A., and Ogawa, M. (2001) "Active Labor Market Policies: Issues for East Asia," in: G. Betcherman and R. Islam (eds), *East Asian Labor Markets and the Economic Crisis* (Washington, DC: World Bank), pp. 295–344.

Betcherman, G., Olivas, K., and Dar, A. (2004) *Impacts of Active Labor Market Programs: New Evidence from Evaluations with Particular Attention to Developing and Transition Countries*, Social Protection Discussion Paper Series no. 0402 (Washington, DC: World Bank).

Blanchard, O. and Wolfers, J. (2000) "The Role of Shocks and Institutions in the Rise of European Unemployment," *Economic Journal*, vol. 110, pp. 1–33.

Blanchard, O.J. and Diamond, P. (1990) "The Aggregate Matching Function," in P. Diamond (ed.), *Growth–Productivity–Unemployment* (Cambridge, MA: MIT Press), pp. 159–201.

Calderon, C. and Servén, L. (2010) *Infrastructure in Latin America*, Policy Research Working Paper no. 5313 (Washington, DC: World Bank).

Calvo, G.A. (1978) "Urban Unemployment and Wage Determination in LDCs: Trade Unions in the Harris–Todaro Model," *International Economic Review*, vol. 19, pp. 65–81.

Ceglowski, J. and S. Golub, 2011. *Does China Still Have a Labor Cost Advantage?*, CESIFO Working Paper no. 3579, September.

Chandra, V., Lin, J.Y., and Wang, Y. (2012) *Leading Dragons Phenomenon: New Opportunities for Catch-Up in Low-Income Countries*, Policy Research Working Paper no. 6000 (Washington, DC: World Bank).

Cissé, D.A. (1988) *Histoire économique de l'Afrique noire*, 3 vols (Paris : L'Harmattan).

Deininger, K., Lindsay, J., Norton, A., Selod, H., and Stickler, M. (2011) "Rising Global Interest in Farmland: Can It Yield Sustainable and Equitable Benefits?," in *Agriculture and Rural Development* (Washington, DC: World Bank).

Devarajan, S., and de Melo, J. (1991) "Membership in the CFA Zone: Odyssean Journey or Trojan Horse?," in A. Chibber and S. Fischer (eds), *Economic Reform in Sub-Saharan Africa* (Washington, DC: World Bank), pp. 25–33.

Dinh, H., et al. (2011) *Light Manufacturing in Africa*, vol. 2 (Washington, DC: World Bank).

Dornbusch, R., Fischer, S., and Samuelson, P.A. (1977) "Comparative Advantage, Trade and Payments in a Ricardian Model with a Continuum of Goods," *American Economic Review*, vol. 65, no. 5, pp. 823–839.

Economist (2012) "Petrodollar profusion," April 28.

Economist (2011) "Moving Back to America," May 14–20, pp. 79–80.

Edwards, L. and Golub, S.S. (2004) "South Africa's International Cost Competitiveness and Exports in Manufacturing," *World Development*, vol. 32, no. 8, pp. 1323–1339.

Ela, J.-M. (1990) *Quand l'Etat pénètre en brousse: les ripostes paysannes à la crise* (Paris: Karthala).

Ela, J.-M. (1980) *Le cri de l'homme africain* (Paris : L'Harmattan).

Firestein, S. (2012) *Ignorance: How it Drives Science* (New York: Oxford University Press).

Fox, L. and Gaal, M.S. (2008) *Working out of Poverty: Job Creation and the Quality of Growth in Africa* (Washington, DC: World Bank).

Fox, L. and Sohnesen, T.P. (2012) "Household Enterprise in Sub-Saharan Africa: Why They Matter for Growth, Jobs, and Livelihoods," mimeo (Washington, DC: World Bank).

Harris, J.R. and Todaro, M. (1970) "Migration, Unemployment, and Development: A Two-sector Analysis," *American Economic Review*, vol. 40, pp. 126–142.

Hausmann, R., and Hidalgo, C. (2012) "Economic Complexity and the Future of Manufacturing," in World Economic Forum, *The Future of Manufacturing: Opportunities to Drive Economic Growth* (Cologny/Geneva: WEF), p. 13.

Hausmann, R., Hidalgo, C., et al. (2011) *Atlas of Economic Complexity: Mapping Paths to Prosperity* (Cambridge, MA.: Harvard Center for International Development).

Hausmann,, R., Rodrik, D., and Velasco, A. (2008) "Growth Diagnostics," in N. Serra and J.E. Stiglitz (eds), *The Washington Consensus Reconsidered: Towards a New Global Governance* (New York: Oxford University Press), pp. 324–354.

Iliffe, J., (1983) *The Emergence of African Capitalism* (New York: Palgrave).

Karnassou, M., H. Sala, and D. J. Snower, 2002. *Unemployment in the European Union: A Dynamic Reappraisal*, Discussion Paper no. 531 (Bonn, Germany: IZA). Available online at www.iza.org.

Kennedy, P. (1988) *African Capitalism: The Struggle for Ascendency* (Cambridge: Cambridge University Press).

Krueger, A.B. (2011) *Presentation at World Bank Seminar for Executive Directors* (Washington, DC: World Bank).

Layard, R., Nickell, S., and Jackman, R. (1991) *Unemployment: Macroeconomic Performance and the Labour Market* (Oxford: Oxford University Press).

Lin, J.Y. (2012 a) *New Structural Economics: A Framework for Rethinking Development and Policy* (Washington, DC: World Bank).

Lin, J.Y. (2012b) *The Quest for Prosperity: How Developing Economies Can Take Off* (Princeton, NJ: Princeton University Press).

Lin, J.Y. (2011) *From Flying Geese to Leading Dragons: New Opportunities and Strategies for Structural Transformation in Developing Countries*, Policy Research Working Paper no. 5702 (Washington, DC: World Bank).

Lin, J.Y. and Monga, C. (2011) "Growth Identification and Facilitation: The Role of the State in the Dynamics of Structural Change," *Development Policy Review*, vol. 29, no. 3, pp. 259–310.

Lindauer, D.L. and Velenchik, A.D. (1994) "Can African Labor Compete?," in D.L. Lindauer and M. Roemer (eds), *Asia and Africa: Legacies and Opportunities in Development* (San Francisco: Institute for Contemporary Studies), pp. 269–304.

Lindbeck, A. and Snower, D.J. (1985) "Explanations to Unemployment," *Oxford Review of Economic Policy*, vol. 1, no. 2, pp. 34–69.

Monga, C. (1997) "A Currency Reform Index for Western and Central Africa," *The World Economy*, vol. 20, no. 1, January, pp. 103–125.

Monga, C. (2011) "Post-Macroeconomics: Lessons from the Crisis and Strategic Directions Ahead," *Journal of International Commerce, Economics and Policy*, vol. 2, no. 2, pp. 1–28.

Monga, C. (2012a) "Shifting Gears: Igniting Structural Transformation in Africa," *Journal of African Economies*, vol. 21 (Supplement 2), pp. ii19–ii54.

Monga, C. (2012b) "The Hegelian Dialectics of Global Imbalances," *Journal of Philosophical Economics*, vol. 6, no. 1, pp. 1–52.

Page, J. (2012) "Can Africa Industrialise?," *Journal of African Economies*, vol. 21 (Supplement 2), pp. ii86–ii124.

Perkins, D.H. and Roemer, M. (1994) "Differing Endowments and Historical Legacies," in D.L. Lindauer and M. Roemer (eds), *Asia and Africa: Legacies and Opportunities in Development* (Cambridge and San Francisco: HIID and Institute for Contemporary Studies), pp. 25–58.

Roemer, M. (1994) "Industrial Strategies: Outward Bound," in D.L. Lindauer and M. Roemer (eds), *Asia and Africa: Legacies and Opportunities in Development* (Cambridge and San Francisco: HIID and Institute for Contemporary Studies), pp. 233–268.

Spence, M. (2011) "The Impact of Globalization on Income and Employment: The downside of Integrating Markets," *Foreign Affairs*, July–August, pp. 28–41.

Stiglitz, J.E. (1974) "Alternative Theories of Wage Determination and Unemployment in LDCs: The Labor-Turnover Model," *Quarterly Journal of Economics*, vol. 88, pp. 194–227.

Taylor, L. (1983) *Structuralist Macroeconomics: Applicable Models for the Third World* (New York: Basic Books).

Taylor, S.D. (2012) *Globalization and the Cultures of Business in Africa: From Patrimonialism to Profit.* (Bloomington, IN: Indiana University Press).

UNIDO (2009) *Industrial Development Report 2009 – Breaking In and Moving Up: New Industrial Challenges for the Bottom Billion and the Middle-Income Countries* (New York: UNIDO).

World Bank (2012) *World Development Report 2013: Jobs* (Washington, DC: World Bank).

World Bank (2008) *World Development Report 2009: Reshaping Economic Geography* (Washington, DC: World Bank).

World Economic Forum (2012) *The Future of Manufacturing: Opportunities to Drive Economic Growth* (Cologny/Geneva: WEF).

3.2

Walking (Stumbling?) on Two Legs: Meeting SSA'S Industrialization Challenge*

Raphael Kaplinsky
The Open University, Milton Keynes, UK

3.2.1 Introduction

Industrial development in the current era in Sub-Saharan Africa (SSA) is bounded by two major framing dynamics. The first is the issue of exclusion. Hitherto, the growth process in general, and industrial development in particular, have led to an outcome in which the fruits of accumulation are heavily skewed, in terms of both participation in the process of production (and hence the distribution of income streams which are generated) and also the nature of the products and services which are produced. Second, many countries in SSA are benefiting from the sustained boom in commodity prices, and this has important implications for industrial development. These framing dynamics present both threat and opportunity to future industrial development, and are subject to policy intervention.

This paper assesses the implications of these two framing dynamics for industrial policy in SSA. Section 3.2.2 begins with a brief review of the exclusionary character of growth in SSA. This is followed with a discussion of the commodity price boom. Building on this, section 3.2.3 addresses the disruptive character of southern-based innovation systems and the potential this holds for more inclusive patterns of industrial development and section 3.2.4 focuses on the unrecognized potential for promoting industrial development through linkages to the commodity sector. Section 3.2.5 considers the composition problem, that is, the prospects for walking (and perhaps even jogging or sprinting) on two legs. The paper concludes in section 3,2.6 with a discussion of the politics underlying the development of an integrated strategy towards industrial development in SSA.

The analysis in this paper is a subset of a broader issue, that is, the significance and impact of the emergence of the Asian Driver economies

* I am grateful to Carlota Perez and David Kaplan for comments on an earlier draft.

(particularly China, but also India) on SSA. As we will see, their rapid growth is key to an understanding of both disruptive technological change and the commodity price boom. But their impact is, of course, much larger than this, and is increasingly recognized in burgeoning literatures on the Asian Drivers, on the impact of China, on "Rising Powers" and on "Emerging Economies." One aspect of these literatures is the impact of China and other rapidly growing emerging economies on industrial development in Africa. This is a literature which largely sees the impact as being negative, with respect to both the indirect impact on export-oriented industrialization and the direct impact on industrial production destined for the domestic economy (Jenkins and Edwards, 2005: Kaplinsky and Morris, 2008; Kaplinsky, 2009). There is, however, a (wishful) expectation that as wages rise in the East Asian production network (particularly in China) SSA will take its place in global value chains. However, high unit wage costs, low levels of systemic efficiency, and low levels of capabilities in SSA contrast with the corresponding efficiency parameters in Asia, Whilst China may soon begin to deplete its reserve army of labor in the medium term (although there is substantial scope for moving production into the interior regions), there is a large pool of surplus labor and capabilities in the Asian production system as a whole. SSA is unlikely to become a large cog in the extension of global value chains. The policy challenge is thus to focus on a more inward-oriented industrial strategy – "inward" as much to the African region as to individual economies.

3.2.2   The framing environment for industrial development in SSA

3.2.2.1   Development as an exclusionary process

The first decade of the 21st century witnessed an acceleration of growth in many low- and middle-income countries. These rates were high by comparison with the last decade of the 20th (and even more so in comparison to the lost development decades of the 1980s), and by comparison with global average growth rates in the same periods (Table 3.2.1). Rapid and accelerating growth was most pronounced in China and India, but was also evidenced in middle income countries as a whole, as well as in SSA. At the same time, the numbers living globally below the MDG1 $1.25pd benchmark fell by 339m between 1988–90 and 2007–08. This is often taken as an indication of the power of globalization to reduce global poverty. Yet the decline in the poverty number in China (516m) exceeded the global total (339m), which means that outside of China, the number living globally below MDG1 increased by 177m. In SSA, a more than doubling of the annual average growth rate in the two decades resulted in a 59 percent increase in absolute poverty numbers. In India, the recent growth miracle has been associated with an additional 42m people living below MDG1.

Table 3.2.1 GDP growth rates and numbers living below MDG1, 1990–2008

	GDP growth p.a (%)		Living below $1.25 per day (MDG1) ($2005PPP)	
	1990–2000	2000–2008	1988–90	2007–2008
World	2.9	3.1	1,668	1,329
China	9.9	10.4	724	208
India	5.5	7.0	414	456
SSA	2.2	4.9	224	355

Source: Poverty numbers from Chen and Ravallion (2008) and Sumner (2010). Growth rates from WDI, accessed October 2011.

Strikingly, despite rapid economic growth, there was a more than doubling of the number of the absolutely poor in middle income countries and currently, more than 70 percent of those living below MDG1 live in this rapidly growing group of economies (Sumner, 2010).

What these numbers point to is the structural character of the dominant growth model in which, in many countries, a significant proportion of the population is being excluded from the fruits of growth. This impoverished population is made up of two groups. The first are those living in Lewis's traditional sector, eking out a living in subsistence agriculture or in low-paid formal-sector employment. The second are the truly-marginalised, those living without access to land or formal-sector employment.

Three primary and related reasons explain this structural character of the current dominant global growth trajectory. The first is that it arises as a direct result of deepening globalization (Kaplinsky, 2005). Globalization allows high-income earners who possess various forms of rent (such as natural resources, skills, entrepreneurship, brandnames, privileged access to low-cost capital and patents) to valorize these rents over a larger market. At the same time it exposes those with low incomes and without rents to intensified competition. For example in the case of unskilled labor, the global labor pool has doubled in the past two decades, following the entry of China, India, and the former Soviet Union into the global economy. The second factor underlying the distributional character of this global growth trajectory is the financialization of the global economy (Lazonik, 2010). This has placed a growing emphasis on arbitrage rather than production, with this arbitrage being a function confined largely to the high-income economies and to the capital cities of a selected few middle-income countries. It has led to a change in the terms of trade between producers of goods and non-financial services, and financial services, shifting distributional patterns in favor of the financial sector. It has also led to, and is likely to continue to lead to growing volatility of incomes throughout the global economy not least for the global poor. The financial crisis of 2008 temporarily pushed almost 100 million Indonesians into absolute poverty. The third factor which explains why enhanced growth coexists with, and indeed in some cases causes absolute poverty arises from the dominant trajectory of innovation. Its capital-intensive nature, its scale intensity, its dependence on high-quality networked infrastructure, its reliance on skilled labor and its product portfolio (producing products which meet the needs of the rich) all have the effect of disadvantaging the poor, both as consumers and producers, and of excluding large segments of the population in many countries from productive employment. Moreover, much contemporary technology is also destructive of the environment, not least in relation to its energy-intensity, and this has disproportionately negative impacts on the global poor. Whilst innovation is only a partial contributor to the persistence of global poverty it is an important one, and one which is largely neglected in the theorisation of innovation (Cozzens and Kaplinsky, 2009).

3.2.2.2   The commodities super cycle (and perhaps structural break) in the terms of trade

Since 2002 the global economy has witnessed the emergence of a long-lived commodity price boom (Figure 3.2.1), that is, it is long-lived by comparison with the two previous price booms in the early 1950s and early 1970s. The price surge was initially limited to hard and energy commodities, but after 2005 also began to affect the soft commodities sectors. Although commodity prices continued to be very volatile by comparison with the prices of manufactures, and

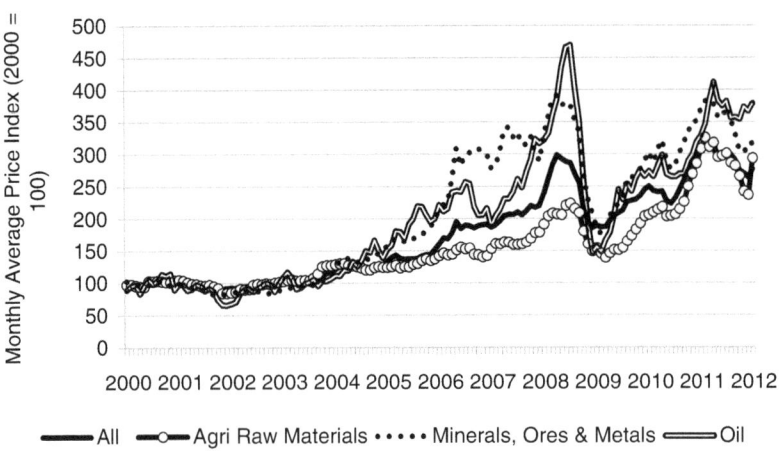

Figure 3.2.1   United Nations Conference on Trade and Development (UNCTAD) monthly average price index, 2000 = 100 (2000 to Jan. 2012)

Source: Compiled from UNCTAD stat. data. Online <http://unctadstat.unctad.org/> (accessed April 2012).

witnessed a sharp (albeit temporary) price fall after the 2008 global financial crisis, they have been on a sustained upward trend for a decade, a unique trend by comparison with the economic history of the 20th century.

The short-lived commodity price booms of the 1950s and 1970s were based on a combination of temporary interruptions to supply (anticipated threats to supply from the Korean War in the 1950s and the surge in oil prices after the 1973 oil crisis) and unrealistic expectations of a sustained growth in demand. But neither of these circumstances endured. Supply threats from the Korean War failed to materialize in the 1950s, and global economic growth adjusted to the higher oil prices by the early 1980s.

By contrast, the post-2002 commodity price boom has resulted from a combination of events which make it highly likely that prices will remain high and, in many cases, grow for some years to come (Farooki and Kaplinsky, 2012). On the demand side, China, India, and other low- and middle-income emerging economies are at an early stage of their per capita consumption of most hard and energy commodities. Although their demand growth is often thought to arise from their rapidly growing export-oriented manufacturing sector, in fact most of their demand for commodities has resulted from the massive investments in infrastructure and construction. The demand for soft commodities will also expand in the future, as incomes and per capita consumption of food (particularly animal proteins) continue to grow and as agricultural land is used to produce biofuels.

On the supply side, there are constraints in each of the three families of commodities to the expansion of low-cost supplies. In energy commodities, low-cost deposits of oil have reached their limits and the marginal price, of what are often substitutable sources of supply, is set by the costs of deep-sea oil production and shale oil and gas production. The days of cheap energy are therefore over. The supply response in soft commodities is limited by the high costs of investment in irrigation, slowing rates of productivity growth, the growing cost of hydrocarbon-based agrochemicals, the global shortage of water, and climate change and climate chaos. With regard to hard commodities, there are large unexploited deposits of most minerals, but these are generally in inaccessible areas, and in countries of high political risk including in SSA. Moreover, for a combination of reasons, exploration budgets have been low for much of the past two decades and mines have a long gestation period between exploration and production (frequently this can be more than twenty years).

Consequently, commodity prices are likely to consolidate their gains of the last decade, and perhaps also to remain on a rising trend for some years to come. At the same time, the growing global diffusion of manufacturing capabilities has meant that competition in many manufacturing sectors – particularly in low-technology and labor-intensive manufactures – has continued to grow. Hence the declining commodities-manufactures terms of trade which bedevilled commodity producers for many decades has begun to shift in favour of commodities, a process which is likely to be sustained for some years to come.

3.2.3   The disruptive character of southern-based innovation systems[1]

Returning to the discussion in section 3.2.1 above, we now focus on the contribution of technological change to exclusionary growth. The theory of induced innovation provides a framework for understanding how this exclusive technological trajectory has evolved. It identifies three factors which determine the nature and trajectory of technological progress (Ruttan, 2001). The first is the nature of demand, with innovators responding to the effective demand of consumers with disposable cash incomes. The large and growing markets in the post-war era were of high-income consumers in developed economies rather than low-income consumers in developing economies. It is not surprising, therefore, that the products emerging from the dominant innovation system have increasingly been focused on meeting the needs of higher-income consumers, including for diversified products, positional consumption goods, and "high-quality", high-acquisition-cost products. The second inducing determinants of innovation are factor prices and the quality, nature, and price of infrastructure. Innovation occurring in high-income economies reflects these operating conditions and has been capital intensive, large in scale, and dependent on reliable, widely-diffused and centralized infrastructure. The third innovation-inducing factor identified by Ruttan – based on insights from institutional economics (Dosi, 1982) – reflects the path-dependencies of innovating firms. Their bounded rationality means that northern-based firms innovated in areas closely related to their past success, reinforcing a trajectory of innovation which was largely focused on meeting the needs of high-income consumers and operating conditions in high-income economies. We can add to Ruttan's threefold induced innovation framework the role of regulatory systems. An increasingly tight and enduring system of global intellectual property rights has created major barriers to the entry to new innovators. The underpricing of the real cost of energy and environmental externalities (a reflection of regulatory systems) has led to the development of energy-intensive and polluting innovation streams.

We are now witnessing the emergence of a series of trends which are beginning to threaten the dominance of a global innovation system which target the needs of high-income consumers by utilizing capital-, scale- and standards-intensive technologies which are sensitive to the quality, reliability, and ubiquity of infrastructure. They are beginning to provide "appropriate technologies" which are efficient and which are increasingly diffused through profit-seeking and market-driven innovation. Four of these emerging disruptive factors can be identified – the dynamism of low-income markets, the availability of new radical technologies, the global diffusion of innovative capabilities, and the emergence of new innovation actors.

3.2.3.1 The character and dynamism of low-income markets

With the North increasingly likely to be mired in economic stagnation, the driver of global demand will shift to the South in general, and to the two rapidly growing and very large Asian Driver economies of China and India in particular. In 2010 the Africa-Asia-Central Europe head of Unilever estimated that, by 2020, nearly 80 percent of incremental consumption growth will come from emerging economies.

These growing low-income economy markets are distinctive. On the one hand, they reflect a rapid growth in demand by an urban middle class which is not very different from most consumer markets in the north, searching for globally-branded, differentiated and high-quality positional goods. But, on the other hand, there is a rapidly expanding and very large market of poor consumers. In particular, in both China and India, there is a clustering of households with total household incomes of less than $5,000 in 2009.[2] In 2009 they comprised 56 percent of all households in China, and 71 percent in India . According to McKinsey calculations, the number of Indian households with an annual income between $7,000 and $10,000 will catapult from 14m to 200m between 2010 and 2015 (*Financial Times*, January 5, 2011). Critically, incomes in this category of income recipients are growing rapidly.

In all probability, or at least by hypothesis (drawing on Ruttan's induced innovation framework), the driving of consumption by low-income households will induce a different set of products compared to high-income earners in northern economies. These product innovations are likely to be differentiated to meet the environments in which they are developed. As McKinsey advises its clients, these innovations will be distinctively different from those produced for high-income global consumers, somewhere between the positional goods of high-income consumers and the basic functions and low acquisition-cost goods of the very low income defined by Prahalad (2005) as those at the "bottom of the pyramid". It is this "bottom of the pyramid" market which has begun to draw the attention of many of the world's largest TNCs, particularly those selling final consumer goods such as Unilever, Proctor and Gamble and Nestlés. Low-income consumers may prefer and aspire to "high-quality" branded goods, but they lack the incomes required to both acquire and then consume these more expensive goods. In these circumstances they will make do with what they can afford, rather than what they would prefer to consume.

A further important reflection of the changing geography of global consumption has been the shift of final market in many sectors from high-income countries to low-income countries. This has had important implications for the role of standards in global value chains. Products destined for high-income consumers and countries have tended to involve the extensive use of both product and process standards. There is considerable evidence that these standards have acted to exclude low-income producers from global value chains. By comparison, products destined for low income markets have been relatively devoid of standards (Kaplinsky, Terheggen and Tijaja, 2011), removing some of the barriers to entry for small-scale producers. However, insofar as these standards have protected the environment and the exploitation of vulnerable labor, there has been some trade-off between the various consequences of production processes and products which affect poor producers and consumers.

3.2.3.2   The emergence of new radical technologies

The literature on long-wave cycles and innovation distinguishes a spectrum between incremental changes on the shopfloor and farm and the revolutionary heartland technologies which sweep across sectors rapidly in disruptive waves of creative destruction (Freeman, 1993). Somewhere in between these extremes are a series of radical technologies which provide the opportunity for new, higher-quality and multifunctional products produced with different technologies and delivered through new business models and which are applicable across a range of sectors Historically, plastics is an example of this form of radical technical progress.

In the current era, we can witness the emergence of new technological families which are applicable across a range of economic sectors, each of which has widespread potential significance for producing products for poor consumers and/or for including poor producers in efficient production processes. The first of these is the rapid growth and diffusion of information and communication technologies. Perhaps the most pro-poor innovation-relevant outcome has been the benefits provided by mobile telecommunications for low-cost and distributed information diffusion (that is, in the form of capital goods). The second relevant emerging technology are the new forms of energy production, renewables such as solar and windpower, and biomass. Again, as in the case of mobile telephony, these new technologies both enhance consumer welfare and provide the potential for low-cost and distributed energy supply. The distributed character of both mobile telephony and renewable energy is particularly relevant for poor consumers who were previously prevented from benefitting from these services because with previous technologies, access followed from large and capital-intensive investments in network-intensive infrastructure. By contrast, the new technologies allow access to small-scale consumers and producers, particularly those living in non-urban areas. The final two sets of emerging pro-poor relevant technologies are nanotechnology and biotechnology (Singer and Daar, 2001). Both of these provide the scope for radically new technologies which have important potential applications in meeting the needs of poor people, and small-scale applications through, for example, new diagnostic kits and new water purification systems. Each of these discrete families of technological applications (including those which are specifically designed for the poor) are underwritten by the diffusion of the revolutionary "heartland" technology of microelectronics (Freeman and Perez, 1988).

3.2.3.3   The global diffusion of innovative capabilities

Recent decades have seen a substantial increase in the share of global manufacturing value added in low-income countries in general, and in China in particular. The global diffusion of manufacturing value added has been associated with a pervasive increase in capabilities in many low-income economies. These capabilities have been built on a number of strands of activity. The first has been the relatively passive processes of learning-by-doing, and the more active processes of "learning by adaptation" and "learning by capacity expansion" (Katz, 1987; Bell, 2007). These firm- and farm-level activities – generally associated with efforts to make maximum use of purchased, and often imported technologies – arise out of incremental changes undertaken in the operation of equipment. They are often also acquired through participation in global value chains (Kaplinsky and Morris, 2001; Gereffi, Humphrey, and Sturgeon, 2005). Formally constituted R&D is another important component of innovation (although its importance if often overestimated), By 2000, more than one-fifth of global R&D was located in the developing world (Hollanders and Soete, 2010), an increase of major significance given the estimated share of only 2 percent in 1970 (Singer et al, 1970). An increasing share of this dispersed R&D occurs as a result of outsourcing by global TNCs, particularly to China and India (Bruche, 2009). This global diffusion of capabilities to countries with large populations of low-income consumers provides the scope for a new source of innovation, potentially disruptive to the historic dominance of northern-sourced technological change.

3.2.3.4   Disruptive entrepreneurs

The existence of capabilities, the availability of radically new technologies, and the growth of effective demand from poor people do not in themselves result in innovation. Instead, as Schumpeter highlighted, innovations arise as a consequence of purposive action by entrepreneurs developing and utilizing inventions in product, process, and organization in the search for supernormal profit.

We can distinguish a number of different categories of entrepreneurs who might play a role in the innovation of pro-poor products and services and process technologies. One key set of actors are the established global TNCs seeking to capture the "fortune at the bottom of the pyramid," particularly in the FMCG (fast-moving-consumer-goods) sectors, but also in medical instruments (where General Electric is increasingly using India and China as sources of low-cost innovation. Prahalad believed that this provided a profitable market opportunity for transnational corporations (TNCs) rather than for the small-scale and locally-owned firms long identified in the appropriate technology and informal sector literature as being key providers for low income consumers. He argued that TNCs "…need only act in their own self interest, for there are enormous business benefits to be gained by entering developing markets" (Prahalad and Hammond, 2002: 4).

But this belief that northern TNCs would be able to grasp this market is an untested assertion. As Christenson's widely cited work has pointed out (Christenson, 1997), large firms which dominate industries are often extremely good at hearing the demands of their existing customers, but very poor at hearing the needs of new customers. He argued that when new markets emerge established producers who know their existing markets intimately, tend to miss out on the new opportunities. He referred to this as a process of disruptive innovation. TNCs are largely attuned to high income customer needs. If the leading northern-origin TNCs are unable to exploit this emerging low-income market effectively, there are a variety of domestic firms in low income economies which recognise the potential for profitability in targeting the needs of low income consumers, and addressing these needs through innovations of basic, labor-intensive technologies. A widely-cited example (which is not without its teething problems) is the Tata Nano in India, a basic car priced at less than $2,500 and aimed at low-income consumers moving up from a two-wheeled scooter. One conception of this car is also to produce it in kit form to enable consumers to tailor the body to meet their needs (adding trailers, for example) so that the car becomes a capital good. In China, Haier (which is now the world's second-largest producer of white goods), discovered that some rural consumers used their washing machines both for clothes and to wash potatoes, so they redesigned their machines to make them more robust and to serve both consumer needs more effectively.

Less visible, and below the radar, are a plethora of small- and medium-scale entrepreneurs in the South who are introducing small-scale innovations without the input of formal R&D, and with little attention being paid to intellectual property rights or product and process standards. For example, DMT Mobile Toilets is a commercial enterprise that produces, rents, and maintains safe, sanitary portable toilets in West Africa. Lifeline Energy conducts extensive end-user research and then develops and distributes appropriate, clean energy products, including radios, a range of lights, solar panels, and MP3-enabled Lifeplayers that allow pre-loaded educational content as well as internet access.

3.2.3.5   The combined impact of disruptive forces on the innovation trajectory

The single most important conclusion which emerges from the above analysis is that there has been a sea-change in the determinants of pro-poor innovation. In the past appropriate technologies were often inefficient, were promoted by not-for-profit aid and civil society organizations and were scorned by both consumers and formal sector producers. By contrast, as a result of the disruptive factors discussed above, pro-poor innovations have moved from the margin of economic accumulation. Critically, their diffusion is driven by a profit-seeking Schumpeterian rather than a normatively-driven Schumacherian motor.

There is widespread evidence that market-driven diffusion is occurring and that this has resulted in pro-poor outcomes. For example, in the Cameroons (Khan and Baye, 2011). Chinese motorcycles are less durable than Japanese motorcycles and require more repairs. However, they cost one-third of the cost of the higher-quality products and this has provided the opportunity for low-income school-leavers to enter the market as taxi drivers and logistics providers. Similarly, Chinese-produced batteries have half the operating-life of northern-branded products, but cost only one-third as much. In both cases, the Chinese products both lower the entry-costs for purchases and reduce the unit costs of consumption. Similarly, as a recent article in the *Economist* documents, there is also a rapid development and diffusion of a range of pro-poor innovations in South Africa, and through South African firms, in SSA – "South African companies are ... discovering the "bottom of the pyramid" in their own country. Several companies have pioneered the art of using cell phones to map the distribution of informal shops (spaza) and truck stops. Blue Label Telecoms, which sells pre-paid tokens, has blazed a trail in forming relationships with tribal chiefs and popular gospel singers to help sell its products. Knowledge of the bottom of the pyramid is now being used to expand in emerging markets. SABMiller produces beer for Uganda using cheap local ingredients rather than expensive imported malt. MTN provides solar-powered phones to fishermen" (*Economist*, September 10, 2011).

3.2.4 One thing leads to another – industrial development through linkages to the commodity sector[3]

We now turn to the impact of the commodities price boom on industrial development. There is a widespread belief that the hard and energy commodities sectors operate as enclaves, with limited spillovers to the local economy. This perception has deep roots in development strategy thinking. Singer observed the virtual absence of linkages from these commodity sectors in the decades after World War II (Singer, 1950). It was a view which was reinforced by studies of corporate strategy which showed why a series of market failures led firms to internalize the greater part of their value chains. However, in recent decades there has been a sea-change shift in the corporate strategy of leading global firms, and this has substantially altered the pattern of linkage development across industrial, agricultural and service sectors as well as in the commodities sector.

The deepening of globalization after the 1970s led to intensified competition as firms were subject to a larger pool of competitors. One of the most important responses to this was the drive by firms to concentrate on their core competences, namely those activities in which they had distinctive competences, where there were barriers to entry, and which were valuable in the marketplace (Hamel and Prahalad; 1994). As a consequence there was a growing trend for non-core activities to be outsourced to low-cost suppliers and for firms and economies to specialize in capabilities rather than wholly manufactured products (Kaplinsky and Morris, 2001; Gereffi, Humphrey, and Sturgeon, 2005). This is the antithesis of the pressures for internalization which had previously played an important role in driving foreign direct investment in integrated value chains (Dunning, 2000; Williamson, 1985).

Once the lead firm has made the decision in principle to outsource non-core activities, the first task is to find the lowest-cost suppliers who can produce to the required quality and meet delivery schedules reliably. Suppliers able to offer unique technological competences of their own are particularly attractive, especially in the first tier of suppliers. The logic is wherever possible to have these suppliers locate production and service delivery close to the doorstep, rather than abroad, or some distance from the lead firm's activity. An efficient proximate supplier provides the capacity for flexible and tailored responses to the needs of the lead firm, allows for value chain inventories to be reduced, and removes uncertainties associated with extended logistics. This unfolding process of initial outsourcing to seek the lowest-cost supplier ("global sourcing") then extends in requiring the supplier to locate proximate to the factory ("follower supply") was initiated in the automobile industry (Barnes and Kaplinsky, 2000). Global value chains now dominate most manufacturing sectors and many service sectors.

The global mining and oil and gas industries are relatively late entrants to this trend towards specialization and outsourcing. Although undocumented as a general phenomenon, there is evidence that this has been occurring across a range of commodity sectors. Mines have moved away from a high level of vertical integration toward outsourcing almost every stage in the mining process to independent firms, including the provision of capital goods and intermediate inputs such as chemicals (Urzua, 2007). The desirability of finding an efficient local supplier is particularly attractive in Africa and Central Asia. This is because transport and logistics are poorly developed, because goods brought in from outside may be subject to long and unpredictable delays and because government policies have often mandated the deepening of local value added. Supplier firms have responded to these opportunities to be incorporated in the chain. For example, Bell Equipment in South Africa built competences in the domestic mining sector, and then became a supplier of these machines into a number of global markets, including the mining, construction, sugar, and forestry sectors (Kaplinsky and Mhlongo, 1997; Walker and Jourdan, 2003). There has also been growth in the outsourcing of knowledge-intensive services, and this has led to the emergence of specialized knowledge intensive mining services providers (SKIMS), offering not only specialized services but also other high-technology inputs (Kaplan, 2012). Companies such as SRK in South Africa, which started as a service provider to Anglo American, have grown into global mining consulting firms. The development of local suppliers is more advanced in Chile where global mining companies are actively involved in building capabilities in their suppliers. BHP Billiton, for example, has an extensive supplier development program in Chile (Barnett and Bell, 2011). In Ghana, there is an increasing trend for knowledge-intensive service providers to the gold sector to also sell these services to the emerging gold industry in neighboring West African economies (Bloch and Owusu, 2012).

Although all of the above examples relate to the hard and energy commodities sectors and primarily involve backward linkages, there have also been important linkage developments in the soft commodities sectors and in the extension of forward linkage processing industries. Many agricultural commodities are being increasingly processed in commodity-producing economies (such as timber being converted into veneer and plywood in Gabon and into pulp in South Africa), new plants are under construction to process copper in Zambia, a new refinery and a liquid gas plant are under construction in Angola, and diamonds are being cut and polished in Botswana.

It is possible thus to construct a general model of linkage development (Figure 3.2.2) taking account both of the localization of what was previously

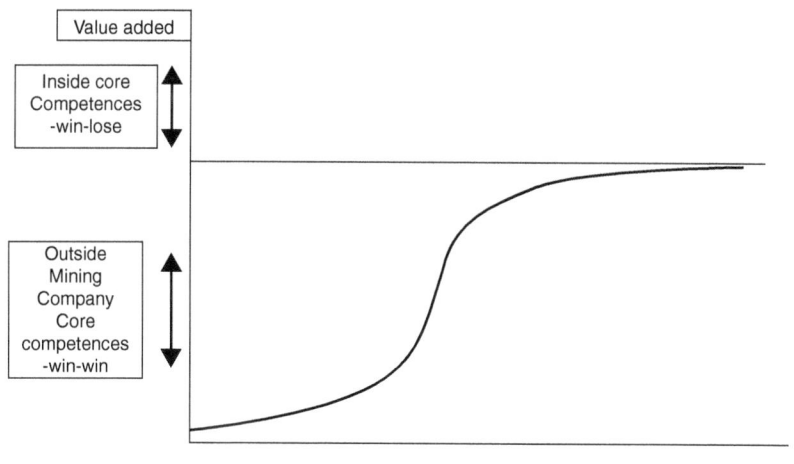

Figure 3.2.2 Market-driven linkages over time
Source: Morris, Kaplinsky and Kaplan, 2012.

imported and also the growing trend toward outsourcing by lead commodity firms. The vertical axis in Figure 3.2.2 represents the accretion of value added in the provision of inputs into the production of a commodity. Based on the insights drawn from the core competences framework we can distinguish on the one hand inputs which the lead commodity producers have no intrinsic interest in maintaining in-house since they do not reflect their core competences. We characterize these as win–win linkages – where lead commodity producing firms and local suppliers and customers have a common interest in developing local linkages. On the other hand, there are a range of inputs which are central to the firm's competitiveness and which it is reluctant to see undertaken by a competitor. We consider these to be win–lose linkages. We can take the diamond value chain as an example to illustrate these two categories of inputs into a commodities value chain (Mbayi, 2011). The cutting and polishing firms may actively want auditing, office provisions, and utilities to be provided by outsiders, undertaken in the best of all cases, by reliable and low-cost suppliers based as close to their operations as possible. On the other hand, they are very reluctant, and have to be forced, to allow customers to participate in the cutting and polishing of diamonds, and in the logistics, branding, and marketing which guarantee their control over the profitable segments of the diamond value chain. These are their core competences. The horizontal axis of Figure 3.2.2 reflects the passage of time. The curve shows that, as a general consequence of the outsourcing of non-core competences, there is a market-driven process of linkage development. Initially, the pace of outsourcing is low, it then speeds up and subsequently tails off as the easy hits are exhausted. This discussion of Figure 3.2.2 has given examples of backward linkages, but analogous examples can be provided for forward linkages, as core firms jettison non-core processing activities form their operations.

There are a number of factors which determine the shape of this curve. It is helpful to distinguish between intrinsic and contextual determinants of linkage development, although, of course, these are not watertight distinctions.

There are a number of intrinsic factors which reflect the technological specificities of the sector in question and which provide the opportunity for domestic linkages. The first is the imperative of achieving lean production. Central to lean production are low inventories, "zero defect" suppliers who can be trusted to deliver reliably in smaller batches. This places a premium on *near-sourcing* within the outsourcing process. Second, further to this logistical imperative to local sourcing, a key characteristic of virtually every mining or energy resource is that it is location specific. No two deposits will be identical. The technology and the accompanying knowledge and skill inputs required for efficient identification and exploitation of the resource therefore are of necessity to be applied locally on site. This provides the possibility of drawing on local skills and knowledge as well as presenting the potential for local technological spillovers. But, third, these imperatives to local sourcing are, of course, circumscribed by the technological and scale complexity of the commodity sector. In general, technological barriers to entry are less evident in the soft commodities sectors, where technological complexity and learning spillovers are less limited than in the hard and energy commodities sectors. But even in the scale- and technology-intensive hard and energy commodity sectors there are multiple inputs which are relatively low in technological content and are characterized by few barriers to entry. At the most basic level this includes the provision of food and accommodation for the workforce, transport and logistics, security, some utilities, and simple maintenance and repair. How feasible low-cost and flexible local supply is will, of course, reflect not only the intrinsic technological complexity of the resource sector in question, but also the extent of capabilities in the local economy – that is, the technological gap. Finally, many soft commodities (such as sugar) have a short shelf life after extraction and require rapid processing, providing powerful incentives for the localization of these activities. Other soft commodities, as well as many hard and energy commodities involve significant weight and volume loss in processing, and this, too, predisposes them to local processing.

Beyond these intrinsic drivers to linkage development are contextual factors which determine the economic feasibility of local linkage development. These reflect a series of social and political factors, as opposed to technical determinants of linkage development, and are, as a consequence, more open to the influence of policy. Based on the research conducted on linkage development in the resource sector in eight SSA economies (Morris, Kaplinsky, and Kaplan, 2012) four dominant contextual factors can be identified. The first is ownership, particularly of the lead commodity firms but also of suppliers. In many cases the embeddedness of locally owned firms is an important influencing factors (Morris, Staritz, and Barnes, 2011), but there are also significant differences between individual firms and in the behavior of lead firms emanating from different countries (including the distinctiveness of Chinese and Indian firms – Fessehaie, 2012). A second factor of significance is the quality of hard and soft infrastructure. This is a complex linkage determinant, since poor infrastructure both acts as a form of protection to local producers, and also undermines their competitiveness, The third exogenous factor is the level of capabilities in the local economy, the character of the National System of Innovation and the gap between these capabilities and the particular demands of the commodity sector in question. Finally, a factor of pervasive importance – to which we will return below – is the nature of the policy environment and the willingness and the capacity of the state to define and implement an effective strategy to promote linkages.

3.2.5   Walking on two legs: developing a strategy toward industrial development

I have argued in previous sections that industrial development in SSA is bounded by two critical framing dynamics – the exclusionary character of growth paths and the likely persistence of the commodities boom. In turn, I have identified four sources of disruption – the growing consumption power of low-income consumers, the emergence of radical new technologies, the global diffusion of innovative capabilities, and the emergence of new forms of entrepreneurship. How do these two sets of developments influence the industrial policy agenda in SSA?

3.2.5.1   Policies to promote the diffusion of market-driven pro-poor innovations[4]

Policies designed to promote the diffusion of pro-poor innovation begin with the recognition that the development and diffusion of labor-intensive, small-scale, infrastructure-robust process technologies producing products for low-income rather than high-income consumers is increasingly market-driven. As observed above, diffusion is increasingly driven by a Schumpeterian rather than a Schumacherian motor.

The first key policy intervention is to correct for market failures. The task is to identify those market imperfections which are intrinsic to pro-poor innovation. Perhaps the most widely cited imperfection noted in the literature on AT is that which relates to factor prices, where it is widely considered that the wages of the organized sector's working class in low-income countries are higher than their opportunity cost, that the cost of capital is lower than its opportunity cost and that environmental and social externalities are either not represented in the price system or the prices at which they are represented do not reflect their true environmental cost. Clearly, factor pricing is an important issue with regard to the diffusion of these pro-poor innovations, but the policy conclusions are not always as clear-cut as they seem. For one thing, in many low-income economies high formal sector wages support a large number of people and are consumed as extended family household incomes rather than as personal incomes. For another thing, investment in pro-poor innovation will undoubtedly be furthered by low-cost capital; the trick is to direct this low-cost capital to investors in pro-poor technologies, and this may involve innovations in the delivery of investment (as in the case of micro-credit) which is in itself a form of appropriate technology. The point is not that different factor prices will not make a difference, but rather that – contra mainstream economics – they will only make a limited difference.

Second, since poor producers and consumers are often illiterate and/or lack access to the internet and print media they are particularly prone to knowledge imperfections. For example, users of innovations will characteristically lack knowledge of the nature and extent of relevant innovations. Mirroring this are producers of innovations who lack knowledge of final markets, particularly those which are not geographically proximate. These knowledge imperfections are especially problematic in the case of pro-poor innovations since, by their nature, many are produced by SMEs in rural areas, unconnected to high-quality infrastructure and emerge "below the radar." A mechanism needs to be established to fill these knowledge gaps within countries and in trade between countries. Unlike the existing policy trajectory which seeks to connect poor producers to rich consumers, the task is to connect poor producers to poor consumers, particularly those outside of their region.

A second area for policy development is in the reorienting of national, regional, and sectoral innovation systems. Optimizing the flow of pro-poor technologies requires an alignment of the relevant actors in the innovation system. This recommendation slips off the tongue easily, but is a more daunting task than is often recognized. Connecting private sector firms in the innovation value chain is relatively easy and is generally an outcome of market forces. But getting the supportive institutions aligned to meet the needs of poor producers and to develop products and services for poor consumers is more difficult, since the price-system plays only a marginal role. Often "quality" standards and curricula – let alone the direction of research – reflect connections in the system of innovation with the global community of peers rather than with the needs and capabilities of the marginalized domestic populations.

The third policy agenda is a strengthening of the role of non-market actors, particularly with regard to the provision of public goods. Public–private partnerships such as GAVI have demonstrably played an important role in developing technologies to meet the needs of the poor, despite the fact that there is also evidence that the emphasis on hard technologies and a laser focus on particular diseases (rather than the functioning of the health system) may simultaneously also have constrained effective policy design and delivery.

The final policy agenda furthering the development and diffusion of efficient pro-poor innovation is the redistribution of income. As we have seen, the character of the market is a major factor inducing and biasing the trajectory of innovation. It stands to reason that the faster this market of poor consumers grows, and the larger this market, the greater will be the inducement for pro-poor innovation. We can therefore anticipate a self-reinforcing virtuous circle in which pro-poor growth stimulates pro-poor innovation which, in turn, reinforces pro-poor growth. Nevertheless, although redistribution will hasten the pace of pro-poor innovation, I have argued that the growth of incomes amongst the poor is a fact behind the rapid growth of both China and India and that these incomes will provide an inducing source of demand with or without income redistribution.

3.2.5.2 Policies to broaden and deepen linkages with the resource sector

Policy designed to foster linkages to the resource sector can have a range of outcomes (Figure 3.2.3). The first two are positive – speeding up and deepening linkages, including in advanced cases by becoming world-leading sources of core competences in the sector (as occurs in South Africa's mining sector and, arguably, in Kenya's horticulture sector). The second two are

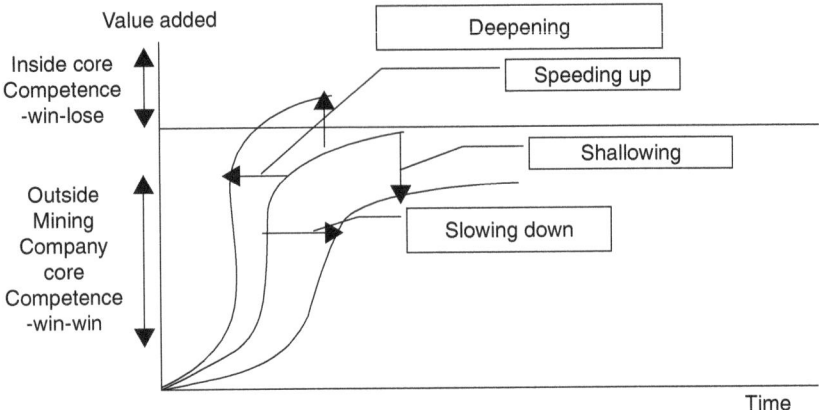

Figure 3.2.3   Different trajectories of linkage development
Source: Morris, Kaplinsky and Kaplan (2012).

negative, slowing down and shallowing linkages. The trick, of course, is to make policy speak to the first two of these, rather than to the latter two. Unfortunately, many African countries have policy agendas which promote the latter rather than the former set of outcomes.

Because there is little that most SSA economies can do to affect the intrinsic factors driving linkage development, policies to promote linkages need to focus on the contextual exogenous factors identified in section 3.2.4 – ownership, infrastructure, the national system of innovation, and the efficacy of policy design and delivery. Given the contextual nature of these policies, it is difficult to make any routinely general policy prescriptions. However, three general policy conclusions are evident.

First, there has been a pervasive tendency in many SSA economies to conflate local sourcing with local ownership and, in some cases, as in contemporary South Africa and Madagascar, to promote local ownership by particular segments of the society. Insofar as local owners are demonstrably embedded, have longer time horizons and deeper ambitions for extended local sourcing than foreign-owned firms, there need be no conflict between these two policy objectives. The reality, however, is that this coincidence of ownership and ambition is often not observable. For example, in South Africa, world-leading capabilities built up over decades are rapidly depleting in the face of the migration of scarce skills to Australia and other resource-rich economies (Kaplan, 2012). New entrants into this sector appear to be more concerned with short term rent extraction than with longer term capability building.

The second generalized policy conclusion is that in many cases policies to broaden and deepen linkages are ill-informed about sectoral and technological dynamics. Whilst the pursuit of dynamic comparative advantage is a *sine qua non* of industrial policy, this does not mean that everything is possible. Countries have to scale their ambition through a careful and informed calibration of dynamic capabilities and sectoral and technological dynamics over time. Through overambition, it is possible to waste large sums of investment and to squander policy space and legitimacy. The fixation in many SSA countries (most markedly in South Africa) with "beneficiation" sometimes reaches absurd proportions, for example that because a country possesses iron ore it should seek to manufacture the full range of final products and components with a steel content.

Third, and related, is the need to develop the strategic capacity to target feasible linkages. This requires an *informed* process in which stakeholders cooperate in identifying three broad families of linkages in the context of a moving global innovation frontier. The first family are the *"low-hanging fruit,"* linkages which provide short-term returns to lead commodity firms (Figure 3.2.4). In these cases, suppliers and customers are able to produce quality products reliably at prices which are near the global price frontier. In the case of backward linkages, we can term these "commodity gate prices," that is the cost of inputs at the mine/farm/well gate, including both the costs of transforming inputs into products and the costs of hard infrastructure (for example, transport) and soft infrastructure (for example, import permits). In the first instance, linkage development policies should be designed to grasp these win–win low-hanging fruit opportunities. Beyond this are linkages

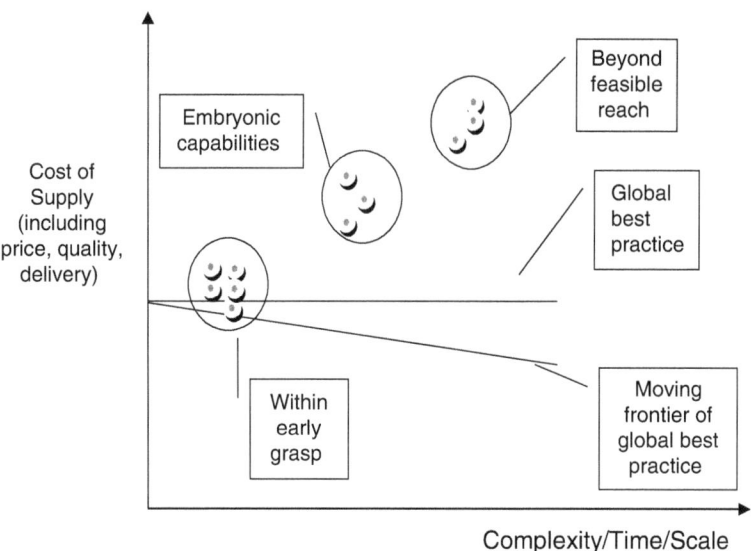

Figure 3.2.4   The trajectory of local supply
Source: Morris, Kaplinsky and Kaplan, (2012).

where *embryonic* capabilities exist and where there is some prospect that, with reasonable time-bound support, local producers will be able to compete with foreign producers. The response in this category of products is to develop targeted interventions which enable local producers to compete with foreign producers over time. The final family are ambitious and often high-profile linkages which are *beyond feasible reach* in the short to medium term. Policy here should be focused on resisting the political pressures often exerted by local stakeholders (such as segments of industry, local scientists, and engineers and politicians) to promote these overly ambitious linkages.

3.2.6   The politics of walking on two legs

Section 3.2.5 sets out a two-legged structure for industrial policy in SSA. The first leg is the promotion of efficient pro-poor innovations incorporating the poor in processes of production and producing goods and services for poor consumers. The second is a set of policies designed to promote linkages from the resource sector. The trick is to address both policy agendas in an integrated manner. Similar conclusions have been drawn by the Venezuelan economist Carlota Perez (Perez, 2010). She focuses on Latin America and calls for a "dual integrated strategy." Given the greater level of capabilities in Latin America her policy prescriptions are nuanced in different directions. She sees, at the top end, possibilities for building innovative networks around the natural resource endowment capable of competing at the international technological frontier and increasing the value of the export mix. At the other end of the dual strategy she envisages the potential for distributed small-scale production by SMEs, producing final products both for domestic markets and for niche export markets, and providing inputs into the commodities sector and engaging in specialized processing of sub-products within the commodities value chain.

Before (briefly) considering the politics of this integrated strategy, it is helpful to begin by setting out a sequenced unfolding of policy which addresses all effective policy design and delivery, not just with regard to industrial policy. The first stage is the development a strategic agenda – a vision for the future. (In terms of the analysis embodied in the discussion above, this targets the simultaneous development and diffusion of pro-poor innovation and the broadening and deepening of linkages to the resource sector.) Beyond the development of a vision is the specification of policies designed to achieve specific ends (for example, promoting better information flows between AT innovators and SMEs; policies designed to promote more embedded firms in the resource and linkage sectors). It is critical that these policies move beyond rhetoric (which is the agenda of strategy) to embody both incentives and sanctions. Third, policies must be mutually consistent. This sounds self-evident, but conflicting policies are an unfortunate outcome of political processes, through a combination of competing interests, poor communication, and the absence of an evidenced-based policy process. Fourth, policy must be attuned to capabilities in the state. This, too, is self-evident. But weak policy implementation capabilities are an unfortunately common fact of life in African economies where the state has been systematically undermined by Washington Consensus policies. Linked to capabilities is the question of policy will (often undermined by rent-seeking behavior) – is the political class and the state apparatus genuinely interested in achieving the ends of industrial strategy policy, or is industrial policy a mask for kleptocracy? Finally, effective policy deployment requires policy legitimacy, which brings us to the issue of the politics of industrial policy.

So, what constituencies are required to implement each of these two legs for emerging industrial policy? The first leg – the development and diffusion of pro-poor innovation – involves the politics of income and consumption on the one hand, and the constellation of forces of production on the other. As we argued in earlier discussion, a necessary component is the growth of incomes amongst the poor which provides an inducement to technological progress. The greater these incomes, the greater the inducement to the development of efficient pro-poor innovations. Hence our earlier observation of the importance of income-redistributive policies in reinforcing the conditions in which innovation may act to further redistribute income. Put this way, it suggests little possibility of progress since the pressure for income-redistribution policies is somewhat remote at present in SSA. However, we have also argued that, de facto, incomes are growing rapidly amongst poor consumers, in SSA and especially in other low- and middle-income economies. Moreover, there is no necessary reason why, in the first instance, the diffusion of efficient pro-poor innovations should not draw on the technological shelf of innovations produced in other low- and middle-income economies outside of SSA where the incomes of poor consumers are growing rapidly.

With regard to the forces of production, the extension of this pro-poor innovation leg of industrial development is essentially an agenda for accumulation by SMEs. In Africa, a particularly vibrant set of small-scale entrepreneurs are returning migrants, often highly educated. Another dynamic source of small-scale entrepreneurship is the rapid influx of Chinese migrants (Mohan and Tan Mullins, 2009: Mohan, Cheng, and Lampert, 2011), although there is growing political opposition to these migrants from indigenous entrepreneurs who seek to fill the same economic space (MacNamee et. al., 2012).

The political coalition required to walk on the second leg may in some cases overlap with the first leg, particularly in the soft commodities sectors, where linkages are often less technologically intensive and are smaller in scale. In both cases it is possible to envision a SME, petite bourgeoisie accumulation trajectory. But, more often, linkage development involves large-scale capital and higher levels of scale and technological intensity. This draws on a different political constituency, often closely linked to the state and frequently closely associated with rent-seeking behavior. An exemplar of this constituency – perhaps in extreme form – is Sonangol in Angola which is tasked with deepening linkages into the oil sector and which has been characterized by corruption. South Africa represents an associated development in which under the name of the pursuit of dynamic comparative advantage and the redressing of historical wrongs, effective linkage development is being undermined by a rent-seeking unproductive politically connected consuming class. A further characteristic of the linkage path is that it involves value chains – both supply and customer chains – and hence an ensemble of actors. The task here is one of value chain alignment, bringing together the constituent parts of the chain to achieve chain efficiency. The lesson of international experience is that these coalitions require the involvement of both sets of actors (and, in some cases, civil society actors) (Rodrik, 2004). In some cases the driving convening energy might be in the state, in other cases, in the private sector.

Where these two legs are of similar "size" and are able to march in tandem, there is scope for walking – perhaps even jogging or sprinting – on two legs on a path of rapid income-augmenting industrial development involving the poor as producers, the poor as consumers, and the poor producing products which the poor can afford. That is the desired outcome. The problem is that the political coalitions required to walk on both legs are of a rather different nature. The first leg is predominantly a coalition of small-scale capital working fairly independently from the state and living in a world of narrow income differentials. The second is predominantly a coalition of large scale, and often foreign capital, with ready access to a large slice of the resource rents which arise in commodity production and which are a driver for increasing income inequality.

Can the balance be maintained, and at what speed? The answer is, of course, contextual, specific to particular countries and particular periods. But, at least in principle, there is the scope for a synergistic and reinforcing trajectory of a pattern of industrial development which will simultaneously promote rapid growth, spread the fruits of growth more equitably, and use natural resources more effectively. Ultimately, from the policy perspective, it raises the issue of the nature and determinants of the Developmental State. But that is another discussion.

Notes

1. This discussion is treated in more detail in Kaplinsky (2014).
2. Compiled from http://www.portal.euromonitor.com, accessed July 2010.
3. The discussion in this section is drawn from Morris, Kaplinsky and Kaplan (2012), UNIDO (2012) and a forthcoming Special Issue of *Resources Policy*.
4. The discussion in this section is elaborated in Kaplinsky (2014).

References

Barnes J. and Kaplinsky R (2000) "Globalisation and the Death of the Local Firm? The Automobile Components Sector in South Africa," *Regional Studies*, vol. 34, no. 9, pp. 797–812.

Barnett, A. and Bell, M. (2011) *Is BHP Billiton's Cluster-Programme in Chile Relevant for Africa's Mining Industry?*, Policy Practice Brief No. 7. Retrieved from www.thepolicy practice.com.

Bell, R.M. (2007) "Technological Learning and the Development of Productive and Innovative Capacities in the Industry and Infrastructure Sectors of the Least Developed Countries: What Roles for ODA?," paper prepared for UNCTAD Division for Africa, Least Developed Countries Specialised Programme (Brighton: Science Policy research).

Bloch, R. and Owusu, G. (2012) "Linkages in Ghana's Gold Mining Industry: Challenging the Enclave Thesis, *Resources Policy*.

Bruche, G. (2009) "'A New Geography of Innovation – China and India Rising,'", *Columbia FDI Perspectives*, no. 4, April 29.

Chen, S. and Ravallion, M. (2008) "The Developing World Is Poorer Than We Thought, But No Less Successful in the Fight against Poverty," Policy Research Working Paper 4703 (Washington, DC: The World Bank Development Research Group).

Christenson, C. (1997) *The Innovator's Dilemma* (Cambridge, MA: Harvard Business School Press).

Cozzens, S.E. and Kaplinsky, R. (2009) "Innovation, Poverty and Inequality: Cause, Coincidence, or Co-evolution?," in B.-A. Lundvall, J.K. Joseph, C. Chaminade, and J. Vang (eds), *Handbook of Innovation Systems and Developing Countries: Building Domestic Capabilities in a Global Context* (Cheltenham: Edward Elgar).

Dosi, G. (1982) "Technological Paradigms and Technological Trajectories," *Research Policy*, vol. 11, no. 3, pp. 147–162.

Dunning, J. (2000) "The Eclectic Paradigm as an Envelope for Economic and Business Theories of MNE Activity," *International Business Review*, vol. 9, no. 1, pp. 163–190.

Farooki, M. and Kaplinsky, R. (2012) *The Impact of China on Global Commodity Prices: The Global Reshaping of the Resource Sector* (London: Routledge).

Fessehaie, J. (2012) "What Determines the Breadth and Depth of Zambia's Backward Linkages to Copper Mining? The Role of Public Policy and Value Chain Dynamics," *Resources Policy*, vol. 37, no. 4, pp. 443–451.

Freeman, C. (1993) "Technical Change and Future Trends in the World Economy," *Futures*, October, pp. 621–635.

Freeman C. and Perez, C. (1988) "Structural Crises of Adjustment: Business Cycles and Investment Behaviour", in Giovanni Dosi et al. (eds), *Technical Change and Economic Theory* (London: Frances Pinter).

Gereffi G., Sturgeon, T., and Humphrey, J. (2005) "The Governance of Global Value Chains," *Review of International Political Economy*, vol. 12, no. 1, pp. 78–104.

Hamel, G. and Prahalad, C.K. (1994) *Competing for the Future* (Cambridge, MA: Harvard Business Press).

Hollanders, H. and Soete, L. (2010) "The Growing Role of Knowledge in the Global Economy," *A World of Science*, vol. 8, no. 4, pp. 2–10.

Jenkins, R. and Edwards, C. (2005) "The Effect of China and India's Growth and Trade Liberalisation on Poverty in Africa," DCP 70 (London: DFID)

Kaplan, D. (2012) "South African Mining Equipment and Specialist Services: Technological Capacity, Export Performance and Policy," *Resource Policy*, vol. 37, no. 4, pp. 405–484.

Kaplinsky, R. (2005) *Globalisation, Poverty and Inequality: Between a Rock and a Hard Place* (London: Polity).

Kaplinsky, R. (2008) "What Does the Rise of China Do for Industrialisation in Sub-Saharan Africa?," *Review of African Political Economy*, vol. 35, no. 115, pp. 7–22.

Kaplinsky, R. (2010) *The Role of Standards in Global Value Chains and their Impact on Economic and Social Upgrading*, Policy Research Working Paper 5396 (Washington, DC: World Bank).

Kaplinsky, R. (2014 forthcoming) "Innovation for Pro-Poor Growth: From Redistribution with Growth to Redistribution through Growth," in G.A. Cornia and F. Stewart (eds), *Towards Human Development: New Approaches to Macroeconomics and Inequality* (Oxford: Oxford University Press).

Kaplinsky R. and Mhlongo, E. (1997) "Infant Industries and Industrial Policy: A Lesson from South Africa," *Transition,* vol. 34, pp. 57–85.

Kaplinsky, R. and M. Morris (2001) "A Handbook for Value Chain Research." Available online at http://asiandrivers.open.ac.uk/documents/Value_chain_Handbook_RKMM_Nov_2001.pdf.

Kaplinsky, R. and Morris, M. (2008) "Do the Asian Drivers Undermine Export-Oriented Industrialisation in SSA?", *World Development Special Issue on Asian Drivers and their Impact on Developing Countries*, vol. 36, no. 2, pp. 254–273.

Kaplinsky, R., Terheggen, A., and Tijaja, J.P. (2011) "China as a Final Market: The Gabon Timber and Thai Cassava Value chains," *World Development*, vol. 39, no. 7, pp. 1177–1190.

Katz, J. M. (1987) "Domestic Technological Generation in LDCs: A Review of Research Findings," in J. M. Katz (ed.), *Technology Generation in Latin American Manufacturing Industries* (London: Macmillan).

Khan, S.A. and Baye, R.M. (2011) "China–Africa Economic Relations: The Case of Cameroon," Report Submitted to the African Economic Research Consortium, Dept. of Economics and Management, University of Yaounde II.

Lazonick, W. (2010) "The Fragility of the US Economy: the Financialized Corporation and the Disappearing Middle Class." Available online at http://www.theairnet.org/files/research/lazonick/Lazonick%20FUSE%2020101003.pdf.

MacNamee, T., with Mills, G., Manoeli, S., Doran S., and Chen, E. (2012) "Africa in Their Words: A Study of Chinese Traders in South Africa, Botswana, Zambia and Angola," Brenthurst Foundation Discussion Paper 2012/03 (Johannesburg: Brenthurst Foundation).

Mbayi, L. (2011) "Linkages in Botswana's Diamond Cutting and Polishing Industry," MMCP Discussion Paper no. 6 (Cape Town, South Africa, and Milton Keynes, UK: University of Cape Town and Open University).

Mohan, G. and Tan Mullins, M. (2009) "Chinese Migrants in Africa as New Agents of Development? An Analytical Framework," *European Journal of Development Research*, vol. 21, no. 4, pp. 588–605.

Mohan, G., Lampert, B., and Chang, D. (2011) "Chinese Diaspora, African Development? Chinese Business Migrants in Angola, Ghana and Nigeria," Paper presented at the DSA/EADI conference: Rethinking development in an age of scarcity and uncertainty, York, UK, September 19–22.

Morris, M., Kaplinsky, R., and Kaplan, D. (2012 forthcoming) "'One Thing Leads to Another'" – Commodities, Linkages and Industrial Development, *Resources Policy*, vol. 37, no. 4, pp. 408–416.

Morris, M., Staritz, C., and Barnes, J. (2011) "Value Chain Dynamics, Local Embeddedness, and Upgrading in the Clothing Sectors of Lesotho and Swaziland,"

International . *Journal of Technological Learning, Innovation and Development*, vol. 4, nos 1–3, pp. 96–118.

Perez, C. (2010) "Technological Dynamism and Social Inclusion in Latin America," *CEPAL Review*, no. 100, pp. 121–141.

Prahalad, C.K. (2005) *The Fortune at the Bottom of the Pyramid: Eradicating Poverty through Profits* (Upper Saddle River, NJ: Pearson Education/Wharton School Publishing).

Prahalad, C.K. and Hammond, A. (2002) "Serving the World's Poor Profitably," *Harvard Business Review*, September, pp. 4–11.

Rodrik, D. (2004) "Industrial Policy for the Twenty-first Century," mimeo (Cambridge, MA: John F. Kennedy School of Government).

Ruttan, V.W. (2001) *Technology, Growth and Development: An Induced Innovation Perspective* (New York: Oxford University Press).

Singer, H.W. (1950) "The Distribution of Gains Between Investing and Borrowing Countries," *American Economic Review*, vol. 40, no. 2, pp. 473–485.

Singer, H., Cooper, C., Desai, R.C., Freeman, C., Gish, O., Hall, S., and Oldham, G. (1970), *The Sussex Manifesto: Science and Technology for Developing Countries during the Second Development Decade*, IDS Reprints no. 101 (Brighton: Institute of Development Studies).

Singer, P. and Daar, A. (2001) "Harnessing Genomics and Biotechnology to Improve Global Health Equity" Science 5 October 2001 Vol. 294(5540) 87–89

Sumner, A. (2010), Global Poverty and the New Bottom Billion: What if Three-Quarters of the World's Poor Live in Middle Income Countries?, mimeo, Brighton: Institute of Development Studies.

UNIDO (2012) *Promoting Industrial Diversification in Resource Intensive Economies: The Experiences of Sub-Saharan Africa and Central Asia Regions* (Vienna: UNIDO).

Urzua, O. (2007) "Emergence and development of Knowledge-Intensive Mining Services (KIMS)", Mimeo, background paper prepared for UNCTAD (Brighton, UK: University of Sussex).

Walker, M. and Jourdan, P. (2003) "Resource-based Sustainable Development: An Alternative Approach to Industrialisation in South Africa," *Minerals and Energy*, vol. 18, no. 3, pp. 25–43.

Williamson, O.E. (1985) *The Economic Institutions of Capitalism: Firms, Markets, Relational Contracting* (New York: Free Press).

Part IV
Macroeconomics and Governance: Creating an Enabling Environment

4.1

How Macroeconomic Policy Can Support Economic Development in Sub-Saharan African Countries

James Heintz
University of Massachusetts, Amherst

Conventional wisdom has generally held that macroeconomic policy should create an enabling environment for industrial policy and should also maintain conditions which facilitate the structural transformations necessary for economic development. This includes a number of components: keeping exchange rates at levels that support, rather than undermine, industrial development; adopting monetary policies which maintain price and financial stability while insuring the availability of credit for productive investment; providing complementary public investments; and making sure that tax policies promote economic development. After macro policies set the scene, the interaction between macroeconomic and industrial strategies is fairly limited. Industrial policy manages the details of economic development within the environment and boundaries determined by macroeconomic management.

This paper advances a different argument in the context of Sub-Saharan Africa. In many countries of Sub-Saharan Africa, the scope for conducting macroeconomic policy to support industrial development is limited. This is primarily a result of institutional and structural constraints. If these constraints are taken as given, there may be little potential for macroeconomic policy to set the stage for a successful industrial policy. Often, the approach to macroeconomic policy might be described as trying to "do no harm" – that is, avoid unsustainable debts or hyperinflation. This approach to macroeconomic policy shortchanges many African countries in terms of the instruments they have at their disposal to encourage industrial development. In this context, the challenge is to invest in institutional development and to address structural constraints which limit policy effectiveness, thereby replenishing the economic toolkit and allowing macroeconomic policy to play a more developmental role. This involves broadening what we typically mean by macroeconomic policy to take into account the role of institutions, and pursuing a coordinated approach to macroeconomic and industrial policy.

To illustrate this point, the remainder of this paper puts forward examples from three areas of macroeconomic policy that have implications for industrial development. In each of the three areas, we focus on specific questions.

- *Real exchange rate* – real exchange rates are considered important for the allocation of resources between tradable and non-tradable activities in ways that support economic development. How do issues of real exchange rate management for industrial development apply to countries in Sub-Saharan Africa?
- *Monetary policy* – Here we examine two issues: (1) What are the sources of inflationary pressures in Sub-Saharan African countries and do inflation targets (and inflation targeting) constitute an appropriate monetary policy?; and (2) What are the institutional barriers which prevent monetary policy from playing a more developmental role?
- *Fiscal policy* – Fiscal tools often feature in the design of industrial policy – for example, subsidies, tax incentives, and public investment. Rather than focusing on these details, we discuss the question of domestic resource mobilization. Specifically, what are the barriers to better mobilization of domestic resources for industrial policy in terms of tax revenues and domestic public borrowing?

4.1.1   Real exchange rate management and industrial development in Sub-Saharan Africa

The real exchange rate is considered to exert an important influence on growth and economic performance (Frenkel and Rapetti, 2010; Galindo and Ros, 2008; Barbosa-Filho, 2008; Gala and Lucinda, 2006; Frenkel and Taylor, 2005; Ghura and Grennes, 1993; Dollar, 1992; Cottani, Cavallo, and Khan, 1990). The real exchange rate affects the allocation of resources between tradable and non-tradable sectors. The scope for productivity improvements are assumed to be larger in the tradable sector than in the non-tradable sector, due to the potential of technology to raise productivity in industrial activities, the existence of economies of scale and positive externalities, and access to larger markets. Therefore, a real exchange rate maintained at a competitive level should insure that adequate resources are allocated to tradable activities and thereby support the kind of structural transformation associated with industrial development.

An overvalued exchange rate would have the opposite effect – shifting resources to the non-tradable sector where productivity improvements are less promising and the potential for industrial development is significantly weaker. Overvalued exchange rates can be caused by a number of factors. For example, the "Dutch disease" occurs when an increase in natural resource exports leads to an appreciation of the real exchange rate. The prices of non-tradable goods and services rise relative to tradable goods, triggering a reallocation of resources to the non-tradable sector. If the tradable sector possesses greater potential for productivity growth, the result of a boom in natural resource exports may be slower economic growth (Humphreys, Sachs, and Stiglitz, 2007; Sachs and Warner, 1997). In other situations, the management of capital flows can lead to a real appreciation. For example, high interest rates may be used to attract short-term capital inflows which then lead to an appreciation of the real exchange rate (Galindo and Ros, 2008; Barbosa-Filho, 2008).

When considering the issue of real exchange rates in Sub-Saharan Africa, we need to take into account the possibility of a very high pass-through between nominal exchange rates and domestic prices. A vigorous pass-through has been documented in empirical studies of inflation dynamics in Sub-Saharan African countries (for example, Heintz and Ndikumana, 2010; Oladipo, 2007; Nell, 2004). The close relationship between nominal exchange rates and price levels means that there is often a close relationship between exchange rate policy and inflation targets.

This relationship extends beyond Sub-Saharan Africa. For instance, one study of emerging market economies found that inflation-targeting countries pursue a mixed strategy – responding to both inflation rates and real exchange rates (Aizenman, Hutchison, and Noy, 2008). This same study found that policy in emerging markets without a formal inflation-targeting regime tended to respond more strongly to the real exchange rate. The relationship between exchange rates and inflation also raises questions about the level of foreign reserves a country must maintain. Epstein and Yeldan (2008) present evidence suggesting that many countries have accumulated larger stocks of foreign exchange reserves after adopting an inflation-targeting regime. One explanation is that these reserves may be needed in order to defend the currency and control inflation if the economic environment changes in a way that leads to a depreciation, yet maintaining excess reserves can be costly. This raises a number of issues for further investigation: is the exchange rate that is consistent with the inflation target also the exchange rate that is consistent with industrialization and long-run development? If not, is it possible to reconcile inflation targets with attempts to manage exchange rates to support developmental outcomes?

For many countries in Sub-Saharan Africa, the more important question may be: does it make sense to attempt to manage the exchange rate at all? The high level of pass-through to domestic prices suggests that a nominal depreciation will only produce a fleeting depreciation of the real exchange rate. Domestic prices quickly adjust, eroding any competitive advantage granted by the nominal depreciation. The ability to maintain the real exchange rate at a particular level by engaging in an activist exchange rate policy may be limited, particularly if the idea is to influence industrial development in the medium to long run.

This does not mean that concern over the real exchange rate is misplaced when we consider Sub-Saharan African countries. However, the way in which we think about the issue may need to change. Instead of focusing on managing the nominal exchange rate to achieve a desired real rate, a better entry point may be to begin with the domestic price level. The relative domestic price level (that is, the price level in one country relative to another country or an international standard) is an important component of the real exchange rate and a high relative domestic price level can have similar adverse consequences as an overvalued real exchange rate.

Accurate measurement of differences in price levels across countries is notoriously difficult, due to a variety of factors, including differences in consumption patterns, variations in the quality of goods, rural and urban differences, and uncertainties associated with survey data on prices.[1] One commonly used measurement of the relative domestic price level is the PPP (purchasing price parity) conversion factor to nominal exchange rate ratio – such as that contained in the *World Development Indicators* database. This provides an estimate of the national price level relative to a fixed international reference point – in this case, the US economy, which takes on a value of one. The PPP conversion factor to nominal exchange rate ratio tends to increase with the level of per capita GDP, used as a proxy for average labor productivity. Therefore, it is useful to compare the average price levels for countries at similar productivity levels. Specifically, we want to compare the average price level for Sub-Saharan African countries, controlling for per capita income. As with all such indicators, there are potential pitfalls when making comparisons across countries or regions. Therefore, the analysis presented here is meant to be suggestive, rather than definitive.

To do this, we perform a basic exercise. We estimate the following relationship using a simple linear regression:

$$P_i = \alpha + \beta \ln GDP_i + \delta d_i + e_i$$
$$-0.51 \quad 0.14 \qquad 0.11$$
$$(-6.1) \quad (14.6) \qquad (3.4)$$

In the above equation, P_i is the price level of country 'i' (as measured by the PPP/nominal exchange rate ratio), $\ln GDP_i$ is the natural log of per capita GDP, d_i is a dummy variable which takes on a value of one for Sub-Saharan Africa, and e_i is an error term. The regression was estimated using 2010 data for 171 countries.[2] The coefficient estimates are reported below the variables in the equation with the t-statistics in parentheses. The adjusted R-squared equals 0.58. While this analysis is simple and relies on an imperfect measurement of price differences, it does suggest that, controling for per capita GDP, the average price level in Sub-Saharan African countries is higher than countries elsewhere, to the extent that the PPP-based indicator is capturing actual variations in average price levels.

How big is the 0.11 coefficient on the Sub-Saharan African dummy variable? The average price level across all low- and middle-income countries is 0.56. So, one way of interpreting the additional 0.11 is that domestic prices are roughly 20 percent higher in Sub-Saharan Africa compared to other countries at similar levels of development.

If this conclusion is accurate, it has important implications for the competitiveness of the tradable sectors in Sub-Saharan African countries. For example, wages that are competitive with those of other countries with similar levels of productivity would translate into lower living standards in Sub-Saharan Africa because the average price level tends to be higher. Or wages that translate into similar standards of living in Sub-Saharan African countries compared to countries elsewhere would be uncompetitive internationally.

This is an important issue for industrial policy. Sub-Saharan Africa countries may be less competitive because of structural conditions which keep average price levels higher. Because of a strong exchange rate pass-through, a devaluation of the nominal exchange rate cannot compensate for these differences. Prices may be higher in Sub-Saharan African countries for a number of reasons – for example, high transport costs, poor infrastructure, inefficient distribution systems (including for energy), and other related factors. These factors that raise domestic prices relative to those in other countries are associated with the non-tradable sector, that is, the costs cannot be lowered simply by importing cheaper alternatives. In other words, improvements to the productivity of the non-tradable sector may be critical for determining the competitiveness of Sub-Saharan Africa countries relative to others. The implications for industrial policy are parallel to those associated with an overvalued exchange rate.

Improving the productivity of activities and services in the non-tradable sector in order to boost competitiveness sounds more like industrial policy than macroeconomic policy. But this is the core of the argument being advanced in this paper. In Sub-Saharan Africa, industrial policy and macroeconomic policy should be seen as closely intertwined. Structural changes have macroeconomic effects. Moreover, there is a need to think differently about standard categories of macroeconomic interventions. Real exchange rates are important for countries in Sub-Saharan Africa, but the best way of influencing them for long-run development may not be through nominal devaluations.

4.1.2 Monetary policy and financial reform

Next we turn to the issue of monetary policy. Most all Sub-Saharan African countries have adopted inflation targets as the keystone to their monetary policy. In two cases – Ghana and South Africa – the central bank has embraced formal inflation targeting. Managing inflation is important for industrial development, providing a nominal anchor for prices, and facilitating longer-term economic planning. However, strict adherence to inflation targets may have adverse effects in terms of raising the cost of credit and limiting its supply. In this section, we extend the same line of argument developed with regard to exchange rates to monetary policy. Specifically, existing institutions and economic structures determine the ability of monetary policy to support economic development in Sub-Saharan African countries.

One important issue is the extent to which inflationary dynamics in African countries are monetary in origin. In studies of inflation dynamics across Sub-Saharan African countries, increases in the growth rate of the money supply, or, alternatively, the gap between money supply and estimated money demand, has been shown to influence the rate of inflation (Thornton, 2008; Barnichon and Peiris, 2008). However, the effect is not the same for all countries. Thornton (2008) finds that the money supply is significantly more important for explaining high rates of inflation dynamics rather than explaining inflation in countries who average inflation rates are more modest. In a similar cross-country analysis, Heintz and Ndikuman (2010) find that the money supply has a relatively small impact on inflation, but that the nominal exchange rate has a strong effect on domestic prices. All these studies indicate that supply-side factors influence inflation dynamics – negative shocks to economic growth or lower estimated values for potential GDP raise inflation rates.

Country-level studies produce similar findings. In Ghana, the growth rate of the money supply, linked to the financing of public sector debt and an expansion of foreign debt, and structural supply-side factors, including shocks to the agricultural sector, are two common explanations for the persistence of high inflation rates from the 1970s through the 1990s, despite the introduction of stabilization and structural adjustment policies (Aryeetey and Harrigan, 2000). In Ethiopia, high rates of inflation have been linked to agricultural supply shocks and strong inertial dynamics (Loening, Durevall, and Birru, 2009). As already discussed, others have documented the importance of exchange rate pass-through and the price of imports in influencing inflationary dynamics in country-level studies, for example, Nigeria and South Africa (Oladipo, 2007; Nell, 2004). The importance of exchange rate pass-through suggests that inflation dynamics would differ in countries with a fixed exchange rate regime (for example, the CFA countries) relative to countries with more flexible exchange rates.

The literature on inflation dynamics in Sub-Saharan African countries demonstrates that there are multiple factors that influence inflation, and that monetary sources of inflation may not always be the most significant. While the domestic money supply does affect the average price level, supply-side shocks and external price dynamics – for example, fluctuations in global energy prices – play a significant role. Inflation inertia – the impact of past inflation on future prices – also appears to be important.

This raises concerns about the effectiveness of inflation targets and inflation targeting as the primary, or sole, focus of monetary policy. The use of policies to affect the money supply or interest rates in response to inflationary shocks may be pro-cyclical. Supply-side shocks may simultaneously reduce growth and raise inflation. Tightening monetary policy in response to this kind of shock may make the situation worse (as has been noted by Friedman and Kuttner, 1996, among others). Strict inflation targeting introduces a pro-cyclical bias into monetary policy for countries in which supply-side inflation is commonplace, including many Sub-Saharan African countries. The degree of this bias will depend on the relative importance of supply-side factors in determining inflation and the amount of discretion monetary authorities exercise.

To reduce the possibility of introducing a pro-cyclical bias into monetary policy, inflation targets are often formulated with a reference to "core inflation" – that is, the inflation rate which excludes food and energy prices, deemed to be more volatile and more sensitive to external price shocks. The problem with developing indicators of core inflation for Sub-Saharan African countries is that, in many cases, food and energy accounts for a very large share of the consumption basket used to develop price indices. Eliminating these prices results in an emaciated price index. Moreover, the price components which are retained are often sensitive to changes in food and energy prices. One study of the components of the consumer price index for Kenya showed, using a vector autoregression model (VAR), that a shock to food and energy prices caused other components of the CPI to increase (Pollin, Githinji, and Heintz, 2008). Efforts to purge price indices of the effects of food and energy prices will often be unsuccessful in the case of Sub-Saharan African countries.

This discussion suggests that a narrow approach to monetary policy which is formulated in terms of an inflation target may not be appropriate for countries in Sub-Saharan Africa, particularly if non-monetary sources of inflation are prevalent and if a pro-cyclical bias is evident. One alternative to inflation targeting would be to formulate a monetary policy that supports economic development (Epstein, 2007). The primary long-run objective of monetary policy would no longer be price stability, but the kind of economic development supported by industrial policy. The monetary policy regime would identify variables that could be targeted in the short run in order to meet the long-run goals associated with economic development. These short-run targets would include a central role for inflation management, but would also include indicators of the health of the productive sectors of the economy. The challenge of conducting monetary policy would be to strike a balance between these short-term indicators in a way that encourages industrial development.

The growth rate could be one such target. The idea would be to keep policy interest rates within a range that encourages investment and growth and does not lead to excessive inflation. This approach would include a consideration of inflation in the conduct of monetary policy, since the emphasis would be on maintaining positive real interest rates (that is, excessive rates of inflation would violate this constraint). Bernanke et al. (1999) suggest that a monetary policy regime which targets the nominal GDP growth rate, for example, would operate quite similarly to an inflation-targeting regime with sufficient discretionary scope to address economic objectives other than inflation.[3] The difference with the growth target is that it would place more emphasis on real economic performance than would an inflation targeting approach.

Introducing a broader set of targets for the conduct of monetary policy does not get around one of the principal constraints to creating a "developmental monetary policy" for Sub-Saharan Africa. Suppose monetary policy were formulated to increase the availability of credit and lower its cost, thereby encouraging investment and laying the foundation for long-run growth. The success of this strategy rests on a critical assumption: that the banking sector will allocate the additional credit in such a way as to support productive investments. In many African countries, the banking sector is characterized by excess liquidity and a shortage of stable long-term resources for extending credit to finance long-term investment (Sacerdoti, 2005; Mkandawire, 1999; Steele et al., 1997). It is unclear that injecting more liquidity into these banking systems will lead to more investment. The barrier is not monetary policy, but rather the institutional reality of the banking sector in which the incentive structure encourages holding high levels of liquid assets.

Banks frequently prefer to hold low-risk assets with strong real returns rather than extending loans to borrowers whom they perceive to be high-risk. Short-term government securities are often the asset of choice because returns are often high and such investments are virtually risk-free. Under these conditions, credit to the private sector is rationed.

An example from Ghana illustrates the problem of excess liquidity in the context of monetary easing. In July 2005, the Bank of Ghana lowered the level of required reserves (primary + secondary) from 44 percent to 24 percent of the level of deposits. Prior to the change, in June 2005, the actual level of reserves was 60.5 percent. By December 2005, the actual level of reserves had fallen by a very small amount, given the size of the reduction in the reserve requirement, down to 56.9 percent. By the following year (December 2006), actual reserves had dropped to 47.4 percent, but this was still greater than the original reserve requirement, of 44 percent, and nearly twice the level of reserves required under the new rules.[4] A looser monetary policy had little effect on the level of reserves held, and hence the amount of credit extended. The Bank of Ghana noted that rural and community banks had been shifting investment into holding government bonds and bills, a trend that "can be explained by the apparent high risk associated with lending vis-à-vis the guaranteed return and risk-free nature of Treasury bills" (Bank of Ghana, 2005: 53–4).

A developmental financial system channels resources to productive uses and facilitates the management of risks associated with the process of development. However, in most African countries, the developmental role of the financial sector is circumscribed by limited access to the appropriate type of financial services that would encourage an expansion of productive activities. Barriers to credit and financial markets are a particularly severe problem for smaller enterprises, those operating in the informal economy, and agricultural activities. However, not only is access to credit limited, but the cost of credit is also typically high throughout Africa. This represents a significant constraint for many investors, large and small, both in terms of direct costs and cash flow management. Many factors are frequently identified as contributing to the high cost of credit: large interest rate spreads, poor information systems, the asset portfolio of banks (including reserves), and high transactions costs, in some cases linked to inadequate information.

A mismatch in terms of the maturity structure of loans is also a potential problem (Mkandawire, 1999). In African banking sectors, most of the credit that is extended is of a short-term nature. However, productive investments often require access to medium- or long-term credit. A number of factors constrain the availability of longer-term credit, one of the most important being the term structure of deposits. As a result of a high prevalence of short-term deposits, banks are reluctant to make long-term loans. A lack of long-term credit represents a potential constraint on industrial development.

The more general point is that the institutional structure of the banking sector prevents monetary and financial policy from playing a developmental role. Institutional reforms had favored financial liberalization, but liberalization often failed to solve the problems sketched above. As a study by Reinhart and Tokatlidis (2003) puts it, "liberalization policies have seemed insufficient in mobilizing savings, deepening intermediation through the financial sector, or raising investment" (p. 54). Steele et al. (1997) show that financial depth (that is, the money supply relative to GDP) fell following reforms in Ghana, Malawi, Nigeria, and Tanzania and there was little improvement in the share of credit going to the private sector. Financial liberalization in Sub-Saharan Africa has frequently meant significant increases in the real interest rate (Reinhart and Tokatlidis, 2003). According to the financial repression hypothesis, higher real interest rates should have mobilized domestic savings in Africa, but any increase in domestic savings as a result of liberalization has been modest at best (Mkandawire, 1999).

What is needed is financial reform which overcomes these institutional constraints and this process should be seen as complementary to industrial policy. Effective reforms would have a variety of components which may include: developing better information systems for small-scale lenders; linking formal and informal credit institutions; introducing longer maturity deposit instruments; introducing incentives to support the extension of credit for productive investment; considering well-designed loan guarantees which could lower risk premiums; and revisiting the question of development finance institutions in Sub-Saharan Africa. The precise mix of interventions would vary from one institutional setting to the next, and not all of these reforms may be appropriate or successful. Development finance has had a bad reputation in many African countries. In many cases, policies have been inefficient, hindered by favoritism and rent seeking (Mkandawire, 1999). However, these problems are problems of institutional design and implementation. With appropriate governance institutions in place, development finance, in various forms, has a role to play in African countries, and is directly linked to the goals of industrial policy.

4.1.3   Mobilizing domestic resources

Fiscal policy tools are the bread and butter of many industrial policies, including tax breaks, subsidies, and targeted public investment. There is much to say about the details of tax and budgetary policies that relate directly to industrial policy. However, for the purposes of this paper, we bypass these details and instead raise issues relating to the size of the fiscus and the dynamics of public credit. Given the centrality of taxation and budgets in the implementation of key aspects of industrial policy, the ability to mobilize domestic resources to support these interventions is critical.

The issue of domestic resource mobilization as a pivotal issue for Sub-Saharan Africa has been examined at length in the *2010 African Economic Outlook*. Pressure to rethink tax systems in Sub-Saharan Africa has increased as there has been a fall in revenue from traditional tax sources, such as trade taxes (Keen and Mansour, 2009; Di John, 2009). Institutional weaknesses and poor tax administration often constitute the central barriers to mobilizing resources through tax systems in the region. High levels of informality and significant levels of employment in subsistence agriculture compound these difficulties. This is not to suggest that the tax structure is irrelevant, but rather to emphasize that increases in public resources can be achieved simply by strengthening institutions and improving administration (OECD and ADB, 2010). In addition, administrative competencies influence the tax structure. Income taxes make more significant institutional demands than taxes on goods and services which are perceived to be easier to administer. In this way, a lack of institutional capacity affects the mix of feasible tax policies.

Tax revenues in Sub-Saharan Africa, as a share of GDP, have increased since the 1980s, but analysis of these trends suggest that much of this improvement has been driven by the growth in revenues from natural resource exploitation (Keen and Mansour, 2009). Removing the contribution of resource-based revenues reveals a less impressive record with little improvement in resource mobilization. Revenues from natural resources could support industrial policy in countries with ample natural resource endowments. However, a heavy reliance on exports of these commodities frequently limits the incentives to develop a more diversified tax base. Reliance on natural resource exports can also squash the motivation to introduce policies that support industrial development, since it reduces pressures to diversify exports (Palma, 2005). If other sources of revenues are cultivated, commodity exports can be used to address other constraints to industrial development – such as limited foreign exchange – or to smooth out the volatility associated with commodity markets (Humphreys, Sachs, and Stiglitz, 2007).

The more significant point is that, excluding revenues from natural resource-based activities, there has not been a significant improvement in the domestic mobilization of tax revenues in Sub-Saharan Africa countries as a whole. Individual countries have made advances in reforming their tax systems (see, for example, the case studies in Di John, 2009). With regard to improvements in tax administration, two categories of reforms have proven to be effective. First, reorganizing the administration of tax collection on a functional basis (for example, developing a specific administrative unit for corporate taxes) instead of having a single administration to deal with all types of taxes. Second, the establishment of semi-autonomous statutory bodies which specialize in tax collection, but not the formulation of tax policies (OECD and ADB, 2010).

Again – the central theme of this paper re-emerges. Fiscal policy is important for supporting industrial policy initiatives in Sub-Saharan Africa. However, the effectiveness of fiscal policy – including the ability to mobilize domestic resources to support economic development – depends on existing institutions. In many cases, this represents a major constraint to developing macroeconomic policies which support industrial development.

The ability to mobilize domestic credit to the public sector in order to support industrial development in Sub-Saharan Africa is similarly constrained. Issues of debt management and sustainability have an important bearing on the question of when to use public borrowing to finance the expenditures relevant for industrial development (for example, infrastructure investments). However, the management of debt depends on the availability of public credit and the conditions under which such debt is taken on board. Much of the focus on debt in Sub-Saharan Africa has been on external sources of debt. Here, in the context of domestic resource mobilization, we highlight issues concerning domestic debt.

In African countries, public debt from domestic sources is frequently much more costly than borrowing from international financial institutions (Beaugrand, Loko, and Mlachila, 2002). For example, in 2011, Kenyan public debt was nearly equally split between external debt (49.7 percent) and domestic debt (50.3 percent). However, monthly interest payments on external debt were 0.8 billion Kenyan shillings compared to 8.6 billion shillings on domestic

212 The Industrial Policy Revolution II

debt.[5] The high costs of servicing domestic public debt constrains the ability of government to turn to domestic sources for debt financing. Moreover, high debt servicing costs can crowd out other budgetary expenditures.

In many Sub-Saharan African countries, much of government debt is short-term, raising the costs of debt management due to the need to rolling over existing debt. Moreover, the ownership of government bonds is typically concentrated in the commercial banking sector and other financial institutions (for example, large insurance companies). In many countries, the commercial banking sector had traditionally extended credit to the state. Although direct lending is far less common today, banks still lend to governments by holding public debt instruments. The fact that there are a limited number of buyers of domestic government bonds in Sub-Saharan African countries, primarily located in fairly concentrated banking and financial sectors, contributes to the high cost of domestic borrowing. As discussed earlier, this allows banks to use excess reserves to buy government bonds with high yields as an alternative to extending riskier loans which may support industrial development.

Once again, institutional realities constrain the use of fiscal policies – in this case, forms of deficit finance – to support industrial policies. Reforms could change this situation, for example, by expanding the range of public credit instruments available through the introduction of longer-term bonds and by developing innovative ways to diversify the base of bondholders as a way of adding depth to the market.[6] In a historical analysis of the evolution of domestic debt, Reinhart and Rogoff (2008) show that in high-income countries, the share of domestic debt in total public debt grew most rapidly during the first half of the 20th century, a time of rapid industrial development. This may suggest that the ability to mobilize domestic resources, including domestic public borrowing, represents an important aspect of industrial growth.[7] However, this capacity does not exist automatically, and must be cultivated over time.

4.1.4 Conclusions

This paper has argued that in order for macroeconomic policies to support industrial development in Sub-Saharan African countries, institutional reforms are needed to address problems which limit their effectiveness. This implies that structural transformation is required to enhance and deepen the scope of macroeconomic management. These institutional innovations should be conceived as part of a larger set of policies which aim to facilitate and accelerate economic development, including more traditional industrial policies. The standard approach would use the commonly accepted levers of macroeconomic climate control – for example, the money supply, policy interest rates, the budget deficit, and the nominal exchange rate – to create the right environment for the more micro-level interventions of industrial policy. However, this is unlikely to be the best approach for Sub-Saharan

Africa, because of the more immediate need to strengthen and diversify the macroeconomic toolkit.

The exact nature of the institutional and structural reforms is beyond the scope of this paper, and would necessarily vary from one context to the next. However, we have suggested a number of areas deserving of attention: exploring ways of enhancing competitiveness by reducing the average price level and enhancing the productivity of non-tradable goods and services; pursuing a broader mandate for monetary policy which takes into account real economic performance; exploring financial sector reforms which would support industrial development; and improving the capacity for mobilizing public resources domestically. In all these areas, the scope of the structural transformations necessary for economic development must be broadened to include the institutional reforms that will allow macroeconomic policy to reclaim its developmental role.

Notes

1. For a much more detailed discussion of these and other issues concerning cross-country price comparisons, see Deaton and Heston (2010).
2. Purchasing power parity adjustments are based on data from the International Comparison Program (IPC). The 2010 estimates from the World Development Indicators are based on the 2005 round of the IPC.
3. Some of the reasons that Bernanke et al. (1999) give for not focusing on nominal GDP growth as a monetary target is that (1) people may not understand nominal GDP growth in terms of formulating expectations and (2) data on GDP is produced less frequently than data on prices, making it more difficult to formulate immediate responses to changing economic conditions.
4. Figures come from the Bank of Ghana *Statistical Bulletin*, various years.
5. Figures refer to August 2011 and were taken from the Ministry of Finance, Kenya *Monthly Debt Bulletin*, August 2011.
6. In countries like Kenya, initial public offerings in companies such as KenGen attracted a range of investors, including very small scale investments. This suggests that individuals with small amounts of savings may be interested in buying securities, including government bonds, if the right vehicles for such investments were developed.
7. There are other contributing factors to the rise of domestic debt, including the need to finance major wars.

References

Aizenman, Joshua, Hutchison, Michael, and Noy, Ilan (2008) "Inflation Targeting and Real Exchange Rates in Emerging Markets," NBER Working Paper 14561 (Cambridge, MA: National Bureau of Economic Research).
Aryeetey, E. and Harrigan, J. (2000) "Macroeconomic and Sectoral Developments since 1970," n Ernest Aryeetey, Jane Harrigan, and Machiko Nissanke (eds), *Economic*

Reforms in Ghana: the Miracle and the Mirage (Oxford: James Currey and Woeli Publishers), pp. 5–31.

Bank of Ghana (2005) *Quarterly Economic Bulletin*, April-June (Accra, Ghana: Bank of Ghana).

Barbosa-Filho, Nelson H. (2008) "Inflation Targeting in Brazil: 1999–2006," *International Review of Applied Economics*, vol. 22, no. 2, pp. 187–200.

Barnichon, Régis and Peiris, Shanaka J. (2008) "Sources of Inflation in Sub-Saharan Africa," *Journal of African Economies*, vol. 17, no. 5, pp. 729–746.

Beaugrand, Philippe, Loko, Boileau, and Montfort, Mlachila (2002) "The Choice Between External and Domestic Debt in Financing Budget Deficits: the Case of Central and West African Countries," IMF Working Paper, WP/02/79 (Washington, DC: International Monetary Fund).

Bernanke, Ben S., Lauback, Thomas, Mishkin, Frederic S., and Posen, Adam S. (1999) *Inflation Targeting: Lessons from the International Experience* (Princeton, NJ: Priceton University Press).

Cottani, Joaquin, Domingo Cavallo and Khan, M. (1990) "Real Exchange Rate Behavior and Economic Performance in LDCs," *Economic Development and Cultural Change*, vol. 1, pp. 61–76.

Deaton, Angus, and Heston, Alan (2010) "Understanding PPPs and PPP-Based National Accounts," *American Economic Journal: Macroeconomics*, vol. 2, no. 4, pp. 1–35.

Di John, Jonathan (2009) "Taxation, Governance and Resource Mobilisation in Sub-Saharan Africa: A Survey of Key Issues," Elcano Royal Institute Working Paper 49/2009 (Madrid: Elcano Royal Institute).

Dollar, David (1992) "Outward-oriented Developing Economies Really Do Grow More Rapidly: Evidence from 95 LDCs, 1976–1985," *Economic Development and Cultural Change*, vol. 3, pp. 523–44.

Epstein, Gerald. (2007) "Central Banks as Agents of Employment Creation," in J.A. Ocampo and K.S. Jomo (eds), *Towards Full and Decent Employment* (London and New York: Zed Books).

Epstein, Gerald and Yeldan, Ervinç (2008) "Inflation Targeting, Employment Creation, and Economic Development: Assessing the Impacts and Policy Alternatives," *International Review of Applied Economics*, vol. 22, no. 2, pp. 131–144.

Frenkel, Roberto and Taylor, Lance (2006) "Real Exchange Rate, Monetary Policy, and Employment: Development in a Garden of Forking Paths," Working Paper 19 (New York: UNDESA).

Frenkel, Roberto and Rapetti, Martin (2010) "A Concise History of Exchange Rate Regimes in Latin America,". Research Report (Washington, DC: Center for Economic and Policy Research (CEPR)).Available online at http://www.cepr.net/documents/publications/exchange-rates-latin-america-2010-04.pdf.

Friedman, Benjamin and Kuttner, Kenneth (1996) "A Price Target for U.S. Monetary Policy? Lessons from Experiences with Money Growth Targets," *Brookings Papers on Economic Activity*, vol. 1 pp. 77–125.

Gala, Paulo and Lucinda, Claudio (2006) "Exchange Rate Misalignment and Growth: Old and New Econometric Evidence," mMimeo (São Paulo, Brazil: São Paulo School of Business Administration and São Paulo School of Economics).

Galindo, Luis Miguel and Jaime, Ros (2008) "Alternatives to Inflation Targeting in Mexico," *International Review of Applied Economics*, vol. 22, no. 2, pp. 201–214.

Ghura, Dhaneshwar and Grennes, Thomas (1993) "The Real Exchange Rate and Macroeconomic Performance in Sub-Saharan Africa," *Journal of Development Economics*, vol. 1, pp. 155–174.

Heintz, James and Ndikumana, Léonce (2010) "Is There a Case for Formal Inflation-targeting in Sub-Saharan Africa?," *Journal of African Economies*, vol. 20, pp. ii67–ii103.

Humphreys, Macartan, Sachs, Jeffrey D., and Stiglitz, Joseph (2007) "Introduction: What is the Problem with Natural Resource Wealth?," In M. Humphreys, J.D. Sachs, and J.E. Stiglitz (eds), *Escaping the Resource Curse* (New York: Columbia University Press), pp. 1–20.

Keen, Michael and Mansour, Mario (2009) "Revenue Mobilization in Sub-Saharan Africa: Challenges from Globalization," IMF Working Papers 09/157 (Washington, DC: IMF).

Loening, Josef L., Durevall, Dick, and Birru, Yohannes A. (2009) "Inflation Dynamics and Food Prices in an Agricultural Economy: the Case of Ethiopia," Policy Research Working Paper 4969, Africa Region (Washington, DC: World Bank).

Mkandawire, Thandika (1999) "The Political Economy of Financial Reform in Africa," *Journal of International Development*, vol. 11 pp. 321–342.

Neary, Peter J. and van Wijnbergen, Sweder (1986) "Natural Resources and the Macroeconomy: a Theoretical Framework," in P.J. Neary and S. van Wijnbergen (eds), *Natural Resources and the Macroeconomy* (Cambridge, MA: The MIT Press), pp. 13–45.

Nell, Kevin S. (2004) "The Structuralist Theory of Imported Inflation: an Application to South Africa," *Applied Economics*, vol. 36, pp. 1431–1444.

OECD and ADB (2010) *African Economic Outlook 2010* (Paris: Organization of Economic Cooperation and Development and Tunis: African Development Bank).

Oladipo, Olajide (2007) "Exchange Rate Pass Through: a Case Study of a Small Open Economy," *Global Economy Journal*, vol. 7, no. 3, pp. 1–24.

Palma, José Gabriel (2005) "Four Sources of 'Deindustrialization' and a New Concept of the 'Dutch Disease'," in J.A. Ocampo (ed.), *Beyond Reforms: Structural Dynamics and Macroeconomic Vulnerability* (Washington, DC: ECLAC).

Pollin, Robert, Githinji, Mwangi, and Heintz, James (2008) *An Employment Targeted Economic Program for Kenya* (Cheltenham, UK: Edward Elgar).

Reinhart, Carmen M. and Kenneth S. Rogoff. 2008. "The forgotten history of domestic debt" NBER Working Paper, 13946. Cambridge, MA: National Bureau of Economic Research.

Reinhart, Carmen M. and Tokatlidis, Ioannis (2003) "Financial liberalization: the African Experience," *Journal of African Economies*, vol. 12, no. S2, pp. 53–88.

Sacerdoti, Emilio (2005) "Access to Bank Credit in Sub-Saharan Africa: Key Issues and Reform Strategies," IMF Working Paper 166 (New York: International Monetary Fund).

Sachs, Jeffrey D. and Warner, Andrew M. (1997) "Natural Resource Abundance and Economic Growth" (Cambridge, MA: Center for International Development and Harvard Institute for International Development).

Steele, William, Aryeetey, Ernest, Hettige, Hemamala and Nissanke, Machiko (1997) "Informal Financial Markets Under Liberalization in Four African Countries," *World Development*, vol. 25, no. 5, pp. 817–830.

Thornton, John (2008) "Money, Output, and Inflation in African Economies," *South African Journal of Economics*, vol. 76, no. 3, pp. 356–366.

4.2

Competition Policy, Industrial Policy, and Corporate Conduct

Simon Roberts[1]
University of Johannesburg

4.2.1 Introduction

There has been a phenomenal growth in the adoption of competition laws, with the number of countries having such legislation increasing to over 100 in 2011 (ICN, 2011).[2] The growth has been strongly promoted by international financial institutions and donors as part of programs to "make markets work" and must rank (in terms of adoption) as one of the more successful of such policy pushes by the Washington institutions.[3] There was also considerable pressure to adopt a particular legal framework with the OECD and World Bank jointly developing a "model" competition law (World Bank/OECD, 1999). In reality, however, there is considerable diversity in the legal and institutional regimes that countries have adopted.[4] From a quite different starting point, recent work on how countries develop and evolve to "open access" regimes with more inclusive economic institutions and markets has also identified the importance of competitive markets although with strikingly little analysis of what this actually means (North et al., 2009; Acemoglu and Robinson, 2012).

Competition law has been located as a component of microeconomic reform packages to "correct" market distortions.[5] This implies it is in opposition to industrial policy, which deliberately introduces distortions. For example, Evenett and Brooks (2005) argue that the rise to prominence once more of industrial policy works against the increased acceptance of competition policy. This relies on a particular view of both competition law, as primarily about deterring cartels, and industrial policy, as about creating national champions not subject to competitive discipline.

I argue that competitive rivalry is very important both for industrial development and for industrial policy and, in turn, industrial policy is important for ensuring effective rivalry, especially in developing countries. Aside from the typical focus on allocative efficiency, I am more concerned with the links between rivalry and the development of productive capabilities, the evolution of countries' comparative advantages and the realization

216

of dynamic comparative advantages (Lin and Chang, 2009; Amsden, 1989). In this, it is critical to recognise the role that large corporations play in the paths taken (Chandler, 1990; Chandler et al., 1998). My discussion is therefore concerned with competition regimes as part of the engagement with the strategies and decision-making of such corporations, and the links with other policies and institutions.[6] In this regard, the passing of competition laws is not equivalent to ensuring competitive rivalry. And the emphasis on simply passing competition laws in developing countries has been criticized as not taking account of political and institutional realities (Rodriguez and Menon, 2010; Mateus, 2010).

At the outset it is important to recognise that African countries are highly heterogeneous. The chapter draws mainly on the South African experience which is in no sense representative but from which insights can be drawn on the wider question of competition law, industrial policy and development.

I start in section 4.2.2 by briefly reviewing issues of competition and industrial development. In section 4.2.3 I take South Africa as a case study. Section 4.2.4 discusses issues of competition at the regional level (southern and east Africa), taking examples from several industries. Section 4.2.5 concludes.

4.2.2 Competition and industrial development[7]

In all countries that have undergone rapid industrialization and "catch-up" large firms have had a crucial role in developing key industries such as consumer electronics, automobiles, shipbuilding, steel, and basic chemicals. It is well recognized that the orientation of big businesses and the ways in which they interact or compete are a central part of countries' development trajectory (Chandler et al., 1997). The internal organizational capabilities of firms are an essential element in the ways in which they adopt and exploit new technologies, and realize economies of scale and scope. Firms can be understood in terms of their productive resources and capabilities which together explain differences in firms' competitiveness and, at the systemic level, the evolution of "business-enterprise systems" (Penrose, 1995; Chandler et al., 1997). For example, interrelationships between firms within large corporate groupings in Japan and South Korea have enabled the necessary support and cooperation to build dynamic competitive capabilities in industries such as electronics, cars, and steel (Amsden, 1997). Large internationalized corporations also control much of resource extraction and processing around the world, crucial to the development of many African countries.

Critical in the East Asian newly industrialized countries was linking the state support and intervention to drive investment in improved industrial capabilities with disciplining mechanisms to ensure that the outcomes were in line with performance expectations (Amsden, 1989; Chang, 1996; Wade, 1990). In this regard, an important aspect was making support for firms contingent on their competitive performance in export markets, to provide a source of discipline at the firm level and a way of measuring firms against each other even while offering protection in the domestic market (Rodrik, 1995; Singh, 2004). It also ensured that firms were forced to adopt and adapt more advanced technologies, production, and marketing methods, as they were being pitched against the international industry leaders in export markets. Using export targets as conditions for incentives and support can thus be interpreted as a tool of competitive discipline. In a similar way, contests were set up for state support around other targets, such as investment, as part of the state supporting rivalrous oligopolies rather than individual national champions.

More generally, ensuring competitive rivalry between big business groups is a very important disciplining and motivating factor to ensure that state support does not lead to collusion and rent extraction. Analyses have highlighted the importance of competitive discipline in the industrial development of East Asian countries such as Japan and South Korea (Amsden and Singh, 1994; Sakakibara and Porter, 2001). The dynamic rivalry that constitutes competition is thus a very important element of Chandler's (1990) characterizations of different capitalisms. In the framework of North et al. (2009) it is part of the evolution of limited access orders to be more impersonal, and can be understood as part of elites committing to longer-term investments rather than prioritizing short-term profits.

Competition understood in this way clearly relates to behavior and not structure. We are not looking to some textbook ideal of maximum or perfect competition with many firms. Rather, the significance of economies of scale, as well as the investments required in acquiring technological capabilities, means that there will normally be few firms in these industries. It should be noted that while there is an extensive literature on competition and innovation, in developing countries we are concerned more with adoption and adaptation of capabilities rather than incentives for frontier R&D. Singh has argued for understanding the competitive discipline provided by vigorous rivals as "optimal competition" (Singh, 2004). It is about effective rivalry, in dynamic as well as static terms. The absence of such rivalry also relates to a dominant firm being able to entrench its monopoly position and the rents derived from it (Rey and Tirole, 2006). If there are strategies through which such firms can protect their position and build barriers to entry then these strategies – rather than efforts to generate improved capabilities and new competitive advantages – may be the firms' primary focus. Similarly, government policies may reward lobbying efforts or may reward performance against well understood industrial development goals.

Particularly in small, industrializing economies, the differing possible behavior of large firms therefore has huge implications for economic development. In South Africa, apartheid industrial policies bequeathed a highly skewed industrial structure and dominant firms in key sectors (Chabane et al., 2006). These firms had developed significant capabilities on the back of state support and under state ownership. Their behavior and orientation, including whether subject to effective competitive discipline, in many regards determines the development of whole sectors of industry.

Industrial policies to alter a country's development path need to realize external economies from stronger linkages, collective learning, and governance (Helmsing, 2001; Kaplinsky, 2000). Processes of learning and technical change involve the firm, its institutional structure and organizational routines (Lall and Teubal, 1998). However, the evolution of firms' capabilities is not necessarily the outcome of "efficient" institutional arrangements, but rather to do with their strategic choices and orientation (Teece and Pisano, 1998). The importance of understanding the types of organization, including the large firms themselves, that are required to successfully exploit technologies has been highlighted by Chandler and others (Chandler et al., 1997). Industrial policy must engage with this, with attention to deliberate and purposeful joint action and the building of local institutions.

4.2.2.1 The practice of competition law in developing countries

I argue that the competition regime and industrial policy should be viewed as complementary. Dynamic competitive rivalry is a central concern of both, especially with regard to its role in inducing dynamic efficiency, technical progress and investment (Singh, 2004; Possas and Borges, 2009).

Competition law typically seeks to address uncompetitive practices and the exercise of market power. In addressing the behavior of firms and taking into account market structure, competition law aims to affect economic outcomes. This does not necessarily mean that the scope of enforcement under the competition law will be wide-ranging. The opposite may be true, in that only a very narrow scope may be identified for the competition authorities. Rather, the actual scope identified for the competition regime in legislation and institutional guidelines indicates a particular choice. In addition, the particular choice may include making competition authorities independent from government to "de-politicize" their practice, based on a narrow conception of the political, which ignores the interplay of interests through institutions.

Choices should take into account country conditions. In his comparison of the USA and Europe, Vickers (2007) finds that differences in the approach to the abuse of dominance are to be expected given the different economic history and Europe being "more monopolized" than the USA. Considering the economies of developing countries we would expect much bigger differences. Developing country economies are, with some notable exceptions, relatively small. Due to poor transport infrastructure, there are also likely to be localised markets within the larger economies, where there would be much wider markets in Europe or North America (Brusick and Evenett, 2008; Gal, 2009). Scale economies are that much more important, as are dynamic issues to do with the process of competitive rivalry in building production capabilities and accessing inputs and markets (Gal 2003, 2009; Hur, 2004).

There are more likely to be entrenched incumbents and higher entry barriers than in developed economies. Access to government in the past has commonly enabled many companies to entrench their position through favorable treatment, including licences, regulatory provisions, and privileged energy and transport infrastructure provision. And these companies may often now be in the hands of multinationals (Brusick and Evenett, 2008). The effects of prior lobbying and patronage, often linking local elites and multinationals, are quite different from the operation of a coherent industrial policy. The latter looks to provide temporary support to build capabilities and is consistent with rivalry.

Higher barriers to entry include weaker and shallower financial systems and other obstacles to new entrants like difficulties in establishing distribution networks and ensuring supply of inputs, as well as factors already identified such as the relationship of scale economies to market size, and less developed transport infrastructure. These factors imply that abuse by dominant firms is more widespread, more persistent and more damaging in developing countries (see also Dabbah, 2010; Fingleton and Nikpay, 2009). On the other side, it could be argued that the greater need to incentivize investment means there are greater costs from over-enforcement as, by penalizing those who have attained a dominant position, the incentives to invest to achieve such a position would be diminished. However, the focus here is on firms who have already attained an entrenched position and held it for many years.[8] It is investment by entrants and much smaller rivals that is more likely to be required, as part of the competitive process, but may be being dis-incentivized by dominant firm conduct (Fox, 2008).

Alongside the factors affecting the likelihood of abuse, and its costs, developing countries generally have weaker and less mature institutions, at least in terms of skills and technical capacity. There is little point in designing a regime assuming that there will be an advanced institution to run it.[9] But this does not imply a minimalist approach to enforcement. Rather, it implies a careful country by country evaluation against what is required for clear and administrable standards. Using the same analytical framework may mean different answers on the presumptions and tests because of the different conditions, as well as different levels of investment in detection and punishment (Evans, 2009).

Different developing country experiences highlight the importance of moving beyond the formal regulatory framework in considering countries' competition policy choices, and they reveal a diversity of approaches in practice. It is also important to remember that competition regimes evolve reflecting countries' different historical, cultural and political economy contexts (Fox, 2003; Singh, 2004). In general, it is the criteria that are applied, the implementation approach, and the overall level of commitment that are most influential (Hoekman, 1998).

Several developing countries emphasize measures addressing the behavior of dominant firms. In the context of small domestic markets, this is consistent with the significance of economies of scale, dynamic effects related to technology, and the importance of production linkages in processes of industrialization (Gal, 2009; Hur, 2004). For example, the objectives of the South Korean Fair Trade Commission (KFTC) are to encourage free and fair competition, prevent the concentration of economic power and thereby promote "balanced development" (Wise, 2000). This is given that the early stages of rapid industrialization were viewed as "unbalanced," requiring an active competition policy addressed at dominant firms in that country (see Fox, 2002, 2003).

With enactment of the Monopoly Regulation and Fair Trade Act in 1981, the KFTC has been oriented to addressing monopoly power and its effects, including "unreasonable" practices and "unjustifiable" restrictions on competition (Fox, 2003). Amendments to the law in 1987 provided for further powers to address the concentration of economic power in the *chaebol* (Hur, 2004). This orientation is consistent with a broad definition of free and fair competition, in the sense of a competitive industrial structure and the control of potential abuses and imbalances in the bargaining power between parties – in particular, subcontracting relationships to protect against exploitation of smaller firms (Hur, 2004). Typically, in the short run such subcontracting arrangements would lower prices and hence not harm consumers. In the longer term, however, unfair subcontracting arrangements by large firms militate against the development of a dynamic base of small and medium-sized firms able to invest in their own independent production capabilities. The KFTC has pursued an explicit strategy of promoting "shared growth" of large firms and small and medium-sized enterprises (KFTC, 2011). In addition, there have been high levels of activity in cartel detection.[10]

In South Korea, as in Japan, the focus on dynamic competition processes and rivalrous behavior rather than structure per se is despite having competition laws strongly influenced by USA law (Amsden and Singh 1994). Rather than emphasizing legal independence, the KFTC derives influence from its position within the institutions of government. The chairperson has the right to participate in cabinet meetings and, by law, ministries are required to consult with the KFTC about measures that may impact on competition. The interpretation of "unreasonable" practices by dominant companies and "unjustifiable" restrictions on competition allow the KFTC substantial discretionary power. As important, perhaps, for the ability to exercise this power is the close links of the KFTC with the powerful Economic Planning Board, within which it fell until 1994 (Sanekata and Wilks, 1996; Wise, 2000). The KFTC case well illustrates the importance of de facto autonomy rather than a preoccupation with de jure independence.

In many countries, by comparison, the competition authorities may be independent in theory but their effectiveness is hampered by lack of resources and political economy factors within the countries. The importance of appropriate implementation mechanisms is further highlighted by the many examples of countries with competition laws but no effective mechanisms for their realization. The Philippines has had anti-monopoly laws since 1935 but there was no central agency to oversee the legislation and no administrative mechanisms to give effect to the provisions. Countries with legislation that was not being implemented until the 1990s include Mexico, Argentina and Brazil, highlighting the importance of political will and the appropriate institutional framework. There are also countries which have achieved rapid growth, such as Malaysia, that have not prioritized competition policy. Alternative policy instruments have been used to impact on the behavior of large companies.

Appropriate and effective competition regimes must also take account of countries' institutional capabilities. A highly litigious, prosecutorial system, drawing on large numbers of lawyers and economists, is not an optimal use of scarce expertise and will favor well-organized interest groups and large corporations (Stevens, 1995; Laffont, 1998). Given the information asymmetries in favor of the firms on which judgments are to be made, the provisions must allow agencies enough flexibility to make and enforce their determinations.

There has been a tendency to overemphasize the legal independence of competition authorities. In reality, the commitment of government is necessary for the effectiveness of competition institutions, regardless of the exact nature of their independence or autonomy.

4.2.3   South Africa competition law case study

South Africa is a useful case study having adopted a new competition law in 1998 (coming into force in 1999) very much as part of an economic reform strategy. The impact of the competition regime provides insights into the role of competition law as well as allowing an assessment of the choices made in terms of the particular legal provisions and institutional setup. While the objectives of the South African law are framed in terms of addressing the apartheid legacy of the concentration of control and the need to open up access to small businesses and those owned by historically disadvantaged persons, the practice has been a focus on merger control and cartel enforcement. Addressing abuse of dominance has proved relatively difficult.

4.2.3.1   Law and institutions

Competition law in post-apartheid South Africa had two main motivations. The first was the imperative of addressing the apartheid legacy of concentration of control, as was reflected in its position in the Reconstruction and Development Programme (ANC, 1994). The second was the emphasis on removing market distortions as part of the programme of economic liberalization (see, for example, the reference to competition in Department of Finance, 1996).

The tension between addressing the apartheid legacy and the liberalization agenda is reflected in the combination of the relatively expansive objectives of the Act with the specification of the provisions in the legislation being quite restrictive, especially regarding the abuse of dominance (the provisions that address monopoly power) (Roberts, 2012). The objectives of the Act emphasize the ability to participate in the economy, including by small and medium-sized enterprises and by historically disadvantaged persons. They also identify the need to address the legacy of apartheid in terms of concentrated ownership and control. The particular provisions of the Act stipulating the tests to be done in evaluating mergers and most anti-competitive conduct specify effects-based tests, framed as whether there is a substantial prevention or lessening of competition. Mergers are also subject to a separate public interest test.

The framework for the legislation itself had been negotiated between business, government, and labor. The narrow framing of specific provisions was strongly argued for by business, in terms of the need for "certainty" (Roberts, 2000). The business constituency also strongly supported independent institutions and a limited role for the Minister in proceedings. This emphasis accorded closely with the policy stance taken by the government following the sharp depreciation in the Rand in 1996 and perceived need to maintain the confidence of business and international markets.

Under the Act the Competition Commission has the responsibility to investigate mergers and anti-competitive conduct, and the Competition Tribunal rules on cases. The Competition Appeal Court was also established, as a specialist division of the High Court. The Tribunal members typically have a legal or economics background, and a panel of three members is formed to hear and decide on each matter.[11]

The Tribunal hearings are legal in nature, with the discovery of relevant information, factual and expert evidence being led and subject to intense cross-examination, and extensive legal argument. While the Tribunal has inquisitorial powers, in practice the Tribunal processes have been intensely adversarial in nature. Many successful legal challenges have been brought on procedural or narrow technical grounds, limiting the scope of the Commission and Tribunal to inquire into the multifaceted aspects of conduct and to frame their decisions.[12]

The main test for merger evaluation is whether there is a likely substantial lessening of competition, with particular factors identified in the law that need to be considered. If the merger is likely to have anti-competitive effects then it is necessary to consider whether there are any technological and/or efficiency gains that may offset this. The Tribunal is also required to consider public interest issues in all mergers.

The Competition Act prohibits horizontal restrictive practices, with per se prohibitions on price fixing, dividing markets by allocating customers, suppliers, or territories, and colluding on tenders. The Competition Act allows for a financial penalty up to a maximum of 10 percent of one year of a company's affected turnover for these conducts. There is an effects-based test for other horizontal arrangements for which there are no penalties for a first-time contravention. This is also the case for vertical restrictive practices.

A dominant firm is prohibited from charging an excessive price to the detriment of consumers. An excessive price is defined under the Competition Act as a price which bears no reasonable relation to the economic value of the good or service, and is higher than such value. Economic value is not defined in the Act.

Exclusionary abuse of dominance is assessed in effects-based tests. There are also explicit pro-competitive, efficiency, and technology defenses for most of the abuse prohibitions. Particular types of exclusionary acts are identified where a penalty may be imposed for a first contravention. There is also a prohibition on a dominant firm engaging in exclusionary conduct defined in general terms, with no penalty for a first contravention and with the onus on the complainant to demonstrate that the anti-competitive effect outweighs its technological, efficiency, or other pro-competitive benefits. Prohibited price discrimination, for equivalent transactions and with the effect of substantially preventing or lessening competition, has no penalty for first offence.

4.2.3.2 The record

A very large part of the Commission's work in the first five years was taken up with merger evaluation as compulsory pre-merger notification meant that a large number of deals had to be evaluated right from the commencement of operations. The Commission has assessed around 400 mergers per year, most of which raised no competition or public interest concerns. Public interest concerns have, in almost all cases, been to do with potential job losses associated with the merger and typically this has led to the imposition of conditions limiting retrenchments and/or providing retraining and other opportunities for affected employees. Other public interest concerns addressed have been to do with the effect of the mergers on the development of industries and local suppliers.

The Commission has referred an average of nine cases of anti-competitive conduct per year. Since the mid-2000s, cartel enforcement has increased, while the number of abuse of dominance cases referred by the Commission has averaged just 1.5 per year. The relatively large number of cartel cases in recent years is due largely to the success of the corporate leniency policy and a proactive stance to investigating areas of likely collusion (Makhaya et al., 2012). This involved the Commission, from around 2007, identifying priority sectors of the economy and, based on initial research and information gathering, initiating investigations. The uncovering of two cartels, in particular, in bread and in concrete pipes, led to wider investigations as the same companies were found to be implicated in conduct in related products.

The abuse of dominance cases are notable for the fact that most have been against a former state-owned company (or a currently state-owned one, as in the case of South African Airways). These include referrals against Telkom (two cases), South African Airways (SAA) (two cases), Sasol (three cases), Mittal Steel, Foskor (owned by the Industrial Development Corporation), and Safcol. Moreover there have been several involving firms whose position is based in historic state support and/or regulation in agriculture markets – namely, Senwes, Rooibos, Patensie.

Of the 19 abuse of dominance cases referred to the Tribunal in the 13 years to end-August 2012, 11 had been ruled on by the Tribunal, three have been settled, and five are still to be decided. The Tribunal found abuse had occurred in seven, of which two were overturned on appeal. This means there are five cases in which findings of abuse of dominance have been sustained – SAA (two cases), Patensie, Senwes, and Telkom.[13] In the SAA and Telkom cases there have been penalties. The Senwes matter was ultimately upheld by the Constitutional Court, although there are no penalties under the particular section of the Act.[14] There have been five settlements in all (two of which were settled before referral), of which three had substantive undertakings. These were the settlements by GlaxoSmithKline and Boehringer-Ingelheim, Sasol Nitro, and Foskor.

In cartel enforcement, the work of the competition authorities has achieved notable successes. Since the Competition Commission adopted a more proactive approach to enforcement in 2006 a slew of cartels has been identified, many of them involving established firms in industrial products continuing a quiet life and protecting their rents (Makhaya et al., 2012). In several important cases these include cartels that operated across southern Africa such as in cement and concrete pipes. Multi-level cartels have also been identified in several value chains, apparently to raise entry barriers to protect the collusive arrangements.

In summary, while the competition authorities have stopped insiders colluding and have blocked anti-competitive mergers, the competition regime has not generally worked to open up markets to new competitors. Instead, the distinction between a substantial lessening of competition and the effect on an individual competitor has been emphasized, at least when the final decisions of the appeal courts are taken into account. The Competition Appeal Court (CAC) overruled the Tribunal decision on price discrimination by Sasol against Nationwide Poles precisely because the effect on the small firm in question, despite it being efficient, was not enough to demonstrate an effect on competition. In Netstar-Tracker, the ability of smaller firms to enter the industry and the effect of rules setting up obstacles to them doing so was discounted by the CAC due to there already being a few large competitors. In the SAB case brought by the Commission, and dismissed by the Tribunal due to the decisions of higher courts, the role of smaller participants in the distribution chain was effectively dismissed.

Viewed from the perspective of addressing the power of entrenched dominant firms with their roots in apartheid policies, the competition enforcement record does not look good (see Roberts, 2012, for a fuller assessment). The government's industrial policies have repeatedly identified the power of such corporations in sectors such as steel and basic chemicals as an obstacle to the growth of diversified industrial development. But, as reflected above, there has been almost no successful measures taken under the abuse of dominance provisions against these firms. To better understand the issues I look at the example of basic chemicals, an industry at the heart of industrial development.

4.2.3.3 Influencing the decisions of large corporations – an illustrative example of chemicals, fuels, fertilizer

The development of the chemicals industry in South Africa is closely related to two requirements: first, the demand for explosives and fertilizer inputs by mines and farmers; and, second, the apartheid state's concern to reduce its dependency on crude oil imports (see Dobreva et al., 2005; Fine and Rustomjee, 1996; Roberts and Rustomjee, 2009). Two firms dominated the growth of the sector. The leading producer for much of the 20th century was African Explosives and Chemical Industries (AECI), part of the mining-based Anglo-American Corporation. Sasol, which now dominates the industry, developed out of state intervention.

After World War II the state used the enabling 1947 Liquid Fuel and Oil Act to create the first Sasol oil from coal plant (utilizing adapted German World War II technology) in the 1950s with financing from the state's Industrial Development Corporation. Following the increases in oil prices in 1973, it was decided to construct Sasol 2 in Secunda. A further increase in global pricing prompted the decision in 1979 to construct Sasol 3, following immediately after the commissioning of Sasol 2 at Secunda. At the same time, Sasol was partially privatized, partly in order to raise the capital required to construct Sasol 3.

Sasol employs the Fischer–Tropsch process for the gasification of coal to produce synthetic liquid fuels. The development of the technologies had a range of spin-offs, and resulted in a major industrial chemicals complex founded on organic chemicals from the processing and refining. Sasol has grown to dominate the basic chemical sector and has become a major domestic supplier of liquid fuel. In the Gauteng region, Sasol created an industrial gas pipeline network during the 1980s, expanding this to the Durban region by leasing the disused crude oil pipeline, owned by the transport parastatal.[15]

It is important also to note that the development of chemicals was not motivated by the normal import-substituting industrialization strategy. The strategic goals of the apartheid state meant that it was concerned only with key industries (mining, agriculture) and key products (liquid fuels). The strategy was generally not concerned with developing competitive manufacture of downstream consumer chemicals. The extremely skewed nature of income and consumer demand reinforced this pattern and the bias to heavy upstream industrial chemicals.

The developments over the past two decades under liberalization have been heavily influenced by Sasol's position of market power in the domestic industry. This resulted from state support, implemented in pursuit of strategic aims rather than profit-maximizing objectives. The support included infrastructure provision, the regulation of markets including the petrol and diesel markets, and a major R&D effort including centers of science and technology across the country. Sasol's oil from coal project led to unique technological capabilities being developed. These capabilities have provided the base for it to become an internationally competitive and internationalized industrial chemicals company, with operations on five continents, and secondary listing on the New York Stock Exchange.

Since 1990, capabilities have been strengthened in some areas (largely around Sasol) and weakened in others. In the 1990s, Sasol invested in the Mozambique gasfields and, in partnership the South African state's Central Energy Fund, constructed a gas pipeline to transport the gas to its plants in Sasolburg and Secunda, diversifying its input away from coal. The new natural gas feedstock coming onstream from 2004/5 has underpinned Sasol's growth.

Sasol has also consciously internationalized and has sought to diversify globally, buying into the downstream chemical industry in Europe and initiating two capital-intensive gas-to-liquid (GTL) plants in Nigeria and Qatar and a petrochemical complex in Iran in partnership with other transnational corporations. It also has a polymers joint venture in Malaysia with Petronas.

4.2.3.3.1 *Dominant firm strategies, competition law, and industrial policy*

Under apartheid it appears that the industry was disciplined by industrial policies, broadly understood, influenced by the key interests it had been developed to serve, as these were powerful constituencies. The mining industry, for which explosives production had been developed, was at the heart of the economy. The main explosives producer, AECI, was also a subsidiary of the largest mining house, Anglo-American. The interests of large commercial agriculture were also very influential, and until the 1980s fertilizer was subject to regulation which ensured the interests of farmers were protected.

Similarly extensive regulatory arrangements were in place in the area of liquid fuels. The regulation here effectively represented a bargain between the multinational refiners present in the country (including Shell, BP, Total, and Chevron) and Sasol together with the South African state. The arrangements under the Sasol Supply Agreements of 1954, subsequently known as the Main Supply Agreement, meant the crude oil refiners agreed to purchase all Sasol's output in exchange for guaranteed refining and marketing margins, while Sasol agreed not to enter marketing.[16] Competition between fuel producers was removed in the interests of supporting Sasol's profitability.

Sasol was also supported by a dispensation whereby synthetic fuel producers received tariff protection when crude oil prices fell below a defined floor price of $23/barrel (the level at which it was estimated they would earn a 10 percent return on assets). When oil prices rose above $27.7/barrel the producers had to pay back 25 percent of the additional revenue into the "Equalisation Fund" until the quantum of state protection previously received had been repaid (see Rustomjee, 2012).

At the end of 1998, Sasol gave the required five-year notice to end the Main Supply Agreement, with the intended date of December 2003. In 1998 the government also released Sasol from the obligation to repay any outstanding subsidies it had received during the earlier dispensation (National Treasury, 2007). This meant that from the end of 2003 Sasol has been free to enter and expand into the marketing and retailing of fuel, and the Other Oil Companies (OOCs) have not been required to buy Sasol products. Price regulation remains on some products, principally retail petrol where the pump price is set.[17] These prices are set with a view to ensuring a rate of return for the industry on marketing assets.

It appears that Sasol's termination of the MSA was linked to its anticipation of deregulation by government and the related competitive pressure (Competition Tribunal, 2006: para. 123). Sasol wanted to be able to enter and expand in the downstream, retail markets (para. 125). In the absence of such a presence, despite being the dominant producers of fuel, especially in the inland market, it could be subject to countervailing bargaining power on the part of the OOCs (see Corbett et al., 2011).

Sasol's main strategy to respond to actual and expected changes in regulation and protection was intended to consolidate its position through mergers and ensure that it continued to occupy a national champion position, making it indispensable for the country's security of supply. At the same time it promised to continue to invest to ensure supply met demand and to develop petrochemicals production. Other chemicals producers faced with declining levels of protection generally sought to restructure and narrow their production to achieve scale economies and to develop their trading activities, drawing on imports.

Merger regulation under the competition authorities did block deals aimed at further strengthening Sasol's position; however, its existing position has not been undermined nor has the power been substantively constrained. I argue that in the context of the challenges of addressing entrenched dominance in developing countries this is where the combination of competition law and industrial policy ought to be working. Instead, the challenge has been passed to a relatively ineffective competition regime instead of being the object of industrial policy instruments.

Sasol tried two significant mergers – the first blocked by the old Competition Board in 1998 and the second blocked by the Competition Tribunal in 2006. In the second half of the 1990s, Sasol and AECI sought to merge their interests in ammonia, fertilizers, explosives, and polymer chemicals on the basis that major new investment could only be made in world-scale plants under a single entity. The then Competition Board prohibited it in the areas of fertilizer and explosives and imposed conditions on other products, including stipulations regarding the supply and pricing of ammonia, phosphoric acid, nitrogenous derivatives, and nitrogenous/phosphoric acid combinations.[18] Rather than agree to these conditions, the parties abandoned the merger and achieved the desired restructuring in other ways.[19]

The second industry-reshaping merger planned by Sasol was with Engen and would have combined inland and coastal refining capacity and the largest distribution network. The Tribunal prohibited the merger as it would have meant Sasol could credibly threaten to foreclose the other oil companies as customers for bulk supply of fuels and its competitors in retail and commercial markets (Competition Tribunal, 2006). The former Minister, Penuell Maduna, was now employed by Sasol and had been intimately involved in drawing up the deal (Lewis, 2012).

The system of regulation which protects the profitability of the upstream industry has, however, remained in place. Nor has industrial policy effectively altered the balance from the heavy chemicals bias of the apartheid strategy. This is despite successive policies having this as a key objective (Machaka and Roberts, 2003; Roberts and Rustomjee, 2009). The industrial policies since 2007 have identified the pricing of key intermediate or strategic inputs as an issue for the growth of downstream industries and the need to address this through a strengthened competition regime (DTI, 2007 and 2010). In 2007 the Department of Trade and Industry requested the Competition Commission to investigate the pricing of polymer chemicals, the key input to the manufacture of plastic products.

While some other measures were identified in industrial policy action plans (see, for example, DTI, 2007), there has been little concrete progress, possibly because the competition regime was viewed as the answer. In addition, a mooted windfall tax on excessive profits of Sasol, supported by a National Treasury task team, was rejected by the government (National Treasury, 2007). The grounds included the fact that Sasol had promised to invest to ensure security of supply and the development of petrochemicals.

In 2010, following the request by the Department of Trade and Industry, the Competition Commission referred a case of excessive pricing of propylene and polypropylene on the part of Sasol. The Tribunal hearing is set down for mid-2013, with any finding likely to be appealed. The Competition Commission is also evaluating the conduct of the oil companies focused on information exchange (with a case of collusion subsequently referred). By exchanging information on sales, at a very disaggregated level, it appears as if the oil companies undermined incentives to compete (Das Nair and Mncube, 2012).

In the meantime, Sasol's continued hold over supply of fuels in the inland market in particular has been reinforced by their position as joint owner in the exploitation of the large Mozambican gas reserves and in the pipeline delivering it to Secunda. The pricing of the gas has been subject to maximum regulation, for the first ten years from 2004 to 2014, with the volume-weighted price not to exceed an average price of selected European countries, while individual customers can be charged up to a maximum determined as the price of their alternative energy source (including the cost of physically switching to gas). This latter provision is effectively the monopoly price in any case as it is the maximum price that Sasol would have to offer in order to attract the individual buyer to switch to natural gas.

4.2.3.3.2   *Fertilizer cases*

The nitrogenous fertilizer value chain runs from ammonia through to the supply of blended fertilizer products (including other nutrients in addition to nitrogen) to farmers. Ammonia is typically produced from natural gas.[20] In South Africa it is produced by Sasol, approximately half as a by-product of the coal to liquid fuels production, and half from natural gas piped from Mozambique. The reaction of ammonia with nitric acid produces ammonium nitrate. This compound has two main uses – in fertilizers and explosives. In South Africa Sasol, Omnia and AECI produce ammonium nitrate. The main fertilizer derivative, limestone ammonium nitrate (LAN), is only manufactured by Sasol and Omnia. AECI concentrates on explosives and sold its fertilizer business, Kynoch, to the multinational fertilizer manufacturer, Yara, although it has subsequently been resold to local interests.

Following the Competition Board's decision to block the Sasol–AECI merger, AECI shut down its ammonia operations in 2000, including the production of LAN, and bought ammonia from Sasol instead. AECI retained its operations in explosives, with which there were strong linkages to mining, but spun off the fertilizer activities. Sasol became the sole producer of ammonia and remains the only player in the market that is vertically integrated from ammonia to ammonium nitrate and derivative products such as LAN. The example of nitrogenous fertilizer illustrates how an entrenched position, in this case at the upper levels of the value chain, can lead to exclusion of smaller and "outsider" firms at lower levels of the supply chain, as well as the limited efficacy of competition law in addressing such a situation.

In terms of participation in the value chain, entry barriers are relatively low at the level of blending and supply of fertilizer, in terms of scale economies and the initial investments that were required. Firms can build a business involving a mix of advisory services (such as agronomists), and the manufacturing and supply of fertilizer in liquid and granular form, without necessarily being part of a large chemicals business. However, this level had been dominated by Sasol, Omnia, and Kynoch/Yara.

In the early 2000s two relatively small firms, Nutriflo and Profert, began to grow their businesses aggressively. Nutriflo was based in KwaZulu-Natal and focused on sugarcane farmers. Profert was a group of people who had worked in the major fertilizer companies. These companies bought the key nitrogen fertilizer components, principally LAN and ammonium nitrate solution (ANS), from Sasol (as Omnia self-supplied) and blended them in order to on-sell to farmers. Both laid complaints in 2002 and 2003 that they were being subjected to exploitative and exclusionary conduct on the part of Sasol, while Nutriflo also complained that there a cartel of Sasol, Omnia, and Yara was operating across a range of fertilizer products.

The Competition Commission's investigation identified Sasol abusing its dominant position upstream, together with cartel arrangements on the part of Sasol, Omnia, and Kynoch governing supply of fertilizer products to both South African and regional markets in the "Import Planning Committee," "Export Club," and "Nitrogen Balance Committee."[21] The competition cases, and the Competition Commission's analysis, indicated that ammonia is priced on an import parity basis by Sasol using a benchmark Ukraine price plus all related transport costs (including overland railage) to determine the price for Sasol's internal "sales" as well as sales to third parties such as Omnia. These arrangements meant simply that farmers in southern Africa have been paying substantially higher prices than farmers in Europe for locally made fertilizer, despite relatively low local costs and extensive government support over the years.

The cases highlight the links between the protection of a monopoly position and coordination by a small group of insider firms to exclude others and exploit buyers. Sasol was potentially subject to bargaining power on the part of buyers as it has few alternatives for its ammonia other than it being sold into fertilizer and explosives. Its ability to charge the full monopoly price ceiling (represented by inland import parity) depended on not being credibly threatened by buyers to withhold purchases by turning to downstream alternatives in the form of blended products (which could be more readily imported) or alternative types of fertilizer (such as urea). Buyers could also sponsor entry upstream, as such an entrant would require a sales base to justify the large capital investment. The arrangements with Omnia and Kynoch can be seen in this light. Omnia was vertically integrated and so did not offer its product to other blenders, but rather sold it to end-users (farmers). Kynoch (AECI having closed its ammonia facility) could import downstream fertilizer products on a large scale due to the size of its parent company. By tying both of these firms into a coordinated arrangement they were rewarded with collusive margins while at the same time paying Sasol the monopoly prices on upstream products.

In these circumstances competition is obviously not simply about removing the obstacles to entering and growing in a market. Nor is the enforcement of competition law necessarily a quick remedy. The Commission referred the cases in 2005 and 2006. After much litigation, they were due to be heard in 2010 when Sasol settled without an admission but with substantive remedies around non-discrimination and withdrawal from fertilizer distribution apart from close to their main production site. Interestingly, Omnia has subsequently invested in an expanded production facility for which it is seeking to import ammonia on a large scale.

4.2.3.4 Conclusions

The case of fuel and basic chemicals highlights the danger of equating competition with absence of constraints. The liberalization of restrictions may well mean consolidation under the largest firm, especially where it is able to leverage off its existing advantages.

Competition law has not been a very effective answer to the challenges of entrenched dominant firms. While the two planned large mergers by Sasol were blocked by the competition authorities, ultimately similar outcomes (consolidation under Sasol) were achieved in any case through industry shifts, restructuring, and Sasol securing gas as an additional feedstock. The fertilizer case demonstrates both how a firm such as Sasol can protect its powerful position and the exploitation of it, and at the same time the potential for smaller independent firms to be the drivers of change if they are not excluded.

Various reviews of South African economic policy (for example, Rodrik, 2006; OECD, 2010) have identified anti-competitive conduct and entrenched dominant firms as an important impediment to broader-based industrialization but have simply recommended a strengthened competition law. This ignores the wider set of tools and levers that exist in industrial policy and regulation. South Africa has failed to use such mechanisms to discipline the power of firms such as Sasol. It bears noting that both propylene and a substantial proportion of ammonia are produced as by-products of Sasol's liquid fuels operation which is still subject to regulation.

Admittedly, merger regulation by the competition authorities has prevented even greater dominance by Sasol over the South African, and southern African, economy. Sasol has also been penalized for participating in several cartels.[22] It is critical, however, to recognize that both merger regulation and cartel enforcement works on the premise that in the absence of such arrangements competitive outcomes will prevail. This is quite different from addressing unilateral market power. While the Competition Commission did reach a settlement of the abuse of dominance charges in ammonia and ammonium nitrate derivatives, with substantive undertakings and divestiture on the part of Sasol, this was without an admission or penalty and came at a time when the ending of the cartel arrangements in any case meant it was affected by changes on the part of other firms such as Omnia.

4.2.4 Competition law and corporate conduct in southern and east Africa

Most of the countries of southern and east Africa have established competition authorities.[23] These principally follow the continental European rather than the South African (or Anglo-Saxon) model. Comesa has also established a regional competition authority. I consider here what the approach should be for competition enforcement to foster industrial development with specific reference to examples from this broad region of Africa.

It is important to recognize at the outset the substantial extent to which companies in many industries are operating regionally, notwithstanding remaining barriers to trade. Aside from the ability to move goods around the region (albeit impeded by poor infrastructure and inefficient border controls), it is relatively easier for companies to migrate from one country to another in the same region, transferring business models and skills, than to another region, whether the companies' home base is in the region, or they are transnationals with home bases on another continent.

Companies are also able to coordinate across the region. At the same time, competitive discipline at a regional level can also be more effective in industries with scale economies than at a national level. However, the colonial and apartheid legacy is of a region divided up largely in the interests of resource exploitation, as is evident in a transport infrastructure not oriented to intraregional trade but by the need to move minerals from the hinterland to ports. This is a reminder that the decisions of companies and the nature of rivalry between them are shaped by this past and by industrial policies and infrastructure provision. Colonial borders are also not along the lines of natural markets.

I highlight several examples of the way apparently anti-competitive arrangements operate at a regional level, before reflecting on some implications for competition law and industrial policies.

- The major *beer* multinationals, led by SABMiller and Castel, appear to have effectively allocated countries amongst themselves (see Jenny, 2009). Referring to the relationship between SABMiller and Castel:

  "This agreement enabled us to develop opportunities," justified, Najil Fairbass,[24] SABMiller Communications Director. Before adding: "There may be antitrust laws at the national level, but none covering the continent. I don't see what the problem is."

  (Philipp. Perdrix Le marché de la bière africaine monte en pression Jeune Afrique 10/09/2008, cited in Jenny, 2009).

  Indeed, SABMiller enforced an agreement restricting competition in East Africa with Diageo in a London court.[25]
- According to the settlements in the South Africa *cement* cartel investigation of PPC, Lafarge and Afrisam (formerly Holcim-) after the end of the legal South African cartel in 1996 the cement producers agreed to

specific market shares for the SACU region and effectively divided markets by geographic area.[26]

- Similarly, the subsidiaries of two main South African *construction* companies that make cast concrete products such as pipes, culverts, and railway sleepers effectively allocated the countries to one or other of them, as far as East Africa. South African construction companies have also been found to have been engaged in extensive rigging of construction contracts.[27] Cartels have also been identified in South Africa in several other infrastructure inputs such as steel rebar and wire mesh and it is likely that there were arrangements across the region.

- The *fertilizer* cartel of Omnia, Yara and Sasol also operated across the region, via an "Export Club," alongside the "Nitrogen Balance Committee." These companies sold overland, supplying into countries such as Zambia and Malawi.

In contrast, there are several examples which illustrate that market entrants are most likely to be those with existing capabilities, such as firms in the region or in related areas, including upstream or downstream activities.

The main entrant that challenged the *poultry* duopoly in South Africa has its origins in Zimbabwe, and expanded to Zambia and Botswana, establishing a capabilities and business base that enabled it to challenge in South Africa from the mid-2000s.[28]

Similarly an entrant into the steel industry, just downstream from primary steel manufacture in a rolling mill and processing operation, is an offshoot of an East African business with operations spreading across the region. However, in contrast, the dominant producer in South Africa, ArcelorMittal, acquired a steel mill in Mozambique which it subsequently closed down, and has been involved in bidding for Zimbabwe's producer, Zisco. As discussed above, by ensuring it controls access to the major exploited gas reserve in Mozambique, Sasol has prevented a potential rival emerging using this as a feedstock.

In industries with significant scale economies, such as many of those involved in processing natural resources, there is greater scope for competitive rivalry across the region. This points to the linkages between the integration of regional markets, provisions governing access to mineral inputs, the provision of development finance, and industrial policies. For example, lack of coordinated action in telecommunications means that roaming charges are kept at extremely high levels, and prices in some countries are greatly in excess of others.

4.2.5 Concluding reflections

Competition laws can play an important part in the economic development of African countries. Whether they do or not, depends on several important considerations, as is highlighted by the South African experience.

First, competition regimes are part of the framework of regulating business conduct, especially of large corporations. This framework shapes the norms of business conduct, including formal rules and informal conventions and values. Industrial policy is closely related and should be complementary, if it is understood as the incentive regime to deliberately influence businesses to build capabilities and prioritize longer-term investments over short-term rent seeking. The South African case study illustrates a failing to understand the linked roles of competition law and industrial policy in addressing the behavior of large companies. Instead, such companies have been able to retain their historic positions and the rents earned from them by adopting strategies that undermine potential rivals.

Second, the competition regime cannot be limited to the assumption that, in the absence of cartels and by preventing horizontal mergers, competitive outcomes will be realized. Markets in developing countries are small, while economies of scale and scope along with network effects and learning-by-doing are all important. This means that it is the interactions and decisions of a small number of large firms, likely vertically integrated, which will determine the development of whole sectors. In short, the nature of competitive rivalry is crucial to the industrial development path, as illustrated by the examples above. I am not arguing that this should all be loaded onto the plate of the competition authorities. But, if the issues are not framed in these terms, the ability to have a positive influence on the decisions of the corporations will be severely limited, as in the example of South Africa.

Third, the choice of model for the competition regime is important. Those that place greater emphasis on fair competition, in terms of outcomes rather than the number of competitors, and on the ability of smaller firms and potential entrants to be effective competitors where scale economies are not overwhelming, are more appropriate. The examples of Germany and South Korea are more appropriate than the Anglo-Saxon models, such as the USA. This is not simply about the law, especially if the law is cast in broad terms. Rather it is about the location of the authority within the wider policy framework, and the prominence and autonomy it is accorded.

Fourth, the type of regime also depends on the institutional capabilities. For some countries it makes little sense to establish a competition regime when the skills and expertise are better placed in government departments responsible for developing appropriate regulations. While South African lawyers and consultants (many already being part of international groups) may be licking their lips at the prospect of the opportunities that protracted litigation of competition cases may open up across the continent, they are likely to be the greatest beneficiaries, rather than consumers or industrial development, if regimes are simply transplanted.

Fifth, what about the likelihood that in countries with relatively low levels of development and with concentrated economic interests the competition authority will simply be undermined? This applies to any policy to discipline large business interests. It therefore misses the point, as what needs to be understood is not whether there will be such pressure but, as with corruption (see Khan, 2006), how the pressures are mediated. In this regard, the competition authority can be an important forum for business to account for short-term rent protection as against longer-term investment. Competition authorities are acknowledged to require strong powers to obtain information from firms. Indeed, arguably this has been one of the greatest benefits of competition law in South Africa – the light that is shed on industries through cases. It is important that matters are addressed transparently such that they can be reported in the press, while specific information is kept confidential. This should not be conflated with de jure independence which can in any case be undermined such as through the allocation of funding. Rather, it is about how the institutions establish autonomy, and a following from constituencies that support their work, including sections of the elite, to ensure their work remains impersonal.[29] Transplanting institutional models from western economies is also not an answer.[30]

Sixth, the information and analysis of industries and firm behavior should not necessarily be matched with the powers to address the conduct. It may be the case that regulatory provisions and industrial policies are more appropriate to discipline the firms. In considering the respective roles of the competition regime, industrial policy, and regulatory bodies what must be avoided is drawing false boundaries and oppositions that then generate misleading answers. For example, the South African fuel and chemicals firms are subject to a range of regulatory provisions, while also being investigated under the competition law. The starting point must be to understand the role of large firms, the influences on their decisions in terms of a longer-term orientation over short-term rent seeking, and how their power over the political process can be mediated.

Lastly, the work of competition authorities in countries such as Kenya, Tanzania, and Zambia, as well as more recently in Botswana and Namibia, point to the potential for building popular support and embedding these institutions. Kenya and Zambia have also both passed laws strengthening the powers of the institutions in recent years. Comparisons across the region provide useful benchmarks. For example, Tanzania has addressed exclusionary conduct by the local subsidiary of SABMiller, similar to that which the South African Competition Commission has failed to tackle.[31] The South African experience, however, demonstrates the way in which uncovering cartels, especially in basic consumer goods such as bread, can raise the public recognition of such institutions. The internationalized nature of businesses operating across the region must also be recognized. This is a challenge to the work of competition authorities, including the newly established Comesa authority. This is equally true for industrial policy where, for example, South African industrial policy must pay attention to the dynamics of regional industrialization.

Notes

1. This chapter is written in a personal capacity and does not represent the view of the Competition Commission South Africa. I have acted as an economic expert in several of the cases discussed here.
2. The International Competition Network had 117 member agencies in 103 jurisdictions by 2011. As of 2011 24 African countries had competition laws.
3. It has also been strongly encouraged by the International Competition Network, which grew out of the USA's ICPAC initiative after the negotiations to include competition under the WTO broke down (Souty, 2011).
4. Such diversity has been welcomed by economists from different schools of thought (Evans, 2009; Christiansen and Kerber, 2006; Budzinski, 2008).
5. As in South Africa (Department of Finance, 1996).
6. Sometimes the wider set of policies is subsumed within a catch-all "competition policy" category, but it is unclear what is and is not included. I focus on competition law and the competition regime (including the institutions and their rules and workings).
7. Draws from Roberts (2010).
8. In developing countries these are also mainly in mature industries, not ones characterized by high levels of innovation. Scherer (2008) also points to the lack of evidence in the USA that antitrust enforcement has had an adverse impact on investment in innovation.
9. For a strong critique of the vigorous promotion of competition law for developing countries without regard to the political and institutional realities see Rodriguez and Menon (2010).
10. From 1998 to 2007, the KFTC made 303 findings of illegal cartel conduct, 48 findings of abuse of market dominance, and 1938 findings of unfair business transactions including subcontracting arrangements (KFTC, 2011).
11. Intermediate mergers are decided by the Commission, appealable to the Tribunal.
12. However, the 2012 Constitutional Court judgment in the *Senwes* case found that the Tribunal does have considerable scope to determine its own process and the evidence it requires to make a decision (Case CCT 61/11 [2012] ZACC 6).
13. The Telkom decision by the Tribunal is under appeal to the Supreme Court of Appeal.
14. There are possible remedies, still to be determined by the Tribunal.
15. This had previously been used to route oil into the strategic stock reserves in disused coal mines in Mpumalanga province.
16. The Other Oil Companies also attained their goal of having single branded petrol stations.
17. See: Windfall Tax Report (National Treasury, 2007); Competition Tribunal (2006).
18. Para. 146 of the Competition Board's decision.
19. These included AECI shutting down its ammonia operations in 2000, for which it was allegedly paid by Sasol, and entered into long-term supply arrangements with Sasol instead.
20. Ammonia is a gas at room temperature and is usually transported and stored in chilled liquid form in refrigerated and pressurized tanks and ships. The handling and storage of ammonia is capital intensive, as it needs to be stored at minus 33 degrees centigrade.
21. This section is based on cases referred to the Competition Tribunal by the Commission. The consent and settlement agreement between the Competition

Commission and Sasol Chemical Industries Ltd relating to the cartel conduct was confirmed by the Competition Tribunal in June 2009 and Sasol paid a penalty of R250.7mn. The consent and settlement agreement relating to the abuse of dominance by Sasol was confirmed by the Tribunal on 20 July 2010. Sasol agreed to divest all but one of its blending plants and made commitments regarding non-discriminatory pricing. There was no penalty or admission.

22. Sasol has paid penalties for collusion in fertilizer, phosphoric acid and polypropylene.
23. There are now authorities in South Africa, Swaziland, Botswana, Namibia, Zambia, Kenya, Tanzania, Rwanda, Mauritius.
24. This appears to be a misspelling of Nigel Fairbrass.
25. EABL's attempt to acquire Serengeti Breweries, the rival in Tanzania, was blocked by a London high court injunction on August 18, 2009 (see Press Statement, August 18, 2009. Available online atwww.sabmiller.com).
26. See confirmation of settlements between the Competition Commission and Afrisam and Lafarge. Available online at www.comptrib.co.za.
27. Competition Commission Annual Reports, 2010, 2011, 2012.
28. The firm, Country Bird, brought a complaint of exclusionary abuse of dominance, referred by the Competition Commission in 2008 (press release on poultry referral. Available online at www.compcom.co.za).
29. In this regard, it is interesting to note that the popular pressure for stronger legal provisions in South Korea came in response to companies exploitation of control over the "three powders," cement, flour, and sugar (KFTC, 2011), while in the USA the pressure to address the power of the trusts, that led to the Sherman Act, came largely from farmers (Acemoglu and Robinson, 2012).
30. As Mkandawire (2010) has characterized it, drawing from Evans, "monocropping" and "monotasking."
31. Fair Competition Commission of Tanzania (2010).

References

Acemoglu, D. and J. Robinson (2012), *Why Nations Fail* (New York: Random House).

African National Congress (ANC) (1994) *The Reconstruction and Development Programme: A Policy Framework* (Johannesburg: Umanyano Publications).

Amsden, A. (1989) *Asia's Next Giant* (Oxford: Oxford University Press).

Amsden, A. (1997) "Editorial: Bringing Production Back In – Understanding Government's Economic Role in Late Industrialization," *World Development*, vol. 25, no. 4, pp. 469–480.

Amsden, A. and Singh, A. (1994) "The Optimal Degree of Competition and Dynamic Efficiency in Japan and Korea," *European Economic Review*, vol. 38, nos 3/4, pp. 940–951.

Brusick, P and Evenett, S. (2008) "Should Developing Countries Worry About Abuse of Dominant Power?," *Wisconsin Law Review*, vol. 2, pp. 269–294.

Budzinksi, O. (2008) "Monoculture Versus Diversity in Competition Economics," *Cambridge Journal of Economics*, vol. 32, pp. 295–324.

Chabane, N, Goldstein, A., and Roberts, S. (2006) "The Changing Face and Strategies of Big Business in South Africa: Ten Years of Political Democracy," *Industrial & Corporate Change*, vol. 15, pp. 549–578.

Chandler, A. Jr. (1990) *Scale and Scope: The Dynamics of Industrial Capitalism* (Cambridge, MA: Harvard University Press).

Chandler, A. Jr., Amatori, F., and Hikino, T. (eds) (1997) *Big Business and the Wealth of Nations* (Cambridge: Cambridge University Press).

Chandler, A. Jr., P. Hagström, and Ö. Sörvell (eds.) (1998) *The Dynamic Firm* (Oxford: Oxford University Press).

Chang, H.-J. (1996) *The Political Economy of Industrial Policy* (London and Basingstoke: Macmillan).

Christiansen, A. and W. Kerber (2006) "Competition Policy with Optimally Differentiated Rules Instead of 'per se Rules vs. Rules of Reason'," *Journal of Competition Law and Economics*, vol. 2, no. 2, pp. 215–244.

Competition Board (1998) *Investigation into the Transaction between Sasol and AECI Limited and Annexures*, Report No.68. (Pretoria: Competition Board).

Competition Commission and Competition Tribunal South Africa (2009) *Unleashing Rivalry – Ten Years of Enforcement by the South African Competition Authorities 1999–2009*. Pretoria. Available online at www.comptrib.co.za.

Competition Tribunal (2006) *Decision in Sasol–Engen Merger*, case 101/LM/Dec04.

Corbett, C., das Nair, R., and Roberts, S. (2011) "Bargaining Power and Market Definition: a Reflection on Two Mergers," *Journal of Economic and Financial Sciences*, vol. 4, pp. 147–166.

Dabbah, M. (2010) "Competition Policy, Abusive Dominance and Economic Development: Some Reflections," presented at 37th Annual Conference on International Antitrust Law and Policy, Fordham Competition Law Institute, New York, September 24.

Das Nair, R. and L. Mncube (2012) "The Role of Information Exchange in Facilitating Collusion – Insights from Selected Cases," in K. Moodaliyar and S. Roberts (eds), *The Development of Competition Law and Economics in South Africa0* (Pretoria: HSRC Press).

Department of Finance (1996) *Growth, Employment and Redistribution – A Macroeconomic Strategy* (Pretoria: Government Printers).

Department of Trade and Industry (2007) *Implementation of Government's National Industrial Policy Framework: Industrial Policy Action Plan*, August 2007. Available online at www.thedti.gov.za (downloaded September 2, 2012).

Department of Trade and Industry (2010) *Industrial Policy Action Plan (IPAP) 2012/12–2014/15* (Pretoria: Department of Trade and Industry).

Dobreva, R., Makrelov, K., May, C., and Mohamed, G. (2005) "A Case Study of the Impact of Competition Law and Policy on South Africa's Investment Climate and Competitiveness: the Industrial Chemicals sector," report for World Bank/DTI review of Competition Law in South Africa.

Evenett, S. and Brooks, D. (2005) *Competition Policy and Development in Asia* (London: Palgrave Macmillan).

Evans, D. (2009) "Why Different Jurisdictions Do Not (and Should Not) Adopt the Same Antitrust Rules," *Chicago Journal of International Law*, vol. 10, no. 1, pp. 161–188.

Fair Competition Commission of Tanzania (2010) *Decision of the Commission in the complaint between Serengeti Breweries Ltd and Tanzania Breweries Ltd*, Complaint No 2 of 2009.

Fine, B. and Rustomjee, Z. (1996) *The Political Economy of South Africa- from Minerals-Energy Complex to Industrialisation* (London: Hurst).

Fingleton, J. and Nikpay, A. (2009) "Stimulating or Chilling Competition," in B. Hawk (ed.), *International Antitrust Law & Policy: Fordham Competition Law 2008* (New York: Juris).

Fox, E. (2002) "What is Harm to Competition? Exclusionary Practices and Anticompetitive Effect," *Antitrust Law Journal*, vol. 70, pp. 372–411.

Fox, E. (2003) "We Protect Competition, You Protect Competitors," *World Competition*, vol. 26, no. 2, pp. 149–165.

Fox, E (2008) "The Efficiency Paradox," in R Pitofsky (ed.), *How the Chicago School Overshot the Mark: The Effect of Conservative Economic Analysis on US Antitrust* (Oxford: Oxford University Press).

Fox, E. (2011) "In Search of a Competition Law Fit for Developing Countries," 5–10 *NYU Law & Econ. Research Paper Series*, Working Paper No. 11-04.

Gal, M. (2003) *Competition Policy for Small Market Economies* (Boston, MA: Harvard University Press).

Gal, M. (2009) "Antitrust in a Globalised Economy: The Unique Enforcement Challenges Faced by Small and Developing Jurisdictions," *Fordham International Law Journal*, vol. 33, no. 1, pp. 1–56.

Helmsing, A.H.J. (2001) "Externalities, Learning and Governance: New Perspectives on Local Economic Development," *Development and Change*, vol. 32, pp. 277–308.

Hoekman, B. (1998) "Competition Policy in the Context of Economy-Wide Reform," paper presented at TIPS Annual Forum 1998.

Hur, J.S. (2004) "The Evolution of Competition Policy and Its Impact on Economic Development in Korea," in P. Brusick, A.M. Alvarez, L. Cernat, and P. Holmes (eds), *Competition, Competitiveness and Development: Lessons from Developing Countries* (Geneva: United Nations Conference on Trade and Development).

International Competition Network (ICN) (2011) "The ICN's Vision for its Second Decade," presented at the 10th Annual Conference of the ICN, May 17–20.

Jenny, F. (2009) "Competition Enforcement in Testing Times: Beyond the National Level," presented at Competition Principles Under Threat, IDRC Pre-ICN Forum on Competition and Development, Zurich, Switzerland, June 2. Downloaded from www.idrc.ca/uploads/user-S/1244752374/Frederic_Jenny.ppt.

Kaplinsky, R. (2000) "Globalisation and Unequalisation: What Can Be Learned from Value Chain Analysis?," *Journal of Development Studies*, vol. 37, no. 2, pp. 117–146.

Khan, M. (2006) "Corruption and Governance," in K.S. Jomo and B. Fine (eds), *The New Development Economics* (London: Zed Press and New Delhi: Tulika).

Korea Fair Trade Commission (KFTC) (2011) *Annual Report 2011 Special Edition 30 Years of KFTC, Looking Back, Moving Forwards* (Seoul: KFTC).

Laffont, J. (1998) "Competition, Information, and Development," *Annual World Bank Conference on Development Economics 1998* (Washington, DC: World Bank), pp. 237–269.

Lall, S. and M Teubal (1998) "'Market-Stimulating' Technology Policies in Developing Countries: A Framework with Examples from East Asia," *World Development*, vol. 26, no. 8, pp. 1369–1385.

Lin, J. and Chang, H.-J. (2009) "Should Industrial Policy in Developing Countries Conform to Comparative Advantage of Defy It? – A Debate between Justin Lin and Ha-Joon Chang," *Development Policy Review*, vol. 27, no. 5, pp. 483–502.

Machaka, J and Roberts, S. (2003) "The DTI's New 'Integrated Manufacturing Strategy'. Comparative Industrial Performance, Linkages and Technology," *South African Journal of Economics*, vol. 71, no. 4, pp. 679–704.

Makhaya, G., Mkwananzi, W., and Roberts, S. (2012) "How Should Young Institutions Approach Enforcement? Reflections on South Africa's Experience," *South African Journal of International Affairs*, vol. 19, no. 1, pp. 43–64.

Makhaya, G. and Roberts, S. (2012) "The Changing Strategies of Large Corporations in South Africa Under Democracy and the Role of Competition Law," mimeo, report for the Agence Française de Développement (AFD).

Mateus, A. (2010) "Competition and Development: Towards an Institutional Foundation for Competition Enforcement," *World Competition*, vol. 33, no. 2, pp. 275–300.

Mkandawire, T. (2010) "From Maladjusted States to Democratic Developmental States in Africa," in O. Edigheji (ed.), *Constructing a Democratic Developmental State in South Africa: Potentials and Challenges* (Pretoria: HSRC Press).

National Treasury (Windfall Task Team) (2007) "Possible Reforms to the Fiscal Regime Applicable to Windfall Profits in South Africa's Liquid Fuel Energy Sector, with Particular Reference to the Synthetic Fuel Industry," report for National Treasury, February 9.

North, D.C., Wallis, J.J., and Weingast, B. (2009) *Violence and Social Orders* (Cambridge: Cambridge University Press).

OECD (2010) *Economic Survey of South Africa 2010* (Paris: OECD).

Penrose, E. (1995) *The Theory of the Growth of the Firm*, 3rd edn (Oxford and New York: Oxford University Press).

Possas, M. and Borges, H. (2009) "Competition Policy and Industrial Development," in M. Cimoli, G. Dosi, and J. Stiglitz (eds), *Industrial Policy and Development* (Oxford: Oxford University Press).

Republic of South Africa (1998) "Competition Act, No. 89," *Government Gazette*, vol. 400, no. 19412.

Rey, P. and Tirole, J. (2006) "A Primer on Foreclosure," in M. Armstrong and R.H. Porter (eds), *Handbook of Industrial Organization III*, (Amsterdam: North-Holland).

Roberts, S. (2000) "The Internationalisation of Production, Government Policy and Industrial Development in South Africa," unpublished PhD thesis, University of London.

Roberts, S. (2004) "The Role for Competition Policy in Economic Development: the South African Experience," *Development Southern Africa*, vol. 21, no. 1, pp. 227–243.

Roberts, S. (2010) "Competition Policy, Competitive Rivalry and a Developmental State in South Africa," in O. Edigheji (ed.), *Constructing a Democratic Developmental State in South Africa: Potentials and Challenges* (Pretoria: HSRC Press).

Roberts, S. (2012) "Administrability and Business Certainty in Abuse of Dominance Enforcement: an Economist's Review of the South African Record," *World Competition*, vol. 35, no. 2, pp. 269–296.

Roberts, S. and Rustomjee, Z. (2009) "Industrial Policy Under Democracy: Apartheid's Grown-up Infant Industries? Iscor and Sasol," *Transformation*, vol. 71, pp. 50–75.

Rodrik, D. (1995) "Getting Interventions Right: How South Korea and Taiwan Grew Rich," *Economic Policy*, vol. 20, pp. 53–108.

Rodrik, D. (2006) "Understanding South Africa's Economic Puzzles," CID Working Paper No.130, Harvard University.

Rodriguez, A. and Menon, A. (2010) *The Limits of Competition Policy: Shortcomings of Antitrust in Developing and Reforming Economies* (The Hague: Kluwer Law International).

Rodriguez, A.E. and Williams, M. (1998) "Recent Decisions by the Venezuelan and Peruvian Agencies: Lessons for the Export of Antitrust," *The Antitrust Bulletin*, vol. 43 (spring), pp. 147–178.

Rustomjee, Z. (2012) Witness Statement in *Competition Commission v Sasol Chemical Industries*.

Sakakibara, M. and Porter, M.E. (2001) "Competing at Home to Win Abroad: Evidence from Japanese Industry," *Review of Economics and Statistics*, vol. 83, no. 2, pp. 310–322.

Sanekata, K. and S. Wilks (1996) "The Fair Trade Commission and the Enforcement of Competition Policy in Japan," in G.B. Doern and S. Wilks (eds), *Comparative Competition Policy – National Institutions in a Global Market* (Oxford: Clarendon Press).

Scherer, F.M. (2008) "Conservative Economics and Antitrust: A Variety of Influences," in R Pitofsky (ed.), *How the Chicago School Overshot the Mark – The Effect of Conservative Economic Analysis on US Antitrust* (Oxford: Oxford University Press).

Singh, A. (2004) "Multi-lateral Competition Policy and Economic Development," UNCTAD Series on Issues in Competition Law and Policy (Geneva: United Nations).

Souty, F. (2011) "From the Halls of Geneva to the Shores of the Low Countries: the Origins of the International Competition Network," in P. Lugard (ed.), *The International Competition Network at Ten – Origins, Accomplishments and Aspirations* (Cambridge: Intersentia).

Stevens, D. (1995) "Framing Competition Law Within an Emerging Economy: the Case of Brazil," *The Antitrust Bulletin*, vol. 40, no.4, pp. 929–971.

Stiglitz, J. (1998) "More instruments and Broader Goals: Moving Towards the post-Washington Consensus," 1998 WIDER Annual Lecture, Helsinki.

Teece, D.J. and Pisano, G. (1998) "The Dynamic Capabilities of Firms: An Introduction," in Dosi, G., D.J. Teece and J. Chytry (eds.) *Technology, Organization, and Competitiveness – Perspectives on Industrial and Corporate Change* (Oxford: Oxford University Press).

Vickers, J. (2007) "Competition Law and Economics: a Mid-Atlantic Viewpoint," *European Competition Journal*, vol. 3, pp. 1–15.

Wade, R. (1990). *Governing the Market: Economic Theory and the Role of Government in East Asian Industrialisation* (Princeton, NJ: Princeton University Press).

Wise, M. (2000) "The Role of Competition Policy in Regulatory Reform – Review of Competition Law and Policy in Korea," *OECD Journal of Competition Law and Policy*, 3, no. 2, pp. 128–180.

World Bank/OECD (1999) *A Framework for the Design and Implementation of Competition Law and Policy* (Washington, DC: World Bank).

References to South African cases

Competition Commission v *Senwes Ltd*, Tribunal case 110/CR/Dec06

Competition Commission v *Senwes Ltd*, Constitutional Court case CCT 61/11 [2012] ZACC 6

Competition Commission v *South African Airways* Tribunal case 18/CR/Mar01

Competition Commission v *Telkom SA Ltd* Tribunal case 11/CR/Feb04

Nationwide Airlines (Pty) Ltd v *South African Airways (Pty) Ltd* Tribunal case 80/CR/Sep06

Competition Commission v *Patensie Sitrus Beherend Beperk* Tribunal case

Nationwide Poles cc v *Sasol Oil (Pty) Ltd*, Tribunal case 72/CR/Dec03

Sasol Oil (Pty) Ltd v *Nationwide Poles cc* Competition Appeal Court Case 49CACApril05

Netstar (Pty) Ltd and other v *Competition Commission and other*, Competition Appeal Court Cases 97/CAC/May10, 98/CAC/May10, 99/CAC/May10

4.3
Political Settlements and the Design of Technology Policy

Mushtaq H. Khan
SOAS, University of London

Technology policies have a dual character. They are technical instruments for addressing important contracting failures affecting technology acquisition *and at the same time* they are interventions that inevitably create new sources of incomes or rents. These two aspects of technology policies are closely related because the intensity and effectiveness of the rent-seeking strategies of different organizations can explain why particular technology policies are effective or ineffective. One of the puzzles in global comparisons of the performance of technology policies is that policies that worked well in one context fared less well in others, and policies with apparently inferior design characteristics worked better in some contexts compared to policies that were more straightforward. We can make sense of these paradoxes by examining the policies in question in the context of the organizations affected by the policy. The "political settlement" is our shorthand for describing the distribution of bargaining power and technical capabilities across the relevant organizations in that society. A specific technology policy generates rents across different organizations and requires these rents to be allocated and managed in particular ways to achieve the desired outcomes. The political settlement describing the relative power of different organizations can therefore help to explain why the outcomes of similar policies can vary significantly across contexts. This analysis can also help to design better policies in countries in Africa and Asia that have had mixed experiences with technology policies in the past.

In their role as technical instruments, technology policies (or industrial policies) address contracting failures constraining the adoption and learning of new technologies. A variety of factors can prevent investors, financiers, technology providers, and firms from privately contracting to transfer new technologies to developing countries. Clearly, the first requirement for a successful technology policy is that the policy should address the specific problem affecting technology acquisition in a country or sector at that time. As there are potentially a number of quite different contracting failures that could affect technology adoption, a policy designed to solve one type of problem may be inappropriate for another. Technology policy can therefore fail if its design does not address the most important problems that are actually constraining technology adoption in that context.

However, even if the policy was technically appropriate it could still fail if it was not effectively implemented and managed. The problem of implementation has been widely recognized, but the problem has been usually explained in terms of a broad binary distinction between the capacities of effective (developmental) states and other ineffective types of states. A common conclusion is that a country without a developmental state should not attempt industrial policy, or it should first construct the relevant aspects of a developmental state. Technology policies clearly played an important role in the East Asian success stories of the 1960s and 1970s and yet similar policies achieved less impressive results in many other developing countries. The differences in outcomes can be linked to differences in the degree to which subsidies and support were linked to the achievement of outcomes, with corresponding penalties for non-performance. The East Asian countries undoubtedly had effective developmental states that could discipline subsidy recipients and enforce performance conditions while providing support for technology adoption (Amsden, 1989; World Bank, 1993; Chang, 1994). The problem is that the construction of significant aspects of a similar developmental state is not a feasible goal for most developing countries. If industrial policy requires such a state, and if East Asian technology policies were the only ones that could accelerate technology adoption, most developing countries should indeed refrain from attempting such policies. This is the conclusion of many economists who do not reject the evidence of successful industrial policies in East Asia but who nevertheless believe that such policies may have a negative effect in most other developing countries.

Fortunately, this conclusion may be too pessimistic. To see why, we need to look at the other aspect of industrial policy: its link with rent generation and "rent-seeking" strategies. The organizations benefiting from technology policy rents can be expected to attempt to capture and protect the streams of income associated with these interventions. However, societies have different configurations of power and capabilities across their economic, political and bureaucratic organizations. As organizations try to capture and protect the rents associated with particular policies, the feasibility of enforcing the conditions that are most likely to yield good results for that policy can vary widely across societies as the relative power of the relevant organizations is different. Thus, the results achieved will depend on the "fit" between the particular policy (and specifically the rent allocation and management that it requires) and the organizational configuration in which it is placed. The "developmental state" describes a particular configuration of power between political, bureaucratic and economic organizations (a particular political settlement) and this allowed the enforcement of a range of ambitious industrial policy instruments. In South Korea in particular, significant rents were allocated to large firms across a number of sectors with performance conditions that were credible. Non-performance resulted not only in changes in the relevant policies and the withdrawal of the rents that were not working, but on occasion involved the re-allocation of entire plants to new managements and ownership.

However, countries like India, Bangladesh, Thailand and Malaysia had different configurations of organizational power and capabilities that were significantly different from the East Asian developmental states (as well as being different from each other). Ambitious industrial policies were also tried in these countries but generally produced less dramatic results. Yet these countries also had other variants of industrial policies at different times that were sometimes quite successful in accelerating technology acquisition in particular sectors (Khan, 2000b; Khan and Blankenburg, 2009; Khan, 2013). Different policies were successful because each policy created a different configuration of rents and had different requirements of rent allocation and management. Some policies were therefore more likely to be effective in creating the required combination of incentives and compulsions for technology acquisition given the different configuration of organizational power in each country. From a policy point of view, this means that the design of an effective industrial policy has to take into account not just the technical question of the specific contracting failures that have to be addressed. It also has to account for the specific "political settlement" in the country because only interventions whose success depends on rents being allocated and managed in ways that are feasible in that context are likely to achieve desirable outcomes. Section 4.3.1 discusses the most important contracting failures that technology policies have to address. Section 4.3.2 locates the problem of policy design in the context of specific political settlements and the rent-seeking strategies of organizations. Section 4.3.3 deals with a particular contracting failure that needs to be addressed to ensure that success of technology acquisition in developing countries: the problem of developing organizational capabilities for using new technologies in competitive ways. Section 4.3.3 develops an analytical framework showing how effective technology policy design has to take into account the non-linear relationships of policy variables with the political settlement. The approach is able to explain the variable success of technology policies across countries and suggests a methodology for policy design in developing countries.

4.3.1   Technology policy and contracting failures

Developing countries face significant constraints and contracting problems that can prevent them from adopting existing technologies. These contracting failures are often the primary impediment to development. Technology policies refer to policies that attempt to overcome or bypass the important contracting failures that may be preventing private parties from contracting to adopt and learn new technologies. Contracting failures occur because technology adoption is subject to a number of externalities and principal–agent problems and private contracting may be unable to overcome these problems, particularly in the governance contexts of developing countries (Khan, 2013). These problems include the externality problems affecting investments in workforce skills, externalities facing technology providers bringing new technologies to developing countries when these technologies still enjoy technology rents, externalities facing first movers investing in sectors that may turn out to be competitive, a variety of coordination problems affecting investments across sectors and the principal–agent problems facing investors who want to ensure high levels of effort when they finance learning-by-doing processes. If private contracting fails to find appropriate solutions to these and other problems, policy interventions are required. But policy can only be effective if it targets a relevant problem and targets it adequately. As each problem is different, interventions that are appropriate for solving one type of problem will not work if the underlying problem was a different one.

The importance of designing policy responses so that they address the most important contracting failure is discussed in Khan (2013). Developing countries have used a variety of mechanisms to accelerate technology acquisition, including the protection of domestic markets for infant industries, subsidizing technology acquisition through a variety of implicit and explicit subsidies like subsidies on the cost of credit, export subsidies and tax breaks on investments in new machinery. Each of these instruments provides different types of rents which are associated with solutions to specific contracting failures. However, the actual underlying contracting failure will determine the conditions that need to be established for different stakeholders if desirable results are to be achieved. For instance, if positive externalities were preventing adequate investments in training, subsidies to firms would have to come with arrangements for monitoring the quality of training, and the terms of the rent allocation would have to include credible withdrawal and penalty arrangements if the training was poor (Dosi, 1988; Khan, 2000a). A very different technology problem emerges if external technology providers feel their technology rents are threatened by illegal imitation. If this slows down the inflow of technologies into the country, the appropriate policy response may be to protect the rents of technology owners through patents or to provide them with compensating rents in the form of incentives or licensing fees. In each case a different set of conditions need to be established on the relevant rents. For instance, if incentives are provided to technology providers, the quality and type of technologies they transfer have to be monitored, including the pace of subcontracting to domestic producers. In the case of patents, regulatory agencies have to have the capability to enforce these restrictions but also to negotiate the time period of patent protection for each sector to maximize the net benefit for that society (Hoekman et al., 2004). In reality, patent protection terms are often determined by more advanced countries and these terms do not necessarily protect the interests of developing countries (Khan, 2000a; Stiglitz, 2007).

The first-mover problem refers to the possibility that the first investors in a sector may discover that the country has a comparative advantage in that sector but may fail to capture sufficient benefits themselves to justify the costs and risks of their investments in discovery (Hausmann and Rodrik, 2003). The discovery of new business opportunities obviously has positive externalities for the country but the initial investors may not be able to capture much of this. Moreover, subsequent entry into the sector can actually reduce their profits by raising wages and input costs. Unlike new innovations, discovery cannot be patented, and therefore the solution to this contracting failure may require temporary subsidies that encourage trials in new sectors. These rents need their own set of effective conditions: they have to be available for short periods, no longer than is needed to set up the trials and discover the presence or absence of comparative advantage in that sector. For this contracting failure, it is critical for the relevant agencies to have the capacity to withdraw rents after fixed periods and in any case to desist from continuing to support experiments that are clearly not going to produce competitive industries.

Coordination of investments may be important because of both demand and supply side complementarities. High transaction costs, information asymmetries and the possibility of opportunistic behavior by second movers may preclude private contracting solutions to solve coordination problems (Rosenstein-Rodan, 1943; Nurkse, 1953; Scitovsky, 1954; Williamson, 1985; Murphy et al., 1989). Public investments in coordination also provide rents to private providers but here a different set of conditions have to be enforced. Government agencies charged with the implementation of coordination policies are in a position to provide rents to firms in promoted clusters. The identification of the clusters to be supported and the complementary investments that private investors have to provide have to be agreed upon, monitored and enforced.

The solutions to all these contracting failures assume that a more fundamental contracting failure has been addressed. Developing countries typically find it difficult to absorb and use existing technologies even when their wages are low and they have sufficient workers with the appropriate formal skills. The missing factor is the *organizational capability* of the production team. Owners, managers, and supervisors do not know how to set up the factory, align the machinery, set up systems for quality control, reduce input wastage and product rejection, manage inventories, match order flows with production cycles, maintain after sales services and a host of other internal coordination and management issues that are essential for achieving competitiveness. As a result, the firm may be able to buy the machinery at international prices, employ the workers and managers at lower wages than the most competitive country, and yet be unable to achieve competitiveness. The development of organizational capabilities requires the acquisition of *tacit knowledge* through learning-by-doing. By definition, learning-by-doing requires opportunities for doing, and this requires periods of loss-financing when the firm produces but is unable to make a profit. This period of learning can help to raise organizational capabilities if the production team is also under pressure to continuously experiment with new internal organizational arrangements to raise productivity. Thus, the "doing" is necessary but does not guarantee learning, unless there is some compulsion on the owners, managers and supervisors to put in high levels of *effort* in the learning process (Khan, 2013).

In theory, sufficiently complex contingency contracts between the private parties involved could address these requirements, but their enforcement is not likely to be credible in the typical developing country. Essentially, financiers need to have credible ways of penalizing non-performance and extracting their capital if the project fails. Private contracting of this type typically does not emerge because financiers cannot credibly ensure that stakeholders within the firm will put in high levels of effort in learning and thereby assure returns on their investments. Technology policy can address this failure by co-financing or sharing the risks involved in the learning provided governance agencies have the appropriate enforcement capabilities to induce appropriate levels of learning effort. The necessary condition for rent allocation here is not just that a firm gets the rent that allows it to engage in learning-by-doing, but also that the conditions of rent withdrawal are clearly set out so that owners, managers, supervisors and others feel the compulsion to put in a high level of *effort* in the learning process. This problem usually cannot be solved by announcing the time period for support in advance. Unlike a trial that is supposed to *discover* comparative advantage (and reasonable time periods for trials can be pre-specified), here comparative advantage is being *created* through learning and the development of organizational capabilities. The creation of comparative advantage can take much longer and the time period may differ from country to country, sector to sector, and perhaps even firm to firm. More complex monitoring and incentives have to be created here to induce the right kinds of effort.

Given the different problems that technology policies may be required to solve, and the very different governance and institutional conditions that each requires, one reason why effective policies cannot have a standard design across countries is simply because they must address different problems and priorities. Without careful attention to identifying the major problems the country faces, and designing the rent monitoring and allocation conditions accordingly, a general policy of supporting infant industries can produce very variable outcomes. In some cases, the requisite conditions for solving the underlying problems could fortuitously be in place, and in others not. In some countries, famously the East Asian ones, ambitious technology policies that provided support simultaneously for many firms and sectors resulted in accelerated technology acquisition and development. In others, similar policies resulted in the proliferation of subsidies to protected industries that refused to grow up. Subsidies kept growing and could not be withdrawn despite the poor performance of the supported firms and sectors. Similarly, in some countries, development banks played a dynamic role, while in others they closed down because their low interest loans were not repaid and their bad debts escalated. In the less dynamic cases, consumers and taxpayers paid the price of these failing policies till they were finally abandoned.

The identification of the relevant contracting failure is the first stage of finding an effective solution to a technology acquisition problem. The second stage is to investigate whether a policy with the requisite characteristics can be enforced given the power and capabilities of the organizations affected. Here again there is a degree of openness, but now the openness can create opportunities as well as problems. On the one hand, obvious policy responses that worked in some other country may not be implementable because the configuration of power may be such that the policy would be excessively distorted by rent-seeking activities and desirable outcomes may not emerge. On the other hand, there are typically multiple solutions to the same problem and each solution implies a different allocation of rents and a somewhat different set of conditions for achieving desirable outcomes. This makes it more likely that an effective solution can be found despite differences in the political settlement. The problem of finding a solution to a contracting failure that is effective within a specific political settlement is a general problem that can affect solutions to any contracting failure. We illustrate the general problem with reference to a particular contracting failure: the problem of developing organizational capabilities through learning-by-doing. There is an additional merit in focusing on the learning-by-doing problem. Attempts to solve any of the other problems affecting technology acquisition are likely to fail if effective organizations that can competitively use the new technologies do not yet exist.

4.3.2 Political settlements and rents

Rents are defined as incomes higher than the minimum a person or organization would have accepted, the minimum usually being defined as the income in the next-best opportunity available to that individual or organization. According to this definition, policies that leave some individuals better off create rents for them. However, policies can also leave some individuals worse off, so that in effect they suffer *negative* rents, though this is not how these losses are usually described in the literature. Taxes for instance leave some individuals worse off, while the corresponding subsidies provide rents for others. Any policy intervention will change income flows and therefore every policy intervention creates rents, both positive as well as negative. In the simple story that is often told in textbooks, in the absence of government intervention a zero-rent general equilibrium is possible and serves as the benchmark for the analysis of rents. This is because if there were no restrictions on entry and exit and all contracts were voluntary, no factor would earn higher or lower returns in any activity than in any alternative activity available to that factor, and consequently no factor could earn a rent or suffer a "negative rent." If we ignore the critical question of where the property rights sustaining a general equilibrium came from, and if we ignore the equally critical question of how in the absence of any rents the information required for market operations can be discovered, we can claim that if such an outcome could be achieved by private contracting, we would also achieve an efficient allocation of resources. An efficient allocation of resources is simply one where re-allocation cannot enhance net social benefit and this would be the case if no factor was earning a higher or lower return anywhere else. Much of the analysis of rents and rent seeking has been hampered by this unnecessary and unrealistic benchmark. If we accept the general equilibrium benchmark, deviations from this benchmark generate rents *and* these deviations signal inefficiency.

In reality, as North (1990) and Stiglitz (1996) argue in different ways, the general equilibrium benchmark is not only unrealistic, it can be very misleading as a guide for policy-making. First, in the institutional economics that North introduced, the creation of property rights (for instance over free-access resources) creates rents for owners because these streams of property incomes did not exist earlier. Since the role of the state is transparent when property rights are newly created, new property rights are clearly the product of "intervention." The incremental income streams associated with them are therefore the product of intervention and appear as "rents." Indeed neoclassical textbooks occasionally describe the income streams that are created when open access natural resources become property as rents. Since the absence of property rights was associated with free access overuse, the creation of property rights and the associated rents are associated with improvements in net social benefits. In fact, free access can destroy the value of *any* asset, not just natural resources, so the incremental creation of property rights always creates new income streams (rents) and in many cases also enhances net social benefits. Paradoxically, once property rights have existed for some time, mainstream economics overlooks the role of the state in maintaining these property rights, and the income from property of all types is no longer seen as the product of "interventions" and therefore are no longer rents. The general equilibrium model extends this to the extreme case where property rights have been defined over all possible assets and all these rights are protected at no cost and without a state. Property ownership in itself is no longer perceived to have anything to do with the state and the returns from property ownership are therefore perceived to be quite different from rents that are now only created by interventions that prevent factors from being freely allocated.

In reality, property rights are always imperfectly developed because of the high costs of defining and protecting many rights. There are differences between advanced and developing countries because of differences in the capacities of their states, but the proposition is true in general for all countries. Partly for this reason and partly because of the high costs of contracting due to asymmetric information and other problems, contracting in incomplete markets is also incomplete. In the real world, we are never in general equilibrium and a wide variety of rents exist, some of them associated with past interventions that enhanced net social benefits and others associated with interventions that reduced them. Stiglitz (1996) therefore argues that incremental interventions can potentially raise net social benefit even though they will be associated with the creation of new rents. We can re-state this as follows: The appropriate benchmark for evaluating rents is not the zero-rent general equilibrium that never existed and can never be reached but the currently existing structure of rights, interventions and institutional solutions that defines a complex structure of rents in the economy. The question is whether an *incremental* intervention that creates an *incremental* rent is associated with a positive or negative *incremental* change in net social benefits in this context. Interventions and rents that are associated with positive incremental outcomes are desirable even if they create rents.

The incremental rents framework should not be confused with an analysis of rents that takes the zero-rents general equilibrium as its benchmark. The alternative framework does not presume either that a general equilibrium is feasible or that movements in that direction are necessarily beneficial. It certainly does not explain rents in terms of market restrictions causing deviations from that (unrealistic) benchmark. Rather, the incremental rents framework seeks to identify and analyse the *changes* in rents associated with specific policies. These rents identify the direct beneficiaries of a policy so that we can begin to assess the plausibility of subjecting them to the conditions theoretically required for the policy to be effective. The actual outcome of the policy depends on how effectively rent seeking by the organizations benefiting from the rents can prevent or distort the imposition of the conditions that are required for socially desirable outcomes to emerge. The likelihood of that in turn depends on the interests and holding power of the organizations involved, and this information is therefore also required.

We describe the configuration of capabilities and holding powers across organizations as a "political settlement." The configuration of organizational power in a society is constantly changing but usually not so rapidly that aspects of continuity cannot be identified. Indeed, there are powerful feedback mechanisms between the distribution of organizational power in one period, the activities of organizations to protect and create institutions and policies to sustain their relative incomes and organizational powers during that period, and the reproduction of organizational power as a result of these activities in the next period. The distribution of organizational capabilities is nevertheless gradually changing but in a path-dependent way, with important aspects of continuity. We describe the currently existing macro-system of organizational capabilities and powers as a political settlement, and at any given time, countries have political settlements with features that are reproducible over time (Khan, 2010).

Combining the incremental rent analysis with a description of the political settlement allows us to analyse the likelihood of a particular policy achieving its expected outcomes. If the organizations affected by that policy are likely to operate as the theory expects them to, the expected outcome may be achieved. However, organizations have their own interests and capabilities and they may want to modify the application of the policy. In particular, they may want to modify the conditions under which they gain or lose the incremental rents created by a policy. For this, they are likely to engage in rent-seeking activities of different types. For instance, the organizations in question may find the formal conditions for acquiring rents to be too difficult relative to the alternative of attempting to distort or overcome these conditions using appropriate rent-seeking activities. The strategy they actually follow will depend on how easy it is to modify or resist the imposition of the formal conditions, and that depends on the bargaining power of these organizations relative to the governance agencies of the state. If they have the capability to modify the policy, the expected outcomes would be unlikely to be achieved. Thus, a policy that attempts to make powerful organizations operate in ways that they are likely to successfully resist is likely to either fail or achieve much more limited results.

Figure 4.3.1 shows the relationship between a technical analysis of expected outcomes of policy and an analysis of the likely responses of organizations to the rents created by the policy. The "standard analysis" of policy outcomes describes the technical analysis of policy responses to contracting failures which typically ignores the problem of enforcing the conditions required for policy success. This is shown in the shaded rectangle in Figure 4.3.1. In theory, policy works by changing the incentives and compulsions of the relevant parties so that more desirable social outcomes can emerge. The changes in incentives and compulsions can be described by the incremental rents that are created by the policy and the conditions that organizations have to fulfil to gain or lose these rents. The vertical chain of causation described as the "incremental rent analysis" is superimposed on this and asks how the organizations affected by these rents are likely to respond, given their interests and their bargaining power relative to other affected organizations and the agencies enforcing the conditions. The result is that the actual rent allocation may differ from the theoretical expectation and organizations can also modify the

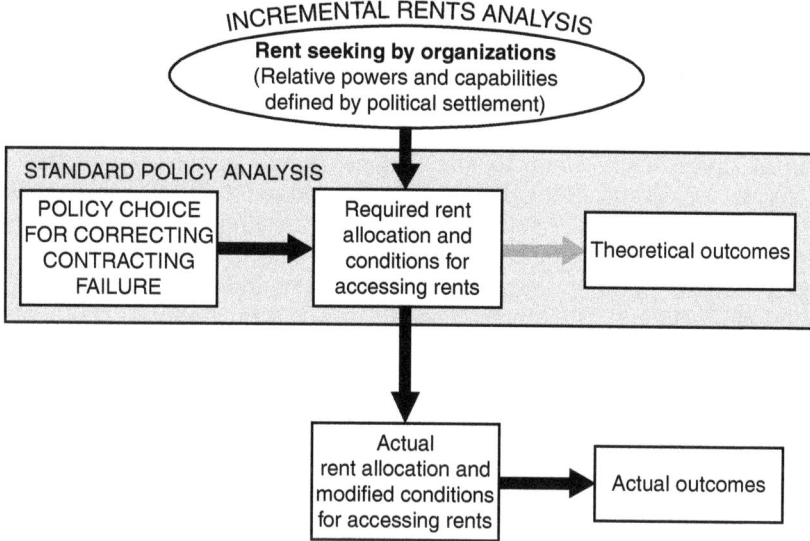

Figure 4.3.1 Rents, political settlements, and policy outcomes

conditions under which the relevant rents can be gained or lost. As a result, the actual outcomes achieved may be quite different from the outcomes that are theoretically expected. Moreover, as political settlements vary across countries, the actual outcomes associated with the same policy could be quite different in different contexts.

These overlapping analytical questions can be illustrated with reference to a simpler set of contracting failures, for instance those that result in persistent pollution externalities. In this case, a number of interventions are possible that could enhance net social benefits for society. One solution to this contracting failure is a tax imposing "negative rents" on polluters. This can reduce the incentive to pollute and result in higher net social benefits. However, the success of the tax depends on its allocation and management: state agencies have to assess the right tax level, monitor polluting activities, collect the appropriate taxes from polluting organizations, and prevent evasion or the passing on of these costs to others. These are the required rent allocation conditions in this case. Not surprisingly, pollution taxes may not produce the desired outcome and a rent analysis may explain why. An obvious problem may be that the theoretical tax allocation and management requirements are not met in practice because the organizations that are polluting can use rent-seeking activities to effectively distort the monitoring of pollution and the collection of taxes. If many polluting organizations have the capability to block the accurate monitoring of their activities, to challenge the tax regime legally, or in developing countries, to buy themselves political or bureaucratic support to block or evade the policy, the actual outcome of the strategy may be far removed from the expected one.

The rent analysis can be extended to policy design and allows us to ask if an alternative policy may have generated better outcomes given the political settlement. In reality, policy *choice* (the independent variable on the left in Figure 4.3.1) is also to some extent the product of the rent-seeking activities of organizations, but to simplify we assume with some realism that policy-makers have sufficient freedom to attempt a number of different types of policy responses to the same problem. For instance, apart from the tax solution, the problem of pollution externalities can be addressed by subsidies or by imposing regulatory restrictions on pollution. Consider the subsidy solution. Instead of taxing polluters, the subsidy strategy offers polluters rewards for reducing pollution. The success of *this* strategy depends on a very different set of monitoring and enforcement capabilities. Some of the monitoring requirements could be more demanding because the government has to estimate the pollution that *would* have been created in the absence of the policy, as well as monitoring current pollution to reward polluters for the reduction. Powerful organizations can obviously attempt to influence this assessment in different ways. However, instead of the difficult task of extracting revenue from powerful organizations, the subsidy strategy has the easier task of providing organizations with subsidies.

Given the configuration of power, this strategy may produce better outcomes relative to a tax strategy, provided some minimal conditions linking the delivery of the subsidy to actual pollution reduction could be enforced. This enforcement is more likely if after the subsidy and the pollution reduction the relevant organizations are better off than they would be if they continued polluting. In contrast, in the tax solution, the enforcement of the tax leaves polluting organizations worse off than they were. While enforcement is not likely to be perfect in either case, we would expect enforcement to be better for the subsidy case if the polluting organizations are powerful. The downside of the subsidy strategy is that the government loses revenue, instead of gaining revenue with a tax strategy. In addition, considerations of justice may politically prevent subsidies being offered to polluters, but if the polluters also happen to be relatively poor, welfare considerations could support a subsidy strategy. The general point is that apart from fiscal, justice and other considerations, the alternative policy solutions need to be compared purely in terms of the enforceability of the conditions required to achieve the desired outcomes. Given the distribution of power across organizations described by the political settlement, this comparison could help to identify the policy solution that is most likely to be effective in enhancing net social benefits.

The general proposition that follows from this discussion is that there are typically several policies that could address any particular contracting failure and an important policy question is to select the best policy for that context.

Policy choices can be motivated by many considerations, for instance, fiscal consequences or distributive justice, and to some extent policy choices are themselves driven by rent-seeking activities of organizations. However, an important consideration for policy-makers is to check that the *requirements* for successful policy outcomes (the required rent allocation conditions shown in Figure 4.3.1) can be plausibly approximated given the political settlement. The relative power of organizations is difficult to influence as this reflects the political settlement describing macro-social characteristics of that society. The political settlement can and does change over time but it is not an immediate policy variable under most circumstances. Normally, the current political settlement is an exogenous variable that may not be amenable to policy choices. This simply means that selecting the policy that is most likely to work in that context is very important for ensuring the best possible policy outcomes.

4.3.3   Technology policies for accelerating learning

The contracting failures affecting pollution are relatively simple compared to the contracting failures that can affect technology acquisition. As discussed earlier, there are potentially several different types of contracting failures affecting technology acquisition, and the first task is to identify the most important ones affecting particular countries or sectors. We will illustrate the general argument with reference to a particular contracting failure affecting technology acquisition: the problem of financing the learning-by-doing necessary for achieving competitiveness with new technologies (Khan, 2013). In developing countries, while domestic innovations may play a role, the main problem of technology acquisition is "learning" the use of existing technologies and building the organizational capabilities for competitively using these technologies. Developing countries find it difficult to set up productive economic organizations even if they can buy the appropriate machines and have low wages for workers with the appropriate formal skills. Learning refers to processes of learning-by-doing required for building the relevant organizational capabilities so that economic organizations can become competitive in using these technologies and implicit or explicit subsidies are no longer required for these operations.

The core problem of achieving competitiveness with new technologies is that competitiveness is determined not only by domestic factor prices but primarily by the productivity of labor, inputs and of the capital stock of domestic economic organizations using these technologies. These productivities depend largely on the organizational setup of the firm and not just on the quality and vintage of its capital stock and the formal skills of its workforce. The firm as an economic organization has to continue to experiment and adapt its internal organizational structures to reduce costs and improve a range of vital input-output ratios. The processes in question include setting up the machines and processes in the workplace to achieve the fastest throughput of production, setting up internal processes to minimize input wastage, processes to minimize the rate of rejection of final products, to minimize inventories without losing production time due to bottlenecks, maximize orders without missing delivery deadlines, managing customer services and after sales support and so on. These vital processes are much more important and more difficult to learn than the operation of individual pieces of machinery. The knowledge in question is also *tacit knowledge* that can only be acquired through learning-by-doing processes and not from manuals or classes, though these can provide some threshold level of knowledge. Moreover, the most effective organizational design for using the same technology may also vary across countries, because organizations have to respond to and find solutions to differences in work patterns, infrastructural constraints, external supply and support systems and so on. Thus, hiring supervisors with experience in foreign factories can reduce the learning time, but organizational innovation is still necessary because the organizational design of a foreign factory will in most cases not achieve the competitiveness that is required.

The challenge for technology acquisition is therefore to adapt the design of organizations, their internal hierarchy structures, incentive systems, monitoring systems and so on, till competitiveness is achieved. If the development of *organizational capability* fails, the plant continues to produce at a higher cost or produces products of a lower quality. This can be sustained for a time using market protection and subsidies of different types but subsidies cannot be sustained forever. Moreover, if organizational capability does not develop, the subsidies required to survive are likely to grow as plants in other countries become even more productive. Thus, the failure to develop productive organizational capabilities is likely to result in a failure of the technology acquisition strategy as a whole. The organizational learning problem has two closely related dimensions. First, during the period of learning the organization is not yet competitive and its low or negative profits have to be financed. Secondly, the financing has to be on terms such that the stakeholders within the firm put in high levels of effort in the learning process to rapidly achieve competitiveness. In principle, the loss-making period of learning-by-doing can be financed with injections of private funds, provided the contracts between financiers and firms create sufficient compulsions on the firm to use the learning space to rapidly raise productivity and product quality. The "doing" is necessary for "learning," but on its own the doing is not sufficient to *ensure* learning. This is unfortunately demonstrated by the many instances of "infant industries" in developing countries that failed to become competitive after years of subsidies financing learning-by-doing.

The important question is why private contracting fails to organize investments in high-effort learning, particularly since all the stakeholders in the firm stand to gain. Several variants of contracting failures can be relevant, and it is important to identify the most plausible ones. One possibility is an appropriability problem. Here the assumption is that a first-mover firm may have an incentive to invest in learning to create a competitive organization because low wages in the country offers the possibility of earning higher-than-normal profits once productivity improves. The appropriability problem is that some of their supervisors and managers can leave with their tacit knowledge to set up competing firms. If these competing firms reduce the profits of the first mover down to the normal level, that can dissuade investments in learning. This is a theoretically plausible argument except that privately financed learning fails to emerge just as frequently in industries and sectors that do not have the characteristics that would make them subject to this type of appropriability problem. For instance, private investments in learning are rare even in sectors with considerable market power or entry barriers, like automobiles or iron and steel in countries which have the formal skills to contemplate these sectors. In addition, at the other end of the scale, there are many sectors like low technology garments in labor surplus countries, where entry does not have any plausible threat of raising wages or global input prices and both first movers and their followers can expect low profit margins to begin with. Here too the fear of entry is unlikely to deter the first mover. On the contrary, in many such industries, including electronic components and light engineering, the first mover may positively welcome new entrants so that clustering happens and foreign buyers are attracted to set up their buying houses. So while the appropriability problem for first movers may affect investments in learning in some sectors, it is not likely to be the general problem.

If first mover fears of losing profits were the relevant problem, this could be addressed with short-term subsidies for new start-ups. With a temporary subsidy for the learning period, the first mover would not have to finance the development of organizational structures on the expectation of high future profits. In that case, even if imitation was expected to reduce profits to the normal level relatively quickly, the first mover would still earn normal profits like anyone else. However, if investments in learning are not happening even in sectors where entry does not pose compelling risks to future profitability, some other type of contracting failure may be relevant. Indeed, we know that subsidizing the loss-making period is not sufficient for ensuring the achievement of competitiveness because many firms and industries never become competitive even after years of external support. This suggests other contracting failures may be at play. Private financiers may not have any credible way of ensuring that when they finance a firm's loss-making period, decision-makers within the firm will be compelled to put in high levels of *effort* in the learning process so that competitiveness is rapidly achieved. What type of contract would ensure this?

When a developing country acquires existing technologies, its firms cannot hope for very high profits in the future, irrespective of the level of domestic entry. The technologies are typically mature, there are countries with higher wages producing these products (but with even higher productivity levels they are more competitive), and many lower wage countries could potentially enter later. The expectation of above normal profits cannot be the main incentive for domestic producers attempting to enter these markets, and this is the main reason why focusing on the appropriability problem may be misleading. In the general case, the firm that is successful in organizing learning can at best look forward to normal profits in a harshly competitive world. The prize, in other words, is not very attractive, and certainly in the general case does not offer the promise of significant or long-lasting rents. Yet learning happens in some of these "normal-profit" sectors with no promise of above-normal profits for first movers, and learning often fails in many sectors despite long-lasting learning rents being allocated to first movers in the form of protected markets and subsidies. The answer to this puzzle must be that normal profits can be incentive enough for many types of learning and the availability of rents on their own is insufficient to ensure successful learning-by-doing. The deeper problem is likely to be one of ensuring high levels of effort in the *process of learning* within the production team. This is particularly likely to be a problem if the learning is financed by financiers who are not in control of the learning process within the firm.

Consider the simplest case of a firm owned by a single individual who is also the manager. This allows us to ignore the principal-agent problems between owners and managers within the firm. The problem we focus on is that the typical owner is unlikely to have the resources or the risk appetite to finance the entire process of technology acquisition and learning without external financing. The external financier on the other hand has little control over the effort that insiders put into the learning process. Neither side can accurately predict how long it will take the firm to become profitable. Finally, the firm is unlikely to make high profits even when it does become profitable. It follows that in the typical case, it is hard to find a contract acceptable to both sides which provides adequate financing for learning and yet creates strong compulsions for putting in high levels of effort. If effort could be easily observed, contracting would be easier. The financier could repeatedly check progress and stick it out despite temporary problems if there was a prospect of a resolution soon. Without this, the financier is likely to demand contracts with exit clauses that allow it to withdraw investments at a later stage if progress is perceived to be slow, but the firm will reject most such contracts if it thinks its effort can go to waste at a later stage because it could not persuade the financier to stick it out for a little longer. Only a relatively complex contract would be acceptable to both sides under these circumstances, but the more complex the contract, the more unlikely that it can be enforced in the typical developing country.

Fixed interest financing will probably not be acceptable to the firm because it exposes it to too much risk. A viable firm engaging in technology acquisition may easily go bankrupt with a fixed interest loan if there were relatively small delays in achieving competitiveness. An *ex post* profit-sharing contract may be acceptable to the firm if the terms were right. But in most cases profit-sharing may be unacceptable for the external financier given the tight limits that have to be set on the learning period for the financing to be viable. It is possible to imagine contingency contracts that may be acceptable to both sides, for instance, setting clearly defined milestones which could be used to trigger credible exit strategies for the financier enabling at least a part of the investment to be withdrawn under different contingencies. This would reduce the risk for the financier and also increase the compulsion on the firm to put in high levels of effort. However, given the weak contract enforcement conditions in most developing countries, plus the uncertainties of evaluating intermediate learning outcomes (for the financier) and of predicting achievable levels of progress in learning in advance (for the firm), it is not surprising that contingency contracts for financing learning are not often observed in practice.

The technical problem that private contracting can fail to address is summarized in Figure 4.3.2. The vertical axis measures the competitiveness of the domestic firm for a product of a specific quality that it intends to produce after acquiring a technology new to the firm and new to the

country. Competitiveness is measured by $\frac{P^{global}}{C^{domestic}}$ where P^{global} is the global

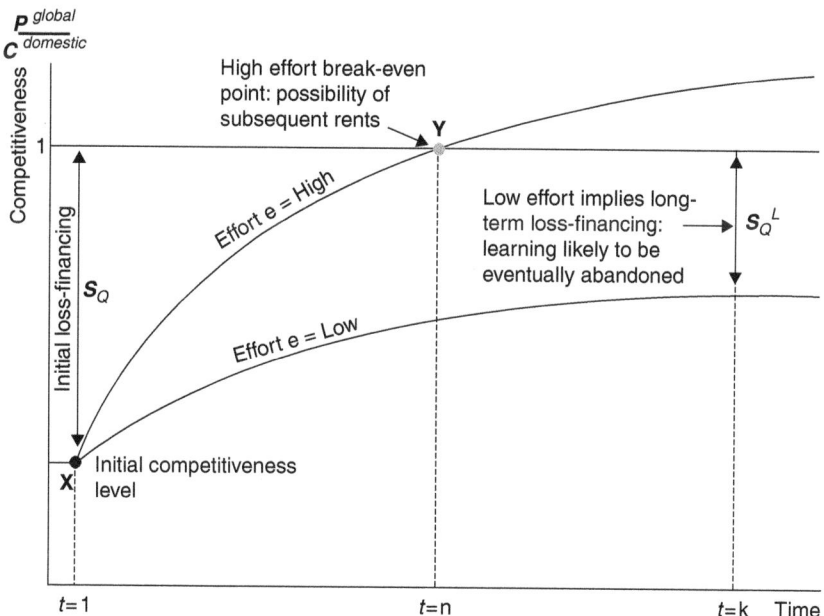

Figure 4.3.2 Effort levels and the viability of the learning process
Source: (Khan 2013: Figure 2.1.2)

market price of a product of that quality and $C^{domestic}$ is the domestic cost of production. The domestic firm becomes competitive only when the competitiveness index becomes greater than 1. At time $t = 1$ when the firm plans to acquire its technology, its low productivity of labor and input usage and possibly also low levels of capacity utilization and capital productivity means that its competitiveness index at point X is far below that required for market viability. For the firm to be able to begin a learning-by-doing process of capability development, the implicit gap in competitiveness has to be covered with loss financing shown in Figure 4.3.2 by the gap s_Q. The contracting problem is that this financing has to be provided by financiers external to the firm on contractual terms acceptable to all parties. If the firm puts in high levels of effort in experimentation and adaptation of its internal organizational routines, the high effort path can lead it to competitiveness by time $t = n$. If on the other hand the firm puts in low levels of effort in learning, it may never achieve competitiveness (or achieve it too late for the financing to be profitable). The financier cannot predict the firm's level of effort in advance, and may even be unable to discern the effort trajectory while organizational capability is being developed. Given the narrow profit margins in most cases and the sensitivity of the returns to the breakeven period, it is not surprising that left to their own devices, financiers with money and firms with potentially good management structures fail to contract to finance the learning required for technology acquisition.

Public policies for technology acquisition in developing countries have responded to this and other contracting failures. One component of most technology acquisition strategies is that states directly or indirectly provide the financing s_Q required for the learning-by-doing to commence. When public policy does this, it effectively provides a "learning rent" to the firm. However, as in the case of private financing, the learning rent is only likely to succeed if by design or accident, the policies create not only opportunities but also compulsions for firms to raise their competitiveness by putting in a high level of effort in the development of organizational capabilities. Without a set of credible conditions on the allocation and withdrawal of subsidies (the rent allocation and management conditions), the outcome is typically a low effort learning strategy on the part of firms, and competitiveness is often never achieved. Thus, with public financing, a different set of incentives and enforcement capabilities come into play, but the underlying problem remains very similar. On the one hand, the state has a wider range of financing instruments and associated enforcement tools than the ones available to private financiers. On the other hand, public financing and policy-induced rents are subject to the rent-seeking activities of powerful economic organizations that now have the incentive to spend time and resources to "politically" protect their rents. We know that some countries have managed to achieve dramatic outcomes through public technology acquisition strategies while others have not. Our contention is that by understanding the different components of this problem and designing policies that are likely to work better in the context of specific political settlements, the probability of success can be improved. In any case, the alternative route of attempting to encourage private contracting to finance learning is likely to be even more difficult given the governance environments in most developing countries and the economic characteristics of the learning process.

The apparently short-sighted rent protection strategies of firms receiving learning rents can be better understood if we keep in mind the limited prize that is available by achieving competitiveness. The social benefit to a country of developing national organizational capabilities can be large because of spillovers and clustering effects. However, for the individual firm receiving a learning rent, there is often a strong incentive compatibility problem in putting in high levels of effort to achieve competitiveness. The firm is very likely already receiving enough rents through the policy mechanism to achieve a normal rate of return for the key stakeholders. Its prize for achieving a higher level of organizational capability is that it will lose its learning rent and instead earn a similar normal profit through the tougher route of production in an uncertain and harsh market environment. Given this adverse incentive, it is not surprising that firms will often use their ingenuity and effort in rent-seeking activities to prolong the period of support or to postpone the withdrawal conditions. The result is "satisficing" behavior by many firms receiving support for learning, where management and key stakeholders within the firm are happy to continue business as usual and exert most of their creative effort in ensuring that the status quo continues. Of course, in the long run this is not a sustainable strategy, but the long run rarely constrains economic decisions. Successful catching-up strategies have to rely on more than the natural incentives of managers, owners and other stakeholders to grab the opportunity provided by the rent to try and achieve long-run competitiveness. High-effort learning strategies require effective short to medium-term compulsions on decision-makers in firms to direct their time and effort into developing productive organizational capabilities. This involves some combination of measures to block unproductive rent-seeking activities and imposing conditions on the allocation of rents to compel high levels of effort in learning. This is precisely why the interface shown in Figure 4.3.1 between the rent allocation conditions required for the success of a policy and the rent seeking strategies of the relevant organizations is so important.

4.3.4 Institutional problems of ensuring effort in learning

The interface between the rent allocation requirement of particular policies and the rent-seeking strategies of organizations is not simple because the outcome depends on non-linear interactions between several variables.

The underlying enforcement success or failure has elements that are similar to principal–agent problems that can result in breakdowns in team effort or in the operation of credit markets (Alchian and Demsetz, 1972; Stiglitz and Weiss, 1981; Shleifer and Vishny, 1997). However, here broader political economy issues are relevant because the *state* is allocating rents and the *political* ability or otherwise of the state to enforce credible conditions for effort becomes salient. This raises issues that go beyond asymmetric information. Rent seeking is now based on the mobilization of organizational and political power and can determine the likelihood of capturing or protecting particular rents without any asymmetric information. In particular, the political power and links of economic organizations and their organizational capabilities can affect the possibility of enforcing effort-inducing conditions on the allocation of particular incremental rents. The problem is that the effect of a rent allocation policy depends not just on the details of the formal rent allocation instrument, but also on its appropriateness for solving the learning problems of firms, on the capabilities of the agencies enforcing it and the political settlement that describes the relative power of the organizations involved. The effect on effort is the outcome of an interaction between these variables that determines the actual conditions of rent allocation and withdrawal, and these determine the real incentives and compulsions of firms to put their effort into productive capability development or unproductive rent maintenance activities. The critical "variables" that determine the level of effort firms put into the learning exercise to raise their productive capabilities are listed in eq. [1]:

$$e = f(FI, GA, FS, PS) \qquad [1]$$

Effort e is defined as the intensity with which organizational learning through experimentation is being carried out, to raise firm-level productivity. The higher the level of effort, the steeper the convergence to global competitiveness levels in Figure 4.3.2. *FI* describes the specific *financing instrument* through which the learning rent is delivered. This is broadly defined as any policy instrument that directly or indirectly allocates rents to firms with a possible effect on their learning strategies. The financing instrument is the immediate policy variable that *formally* defines how the rent should be allocated and defines the formal terms and conditions for withdrawal and the formal responsibilities of the different parties. The formal allocative rules defined by the financing instrument *FI* may of course not correspond very closely to the *actual* allocation and management of rents, which may happen largely in response to political pressures and mobilizations, often operating informally. These informal modifications are hugely important and their nature and extent depends on the interaction of the financing instrument with other variables in the function. *GA* describes the capabilities of the *governance agencies* that monitor and enforce the conditions implicit in the operation of the financing instrument. The enforcement of the formal rules implicit in each instrument can vary widely depending on the enforcement capabilities of the agencies responsible. *FS* describes features of the *firm structure*, referring to characteristics of the firm(s) being supported that are relevant including size, initial productive capabilities, political links and the type of markets (competitive or otherwise) in which they operate. *PS* is the *political settlement* which describes the relative bargaining power of the different types of organizations affected by the operation of the policy. The function f is *not* a differentiable mathematical function, and the variables in this function are unlikely to have additively separable effects. Rather, each of the variables has an effect whose magnitude and even sign can depend on the values of the other variables. This non-linear interdependence makes the political economy of industrial policy particularly interesting.

4.3.4.1 Financing instruments

In the industrial policy strategies of many developing countries in the 1960s and 1970s, very significant learning rents were typically allocated to broadly defined sectors. The financing instruments used included tariff protection to raise domestic prices of particular products thereby providing rents to domestic firms in protected sectors, export subsidies, tax breaks, low interest credit, often from state-owned development banks and subsidized input prices, including utilities and infrastructure. There are important differences in the details of the design of each of these instruments from country to country. However, the general feature of these policies was that a significant portion of these rents were allocated *ex ante*, that is before the firm had established competitive capabilities, and the rents were significant in their scope (in terms of the numbers of sectors and firms supported). A common feature of these policy choices was that the formal pattern of rent allocation, combined with the distribution of power in the political settlement, created strong incentives for recipient firms to spend time and effort in rent-seeking activities to protect the rents once they had been allocated. Very few developing country states had the political capability to enforce the formal conditions on rent allocation that would compel high levels of effort, such as making the rents time dependent or their allocation conditional on performance. In many cases states did not even try to formally define rent allocation conditions, while in the few successful industrial policy states, early successes in attempts at rent allocation resulted in greater formalization of conditions over time.

This was not just an oversight in the less successful industrial policy states. No country began its technology acquisition policies with a complete map of what needed to be done. In the successful countries, trial and error in policy formulation resulted in formal financing instruments moving in the direction of better-defined formal conditions precisely because productivity-enhancing rent allocations were successful. The political and bureaucratic elites in many developing countries where industrial policy was performing poorly were perfectly aware of the problem at a very early stage but in these countries formal policy did not evolve in the direction of greater effectiveness, precisely because the relevant agencies knew that movements in that direction would not be enforceable. For instance, in India, the Dutt Committee recognized by the mid-1960s that the licensing regime that was directing rents to infant industries was primarily helping a small group of large firms who were capturing these rents on their own terms (Government of India 1969). But the politics of responding to this effectively was not simple. To the extent that responses were attempted, they were often blunt and counterproductive. Thus, in India, one response was Indira Gandhi's Monopolies and Restrictive Trade Practices Act (MRTP) of 1969 which set asset limits on the holdings of large business houses that were thought to have unduly prospered under the licensing regime. The new act was largely punitive, was not properly enforced and had little effect on actual levels of concentration. Significantly, it did not seek to address the problem of rent management to achieve better outcomes. The state did not try to set new conditions for achieving competitiveness by changing the broad contours of the policy, including the choice of supported sectors and firms, even though the necessity of such changes was explicitly recognized by the Dutt Committee.

In other words, the failure to move in the direction of better rent management, at least in India in the 1960s, cannot be attributed to ignorance. However, there may have been missed opportunities of a more complex sort. The problem was that the current financing instruments allocating learning rents were giving significant *ex ante* rents to broadly defined sectors and it was difficult to exclude large business houses from these rents. Enforcing effective conditions on *this* financing instrument was clearly beyond the capabilities of the Indian state of the time given the political settlement and it did not attempt to move in that direction. However, other financing instruments may have been more successful and some insights into what may have worked became clearer with the experiences of the 1980s. But thinking through to those options would require a much more open and interactive analytical framework incorporating the effects of the political settlement in assessing policy options. Only in this sense were opportunities of policy reform missed at that time.

Similarly, widespread public disapproval of state supported accumulation and technology strategies emerged in Pakistan in the late 1960s as a result of the concentration of wealth in the hands of Pakistan's "twenty-two families." The weak control over the rent management process led not only to a very high level of wealth concentration, many of the industries that were emerging were not approaching global competitiveness and had the character of industries protected for cronies. Some real capabilities were undoubtedly developed, but the failure of any significant sector to reach global competitiveness undermined the political support for these strategies. The result was widespread nationalizations in Pakistan and the newly created Bangladesh in the early 1970s under Bhutto and Mujib respectively. The nationalized industries were even closer to political power and therefore even more able to distort rent allocation and less likely to put in high levels of effort in learning. This was the prelude to the abandonment of learning strategies and the transition to liberalization.

The types of formal financing instruments used by states are an important determinant of the incentives and compulsions facing firms not only because the formal rent allocations are different, but also because the informal modifications through rent seeking and resistance may be different because different types of organizations are selected or self-select themselves given the incentives. For instance, monitoring requirements are very different depending on whether the learning rents are available *"ex ante"* (before success is established) or promised *"ex post"* (after success is established). The typical patent based Schumpeterian rent that creates incentives for innovation is usually available to successful innovators *ex post*. For rents allocated *ex post*, the public monitoring requirements are less demanding and the institutional requirement is mainly to determine the period of *ex post* rent protection, which primarily determines the magnitude of the prize allocated to the successful innovators (Khan, 2000a). Even if rents are only available as *ex post* prizes, they can still help to make the financing of innovation more viable, because innovators can now offer risk-taking investors higher returns in the future, thereby getting access to longer periods of low-interest or zero-interest financing. However, some Schumpeterian rents may also be allocated *ex ante* by public policy, for instance as subsidies to universities or to industries in the form of innovation grants. These *ex ante* rents require much closer monitoring to ensure progress is being made at different stages of the innovation cycle so that support can be withdrawn and losses minimized if progress is unsatisfactory.

In contrast to Schumpeterian rents, learning rents are typically provided *ex ante* (for instance through tariffs on imports or the provision of low cost credit). Unfortunately, large programmes granting significant learning rents *ex ante* have been associated with low effort in learning in many cases. There are exceptions in countries where the political settlement allowed the state to monitor, manage and withdraw rents from significant economic organizations. Most developing countries did not have state organizations or political settlements that had these characteristics, and as a result these types of financing instruments performed poorly. However, there have been interesting cases of successful technology adoption in countries that did not do well with *ex ante* financing instruments. In the cases of success, the financing often involved the allocation of a significant part of the rent *ex post*, after substantial success in learning had been established. If the financing instrument allocated some of the rent *ex ante* but reserved significant rents as a prize *ex post*, conditional on the achievement of competitive success, these conditions could help to self-select firms that believed they could make the productivity jump as well as creating strong compulsions and incentives for high levels of effort in learning. In addition, if the delivery of the *ex post* rents was sufficiently large and credible, firms engaged in learning could also raise financing on viable terms from investors in the same way as innovators aiming for Schumpeterian rents can raise money for financing innovations.

In the 1980s a number of sectors in South Asian countries made significant progress in technology adoption and in developing organizational capabilities for competitive production. Far from being associated with liberalization, many of these successes were associated with new types of policy-induced rents and rent allocation mechanisms that worked much better. The interesting feature of the new policy environment was that the old financing instruments based on large-scale *ex ante* financing were gradually phased out and new forms of support emerged, many of which provided a significant part of the learning rent as a prize for success *ex post* and targeted rents to more narrowly defined sectors or even to individual firms.

Examples include the rents offered by the Indian state to Suzuki to participate in the Suzuki-Maruti joint venture agreement signed in 1982. Most of the learning rent in this case was accessible *ex post* in the form of access to the protected Indian automobile market which still had tariffs in the region of 85 per cent. But to be able to sell in this protected market, Suzuki first had to make the Maruti–Suzuki car and it had to make it with 60 per cent domestic content within five years. This meant Suzuki had to make a significant investment in improving the organizational capabilities of Indian Tier 1 and Tier 2 component producers to meet the domestic content target and yet produce a car that would be of higher quality than existing Indian cars like the Ambassador. There were additional reasons for not compromising on quality, including the reputation risk for the global Suzuki brand. The design of the financing here clearly created strong incentives and compulsions for effort because Suzuki had no interest in drawing the process out and every interest in completing it quickly. Moreover, there was a very strong likelihood that without fulfilling the domestic content requirement the company could be excluded from the *ex post* rent. Exclusion from the domestic market for contract violation was a condition that could be plausibly enforced on a single foreign company with no domestic political alliances given India's governance capabilities and political settlement at the time. Not surprisingly, the result was a very successful transfer of organizational capabilities, with the rapid development of a broad group of component manufacturers who later became the foundation of a globally competitive Indian automobile industry.

Another example was the garment industry takeoff in Bangladesh in the 1980s which was based on the MFA (Multi-Fiber Arrangement) providing *ex post* rents to producers in Bangladesh provided they achieved sufficient competitiveness to begin to export. The MFA restricted imports into the USA from established garments exporters and this enabled quota-free countries like Bangladesh to temporarily enjoy rents in these markets as a result of the slightly higher prices at which they could sell. This was an *ex post* rent because the prize could only be captured by firms that had already developed enough organizational capabilities to be able to export. The availability of the prize enabled the first garments firms in Bangladesh to raise money for investing in capability development. Here too there were interesting innovations, including an on-the-job training programme for managers from the Bangladeshi company Desh that was conducted in the South Korean plant of Daewoo. Daewoo undertook to host the Bangladeshis at its own expense, to be repaid by the Bangladeshi company with a percentage of its sales revenue. This financing arrangement for transferring organizational capabilities created strong compulsions on both sides to put in high levels of effort as the costs of all parties went up with a low-effort strategy. The result was a very successful transfer of organizational capabilities. Desh became the pioneer of the garments industry in Bangladesh, and contrary to the first-mover disincentive story, it encouraged and allowed its managers to leave and set up new garments firms so that clustering could rapidly happen. Both these examples are discussed in greater detail in Khan (2013).

The general point to be made here is that while the traditional financing instruments providing *ex ante* rents did not work in South Asia, the experience of the 1980s shows that other types of financing instruments did work in successfully financing the development of new organizational capabilities. These capabilities in turn allowed the transfer and adaptation of technologies new to these countries. Indeed both the automobile sector in India and the garments and textile sector in Bangladesh played an important role in driving economic growth in these countries for more than three decades since the 1980s.

4.3.4.2 Governance agencies

Governance agencies are the bureaucracies within the state that are charged with the management of policies including the allocation of the relevant rents. The formal technical capabilities of these agencies to monitor and enforce these allocations clearly matter. Relevant agencies may include central banks, development banks, fiscal agencies and planning commissions charged with monitoring and implementing the allocation of rents associated with particular programmes. However, the actual power of governance agencies depends not just on their technical capabilities and training but also on the political settlement of which they are a part. Governance agencies are organizations and the relative power of these organizations relative to others is an important aspect of the political settlement. The technical capabilities of governance agencies (described in this variable) and the relative power of these organizations relative to others (as described in the political settlement variable) jointly determine the ability of governance agencies to enforce particular sets of rent allocation conditions.

The governance agency that is relevant depends on the financing instrument. For instance, if rents are allocated to firms in the form of cheap credit from industrial banks, the relevant governance agencies are the managements of the banks and the agencies the banks in turn rely on for the enforcement of their contracts (like bankruptcy courts). Do these agencies collectively have the capability to monitor loans effectively; do they have the power to withdraw loans if firms are failing to adhere to agreed conditions? Similarly, if rents are allocated in the form of subsidies, the relevant governance agencies are the ones responsible for administering the subsidies. Do they have the technical capabilities for monitoring performance and withdrawing the subsidies if necessary?

Technical capabilities alone clearly do not ensure that enforcement will be effective. The distribution of power across organizations in the political settlement and the types of rents that are being allocated through the financing instrument jointly determine the degree of enforcement that is achieved. The same governance agencies may be quite effective in enforcing a rent allocation that involves imposing conditions on relatively weak organizations but may fail when enforcing a slightly different policy that requires them to discipline organizations that happen to be powerful within the current political settlement. For instance, a policy of granting temporary export subsidies to firms using new technologies could create compulsions for high levels of effort if the affected firms had no means of prolonging these subsidies but not if they had the political ability to override the time limits using their political alliances. Industrial development banks are likely to have higher levels of credibility for enforcing threats of capital withdrawal from failing firms if the firms do not have powerful political allies and the bank is supported by a strong president rather than if the bank is operating in a context of divided political authority where powerful political factions can prevent the enforcement of discipline on their client business houses. The contribution of the governance agency to the achievement of a high-effort outcome therefore depends not just on the technical competence of the relevant agency but also on the financing instrument that defines the distribution of rents and the political settlement that defines the relative power of the affected organizations: another example of the non-linear interaction between these variables.

4.3.4.3   Firm structure

The outcome of a particular policy framework also depends on the characteristics of the firms that are benefiting from a learning strategy. A number of features of the firms targeted by policy may be relevant. What is their initial productive capability, how are they connected to different types of political organizations, how does this affect their bargaining power to protect rents, what kind of markets do they operate in and are there competitive pressures coming from these markets to raise their productivity? These and other features of the firm structure can affect the "fit" between the expected outcomes of a formal rent allocation policy and its actual outcome in terms of the effort put in by firms in raising productive capabilities. Once again, there are many non-linear interactions to be aware of that can produce unexpected outcomes if we are not careful.

The productive capabilities of firms can have two contradictory effects on their rent capture strategies. First, more productive firms have more resources to invest in rent-seeking activities. This increases the likelihood that these firms will be more able to protect any incremental rents they get. On the other hand, productive firms that are already close to the competitiveness frontier may find that putting their effort into becoming competitive may be a safer and more viable strategy than focusing on rent protection alone. In contrast, for firms that are far away from the competitiveness frontier, high effort in developing the appropriate organizational capabilities only makes sense if they can be assured of long-run support for learning and if the easier strategies of rent protection are ruled out by effective limits on their rent-seeking activities. By definition, most firms in developing countries initially do not have high levels of technological and organizational capabilities (this is why the country is still developing). Most firms still have to learn how to learn before they actually start learning (Stiglitz, 1987). This creates adverse incentives for many firms to invest in political connections because if they had to rely solely on their productive capabilities they would be very vulnerable. Older or larger firms, particularly when they are not very productive are more likely to be well-connected to political organizations and their prosperity is likely to be dependent on these connections. Consequently it may be difficult to discipline such firms in a context where significant learning rents are being provided by the state. One of the advantages of financing mechanisms that provide significant *ex post* rents is that this induces a degree of self-selection in the firms taking up these schemes. A firm that has little chance of becoming competitive in a new technology is unlikely to participate in a scheme that requires it to invest up-front in organizational capabilities based on the promise of significant *ex post* rents.

The political connections and networks of firms are very important for explaining their bargaining power in protecting their rents or subverting conditions attached to these rents, but these connections cannot be read off from their economic characteristics. This is why we need independent data on the overall political settlement which describes the relative power of different types of organizations. The political settlement variable has an interactive effect in determining why apparently similar types of firms may respond differently to similar types of financing instruments. For instance, the modern manufacturing sector in both Pakistan and South Korea in the

1960s was dominated by a small number of large diversified holding companies that each included plants in different manufacturing sectors. In both countries, public policy provided learning rents to these conglomerates to acquire new technologies and move into exports through similar financing instruments like domestic market protection, subsidized credit, and export subsidies. However, high levels of effort could not be achieved for firms of this type in Pakistan but were achieved in South Korea. To a significant extent this was because large conglomerates in Pakistan acquired the political capacity to protect their rents from threats of withdrawal in a way that South Korean *chaebols* could not. To understand this we need to look at the relationships between the firm structure and political organizations within the context of a political settlement. In Pakistan, there were many *political* sub-organizations that were not under the centralized control of the ruling coalition, despite the ruling coalition being a military-led government in the 1960s, just as in South Korea. Behind the formal structure of a unified ruling coalition, the Pakistani political settlement described a distribution of organizational power that was significantly fragmented. Many political and bureaucratic organizations were independently powerful and they could deploy their power to benefit themselves independently of the wishes of the President.

The consequence was that firms in Pakistan that wanted to protect their rents could easily make arrangements to share rents with one or more of these political or bureaucratic sub-organizations. This involved kicking back some of their subsidies to these lower-level organizations and in exchange the latter would assist by effectively protecting their rents. This arrangement benefited the firm and their allied political and bureaucratic organizations but adversely affected the overall industrial strategy and the net social benefits of the country. The interface between the firm structure and the specific political settlement meant that financing instruments that provided a significant part of the rents *ex ante* could not be effectively disciplined in Pakistan. Not so in South Korea. The large *chaebol* were the descendants of Japanese companies and after the defeat and departure of Japan, these companies enjoyed little popular sympathy or support. Moreover, even if the *chaebol* had some legitimacy, they would have found it very difficult to make similar political connections. The ruling coalition in South Korea was differently structured, and could impose its authority on its own lower levels. Political organizations outside the ruling coalition had very limited power to protect the rents of firms. This meant that firms receiving rents would have to satisfy the calculations of the highest authorities to retain their rents. The highest authorities had no incentive to tolerate rent capture by organizations that were not enhancing productivity. This is because a secure ruling coalition that could take a view over several years would always find more productive organizations more attractive to support because the latter could provide greater benefits over time, whether legally in the form of taxes or illegally in the form of kickbacks. The threat of rent withdrawal from low-effort firms was therefore credible in South Korea and because it was credible, this threat rarely had to be used. High levels of organizational effort were always forthcoming (Khan, 1999).

Although Taiwan is often loosely included in the "East Asian" model, its firm structure and financing instruments were quite different from South Korea in the 1960s and 1970s. In Taiwan, financing instruments allocated rents to much smaller firms and once we look at Taiwan's political settlement, it is possible that a strategy of building up very large conglomerates may have failed at that time. The Kuomintang (KMT) was a foreign political force in Taiwan, having been forced there after their defeat in mainland China at the hands of Mao's forces in 1949. Given its external origins, the KMT was clearly unwilling to allow domestic economic conglomerates to become too big because they may well have used their economic power to challenge the political authority of the outsiders. In any case, large Taiwanese conglomerates may have been difficult to discipline in this political settlement. Fortunately for Taiwan, the financing instruments used by the government in its strategies of technology acquisition focused on smaller firms in high technology sectors. These firms had sufficient organizational capabilities to be interested in investing in productive capacity development, but were politically unable to link up with sub-organizations within the KMT or to challenge its authority entirely. As a result, the Taiwanese state's ability to enforce discipline in the form of conditions on its rent allocation decisions was not impaired. The interesting counterfactual is whether countries like Pakistan and India may have fared better if they had designed support schemes for smaller firms who may have found it more difficult to capture policy in the way in which the "twenty-two families" of Pakistan or the big business houses of India did (Wade, 1988; Amsden, 1989; Wade, 1990; Whitley, 1992; Khan, 1999; Khan and Blankenburg, 2009).

The pressure on firms to invest in productivity growth is likely to be enhanced if some part of their activity is in competitive markets. Firms that are exporting, even with subsidies, will soon find that without productivity growth, the existing level of subsidy will be insufficient for their continued survival. In contrast firms producing for protected domestic markets or with considerable market power may ignore productivity growth for much longer. This is yet another reason why countries with political settlements where large established firms have many links with political organizations should focus their financing on smaller firms operating in more competitive markets. Apart from the greater difficulty such firms may find in establishing political linkages, their market operations can add to their compulsions for enhancing organizational capabilities. Market competition is not enough on its own, because learning still requires rents and the rents dampen competitive pressures for a while. This is precisely because at existing market prices these firms could not enter production at all given their current capabilities.

But some market exposure can reduce the challenges of monitoring and enforcing conditions to compel high levels of effort. Of course, for some products, scale economies mean that a small-firm strategy is implausible. In these cases, policy design has to be aware of the difficulties of disciplining large well-connected firms. Compensatory measures to prioritize the strengthening of governance agencies may be a partial solution. In some cases the answer may be to delegate the governance of learning rents to more independent external agencies like industrial banks. If the management of the industrial bank is less accessible to political pressure, the credibility of withdrawal may be high enough to compel learning. Finally, in some cases, *ex post* rents can work, as in the case of the Maruti–Suzuki partnership in India. Here, the instrument was the offer of large *ex post* rents conditional on the transfer of organizational capabilities to domestic component producers. This led to a large foreign firm self-selecting to participate in the joint venture because it had enough organizational capabilities to believe it could transfer the requisite capabilities to Indian firms and thereby capture the *ex post* rents.

4.3.4.4   The political settlement

The political settlement describes the distribution of organizational and bargaining power across economic, political and bureaucratic organizations in a society (Khan 1995, 2010). The relative power of different organizations develops in path dependent ways, but at any point in time, the description of the political settlement in a country is an important "independent variable" in an analysis of the outcomes associated with incremental policy changes. Each incremental policy change allocates incremental rents to different organizations on specific conditions. The political settlement is relevant for understanding the likely outcomes of the policy because it describes the capability of organizations to challenge or distort the conditions of rent allocation implicit in the formal policy. The outcome in reality may therefore be far removed from what the formal policy set out to do, because the rent allocation that the formal policy required or the conditions of evaluation and enforcement that it depended on could not be enforced in that political settlement.

Rent seeking by powerful organizations refers not just to their expenditure of resources in order to influence bureaucrats and politicians. More importantly, it refers to their political activities through which they develop their holding power and construct coalitions to enhance this holding power. Holding power describes the ability of an organization to hold out in prolonged conflicts and it is this capability that determines the probability of winning. Holding power depends not just on the resources the organization can deploy but also on its power to mobilize support. In a developing country this depends on its links with powerful patron-client political organizations. Rent-seeking contests between organizations have characteristics of "chicken games" in game theory where a prize can be distributed in two very different ways but each requires one side to win and the other to accept defeat. There are thus two Nash equilibria but which one emerges depends on the perceptions of each side of the holding power of the other. It is only when they each think they can win or if they miscalculate the holding power of the other that a conflict ensues which is costly for both sides. Conflicts of this type end when a new distribution of holding power is accepted by both sides and the distribution of rents reflects this distribution.

The political settlement describes the structure of holding power as it has evolved and helps us to understand some of these rent conflicts better. In many developing countries, there are many competing political organizations each based on mobilizing supporters using patron–client politics. The more such political organizations exist, the easier it is for economic organizations to buy themselves holding power at a relatively low price. When political organizations are at the same time powerful and fragmented, economic organizations, certainly the bigger and more resourceful ones, are likely to find it easy to purchase holding power. On the other hand when the ruling coalition includes the most powerful political organizations and the higher levels of the ruling coalition have effective control over the lower levels, economic organizations can find it much harder to buy themselves holding power and protection at an acceptable price. These are the types of differences in the political settlement between South Asia and East Asia in the 1960s that we have already referred to.

We have already seen how differences in political settlements can explain why apparently similar governance agencies, firm structures and financing instruments can result in very different outcomes across countries. South Korea and Pakistan in the 1960s used fairly similar strategies of providing cheap long-term bank credit and export subsidies to large conglomerates in export-oriented sectors. But the outcomes were significantly different because their political settlements were different and the critical conditions that were required for inducing effort through rent allocation could be enforced in one case but not the other (Khan, 1999). Indeed even the evolution of formal policy was affected in South Asia. As we saw in the case of the Dutt Committee report in India, an adverse combination of a particular political settlement and a financing instrument made policy-makers give up on evolutionary developments of formal policy which they knew were pointless given the holding power of powerful economic organizations. Differences in the political settlement can also help to explain why effective financing instruments and governance agencies have *differed* so significantly across *successful* catching-up countries. South Korea, Taiwan, China and Malaysia display significant differences in their catching up strategies and instruments. The general framework outlined here can explain why a different ensemble of instruments and agencies would be effective in inducing high-effort learning given the differences in their structures of firms and their political settlements (Khan, 2000b, 2008; Khan and Blankenburg, 2009).

4.3.4.5   Interdependencies affecting policies for learning

Effective learning strategies require as a precondition an ensemble of conditions to ensure high levels of effort. This is not always easy to achieve, and the failure to address or even understand these problems has been responsible for the abandonment of many learning and technology acquisition strategies across developing countries. An important reason why effective policies have been difficult to devise is because the variables in eq. [1] have interdependent non-linear effects on effort. This means that the best financing instrument, for instance, may depend on the type of political settlement and firm structure that a country has inherited. The same instrument may be ranked lower than others in its effects on effort in a context with a different political settlement and firm structure. As a result, there is no single set of financing instruments and governance arrangements that characterize all successful catching up countries. It also follows that it is not possible to simply imitate the policies or governance structures of more successful developers.

Some of the interdependencies between the variables affecting effort in eq. [1] are shown in Figure 4.3.3. From a policy perspective, it is important

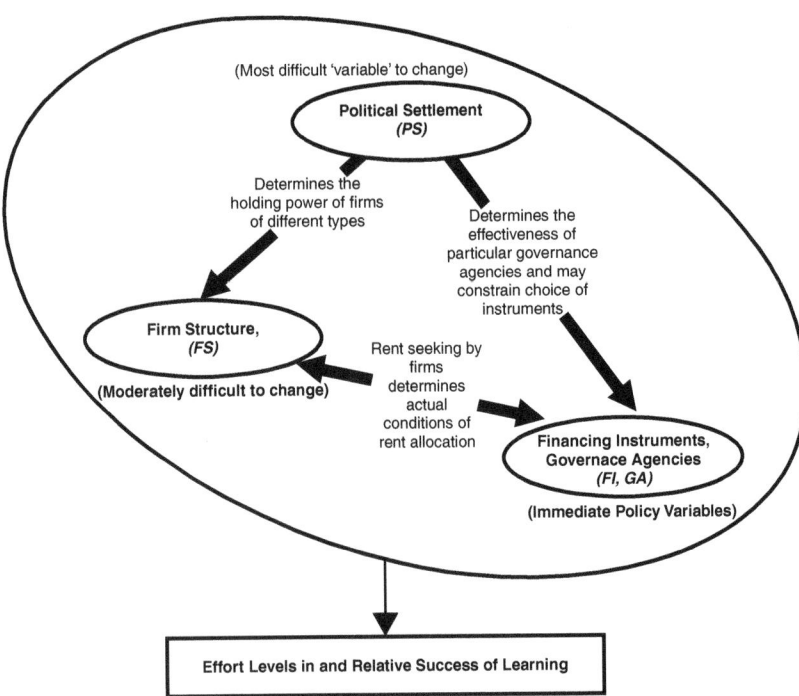

Figure 4.3.3   The interdependence of variables determining effort

to distinguish between variables that are very difficult to change and which can therefore only be the targets of policy in the long term and variables that are easier to change and are more immediate policy variables. The variables that are most difficult to change are effectively "exogenous" in the short term and policy is likely to have to accept them as given. In Figure 4.3.3, the political settlement, *PS*, appears at the top of the list as it is likely to be the variable that is most difficult to change. However, even the political settlement can of course change, and it can change as a result of political policy, for instance through the organization of new political coalitions or movements. Indeed, if the political settlement is very unfavorable for organizing any serious process of learning, the only meaningful policy would be to begin the process of changing the political settlement. Of course, this is a process with unpredictable outcomes and one that only political organizations with legitimate leaderships can hope to achieve.

Next in terms of difficulty of changing is the firm structure, *FS*. The overall firm structure may be very slow to change, but policy can still select different groups of firms to support, so the firm structure that is targeted by policy is not necessarily fixed. Finally, the variables that are usually the most direct targets for policy appear at the bottom, the financing instruments, *FI*, and the associated governance agencies, *GA*, though governance agencies too may not necessarily be easy to set up or change. However, even if the policy relevant financing instruments are the only entry points for most policy purposes, the most appropriate financing instruments cannot be identified without at least identifying the other variables and the implications for rent management in the context defined by those variables. What is ruled out is the hope that these variables are "additively separable," so that good financing instruments or effective governance agencies can be identified independently of a political economy analysis of the interactions between these variables in particular contexts.

4.3.5   Policy conclusions

The complexity of the relationships between financing instruments, governance agencies, firm structures and political settlement can explain why many plausible strategies of learning often failed. In many developing countries, strategies of learning and catching up between the 1950s to the late 1970s failed because while many new sectors and firms emerged, the progression to global competitiveness was too slow. Financing costs multiplied and found expression in growing budget deficits or in growing non-performing assets of state-owned industrial development banks. Eventually, many of these strategies were abandoned, partly because of internal reasons, partly because of the global intellectual and policy consensus in favor of cutting back subsidies in developing countries in the 1980s.

An intriguing question is whether the countries which eventually abandoned learning strategies could have done significantly better had they followed a different approach for identifying and addressing the market failures that affected their learning. India and Pakistan (of which Bangladesh was a part at that time) attempted ambitious "East Asian" industrial policies but without the political settlements that would allow effective compulsions for high levels of effort. Large, relatively well-connected firms benefited from different types of "learning rents" but managed to buy themselves sufficient protection from different factions to prevent threats of subsidy withdrawal to be credible. The result was significant industrialization but slow growth towards global competitiveness levels (Khan, 2000b).

Figure 4.3.3 suggests that there could have been two types of responses to this problem (apart from abandoning the strategy). The first and more ambitious response would have been to use policy to change aspects of the political settlement that were preventing the imposition of credible compulsions on the firms receiving rents for learning. The political settlement may be difficult to change rapidly, but it is always changing endogenously. Could the relevant aspects of the political settlement that constrained growth have been addressed by political entrepreneurs if they had a better understanding of the constraints? This is a tempting idea but it is not a direction in which we should readily go without understanding the dangers. Political settlements are complex systems like biological organisms or weather systems. We can understand and describe the macro-level features of biological organisms or weather systems and this may help us to design microinterventions like medicines or when to take out our umbrellas. However, we are far away from understanding these complex systems well enough to attempt to change a biological organism or a weather system into another with predictable results. The same is true of political settlements. A political intervention like a new party or administrative decentralization will change the distribution of power across organizations over time, but we may be surprised at the direction of the evolution. To say the least, attempts to change the political settlement are highly risky and the results are too uncertain for this to be policy advice that can be given with any confidence. Nevertheless, it is equally clear that political movements and struggles as well as economic changes that are going on all the time are constantly changing the political settlements of countries.

A second and apparently less ambitious response may be more appropriate. This would be to focus on policy choice, but to do so with a fuller understanding of the non-linear relationships between the relevant variables. The response would be to consider other policy mechanisms for supporting learning in the context of the existing political settlement, and feasible changes in governance agencies and firm structures such that the incremental rents effectively created a combination of incentives and compulsions for learning. We know that in the 1980s a number of developing countries that had not performed strongly with "traditional" industrial policy nevertheless achieved effective learning outcomes in some sectors. They did this because (largely serendipitously) they attempted financing instruments, which given the firm selection and the technologies they were acquiring, resulted in credible incentives to enhance or transfer organizational capabilities in these sectors. The policy challenge in developing countries is to do this matching of compatible combinations of variables in a more deliberative and purposive way so that we do not have to wait for the next lucky accident to happen.

Much of the policy discussion on technology policy identifies a variety of contracting failures but the critical contracting failures that constrain the development of competitive organizations have often been ignored. The starting point for any policy analysis of technology acquisition is to understand that almost every effective learning strategy must involve a component of rent management for developing appropriate organizational capabilities. For this, it is not enough to create rents to support learning, we have to be sure that these rents come with appropriate and enforceable conditions that create credible compulsions for effort. Here a background understanding of the current macro-level distribution of power across organizations (the political settlement) helps to identify the clusters of firms that are politically powerful and therefore likely to present the most serious challenges for effective rent management. This does not mean that these firms should be avoided by technology policy, but it does mean that technology policy has to give particular attention to how issues of effort and rent withdrawal can be managed for these types of firms. It may be much easier to drive growth with a different set of firms or sectors where the political linkages are less problematic. Indeed, if political stability requires giving something to the politically well-connected enterprises, that should be seen as a part of political stabilization strategies and not technology policy. Even at the height of its reform process, China allowed a number of less efficient public sector enterprises to continue operating and receiving rents, as these enterprises protected employment and distributed rents to important constituencies even if they had no chance of becoming economically viable. These types of redistributive policies are fine as long as we do not confuse them with technology policy. In China policy support for enterprises that could become globally competitive used other instruments and focused on other sectors.

If governance agencies are weak and particularly if the weakness is related to characteristics of the political settlement, then financing strategies need to be considered which further reduce the monitoring and enforcement requirements for governance agencies. For instance, if the political settlement describes a distribution of power across political organizations that results in intense political competition between parties and factions, the imposition of hard rent allocation conditions on powerful industrial groups is likely to be difficult as different parties and factions are likely to strongly protect their client businesses. An interesting variant of financing instruments that can significantly reduce monitoring requirements are those providing a significant part of the rents *ex post*. We have seen a few examples of these in developing countries. These financing instruments are not suitable for all sectors and technologies but they may be for some. The advantages include self-selection of the more appropriate economic organizations to participate in these policies. In addition, this type of financing can create strong internal incentives and compulsions for effort within the firm because it is investing first and relying on the achievement of competitiveness to get the prize of rents later. In some cases, like the Indian automobile and Bangladeshi garments cases that we discussed, the financing instrument also involved a small number of initial participants or even only one, so that the monitoring of the rent allocation conditions was even easier.

Finally, an important general result that can be derived is that the next set of successful financing instruments for successful technology acquisition and learning in the next developing country will not look exactly like any previous ones. This is precisely because of the non-linear interdependencies that we have discussed, which make technology policy so challenging. The framework discussed does not give us blueprints for financing instruments that can be used in different contexts because such blueprints do not exist. However, it goes beyond general recommendations for context-specific analysis. It provides a broad analytical framework for discussing issues and checking the plausibility of a particular set of financing instruments by looking for interdependent relationships that may help or hinder the enforcement of conditions for high-effort learning.

References

Alchian, Armen A. and Demsetz, Harold (1972) "Production, Information Costs, and Economic Organization," *American Economic Review*, vol. 62, no. 5, pp. 777–795.

Amsden, Alice (1989) *Asia's Next Giant: South Korea and Late Industrialization* (Oxford: Oxford University Press).

Chang, Ha-Joon (1994) *The Political Economy of Industrial Policy* (London: Macmillan).

Dosi, Giovanni (1988) "The Nature of the Innovative Process," in Giovanni Dosi, Christopher Freeman, Richard R. Nelson, Gerald Silverberg, and Luc Soete (eds), *Technical Change and Economic Theory* (London: Pinter Publishers).

Government of India (1969) *Report of the Industrial Licensing Policy Inquiry Committee (Main Report)* (Chairman Shri Subimal Dutt) New Delhi: Ministry of Industrial Development).

Hausmann, Ricardo and Rodrik, Dani (2003) "Economic Development as Self Discovery," *Journal of Development Economics*, vol. 72, no. 2, pp. 603–633. Available online at http://ksghome.harvard.edu/~drodrik/selfdisc.pdf.

Hoekman, Bernard M., Maskus, Keith E. and Saggi, Kamal (2004) *Transfer of Technology to Developing Countries: Unilateral and Multilateral Policy Options*, World Bank Policy Research Working Paper No. 3332 (Washington, DC: World Bank).

Khan, Mushtaq Husain (1995) "State Failure in Weak States: A Critique of New Institutionalist Explanations," in John Harriss, Janet Hunter, and Colin M. Lewis (eds), *The New Institutional Economics and Third World Development* (London: Routledge).

Khan, Mushtaq Husain (1999) *The Political Economy of Industrial Policy in Pakistan 1947–1971*, SOAS Department of Economics Working Paper No. 98, School of Oriental and African Studies, University of London.

Khan, Mushtaq Husain (2000a) "Rents, Efficiency and Growth," in Mushtaq H. Khan and K.S. Jomo (eds), *Rents, Rent-Seeking and Economic Development: Theory and Evidence in Asia* (Cambridge: Cambridge University Press).

Khan, Mushtaq Husain (2000b) "Rent-seeking as Process," in Mushtaq H. Khan and K.S. Jomo (eds), *Rents, Rent-Seeking and Economic Development: Theory and Evidence in Asia* (Cambridge: Cambridge University Press).

Khan, Mushtaq Husain (2008) "Governance and Development: The Perspective of Growth-Enhancing Governance," in GRIPS Development Forum (ed.), *Diversity and Complementarity in Development Aid: East Asian Lessons for African Growth* (Tokyo: National Graduate Institute for Policy Studies). Available online at http://eprints. soas.ac.uk/9853/1/GRIPS.pdf.

Khan, Mushtaq Husain (2010) *Political Settlements and the Governance of Growth-Enhancing Institutions*, Research Paper Series on Governance for Growth. School of Oriental and African Studies, University of London: London. Available online ate http://eprints.soas.ac.uk/9968/1/Political_Settlements_internet.pdf.

Khan, Mushtaq Husain (2013) "Technology Policies and Learning with Imperfect Governance," in Joseph Stiglitz and Justin Yifu Lin (eds), *The Industrial Policy Revolution I. The Role of Government Beyond Ideology* (London: Palgrave).

Khan, Mushtaq Husain and Stephanie Blankenburg (2009) "The Political Economy of Industrial Policy in Asia and Latin America," in Giovanni Dosi, Mario Cimoli, and Joseph E. Stiglitz (eds), *Industrial Policy and Development: The Political Economy of Capabilities Accumulation* (Oxford: Oxford University Press).

Murphy, Kevin M., Andrei Shleifer, and Robert W. Vishny (1989) "Industrialization and the Big Push," *Journal of Political Economy*, vol. 97, no. 5, pp. 1003–26.

North, Douglass C. (1990) *Institutions, Institutional Change and Economic Performance* (Cambridge: Cambridge University Press).

Nurkse, Ragnar (1953) *Problems of Capital Formation in Underdeveloped Countries* (Oxford: Oxford University Press).

Rosenstein-Rodan, Paul N. (1943) "Problems of Industrialisation of Eastern and South-Eastern Europe," *The Economic Journal*, vol. 53, nos 210/211, pp. 202–211.

Scitovsky, Tibor (1954) "Two Concepts of External Economies," *Journal of Political Economy*, vol. 62, no. 2, pp. 143–151.

Shleifer, Andrei and Vishny, Robert W. (1997) "A Survey of Corporate Governance," *Journal of Finance*, vol. 52, no. 2, pp. 737–783.

Stiglitz, Joseph E. (1987) "Learning to Learn, Localized Learning and Technological Progress," in Partha Dasgupta and Paul Stoneman (eds), *Economic Policy and Technological Development* (Cambridge: Cambridge University Press).

Stiglitz, Joseph E. (1996) *Whither Socialism?* (Cambridge, MA: MIT Press).

Stiglitz, Joseph E. (2007) *Making Globalization Work* (London: Penguin).

Stiglitz, Joseph E. and Weiss, Andrew (1981) "Credit Rationing in Markets with Imperfect Information," *American Economic Review*, vol. 71, no, 3, pp. 393–410.

Wade, Robert (1988) "The Role of Government in Overcoming Market Failure: Taiwan, Republic of Korea and Japan," in Helen Hughes (ed.), *Achieving Industrialization in East Asia* (Cambridge: Cambridge University Press).

Wade, Robert (1990) *Governing the Market: Economic Theory and the Role of Government in East Asian Industrialization* (Princeton, NJ: Princeton University Press).

Whitley, Richard (1992) *Business Systems in East Asia: Firms, Markets and Societies* (London: Sage).

Williamson, Oliver E. (1985) *The Economic Institutions of Capitalism* (New York: Free Press).

World Bank (1993) *The East Asian Miracle: Economic Growth and Public Policy.* (Oxford: Oxford University Press).

4.4

Infant Capitalists, Infant Industries and Infant Economies: Trade and Industrial Policies at Early Stages of Industrialization in Africa and Elsewhere

Akbar Noman
Columbia University

4.4.1 Introduction

Adam Smith explicitly assumed the existence of a class of capitalists. He spoke of a "previous accumulation" of wealth in the economy into the nature and causes of whose wealth he was inquiring. This "previous accumulation" predated and preconditioned his analysis: "the accumulation of [capital] stock must, in the nature of things, be previous to the division of labour, so labour can be more and more subdivided in proportion only as stock is previously more and more accumulated."[1]

Karl Marx can be said to have followed Smith in making that assumption, translating "previous" as "*ursprunglich*" in German, which his translator rendered back into English as the famous "primitive" accumulation.[2] By being embellished by Marx and becoming part of the Marxist lexicon, "primitive accumulation" presumably acquired the connotations that perhaps led to its neglect by economists of other persuasions. Marx criticized Smith for being ahistorical in his explanation but agreed on its essentiality.[3]

The fundamental point on which Smith and Marx agree is that the accumulation of capital, at any point in time, depends on some already existing capital accumulated earlier to invest in the production process.

Hoff and Stiglitz remark that "in leaving out institutions, history and distributional considerations, neo-classical economics leaves out the heart of development economics."[4] But even the recent large literature on institutions, including notably those required for the existence and proper functioning of markets, ignores the institution implied by "previous" or

---

*The valuable help and comments of Kay Kastnet and Sanjay Reddy are gratefully acknowledged, with the usual caveats about responsibility.

"primitive" accumulation. In other words, it implicitly assumes the existence of economic agents who have monies to invest and the ability to do so – capitalists and entrepreneurs. Incentives simply determine their willingness, but not their ability, to invest how much and where.

But almost by definition that assumption is of dubious validity for economies at early stages of development like many countries in Sub-Saharan Africa today or many in East and South Asia yesterday and elsewhere the day before yesterday.

Some of the earlier literature on development with its emphasis on capital accumulation as being central to development did pay some attention to the issue of the absence or weakness of the institution implied by Smith's "previous" or Marx's "primitive" accumulation.[5]

More often than not, the focus was not so much on the complete absence of capital and capitalists as their inadequacy. As Peter Evans remarks,

> Gerschenkron's work on... late industrializers confronting... technologies with capital requirements in excess of what private markets were capable of amassing were forced to rely on the power of the state to mobilize... resources... The crux of the problem faced by late developers is that institutions that that allow large risks to be spread across a wide network of capital holders do not exist... Hirschman takes up this emphasis on entrepreneurship as the missing ingredient for development in much more detail.[6]

But, as noted above, the large literature on the economic role of institutions that has emerged rapidly in recent years, implicitly assumes the existence of capitalists/entrepreneurs in adequate measure.[7] Thus, Dani Rodrik in answering the question of which institutions matter according to the new institutional literature identifies the following five: (a) property rights, (b) regulatory institution; and institutions for (c) macroeconomic stabilization, (d) social insurance, and (e) conflict management, (whilst adding that in his view participatory politics is a "meta institution").[8]

An exception has been the attention given to this prerequisite of successful privatization in the transition economies of Eastern Europe and the former Soviet Union. This was reflected in the schemes for voucher privatization in some of these countries. Some of the critics of privatization, particularly the Russian privatization of the 1990s, blamed the disaster not only on the absence of the "standard" institutions of property rights and contract enforcement that figure so prominently in the institutional literature but also, in effect, of capitalists.[9] This has also been an issue in some of the reform programs of Africa that have also been beset by cases of privatization without the requisite institutional underpinnings.

This essay focuses on the implications of the neglect of the institution of capitalist-entrepreneurs for economic policy in countries at early stages of development. In particular, it is concerned with the fact that whilst the past decade or so has witnessed a reversal in the collapse of growth in Sub-Saharan Africa (hereinafter simply referred to as Africa) that resulted in its "lost quarter-century," progress in bringing about economic transformation of the sort that lays the foundations for sustained growth and development remains very limited. Indeed, the share of manufacturing and formal sector employment has been generally declining since 1980.

On average, the share of manufacturing in GDP in Africa fell from 17.5 percent in 1965 to 12.9 percent in 2009. Relatedly, as Noman and Stiglitz point out "there has been little success in exporting manufactures and in attracting foreign direct investment in non-extractive activities. Much of the growth of the past decade or so is accounted for by extractive activities in non-renewable resources – minerals, metals and above all, oil..."[10]

In section 4.4.2, we attempt a diagnosis of this phenomenon of deindustrialization or "detransformation" of African economies. Much of it is necessarily speculative and more in the nature of hypotheses than established results of research. Before that, in the next section, we sketch a formal case for infant capitalist protection with minimal mathematics to keep it accessible to a wider audience. The final section makes concluding remarks.

4.4.2 The infant capitalist argument

The explicit assumption of Adam Smith and Karl Marx and the implicit one of much (all?) recent institutional literature acquires particular salience at early stages of development. Formally, this can be characterized, along the lines of Greenwald and Stiglitz,[11] as the stage when the economy is embarking on *development aimed at moving beyond simple agriculture and crafts to producing output for which capital and learning are important.*

By definition, the "modern" private sector and its capitalists/entrepreneurs are absent at this stage and all output emanates from sector A which comprises agriculture and crafts, using only labor L (including skills) and M, which consists of modern manufacturing and employs both L and capital, K, which is owned and operated by capitalists, C.

$$Y = A = f_1(L)$$

M, which consists of modern manufacturing and employs both L and capital, K, which is owned and operated by capitalists, C.

$$M = f_2(L,K) = f_3(L,C) \{\text{i.e.} = f_4(C)\}$$

With both sectors, total output

$$Y = A + M = f_1(L) + f_3(L,(f_4 C))$$

C either exists on account of primitive/previous accumulation or must be acquired. There is no foreign capital or capitalist.[12]

The argument that is elaborated below on the acquisition of C and its impact on Y can be summarized as:

$$C = f_5(T,F)$$
$$Y = f_1(L) + f_3(L,(f_5(T,F)))$$

Where T stands for tariffs (implicit and explicit) and F for investment finance. With no protection and no finance for investment there is no capital accumulation and hence no capitalists and no output in M.

The relationship is not monotonic, especially with respect to T. Indeed it can be thought of as having a threshold below which and another above which there is no relationship between C and T (or indeed even a negative one beyond a point as the static efficiency costs outweigh dynamic gains) i.e. $T \geq T_a \leq T_b$

Inevitably at early stages of development, the form of industrial organization is characterized by an absence of divorce between ownership and management of capital. *The capitalist and the entrepreneur are one and the same.* So protection stimulates both accumulation and entrepreneurship.

Industrial (or modern sector) entrepreneurship requires capital, which can be borrowed – and much of it typically is, especially at early stages of industrialization – or saved out of profits.

Again, inevitably the financial sector is very weak and highly imperfect at the stage we are concerned with. Stock and bond markets do not really exist and the availability of long–term finance is largely characterized by its absence, especially at rates of interest that would allow borrowing for investment that does not yield immediate and very high returns.

The venerable infant industry argument used by Alexander Hamilton, the first Treasury Secretary of the United States, to establish the system of protection under which US industrialized[13] can be said to have matured some six years with the infant economy argument of Greenwald and Stiglitz.[14]

The essence of these arguments is well known and revolves around learning and spillovers. Activities in countries at an early stage of development cannot compete with those already well established in more advanced economies and protection is necessary to help them grow, learn, and become competitive. That case is extended or adapted in this essay to what we refer to as the *infant capitalist argument: protection by reducing risks and boosting profits can help create and nurture capitalists and enable learning.* It does so by facilitating both higher accumulation (savings) out of profits and bigger borrowings – as larger profits and reduced risks in the protected activities enhance creditworthiness.

If the capitalist and the entrepreneur are one and the same then capital accumulation and entrepreneurship are intertwined at "infancy" and physical and human capital are accumulated jointly. Acquiring physical capital is necessary for learning, which in turn facilitates further accumulation.

Moreover, as argued below, a well-designed structure of protection can also help to improve the quality of rents by directing them into industry and entrepreneurship from arguably the more wasteful forms that rents have often taken, particularly after trade liberalization in many countries, notably in Africa.

4.4.3 Infant capitalism in Africa: facts, speculations, and hypotheses

At the time of independence, African countries typically can be characterized as lacking a class or private sector with the wherewithal to become entrepreneurs in "modern" activities. More precisely, to the extent such groups existed, they predominantly comprised foreigners or ethnic minorities of relatively recent origin (such as Indians and Lebanese in parts of East and West Africa, respectively).[15]

Arguably, at independence there was probably a greater divorce between economic and political elites in Africa than anywhere else. This would seem to underlie the emergence of the political economy of what Meles Zenawi calls the "predatory state" in Africa.[16] At any rate, this is likely to have provided the basis for an attitude of ambivalence, at best, toward the private sector and of resort to public ownership of industries that characterized much of Africa, especially in the 1960s and 1970s.

Many countries in the region still feature predominantly infant or toddler indigenous capitalists in manufacturing or modern services. There is a clear political economy case to protect, create or nurture them.

Whilst some individuals and groups have acquired significant wealth from rent seeking, it does not serve the purpose that previous or primitive accumulation performed in Adam Smith's and Karl Marx's economy. That is to say, there is little or no incentive to invest in modern, transformational sectors in which learning is important or indeed to invest domestically as opposed to transferring assets abroad.

The sources of wealth are predominantly trading or unproductive rents in a system of incentives that emerged from the economic reforms that are commonly referred to as of the Washington Consensus (WC) variety.[17] Typically, rents have taken the form of kickbacks on government contracts, insider wheeling and dealing associated with contracts for mineral resources or real estate or privatization or just plain theft. Such wealth is also more likely to end up overseas than that emanating from investment in industry.

Trade and financial sector reforms aimed at liberalization have often taken away the incentives to invest in domestic production activities. As Azizur Rehman Khan put it, such reforms have often taken away bad incentives but replaced them with worse ones.[18]

Nicholas Stern argues that the

> central policy question here is: How can a country develop governance
> and institutions to support entrepreneurship and well-functioning mar-
> kets... The policy challenge is thus the promotion of growth through
> improvements in the investment climate: it is about creating conditions
> so the pie keeps expanding. It is not just a question of how to avoid or
> limit losing slices of the pie as measured by Dupuiy-Harberger triangles
> or even rent-seeking quadrilaterals...[19]

However, the investment climate and related governance reforms of the
type that have become the fashion or part of donor conditionalities have
been very imperfect substitutes for the sort of trade and industrial policies
that attract investments in productive, learning activities. More often than
not the reform programs ended up by not so much reducing rents as diverting them into unproductive forms.

In contrast, rents acquired via incentives for infant industrialists to invest
in infant industries can contribute to structural transformation and learning
of the type that succeeded so spectacularly in East Asia and to varying degree
elsewhere in Asia and in Latin America.[20]

4.4.4 Lessons of success: infants who grew up

Much of the literature on policies for developing countries to catch up
revolves around the interpretation and lessons of the astounding success in
several East Asian countries that has been labeled the East Asian miracle.[21]

The replicability of the East Asian "model," especially with regard to
trade, industrial, and financial policies has been much debated essentially
on account of its "governance" requirements. The "developmental state"
to which is attributed the success of East Asian-style public policy interventions is held to be very difficult to emulate. However, others, such as
Ha-Joon Chang, Mushtaq Khan, Noman and Stiglitz, and Meles Zenawi,
have emphasized that governance is not entirely exogenous and argued that
the non-replicability of East Asian policies in Africa and elsewhere is much
exaggerated.[22]

Whatever one's views on the replicability of East Asian-style policy interventions, the feasibility of success with the sort of infant capitalist promotion outlined above is demonstrated by a highly relevant non-East Asian
case: that of Pakistan. An excellent, detailed study by Gustav Papanek[23]
shows how Pakistan created a class of "capitalist-industrialist-entrepreneurs"
pretty much from scratch almost overnight: in not much more than five
years. Protection played a key role.

Papanek notes that "Pakistan like other countries in Africa and Asia, not
only lacked industrial entrepreneurs; it seemed unlikely to develop them in

the short run... [but] in fact industry grew rapidly, indeed and was largely developed by private entrepreneurs."[24] He attributes it at the most proximate level to "annual profits of 50–100 percent on investment" in industry[25] in the early 1950s (which moreover "helped to restrict both capital flight and consumption").[26] By the late 1950s, Papanek reports, such profit rates had fallen to 20–50 percent. Nonetheless by then enough of a class of industrial entrepreneurs and momentum had been created for industrial growth to continue at heady rates.

Stephen Lewis (1970) and Akbar Noman (1991) also examine how industrialists/entrepreneurs/capitalists emerged and blossomed. At the center of a host of incentives for investment in manufacturing, were rates of protection that provided high and assured profits.[27] With long-term credit at modest interest rates provided in ample measure by two development banks – the Pakistan Industrial Credit and Investment Corporation (PICIC) for large industries and the Industrial Development Bank of Pakistan (IDBP) for medium-sized industries – in a context of reasonable macroeconomic stability, investment and accumulation boomed.

The aforementioned Lewis study was undertaken under the rubric of the highly influential OECD research program on trade and industry directed by Little, Scitovsky, and Scott (LSS) that resulted in their seminal synthesis volume and accompanying country studies.[28] Even as LSS noted and criticized the many pitfalls of the protection regime they pointed out that "within our seven countries, only Pakistan had to discover an entrepreneurial class" and as is shown by the accompanying country study, Lewis (1971), it had done so well within a decade.

LSS and Lewis agree with Papanek (1967) on this count but they differ from his analysis, in emphasizing the static inefficiencies generated by protection. Indeed, LSS go as far as to suggest that the rapid industrialization that Pakistan experienced was so inefficient that value added at world prices remained almost negligible. However, this claim of LSS has been subjected to critical scrutiny with the upshot that there is little doubt that these inefficiencies are much exaggerated.[29] The system of protection in Pakistan had many excesses and irrationalities and attendant inefficiencies but they were nowhere near as bad as claimed by LSS and Balassa (1971).[30] Moreover, there was considerable learning with productivity growth and declining inefficiencies over time.[31]

Indeed, Pakistan's GDP and industrial growth accelerated to what came to be known as East Asian miracle levels before Korea, as did the emergence and growth of manufactured exports. In the mid-1960s such exports exceeded those of Korea by a substantial margin. Korea actively sought to learn from Pakistan, including by sending the staff of its economic ministries for training in Pakistan.

Whatever the inefficiencies of Pakistan's industrialization, there are, arguably, some important lessons that can be drawn about creating or building the institution of capitalists/entrepreneurs, albeit whilst avoiding the excesses that vitiated Pakistan's trade and related policies. The rates and variability of protection in Pakistan during the 1950s and 1960s were so high as to leave considerable scope for improvements while still providing the critical level of incentives for the building of a group or class of economic agents with the ability and willingness to invest in modern, transformational activities.

4.4.5   Concluding remarks

The case for infant capitalist or any other rationale for protection has to be tempered in the light of the many failures of interventionist policies for trade and industrialization. But the dangers of excessively high and irrational protection can and should be avoided. We now have lessons of failure that were not available or widely appreciated in the 1950s and 1960s and perhaps even in the early 1970s.

The importance of an experimental approach that quickly scales up successes and abandons failures is one of the lessons of success. However, learning and implementing the lessons of successes and failures well does demand capacities that are not possessed by all governments. More precisely, the risks and rewards depend on the particular circumstances of a country, including its governance. However, governance capabilities are not given and immutable: the question is not only what governance capacities exist at any point in time but also what need to be and what can be built up at what speed. This way of posing the question is all too often ignored or neglected.

As noted above, the absence of protection of infants also carries risks. Inevitably, there are and will be rents and corruption everywhere. The questions are what forms of corruption are most intolerable, what forms can be eliminated and how to minimize the negative effects of corruption and rents and channel them into productive activities and learning. A blanket attempt to eliminate all corruption and rents, which is the avowed aim of the good governance agenda that has become the fashion, may make the pursuit of the best the enemy of the good through a failure to prioritize and by unintended consequences.

Diverting rent seeking toward rents that accrue from investing in domestic transformational activities such as industry in poor countries can be done by a well-designed system of protection. We have a much better appreciation of the need to avoid extremes of level and variability of protection but some variability is needed: broadly speaking, moderately nigh for simple consumer goods in which low-income countries have comparative advantage, lower on intermediate goods (none for those that are inputs for exports) and very low or none for capital goods.

Trade policies need to be embedded in a vision, a strategy for economic transformation, in *industrialization* policies. Managing the moral hazard emanating from socializing risks of investment and accumulation in industry requires ensuring that infants grow and learn. The successful cases provide ample evidence of the role of exports and competition in achieving that: protection and export promotion can coexist and competition can be gradually increased.

Another challenge is to avoid exchange rate overvaluation in resource-rich and heavily aid-dependent economies. That is beyond the scope of this paper, except to point out that such overvaluation is an argument for protection. Indeed, trade liberalization in such a context can exacerbate the adverse effects of currency overvaluation – and arguably did so in the case of some African economies.

This is reflected in the deindustrialization or "de-transformation" of African economies in the lost quarter-century that has not been reversed even as economic growth has accelerated in the past decade or so. Bringing about that reversal, in particular, the role that trade policies can play in facilitating Adam Smith's "previous" or Karl Marx's "primitive" accumulation or just plain private sector investment in domestic activities that transform the economy, is what we have been concerned with. Infant capitalists establishing infant industries in infant economies need protection. They also need long-term finance at reasonable interest rates. These considerations were neglected in the so-called Washington Consensus-inspired reform programs. The neglect remains to be rectified.

Notes

1. Adam Smith ([1776] 2003) *The Wealth of Nations* (New York: Bantam Dell), p. 350. "Stock" is Smith's term for capital stock. Smith elaborates that for example, in a market society, "a weaver cannot apply himself entirely to his peculiar business, unless there is beforehand stored up somewhere, either in his own possession or in that of some other person, a stock sufficient to maintain him, and to supply him with the materials and tools of his work, till he has not only completed but sold his web. This accumulation must, evidently, be previous to his applying his industry for so long a time to such a peculiar business" (Smith [1776] 2003).
2. Michael Perelman (2000) *The Invention of Capitalism: Classical Political Economy and the Secret History of Primitive Accumulation* (Durham, NC: Duke University Press), p. 25.
3. In highlighting the historical process, Marx developed a different meaning of primitive accumulation in that he linked it to the notion of capital as "class relation" rather than as "stock." Given that "the capital-relation presupposes a complete separation between the workers and the ownership of the conditions for the realization of their labour," it follows that "the process... which creates the capital-relation can be nothing other than the process which divorces the worker from the ownership of the conditions of his own labour." By turning "the social means of subsistence and production into capital, and the immediate producers into wage-labourers," this process is therefore the basis of class formation. Thus, the "so-called primitive accumulation is nothing else than the historical process

of divorcing the producer from the means of production"; Karl Marx, ([1867] 1976) *Capital*, vol. 1 (New York: Penguin), pp. 874–875.

4. K. Hoff and J.E. Stiglitz (2001) "Modern Economic Theory and Development," in G. Meier and J.E. Stiglitz (eds), *Frontiers of Development Economics* (New York: Oxford University Press), p.390.

5. Gerald Meier, for example, remarks that "Believing that [in] a developing country ... the supply of entrepreneurship was limited and large structural changes... were needed the first generation of development advisers... turned to the government... to promote *capital accumulation*, utilize reserves of labor,... undertake policies of deliberate industrialization..." (emphasis added); G. Meier (2001) "The Old Generation of Development Economists and the New," in G. Meier and J. Stiglitz (eds), *Frontiers of Development Economics* (New York: Oxford University Press). Also see, for example, Papanek (1967); Lewis (1971), Little, Scitovsky and Scott (1971), where the issue of creating or strengthening the institution of the private sector or capitalists/entrepreneurs is discussed. Elsewhere, advocates of public sector-led industrialization based their case partly on the weakness of the private sector.

6. Peter Evans (2005) "The State as Problem and Solution: Predation, Embedded Autonomy and Structural Change," excerpted in G. Meier and J. Rauch (eds), *Leading Issues in Economic Development* (New York and Oxford: Oxford University Press), p. 543.

7. For a general overview and critique of this literature, see Mushtaq Khan (2012) "Governance and Growth: History, Ideology and Methods of Proof," in Akbar Noman et al. (eds), *Good Growth and Governance in Africa: Rethinking Development Strategies* (New York and Oxford: Oxford University Press). Also see, in the same volume, Thandika Mkandawire (2012) "Institutional Monocropping and Monotasking in Africa."

8. Dani Rodrik (2007), One *Economics Many Recipes: Globalization, Institutions and Economic Growth* (Oxford and Princeton: Princeton University Press), Chapter 5.

9. See, for example, Joseph Stiglitz................... For other institutional failures that marred privatization in the transition economies of the former Soviet Union and Central Europe, also see Karla Hoff.

10. Akbar Noman and Joseph Stiglitz (2012), "Strategies for African Development," in Akbar Noman et al. (eds), *Good Growth and Governance in Africa: Rethinking Development Strategies* (New York and Oxford: Oxford University Press), p. 8.

11. Bruce Greenwald and Joseph Stigitz (2006) "Helping Infant Economies Grow: Foundations of Trade Policies for Developing Countries," *American Economic Review*, vol. 96, no. 2, pp. 141–146.

12. Alternately, foreign capital/capitalists are very imperfect substitutes for those of the domestic variety or domestic capital/capitalists are a different and necessary factor of production. This is essentially a political economy argument for the need for local capitalists, where "local" could mean a particular ethno-linguistic group like the "bumiputras" in Malaysia.

13. See Ha-Joon Chang (2002) *Kicking Away the Ladder: Development Strategy in Historical Perspective* (London: Anthem Press).

14. Greenwald, B. and Stiglitz, J.E. (2006).

15. This is analogous to the situation in Malaysia that led to the New Economic Policy (NEP) launched in 1971 to promote the development of Bumiputra (indigenous Malay) businesses/capitalists/private sector. Whilst controversial and flawed in some respects, NEP is credited with possibly staving off ethnic conflicts.

16. Meles Zenawai (2006) *African Development: Dead Ends and New Beginnings (excerpts).* Available at http://policydialogue.org/events/meetings/africa_task_force_meeting_manchester_2006/materials/.
17. See, for example Joseph Stiglitz (2008) "The Post-Washington Consensus Consensus" in Narcis Serra and Joseph Stiglitz (eds), *The Washington Consensus Reconsidered* (New York and Oxford: Oxford University Press).
18. A.R. Khan (2009) chapter 4, in Quazi Shahabuddin and Rushidan I. Rahman (eds), *Development Experience and Emerging Challenges: Bangladesh* (Dhaka: University Press), especially pp. 66–72.
19. Nicholas Stern (2003) "Public Policy for Growth and Poverty Reduction," in R. Arnott, B. Greenwald, R. Kanbur, and B. Nalebuff, *Economics for an Imperfect World: Essays in Honor of Joseph E. Stiglitz* (Cambridge, MA and London: MIT Press,).
20. See for example, Robert Wade (1990) *Governing the Market* (Princeton, NJ: Princeton University Press); Alice Amsden (1989) *Asia's Next Giant* (New York: Oxford University Press); Ha-Joon Chang (1994) *The Political Economy of Industrial Policy* (London and Basingstoke: Macmillan); Jose Antonio Ocampo (2012) *The Economic Development of Latin America since Independence* (Oxford: Oxford University Press).
21. The literature is vast. In addition to Amsden (1989) and Wade (1990); see, for example, World Bank (1993) *The East Asian Miracle: Economic Growth and Public Policy* (New York: Oxford University Press); Ha-Joon Chang (2006) *The East Asian Development Experience: The Miracle, The Crisis and the Future,* (London and New York: Zed Books); Bela Balassa (1988) "The Lessons of East Asian Development: An Overview," *Economic Development and Cultural Change,* vol. 36; no. 3, Supplement; Joseph Stiglitz (1996)"Some Lessons from the East Asian Miracle." *The World Bank Research Observer,* vol. 11, no.2; J. Stiglitz (2001) "From Miracle to Crisis to Recovery: Lessons from Four Decades of East Asian Experience," in J. Stiglitz and S. Yusuf (eds), *Rethinking the East Asian Miracle* (Oxford: Oxford University Press). Also see Commission on Growth and Development (2008) *The Growth Report: Strategies for Sustained Growth and Inclusive Development* (Washington, DC: World Bank).
22. See Ha-Joon Chang's contribution to this volume. Also see the following essays in A. Noman, K. Botchwey, H. Stein, and J. Stiglitz (eds) (2012) *Good Growth and Governance in Africa: Rethinking Development Strategies* (Oxford and New York: Oxford University Press): Mushtaq Khan (2012) "Governance and Growth Challenges for Africa"; Akbar Noman and Joseph Stiglitz (2012) "Strategies for African Development" and Meles Zenawi (2012) "Neo-liberal Limitations and the Case for a Developmental State".
23. Gustav Papanek (1967) *Pakistan's Development: Social Goals and Private Incentives* (Cambridge, MA: Harvard University Press), in particular chapters II and III.
24. Ibid., p. 29.
25. Ibid., p. 33.
26. Ibid., p. 36.
27. S.R. Lewis (1970) *Pakistan; Industrialization and Trade Policies* (Paris: OECD). Akbar Noman (1991) "Industrial Development and Efficiency in Pakistan: A Revisionist Overview," *The Pakistan Development Review,* vol. 30, no. 4 (Winter).
28. I.M.D. Little, T. Scitovsky, and M.F. Scott (1970) *Industry and Trade in Some Developing Countries* (Paris: OECD).
29. See Noman (1991) for the compelling reasons for considering the LSS estimates of inefficiency to be grossly exaggerated and references to other relevant

studies, including A.R. Kemal (1974) "The Contribution of Pakistan's Large-scale Manufacturing Industries Towards GNP at World Prices," *The Pakistan Development Review*, vol. 13, no. 1.

30. B. Balassa and Associates (1971) *The Structure of Protection in Developing Countries* (Washington, DC: Johns Hopkins University Press).

31. See, for example, Meekal Ahmed (1980) "Productivity, Prices and Relative Income Shares in Pakistan's Large-Scale Manufacturing," D.Phil. Thesis, Oxford University; and A.R. Kemal (1978) "An Analysis of Industrial Efficiency in Pakistan, 1959–60–1969–70," PhD thesis, University of Manchester.

4.5

Industrial Policies and Contemporary Africa: The Transition from Prebendal to Developmental Governance

Richard Joseph
Northwestern University

Africa has entered a new era of economic growth after decades of sustained efforts to promote reforms. During the 1980s, it was recognized that the economic strategies implemented during the first two decades of the post-colonial period had largely failed. Economies were stagnant or in decline, core institutions were eroding, and there was a steady outflow of intellectual talent and financial resources. An economic recovery became apparent in the mid-1990s and has strengthened over the past 15 years, matching the last sustained period of growth in Africa that began in the mid-1950s (Radelet, 2010). Accompanying the economic downturn was political stasis and decay. Competitive party systems eroded and few countries were even minimally democratic in 1990. The economic and political quandary heightened concerns about the legitimacy, efficacy and even coherence of the nation-state systems bequeathed to Africa by colonialism (Joseph, 1999; Herbst, 2000).

The resumption of economic growth in much of Sub-Saharan Africa, and the stabilizing of political systems after democratic and other reform processes of the 1990s, have re-engaged the attention of economists. Their studies are multiplying and so is the application of theoretical models based on experiences in other regions. Invariably, these analyses take into consideration the state and governmental systems. Even more problematic for many economists are factors involving society, culture, and institutional legacies. The prospect of high sustained growth in Africa raises the possibility of the transformation of these countries from a reliance on primary agricultural production and mineral extraction which have characterized their economies for decades.

John Page, among others, has underscored this fundamental challenge: "In poor countries structural change – the shift of resources from low productivity to high productivity uses – is a key driver of economic growth. In both theory and history, industry has been the sector that leads the process of structural change." However, "on average manufacturing in Africa's low-income countries is smaller as a percentage of GDP than it was in 1985." Consequently, "Africa has experienced very little growth enhancing structural change." "There is little evidence," he further contends, "that significant structural change has underpinned Africa's recent growth" (2012: 86–7).[1] A critical question, therefore, is whether the widely reported GDP increase in a score of African states since the mid-1990s will be more than a transitory episode.

Roger Myerson is an economist who has expressed a keen interest in "the problematic nature of governments in Africa." "The great central question," he suggests, "is what can anyone do to try to improve the quality of governance." What is needed, he continues, is "some conceptual framework for thinking more clearly about the fundamental political problems that impede economic development in so many countries."[2] Some contemporary development economists, however, do not regard "the problematic nature of African governments" as a central concern, nor do they ponder what can be done "to improve the quality of governance." The contention that the "fundamental political problems that impede economic development" require a revamped "conceptual framework" is not always acknowledged. Myerson's comments highlight two contrasting perspectives: one concerned with governance, and other societal, impediments to growth; the other contending that major governance issues can be taken up further along the path of economic progress.[3]

In most African countries, however, it is often difficult to disentangle state, politics, and economy, as excerpts from a commentary by Kenyan anti-corruption crusader, John Githongo, show:

- Kenya's $34 billion economy is the largest economy in east Africa, constituting more than half that of the region and 60 percent of its middle class.
- Some of the most entrenched politicians are facing charges at the International Criminal Court, which has introduced accountability to a class... that has run the country since independence with a mixture of corruption, crony capitalism, repression and a delicate waltz with the west.
- The recent discovery of oil and other mineral deposits has raised the stakes further.
- One of the continent's most venal, ruthless yet sophisticated elites has tended to mobilize according to tribe.
- Despite President Mwai Kibaki's laissez-faire approach to economic management and corruption, Kenya has done well economically. In the past ten years, gross domestic product has risen 33 percent.
- Violence that followed elections in 2007, when Kenya came dangerously close to civil war... The danger of more bloodshed is dangerously high. The effects of violence would reverberate throughout the region and damage hopes of an economic renaissance.[4]

Virtually all African countries must find a path through the state–governance–economy thicket described by Githongo. There is little consensus about how this can be done.

4.5.1 Industrial policies and the developmentalist state

"'Industrial policies', meaning policies by which governments attempt to shape the sectoral allocation of the economy, are back in fashion and rightly so" (Greenwald and Stiglitz, 2012). Martin Wolf provides a useful summary of industrial policies. While recognizing "the decisive contribution of market forces," it acknowledged that the government plays a key role "in prodding those forces in the right direction... guiding the economy and overcoming obstacles to the process of continued economic upgrading."[5] In line with this perspective, Akbar Noman and Joseph Stiglitz (2012 pose specific questions about contemporary Africa:

1. Could government play a more active role in promoting development?
2. If so, what should it do? What are the governance requirements for a more activist state?
3. What lessons could Africa glean from the experience of Asia?
4. "How could one square accusations of corruption...with the tasks to be performed by the developmental state or its more common and feasible variant, the 'developmentalist state'?" (2012: 4)

Different responses to these questions are provided in papers published in *Good Growth and Governance: Rethinking Development Strategies* (2012).[6] At the Pretoria Roundtable on July 3, 2012, Ha-Joon Chang gave one of the most affirmative responses: "The advanced economies all suffered from these problems in the past. When they were at levels of economic development comparable to today's African countries, today's developed countries were actually much worse in terms of suppression of democracy, corruption, state capture, incoherence of the state machinery, nepotism, and other 'pathological' forms of politics. [These problems] "should not make us believe that we have to wait for a perfect state to emerge before doing anything." The Taiwanese model, Chang argues, shows how "islands of competence" can be constructed within a bureaucracy, given greater responsibilities as they succeed, and increase their legitimacy and status until they supplant much of the old bureaucracy (2012). Implied in his formulation is the presence of an interventionist regime which, in a directive fashion, rebuilds the state machinery from the inside out.[7] Are such regimes, we should ask, evident in the current growth spurt in Africa? If not, what is the likelihood of their emergence?

Mushtaq Khan adds several refinements to the industrial policy perspective (2012a, 2012c):]

1. The governance capabilities required to pursue new growth trajectories need not be optimal. They may be far from "developmental state capabilities."
2. A dual "learning-by-doing" process ensues in which actions are taken to overcome market failures while increased capabilities are acquired.
3. The capabilities cannot be transferred from outside. The learning process involves drawing on "tacit knowledge" which differs among countries. Good outcomes can be obtained in different industries organized differently in the same countries.
4. The learning process is not determined *ab initio* and then implemented. Growth requires a continuous adaptation to changing economic and political circumstances.
5. The nature of a country's politics constrains how ambitious it can be. Attention must be paid to institutions "that will work in different countries" and the "macro-political order" that determines how such institutions function.
6. No country achieved significant "good governance" capabilities before it developed. So "good governance" should not be considered a "precondition for development."
7. Economically successful countries did not begin with "good governance capabilities." What they had were "growth-producing" governance capabilities that allowed them to sustain growth. The challenge therefore becomes that of identifying the "vital growth-enhancing capabilities."
8. Ultimately, societies have to devise their own political compromises and government institutions that can pragmatically address their growth challenges given their historical and political constraints.

Khan has provided a number of important insights, drawing notably on the Bangladesh experience. There are certain assumptions embodied in his framework. First, it implies the presence of a "growth-enhancing" state, a Janus entity that can see both backward and forward, make adjustments as needed, and direct the activities of a range of economic agents in society. This entity contrasts with the state familiar to students of African politics, which has been described as evincing "deeply rooted manifestations of weakness and ineffectiveness arising from decades of postcolonial authoritarian and corrupt stewardship" (Harbeson, 2013). How the gap will be bridged between such state systems and the ones that would play the development-promoting role outlined by Chang, Khan, and others is a question to be confronted.

4.5.2　The learning agenda

The industrial policy framework includes, at its very core, a learning agenda. These suggestions draw on earlier work by Joseph Stiglitz that emphasized the importance of educational development and especially of the tertiary sector ([Chang, 2001). Greenwald and Stiglitz note the significance of understanding how economies best learn, and how they can be organized to increase the production of knowledge considered a central component of growth and development. Moreover, this learning process must be largely endogenous: "Learning takes place locally and must adapt to local differences in culture and economic practice" (2012). The weakness of African universities, and their significant decline in quality and capacity even while rapidly increasing in number, as in Nigeria, show how much of a challenge this recommendation implies.

Greenwald and Stiglitz echo Khan and others on points whose problematic nature can be indicated. One of these is the significance of drawing on "tacit knowledge." "There are numerous aspects of tacit knowledge," they claim, "about how individuals interact with each other, and norms of behavior that affect economic performance, and most particularly, how (and whether) they learn and adapt." The learning that is essential to the growth process has implications for the state and governmental systems required to facilitate this course: "Each country makes, effectively, decisions about what it will learn about." "Where does it want to go? What must be learned?" The "tacit knowledge" that guides behavior that impacts economic activities may, however, be non-developmental and generate suboptimal outcomes, a point to be taken up later. The state and governmental system described by John Githongo, and which is present in many African countries, is the agent implied in the statement that "the country makes, effectively, decisions..." Who, it should be asked, speaks and acts on behalf of "the country"? There is a great gap between the self-serving, unaccountable, "agent" represented by many post-colonial African regimes and the "smart state" implied by the industrial policy framework.

The developmentalist state conceived by Khan, or the more modest notion of a "facilitating state" by Justin Yifu Lin (2012), is a sagacious entity. It systematically promotes learning about market opportunities and explores how to seize them. It learns how to strengthen its own operational capabilities, and endeavors to "discover and find solutions appropriate" to the country's conditions (Khan, 2012a: 55). Khan sums up his vision and analysis in a complex sentence: "The answer may be we need to achieve some intermediate and immediate growth-promoting governance capacities to sustain growth which will eventually provide the resources to improve some of these market-enhancing capabilities as well as achieve other development objectives" (2012a: 73–4). To highlight the steps envisaged by Khan, I have distilled his sentence into a diagram (see Figure 4.5.1).

Assumed but not examined are the sociocultural and historical factors that facilitate the emergence of a developmentalist/facilitating state; or, conversely, that may impede or render unlikely its emergence without some extra-systemic intervention. The pertinent writings of Dani Rodrik

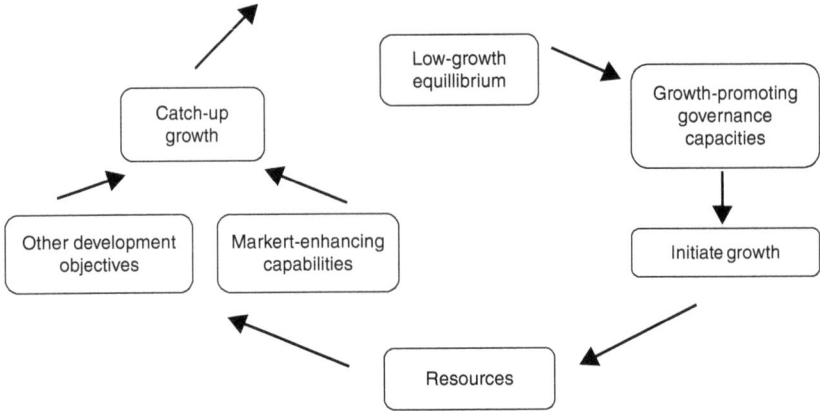

Figure 4.5.1   Growth-promoting governance

can be applied to this model. Rodrik agrees that the initiation of economic growth – the growth spurt or acceleration – is relatively easy to do. It has happened before in many African countries but just as often fizzled out. This phase does not require significant institutional innovations. However, achieving catch-up growth so that a country escapes the low-growth equilibrium, and the economy undergoes structural transformation in its levels and sectors of productivity – and generates increased employment, incomes and livelihoods – requires new and appropriate institutions ([2007: 43–51). Unlike some contemporary political economists, Rodrik emphasizes the value of democracy – which he calls a meta-institution – in the building, extension and expansion of such institutions (2007: 51, 155).

4.5.3   The developmentalist option: confronting complexity

The developmental state, as theorized by Chalmers Johnson and elaborated by several others, was a superb modeling exercise. Complex developments in several Asian countries were distilled into a half-dozen key elements. On the basis of this model, Johnson made a rather biblical injunction: "A state attempting to match the economic achievements of Japan must adopt the same priorities as Japan. It must first be a developmental state." In an edited book devoted to this framework, it is interesting to note the chapter by Juhana Vartiainen which opened a few windows to the real-world complexities in latecomer countries (1999). Vartiainen brings to the developmental state debate the experiences of Finland and other Nordic countries in which an "all-encompassing corporatist mobilization of the major agents of the economy was undertaken from the turn of the century onward" (1999: 209). We will take up the "Nordic Advantage" while reviewing the ongoing work of Bo Rothstein and his colleagues in the Quality of Government Institute (QOG), Sweden.

Here I want to consider Vartiainen's statement that "the incredibly complex system of implicit and explicit contracts and moral rules of which a mature economy consists contains a substantial hidden order that has developed... over decades and centuries" (1999: 234). It is this "substantial hidden order" which can facilitate or obstruct the developmental process and should not be minimized. Some of the attempts to apply the developmental state experience in East Asia to Sub-Saharan Africa tend to gloss over this "hidden order" in the former, and the "drag" of social, economic, and political behaviors in the latter. By contrast, Vartiainen acknowledged "the importance of social and political institutions and cultural norms in fostering economic development and sustaining exchange transactions" (1999: 201). Some scholars engaged in this debate over a decade later are similarly wary of minimizing the behaviors and institutions of long duration that produce suboptimal outcomes in education, health, and infrastructure, as well as in commercial and other economic ventures.

In *Good Growth and Governance*, Banji O. Oyeyinka and Padmashree Gehl Sampath reflect the cautionary perspective of Vartiainen. "Most latecomers," they argue, "have weak or non-existent state capacities." They therefore require "an even larger dose of state action, but also of policy competence," and stronger governmental interventions (2012: 274). How can that be done in such circumstances? The process of creating institutions that override market forces, they point out, are often stymied by self-interested behaviors of the very persons responsible for designing and/or implementing these policies which contribute to repetitive suboptimal outcomes. "State-led development and lessons learned from East Asian successes" therefore must "be broadened to include factors specific to latecomer contexts." The developmental discourse must, Oyeyinka and Sampath further contend, be "broadened to capture a wider array of issues than those simulated by the East Asian experiences" (2012: 277). They identify obstacles which would be familiar to persons who have overseen development projects in Africa: "low-level information regimes," "low-level knowledge and poor skills for policymaking choices," domestic structures and socioeconomic forces that "are powerful enough to induce socially suboptimal policy choices to retain the status quo" (2012: 277–8). Next to each of these impediments I can affix a specific set of endeavors in Nigeria that accounted for suboptimal choices, performance, and outcomes and the wastage of enormous human and capital resources.[8]

Justin Yifu Lin's formulation of the "facilitating state" is a balanced one. He identifies the tasks to be performed in the state-led model that include "addressing the information gap and externalities," "targeting industries in line with comparative advantages," devising industrial policies based on industries and countries which are a step up in the chain of production, and then the judicious use of rents and protection (2012). But there is no certainty, Lin acknowledges, that the process will unfold in a beneficial manner. The risks are substantial: subsidies and protection could go to firms that prove not to be viable or fail to achieve global competitiveness. The allocation of rents and subsidies could add fuel to already existing rent-seeking behaviors. The attempt to pick winners can result in the picking of losers; and crony instead of competitive capitalism can be fostered. This cautious approach reflects the high uncertainty of successful implementation and thus outcomes.

Stiglitz asks whether some African states have the capacity to fulfill the roles assigned to them by the industrial policy framework. He and Noman distinguish "developmental states," such as Japan, Korea, Taiwan, and Japan, from "developmentalist states," such as Indonesia, Malaysia and Thailand, where state interventionism was less stringent (2012: 33). This is a helpful point of departure. Izuji Ohno and Kenichi Ohno carry forward this inquiry by noting the considerable variety among East Asian states normally cited (2012: 222–4). These countries advanced at different speeds, used different mechanisms, and focused on different sectors of their economies. What they all did was develop capacities through learning and discovery. They identified the ultimate goals, but not the paths to achieving them. There were missteps, mistakes, and the learning process was endogenous. They encountered weak policy capability, as discussed by Oyeyinka and Sampath, but overcame them through "focused hands-on endeavors to accomplish concrete objectives" (2012: 242). "Capabilities were built in the process of industrialization; they were not prepared *ex ante* as the precondition for growth" (2012: 225). Ohno and Ohno describe this process as "dynamic capacity development: building industrial policy capability through a joint process of tackling the political and economic factors" (2012: 234).

These insights are also reflected in the attitudes of some contemporary scholars of African development, and development practitioners, which focus on "learning-by-doing." Deborah Brautigam, one of the leading scholars of China's economic engagement with Africa, criticizes US aid policies for being overly skewed to addressing social sectors, such as health, while "not doing much to provide jobs." Six Chinese firms, she points out, "have now invested in Ethiopia's thriving leather products sector but none from the U.S." "We could do a lot more," she concludes, "to help Africans build their own economic pathway to better governance."[9] An "economic pathway to better governance" would, not too long ago, seem like an oxymoron. Others are chiming in, such as Jacqueline Novogratz, CEO of the Acumen Fund, which works directly to help small entrepreneurs in poor countries: "Just start, and let the work teach you," she states.[10] Two quite different modes of thought are in confrontation. While Ohno and Ohno see a "confusion of causality between growth and governance," another voice claims that better governance *is* "the change that can unlock Africa's potential."[11]

We have to work with, and indeed seek to harmonize, these contrasting but equally important perspectives. One claims that growth-enhancing govern-ance capabilities can be acquired through concrete economic endeavors; the other contends that bad governance, and deficient governments, will obstruct and corrupt even the suggested growth-enhancing process.

4.5.4 The low-growth equilibrium and the social trap

What development economists discuss as a low-growth equilibrium, other social scientists have viewed from combined sociological, political, and cultural perspectives (Hyden 1983; Sandbrook 1985; Englebert 2000). One of the most innovative efforts in this regard is the current work of Bo Rothstein and his colleagues in the Quality of Government Institute (QOG) of the University of Rothenberg, Sweden.[12] QOG's work centers on how the African predicament of pervasive corruption, and clientelistic and patrimonial politics have yielded governments incapable of producing core public goods and services, much less achieving high sustained growth.[13] They describe such countries as having "severely corrupt environments" and their economies as hindered by the reinforcing dimensions of a "social trap." Instead of the standard definition of corruption as "the abuse of pub-lic office for public gain," they propose a norm of "impartiality" for public officials. Corruption is its violation "to achieve a private gain" (Rothstein, 2011b). The ultimate challenge is the creation of an impartial and universal state which treats all citizens fairly.[14] While QOG criticizes the limited atten-tion social scientists have devoted to studying corruption, Justin Yifu Lin and Celestin Monga provide a summary of the many innovative approaches to this issue (2012: 2–3).

Similar to the development economists, QOG is critical of the "interna-tional good governance regime," or what the former calls the good govern-ance agenda, not because its usual objectives – accountability, transparency, human rights, and the rule of law – are not worthy in themselves, but because their pursuit has often been ineffective.[15] Many reasons for the inef-fective implementation of this agenda are given. A key one, they suggest, is because it is usually based on a principal–agent model. The principal agent, the government leaders, are induced and incentivized – usually by external donors – to get the agent, the bureaucracy, to be non-corrupt. These efforts have produced little change in the perception-of-corruption rankings of the countries concerned. Transitions to electoral democracy, according to QOG, have also not served to effect change, as ordinary citizens are also caught in the "social trap" and reinforce it through their voting behavior.[16]

There is limited knowledge, QOG contends, regarding how the transi-tion from a severely corrupt environment to a less corrupt one can be made.[17] The main reason is because the problem tends to be mischaracter-ized. Usually absent is the willingness of principals to hold corrupt officials

302 The Industrial Policy Revolution II

accountable. Lin and Monga make the same point: "the social sciences literature does not provide an incentives-compatible mechanism for political leaders to improve governance and eliminate corruption" (2012: 3). At all levels of society, according to QOG, individuals and groups calculate that the immediate benefits to them of corruption outweigh the costs of behaving differently. Transforming these systems would require collective action that is difficult, and often impossible, to engineer. Two questions converge. How to break out of the low-growth equilibrium? How to break out of the "social trap"?

If the historical experience usually referenced by development economists is that of East Asian economies, for QOG it is that of the Nordic countries. What occurred in Sweden within a few decades in the late 19th-century parallels similar developments elsewhere in the region. A transition from corrupt patrimonial governance took place, often in response to military defeat, to effective and non-corrupt bureaucratic systems as a consequence of deliberate actions by political reformers. Rothstein refers to what occurred as a "big bang." This notion might at first appear inappropriate to characterize changes that occurred over a few decades. However, according to the cosmological model, the big bang was followed by "inflation" in which the cosmos emerged very rapidly, and then settled into evolutionary processes over eons. The key point is that a sharp transition occurred from one mode of governance in both the Nordic and East Asian countries, and this facilitated the expansionary and structural growth that followed. Growth-enhancing governance, in other words, is made possible by a rupture within the macro-institutional framework.

We have two contrasting models, both of which start from similar observations and share similar objectives: exploring how countries trapped in a low-growth equilibrium can experience accelerated growth, and sustain it over the decades necessary to transform economies and social wellbeing. Where they differ is significant. QOG speaks of a social trap which cannot be gradually pried open – efforts to do so usually end up reinforcing the same harmful behaviors – but must be busted open. In this regard, their views are consonant with that of Francis Fukuyama in his explanation of how countries have historically moved from patrimonial to modern state systems (2011). According to Fukuyama, a bright line separates two fundamentally different ways of regarding and using state offices: one essentially for the private benefit of their occupants, cronies and kin-groups, and the other to advance the public welfare of citizens.

Three decades ago I first published an analysis of Nigeria's political sociology which I characterized as prebendalism. Here is a summary of this perspective which is consonant with both that of Fukuyama and QOG:

In my adaptation of this concept to Nigerian politics as well as many peripheral capitalist nations, the term prebendal refers to patterns of political behavior which reflect as their justifying principle that the offices of the existing state may be competed for and then utilized for the benefit of office-holders as well as that of their reference or support group. To a significant extent, the "state" in such a context is perceived as a congeries of offices susceptible to individual *cum* communal appropriation. The statutory purposes of such offices become a matter of secondary concern however much that purpose might have been codified in law or other regulations or even periodically cited during competitions to fill them. (Joseph 1983)

In *Origins of Political Order*, Fukuyama similarly applies the fundamental insights of Max Weber: "The hallmarks of the modern office are a separation between the office and the officeholder; the office is not private property; the office-holder is a salaried official subject to the discipline of the hierarchy within which he is embedded; offices are defined functionally; and office-holding is based on technical competence" (2011: 270). Although Fukuyama carries his analysis up to the French Revolution in the first volume of his study, he has set forward the framework that will no doubt feature in the second volume: "Impersonal modern states are difficult institutions to both establish and maintain, since patrimonialism – recruitment based on kinship or personal reciprocity – is the natural form of social relationship to which human beings will revert in the absence of other norms and incentives" (2011: 450). Fukuyama and QOG concur, both in the analysis of the central dilemma and even in their regional frame of reference. Fukuyama calls the transformation process, "Getting to Denmark": a state system that is "stable, democratic, peaceful, prosperous, inclusive and...[has] extremely low levels of political corruption" (2011: 14).

Fukuyama's description of governance in pre-revolutionary France could be applied virtually unchanged to many African countries during the post-colonial era: "The system created by the French government was an absolute nightmare. It virtually legitimized and institutionalized rent seeking and corruption by allowing agents to run their public offices for private benefit" (2011: 339). "A modern France could not arise until venal office-holding was replaced by impersonal, merit-based bureaucracy" (2011: 349). Fukuyama and QOG share a fundamental conviction: this change is not brought about incrementally but reflects a rupture that usually requires the control of state power by a leader and regime determined to execute such a transformation:

The French Revolution was able to reestablish a bright line between public and private interest by simply expropriating all of the old venal officeholders' patrimonies and lopping off the heads of the recalcitrant ones. A new political system in which recruitment into political office was to be based on merit and impersonality – something the Chinese had discovered nearly two millennia earlier – was then brought to the rest of Europe by the man on horseback... The nineteenth-century German bureaucracy that became Max Weber's model for modern, rational public administration did not evolve out of patrimonial officeholding, but rather styled itself as a conscious break with that tradition. (2011: 371)

The analyses of QOG and Fukuyama help sharpen the contrasting perspectives mentioned above. One argues the need to wrest government systems, societies, and economies out of an institutional and behavioral matrix characterized by prebendalism and suboptimalism. Another, based on interpretations of the East Asian experience, suggests otherwise. Ha-Joon Chang addresses and, in effect, dismisses the perspective advanced by the QOG. Many believed, he asserts, that "high-quality bureaucracies are very difficult to build and that the East Asian countries were exceptionally lucky to have them from history. However, a high-quality bureaucracy can be built pretty quickly as shown by the examples of Korea and Taiwan" (2012). Korea in the mid-20th century, he contends, was characterized by poor governance, high corruption, and low capabilities, just as many African countries today. Other scholars, however, are providing a more nuanced understanding of governance, growth, and social welfare in South Korea, even during the years of dictatorship (Kim, Kwon and Yi 2011). It may prompt similar re-examinations of other East Asian cases.

Many political economists, when they wish to show that African countries can have state/society/economy experiences that replicate East Asia, often point to the examples of Botswana and Mauritius. But these two countries, which avoided the low-growth equilibrium and social trap, have long been regarded by Africanist social scientists as exceptions whose impressive achievements have few carry-over implications for most of the continent. Mauritius, with a heterogeneous racial composition, diverse colonial heritage, and sustained competitive party politics, adopted *dirigiste* economic management and welfarism. However, it is so distant from the African landmass that it often does not even appear on maps of the continent. Botswana has benefited from an unusual combination of a small population, exceptional leadership, a core ethnic configuration, and well-managed resource wealth.[18] (Samatar 1999, 2002). Daron Acemoglu and James Robinson, in elaborating their distinction between inclusive and exclusive political and economic institutions, use Botswana and the Congo to represent these alternatives in Africa (2012). But they are outliers. The challenge in Africa today is exiting the default prebendalist systems and transiting to developmentalist political economies, as represented by Figure 4.5.2.

4.5.5   Prebendalism to developmentalism

Considerable work has been done in defining the developmental state and explaining its key features. The elements of this model, however, constitute

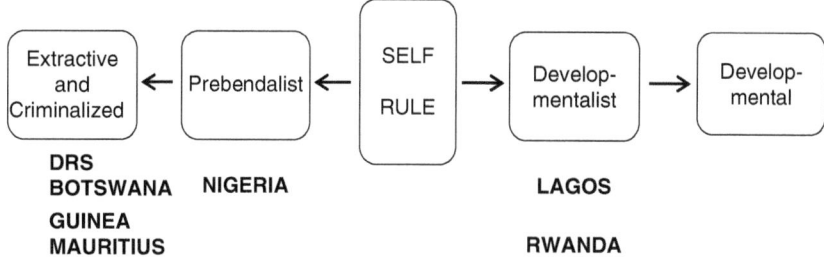

Figure 4.5.2 Prebendalism vs developmentalism[19]

"too ambitious" a project for most African countries where core infrastructures have atrophied along with the bureaucracies needed to maintain them.
To imagine such entities "governing the market", as Robert Wade describes
the developmental state, is not a realistic proposition (2004, 2012). Among
the score of African countries now experiencing accelerated growth, more
feasible are the developmentalist variants suggested by Noman and Stiglitz.
From Justin Yifu Lin, we can also think of the developmentalist state as a
"facilitating state." Four sets of "facilitating factors" appear critical:

1. Growth and Development Leadership
2. Growth and Development Institutions
3. Growth and Development Society and Culture
4. Growth and Development Resources (Human/Natural/Financial)

A country such as Nigeria could be well endowed with the fourth factor –
human, natural, and financial resources – but all of the other three could
become warped away from developmentalism. How these four factors are
dynamically coordinated is the challenge to be confronted in all African
countries, if an exit from the low-growth equilibrium/social trap is to be
negotiated. South Africa, approaching the end of the second decade of post-
apartheid rule, is facing the same dilemma.[20] As Oyeyinka and Sampath
contend, this is a more daunting scenario than the one considered in the
growth-enhancing governance model based on a "simulation" of the East
Asian experience.

In my introduction to the edited volume, *State, Conflict and Democracy in
Africa* (1999), while discussing Deborah Brautigam's chapter on Mauritius,
I remarked: "The challenge of explaining how a dysfunctional state can be
transformed into one that enjoys authority and legitimacy while facilitating
socioeconomic development can prompt exercises in conjecture and advocacy" (1999: 13). After summarizing her chapter, I concluded: "Since 1989,
many political experiments have been launched in Africa. Identifying the
ones that are likely to combine state building, democracy, and economic

growth is a vitally important project that requires similar studies of the *actual exercise of power and the building of institutions* in a range of countries" (italics added). After another decade marked by resumed growth, we are in a position not just to hypothesize about how to sustain these processes, based on the quite different societies and cultures of Scandinavia and East Asia, but by examining how they are being actually executed in Africa. A shift can therefore be made from conjecture and advocacy to analysis and interpretation based on how these processes are unfolding.[21]

Space does not permit a full discussion of these models. However, two contrasting cases, Rwanda and Lagos State in Nigeria, can be summarized briefly from the optic mentioned above: "growth-enhancing governance is made possible by a rupture within the macro-institutional framework." They illustrate models of developmental governance that can be characterized as authoritarian and democratic. Developmentalism is propelled by leaders and regimes that are committed to moving their societies out of the low-growth equilibrium, building globally competitive economies, and avoiding replicating the "modal pattern in sub-Saharan Africa... in which 'rent-seeking' is widespread and uncontrolled, and associated with both political and administrative corruption" Booth and Golooba-Muteba, 2012: 7).[22] The governments concerned do not just rely on indigenous "tacit knowledge." Rather, they assess what the knowledge needs are and contract with foreign institutions to provide technical and organizational knowledge to supplement what is locally available. In view of their different histories, ethnic composition, and colonial experiences (Belgian/ British), their leaders have considerably different social and political forces with which to contend.

David Booth and Frederick Golooba-Muteba label Rwanda under the rule of Paul Kagame and the Rwanda Patriotic Front (RPF) a case of "developmental patrimonialism."[23] Through RPF-controled holding companies, "politically-generated opportunities for profit are comprehensively institutionalized and centralized" (2012: 9). Using the regime's monopoly powers, Fukuyama's bright line could be instituted and enforced. As a consequence, "recruitment and promotion decisions are able to be based to a large extent on merit and effectiveness," a wide range of public goods could be generated, and "corruption is quite uncommon in [the] public service at any level" (2012: 14). In Lagos State, one of Nigeria's 36 states with a population comparable to Rwanda's of over 10 million, a comprehensive state-directed transformational exercise has been pursued since 1999 under former state governor Bola Tinubu (1999–2007), and especially his previous chief-of-staff and now governor, Babatunde Fashola.[24]

Unlike Rwanda, growth and development in Lagos State is taking place in a highly democratic environment. While the business–politics relationship in Rwanda "rests on a centralized management of rents," Lagos State pursues a vast array of public–private partnerships along with a multiplicity of state-created ventures in power generation, transportation, water supply, environment, and physical security. There is no equivalent in Lagos State of the holding companies, allied with the ruling party, that control major business ventures in Rwanda. There are areas of overlap between the two systems. In Rwanda, the UK-trained Rwanda Revenue Authority is seen as "harsh and inflexible [and]... unlikely to make concessions to anybody" (2012: 18n). The Lagos State growth model was propelled by the creation of a taxation system which generates so much income from individuals and corporations that the state covers a substantial proportion of its operating budget from internally generated revenues.[25] It has also tapped into international capital markets.

On the issue of financial probity, words used to describe Babatunde Fashola could be equally applied to Paul Kagame: "Fashola has acquired a reputation that embodies the very qualities Nigerians often complain have been lacking in their leaders: technocratic competence, commitment to results and above all, integrity."[26] Rwanda and Lagos both exemplify growth-enhancing governance; both are seeking to build regionally and internationally competitive market economies; and both are making considerable use of global partners. None of this would be possible without a macro-institutional rupture. The Rwandan case is well known as a consequence of the 1994 genocide and the publicity brought to the regime by its foreign advocates, such as former US president Bill Clinton. The macro-institutional rupture followed armed conquest by the RPF, the battles and interventions in neighboring Congo, and the determination of this regime to keep all opposition forces at bay using whatever draconian measures it deems necessary.[27] The macro-institutional rupture in Lagos State is based on the developmentalist/ welfarist policies and philosophy of Chief Obafemi Awolowo, who served as Premier of Nigeria's former Western Region and Federal Commissioner of Finance and Vice-President of the Federal Executive Council during the Nigerian Civil War.[28]

The political success of the Action Congress of Nigeria (formerly Action Congress) in Lagos State since 1999, and the recapture of control by Awoist parties of most of the states of southwest Nigeria in recent elections, have enabled Tinubu and Fashola to implement their transformational policies. The Lagos State government is demonstrating that economic restructuring, accompanied by major infrastructural developments, can take place while adhering, in significant measure, to a "good governance agenda" of accountability, transparency, the rule of law, and operational efficiency. As many microfinance institutions, public health, and worker training schemes are introduced, the government is also showing that industrial policies favorable to corporate growth can be combined with major social welfare programs.

What this brief summary of these two cases of developmental governance demonstrates is that the four facilitating factors – leadership, institutions, society/culture, and resources – can appear in different configurations in contemporary Africa. Prebendalism is so endemic to Nigeria that it would be unreasonable to expect that it would be curtailed in half-a-generation in the multi-ethnic and multi-religious megalopolis of Lagos State.[29] However, it has not been of a level to hinder the significant socioeconomic and infrastructural advances. Moreover, opportunities for initiatives in developmental governance have been encouraged at many levels and in many sectors (Fashola, 2009). As the main locus of Nigeria's vigorous and diverse media, innumerable civil society groups, and vibrant party politics, many instruments of vertical and horizontal accountability are available to the populace to limit the abuse of power. Given its particular circumstances Rwanda cannot replicate the Lagos model (although it may eventually have to adjust to growing international criticism). Nigerians would not tolerate a RPF-style regime, and a system based on generating and "managing rents in a centralized way," even if this is done "with a view to the long term" (Booth and Golooba-Mutebi, 2012: 9). To adapt a comment once made by Richard Sklar (1983) about African democracy, Africa is today a workshop of developmental governance. Before long, the issue of whether or not East Asian growth models can be adopted there may be less salient as the continent continues to generate viable ones of its own.

4.5.6 *Good Growth* and *Good Governance*

Countries cannot achieve sustained and transformative growth, involving the shift from largely subsistence agricultural economies to globally competitive ones, and the generation of well-paying jobs for their urbanizing populations, without significantly improving ways of managing their collective affairs through appropriate institutions.[30] Justin Yifu Lin and Célestin Monga are seeking to formulate an approach that does not minimize the political and social constraints in Africa while pursuing growth-enhancing governance. They acknowledge the correlation between Africa's stalled development and the low quality of governance (2012: 5). Yet, in line with Chang and Khan, they believe that "the dominant view of good governance as a precondition for economic success is ... misguided" (2012: 2). Similar to most participants in the Pretoria Roundtable on Industrial Policy, they recommend shifting the focus from the many items on the "good governance agenda" to "actionable policies that poor countries could implement to foster inclusive growth in a pragmatic and incentives-compatible way" (2012: 2). Lin and Monga believe they have an answer to the growth–governance conundrum:

> The observation that the generally low quality of governance in Sub-Saharan African countries (at least as measured by available perception indicators) is correlated to their level of economic development may be a first step in solving an apparent mystery. What is crucially needed to

fight corruption and improve governance in low-income countries is *a development strategy that offers few opportunities for state capture and rent-seeking activities.* In other words, the main solution to corruption is to create a policy environment where there are few opportunities and gains for such externality-generating activities. We suggest economic development strategies be geared towards industries, sectors, and policies with few opportunities for rent-seeking.[31] (italics added)

However, as was shown earlier regarding Mushtaq Khan's "answer," resolving the mystery of the growth–governance nexus in Africa can generate further conundrums. The Lin/Monga formulation hovers on a tautology: "the main solution to corruption is to create a policy environment" where there is reduced corruption ("few opportunities for rent-seeking"). Yet, "severely corrupt environments," as Rothstein and his colleagues argue, are characterized by "state-capture and rent-seeking." Industrial policy strategies usually require the allocation of subsidies and rents to enable indigenous firms to get started and grow until the subsidies and rents can be phased out. As mentioned earlier, Rodrik contends that high-quality institutions are needed for countries to advance beyond the growth acceleration stage. By contrast, Lin and Monga state that "the dynamic development of competitive firms and industries *eventually leads* to institutional development"(italics added; 2012: 2). Their hypothesis corresponds to the one cited above from Deborah Brautigam that economic growth can provide a path to better governance. The "answer" proposed by Lin and Monga that state responsibilities must be carried out in ways that reduce "risks of state capture and rent-seeking" (2012: 6) would be agreed to by John Githongo and all anti-corruption crusaders. To avoid a tautological exercise – reducing corruption by reducing opportunities to be corrupt while providing the very instruments and resources that, *pace* Oyeyinka and Sampath, fuel corruption – a "macro-institutional rupture" cannot be avoided.

The QOG contention, supported by Oyeyinka and Sampath, that you cannot achieve "growth-enhancing governance" within "severely-corrupt environments" by just "doing things differently" must be directly confronted. "State-capture and rent seeking" *is* the system in many African countries. Systemic change (and structural economic growth), I would argue, require multi-level as well as multi-sectoral strategies. This is what each of the emerging models of developmental governance in Africa must seek to accomplish. Lagos State is making demonstrable advances with such an approach: combining a macro-institutional "rupture" with growth-enhancing changes at all levels and in all sectors subject to state action, or through guidance and prodding by the state of private actors.

What we do know from decades of post-colonial rule in the continent confirms Fukuyama's observation that "the most universal form of human political interaction is a patron–client relationship in which a leader exchanges favors in return for support from a group of followers." Even when political upheavals take place, "there is constant pressure to repatrimonialize the system" (2011: 453).[32] Despite major political transitions, and the availability of abundant external assistance, Frederick Chiluba as president of Zambia (1991–2001) and Abdoulaye Wade as president of Senegal (2000–12) used their power and authority largely to replicate autocratic, corrupt, and nepotistic systems. The same appears to be happening under Alpha Condé in Guinea, a country whose abundant natural resources have been used to sustain predatory systems over a half-century, condemning its people to widespread poverty and the depredations of transnational crime networks.[33] The record of the post-1990 period in Africa is clear: If a new government arrives with a Chiluba, Kibaki, Wade, Zuma, or Condé at the helm, who is not determined to engineer a pro-development rupture in the state/politics/economy fabric but is content to manage ethno-prebendalist networks, suboptimal rather than transformative outcomes are inevitable.

The Pretoria Roundtable and *Good Growth and Governance* brought to my attention an important wave of work by political economists concerned with how Africa could exit the labyrinth of low productivity and multiple social ills. After reading and reflecting on these studies, I find the proposal that governance capabilities will be "discovered" in the growth process as insufficient as the one being rejected, namely, that improvements in governance will open the door to accelerated growth. Neither perspective, as it concerns contemporary Africa, is compelling on its own. I suggest instead the need to harmonize them, in theory and practice. Moreover as mentioned above, such syntheses *are* occurring in multiple arenas in Africa. Some ideas for follow-up work emerge from this exercise. First, the frontiers of political economy and social science regarding structural economic transformation in Africa represent a gray zone in which theories and arguments often fade into speculation. A determined effort should be made to bring together political economists concerned with Africa and their Africanist counterparts.[34] They can work collaboratively on a new body of research that carries forward the "juxtaposition" initiated in this chapter. Moreover, a research center has been created with the requisite financial and institutional support, within an educational institution, to help unravel the "quality of governance" issues.[35] QOG can contribute significantly to such a collaborative project, especially as its researchers have the statistical capabilities of modern economists.

The developmentalist models being formulated in actual governing practice in Africa provide an opportunity to focus on what is required to help these incipient efforts succeed. "Islands of excellence" can be created in particular sections of national and provincial bureaucracies. But they can, as often happened in the past, be swamped by waves of prebendalism and political repression. In country after country in Africa, development initiatives have been undermined by such practices. Regarding South Africa,

Africa's largest economy, where the growth rate is now less than half that of the rest of Sub-Saharan Africa, two recent commentaries show how South Africans are beginning to characterize the post-apartheid system. Oxlela Mangcu: "Our government has become the closest thing to what Richard Joseph called prebendalism – a term he borrowed from the sociologist Max Weber and applied to Nigeria. A prebendal government is one in which politicians reward their families, friends and supporters with loads of money."[36] Morris Sello: 'I am very disappointed in this government. I lost faith in them. They are stealing too much and leaving us with nothing."[37]

Lin and Monga contend that African policymakers are provided "few actionable prescriptions on how to design policies to achieve their economic and governance goals" (2012: 3). This is certainly true. With regard to the Bola Tinubu/Babatunde Fashola developmentalist model in Lagos State over the past 13 years, however, actionable prescriptions are being fashioned interactively by leaders who, Janus-like, know where their societies have come from, and can convert societal visions into appropriate programs and institutions. A prerequisite that cannot be skirted in such scenarios is a governing entity committed to facilitating/enabling such a process. It may replicate aspects of the developmental state as in Botswana and Mauritius; pursue developmentalism as in Lagos State and Rwanda; or be semi-facilitative, the current situation in several countries. Ghana and Uganda are in the latter category, with developmentalism coexisting with prebendalism. In Ghana, revenues from petroleum export complicate a two-party dominant system in which power can change hands every four years. In Uganda, President Yoweri Museveni and his government have blocked the transition to an electoral democracy. With oil revenues on the horizon, a developmental scenario is even more problematic.

4.5.7 Conclusion: optimizing the growth and governance transitions

Despite the optimism generated by Africa's recent growth, its manufacturing sector, as John Page shows, "is smaller, less diversified and less sophisticated than it was in the decade following independence." "Without an acceleration of structural change," Page argues, "the region's recent growth turnaround runs the risk of not sustaining its momentum into a middle-income status" (2012: 121). Jeffrey Herbst and Greg Mills also caution about the hurdles to be surmounted: "The boom has not led to much investment to boost businesses and start a virtuous cycle of true poverty reduction through job creation."[38] Moreover, not to be overlooked are three challenges to which, as Fukuyama contends, all countries must respond, or see their progress stymied: building an effective state authority, achieving law-based governance, and enhancing public accountability (2011). Wherever African countries begin in the process based on their colonial and post-colonial experiences, they cannot advance as modern states without fashioning institutional responses to these imperatives. They may not, in this era, "get to Denmark," and acquire a state system that is "stable, democratic, peaceful, prosperous, inclusive and... [has] extremely low levels of political corruption." But that is the direction in which their people, given a choice, would want to go.[39]

The pace of population growth, urbanization, climate change, and the coming on stream of petroleum, gas, and other mineral resources – together with achieving structural economic transformation – will require more effective, law-based and accountable governments. Industrial policy strategies prompt questions about state coherence, legitimacy, and efficacy, the Achilles' heel of countries with multiple ethnicities and uneven access to education and other fundamental resources and services. The increased attention being paid by myriad institutions and agencies to reducing corruption is particularly important for African countries seeking to make their economies more attractive for investments outside the extractive sector. Acquiring governments capable of "guiding the economy and overcoming obstacles to the process of continued economic upgrading" (Wolf, 2012) should not be minimized; nor should the importance of *simultaneously* improving the quality of growth and governance.[40] To repeat the contention of Lin and Monga, there are "few actionable prescriptions on how to design policies to achieve their economic and governance goals" that can simply be handed to African leaders in government, business, and society. Our era, however, makes it possible for such policies to be designed interactively using methods of "informed experimentation" available through enhanced modes of communication within and among countries (M. Joseph, 2012). In the absence of governments determined to move their societies decisively from prebendalism to developmentalism, it is difficult to see how the structural transformation of African economies, and the elimination of mass poverty, will be achieved.

Notes

1. These key challenges were also addressed by Célestin Monga in his presentation, "The Globalization Jackpot: Job Dividends from a Multi-Polar World," at the WorldBank/IEA Roundtable, July 2012.
2. These comments are excerpted from a personal message of June 19, 2012.
3. A helpful summary of different definitions of governance is provided in Lin and Monga (2012).
4. John Githongo, "Violence Threatens to Drag Kenya Back into Despair," *The Financial Times*, October 17, 2012.
5. Martin Wolf, "Pragmatic Search for Path to Prosperity," review of Justin Yifu Lin, *The Quest for Prosperity: How Developing Economies Can Take Off, Financial Times*, October 14, 2012.

6. As several authors of papers in this collection were also presenters at the International Roundtable, "New Thinking on Industrial Policy: Implications for Africa," in Pretoria, July 3–4, 2012, I was able to obtain access to a wide range of their ideas, arguments and analyses.
7. Page briefly describes how African countries are experimenting with this approach, such as the launching of a cut-flowers industry in Ethiopia (2012: 121).
8. For a discussion of these pervasive constraints in Nigeria, see Daniel J. Smith (2007), Wale Adebanwi (2011), and W. Adebanwi and E. Obadare (2013). South Africa is experiencing the replication of the same syndromes that stymied growth and development in post-colonial Africa. See Lydia Polgreen, "South Africans Suffer As Graft Saps Provinces," *New York Times,* February 18, 2012.
9. Deborah Brautigam, "It's Business as Usual for China," *New York Times,* September 20, 2012.
10. Quoted in an interview by Adam Bryant, "When Humility and Audacity Go Hand-in-Hand," *New York Times,* September 29, 2012.
11. President Barack Obama in his Address to the Ghanaian Parliament, Accra, July 11, 2009.
12. The summary of the analyses and arguments of QOG is based on Rothstein (2011a and b), Uslander and Rothstein (2012), and Persson, Rothstein and Teorell (2012).
13. Two studies that sounded the alarm about non-developmental politics in newly independent Africa were René Dumont, *l'Afrique noire est mal partie* (Editions du Seuil, 1962), and Stanislav Andreski, *The African Predicament: A Study of the Pathology of Modernisation* (Atherton Press, 1968). An English translation of Dumont's book appeared as *False Start in Africa* (Praeger, 1966), and in a revised edition in 1969.
14. Larry Diamond, in a number of publications, has called attention to how bad governance, and especially corruption, has hindered economic and political progress in many countries, as well as the provision of basic public goods. See Diamond (2008, 2011).
15. There is a contrast here with the contention of Steven Radelet (2010) who contends that the emergence of more democratic and accountable governments is the first of five fundamental changes responsible for the economic turnaround in Africa.
16. These entrenched patterns are discussed in the epilogue, "The Logic and Legacy of Prebendalism in Nigeria," I contributed to Wale Adebanwi and Ebenezer Obadare, *Democracy and Prebendalism in Nigeria: Critical Interpretations* (Basingstoke: Palgrave Macmillan, 2013).
17. There are analyses characterized as "Afro-pessimism," which have regarded the "social trap" as one firmly bolted against efforts at political and economic reforms. Bruce Berman, for example, presents African society as trapped in ethnically driven patrimonial politics that has led to the "fragmentation and privatization of state power [and] undermines its ability to act as the agent of such a project of national development" (2004: 48).
18. For an application to Botswana of the developmental state model, see Ian Taylor (2012). It is important for scholars to avoid simply repeating "miracle stories" about contemporary Botswana and pay attention to how the system has tilted in recent years toward the autocratic patrimonial model. See the report of a talk by Amy Poteete, a leading student of Botswana politics and development: "Canadian Professor Decries Botswana 'false democracy'," *The Botswana Gazette,* February 4, 2012.

19. Countries are listed according to the preponderant dynamics of their political/ economic systems. Whether prebendalist practices in South Africa, for example, now merit its inclusion along with Nigeria in that category is an assessment for South African scholars and analysts to make.

20. 18 years after the first post-apartheid government came to power in 1994, the fraying system in South Africa is reminiscent of Nigeria, 18 years after the end of colonial rule. See R. Joseph, "Affluence and Underdevelopment" (1978). That article was followed by the conceptualizing of the Nigerian system as a case of prebendal governance, a concept now increasingly applicable to South Africa, especially the use of governmental offices in provincial administrations.

21. A new wave of works by Africanist political scientists is doing just that. See, for example, Anne Pitcher (2012) and Scott Taylor (2012).

22. The timely article by David Booth and Frederick Golooba-Mutebi reference the formulations of Mushtaq Khan, including his contribution to *Good Growth and Governance*, so there is an overlap with this chapter in the questions they address.

23. The politics–business relations they describe, however, could also be character-ized as a form of corporatism and an analysis made based on an extensive litera-ture not limited to the developing world.

24. There is considerable variation in estimates of the population of Lagos. The issue has now become politicized, with the state government's citing a figure several million higher than that of the federal authorities.

25. In a country notable for tax-avoidance, along with other financial misdeeds, the success in obtaining compliance with tax obligations by Lagos inhabitants and corporate bodies is a remarkable achievement in contemporary Nigeria. However, the presumed ownership by former Governor Tinubu of the private company which manages tax collection, and gets a hefty commission, has been a highly controversial aspect of these operations.

26. Matthew Green, "The Man who would tame Nigeria's Megacity," *Financial Times*, August 7, 2009.

27. Victoire Ingabire, leader of the opposition in Rwanda, was sentenced on October 30, 2012 to 8 years' imprisonment for "treason and genocide denial." The RPF's treatment of critics in the media and opposition parties is similar to that of another authoritarian developmentalist regime, the EPRDF in Ethiopia.

28. Awolowo came to be recognized as the premier political leader among the Yoruba people, predominant in the southwest, although he failed to win the presidency in the 1979 and 1983 elections.

29. In a forthcoming study by R. Joseph, Kelly Spence, and Abimbola Agboluaje, "Corporate Social Responsibility and Latecomer Industrialilzation in Nigeria," we discuss the daunting obstacles to creating and expanding manufacturing firms in Nigeria. The recent improvement in GDP statistics does not reflect employment growth in the industrial sector or poverty reduction.

30. "Improved ways of managing their collective affairs through appropriate institu-tions" captures the essence of my understanding of good governance.

31. This is a fuller version, provided in a personal message of the statement made in Lin and Monga (2012: 5).

32. A few scholars remain dismissive of the now considerable body of work that has been done on personalist and patrimonial political systems in Africa. See Mkandawire (2012).

33. Guinea is a "nation-space" in which multinational firms contract with whoever occupies the seat of government for the rights to exploit its abundant mineral

wealth, with little benefit accruing to the population. See the exposé in *The Financial Times* of November 3–4, 2012. For the distressing neighboring case, Guinea-Bissau, which emerged from valiant armed struggle against Portuguese rule only to collapse into unstable and predatory governance, see Adam Nossiter, "Leader Ousted, Nation is Now a Drug Haven," *New York Times*, November 2, 2012.

34. The latter group would include such scholars as Wale Adebanwi, Deborah Brautigam, Peter Lewis, Anne Pitcher, Amy Poteete, and Scott Taylor.
35. QOG makes a case for focusing on the quality of "government" rather than "governance." The latter, in my understanding, includes the former.
36. Xolela Mangcu, "Leaders Don't Plunder," *Sowetan* (South Africa), August 14, 2012.
37. Quoted in Lydia Polgreen, "Upheaval Grips South Africa as Hopes for its Workers Fade," *The New York Times*, October 13, 2012.
38. Jeffrey Herbst and Greg Mills, "The Future of Africa's Youth Hinges on Creating Employment," *The Financial Times*, November 1, 2012.
39. This point has been repeatedly confirmed in Afrobarometer surveys; www.afro barometer.org.
40. For a report on the failure of white Zimbabwean farmers, expropriated at home, to succeed in launching commercial agriculture in Nigeria because of their inability to secure basic inputs, see Xan Rice, "Zimbabwean Farmers Lured to Nigeria Struggle for Survival," *The Financial Times*, November 2, 2012. Nigeria's food import bill of $10 billion is increasing by 11 percent annually, although many of the items could be produced locally.

References

Acemoglu, D. and Robinson, J. (2012). *Why Nations Fail: The Origins of Power, Prosperity, and Poverty* (New York: Crown Publishers).

Adebanwi, W. (2011). *Authority Stealing: Anti-Corruption War and Democratic Politics in Post-Military Nigeria* (Durham, NC: Carolina Academic Press).

Adebanwi, W. and Obadare, E. (2013) (eds) *Democracy and Prebendalism in Nigeria: Critical Interpretations* (Basingstoke: Palgrave Macmillan).

Andreski, S. (1968). *The African Predicament: A Study in the Pathology of Modernisation* (New York: Atherton Press).

Berman, B. (2004) "Ethnicity, Bureaucracy & Democracy: The Politics of Trust," in B. Berman, D. Eyoh, and E. Kymlicka, *Ethnicity & Democracy in Africa* (London: James Currey Ltd; Athens: Ohio University Press).

Fashola, B. (2009). "Leadership, Followership, Good Governance and Development in Nigeria". Faculty Distinguished Lecture, No. 3. Faculty of the Social Sciences. University of Ibadan, Nigeria.

Booth, D. and Golooba-Mutebi, F. (2012) "Developmental Patrimonialism? The Case of Rwanda," *African Affairs*, vol. 111, no. 444, pp. 379–403.

Brautigam, D. (2012) "It's Business as Usual for China," *New York Times*, September 12.

Chang, H.-J. (2001). *The Rebel Within: Joseph Stiglitz and The World Bank* (London: Anthem Press).

Chang, H.-J. (2012) "Industrial Policy: Can Africa Do It?" IEA/World Bank Roundtable. New Thinking on Industrial Policy: Implications for Africa." Pretoria, South Africa. July 3–4.

Diamond, L. (2008) "The Democratic Rollback: The Resurgence of the Predatory State," *Foreign Affairs*, vol. 87, no. 2, pp. 36–48.

Diamond, L. (2011) "Why Democracies Survive," *Journal of Democracy*, vol. 22, no. 1, pp. 17–30.

Dumont, R. (1962) *L'Afrique noire est mal partie* (Paris: Editions du Seuil).

Engelbert, P. (2000) *State, Legitimacy and Development in Africa* (Boulder and London: Lynne Rienner Publishers).

Fukuyama, F. (2011) *The Origins of Political Order: From Prehuman Times to the French Revolution* (New York: Farrar, Strauss and Giroux).

Githongo, J. (2012) "Violence Threatens to Drag Kenya Back into Despair," *Financial Times*, October 17.

Greenwald, B. and Stiglitz, J. (2012) "Industrial Policies, the Creation of a Learning Society, and Economic Development," IEA/World Bank Roundtable, "New Thinking on Industrial Policy: Implications for Africa," Pretoria, South Africa, July 3–4.

Harbeson, John W. (2013) "Democracy, Autocracy and the Sub-Saharan African State," in John W. Harbeson and Donald Rothchild (eds), *Africa in World Politics: Engaging a Changing Global Order* (Boulder: Westview Press).

Herbst, J. (2000) *States and Power in Africa: Comparative Lessons in Authority and Control* (Princeton, NJ: Princeton University Press).

Hyden, G. (1983). *No Shortcuts to Progress: African Development Management in Perspective* (London: Heinemann Educational Books).

Johnson, C. (1999) "The Developmental State: Odyssey of a Concept" in M. Woo-Cumings (ed.), *The Developmental State* (Ithaca and London: Cornell University Press).

Joseph, R. (1978) "Affluence and Underdevelopment: The Nigerian Experience," *Journal of Modern African Studies*, vol. 16, no. 2, pp. 221–239.

Joseph, R. (1983) "Class, State and 'Prebendal Politics' in Nigeria," *Journal of Commonwealth and Comparative Studies*, vol. 21, no. 3, pp. 21–38.

Joseph, R. (1987) *Democracy and Prebendal Politics in Nigeria: The Rise and Fall of the Second Republic* (Cambridge: Cambridge University Press).

Joseph, R. (2013) "The Logic and Legacy of Prebendalism in Nigeria," in W. Adebanwi and E. Obadare (eds), *Democracy and Prebendalism in Nigeria: Critical Interpretations* (Basingstoke: Palgrave Macmillan).

Joseph, R. (ed.) (1999) *State, Conflict and Democracy in Africa* (Boulder and London: Lynne Rienner Publishers).

Joseph, R. and Gillies, A. (eds) (2008) *Smart Aid for African Development* (Boulder and London: Lynne Rienner Publishers).

Joseph, R., Spence, K, and Agboluaje, A. (forthcoming) "Corporate Social Responsibility and Latecomer Industrialization in Nigeria." Available online at http://africaplus.wordpress.com/2013/07/21/corporate-social-responsibility-and-latecomer-industrialization-can-nigeria-do-it/.

Joseph, M. (2012) "Make Mistakes Ahead of Time," Interview. Insights Lab. September.

Khan, M. (2012a) "Governance and Growth: History, Ideology and Methods of Proof," in A. Noman et al. (eds), *Good Governance and Growth in Africa: Rethinking Development Strategies* (Oxford: Oxford University Press).

Khan, M. (2012b) "Governance and Growth Challenges for Africa," in A. Noman et al. (eds), *Good Governance and Growth in Africa: Rethinking Development Strategies* (Oxford: Oxford University Press).

Khan, M. (2012c) "Governance Issues," IEA/World Bank Roundtable, "New Thinking on Industrial Policy: Implications for Africa." Pretoria, South Africa. July 3–4.

Kim, T., Kwon, H., and Yi, I. (2011) "'Mixed Governance' and Welfare in South Korea," *Journal of Democracy*. vol. 22, no. 3, pp. 120–134.

Lin, J. (2012) "Comparative Advantage". IEA/World Bank Roundtable. New Thinking on Industrial Policy: Implications for Africa." Pretoria, South Africa. July 3–4.

Lin, Y. and Monga, C. (2012) "Solving the Mystery of African Governance," *New Political Economy*, vol. 17, no. 5, pp. 659–666.

Mkandawire, T. (2012). "Institutional Monocropping and Monotasking in Africa," in A. Noman et al. (eds.), *Good Governance and Growth in Africa: Rethinking Development Strategies* (Oxford: Oxford University Press).

Monga, C.. (2012). "The Globalization Jackpot: Job Dividends from a Multi-Polar World". IEA/World Bank Roundtable. New Thinking on Industrial Policy: Implications for Africa." Pretoria, South Africa. July 3–4.

Noman, A. and Stiglitz, J. (2012). "Strategies for African Development" in A. Noman et al. (eds.), *Good Growth and Governance in Africa: Rethinking Development Strategies* (Oxford: Oxford University Press).

Noman, A. et al. (eds) (2012) *Good Growth and Governance in Africa: Rethinking Development Strategies* (Oxford: Oxford University Press).

Ohno, I. and Ohno, K. (2012). "Dynamic Capacity Development: What Africa Can Learn from Industrial Policy Formulation in East Asia," in A. Noman et al. (eds.), *Good Governance and Growth in Africa: Rethinking Development Strategies* (Oxford: Oxford University Press).

Oyeyinka, B. and Sampath, P. (2012) "Institutional Capacity and Policy Choices for Latecomer Technology Development," in A. Noman et al. (eds.), *Good Governance and Growth in Africa: Rethinking Development Strategies* (Oxford: Oxford University Press).

Pitcher, A. (2012) *Party Politics and Economic Reform in Africa's Democracies* (Cambridge: Cambridge University Press).

Page, J. (2012) "Can Africa Industrialise?," *Journal of African Economies*. 21 (AERC Supplement 2): 86–125.

Persson, A., Rothstein B, and Teorell, J. (2012) "Why Anti-Corruption Reforms Fail – Systemic Corruption as a Collective Action Problem," *Governance*, vol. 26, no. 3, pp. 449–471.

Radelet, S. (2010). *Emerging Africa: How 17 Countries Are Leading The Way* (Washington, DC: Brookings Institution Press/Center for Global Development).

Rodrik, D. (2007) *One Economics Many Recipes: Globalization, Institutions, and Economic Growth* (Princeton, NJ: Princeton University Press).

Rothstein, Bo. (2011a) *The Quality of Government: Corruption, Social Trust, and Inequality in International Perspective* (Chicago and London: The University of Chicago Press).

Rothstein, Bo. (2011b) "Anti-Corruption: The Indirect 'Big Bang' Approach," *Review of International Political Economy*, vol. 18, No. 2, pp. 228–250.

Samatar, A. (2002) "Botswana: Comprehending the Exceptional State," in Abdi Samatar, and Ahmed Samatar (eds), *The African State: Reconsiderations* (Portsmouth, NH: Heinemann).

Samatar, A. (1999) *An African Miracle: State and Class Leadership and Colonial Legacy in Botswana Development* (Portsmouth, NH: Heinemann).

Sandbrook, R. (1985) *The Politics of Africa's Economic Stagnation* (Cambridge: Cambridge University Press).

Sklar, R.L (1983) "Democracy in Africa," *African Studies Review*, vol. 26, nos 3–4, pp. 11–24.

Smith, Daniel J. (2007) *A Culture of Corruption: Everyday Deception and Popular Discontent* (Princeton, NJ: Princeton University Press).

Taylor, S.D. (2012) *Globalization and the Cultures of Business in Africa: From Patrimonialism to Profit* (Bloomington, IN: Indiana University Press).

Taylor, I. (2012) "Botswana as a 'Development-Oriented Gate-Keeping State'," *African Affairs*, vol. 111, no. 444, pp. 466–476.

Uslander, E. and Rothstein, B. (2012) "The Roots of Corruption: Mass Education, Economic Inequality and State Building," The Quality of Government Institute (typescript).

Vartiainen, J. (1999). "The Economics of Successful State Intervention in Industrial Transformation," in Woo-Cumings (ed.), *The Developmental State*.

Wade, R. (2004) *Governing the Market* (Princeton, NJ: Princeton University Press).

Wade, R (2012). "How can Low-Income Countries Accelerate their Catch-Up with High-Income Countries? The Case for Open-Economy Industrial Policy," IEA/World Bank Roundtable, "New Thinking on Industrial Policy: Implications for Africa," Pretoria, South Africa. July 3–4.

Wolf, M. (2012) "Pragmatic Search for Path to Prosperity," review of Justin Yifu Lin, *The Quest for Prosperity: How Developing Economies Can Take Off, Financial Times*, October 14.

Woo-Cumings, M. (ed.) (1999) *The Developmental State* (Ithaca and London: Cornell University Press).

Part V
Trade, Finance, and Sectoral Policies

5.1

Does Financial Market Liberalization Promote Financial Development?: Evidence from Sub-Saharan Africa[1]

Hamid Rashid
United Nations Department of Economic and Social Affairs

5.1.1 Introduction

Since 1990s, many Sub-Saharan African economies have liberalized their financial sectors in the expectation that liberalized financial markets will promote financial development and spur economic growth. In this respect the African economies followed the footstep of their Latin American counterparts who began to liberalize their financial markets in the 1980s, following a period characterized by hyperinflation, stagnant growth, and debt crisis. While the influential papers of Mckinnon (1973) and Shaw (1973) provided theoretical justification for financial liberalization, it was the thrust for broader market-based reforms that promoted wholesale liberalization and privatization and triggered rapid financial market liberalization in the continent. Ignoring both the more nuanced theoretical work[2] and the growing body of empirical evidence on why and when financial liberalization may not promote financial development, Levine (1997) and King and Levine (1997) claimed a positive, first-order relationship between financial development and economic growth. This strand of literature made emphatic claims, albeit not necessarily supported by robust empirical evidence, that the development of financial markets and institutions is a critical and inextricable part of the growth process. They went further to that "the level of financial development is a good predictor of future rates of economic growth, capital accumulation, and technological change" (Levine, 1997), without addressing the more critical issue as to whether financial market liberalization was necessary to promote financial development, with the latter touted as a *sine qua non* for economic growth.

In this paper, we specifically focus on the association between financial market liberalization and financial development, broadly defined in terms of domestic savings rate, real interest rate, interest rate spread and credit to the private sector. Our investigation into this critical – yet largely unexplored issue – is aided by the availability of a robust and comprehensive new database on financial reforms developed by Abiad et al. (2008). The dataset not only provides a wide coverage – 91 countries, spanning 33 years, but also offers a more comprehensive measure of financial market liberalization that covers seven dimensions of financial market operations: 1. credit controls and reserve requirements; 2. interest rate controls; 3. entry barriers; 4. state ownership in the banking sector; 5. capital account restrictions; 6 prudential regulations and banking supervision; 7. securities market policies. The database combines the liberalization scores for each category – which ranges from 0 denoting fully repressed and 3 meanng fully liberalized. They combine them in a graded index that is normalized between zero and one. This marks a significant improvement over other existing measures of financial market liberalization, which code liberalization as binary dummy variables. The use of binary variables treats liberalization as a discrete event and ignores various intermediate stages of liberalization. The Abiad et al. (2008) financial market liberalization index (FML index) provides a more comprehensive and continuous measure of financial market liberalization, comparable across countries and over time. The use of FML index allows our analysis to directly measure for the first time the association between two continuous variables – financial market liberalization and financial development.

The paper adds value to the existing debate as to whether financial market liberalization is necessary for financial development. Our empirical analysis covering other regions – namely South Asia, East Asia, Latin America, the Middle East and North Africa and Transition countries – find no significant relationship between financial liberalization and financial development. Many countries in East Asia, South Asia, and Latin America achieved significant financial development, which cannot be directly attributed to financial liberalization. While the effect of financial liberalization on financial development is mixed, if not non-existent, in other regions, the effect is unambiguously adverse in Sub-Saharan Africa. This suggests the possibility that the effect of financial liberalization on financial development can be outright negative if the initial level of financial and economic development is very weak.

The rest of the paper is organized as following. Section 5.1.2 provides a review of the theoretical and empirical literature on financial market liberalization. Section 5.1.3 introduces the dataset and reports a few descriptive statistics on various measures of financial development in Sub-Saharan Africa and other benchmark regions, while section 5.1.4 discusses the regression results and parameter estimates of our key explanatory variables. Finally, section 5.1.5 presents a few concluding remarks and identifies the need for further research.

5.1.2   Literature review

Discussions on financial market liberalization usually begin with the influential work of Ronald Mckinnon (1973) and Edward Shaw (1973), who made a strong case for liberalizing financial markets to ease financing constraints and promote financial development and economic growth. Their argument was predicated on a state of financial repression – commonplace in both developed and developing countries in 1973 – where government decided who gets credit and at what price. In financial repression regimes, government can determine the price and volume of credit, either by directly owning and controlling the financial system, as was the case in the former Soviet Union and other communist bloc countries, or indirectly by imposing ceilings on deposit or lending interest rates and the level of credit to various sectors and subsectors of the economy. The second form of financial repression was prevalent in the industrialized countries until the 1970s. Following the collapse of the fixed exchange rate regime and the liberalization of capital account transactions, industrialized countries paced and sequenced the liberalization of their financial markets over a three-decade period between the 1970s and the 1990s. The Shaw–Mckinnon hypothesis argued that placing a ceiling on interest rates kept real interest rates low and reduced the incentives for savings, prevented capital accumulation and discouraged efficient allocation of scarce financial resources. If the market forces are allowed to determine real interest rates, Shaw and Mckinnon argued, real interest rates would rise to competitive equilibrium leves, encouraging households to postpone consumption and increase savings. Financial liberalization often also meant government allowing unhindered entry to the financial sector for any firm meeting certain criteria and withdrawals of restrictions on current and capital account transactions. As such, financial liberalization came to be broadly defined along the following dimensions (Williamson, 1998):

1. The elimination of credit controls.
2. The deregulation of interest rates.
3. Free entry to the financial sector.
4. Bank autonomy and private ownership of banks.
5. Liberalization of international capital flows.

The claims of the Shaw–Mckinnon hypothesis were soon challenged in both the theoretical and the empirical literature. Campbell and Mankiw (1990) show that the positive effect of interest rate liberalization on the savings rate is based on the assumption that all households have free access to capital market in the domestic economy. For credit-constrained households, the liberalization of interest rates or the easing of liquidity constraints may instead propel a consumption boom and reduce domestic credit. Ostry and Reinhart (1992), on the other hand, shows that sensitivity of savings to an increase in real interest rates, following financial market liberalization, will depend on the level of household income in the economy. If the average household income is close to the subsistence level of consumption, the domestic savings rate will not respond to the rise in the real rate of interest and financial market liberalization will not lead to a higher level of domestic savings. Stiglitz, Hellman, and Murdock (1998) show that policies of financial restraint, with the government providing correct incentives to prevent market failures, can promote financial development. They argue that ceilings on deposit interest rate and restrictions on competition and free entry into the financial sector can help to increase the franchise value of banks and reduce the incidence of moral hazards among financial intermediaries. Stiglitz et al. (1998) also argue that caps on lending rate controls may increase the efficiency of intermediation by reducing agency cost in loan markets. Broner (2010) presents a model to show how financial market liberalization may induce domestic capital flight and have ambiguous effects on net capital flows, investment, and growth and make the capital flows more volatile and make domestic financial markets unstable and shows how these outcomes depend on the initial level of development, the depth of domestic financial markets, and the quality of institutions.

Empirical evidence on the relationship between liberalization and financial development is at best mixed. Giovanni (1985), in a study of 18 developing countries, found an insignificant response of domestic savings to an increase in real interest rates. Ogaki et al. (1996) show that subsistence considerations largely determine consumption decisions in developing countries, particularly in extremely low-income countries. They find that the intertemporal elasticity of substitution and the interest-rate sensitivity of private saving will be close to zero in countries where average per capita income is at or near subsistence consumption levels. Both inter-temporal substitution between consumption and saving and sensitivity to real interest rates are likely to rise once a country crosses the threshold of subsistence level of per capita income. Bandiera et al. (2000) studies the effect of liberalization on financial development in Chile, Ghana, Indonesia, Korea, Malaysia, Mexico, Turkey, and Zimbabwe and finds no evidence of positive effect of real interest on domestic savings rate. The relationship between their liberalization index and savings rate is mixed – negative and significant in Korea and Mexico, positive and significant in Ghana and Turkey and insignificant in other countries. Loayza et al. (2000) also find no direct positive effects of financial liberalization on the saving rate. In a study covering 14 developed and 16 developing countries, Reinhart and Tokatlidis (2001) find that financial liberalization is associated with higher real interest rates, a higher level of foreign direct investment and high gross capital flows. They, however, find no negative correlation between liberalization and growth possibly because higher real interest rates may lead to allocation of resources into more productive and higher return projects. They also find that liberalization may increase private credit (as a percentage of GDP) but not necessarily in low income countries.[3]

On the other hand, there is hardly any empirical paper that shows that financial market liberalization leads to financial development measured in terms of both higher levels of savings and private credit and lower levels of intermediation cost, such as the spread between borrowing and lending rates of interest. Generally ignoring the theoretical expositions and empirical evidences that refute the claims of unambiguous benefits of financial market liberalization, a strand of literature moved in a different direction and took a quantum leap to claim that financial development is both a necessary and a sufficient condition for economic growth. King and Levine (1993) show that "higher levels of financial development are significantly and robustly correlated with faster current and future rates of economic growth, physical accumulation and economic efficiency improvements." Their measure of financial development includes the ratio of liquid liability (M2) to GDP and the ratio of private credit to GDP. Partly in response to offset the empirical evidences that found either weak or no evidence that financial liberalization increased domestic savings and credit, Levine (1997) adopts a broader definition of financial development as the narrow focus on money "can restrict the analysis of the finance-growth nexus." He argues that financial intermediaries reduce information, transaction and enforcement costs and hence the broader definition of financial development must take into account the functions that financial intermediaries perform to ameliorate information and transaction related frictions. Financial development must therefore mean improvements in the financial system that:

1. facilitate the trading, hedging, diversifying, and pooling of risk.
2. allocate resources efficiently,
3. monitor managers and exert corporate control,
4. mobilize savings, and
5. facilitate the exchange of goods and services.

Shifting away from analyzing the relationship between financial liberalization and financial development, a growing body of literature began to focus on the determinants and necessary preconditions for liberalization to deliver financial development. This body of research generally argues that financial liberalization can lead to financial development provided there is a reasonable level of legal and institutional development. Specifically, they argue that financial development is likely to be weak in countries where the legal system does not give a clear definition of property rights or guarantee the enforcement of contracts. It is also argued that the level of credibility and transparency of accounting rules are likely to determine financial development. La Porta et al. (1997) argue that differences in national legal systems largely explain the differences in the levels of financial development in these countries. La Porta (2002) further show that higher degrees of public ownership of banks are associated with lower levels of financial development while Claessens et al. (2003) and Caprio, et al. (2000) find that greater creditor rights are positively associated with financial development. Rajan and Zingales (1998), for example, argue that financial liberalization can lead to financial development only when the economy is open in both cross-border trade and capital flows because economic openness can weaken the political power of incumbent financial institutions to oppose competition and further financial development.

The research on both the determinants of financial development and the nexus between financial development and economic growth, pending any conclusive evidence that financial liberalization promotes financial development, serves an important "policy advocacy role" to convince developing countries to ignore the adverse effects and further liberalize their financial markets. This policy-influencing motivation of these types of research is succinctly presented in Levine (2005) where he suggests, "Research that clarifies our understanding of the role of finance in economic growth will have policy implications and shape future policy-oriented research. Information about the impact of finance on economic growth will influence the priority that policy makers and advisors attach to reforming financial sector policies. Furthermore, convincing evidence that the financial system influences long-run economic growth will advertise the urgent need for research on the political, legal, regulatory, and policy determinants of financial development."

5.1.3   Data and summary statistics

Our analysis considers the impact of financial market liberalization on financial development in 14 Sub-Saharan countries. The financial reform database developed by Abiad et al. (2008) incudes data on only 14 Sub-Saharan countries – Burkina Faso, Cameroon, Côte d'Ivoire, Ghana, Ethiopia, Kenya, Madagascar, Mozambique, Nigeria, Senegal, South Africa, Tanzania, Uganda, and Zimbabwe. Collectively, they represent more than 80 percent of the total Sub-Saharan GDP. We compare the effect of financial liberalization on financial development in Sub Saharan Africa, with that of other comparable regions, namely South Asia (five countries), Emerging East Asia (seven countries), Latin America (17 countries), Middle East and North Africa (MENA – six countries) and Transition economies (16 countries). The full list of countries is included in Annex I.

Our key explanatory variable – the financial market liberalization Index (FML index) – is drawn directly from the Abiad et al. database. The set of dependent variables – gross domestic savings (% of GDP), real interest rate (%), interest rate spread (%), domestic credit to the private sector (% of GDP) – are taken from the World Development Indicators (WDI) of the World Bank. The macroeconomic controls are also taken from the WDI database. The data covers the period 1973–2005, following the data coverage of the Abiad et al. database. Most of the variations in the FML index, both within and across countries, have been observed since 1990 as financial sector liberalization in Africa, Asia and Latin America occurred during the late 1980s and the early 1990s. Hence, our analysis is primarily focused on financial development during this period.

In 1990, the GDP per capita income of our sample of 14 Sub-Saharan economies (please see Annex I) was $455 compared with $335 in South Asia (Figure 5.1.1). By 2005, the average per capita income of the Sub-Saharan and South Asian economies rose to $521 and $678 respectively. In nominal terms, the per capita income of our sample Sub-Saharan countries grew by less than 1 percent a year while the per capita income in comparable South Asian economies grew by 5.3 percent a year between 1990 and 2005. In both nominal and real terms, Sub-Saharan countries experienced the lowest growth rates in GDP per capita income during this period. In 1990, the average per capita income of the sample Latin American countries was four times higher than the Sub-Saharan per capita income. By 2005, it was seven times higher. The gap between the East Asian and Sub-Saharan per capita incomes widened even further, increasing from 3.7 times in 1990 to 8.3 times in 2005. Despite the low level of per capita income and overall economic development, the Sub-Saharan countries liberalized their financial markets faster and deeper than their counterparts in South and East Asia.

Both East and South Asian economies pursued a gradualist approach to the liberalization of their financial sectors. East Asia began liberalizing their financial sector during the 1980s but slowed the liberalization process in the early 1990s and somewhat reversed the trend following the Asian financial crisis in 1997–98. Historically, the Sub-Saharan financial sector was more liberalized than their counterparts in South Asia largely because of strong foreign presence of foreign financial institutions in the former. SSA economies started liberalizing in the early 1990s and, albeit after a later start, exceeded the liberalization levels of the East Asian countries by the

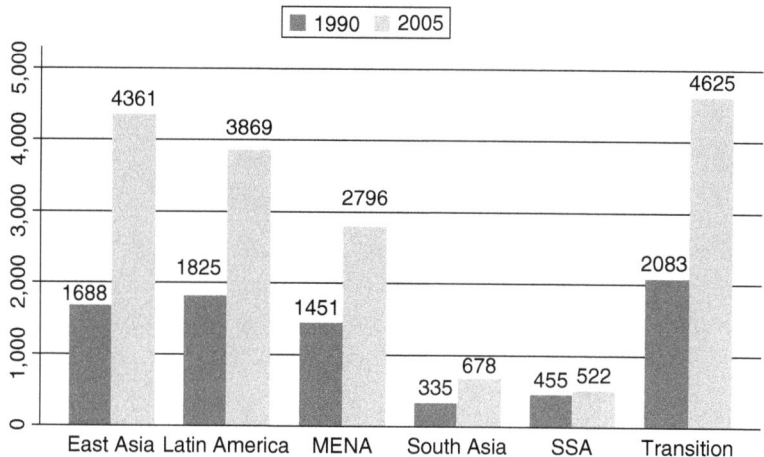

Figure 5.1.1 Per capita GDP in 1990 and 2005
Source: WDI.

mid-1990s. By 2005, only the Latin American financial sector was more liberalized than that operating in Sub-Saharan Africa (Figure 5.1.2).

Figure 5.1.3 shows the FML index scores for our sample countries. If we exclude Ethiopia, all of the SSA financial sectors were more liberalized than the financial sectors in either South Asia or Latin America. The financial sector

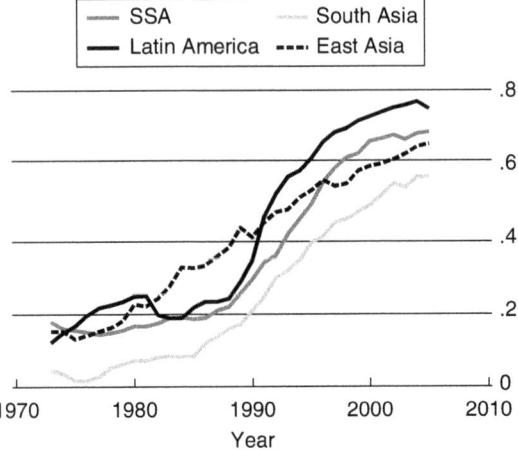

Figure 5.1.2   Trend in financial market liberalization
Source: Constructed from database of Abiad et al (2008).

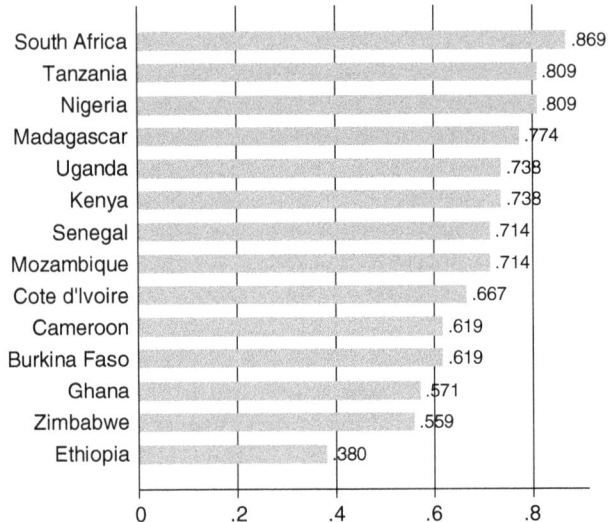

Figure 5.1.3   State of financial market liberalization in Sub-Saharan Africa, 2005
Source: Abiad et al (2008).

of Côte d'Ivoire or Mozambique – both least developed countries – became more liberalized than the financial sectors of Brazil, China or India (Please see Figure 5.1.3a in Annex II). In 2005, Nigeria or Tanzania – both low-income countries – had their financial sectors as liberalized as the financial sectors of Germany in 1992, Japan in 1997, Greece in 2002 and Finland in 2005.

Disaggregation of the FML index shows that the Sub-Saharan African economies achieved financial liberalization largely through: 1. removing barriers to entry; 2. privatization of the banking sector; and 3. ending the policy of directed credit. More than three-quarters of our sample Sub-Saharan countries removed all barriers to financial sector entry by 2005 compared to only 25 percent of countries eliminating the entry barriers in South Asia (Figure 5.1.4a). South Asian economies largely limited the entry of foreign banks which afforded them greater control over their financial sector and possibly more influence to promote financial development. Both South Asia and East Asian economies also maintained a sizable government ownerhip of banks, significantly more so than in Sub-Saharan countries (please see Figure 5.1.4b in Annex III), even though they eased controls on credit ceilings and interest rates as much as their counterparts in SSA (Figure 5.1.4c in Annex III). Retaining ownerhship of banks allowed the governments in some South Asian and East Asian countries – notably in India, China, Vietnam, and Bangladesh – to channel credit to priority sectors of the economy while market forces to determine the interest rates. In contrast

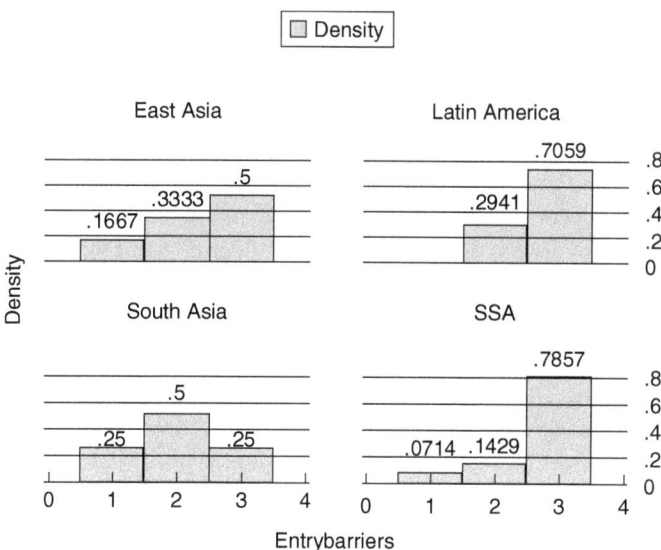

Figure 5.1.4   The status of entry barriers in SSA (% of countries) in 2005
Source: Constructed from database of Abiad et al (2008).

with SSA, East and The disaggregate level differences in the FML index – in terms of the level of entry barriers, privatization, and credit controls – can possibly explain some of the differences in financial development in SSA and South or East Asia. There is a clear need for further research on this issue, which is not addressed in this paper.

5.1.4   Econometric analysis

Our econometric models estimate the effect of financial market liberalization (FML index) on four dimensions of financial development in Sub-Saharan Africa. The four measures of financial development are:

1. Real interest rates (%).
2. Gross domestic savings rate (% of GDP).
3. Interest rate spread (%).
4. Domestic credit to the private sector (% of GDP).

To account for observed heterogeneity in country-level attributes, we include a set of macroeconomic control variables – log of GDP per capita, GDP growth rate (%), annual rate of inflation (%), household consumption (% of GDP), government budget balance (% of GDP), mineral rent (% of GDP) and population growth rate (%). Understandably, these controls do not control for all unobserved country-level heterogeneity that affects both our regressors and our dependent variables. To account for unobserved country-level differences and reduce the omitted variable bias, we estimate our models in generalized least squares (GLS) with country-level fixed effects. Unobserved heterogeneity at the country level may include the political and legal system, the culture of corporate governance, religious and cultural practices, which we believe remain fixed over time but vary across countries. The Hausman specification test confirms the presence of country-level fixed effects in our models. The high Chi2 value in Hausman tests for each model rejects the null that the differences in coefficients are not different from coefficients estimated with random effects. For robustness checks, we also estimate our models in OLS and Feasible Generalized Least Squares (FGLS). As we know, OLS estimates of panel data typically yield biased estimates – usually biased downward – because of heteroskedasticity and serial correlation in the data. We correct we correct the problems of heteroskedasticity and serial correlation by estimating our model in Feasible Generalized Least Square method but the larger problems of omitted variable biases and endogentiy are addressed with fixed effects.

We recognize that our regressors are not strictly exogenous. For example, the growth rate can affect inflation and inflation can affect growth rates and savings rate and both can in turn influence our key explanatory variable – the FML index in the long run. But in the short run – we estimate short-run models which cover 10 to 15 years – the FML index, an index of policy variables, can be treated as exogenous in the model. It is unlikely that policy-makers in Sub-Saharan Africa (or in any other region) will observe the inflation, growth or savings rates and adjust the level of financial market liberalization in the short-time horizon. However, this does not solve the problem of simultaneity biases in the models with respect to our macro-economic controls. Our controls – growth rates or savings rate – can affect, for example, our dependent variable – real interest rates – but real interest rates can also affect the growth and savings rate. To reduce the problem of simultaneity, we estimate our models with lag-dependent variables as one of the regressors. In dynamic panels, we know that the past realization of a dependent variable largely determines its future values. Because of the small sample size (small N relative to the time span of the data), we do not estimate our models in system GMM to address the simultaneity biases in our data. Given that we are simply investigating the association between financial market liberalization and financial development, and not necessarily addressing the question of whether financial market liberalization "causes" financial development, the problem of simultaneity is less of an issue in our estimations. Our regression results do not claim or prove a causal relationship between financial liberalization and financial development.

Our models exhibit good fits and strong explanatory powers, as evident in high adjusted R-squared obtained in the regression results. Fixed effect estimates yield adjusted R-squared in the range of .6 and .8, suggesting that as much as 60 percent to 80 percent of observed variations in the dependent variables are explained by our models. Adjusted R-squared of OLS estimates are even higher, confirming that our models are generally good fit to explain the variations in our dependent variables. The high log likelihood measures obtained in FGLS estimates also confirm that our models possess strong explanatory powers.

In order to compare the regional differences in the association between liberalization and financial development, we estimate our models for other regional groups – namely South Asia, East Asia, Latin America, MENA and Transition economies. We also estimate the models with and without SSA countries to capture whether financial liberalization is associated with differential financial development outcomes in different regions. Our results generally show that liberalization shows the least positive effect, and mostly negative effects, on financial development in Sub Saharan African countries. The association between FML and financial development is somewhat mixed in other regions of the world.

5.1.4.1   Real interest rates

In 1990, Sub-Saharan Africa had one of the highest real interest rates. By 2005, average real interest rates in the region had fallen from from 10.8 percent to 7.9 percent (Figure 5.1.5). Only in the East Asia region was there was a similar fall in real interest rates. In other regions of the world, we observe a steady rise in real interest rates consistent with the prediction that interest rates will typically rise when financially repressed economies allow market forces to determine real interest rates. Latin America, however, presents an extreme case where average real interest rate soared from 0.11 percent in 1990 to 10.7 percent in 2005. In South Asia, average real interest rose from 2.9 percent to 4.1 percent between 1990 and 2005. Commensurate with its high real interest rates, Sub-Saharan African economies continued to have one of the highest interest rate spreads in the world.

Our basic model (column 1 in Table 5.1.1) regresses log GDP per capita, GDP growth rate, annual inflation and FML index on real interest rates. We find strong and positive correlation between real interest rate and FML index, significant at the 1% level. The finding is consistent with the prediction of standard models of financial market liberalization (for example, Shaw, 1973) that liberalization of controls on interest rates and other factors that affect the price of money can lead to higher real interest rates. Incrementally, we include domestic savings rate (percentage of GDP), current account balance (percentage of GDP) and mineral rent (percentage of GDP) as additional controls to check for robustness of our key explanatory variable – FML index. The sign and significance of the coefficient of FML remain same – positive

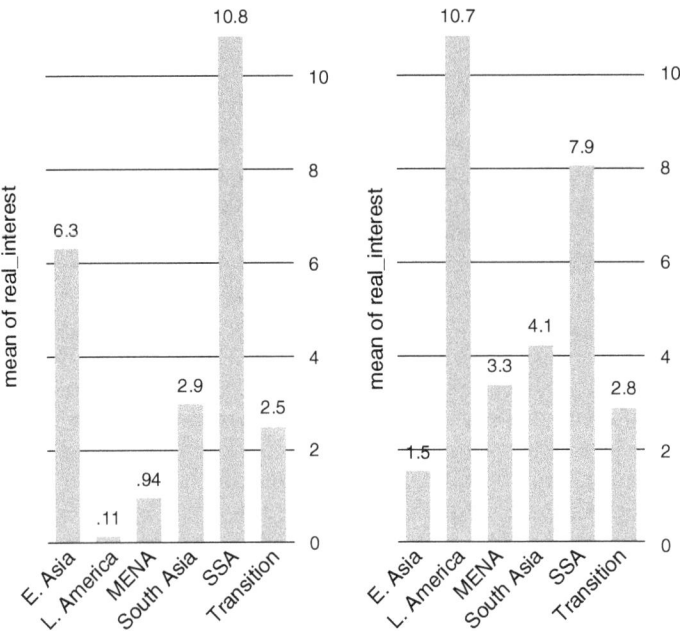

Figure 5.1.5   Real interest rates in different regions, 1990 and 2005
Source: WDI.

Table 5.1.1 Dependent variable: real interest rate (%)

Variables	(1) FE	(2) FE	(3) FE	(4) FE	(5) FE¹	(6) OLS	(7) FGLS
Lag Real Interest	0.67***	0.69***	0.28***	0.28***	0.17***	0.19***	0.14***
	(0.057)	(0.060)	(0.054)	(0.055)	(0.052)	(0.048)	(0.048)
Log GDP per Capita	-4.35	-8.63*	-2.97	-2.94	-1.19	2.27**	2.32***
	(3.696)	(4.452)	(2.085)	(2.086)	(2.127)	(0.905)	(0.779)
GDP Growth Rate (%)	0.27	0.42*	0.05	0.06	0.18*	0.19*	0.19***
	(0.211)	(0.234)	(0.113)	(0.113)	(0.103)	(0.097)	(0.074)
Annual Inflation (%)	0.12***	0.11***	-0.26***	-0.26***	-0.29***	-0.29***	-0.31***
	(0.026)	(0.028)	(0.024)	(0.024)	(0.021)	(0.019)	(0.022)
Financial Market Liberalization Index	15.78***	15.33**	10.97***	10.77***	11.09***	9.46***	10.64***
	(5.533)	(6.424)	(3.470)	(3.480)	(3.474)	(2.103)	(1.917)
Gross Domestic Savings (% of GDP)		-0.38*	-0.03	-0.07	-0.04	-0.11*	-0.10*
		(0.230)	(0.113)	(0.119)	(0.108)	(0.064)	(0.057)
Current Account Balance (% of GDP)			-0.24*	-0.23*	-0.08	-0.00	0.01
			(0.130)	(0.130)	(0.120)	(0.091)	(0.087)
Mineral Income (% of GDP)				0.42	-4.17***	-4.46***	-4.81***
				(0.485)	(1.926)	(1.214)	(1.193)
Constant	21.11	53.49*	22.52*	22.64*	12.65	-6.22	-6.25
	(22.978)	(28.410)	(13.206)	(13.214)	(12.700)	(5.129)	(4.700)
Observations	277	245	233	233	185	185	185
R-squared	0.52	0.57	0.66	0.66	0.77	0.83	
Number of country_id	14	13	13	13	11		11
Adj. R-squared	0.49	0.54	0.63	0.63	0.74	0.82	
Hausman Specification Test for Fixed Effects	Yes	Yes	Yes	Yes	Yes		

Note: ¹Excludes South Africa and Zimbabwe.
Standard errors in parentheses.
*** p < 0.01, ** p < 0.05, * p < 0.10.

and significant at the 1% level, in each stage of the model build-up. Adjusted R-squared increases from 0.49 in model (1) to 0.74 in the full model (column 5) confirming that addition of these controls increase the overall explanatory power of the model. The full model suggests that one unit increase in the FML index can be associated with an 11.09 percent increase (over the base rate) in real interest rate. That is, if a country liberalized its FML index by one unit, real interest rate may increase, say, from 8 percent to 8.9 percent (that is, an 11.25 percent increase from the base level). OLS (column 6, with adjusted R-square of 0.82) and FGLS (column 7) estimates yield similar results. The coefficient of FML index is positive – though the absolute value is lower – and significant at the 1% level. We find that inflation is negatively and significantly correlated to real interest rates in all seven estimations (column 1 through 7).

We estimate the same full model for other regions (Table 5.1.2). In contrast to the earlier estimates, the FML coefficient is negative and insignificant for South Asia (column 1), East Asia (column 2) and Transition countries (column 5) while it is positive and insignificant for Latin America (column 4) and MENA countries (column 3). Inflation is negatively and significantly correlated to real interest rates in all regions. In the full sample, the coefficient of FML index is positive and significant at the 1% level, suggesting the possibility that the robust and positive association between FML index and real interest rates dominate the result of the full sample (column 7).

5.1.4.2   Domestic savings rate

In 1990, the gross domestic savings rate, one of the lead indicators of financial deepening and development, was 7.7 percent in SSA compared to 13.1 percent in South Asia and 28.3 percent in our sample of East Asian economies. By 2005, the savings rate had marginally increased to 8.2 percent in Sub-Saharan Africa, while it increased by nearly 50 percent to 18.9 percent of GDP in South Asia. During the same period, the ratio rose from 32.8 percent to 52.8 percent in South Asia (please see Figure 5.1.7).

Our initial model (Table 5.1.3, column 1) controls for log GDP per capita, household consumption (percentage of GDP) and real interest rate (percentage). FML index is significantly (5% level) and negatively correlated to the domestic savings rate. Both real interest rates and household consumption are negatively and significantly correlated to savings. The adjusted R-squared is 0.86. While we include additional macroeconomic controls in the model, FML index remains negatively and robustly correlated to domestic savings rate at the 1% significance level (columns 4 and 5). The result of the full model suggests that one unit increase in FML index can reduce domestic savings rate by 7.58 percent from its base level. This means if a country had a domestic savings rate of 10 percent and the FML index increased by one unit, its savings rate may fall from 10 percent to 9.25 percent. In all specifications (column 1 through 5), household consumption is negatively correlated to savings rate at the 1% significance level. But in the presence of additional

Table 5.1.2 Dependable variable: real interest rate (%)

Variables	(1) South Asia	(2) Emerging Asia	(3) MENA	(4) Latin America	(5) Transition	(6) Full Sample without SSA	(7) Full Sample
Lag Real Interest	0.16*	−0.13*	0.17	0.51***	0.26***	0.41***	0.42***
	(0.088)	(0.065)	(0.119)	(0.049)	(0.053)	(0.029)	(0.026)
Log GDP per Capita	−1.35	−1.04	0.18	−3.29	−1.09	−0.19	−2.34*
	(2.190)	(1.244)	(2.937)	(3.240)	(4.640)	(1.708)	(1.370)
GDP Growth Rate (%)	0.18	−0.31***	−0.08	0.17	−0.69**	0.07	0.14
	(0.161)	(0.102)	(0.133)	(0.223)	(0.293)	(0.114)	(0.091)
Annual Inflation (%)	−0.42***	−0.63***	−0.38**	−0.00***	−0.05***	−0.01***	−0.01***
	(0.091)	(0.057)	(0.161)	(0.001)	(0.006)	(0.001)	(0.001)
Financial Market Liberalization Index	−1.73	−3.06	5.04	8.36	−1.61	5.89	9.77***
	(3.771)	(3.266)	(4.529)	(5.426)	(12.658)	(3.322)	(2.574)
Gross Domestic Savings (% of GDP)	0.10	−0.01	0.23	−1.43***	−0.08	−0.51***	−0.32***
	(0.159)	(0.099)	(0.143)	(0.308)	(0.234)	(0.117)	(0.092)
Current Account Balance (% of GDP)	0.01	−0.25***	0.00	0.12	−0.29	−0.12	−0.18*
	(0.155)	(0.081)	(0.109)	(0.291)	(0.267)	(0.114)	(0.095)
Constant	14.60	21.23***	0.32	49.73**	19.39	12.88	21.55**
	(11.713)	(6.632)	(19.371)	(24.040)	(28.963)	(10.931)	(8.738)
Observations	98	139	74	275	165	776	1,009
R-squared	0.25	0.54	0.52	0.56	0.46	0.38	0.39
Number of countries	5	6	6	15	15	47	60
Adj. R-squared	0.16	0.50	0.42	0.52	0.38	0.34	0.34
Hausman Specification Test for Fixed Effects	Yes	Yes	Yes	Yes	Yes	Yes	Yes

Notes: Standard errors in parentheses.
*** p < 0.01, ** p < 0.05, * p < 0.10.

Table 5.1.3 Dependent variable: domestic savings rate (% of GDP)

Variables	(1) FE	(2) FE	(3) FE	(4) FE	(5) FE	(6) OLS	(7) FGLS
Lag Domestic Savings Rate	0.18***	0.18***	0.16***	0.20**	0.12	0.33***	0.18**
	(0.036)	(0.035)	(0.035)	(0.084)	(0.079)	(0.097)	(0.086)
Log GDP per Capita	-0.00***	-0.00***	-0.00***	-0.00	-0.01***	0.00	-0.00*
	(0.000)	(0.000)	(0.000)	(0.001)	(0.003)	(0.000)	(0.000)
Household Consumption (% of GDP)	-0.65***	-0.63***	-0.63***	-0.73***	-0.73***	-0.47***	-0.69***
	(0.028)	(0.028)	(0.027)	(0.074)	(0.068)	(0.078)	(0.067)
Real Interest Rate (%)	-0.02***	-0.01**	-0.02**	-0.00	-0.01	0.05	0.00
	(0.006)	(0.006)	(0.006)	(0.035)	(0.034)	(0.042)	(0.027)
Financial Market Liberalization Index	-1.57**	-1.84**	-1.67**	-6.09***	-7.58***	-4.71***	-4.86***
	(0.754)	(0.734)	(0.725)	(2.108)	(2.184)	(1.540)	(1.346)
GDP Growth Rate (%)		0.10***	0.10***	0.06	0.01	0.04	0.01
		(0.025)	(0.025)	(0.048)	(0.044)	(0.060)	(0.048)
Mineral Rent (% of GDP)				0.03	-6.47	-0.44	-0.40
				(0.376)	(8.828)	(0.300)	(0.324)
Government Budget Balance (% of GDP)			0.33***	0.53***	0.43***	0.24	0.25**
			(0.117)	(0.139)	(0.139)	(0.150)	(0.113)
Constant	59.68***	58.31***	58.24***	68.66***	73.14***	45.25***	64.21***
	(2.473)	(2.422)	(2.387)	(6.082)	(5.824)	(6.803)	(6.120)
Observations	257	257	257	63	49	63	63
R-squared	0.87	0.88	0.88	0.81	0.90	0.84	
Number of countries	13	13	13	7	5		7
Adj. R-squared	0.86	0.87	0.88	0.76	0.86	0.81	–
Hausman Specification Test for Fixed Effects	Yes	Yes	Yes	Yes	Yes		

Notes: Standard errors in parentheses.
*** p < 0.01, ** p < 0.05, * p < 0.10.

controls (column 4) and the full model (column 5), the coefficient of real interest rate becomes negative and insignificant. This confirms the hypothesis that a raise in real interest rate is unlikely to boost savings rate if the average income in the economy is at persistence level, as is the case in SSA. The negative sign of the real interest rate also suggests that income effect of higher real interest is likely to dominate the inter-temporal substitution between consumption and savings and may actually reduce savings rate. OLS (column 6) and FGLS (column 7) estimates also yield negative and significant (at the 1% level) coefficients, through biased downward, for the FML index.

We find no statistically significant association between financial market liberalization and domestic savings rate in other regions of the world (Table 5.1.4). The coefficient of FML index is positive and insignificant for the sample of South Asian (column 1), East Asian (column 2), and Latin American (column 4) countries and negative and insignificant for MENA (column 3) and Transition countries (column 5). It is also insignificant for the full sample with or without SSA. We, however, find a positive and significant (at the 1% level) correlation between real interest rate and savings rate for the Latin American countries. This perhaps suggests that at a relatively higher level of per capita income, an increase in real interest rate can trigger the substitution effect and encourage households to save more. This is, however, not evident in the Emerging Asian economies, where we observe a negative and weakly significant (at the 10% level) relationship between real interest rate and domestic savings rate.

5.1.4.3 Interest rate spreads

The interest rate spread is an important measure of financial development as it implicitly measures the efficiency of the financial sectors in intermediating savings and borrowings. A high interest rate spread between lending and borrowing interest rates is clearly a sign of inefficacy. Financial intermediaries can manage to reap high spreads if there are controls on deposit rates but not on lending rates or when the competition in the financial sector is too limited. In SSA sample countries, interest spreads maintained a upward trend throughout the 1990s and started following only since early 2000 (Figure 5.1.6). The interest spread in SSA remained higher than the spreads in any other regions of the world.

The fixed-effect models estimated in Table 5.1.5 (column 1 through 5) find a positive and strong association, at the 1% level, between financial market liberalization and interest rate spreads in the Sub-Saharan countries. The coefficient of the FML index remains robust and the sign remains positive in different model specifications. Adjusted R-squared of these models vary from 0.59 and 0.73, confirming these models explain a significant portion of variations in the interest rate spreads both within a country over time and across countries. In the final model (column 5), the FML coefficient is 5.06, suggesting that one unit increase in the financial liberalization

Table 5.1.4 Dependent variable: gross domestic savings (% of GDP)

Variables	(1) South Asia	(2) Emerging Asia	(3) MENA	(4) Latin America	(5) Transition	(6) Full Sample without SSA	(7) Full Sample
Lag Domestic Savings Rate	0.26***	0.15**	-0.05	0.35***	0.07*	0.23***	0.23***
	(0.075)	(0.060)	(0.072)	(0.056)	(0.039)	(0.028)	(0.027)
Log GDP per Capita	-0.01***	-0.00**	0.00**	-0.00	0.00	-0.00	-0.00
	(0.002)	(0.000)	(0.001)	(0.000)	(0.000)	(0.000)	(0.000)
Household Consumption (% of GDP)	-1.06***	-0.86***	-0.89***	-0.66***	-0.88***	-0.74***	-0.74***
	(0.088)	(0.048)	(0.059)	(0.063)	(0.043)	(0.030)	(0.027)
Real Interest Rate (%)	0.05	-0.04*	-0.02	0.03***	-0.01	0.02***	0.02***
	(0.041)	(0.019)	(0.060)	(0.012)	(0.010)	(0.007)	(0.007)
Financial Market Liberalization Index	0.46	0.71	-2.26	0.73	-2.18	0.03	-0.72
	(1.380)	(1.476)	(1.785)	(1.745)	(1.833)	(0.860)	(0.782)
GDP Growth Rate (%)	0.01	-0.02	0.07	0.02	0.03	0.01	0.02
	(0.070)	(0.026)	(0.066)	(0.053)	(0.047)	(0.027)	(0.024)
Government Budget Balance (% of GDP)	0.31*	0.17**	0.24***	0.39***	-0.03	0.33***	0.33***
	(0.169)	(0.065)	(0.072)	(0.071)	(0.075)	(0.038)	(0.036)
Constant	92.60***	76.86***	73.52***	58.98***	73.45***	64.56***	65.10***
	(7.150)	(4.269)	(4.475)	(5.480)	(3.156)	(2.420)	(2.224)
Observations	41	53	33	138	114	383	446
R-squared	0.93	0.94	0.96	0.80	0.87	0.80	0.79
Number of countries	5	6	4	14	13	42	49
Adj. R-squared	0.90	0.92	0.94	0.76	0.85	0.77	0.76
Hausman Specification Test for Fixed Effects							

Notes: Standard errors in parentheses.
*** p < 0.01, ** p < 0.05, * p < 0.10.

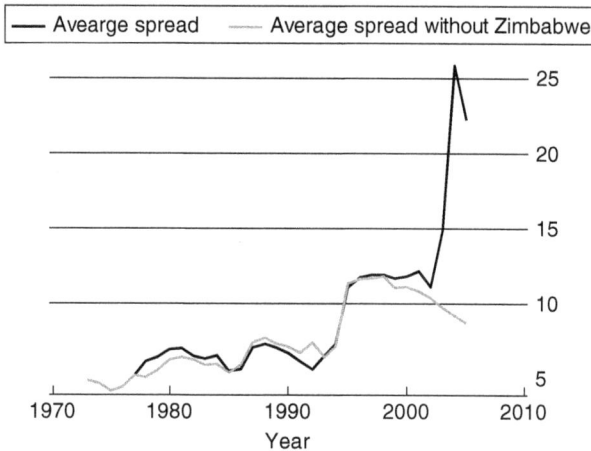

Figure 5.1.6   Trend in interest rate spread in SSA
Source: WDI.

index can increase interest rate spreads by 5 percent from its base level. That is, if the interest spread is 8 percent, then one unit increase in the FML index may raise the spread to 8.4 percent. As expected, inflation is positively and significantly correlated to interest spread in all model specifications. OLS (column 6) and FGLS (column 7) estimations also yield positive and statistically significant, albeit biased downwards, coefficients for the FML index.

Among other regions of the world, only in East Asia (Table 5.1.6, column 2) did we observe a negative and statistically significant relationship between financial market liberalization and interest rate spreads. This perhaps suggests the possibility of a negative "threshold effect" of financial liberalization. Liberalization of the financial sector – particularly interest rate deregulation and increased competition – may contribute to reducing interest rate spreads provided the financial sector has attained a threshold level of financial development. This is perhaps the case with East Asia (column 3), Latin America (column 4) and Transition countries (column 5) as we observe a negative sign (though not significant for Latin America and Transition countries) for the FML coefficient but a positive sign for the FML coefficient when we estimate the model for SSA (Table 5.1.5) and South Asia (column 1, Table 5.1.6). Both South Asia and Sub-Saharan African countries have very low level of financial development and hence liberalization of the sector is unlikely to promote financial development.

5.1.4.4   Domestic credit to the private sector

Domestic credit to the private sector as percentage of GDP is another important measure of financial development. It provides an aggregate measure of

Table 5.1.5 Dependent variable: interest rate spread

Variables	(1) FE	(2) FE	(3) FE	(4) FE	(5) FE¹	(6) OLS	(7) FGLS
Lag Interest Rate Spread	0.74***	0.71***	0.68***	0.68***	0.65***	0.75***	0.76***
	(0.047)	(0.053)	(0.048)	(0.048)	(0.057)	(0.049)	(0.047)
Log GDP per Capita	-1.83	-4.71*	-0.40	-0.45	-0.57	0.83**	0.73***
	(1.974)	(2.773)	(0.840)	(0.847)	(0.830)	(0.340)	(0.223)
GDP Growth Rate (%)	0.04	0.11	0.02	0.02	-0.02	-0.03	-0.03*
	(0.103)	(0.127)	(0.036)	(0.036)	(0.033)	(0.032)	(0.019)
Annual Inflation (%)	0.12***	0.12***	0.02**	0.02**	0.02***	0.01**	0.01
	(0.014)	(0.015)	(0.007)	(0.007)	(0.006)	(0.005)	(0.006)
Financial Market Liberalization Index	7.89***	9.44***	3.54***	3.56***	5.06***	2.49***	1.75**
	(2.509)	(3.151)	(1.063)	(1.066)	(1.255)	(0.892)	(0.768)
Gross Domestic Savings (% of GDP)		-0.11	-0.01	-0.01	-0.04	-0.03	-0.04**
		(0.126)	(0.038)	(0.040)	(0.037)	(0.023)	(0.015)
Current Account Balance (% of GDP)			0.03	0.02	-0.00	0.03	0.03
			(0.044)	(0.044)	(0.039)	(0.031)	(0.022)
Mineral Income (% of GDP)				-0.07	-0.52	-0.18	0.11
				(0.157)	(0.603)	(0.379)	(0.352)
Constant	8.25	27.28	3.57	3.81	4.67	-3.22*	-2.40**
	(12.310)	(17.766)	(5.244)	(5.281)	(4.854)	(1.846)	(1.174)
Observations	261	228	216	216	172	172	172
R-squared	0.75	0.75	0.63	0.63	0.73	0.81	
Number of countries	14	13	13	13	11		11
Adj. R-squared	0.73	0.73	0.59	0.59	0.70	0.80	–
Hausman Specification Test for Fixed Effects							

Notes: ¹Excludes South Africa and Zimbabwe.
Standard errors in parentheses.
*** p < 0.01, ** p < 0.05, * p < 0.10.

Table 5.1.6 Dependent variable: interest rate spread

Variables	(1) South Asia	(2) Emerging Asia	(3) MENA	(4) Latin America	(5) Transition	(6) Full Sample without SSA	(7) Full Sample
Lag Interest Rate Spread	0.62***	0.40***	0.89***	0.26***	0.07**	0.26***	0.27***
	(0.113)	(0.072)	(0.054)	(0.050)	(0.032)	(0.030)	(0.026)
Log GDP per Capita	0.22	0.98**	0.34	-12.67	-4.22	0.32	-3.27
	(2.292)	(0.477)	(0.534)	(30.469)	(6.290)	(11.023)	(8.345)
GDP Growth Rate (%)	-0.11	-0.04	0.02	-1.77	-0.99**	-0.48	-0.32
	(0.130)	(0.038)	(0.028)	(2.154)	(0.395)	(0.733)	(0.550)
Annual Inflation (%)	-0.09	-0.07***	0.03	0.09***	0.03***	0.09***	0.09***
	(0.064)	(0.020)	(0.031)	(0.009)	(0.009)	(0.005)	(0.005)
Financial Market Liberalization Index	4.42	-2.89**	0.24	-14.86	-12.85	-19.03	-9.69
	(6.207)	(1.319)	(0.918)	(51.363)	(17.349)	(22.309)	(15.732)
Gross Domestic Savings (% of GDP)	-0.02	-0.07*	0.04	-2.53	0.08	-0.72	-0.55
	(0.128)	(0.037)	(0.028)	(3.087)	(0.319)	(0.762)	(0.562)
Current Account Balance (% of GDP)	-0.05	0.03	0.03	0.83	0.26	0.22	0.14
	(0.113)	(0.030)	(0.020)	(2.909)	(0.366)	(0.726)	(0.569)
Constant	0.12	-0.90	-2.82	157.96	57.34	29.99	45.12
	(11.794)	(2.531)	(3.522)	(222.967)	(39.414)	(70.490)	(53.143)
Observations	68	135	69	270	166	729	945
R-squared	0.64	0.38	0.91	0.39	0.32	0.38	0.37
Number of countries	4	6	6	15	15	46	59
Adj. R-squared	0.58	0.32	0.89	0.33	0.22	0.33	0.33
Hausman Specification Test for Fixed Effects							

Notes: Standard errors in parentheses
*** p < 0.01, ** p < 0.05, * p < 0.10.

credit availability to the private sector. In developed economies with more developed financial sectors, the share of domestic credit to the private sector as percentage of GDP is usually high. The opposite is true in less developed economies. The share of credit to the private sector of the economy – another oft used indicator of financial development – actually fell from 19.8 percent in 1990 to 15.2 percent in 2005 in Sub-Saharan Africa. In contrast, private credit to GDP ratio increased from 18.4 percent to 33.6 percent in our sample of South Asian economies (Figure 5.1.7).

In Table 5.1.7, we report the regression results for domestic credit to the private sector measured against the level of financial market liberalization in Sub-Saharan Africa. Our estimates in column 3 through 5, show a robust and statistically significant negative relationship between financial market liberalization and private sector credit (Figure 5.1.8). In the full model (column 4), we find that one unit increase in the FML index is associated with 3.16% decline in the private credit to GDP ratio (from its base level). The estimated model has an adjusted R-squared of 0.82. OLS (column 6) and FGLS (column 7) estimates also confirm the negative association between private credit and financial market liberalization in SSA. As expected and observed in other estimations, OLS and FGLS estimates are biased downward because of heteroskedasticity and fixed effects of omitted variables.

In Table 5.1.8, we report the relationship between financial market liberalization and private sector credit in other regions of the world. Only in Latin America (column 4), we observe a positive and significant (1% level)

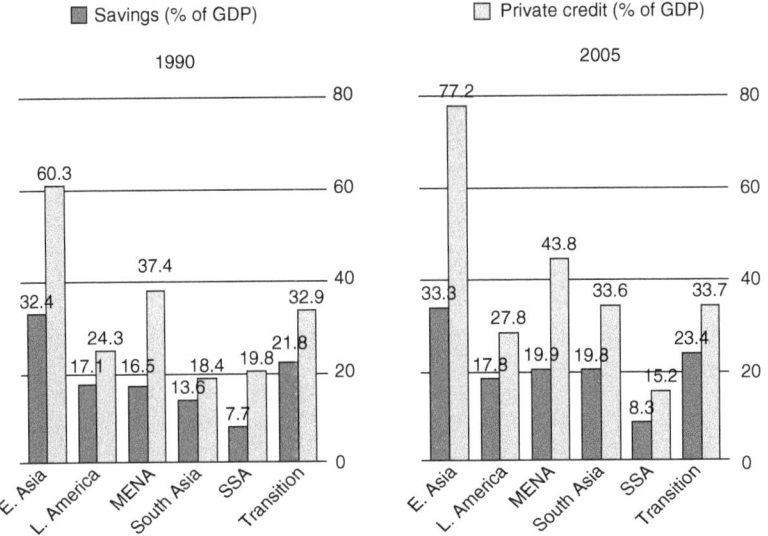

Figure 5.1.7   Domestic savings and credit to the private sector (% of GDP)

Table 5.1.7 Dependent variable: domestic credit to private sector (% of GDP)[1]

Variables	(1) FE	(2) FE	(3) FE	(4) FE	(5) FE	(6) OLS	(7) FGLS
Lag Domestic Credit to Private Sector	0.77***	0.78***	0.83***	0.82***	0.82***	0.91***	0.92***
	(0.042)	(0.044)	(0.029)	(0.029)	(0.029)	(0.025)	(0.022)
Log GDP per Capita	-1.14	-1.42	0.08	0.18	0.19	-0.48	-0.22
	(1.130)	(1.335)	(0.714)	(0.713)	(0.717)	(0.473)	(0.452)
GDP Growth Rate (%)	-0.11*	-0.10	-0.04	-0.04	-0.04	-0.05	-0.02
	(0.061)	(0.070)	(0.036)	(0.036)	(0.036)	(0.046)	(0.029)
Annual Inflation (%)	-0.05***	-0.05***	-0.03***	-0.03***	-0.03***	-0.01	-0.00
	(0.010)	(0.011)	(0.010)	(0.010)	(0.010)	(0.015)	(0.008)
Financial Market Liberalization Index	-2.27*	-2.01	-2.90***	-3.10***	-3.16***	-2.27**	-2.01**
	(1.343)	(1.501)	(0.887)	(0.891)	(0.949)	(1.103)	(0.826)
Gross Domestic Savings (% of GDP)		-0.03	0.13***	0.13***	0.13***	0.06	0.07**
		(0.066)	(0.038)	(0.038)	(0.040)	(0.037)	(0.031)
Current Account Balance (% of GDP)			-0.22***	-0.22***	-0.23***	-0.12**	-0.13***
			(0.044)	(0.044)	(0.047)	(0.051)	(0.037)
Mineral Income (% of GDP)				0.46*	0.45*	0.40	0.03
				(0.261)	(0.267)	(0.273)	(0.357)
Population Growth Rate					-6.00	72.12	22.01
					(37.370)	(44.690)	(38.329)
Constant	12.99*	14.78*	1.53	1.05	1.15	1.81	1.35
	(6.773)	(8.006)	(4.309)	(4.301)	(4.353)	(2.959)	(2.689)
Observations	356	323	301	301	301	206	206
R-squared	0.53	0.53	0.83	0.83	0.83	0.93	
Number of countries	13	12	12	12	12		12
Adj. R-squared	0.51	0.51	0.82	0.82	0.82	0.93	
Hausman Specification Test for Fixed Effects							–

Notes: [1]Excludes South Africa.
Standard errors in parentheses.
*** $p < 0.01$, ** $p < 0.05$, * $p < 0.10$.

Table 5.1.8 Dependent variable: domestic credit to private sector (% of GDP)

Variables	(1) South Asia	(2) East Asia	(3) MENA	(4) Latin America	(5) Transition	(6) Full sample without SSA	(7) Full sample
Lag Domestic Credit to Private Sector	0.86***	0.87***	0.87***	0.68***	0.88***	0.84***	0.86***
	(0.046)	(0.033)	(0.031)	(0.036)	(0.038)	(0.016)	(0.013)
Log GDP per Capita	0.42	-0.09	1.33	-1.45	5.27***	2.74***	2.76***
	(1.312)	(1.876)	(1.247)	(1.434)	(1.702)	(0.740)	(0.565)
GDP Growth Rate (%)	0.11	-0.56***	-0.11	-0.09	-0.30***	-0.01	-0.00
	(0.096)	(0.165)	(0.068)	(0.095)	(0.099)	(0.049)	(0.038)
Annual Inflation (%)	-0.13**	-0.35***	-0.06***	-0.00	-0.03***	-0.00**	-0.00**
	(0.056)	(0.085)	(0.023)	(0.001)	(0.004)	(0.000)	(0.000)
Financial Market Liberalization Index	2.14	6.25	3.02	6.13**	-0.29	1.34	0.73
	(2.225)	(5.007)	(2.083)	(2.433)	(4.686)	(1.398)	(0.987)
Gross Domestic Savings (% of GDP)	0.09	0.71***	-0.04	0.11	0.21**	0.21***	0.14***
	(0.089)	(0.168)	(0.056)	(0.113)	(0.088)	(0.046)	(0.036)
Current Account Balance (% of GDP)	-0.10	-1.01***	-0.23***	-0.28**	-0.18*	-0.34***	-0.30***
	(0.087)	(0.124)	(0.062)	(0.120)	(0.092)	(0.051)	(0.041)
Constant	-0.48	-8.86	-3.21	14.37	-38.02***	-19.09***	-17.96***
	(6.761)	(10.348)	(8.487)	(10.716)	(10.389)	(4.743)	(3.595)
Observations	141	166	185	407	185	1,086	1,417
R-squared	0.85	0.95	0.88	0.52	0.82	0.81	0.82
Number of countries	5	6	7	15	16	49	62
Adj. R-squared	0.84	0.95	0.87	0.49	0.80	0.80	0.81
Hausman Specification Test for Fixed Effects	Positive	Positive	Positive	Positive	Positive	Positive	Positive

Notes: Standard errors in parentheses.
*** p < 0.01, ** p < 0.05, * p < 0.10.

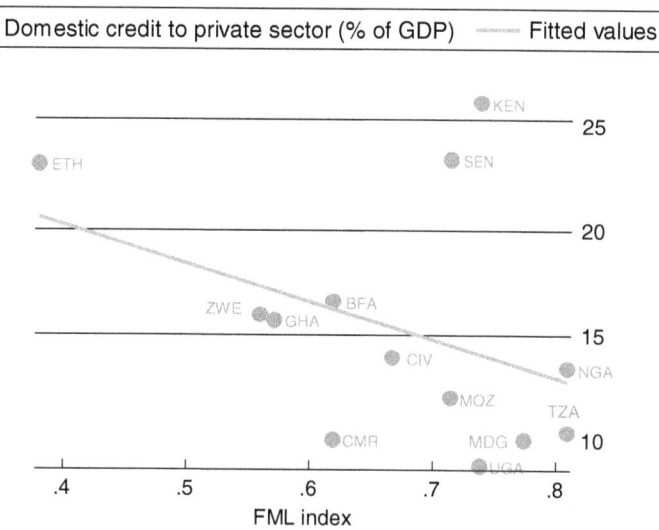

Figure 5.1.8   Financial market liberalization and domestic credit to the private sector

association between financial market liberalization and domestic credit to the private sector. It is positive and insignificant for all other regions, including the full sample. The coefficient for FML index is negative and insignificant for the Transition countries. This suggests that financial market liberalization, in general has, no impact on increasing the availability of credit when we look into a broad set of countries. The association is, however, unambiguous and negative for the Sub-Saharan economies.

5.1.5   Conclusion

Our analysis show that financial market liberalization is unambiguously and negatively associated with financial development in Sub-Saharan Africa, when we measure the impact of liberalization on domestic savings rate and credit to the private sector – the two broad measures of financial development. We also find a very strong and significant positive relationship between financial development and real interest rates and interest rate spreads – two additional measures of financial development used in our paper. These indicators of financial development are by no means exhaustive. But they clearly provide us measurable benchmarks to assess the impact of financial market liberalization. While financial liberalization unambiguously and adversely impacted financial development in Sub Saharan Africa, the relationship is generally ambiguous and/or non-existence in other regions of the world. This helps us draw two plausible conclusions: a. financial market liberalization is neither necessary nor sufficient for financial development; and b. There is perhaps a threshold effect to the extent that financial liberalization can actually be harmful for financial development when the initial level of financial and economic development is very low, which is probably the case with Sub Saharan Africa. While at a higher level of financial and economic development, financial liberalization may or may not render financial development, liberalization can adversely impact financial development if the initial level of financial and economic development is weak. The initial condition is no doubt shaped by political, legal and institutional structures and policy-makers need to take them into account *ex ante*, and not *ex post*.

There is a clear need for further research to determine how various aspects of financial market liberalization – abolition of credit targets and credit controls, deregulation of interest rates, removal of entry barriers, privatization of the banking sector, etc. – affect various dimensions of financial development. As we find, financial liberalization in Sub Saharan Africa was dominated by privatization as well as by removal of entry barriers and credit controls, there is a clear need for policy research to determine whether reversing some of these measures can alleviate the adverse impact of financial liberalization in Sub Saharan Africa. The important issue of capital outflows and capital flights, not addressed in this paper, can also help us better understand why financial liberalization had such negative impact on the financial development in the African continent while it has relatively benign or no effect in other regions of the world. The interaction between financial liberalization, capital account liberalization and capital out-flows - may shed new lights on assessing the impact of financial market liberalization in Sub-Saharan Africa. This clearly warrants further research.

Annex I: List of countries

Sub-Saharan Africa (14): Burkina Faso, Cameroon, Côte d'Ivoire, Ghana, Ethiopia, Kenya, Madagascar, Mozambique, Nigeria, Senegal, South Africa, Tanzania, Uganda, and Zimbabwe
South Asia (5): Bangladesh, India, Nepal, Pakistan, and Sri Lanka

East Asia (7): China, Indonesia, Korea, Malaysia, Philippines, Thailand, and Vietnam

MENA (6): Algeria, Egypt, Jordan, Morocco, Tunisia, and Turkey

Latin America (17): Argentina, Bolivia, Brazil, Chile, Colombia, Costa Rica, Dominican Republic, Ecuador, El Salvador, Guatemala, Jamaica, Mexico, Nicaragua, Paraguay, Peru, Uruguay, and Venezuela

Transition (16): Albania, Azerbaijan, Belarus, Bulgaria, Czech Republic, Estonia, Georgia, Hungary, Kazakhstan, Kyrgyz Republic, Latvia, Poland, Romania, Russian Federation, Ukraine, and Uzbekistan

Annex II

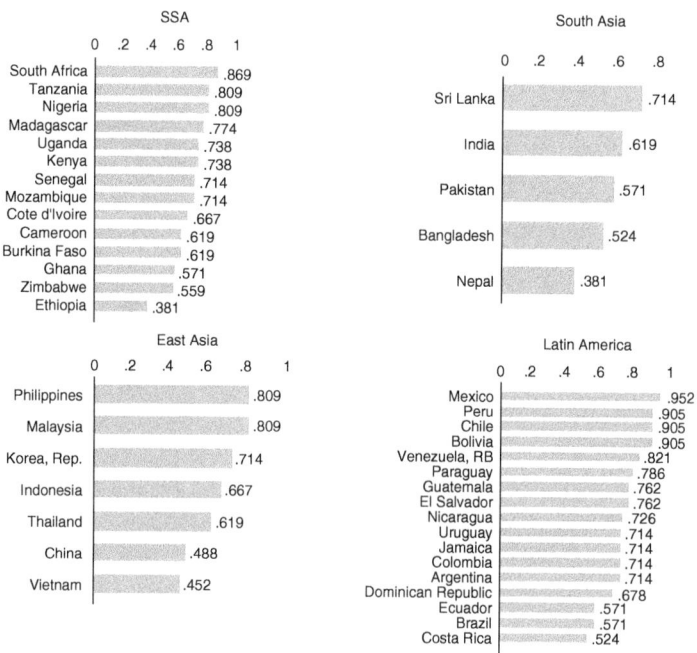

Figure 5.1.3a The status of financial liberalization in SSA, South Asia, East Asia, and Latin America, 2005

Source: Constructed from database of Abiad et al (2008).

Annex III

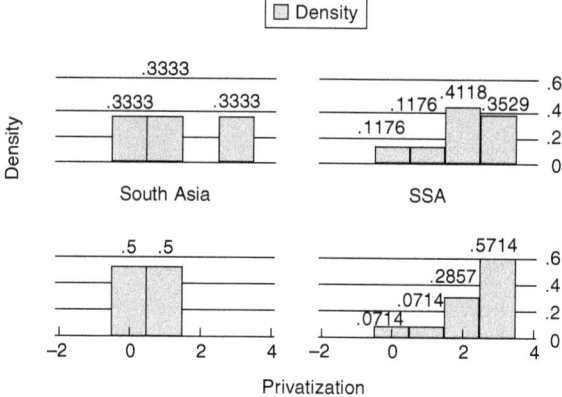

Figure 5.1.4b Status of privatization of the financial sector in various regions (% of countries)

Source: Constructed from database of Abiad et al (2008).

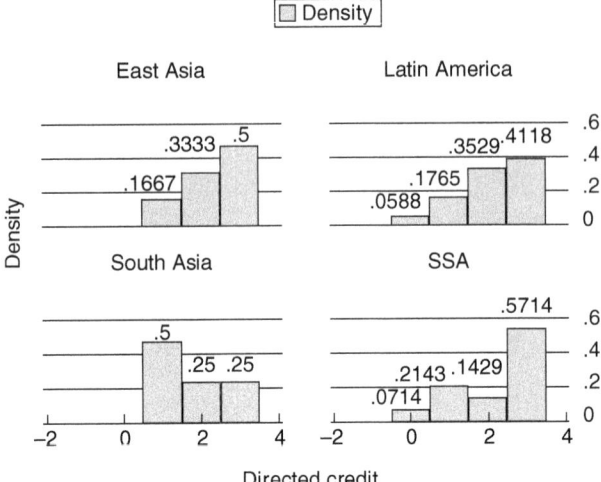

Figure 5.1.4c   Practice of directed credit in various regions (% of countries)
Source: Constructed from database of Abiad et al (2008).

Notes

1. Hamid Rashid is a Senior Adviser at the United Nations Department of Economic and Social Affairs (DESA) in New York. The views and opinions expressed herein are those of the author and do not reflect the views of the United Nations or its member states.
2. See, for example, Campbell and Mankiw (1990), Ostry and Reinhart (1992) and Stiglitz, Hellman and Murdock (1998).
3. See Gemech (2003).

References

Abiad, A., Detragiache, E., and Tressel, T. (2008) "A New Database of Financial Reforms". *IMF Staff Papers*, pp. 1–28.

Bandiera, O. Caprio, G., Honohan, P., and Schiantarelli, F. (2000) "Does Financial Reform Raise or Reduce Saving?," *Review of Economics and Statistics*, vol. 82, no. 2, pp. 239–263.

Bayoumi, T. (1993) "Financial Deregulation and Household Saving," *Economic Journal*, vol. 103, pp. 1432–1443.

Broner, F.A. and Ventura, J. (2010). "Rethinking the Effects of Financial Liberalization," CREI and Universitat Pompeu Fabra.

Campbell, J.Y. and Mankiw, N.G (1990) "Permanent Income, Current Income and Consumption," *Journal of Business and Economic Statistics*, vol. 8, no. 3, pp. 265–79.

Claessens, S. and Laeven, L. (2003) "Financial Development, Property Rights, and Growth," *Journal of Finance*, vol. 58, pp. 2401–2436.

Gemech, F. and Struthers, J. (2003) "The Mckinnon–Shaw Hypothesis: Thirty Years On: A Review of Recent Developments in Financial Liberalization Theory," University of Paisley, Scotland.

Giovannini, A. (1985) "Saving and the Rate of Interest in LDCs," *Journal of Development Economics*, vol. 18, pp. 197–217.

Hellmann, T., Murdock, K., and Stiglitz, J. (1998) "Financial Restraint and the Market Enhancing View," in M. Aoki (ed.), *Proceedings of the IEA Roundtable Conference: The Institutional Foundation of Economic Development in East Asia*, pp. 255–284.

King, R.G. and Levine, R. (1993) "Finance and Growth: Schumpeter Might Be Right," *Quarterly Journal of Economics*, vol. 108, pp. 717–738.

La Porta, R., Lopez-de-Silanes, F., and Shleifer, A. (2002) "Government Ownership of Commercial Banks," *Journal of Finance*, vol. 57, pp. 265–301.

La Porta, R., Lopez-de-Silanes, F., Shleifer, A., and Vishny, R.W. (1997) "Legal Determinants of External Finance," *Journal of Finance*, vol. 52, pp. 1131–1150.

Levine, R. (1997), "Financial Development and Economic Growth: Views and Agenda," *Journal of Economic Literature*, vol. 35 pp. 688–726.

Levine, R. (2004). "Finance and Growth: Theory and Evidence," Working Paper 10766 (Cambridge, MA: National Bureau of Economic Research).

Loayza N., Schmidt-Hebbel, K., and Serven, L. (2000) "What Drives Private Saving Across the World?," *Review of Economics and Statistics*, vol. 82, no. 2, pp. 165–181

McKinnon, R.I. (1973) *Money and Capital in Economic Development* (Washington: The Brookings Institution).

Ogaki M., Ostry, J.D., and Reinhart, C.M. (1996) "Saving Behavior in Low- and Middle-Income Developing Countries: A Comparison," *IMF Staff Papers*, vol. 43, no. 1, pp. 38–71.

Ostry, J.D. and Reinhart, C.M. (1992) "Private Saving and Terms of Trade Shocks: Evidence from Developing Countries," *Staff Papers*, International Monetary Fund, vol. 39, pp. 495–517.

Rajan, R. and Zingales, L. (1998) "Financial Dependence and Growth," *American Economic Review*, vol. 88, pp. 559–586.

Reinhart, C. and Tokatlidis, I. (2000) "Financial Liberalization: The African Experience," African Economic Research Consortium, Nairobi, Kenya, December 2–7.

Shaw, E. (1973) *Financial Deepening in Economic Development* (New York: Oxford University Press).

Williamson, J. and Mahar, M. (1998) "A Survey of Financial Liberalization," *Essays in International Finance*, No. 211 (Princeton, NJ: Princeton University Press).

5.2
Financialization as an Obstacle to Industrialization

C.P. Chandrasekhar
Jawaharlal Nehru University, New Delhi, India

No one can deny that finance has a role to play in industrialization. On the other hand, any process, however short term, in which the financial sector feeds on itself to generate extremely high profits, must be inimical to industrialization. Under the latter, the flow of finance into speculation would, however temporarily, raise returns on financial investments well above returns on investment in real assets and dampen the incentive to undertake real investment. Further, in such a regime, credit to purchase financial assets would fetch higher interest and be privileged over credit for real capital formation.

So theoretical and econometric exercises (King and Levine, 1993; Beck et al., 2000) aimed at assessing whether there should be or does prevail a monotonic relationship between financial expansion and deepening and real economic growth pose the wrong question. This was recognized many years ago by Gurley and Shaw (1967) who suggested, in fact, that while, normally, per capita income growth is accompanied by a faster increase in the volume of financial assets relative to real income or real tangible wealth, beyond a point this would no longer hold.

Yet the issue is not simply one of the absence of a monotonic relationship. Finance is not a homogenous "thing" the availability of which increases or does not as development proceeds. Finance is purchasing power embedded in instruments with different degrees of liquidity (or capability for transformation into goods and services) that are created and transacted by financial institutions of different kinds that populate different financial markets. The proliferation of finance therefore involves the expansion of some combination of markets, institutions, and instruments, whose "functioning" and growth is influenced by the framework of regulation in place. It is this combination of markets, institutions, and instruments, and the framework regulating them that constitutes the financial structure.

There is no logical reason whatsoever to suggest that any given level of financial expansion measured by the ratio of financial assets to GDP or to real tangible wealth should be associated with a specific financial structure. Neither need it be true that the pace and pattern of financial proliferation would be the same in systems with very different financial structures. Thus, right through the period of intensive regulation of the financial sector in the USA, from the Glass–Steagall Act to the 1980s, there was little financial "innovation" in terms of new instruments or institutions, though there were periods characterized by substantial and rapid growth in the financial sector. As a result, in the 1950s, banks and banking activity constituted around 80–90 per cent of that in the financial sector. Even at the end of the 1950, savings accumulated in pension and mutual funds were small and trading on the New York Stock Exchange involved a daily average of three million shares at its peak (Sametz, 1992).

This was to rise to as much 160 million shares per day during the second half of the 1980s (1986–91), when financial liberalization began transforming the US financial structure, generating by the end of the 1990s the Anglo-Saxon model of ostensibly efficient and free financial markets. The relative share of pension funds (public and private) in total financial intermediary assets rose from 9.7 percent in 1960 to 24.6 percent in 1994 and of stock, bond, and money market mutual funds from 2.9 to 15 percent; on the other hand, the share of banks and thrift institutions (Saving and loans, Mutual saving and Credit unions) declined from 58.7 percent to 37.6 percent (Edwards and Mishkin, 1995). That was also the period when instruments like junk bonds and mortgage-backed securities gained currency. There is reason to believe that this change in the structure of the financial system did limit the flow of credit to industry.

5.2.1 Financial institutions and industrial take-off in Europe

The role of financial structures has also been recognised in other contexts. The importance of specific kinds of financial institutions and markets for the success of late-industrialization in Europe was emphasized by Gerschenkron (1962). Finance was important to that process because it required large volumes of capital to be simultaneously invested in capital-intensive capacities in many industries. The presence of certain initial conditions for successful industrial transformation has been emphasized by many analysts. But Gerschenkron believed that certain supposed "prerequisites" for success, such as the prior accumulation of capital or an agrarian transition that released the labor and created the market for industry, were not absolute necessities inasmuch as in the course of development countries that were set for industrialization would find "institutional substitutions" for these prerequisites that ensured the break through.

Principal among these were certain institutional innovations in the financial sector, which played a role in the success of late-industrializers like France and Germany. Using the examples of the Crédit Mobilier of the brothers Pereire in France and the "universal banks" in Germany, Gerschenkron argued that the creation of "financial organisations designed to build thousands of miles of railroads, drill mines, erect factories, pierce canals, construct ports and modernise cities" was hugely transformative. Financial firms based on the old wealth were typically in the nature of rentier capitalists and limited themselves to floatations of government loans and foreign exchange transactions. The new firms, on the other hand, were "devoted to railroadisation and industrialisation of the country" and in the process influenced the behavior of old wealth as well.

These banks, according to Gerschenkron, substituted for the absence of a number of elements crucial to industrialization:

> In Germany, the various incompetencies of the individual entrepreneurs were offset by the device of splitting the entrepreneurial function: the German investment banks – a powerful invention, comparable in economic effect to that of the steam engine – were in their capital-supplying functions a substitute for the insufficiency of the previously created wealth willingly placed at the disposal of entrepreneurs. But they were also a substitute for entrepreneurial deficiencies. From their central vantage points of control, the banks participated actively in shaping the major – and sometimes even not so major – decisions of the individual enterprises. It was they who often mapped out a firm's paths of growth, conceived far-sighted plans, decided on major technological and locational innovations, and arranged for mergers and capital increases. (Gerschenkron, 1962: 137)

In this way, in Austria, Italy, Switzerland, France, and Belgium the banks played a major role in facilitating industrial transformation.

5.2.2   Financial structures and industrial development

What this points to is that the impact that finance and financial proliferation can have on growth and industrialization depends also on the structure within which that proliferation occurs. The relationship between financial structures, financial growth, and overall economic development is, of course, complex. What a regulated financial structure serving as an instrument for development does is that it facilitates the realization of a level and an allocation of investment that is conducive to growth based on capital-intensive industry.

The growth of output and employment in the commodity-producing sectors depends on investment that expands capital stock. Traditionally, development theory had emphasized the role of such investment. It argued, correctly, that given production conditions, a rise in the rate of real capital formation leading to an acceleration of the rate of physical accumulation, is at the core of the development process. Associated with any trajectory of growth predicated on a certain rate of investment is, of course, a composition or allocation of investment needed to realize that rate of growth given the feasible access to foreign exchange.

Once the Keynesian Revolution popularized the notion that the lack of adequate financial savings cannot be the constraint on investment and growth, it appeared that the role of the financial sector in mobilizing and channelling savings was secondary and inevitably fulfilled. As Joan Robinson (1952) put it: "Where enterprise leads, finance follows."

In this perspective, the issue of financing for development was seen as a question of mobilizing or creating real resources: of mobilizing surplus labor (Rosenstein-Rodan, 1943, Nurkse, 1953); of overcoming the wage goods constraint (Kalecki, 1972); or of dealing with the problem that underdevelopment is in part the result of the lack of adequate capital stock to employ the labor force in full and the fact that this capital stock cannot be imported because of a foreign exchange constraint (Mahalanobis, 1955). Finance in the sense of money or financial assets came in only when looking at the ability of the state to tax away a part of the surplus to finance its development expenditures, and address the obstacles to deficit-financed spending, given the possible inflationary consequences if real constraints to growth were not overcome.

In this framework, the financial sector is seen as adjusting to the requirements of the real sector. However, such adjustment is not automatic but the consequence of regulation that subsumes financial policy within the framework of industrial policy. If the financial sector is left unregulated, in economies with substantial private assets and an important role for private agents in investment decision-making, market signals would determine the allocation of investible resources and therefore the demand for and the allocation of savings intermediated by financial enterprises. This could result in the problems conventionally associated with a situation where private rather than overall social returns determine the allocation of savings and investment.

5.2.3 Unregulated finance and investment allocation

To start with, the allocation of investment may not be in keeping with that required to ensure a certain profile of the pattern of production, needed to raise the rate of saving and investment as emphasized by the Feldman–Mahalanobis model. An obvious way in which this happens is through inadequate investments in the heavy industrial or infrastructural sectors characterized most often by lumpy investments, long gestation lags, and (relatively) lower profit. It is precisely such investments that an unregulated financial sector would shun, given the income, capital, and liquidity risks involved. On the other hand, given the "economy-wide externalities" associated with such industries, inadequate investments in infrastructure would obviously constrain the rate of growth. Since unregulated finance would prefer to limit the level of illiquidity associated with its investments, its intermediation would not only direct savings to sectors perceived as more profitable but to those that allow quicker returns. Short-termism in investment is the inevitable result.

The private-profit-driven allocation of savings and investment could also aggravate the inherent tendency in markets to direct credit to non-priority and import-intensive but more profitable sectors, to concentrate investible funds in the hands of a few large players, and direct savings to already well-developed centres of economic activity. Hence, if the government were to want to influence the sectors and agents to whom credit is directed and the prices at which such credit is to be provided, in order to realize a particular allocation of investment, a given rate of investment, and an income-wise and region-wise redistribution of incomes, it may choose to impose restrictions on the financial sector to realize these goals.

Further, even in developing countries which choose – or are forced to choose – a more mercantilist strategy of growth based on a rapid acquisition of larger shares in segments of the world market for manufactures, these segments have not only to be identified by an agency with greater seeing power than individual firms, but that agency must ensure an adequate flow of cheap credit to these entities so that they can not only make investments in frontline technologies and internationally competitive scales of production, but also have the wherewithal to sustain themselves during the long period when they build goodwill in the market, which is a function of time. The state must not merely play the role of investment coordinator, but use the financial system as a means to direct investment to sectors and technologies at scales of production it considers appropriate. Equity investments, directed credit, and differential interest rates are important instruments of any state-led or state-influenced development trajectory. Stated otherwise, although financial policies may not help directly increase the rate of savings and ensure that the available *ex ante* savings are invested, they can be used to influence the pattern of investment.

Such a framework is crucial because in a large number of developing countries development occurs in a mixed economy framework where private initiative and investment are significant. In others, the transition away from planned systems is ensuring a growing role for private agents. This implies that independent of whether or not the government adopts a strategy of growth based on the home market or one of protecting and building the home market while targeting in mercantilist fashion the world market, it would have to play a major role in: (i) channelizing large volumes of cheap capital to the selected units; and (ii) using the leverage provided by this activity to coordinate and influence investment decisions across the industrial sector.

To play these roles the state would have to choose an appropriate institutional framework and an appropriate regulatory structure. That is the financial structure – the mix of contracts/instruments, markets, and institutions – is developed keeping in mind its instrumentality from the point of view of the development policies, especially the industrial policy, of the state. The point to note is that this kind of use of a modified version of a historically developed financial structure or of a structure created virtually anew was typical of most lateindustrializing countries. Financial structures in these countries were created to deal with the difficulties associated with late industrial entry: capital requirements for entry in most areas were high, because technology for factory production had evolved in a capital-intensive direction from its primitive industrial revolution level; competition from established producers meant that firms had to concentrate on production for a protected domestic market or be supported with finance to survive long periods of low capacity utilization during which they could find themselves a foothold in world markets. Not surprisingly, late-industrializers created strongly regulated and even predominantly state-controlled financial markets aimed at mobilizing savings and using the intermediary function to influence the size and structure of investment. This they did through directed credit policies and differential interest rates, and the provision of investment support to the nascent industrial class in the form of equity, credit, and low interest rates.

By dismantling these structures financial liberalization destroys an important instrument that historically evolved in late-industrializers to deal with the difficulties of ensuring growth through the diversification of production structures that international inequality generates.

5.2.4   Financialization and banking behavior

Excessive financialization in developing countries occurs in the aftermath of financial deregulation or liberalization, which inevitably involves the reshaping of relatively "immature" financial systems in the image of the increasingly "market-based" systems characteristic of the developed capitalist world, especially the system that emerged and evolved in the USA since the 1980s. A consequence of that transformation is the erosion of the role played by financial structures in developing countries as instruments of industrial policy. In financial structures geared to play that role, financial institutions and banks are required by policy to direct credit to specific sectors at differential interest rates, and cross-subsidize activity in less profitable markets with surpluses earned in more profitable ones. This does involve some degree of pre-emption of credit through imposition of sectoral targets and by the use of state banking and development banking institutions as instruments for mobilizing savings and directing credit to priority sectors at low real interest rates. Financial liberalization undermines such structures. The role of the financial system as an instrument for allocating credit and redistributing assets and incomes is also thereby undermined.

The process of financialization also affects financial allocation because it is inevitably associated with the transformation of banking. A liberal banking policy is a prerequisite for financialization since financial proliferation requires the prime depository institutions, which are the first port of call for a nation's savings, to leverage agents and operators in non-banking markets experimenting with new institutions and instruments. An inevitable consequence is a sharp rise in credit creation.

This implies that the banking sector cannot rely only on deposit insurance as a guard against risk. Two practices therefore gain importance as a means of managing risk. One is a growing emphasis on capital adequacy, or the requirement that banks should hold capital amounting to a certain proportion of their risky assets in forms that are available and easily accessed to cover losses, if any, incurred on those assets. The second is the sharing of risk, through the transfer of credit risk. This requires bundling together credit assets of different kinds to create securities that are treated as low-risk assets because of the low probability of simultaneous default on credit provided to different geographies, markets and classes of clients.

The problem is that once credit becomes a tradable asset that banks (because of their credibility and reach) can easily create and pass on for a fee and commission income, there is an inevitable tendency toward credit proliferation. Moreover, since the creator of the credit asset is not carrying the risk, there is a tendency to take on excess risk by expanding the universe of borrowers.

Expanding the universe of borrowers requires bringing a larger number of "retail borrowers," borrowing to invest in housing, to buy automobiles or durables, or just enhance current consumption, into the credit net. Since this kind of credit is spread across a large number of borrowers, carries a higher interest rate, and is easily securitized, it is seen as both less risky and more profitable. This creates a banking ethos in which there is less willingness to lend long-term to industrial projects that are considered less lucrative and more risky credit targets, leading to a sharp rise in the share of retail lending in total advances by the banking system. Hence from the supply side this aspect of the process of financialization limits and rations credit for industrial development.

This adverse effect of financial expansion is "tolerated" partly because of the demand-side effects of the proliferation of credit. By expanding the universe of borrowers, financialization does result in an expansion of demand, as long as it does not reverse as the result of a crisis. By permitting agents to consume in excess of their income, for short periods of time the process injects into the system an element of demand that is autonomous of the level of current income.

Recognizing this, in the age of finance, the state, through its central banking arm, has used the financial system to engineer reasonable or even creditable growth in the real economy. It injects liquidity into the system through an easy money policy to sustain a regime with low interest rates and burgeoning credit. With no restrictions on the provision of credit, the loans finance housing investment and consumption, on the one hand, and speculation in stock and real estate markets on the other. The asset price inflation that such speculation generates magnifies the value of the wealth held by households, encouraging them to borrow and spend even further. The outcome is growth in the real sector, which, for a variety of reasons, is not accompanied by inflation in the prices of goods but only in the prices of assets. To keep this process going, however, credit has to go to those who borrow beyond what their incomes would warrant at terms they couldn't afford, making asset price inflation the unstable anchor to which the system is tethered. The system is soon awash with risky assets. When that gives, the edifice collapses.

This tendency implies that the relationship between finance and industrial development depends on the phase of the cycle being observed. During the boom it appears that financialization favours industrial growth. But when the crisis occurs it is clear that this dependence on finance is extremely damaging. Moreover, unlike debt-financed public expenditure, debt-financed private expenditure is not really autonomous. So when the crisis occurs, while public expenditure can be sustained and even expanded as a counter-cyclical measure, there is no reason why private expenditure should revive of its own accord. If that is to occur at all, it requires the rebalancing of household balance sheets, overburdened with debt. A recession is hardly a period when that is easily done, delaying the recovery from the recession substantially.

5.2.5 Financial liberalization and fiscal policy

This difference between debt-financed public and private expenditure is of significance because one feature of financialization is that it tends to *substitute* debt-financed public spending with debt-financed private expenditure as the principal stimulus for growth. Financial liberalization adversely affects industrialization not only by undermining the supportive role that the financial structure plays in allocating investments to "needy" sectors and directing savings to investment projects that may otherwise be ignored but also by tending to undermine what has been an important stimulus for industrial growth: debt-financed public spending.

Inasmuch as financial liberalization leads to financial growth and deepening and increases the presence and role of financial agents in the economy, it forces the state to adopt a deflationary stance to appease financial interests. Those interests are against deficit-financed spending by the state for a number of reasons (Patnaik, 2009). First, deficit financing is seen to increase the liquidity overhang in the system, and therefore is regarded as being potentially inflationary. Inflation is anathema to finance since it erodes the real value of financial assets. Second, since government spending is "autonomous" in character, the use of debt to finance such autonomous spending is seen as introducing into financial markets an arbitrary player not driven by the profit motive, whose activities can render more unpredictable interest rate differentials that determine financial profits. Third, if deficit spending leads to a substantial build-up of the state's debt and interest burden, it may intervene in financial markets to lower interest rates with implications for financial returns. Financial interests wanting to guard against that possibility tend to oppose deficit spending. Finally, the use of deficit spending to support autonomous expenditures by the state amounts to an implicit legitimization of an interventionist state, and therefore, a delegitimization of the market. Since global finance seeks to delegitimize the state and legitimize the market, it strongly opposes deficit-financed, autonomous state spending.

Efforts to curb the deficit obviously result in a contraction of public expenditure, especially expenditure on capital formation, which adversely affects industrial growth by limiting the direct and indirect demands generated by such expenditure.

This macroeconomic fallout and its effects are aggravated by the perception, which accompanies financial reform, that macroeconomic regulation should rely on monetary policy pursued by an "independent" central bank rather than on fiscal policy. The immediate consequence of this perception is the tendency to follow the principle that even the limited deficits that occur should not be "monetized." Fiscal reform is concerned not solely with reducing the size of the deficit, but also with the manner in which any given level of the deficit should be financed. In this regard, fiscal reform involves a sharp reduction of the "monetized deficit" of the government, or that part which is financed with borrowing from the central bank. However, since the interest rate on such borrowing tends to be much lower than the interest rate on borrowing from the open market, its reduction results in a sharp rise in the average interest rate on government borrowing. This worsens the fiscal position of the government, leading to further reduction in public spending and greater reliance on private spending to sustain industrial growth. In the event, if growth has to occur based on domestic demand private credit has to rise sharply.

5.2.6   Institutional change and financial fragility

As noted earlier, associated with the substitution of public spending by debt-financed private expenditure as the principal stimulus to growth is an expansion of overall and retail credit. This process is predicated on a transformation of the financial structure involving institutional changes that unleash a dynamic that endows the financial system with a less regulated, oligopolistic structure, which could increase the fragility of the system. Greater freedom to invest, including in sensitive sectors such as real estate and stock markets, ability to increase exposure to particular sectors and individual clients and increased regulatory forbearance all lead to increased instances of financial failure. In addition, by institutionally linking different segments of financial markets, the process increases the degree of entanglement of different agents within the financial system and increases the impact of financial failure in units in any one segment of the financial system on agents elsewhere in the system. Such possibilities are all the greater because financial transformation follows liberalization, which implies a degree of regulatory forbearance.

Financial markets left to themselves are known to be prone to failure because of the public goods characteristics of information which agents must acquire and process (Stiglitz, 1994). They are characterized by insufficient monitoring by market participants. Individual shareholders tend to refrain from investing money and time in acquiring information about managements, hoping that others would do so instead and knowing that all shareholders, including themselves, benefit from the information garnered. As a result, there may be inadequate monitoring leading to risky decisions and malpractice. Financial firms wanting to reduce or avoid monitoring costs may just follow other, possibly larger, financial firms in making their investments, leading to what has been observed as the "herd instinct" characteristic of financial players. This not merely limits access to finance for some agents, but could lead to overlending to some entities, failure of which could have systemic effects. The prevalence of informational externalities can create other problems. Malpractice in a particular bank leading to failure may trigger fears among depositors in other banks, resulting in a run on deposits there.

Disruptions may also occur because expected private returns differ from social returns in many activities. This could result in a situation where market-driven players take on unnecessary risks in search of high returns. Typical examples are lending for investments in stocks or real estate. Loans to these sectors can be at extremely high interest rates because the returns in these sectors are extremely volatile and can reach extremely high levels. Since banks accept real estate or securities as collateral, borrowing to finance speculative investments in stock or real estate can spiral. This type of activity thrives because of the belief that losses, if any, can be transferred to the lender through default, and lenders are confident of government support in case of a crisis. This could feed a speculative spiral that can in time lead to a collapse of the bubble and bank failures.

These kinds of tendencies effect real investment in two ways. First, inasmuch as speculative bubbles lead to financial crises, they squeeze liquidity, induce distress sales of assets, and result in deflation, all of which impacts adversely on industrial production and employment. Second, inasmuch as the maximum returns to productive investment in agriculture and manufacturing are limited, there is a limit to what borrowers would be willing to pay to finance such investment. Thus, despite the fact that social returns to agricultural and manufacturing investment are higher than that for stocks and real estate, and despite the contribution that such investment can make to growth, credit at the required rate may not be available.

The point is that while financial liberalization leads to these kinds of macroeconomic risks, the evidence suggests that the expected microeconomic gains are not really realized. Even in the USA, the role of stock markets as a source of capital was limited. Between 1970 and 1989, the ratio of profit retention, bank finance, and bonds to the net sources of finance of non-financial corporations in the USA amounted to 91.3, 16.6 and 17.1 percent, respectively. The contribution of equity was a negative 8.8 percent. The first two of these sources played an overwhelming role even in the UK and Germany during this period (Stiglitz, 1994). Thus bond markets play a limited role and equity markets virtually no role at all in financing corporate investment in these countries. The stock market is primarily a site to exchange risks rather than raise capital for investment.

5.2.7   The Japanese experience

Even in Japan, with its predominantly bank-based rather than stock market-based financial system, the financial liberalization that accompanied the rise to dominance of finance proved debilitating. The financial system that underlay Japan's post-war growth was one in which government regulation and control was the key. Interest rates on deposits and loans were controlled, with the government using differential interest rates as a mechanism to target the growth of specific industries. The net result of such control was that: either (i) the government had to ensure financial agents a portfolio of activity that delivered returns adequate for self-sufficiency and growth; or (ii) the government had to channelize resources garnered through taxation or other means to the financial system to ensure the viability of individual financial agents. The government's implicit or explicit guarantee of such viability implied that it guaranteed depositors' savings as well, making bank deposits and insurance products rather than stock market investments the preferred form in which household savings were held.

Inasmuch as the government "permitted" the banks to play this role, Japan saw the emergence of the main bank system where banks provided loans to firms, as well as held their stock (Aoki and Patrick, 1995). This meant that the banks were in a position to use the resulting leverage to ensure that their funds were profitably employed and properly managed. Firms depended on banks for steady, long-term funding support. And the banks were assured of business from these firms which delivered fees and profits.

During the years of high growth this system served the Japanese economy well. It allowed banks and firms to take a long-term perspective in determining their borrowing and lending strategies; it offered entrepreneurs the advantage of deep pockets to compete with much larger and more established firms in world markets; and it allowed the government to "intervene" in firm-level decision-making without having to establish a plethora of generalized controls, which are more difficult to both design and implement. Above all, when the rate of expansion of world markets slowed after the first oil shock, and Japan, which was highly dependent on exports for its growth, was affected adversely both by this and by the loss of competitiveness that an appreciating currency involved, the system allowed firms to restructure their operations and enter new areas so that profits in emerging areas could neutralize losses in sunset industries.

The consequent high levels of gearing of firms and high exposure of banks to risky assets could be "managed" within a closed and regulated financial system, in which the state, through the central bank, played the role of guarantor of deposits and lender of last resort. Non-performing loans generated by failures in particular areas were implicitly seen as a social cost that had to be borne by the system in order to ensure economic success.

The question, however, is why the system also failed to serve Japan during the 1990s. The answer lies in the fact that the system was changed and considerably diluted as a result of external pressures during the 1980s. The pressure came from three sources. First, from international banks and financial institutions that wanted Japan to open up its financial sector and provide them space in its financial system. Second, once these external agents were permitted to enter the system, they wanted a dilution of the special relationship that existed between the government, the financial system, and the corporate world, since that implied the existence of internal barriers to their entry and expansion. Third, these agents and even some Japanese financial institutions affected adversely by the deceleration of growth in the system, wanted greater flexibility in operations and the freedom to "innovate" in terms of both choice of investments and the instruments with which they transact.

There was one principal reason why Japan succumbed to these pressures: its dependence on world, especially US, markets to sustain growth. When faced with US protectionism against Japanese imports, Japanese investors sought to Americanize themselves by acquiring or establishing new production capacities in the USA in areas such as automobiles. In return for the "freedom" to export to and invest in the USA, Japan had to make some concessions. But the US demands were quite damaging. They began by requiring Japan to appreciate its currency. Following the celebrated Plaza Accord, arrived at in New York in September 1985, the yen, which had started to appreciate against the dollar in February 1985 from a 260 yen/US\$ level, maintained its upward trend to touch its April 1995 level of below 80 yen/US\$. Any economy faced with such a huge appreciation of its currency was bound to stall, let alone an export-dependent one such as that of Japan.

This trend, which resulted in the hollowing out of Japanese industry, also undermined the principal area of business of the banks, which were faced with the prospect that some of their past lending could turn non-performing. It was in response to this that the Japanese banks joined the chorus against financial controls, demanding that they be permitted to diversify away from their traditional areas. The government responded by introducing regulatory changes, in the form of a revision of the Foreign Exchange Control Law in 1980 and permission for commercial banks to create non-bank subsidiaries to lend against real estate investments. Besides expanding overseas operations, the principal areas into which the banks diversified were lending against real estate and stock market investments. The rate of growth of real estate lending rose from 7 percent in the second half of the 1970s, to 18 percent in the first half of the 1980s, and 20 percent in the second half.

The result of this was a speculative boom triggered by a mad rush into the new areas. Even as GDP growth was slower in the 1980s than in the 1950s and 1960s, the six-largest-cities-index of real estate prices tripled between end-March 1985 and end-March 1990, from 33.6 to 100. Similarly, there was a massive speculative boom in stock markets with the yearly high of the Nikkei stock market index rising from 12,500 in 1985 to 38,916 in 1989. By 1989 it was clear that the asset bubble was bound to burst, and in a belated effort to halt the frenzy and respond to householder complaints that acquiring housing was virtually impossible, the government stepped in by controlling credit and raising interest rates. The net result was a collapse in both real estate and stock markets.

What followed was a huge build-up of bad debt within the banking system. At the beginning of 2002, the official estimate of the non-performing loans of Japanese banks stood at 8 per cent of GDP. In the past this would not have been a problem, as it would have been met by the infusion of government funds into the banking system in various ways. But under the new liberalized, market-based discipline banks were not getting additional money to finance new NPAs. Accumulation of such bad debt inevitably leads to a credit crunch, as banks are strapped for cash and turn wary in their lending practices. Overgeared corporations with outstanding loans on their books were no more favored customers, resulting in a collapse of investment and a fall in utilization for lack of long- and short-term capital. Added to that, the insecure Japanese consumer chose to hold back on consumption. The point to note is that with growth having slowed and firms finding it increasingly difficult to show a profit before interest and tax, they were unable to meet past commitments. As a result, the bad loans problem has only increased. The net effect is that financial liberalization has triggered a recession that consecutive rounds of reflationary spending by the state have not been able to counteract adequately. It was not the cronyism that regulated finance generated, but rather the speculation and fragility that financial liberalization resulted in, that explains the collapse of industrial policy and the crisis of industrialization in Japan.

Thus while the financial sector plays an important supply-side role as a facilitator of industrialization, the realization of that role requires intervention by the state to ensure that private financial actors serve the requirements of an industrialization process. On the other hand, the financial proliferation that financial liberalization leads to constrains industrialization in a number of different ways. It diverts financial resources away from the financing of investment. It allows the allocation of investment to be governed by private returns that can diverge from social returns. It increases financial fragility, which often leads to crises. And when that occurs the recovery can be slow and painful.

References

Aoki, Masahiko and Patrick, Hugh (1995), *The Japanese Main Bank System: Its Relevance for Developing and Transforming Economies* (Oxford: Oxford University Press).

Beck, T., Levine, R. and Loayza, N (2000) "Finance and the Sources of Growth," *Journal of Financial Economics*, vol. 58, nos 1–2, pp. 261–300.

Edwards, Franklin R. and Mishkin, Frederic S. (1995) "The Decline of Traditional Banking: Implications for Financial Stability and Regulatory Policy," *FRBNY Economic Policy Review*, July, pp. 27–47.

Gerschenkron, A. (1962) *Economic Backwardness in Historical Perspective* (Cambridge, MA: Harvard University Press).

Gurley, John G. and Shaw, E.S. (1967) "Financial Structure and Economic Development," *Economic Development and Structural Change*, vol. 15 no. 3, pp. 257–268.

Kalecki, Michal (1972) "Problems of Financing Economic Development in a Mixed Economy", in *Selected Essays on the Economic Growth of the Socialist and the Mixed Economy* (Cambridge: Cambridge University Press), pp. 145–161.

King, R.G. and Levine. R (1993) "Finance and Growth: Schumpeter Might be Right," *The Quarterly Journal of Economics*, vol. 108, no. 3, pp. 717–737.

Mahalanobis, P.C. (1955) "The Approach of Operational Research to Planning in India," *Sankhya*, December, pp. 3–62.

Nurkse, Ragnar. (1953) *Problems of Capital Formation in Underdeveloped Countries* (New York: Oxford University Press).

Patnaik, Prabhat (2009) "Finance Capital and Fiscal Deficits," *MRZine*. Available online at http://mrzine.monthlyreview.org/2009/patnaik240509.html.

Robinson, J (1952) "The Generalization of the General Theory," in *The Rate of Interest and Other Essays* (London: Macmillan).

Rosenstein-Rodan, Paul N. (1943) "The Problem of Industrialization of Eastern and South-Eastern Europe," *Economic Journal*, vol. 53, pp. 202–211.

Sametz, A.W. (1992) "Financial Innovation and Regulation in the United States," in *Palgrave Dictionary of Finance* (London: The Macmillan Press), pp. 71–75.

Stiglitz, Joseph E. (1994) "The Role of the State in Financial Markets," *Proceedings of the World Bank Annual Conference on Development Economics 1993* (Supplement to the *World Bank Economic Review* and *World Bank Research Observer*) (Washington, DC: World Bank).

5.3
Toward a Resource-based African Industrialization Strategy

Paul Jourdan
Development Consultant

This paper outlines how Africa's unique natural resource base could provide its peoples with an important lever to achieve industrialization and development objectives if the seminal resources linkages industries and clusters are realized. Alternatively, these assets could be squandered under "free entry" resource regimes, such as the "free mining" (FIFA[1]) mineral regimes, and a continued "free market," non-interventionist scenario, which is likely to leave Africa with little more than ghost towns, such as Kabwe, Stilfontein, Yekepa, and Welkom, or with exhausted soils and depleted fisheries, forests, and other natural endowments.

5.3.1 Is development theory in need of rethinking?

Justin Lin (2010) has argued that that the traditional minority world development theories have run out of steam and need radical rethinking. He argues that "a developing country can change its industrial and economic structure by changing its endowment structure" consisting of both its factor endowments (land/natural resources, labour, and physical & human capital) and its infrastructure endowments: both hard/tangible infrastructure and soft/intangible infrastructure (institutions, regulations, social capital, value systems, and so on). Africa has spectacular land/natural resources endowments that could provide the catalyst for building its capital and infrastructure endowments. Lin proposes that "following comparative advantage determined by the endowment structure to develop industries, is the best way to upgrade endowment structure and to sustain industrial upgrading, income growth and poverty reduction" and that the best models are from other countries that managed industrialize with a similar set of endowments. In Africa's case this would entail the identification of the crucial interventions of countries that succeeded in industrializing off their natural resource endowments.[2] This paper attempts to explore such a framework for African resource-based industrialization.

5.3.1.1 Africa's natural resources

Africa's natural comparative advantages lie in its natural resources endowment as well as in its potential, particularly in certain areas: minerals and energy; agriculture and animal husbandry; forestry and biomass; water; fisheries and aquaculture; and tourism.[3]

The continent's energy resources are exceptional, comprising enormous coal reserves, massive hydro-power potential, hydrocarbons, nuclear minerals and potential solar and geothermal energy.

It has spectacular mineral resources such as the platinum group metals, as well as iron, aluminium, copper, nickel, chromium, vanadium, manganese and cobalt. Its resources of ferrous ores (Fe, Cr, Mn, Ti, V, etc.), combined with its reductants (coal, gas) and energy resources could provide it with the most important industrial feedstock, iron/steel, and its fossil fuel resources (hydrocarbons and coal) could also provide the critical polymer feedstocks essential to modern industrialisation.

Africa is well-watered between the tropics, but above and below them its water resources are constrained. Overall, Africa uses less than 4 percent of its water, but water is generally scarce in terms of access, with the rivers and lakes often in deep valleys or rifts, requiring major access infrastructure.[4]

Due to its high variety of climatic zones, geology/soils, and topography, Africa has almost all the biomes necessary for the production of the bulk of agricultural products, both foodstuffs and industrial feedstocks. A Food and Argiculture Organization (FAO) study has estimated the potential land area for rain-fed crops, excluding built-up areas and forests, for the whole of Africa at ~300 million hectares.[5] Fertilizer consumption (kilograms per hectare of arable land) is less than 10 percent of the global average despite Africa possessing large and diverse sources of fertilizer minerals (NPK).[6]

Natural harvesting of sea fisheries has peaked and although Africa's approximate 28,000 km coastline with two major oceanic systems could give it a relative mariculture advantage, this industry is still in its infancy. Natural harvesting of forests is in decline but there is enormous potential for plantation forestry, particularly between the tropics.

Africa has huge tourism potential based on its enormous cultural, ecological, and geographic diversity. This labor-intensive industry is growing rapidly and could become a major job creator if the natural assets are conserved and effectively managed.

Consequently, Africa's natural resource endowment gives it a potential static *comparative* advantage, albeit a declining advantage in the case of finite mineral deposits based on its diminishing mineral resources. A critical endeavor of an Africa's development strategy must be to transform this unsustainable comparative minerals advantage into a sustainable *competitive* advantage.

Africa's natural resources

Agriculture: Contributes 40 percent of African GDP, provides livelihood for 60 percent of the population, but largest user of scarce water. Enormous unrealized potential (low yields and less than half under cultivation). Agri-commodities exported without processing (beneficiation).

Minerals: World's top producer of numerous mineral commodities. Has world's greatest resources of many more. Africa lacks systematic geosurvey: could be greater resources. But exported as ores, concentrates, metals and most inputs imported: need more up- and downstream beneficiation.

Energy: Significant fossil fuels (oil, gas and coal). Large biomass and biofuels potential (ethanol, bio-diesel). Massive hydroelectric potential (Inga 45 GW, Congo River 200 GW).

Forestry: 22 percent of African land is forested (650 million ha = 17 percent of world total). Deforestation: Africa's net change is the highest globally = − 0.78 percent per annum. Huge silviculture potential, but exported as logs/chips: need greater value addition.

Fishing: 28 000 km coastline (1.28 million km^2 continental shelf) with several oceanic systems. Decline in catch rate (international poaching and overharvesting). ~70 percent of marine protected areas under threat. Aquaculture/mariculture still nascent (large potential).

Tourism: Major potential (world's greatest diversity: culture, flora, fauna, geomorphology). Increasingly important source of livelihood.

5.3.1.1.1   Africa's mineral resources

Africa has the world's largest resources of the platinum group metals as well as aluminum, chromium, gold, manganese (high-grade ore), cobalt, and vanadium and large resources of several other minerals. The continent is also a major producer of these minerals (see table). In terms of minerals, including hydrocarbons, Africa has virtually all the important minerals for diversified industrialization, particularly iron/steel and polymers. However, almost all of its mineral wealth is currently exported as ores, concentrates, alloys, or metals with very little transformation into fabricated products.

Africa has ample resources of the two most important mineral inputs into manufacturing, namely iron/steel and polymers (from oil, gas, and coal). Unfortunately, the resources for both are generally exported as crude ores or minerals, severely curtailing manufacturing potential and job creation.

Critical minerals for agriculture are nitrogen (from natural gas or coal), phosphates, and potassium which Africa has considerable reserves of. In terms of infrastructure, the most important materials are cement (limestone, clay, gypsum, energy), construction steel (iron ore, reductant, energy), and copper. Although Africa has ample resources for their cost-effective production, unfortunately they are undeveloped or production is sold at monopoly prices, significantly raising costs.

Common African markets could make a difference in facilitating greater economies of scale, competition and competitive prices for the essential industrialization of mineral feedstocks.

5.3.1.2 Africa's mineral regimes

African mineral regimes are essentially based on the principle of free mining, or "free entry." Legal mining expert Barry Barton (1993) defines free mining as including:

- "a right of free access to lands in which the minerals are in public ownership;
- a right to take possession of them and acquire title by one's own act of staking a claim; and
- a right to proceed to develop and mine the minerals discovered" (p. 193).

The mining laws broadly fit into the African mineral regimes reformulation process initiated and/or sponsored by the World Bank from the late 1980s until the present and in this regard Professor Bonnie Campbell notes in the *Canadian Journal of Development Studies*:

> . . . certain elements of the free mining doctrine that animated the nineteenth-century formulation of mining regimes in the American and British spheres have also guided the liberalisation process of African mining regimes over the 1980s and 1990s. One of the ways this came about was through the retrenchment of state authority, which in turn contributed to the institutionalisation of asymmetrical relations of power and influence that had important consequences for local political processes, local participation, and community welfare. The approach consequently helps explain some of the social, economic, environmental, or human rights impacts of these regimes, and prompts one to question the extent to which current mining regime reform processes in Africa can transform the asymmetrical power relations that have typified mining activities on the continent in the past. (p. 199)

Free mining refers to the mining regimes that were established in the European conquests. Authors Myriam Laforce, Ugo Lapointe and Véronique Lebuis maintain that free mining *'privileges the values and interests of mining companies in contrast to those of Aboriginal groups'*, and that it was primarily designed to attract European settlers to expropriate the land and minerals and to neutralize the indigenous populations in the Americas, Africa, Oceania and elsewhere. The mineral regimes of Canada and Australia are modern equivalents of free-mining regimes, which are unsurprisingly strongly favored by the mining transnational corporations and the World Bank. African mining laws contain many elements of a free-mining regime, particularly the first-come-first-assessed (FIFA) principle, which dispenses the people's mineral assets gratis, rather than seeking price discovery and the maximisation of the developmental impacts. Fundamentally, according to Ugo Lapointe, "The free-mining system limits the authority and discretionary powers of governments, and as such, governments' abilities to discharge some of their responsibilities."

An African industrialization strategy should rather seek to establish a mineral regime that competitively and transparently concessions all 'known' mineral assets as 25–30-year leases to achieve the optimal resource rents and linkages. Price discovery could include both bidding up fiscal criteria (tax rates, such as resource rent taxes) and developmental criteria (industrial linkages, infrastructure and product pricing).

The wholesale handing out of Africa's mineral assets over the last two decades has probably cost more than a million jobs, including those that could have been catalysed in other sectors, particularly in up- and downstream investments. In general, mineral investors will tend to have a much better idea of the value of the state's mineral assets than the state itself, and competitive auctioning (concessions) would be an effective method of achieving fair value and developmental goals, through testing the market's appetite for establishing industrial linkages. However, where there are little or no geodata, an auction is unlikely to flush out fair value and these terrains should first be thoroughly surveyed by the state (geosurvey departments or subcontractors) before auctioning via a time-limited mining concession (licence) or opened up for private exploration (where the asset is considered to be non-auctionable).

Accordingly, following best practice in the oil and gas sector, African states should demarcate their territory into areas of *unknown mineral assets* (high risk), areas of low risk over *known metallogenic terrains* and areas of *partly known deposits*. The first (high risk) would be open to private exploration (FIFA), the second (known assets) would be auctioned off as blocks with the state tax-take (resource rent share) as the main evaluation criteria (price discovery) in order to flush out the optimal net present value over the life of the concession for the state, as well as developmental criteria such as jobs, infrastructure, linkages and local capital participation ("indigenization"). The third category (partly known occurrences) could be reserved for further geosurvey by the respective geosurvey departments, or explored in partnership with private capital.

With increased investment in resource mapping and geodata acquisition, areas would be reclassified from high risk to low risk. Unfortunately, the most geologically prospective parts of the continent have already been concessioned, usually with no attempt at price discovery or the maximization of their industrial development potential. Over 90 percent of all new African mines in the last boom decade were not "discovered," but were based on *known* assets, particularly old mines or workings and old exploration targets.

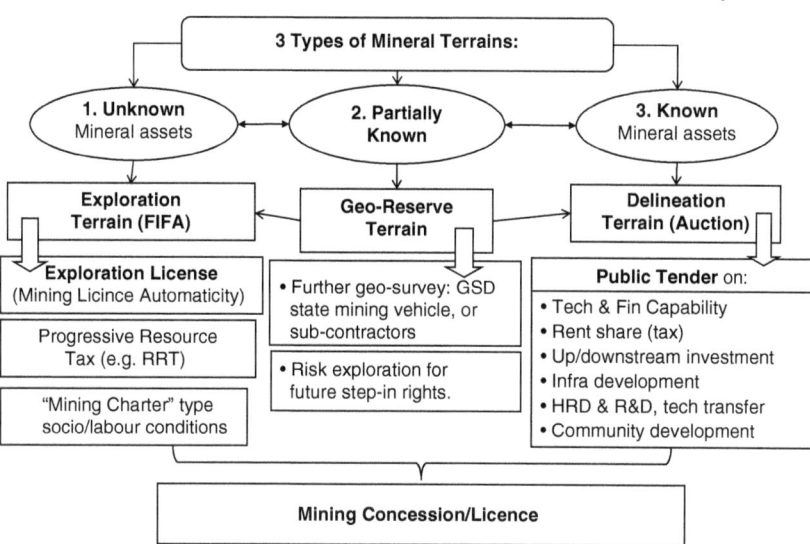

Figure 5.3.1   Possible mineral rights licensing regime

Known and unencumbered mineral terrains could be prepared for public tender by the geo-survey department (the GTK in Finland develops targets for tender[7]) or transferred to a state minerals development vehicle and prepared for competitive concessions. However, oversight of the auctioning process might be best undertaken by an adequately resourced dedicated resources concessions and compliance commission under the respective national treasuries, which could also carry out the ongoing monitoring and evaluation of the concession conditions (including industrial commitments).

However, it remains to be seen whether the juxtaposition of national and international forces will permit the optimization of the developmental impact of Africa's substantial resources endowment. The resource companies and their international allies (particularly the Bretton Woods institutions) appear to have prevailed in subverting the first post-colonial industrialization agenda (particularly through Structural Adjustment Programmes and free mining regimes), but will they prevail again over a new developmental agenda? The counter-agenda has arguably been weakened over the last decade by:

- the exit (relisting) of the main African mining conglomerates (Anglo, Lonrho, Union Minière, Gencor and Goldfields): their control of African economies, particularly in southern Africa, has been dramatically reduced through 'unbundling' and a refocus on their core competence of mining ("dirt-digging");

- the widespread discrediting of the 'free market' non-interventionist ideology by the recent global US toxic debt crisis; and
- the increasing success and importance of China and other Asian economies in the global balance of power and economic strategies (the "Beijing Consensus" versus the "Washington Consensus").

Consequently, the time may be right for establishing a resource-based African industrialization and development trajectory.

5.3.1.3 The current crisis and the underlying commodities boom

Any strategy utilizing a resource endowment clearly requires a degree of comfort that resources demand will be sustained and that prices will not suddenly collapse as happened in the 1980s and 1990s and in the second half of 2008.

From 2002 to 2008, many developing countries displayed strong growth after several decades of stagnation due to the recent commodities boom, which was provoked by robust demand from China and, to a lesser extent, other emerging economies such as India and Vietnam. Many developing countries have significant potential for commodities production, especially minerals, and consequently foreign direct investment (FDI) into the majority world has, according to the UNCTAD World Investment Report (WIR), displayed a marked upturn since 2002/3, mainly into the mineral resources and telecommunications sectors. The commodities boom faltered during the second half of 2008 due to the global recession caused by the US sub-prime debt crisis, but most commodity prices have recovered to 2007/8 the levels and foreign direct investment is reviving.

The resources boom accelerated in 2002/3 with dramatic increases in the prices of minerals, which was followed by agricultural biofuels feedstocks in 2006 and other agricultural commodities in 2007. The lag in the price response of agricultural commodities to Asian demand was most probably caused by the price-depressing effects of minority world agro-subsidies, combined with mineral supply inelasticity.

Nevertheless, the two seminal questions remain: when will the current global US toxic assets and Euro debt recession abate; and how long will the underlying demand last? Or will it peter out like so many earlier commodity booms?

The underlying driver of mineral demand is the metals intensity of global gross domestic product (GDP) growth.

5.3.1.4 Phases of global steel intensity of GDP

The global steel intensity of GDP shows three distinct phases since World War II:

Phase 1 (1950 to ~1970): high intensity – post-World War II minority world (first world) reconstruction and increasing buying power within the minority world, resulting in strong minerals demand and prices and widespread move to greater state control (nationalization) of resources. Negligible majority world (third world) industrialization impact.

Phase 2 (1970 to 2000): low intensity – minority world infrastructure installed, move to services (only Asian Tigers in the high-intensity phase, but too small to impact on global trend). This resulted in over-supply and low prices for most minerals. Stagnation and political instability in resource-exporting states (majority world). Widespread privatization of resources and return to colonial "free mining" regimes, often dictated by Bretton Woods Institutions (SAPs) under minority world "Washington Consensus" ideology. This growth gap reflected a failure of continuous global growth due mainly to minority world hegemony over international trade regimes and widespread use of subsidies.

Phase 3 (2000 to present): High intensity (higher rate than Phase 1) as the majority world takes off (Brazil, Russia, India, China – the BRIC countries) and trade rules are increasingly revised, reflecting a partial loss of minority world hegemony over global trade systems. Period of high demand and prices and a return of "resources nationalism,"but temporarily stalled due to the extraneous US toxic debt crisis, but by the second half of 2009 demand was already showing signs of recovery through stimulus packages and by 2011 most commodity prices had regained their pre-crisis levels.

Global metal intensity would have been on a continuous increasing trend if global growth had been diffused to more of the world's people in the 1980s. Instead, diffusion was only to the "Asian Tigers" with a population of less than 80 million, resulting in a minor impact on global minerals demand. The diffusion of global growth (and intensity) finally only occurred twenty years later (in the so-called BRIC countries), but it was temporarily stalled due to the US toxic debt crisis plunging the world into recession. However, demand appears to be recovering despite the Eurozone debt crisis.

As is apparent from Phase 1 of intensity, sustained by minority world growth for any one country, the intensity tends to fall off once the basic national infrastructure is in place and most domestic markets have been developed and penetrated. Growth from then on is mainly in services accompanied by a falling proportion of employment in manufacturing, as evidenced by almost all mature minority world economies.

The country steel intensity per capita data appears to indicate that, at around $16k–$20k/capita, the metals intensity of GDP growth falls off, no matter when the initial metals consuming 'lift-off' phase occurred. Given that China is only at about one-third up this high-intensity phase, that India is at about a third that of China and given that they have a combined population approaching three times that of the minority world, it would then be reasonable to assume that the current global high metals intensity phase could continue at least as long as Phase 1 or roughly 30 years (1950 to 1980). This assumption excludes growing intensity from other emerging economies, such as Brazil, Vietnam and Indonesia, which if included could make this a 30–50-year high-intensity phase.

In concluding this section, it appears safe to assume that, despite the recent commodities slump, the underlying boom will be an unprecedented long "super-cycle," provided that China and India keep up their robust economic growth. This then leaves us with the fundamental question of how can the current commodities-stimulated high prices be transformed into sustainable growth, industrialization and development in Africa?

5.3.1.5 A resource-based strategy and the resource curse

The resource curse is a much debated and studied phenomenon, but it is clear that a resource endowment is not always a curse and, if well-managed, can be a blessing as evidenced by strong sustained growth in several resource economies such as Sweden, the US, Norway, Malaysia, Finland, Australia, Canada, New Zealand and Botswana. Researchers Paul Collier and Benedikt Goderis's extensive and illuminating analysis of a large sample of countries refines the impact of the resource curse with the following findings:

Empirical evidence suggests that commodity booms have positive short-term impacts on growth, but negative long-term impacts on minority world countries. These adverse long-term impacts are only experienced by exporters of 'high rent' mineral (non-agricultural) commodities. The key determinant as to whether a mineral boom will be a blessing or a curse appears to be the level of governance, particularly the existence of sufficiently good institutions. The main channels of the curse are:

- high public and private consumption;
- low/inefficient investment;
- overvalued (strong) currency (known as "Dutch disease").

What is significant is that all of these channels can be neutralized or ameliorated through appropriate policies and strategies and the resource curse can be turned into a blessing through targeted deployment of the resource rents and opportunities. In this regard, Omano Edigheji also notes that "what sets developmental states apart from mineral-rich countries is primarily the nature of institutions and consequently state capacity" (p. 12).

5.3.1.6 Toward a sustainable resource-based African industrialization and development strategy

Africa's rich and diverse resource base, combined with the strong global resources demand, could underpin a viable resource-based industrialization

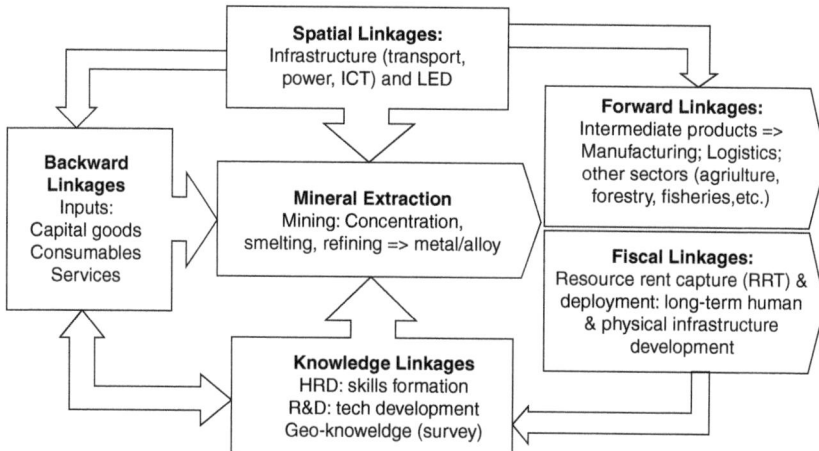

Figure 5.3.2 Maximizing the mineral resources economic linkages

strategy that goes beyond supplying raw materials to the world economy. This could be achieved by utilizing its extensive resource developmental opportunities to establish the requisite economic infrastructure across the region and to create the crucial resource sector linkages into the local, regional and sub-continental economies.

This "deepening" of the resources sector though up-, down- and side-stream (infrastructure) industrial linkages could form core industrialization nuclei for African Regional Economic Communities' economies and will, over time, diversify with increasing human resource development, technology development and skills formation, through the lateral migration of these resource-dependent industrial clusters into resource-independent industrial activities.

In addition to the capture and judicious deployment of resource rents, Africa has a comparative advantage in establishing resource linkage industrial clusters through the following:

1. The immediate market offered by the local and regional resource industries' demand for inputs such as plant, equipment, machinery, consumables, and services. This market can be relatively large for specialized resource industries' demand, ameliorating economies of scale constraints (for example, the region constitutes three-quarters of the global platinum group metals mining and processing inputs market);
2. A potential technological advantage through close proximity to the resource industries' demand for innovation, adaptation, and problem solving (these activities often currently take place offshore in the minority world);

3. A feedstock price advantage for downstream resource-processing industries, particularly mineral processing (smelting, refining, alloying, and fabrication) and agri-processing (food products, leatherwear, meat processing, natural fibres, forestry products, sugar products, and biofuels); and
4. Opportunities to develop the supplier industries for the extensive resource infrastructure requirements.

5.3.1.7   Resource linkages industrial clusters

The development of these resource sector linkages slowly builds integrated resource linkages industrial clusters where the different components reinforce one another and, from initially serving local demand, develop competencies to export goods and services to resource sectors in the region and, ultimately, globally.

The resource linkages industrial clusters are indirectly anchored on the comparative advantage of the resources sectors and are comprised of:

1. Upstream linkage industries: plant, machinery, consumables (inputs), engineering services, financial services, consultancies;
2. Downstream linkage industries: resources processing (value addition) into intermediate products, semi-manufactures, components, sub-assemblies and finished, resource-intensive products. Resource processing usually also produces co-products and by-products, which also constitute potential feedstocks for further downstream linkage industries. These resource beneficiation industries in turn create markets for further upstream industries (capital goods, consumables and services);
3. Sidestream linkages: Power generation and supply, construction, process automation, logistics, marketing, transport infrastructure (rail, road and ports), environmental industries, human resource development and skilling entities and other resource sectors that supply inputs into the resource sector (for example, mineral inputs such as fertilizer and conditioners into agriculture, and chemicals into mining). These, in turn, create new demand for upstream industries.

These linkages were illustrated for the Finnish forestry cluster in the work of Ramos (1998), but similar sector clusters can be developed for Africa's natural comparative advantages.

According to economist Joseph Ramos, the evolution of the resource linkage industrial clusters generally goes through the following four phases.

5.3.1.8   Phasing of resource-based industrial clusters

Phase I: Resource extraction with minimum essential local processing (for example, ore concentration, raw cacao beans, roundwood, and cotton lint). Almost all the inputs (capital goods, consumables, and engineering services) are imported (except for production engineering services) in this phase;

Phase II: Resource processing and export (for example, wood pulp, agri-processing, mineral smelting, and refining) as well as initial import substitution of the lower-technology imported inputs (usually under licence for the local market) and increasing production engineering services;

Phase III: Initial export of some goods and services established under import substitution in Phase II. The engineering services are increasingly based on local intellectual property and the resources are processed into higher value-added products (for example, fine and special papers, metal alloys, semi-manufactures, packaged agricultural products, and textiles);

Phase IV: Exports of a wide range of resource goods and services of increasing complexity and technology, including design engineering services, resource plant and machinery (predominantly based on local intellectual property). Exports of resource-based products of greater variety and complexity and the migration of knowledge-intensive resource services industries, into new, resource-independent sectors.

These phases of resource industrial cluster development are in reality more diverse and complex with some activities moving faster and others slower, but overall there is an increase in product complexity and sophistication (both up- and downstream) that needs to be paralleled with the increasing production of high-level skills (engineers and scientists) and investments into research and development (R&D).

Ultimately, a natural *comparative* advantage (Phase I) has been transformed into a *competitive* advantage (Phase IV) with continuous incremental improvements in productivity and design, and the basis has been laid for the migration of high-tech industries into new, resource-independent (either as a feedstock or market) sectors, and generic diversified industrialization.

Work by Maloney (2007) and the ANC (2012) indicates that the failure of resource-based industrialization is generally due to a lack technological adoption (backward linkages) because of a "deficient national learning or innovative capacity, arising from low investment in human capital and scientific infrastructure." The ANC SIMS study concluded that there appeared to be no resource-based industrialization success story that had not succeeded in dramatically raising their technical HRD (engineers & scientists) capacity and their technology development capacity (R&D), both of which are a prerequisite for fully exploiting the resources backward and forward industrial linkages.

There have been several similar linkages studies done for the minerals sector in both South America and southern Africa. A recent study of the South African platinum group metals sector noted that the engineering, procurement, construction management (EPCM) firms are critical to optimizing the initial linkages, which also impact on the potential ongoing linkages in terms of the technologies and processes selected. In addition, the Mozal (BHPB) linkages program has indicated that the configuration of local subcontracts is important to the success of developing local suppliers. The failure to develop downstream linkages at the Hillside aluminum smelter (Gencor, later BHPB) in Richards Bay is predominantly due to monopoly pricing of the product at an import parity price. The stipulation of competitive pricing of all resource products is seminal to any successful forward linkages (downstream) strategy.

Nevertheless, the development of regional resources inputs industrial clusters is also critically constrained by the small national markets of individual states. Even the South African Customs Union market (Africa's largest market) generally lacks the requisite demand for world-scale viable plants. The establishment of regional common markets would greatly increase the possibility of a successful resource-based development strategy. Other resource-based industrialization success stories either had larger markets (US) or had access to larger markets (the Nordics: USSR, and the EU).

A schematic phasing of a resource-based development strategy is presented in Figure 5.3.3, which displays the decreasing importance of resource exploitation as the resource linkages are developed.

An African resource-based industrialization strategy would typically go through similar phases of industrialization, with decreasing importance of its resources *comparative* advantage and an increasing relative importance of a skills-based *competitive* advantage.

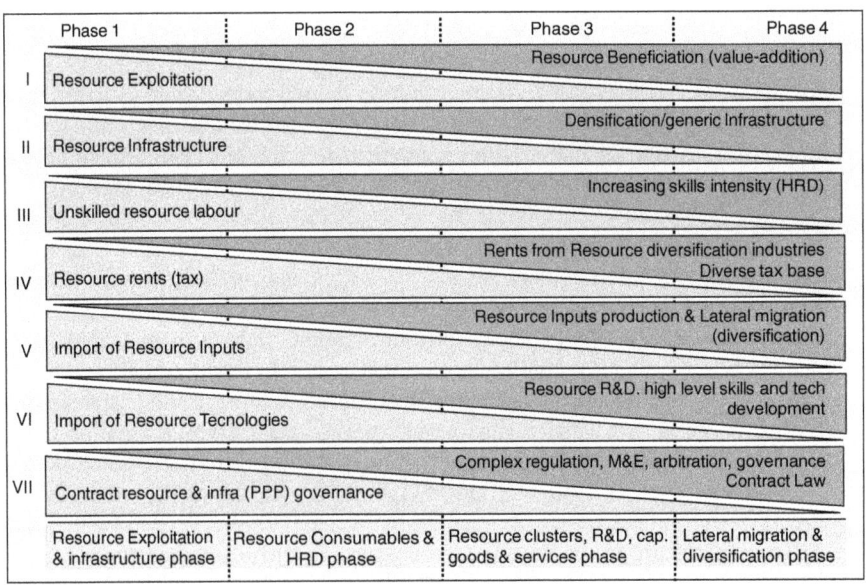

Figure 5.3.3   Schematic resource-based industrialisation phasing
Source: Jourdan (2008).

Almost all African economies can be positioned on this continuum, though most would still be in Phases I or II, while South Africa would probably be positioned somewhere between Phase II and III (though slipping back) and Zimbabwe has possibly slipped from Phase II–III to I–II.

In summary, the key elements of a resource-based industrialization and development strategy are:

1. The realization of a resource comparative advantage by overcoming infrastructure constraints through the establishment of infrastructure networks. This has largely been achieved in southern Africa (though in need of rehab), but not in most other regions of Africa.
2. The 'densification' of the resource-based infrastructure through the establishment of ancillary and feeder infrastructure to enlarge the resources corridor catchments and beneficiary sectors (agriculture, forestry and tourism).
3. The deepening of the mineral sector linkages to the regional economy through beneficiation of these resources and creating supplier and service industries around the minerals sector and developing them into complex resource linkages industrial clusters (up-, side- and downstream industries). However, this is critically dependent on:
4. Dramatically increasing the national quality of human capital and technology development through concerted long-term investment in technical HRD (engineers, scientists, technicians) and R&D (innovation);
5. The capture of resource rents through resource rent taxes and the reinvestment of resource rents into human resource development, skills and R&D for technology development to capitalize on the resource linkages opportunities, as well as into long-term infrastructure, for the development of mature resource industrial clusters, and, ultimately, a competitive advantage, independent of resource endowments.

A comprehensive resource-based strategy should develop the labor-intensive resources upstream sectors as well as going further downstream, beyond capital-intensive intermediate goods, into labor-intensive fabrication, which is often stunted by the widespread practice of monopoly pricing of intermediate industrial feedstocks.

5.3.2 A resource-based African industrialization strategy: optimizing the resource linkages

The key element to a strategy that uses natural resources to catalyse growth and development appears to be, from looking at successful resource-based industrialization, the maximization of the concomitant opportunities offered by a natural resources endowment, particularly the "deepening" of the resources sector through optimizing economic linkages into the local economy.

5.3.2.1   Fiscal linkages: resource rents

Resource rents (returns in excess of the expected/average return on capital) should be used to improve the basic physical and knowledge infrastructure of the nation. Generally, the resource rents are not shared with the resource owner (the state/people) and all African states should consider the implementation of a resource rent tax, possibly to be kept offshore to ameliorate currency appreciation and fiscal shocks, and which could be drip-fed back into long-term (ten to twenty year) regional knowledge and physical infrastructure.

5.3.2.2   Spatial linkages (infrastructure)

The FAO notes that "Only 21 percent of [Africa's] population live within 100 km of the coast or of a navigable river, against 89 percent in high-income countries. The proportion of the population that is landlocked is seven times higher than in rich countries. Landlocked countries in Africa have average freight costs almost three times higher than in high-income countries."[8] Furthermore, over two centuries ago, Adam Smith observed that "There are in Africa none of those great inlets, such as the Baltic and Adriatic seas in Europe, the Mediterranean and Euxine seas in both Europe and Asia, and the gulphs of Arabia, Persia, India, Bengal, and Siam in Asia, to carry maritime commerce into the interior parts of that great continent: and the great rivers of Africa are at too great a distance from one another to give occasion to any considerable inland navigation."[9]

The high-rent resource infrastructure (mainly minerals) should be used to open up other lower-rent, resource potential (such as agriculture, forestry, and tourism), as per the spatial development initiative methodology in order to access zones of economic potential with lower returns that cannot afford their own requisite infrastructure. All resource concessions must include third-party access at non-discriminatory user-tariffs to all the resources infrastructure (transport, power, water, and telecommunications), in order to catalyse the higher development impact resource infrastructure "hitch-hikers" (such as agriculture), which in general have a much higher socio-economic propulsive impact. This condition needs to be configured into all resource contracts (concessions) for all resource infrastructure.

Although most of resource-driven infrastructure is in place above and below the Tropics, there are still opportunities to link in depressed rural areas: for example, through the coal and platinum group metals resources in South Africa's Limpopo Province and Botswana. However, between the Tropics there are huge opportunities for resource-based infrastructure to catalyse wider growth and development in other sectors through resource infrastructure (for example, spatial development initiatives or development corridors[10]).

Resource infrastructure generally relies on state assets (servitudes) or rights (licences) and consequently constitutes a potential lever for encouraging the resource and the infrastructure concessionaires to optimize the local mineral and infrastructure linkages.

5.3.2.3 Downstream value addition (forward linkages)

The locational advantage of producing crude resources should be used to establish resource-processing industries that could then provide the feed-stocks for manufacturing and industrialization. In this regard, the resource contracts or licences need to provide incentives or disincentives for mineral resources downstream beneficiation. However, the widespread practice of monopoly pricing of beneficiated minerals/metals often negates this advantage for the region's manufacturing industry. In addition, the first steps of beneficiation are often energy intensive (smelting), which is currently constrained by Africa's power shortages.

Consideration should be given to much greater intra-regional power trade (through, for example, regional power pools), which could be based on potential low-cost and sustainable hydro-power from the Congo, Zambezi, Niger, Nile and other rivers between the tropics. However, in many cases, African mining companies have encouraged beneficiation offshore. An example would be Anglo American's divestment from its main platinum group metals downstream beneficiator and technology developer, Johnson Matthey Plc in the 1990s (when it was the major shareholder, at more than 40 percent), after investing heavily in it, especially in technology development, over the previous 40 years. This was probably due to its increasing focus on "core competence" (mining) in preparation for its exit and London listing. This appears to indicate that the South African decision to allow Anglo to relist abroad was possibly ill-advised and that the "unfettered" movement abroad of domestic capital should be curtailed. In this regard, Omano Edighedi correctly argues that "by virtue of the listing of key South African conglomerates overseas, South Africa's government has lost influence over the conglomerates and stripped itself of resources that it could have used for its developmental purposes" (p. 22). Similarly, the exit of other African resources companies has had the same consequences (Union Minière and Ashanti Gold, for example).

5.3.2.4 Upstream value addition (backward linkages)

The resources sector market should be used to develop the resource supply/inputs sector (for example, capital goods, consumables and services). This often offers a relatively large market for specific inputs for particular resource exploitation. South Africa, Zimbabwe and the Copperbelt (Zambia and the Democratic Republic of the Congo) used to boast a substantial mineral inputs sector, but these have all but disappeared in the latter two and are diminishing in the former. For example, Zambia Engineering

Services is long gone and EGM Forrest in Lubumbashi relocated to Europe decades ago.

Africa's mineral capital goods are generally imported and of the few capital goods companies that it had, several have been sold to foreign companies over the last decade, in part due to the refocusing of the old southern African mining houses, which used to invest in a plethora of up- and downstream industries. This was in turn due to their relocation after 1994 to offshore stock exchanges (for example, Anglo American, Gencor, Gold Fields and parts of the former JCI). Seeraj Mohamed points out that "these companies were restructured by shareholder pressure, and while there may have been benefits for shareholders, the South African economy lost influence over large, powerful corporations that could have been part of a developmental project to deepen and diversify the country's industrial base" (p. 161).

Local content milestones need to be built into the resource contracts or licences and a first step could be to base local purchasing milestones (for example, black economic empowerment purchases in the South African mining charter) on local value-added rather than value (this would also curtail destructive local supplier 'fronting' for foreign suppliers).

In a Organization for Economic Cooperation and Development (OECD) Development Centre policy brief, Gøril Havro and Javier Santiso point out that both Norway and Chile experienced:

> ... direct efforts to diversify their economy and to support industries associated with the natural-resource sector – such as engineering and supply – as well as non-resource sectors. Norwegian policies in the 1970s were markedly interventionist in this regard... The legal framework emphasised local content until 1990, to develop the infant petroleum supply industry. Norway also pushed for state participation in the same areas, in spite of reluctance on the part of many of the international companies.

Havro and Santiso further contend that:

> ...local-content requirements could potentially have beneficial effects as well, as seen in Norway, since they would contribute to developing domestic economic activity rather than relying on rents, while at the same time increasing human capital through learning-by-doing and technological spillovers. However, there is a need for good co-operation with the foreign companies to ensure that such requirements are not commercially unviable, and at the same time to ensure that they have a real learning impact and are not just seen as another tax payment by companies. Standardised local-content agreements worked out with experts in the field could be useful in achieving this.

The platinum group metals seams of the Bushveld Complex in South Africa and the Great Dyke in Zimbabwe reportedly constitute the world's largest trackless mining opportunity. However, the requisite capital goods will predominantly be supplied by imports, due to the failure to invest in the development of trackless mining equipment, especially after the demise of the Chamber of Mines Research Organisation (COMRO) in South Africa and the Institute of Mining Research (IMR) in Zimbabwe.

5.3.2.5 Technology/product development (knowledge linkages)

Resources exploitation technologies generally need to adapt to local conditions (for example, climate, mineralogy, and terrain) in order to provide opportunities for the development of niche technological competencies in the resources inputs sector. This sector tends to be knowledge-intensive and accordingly needs "priming" through investment in human resource development and R&D. However, several studies have shown that it has the capacity to later "reinvent" itself outside the resources sector to produce new products for other non-resource markets.

African resource exploitation contracts or licences need to facilitate the establishment of a domestic resources R&D capacity, and the requisite human resource development. This type of capacity needs to be rebuilt and resourced across the continent, together with the mining and capital goods sectors to ensure that mineral technology opportunities do not leak away to states such as Sweden and Finland, which offer greater R&D incentives and support.

5.3.3   Developing the linkages industries and clusters

African states should focus on developing their resource linkages firms by applying best practice from more industrialized states had a similar set of endowments. In this regard Justin Lin (2010) proposes six useful steps for "growth identification and facilitation" of firms and clusters that provide several insightful measures for growing these sectors:

Step 1: Find fast growing countries with a similar endowment structure and with about 100% higher per capita income. Identify dynamically growing tradable industries that have grown well in those countries for the last 20 years.

Step 2: See if some private domestic firms are already in those industries (of which may be existing or nascent). Identify constraints to quality upgrading or further firm entry. Take action to remove constraints.

Step 3: In industries where no domestic firms are currently present, seek FDI from countries examined in step 1, or organize new firm incubation programs.

Step 4: In addition to the industries identified in step 1, the government should also pay attention to spontaneous self discovery by private enterprises and give support to scale up the successful private innovations in new industries

(*continued*)

Continued

Step 5: In countries with poor infrastructure and bad business environment, special economic zones or industrial parks may be used to overcome these barriers to firm entry and FDI and encourage industrial clusters.

Step 6: The government may compensate pioneer firms in the listed identified above with: Tax incentives for a limited period, Direct credits for investments, Access to foreign exchanges

---

5.3.4   Conclusions

The Asian boom and concomitant strong demand for Africa's natural resources could provide a window of opportunity for a regional resource-based industrialization strategy. Such a strategy must optimize the developmental impact of resources by ensuring that the resource economic linkages are made (backward and forward). Investment into technical human resource development and R&D is seminal to the optimization of the economic linkages.

The African resource regimes (particularly mineral regimes) need to be overhauled to allow for the competitive concessioning of the region's resource endowments (land, minerals, water, fisheries, and state rights), to maximize price discovery and industrial objectives. Similarly, the developmental impacts of existing ("first-come-first-served") concessions need to be maximized through appropriate legislation and/or contract renegotiation. In this regard, investment in systematic geosurvey is fundamental to the identification of mineral assets.

The development of technical human resources and a technology development capacity is seminal to the realization and growth of the resources backward and forward linkages industries and clusters. Africa should be capturing its resource rents in order to invest them in human and physical infrastructure to underpin the development of its resources related industries.

A resource rent tax of 30–50 percent on all excess profits above a reasonable (expected) return should be imposed on all resource exploitation concessions or licenses and should form the basis of offshore development funds to finance long-term regional physical and human infrastructure. Consideration could be given to placing part of these funds in Regional Development Funds, as virtually none of the African Union member states currently apply a resource rent tax, there would be almost no fiscal loss, especially if the resource rent tax was applied after normal corporate tax and royalty deductions. Such a regional development fund could be a major instrument in facilitating equitable regional economic integration and ameliorating industrial polarization. It would obviously imply a transfer of wealth/rent from resource-rich zones to resource-poor zones, but this wealth/rent is currently untaxed and is generally transferred or remitted to the minority world nations.

Economies of scale and competition would be greatly enhanced by common regional (and, ultimately, continental) markets (customs unions). The success of an African resource-based development strategy would be dramatically compromised without it. A customs union revenue-sharing formula could also contribute to the putative regional development funds and thereby facilitate greater equity in the benefits of integration by prioritizing investment into depressed areas and new industrial nodes. Consideration could be given to merging the national Development Finance Institutions (DFIs) into single regional DFIs (for example, the Industrial Development Corporation and the Development Bank of Southern Africa in southern Africa) in order to develop and facilitate viable investment projects across the regions.

A first step in regional economic integration could be multi-state cooperation in the establishment of regional development corridors to realize latent economic potential through seamless infrastructure provision, which would provide tangible benefits to all the participating parties.

However, only the future will tell whether the balance of local and international forces will permit the realization of an African resource-based industrialization and development strategy, which has the potential to unleash sustainable growth and development and job creation across the continent.

Notes

1. "First-In-First-Assessed."
2. "Find fast growing countries with a similar endowment structure and with about 100% higher per capita income. Identify dynamically growing tradable industries that have grown well in those countries for the last 20 years" (Lin, 2010, ppt).
3. Natural resources based tourism (fauna, flora, cultures, geomorphology, and so on).
4. "… for Africa the percentage of arable land that is irrigated is 7 percent (barely 3.7 percent in Sub-Saharan Africa), the corresponding percentages for South America, East and south-east Asia and South Asia being 10 percent, 29 percent and 41 percent respectively." Available online at http://www.fao.org/docrep/005/y6831e/y6831e-03.htm.
5. http://www.grida.no/graphicslib/detail/current-and-potential-arable-land-use-in-africa_a9fd.
6. http://data.worldbank.org/indicator/AG.CON.FERT.ZS/countries/ZG-1W?display=graph.
7. Mining Journal Supplement, February 2009, "Finland."
8. FAO, "World Agriculture: Towards 2015/2030," p. 27; ftp://ftp.fao.org/docrep/fao/004/y3557e/y3557e.pdf.

9. Adam Smith (1976 [1776]) *An Inquiry into the Nature and Causes of the Wealth of Nations* (Chicago: University of Chicago Press; Cannan's edition of the *Wealth of Nations* was originally published in 1904 by Methuen & Co. Ltd. First Edition in 1776), P. 21.
10. See Jourdan (2008).

References

ANC (2012) "State Intervention in the Minerals Sector (SIMS)," ANC, Luthuli House, Joburg, February. Available online at http://www.anc.org.za/list.php?t=Reports&y=2012.

Barton, B.J. (1993) *Canadian Law of Mining* (Calgary: Canadian Institute of Resources Law).

BHPB (2006) "Where To From Here?" Paper presented to the Merrill Lynch Global Metals, Mining and Steel Conference, Miami, May, available at bhpbilliton.com/bbContentRepository/Presentations/060327CWGML2006ConfMiami.pdf.

Campbell, B. (2010) "Revisiting the Reform Process of African Mining Regimes," *Canadian Journal of Development Studies*, vol. 30, nos 1–2, pp. 197–217.

Collier, P. and Goderis, B. (2007) "Commodity Prices, Growth, and the Natural Resource Curse: Reconciling a Conundrum," CSAE WPS/2007-15, University of Oxford.

Edigheji, O. (ed.) (2010) *Constructing a Democratic Developmental State in South Africa* (Cape Town: HSRC Press).

Havro, G. and Santiso, J. (2008) 'To Benefit from Plenty: Lessons from Chile and Norway'. Policy Brief no. 37 (Paris: OECD Development Centre).

IMF (2009) "Primary Commodity Prices." Available online at imf.org/external/np/res/commod/index.asp.

Index Mundi (2010) "Commodity Prices." Available online at indexmundi.com/commodities.

Jourdan, P. (2008) "Plan of Action for African Acceleration of Industrialisation-Promoting Resource-Based Industrialisation: A Way Forward." Paper prepared for the African Union Commission, Addis Ababa, August.

Jourdan, P. (2010) "Mining for Development: Towards a Resource-based African Development Strategy?" Presentation, RMG, Stockholm, February.

Jourdan, P. (2010) "Africa's Mineral Resources: What Must be Done to Make Them Drivers of Development," in Moeletsi Mbeki (ed.), *Advocates for Change: How to Overcome Africa's Challenges* (Johannesburg: Pan Macmillan SA).

Laforce, M., Lapointe, U., and Lebuis, V. (2009) "Mining Sector Regulation in Quebec and Canada: Is a Redefinition of Asymmetrical Relations Possible?," *Studies in Political Economy*, vol. 84, pp. 47–78.

Lapointe, U. (2009) "Origins of Mining Regimes in Canada and the Legacy of the Free Mining System'. Conference on 'Rethinking Extractive Industry: Regulation, Dispossession, and Emerging Claims," Centre for Research on Latin America and the Caribbean (CERLAC) and the Extractive Industries Research Group (EIRG), York University, Toronto.

Lederman, D. and Maloney, W. (2008) "In Search of the Missing Resource Curse-Comments," *Economia*, vol. 9, no. 1, pp. 1–56.

Lin, J.Y. (2010) "New Structural Economics. A Framework for Rethinking Development," WPS 5197 (Washington, DC: World Bank).

Lydall, M. (2009) "Backward Linkage Development in the South African PGM Industry: A Case Study," *Resources Policy*, vol. 34, no. 3, pp. 112–120.

Maloney, William F. (2007 "Missed Opportunities: Innovation and Resource-Based Growth in Latin America." In *Natural Resources: Neither Curse nor Destiny,* chapter 6.

Mohamed, S. (2010) "The Effect of a Mainstream Approach to Economic and Corporate Governance on Development in South Africa," in O. Edigheji (ed.), *Constructing a Democratic Developmental State in South Africa* (HSRC Press, Cape Town).

Palma, G. (2005) "Four Sources of 'De-industrialisation2 and a New Concept of the 'Dutch Disease'," in J.A. Ocampo (ed.), *Beyond Reforms: Structural Dynamics and Macroeconomic Vulnerability* (Palo Alto, CA and Washington, DC: Stanford University Press and World Bank).

Ramos, J. (1998) "A Development Strategy Founded on Natural Resource-based Production Clusters," *CEPAL Review*, No. 68, 12/1998 (Santiago: ECLAC).

UNCTAD (2011) "WIR: World Investment Report." Available online at unctad.org/en/docs/wir2011_en.pdf.

USGS (2012) "Mineral Commodity Summaries." Available online at minerals.usgs.gov/minerals/pubs/mcs/.

Van der Ploeg, Frederick (2007) "Challenges and Opportunities for Resource Rich Economies," RSCAS Working Papers, European University Institute.

5.4
The Global "Rush" for Land: Does it Provide Opportunities for African Countries?

Klaus Deininger
World Bank

5.4.1 The "land rush": nature and challenges

Growing food demand from an expanding and more affluent population and greater use of land for non–food purposes such as biofuels translated into to higher commodity prices and competition for land and other natural resources. Together with the pricing of environmental amenities, this led to a surge in investments in farmland, often d national borders. In addition to traditional agribusiness investors, demand from actors such as sovereign wealth, pension and private equity funds who traditionally had little interest in agriculture has also increased markedly, mainly in response to land being considered a very desirable asset class in the current volatile environment.

Historical precedents of large–scale land acquisitions following shifts in power, technology, or transport costs raise concerns in three areas. Failure to respect local rights to key natural resources such as land and water often led to conflict and social tension that jeopardized investments' contribution to the sustained improvement of welfare. Lack of a regulatory framework, including clear property rights, ways to bring assets to their best use, and complementary public goods, has often encouraged acquisition of land for short–term extraction of resources rather than sustainable investment to provide local benefits. Finally, without mechanisms to charge investors the full opportunity cost of land or agile mechanisms to transfer land to the highest bidder or the most productive use, land has been held for speculative purposes or owners have resorted to lobbying for subsidies to ensure the viability of their enterprises with undesirable consequences for overall economic growth.

Given the broad social and cultural significance of land, it is unsurprising that processes of large–scale land acquisition have been controversial. Supporters, including governments in target countries, note that, with Africa's long history of agricultural underinvestment, private investment in land, on–farm capital, infrastructure, and applied research offer great opportunities for economic development and poverty reduction especially for countries or region that depend on the primary sector. Denouncing the phenomenon as a modern "land grab" (Pearce, 2012), others point to the enormous risks and the growing body of case studies suggesting that many investments displace local populations, lack economic viability, and fail to comply with basic social and environmental safeguards (Borras and Franco, 2012).

Key concerns revolve around social, environmental, and economic issues. Socially and environmentally, in many target countries, especially in Africa, much of the land of interest to investors is held under customary tenure and may provide environmental public goods. Formal legal frameworks that fail to recognize customary rights, a weak regulatory framework, and gaps in states' enforcement capacity all increase the likelihood of land being acquired or used in ways that undermine existing rights, fail to generate local benefits, and cause environmental damage. This assumes added significance in the light of globally limited supplies of land and water – and with climate change expected to further reduce availability of suitable land and bring about more extreme weather events–. From an economic perspective, large–scale land acquisition has reopened the debate about the most appropriate structure of agricultural production, especially the role of owner–operated vs corporate farms. Disillusion with smallholder–based efforts to improve productivity in Sub–Saharan Africa (Collier and Dercon, 2009) and the apparent export competitiveness of Latin American and Eastern European "mega–farms" led some to the future of global agriculture to lie in large–scale farming with investors as "pioneers" of agricultural globalization – equivalent to the wave of industrial outsourcing that swept the world in the 1980s – who may merit public subsidies rather than opprobrium (Collier and Venables, 2011).

This paper aims to lay out key issues and possible policy responses. Past examples of large–scale expansion of cultivated agricultural area highlight the potential long–term effects of such transfers and the key role of country-level policies in shaping their impacts. The quantification of local potential helps to highlight the trade–off between intensification of production on land that is already cultivated and area expansion, including the fact that potentially high benefits from the latter are associated with high risks. While data on the extent of actual land deals are weak, information on demand expressed at the peak of the "farmland boom" allows us to identify key drivers of such processes, noting in particular that gaps in land governance were associated with a much higher likelihood of a country being the target of investor interest. This allows us to identify measures to increase rural populations' ability to benefit from higher commodity prices and land values while at the same time reducing the risks posed by increased global land demand.

5.4.2   The multifaceted nature of the "land rush"

In the past large–scale land acquisition processes were associated with shifts in power, improvements in technology, or reduced transport costs. Examples show that such investments are risky and that policies often adversely affected size and distribution of the associated benefits. If governance is weak, this could create a danger of such wealth contributing to distortions or a resource curse where rents are squandered rather than used for social and economic development. Recent regional perspectives illustrate the multifaceted nature of this phenomenon as well as the range of options open to investors at a global scale.

5.4.2.1   Historical precedents

During colonial expansion, demand for land was driven less by the desire to produce agricultural commodities than by the need to obtain labor and food for mines. Unequal patterns of land acquisition then often gave rise to distortions that affected social and economic development in the long term (Binswanger et al., 1995). Even in subsequent phases when economic motives, such as elites' desire to "modernize" the economy by bringing "unused" land under production, dominated, outcomes were often unsatisfactory from a social and human rights perspective and failed to contribute to long–term development.

One of the reasons for the failure of such investment was that in many cases large land acquisitions became legally possible only by extinguishing existing communal rights (without compensation) based on the notion that land obviously not used for economic purposes is owned by the state and thus be available for disposal. This was often implemented by requiring land registration within a short time span and subsequent transfer of non–registered land to investors, thereby depriving local populations of a key safety net, this often led to unrest while at the same time reducing the security of property rights and the scope for investment.

Establishing large–scale agriculture from scratch is technically complex and, due to the often long gestation periods involved, risky. Even well–resourced ventures had high failure rates. Historical examples include the "bonanza farms" established in the Dakotas in 1860–1900 (Drache, 1964), Brazilian rubber plantations established by Henry Ford in the 1920s (Grandin, 2009), and alter efforts to establish large–scale agriculture in the Lakeland Downs of Australia's far Northeast (Rogers, 2008). More recently, even not–for–profit ventures that could subsidize loss–making start–ups for a long time managed success rates below one–third (Tyler, 2011). This is unproblematic – and can in fact generate valuable knowledge – if proper safeguards prevent damage to local resources, markets can quickly transfer the assets involved to better uses, and key information can be shared transparently. If not, irreversible resource degradation may inflict losses on local people while resources remain underused and their owners resort to political lobbying so as to be able to continue deriving resource rents from them.

In some cases large farms' lack of economic viability prompted their owners to resort to lobbying and use of monopoly power to keep unskilled labor plentiful and cheap and establish policies, including capital subsidies or tax relief in their favor. Where this was successful, human capital and democratic institutions developed much slower than in countries with a smallholder structure (Nugent and Robinson, 2010). Micro–studies suggest that, land owners' ability to lobby for noncompetitive measures had far–reaching effects (Rajan and Ramcharan, 2011),[1] in line with evidence on long–term effects of unequal asset distribution elsewhere (Banerjee and Iyer, 2005; de Janvry, 1981; Iyer, 2010).

5.4.2.2 Recent regional perspectives

In Latin America, different processes of land expansion and private investment can be distinguished. The best known is forest clearing for extensive livestock ranching in the Amazon motivated in part to establish land rights. Until recently, expansion at the expense of forests was rapid; the cattle population more than doubled from 1990 to 2006 and pasture area expanded by 24 million ha (Pacheco and Poccard Chapuis, 2009). In addition to loss of tropical forests, socioeconomic benefits were often minimal as most of the deforested land was not used productively. Recent policies, including stricter enforcement and monitoring of "legal reserves" (mandates for conserving a certain share of forest on large farms), better delineation of protected areas, environmental zoning, and accelerated land title registration, aim to direct investment primarily towards degraded lands, encourage investment on currently cultivated land, and reduce the detrimental impacts from any area expansion. The slowdown of deforestation in the Brazilian Amazon points towards some success (Nepstad et al., 2009).

A second process is the expansion of soybeans and other crops in the *cerrado* (savannah) region of Brazil, mainly to supply expanding Asian markets. Public investment in research and development was key to allow the cultivation of acid soils that had previously been unsuitable for agriculture, the development of varieties for the low tropics, and the use of conservation tillage. Although a technological success, the economic and social impacts were more limited as weak land policies and large subsidized credit programs that benefited large farmers led to highly mechanized production so that employment generation and poverty impacts remained well below potential levels (World Bank, 2009). This has led many to argue that the development of the *cerrado* region, although successful commercially, was a missed opportunity for broader social development.

Third, building on decades of a proactive policy to promote the sugarcane value chain, Brazil developed the world's leading sugar/ethanol industry. The scope for intensification on currently cultivated land is illustrated by the fact that some two–thirds of the area for sugarcane expansion is former pastureland, 32 percent from other crops, and only 2 percent from natural vegetation. Clear environmental challenges notwithstanding, evidence points towards clear economic and social benefits from sugar compared to the extensive grazing it replaced (Martinelli et al., 2011).

In Argentina, large farm management companies rent most or all of the land they operate and contract with machine operators. Large–scale adoption of the model happened during Argentina's 1990s financial crisis when such companies' ability to access outside capital provided strong advantages. With clear property rights allowing easy contracting, the ten largest companies farm from 100,000 ha to about 1 million ha (Byerlee et al., 2012). Many of these companies are traded publicly, have vertically integrated into processing and marketing, and operate across countries to diversify climatic, price, and political risks. Access to a large pool of highly qualified agronomists who undergo continued training and are organized hierarchically allows adoption of near–industrial methods of quality and cost control. Competitive land lease markets imply that at least part of the savings is passed on to landowners, who may receive lease payments above what they would have been able to earn by self–cultivation.

The case of Peru provides an interesting example for the benefits that can be had from a well–designed and transparent process to bring in competent investors. To divest a rather limited amount of public land, the country established a process of auctions with strong and public technical vetting from the private sector. In the country's Pacific region, this has given rise to the transfer of 235,500 ha of public land over the past 15 years in a way that brought in $50 million in investment and created the basis for the country's emergence as the prime supplier of high value and employment–intensive horticultural products to the North American market.

In South East Asia, the expansion of oil palm, one of the most profitable land uses in the humid tropics, has provided ample scope for positive social impacts and economic diversification (Butler and Laurance, 2009). Eight of the world's largest agricultural production companies are based on oil palm. Commercial oil palm cultivation was pioneered by Malaysia but expanded to Indonesia which, at 20 million tons, is now the world's largest producer. Indonesia's oil palm area more than doubled between 1997 and 2007, from some 2.9 million ha to 6.3 million ha, providing significant gains in employment with an estimated 1.7 to 3 million jobs generated in this labor–intensive industry.

Despite the overall positive impact, social and environmental problems abound. Policies to provide land virtually free implied that over half of the 1990–2005 oil palm expansion is estimated to have been at the expense of natural forests (Koh and Wilcove, 2008). Large areas – up to 12 million ha by some estimates (Fargione et al., 2008) – were deforested to extract timber without ever being planted to oil palm. Land–use change and deforestation are the largest single contributors to Indonesia's greenhouse gas emissions and a moratorium on deforestation has been imposed to limit negative environmental outcomes. On the social side, expansion of palm oil in non–forested areas, especially degraded lands with poorly defined land rights, often infringed on rights of existing users (Barr et al., 2010). Insecure land rights also constrained expansion of smallholder cultivation, which currently accounts for a third of production. It still increased rapidly, partly due to administrative requirements and partly due to the rise of independent growers who, with higher density of mills and other infrastructure, take advantage of this highly profitable opportunity.

In the former Soviet Union (FSU a spectacular, though ultimately unsuccessful, effort to expand cultivated area was Khruschev's "Virgin Lands" campaign that aimed to draw large parts of Kazakhstan into large–scale production. By 1954, 55 million ha were brought under state farms with up to 70,000 ha each. Managerial and incentive problems, exacerbated by marginal agro–ecological suitability, undermined productivity and prompted the abandonment of much of the area (McCauley, 1976).

Since 1990, FSU countries have undergone major transitions from the system of collective and state farms to new agrarian structures. After initial drops, cereal yields increased significantly, though they remain well below potential. Elimination of subsidies to the inefficient meat industry greatly reduced domestic demands for feed–grain, allowing the region to shift from massive grain imports to becoming a major supplier of global grain markets (Liefert et al. 2010).[2] In many countries, Soviet structures evolved into large farming companies that control enormous amounts of land. In Russia, the 30 largest holdings farm 6.7 million ha or 5.5 percent of cultivated area and in Ukraine, the largest 80 firms control about 5 million ha or 14 percent of cultivated area (Deininger and Byerlee, 2012). In an environment with deficient infrastructure, weak governance, non–competitive inputs and output markets, and the high cost of domestic finance, direct access to foreign capital – mainly via listing in foreign stock exchanges – and the credible threat of withdrawal creates advantages for very large operators. In Kazakhstan, inflows of capital have helped to improve the sector's depreciated capital stock, with employment and wage benefits (Petrick et al., 2013). In Ukraine, where land can only be leased, rental prices are very low, in some cases only a tenth of what is observed in Argentina and a brisk pace of structural change in the period before 2005 that saw the exit of a large number of inefficient firms has since slowed significantly (Deininger and Nizalov, 2013).

Policy reforms that ended discrimination against agriculture have accelerated agricultural growth and paved the way for renewed investor interest in a continent where many countries are well endowed with water and land. However, attempts to jumpstart agricultural growth via large–scale farming will benefit from incorporating the lessons from past investment booms.

In most of Africa, adverse policies and weak infrastructure implied that success with export agriculture was limited to high–value crops (>$500/ton) such as cotton, cocoa, coffee, and, more recently, horticulture where good agro–ecological conditions and cheap labor helped offset the disadvantages arising from weak institutions, high transport costs, and weak market development (Poulton et al., 2008). Insecure land rights and poorly functioning land markets limited development impacts irrespectively of how land was operated. For example, in the 1980s, Côte d'Ivoire became the world's largest cocoa exporter based on small and medium–sized producers. About one million ha of forestland was converted to cocoa, mostly based on immigrants under a system that allowed them to gain ownership of part of the plantation once established. Closing of the land frontier and the ensuing competition for land led locals to renege on these promises, prompting conflict and a decade–long civil war that negated much of the progress made (Wood, 2003).

Rent–seeking elites' extractive motives dominated and eventually doomed many ventures into large–scale farming. Semi–mechanized sorghum and sesame production in Sudan, which expanded rapidly in the 1970s when financing from the Gulf States aimed to transform Sudan into a regional breadbasket, is one example. Easy access to land and subsidized credit for machinery attracted many civil servants and businessmen and between 5.5 and 16.5 million ha were converted into arable land with farm sizes averaging 1,000 ha but some much larger (Government of Sudan, 2009). Neglect of small farmers' and pastoralists' traditional rights undermined their livelihoods and led to conflict (Johnson, 2003, Pantuliano, 2007) which prompted a highly extractive mode of cultivation that was ecologically unsustainable and economically uncompetitive.

Other externally driven ventures also ran into technical problems. Efforts to introduce mechanized rainfed wheat in Tanzania on some 40,000 ha of land that was previously prime grazing grounds for pastoralists illustrate this. Pastoralists tried to use litigation to force a benefit–sharing agreement with wheat farmers, with limited success. After a $45 million investment, production became marginally profitable from a private point of view. It was ultimately deemed unprofitable, and production has been declining (Lane and Pretty, 1991; Rogers, 2004).

5.4.3   Assessing the bio–physical potential: land acquisition vs productivity increases

While many analyses focus on demand for large land–related investments, the economic competitiveness of such ventures will be determined by location–specific agro–ecological potential, infrastructure access as a determinant of transport cost, and the ability to add value. The value of potential crop output (net of transport cost) at any location can provide a basis to assess not only whether a country has currently uncultivated areas that might be of interest to investors but also the extent to which there is scope for increasing productivity on areas already cultivated. For the majority of countries, data suggest much higher scope for intensification as compared to area expansion.

5.4.3.1 Potential output as the basis for yield gap and area expansion potential

The starting point for gauging the potential supply of land for rainfed cultivation is an assessment of potential yields that can be achieved on a given plot (approximated by a pixel in the analysis). To do so, we use the global agro–ecological zoning methodology developed by the International Institute for Applied Systems Analysis (Fischer et al., 2002), which predicts potential yield for rainfed cultivation of seven key crops based on simulated plant growth at each stage of the vegetative cycle,[3] taking into account factors including soil, temperature, precipitation, elevation, and slope and allowing simulations for different climate change scenarios. Applying a price vector (net of transport cost) allows us to determine the crop that produces the highest revenue for any cell. Results are illustrated in Figure 5.4.1. For areas that are currently cultivated, the difference between possible output and what is attained provides an estimate of the yield gap. Although

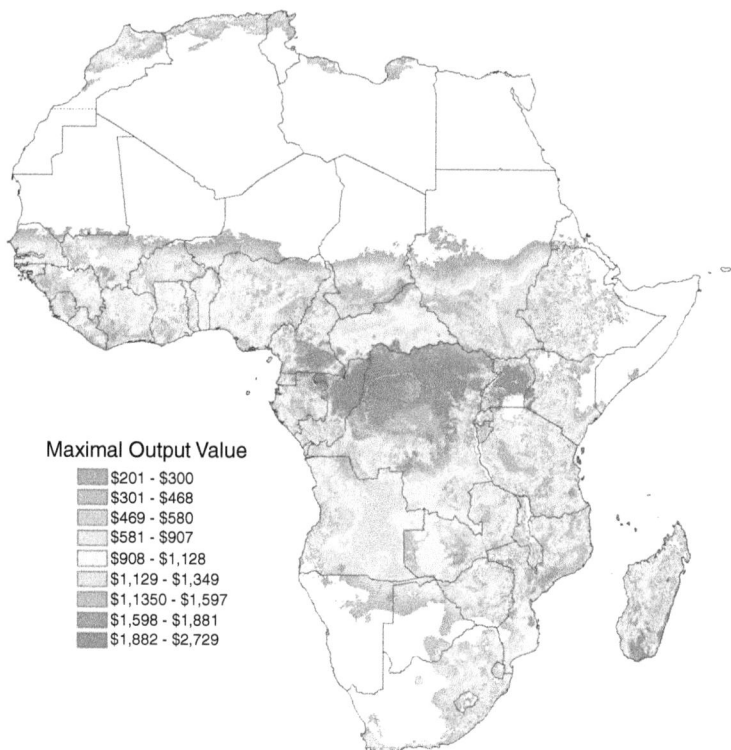

Maximal Output Value

- $201 - $300
- $301 - $468
- $469 - $580
- $581 - $907
- $908 - $1,128
- $1,129 - $1,349
- $1,1350 - $1,597
- $1,598 - $1,881
- $1,882 - $2,729

Figure 5.4.1 Maximum potential value of output ($/ha) for Africa
Source: Based on Fischer and Shah (2010).

there are many reasons for the existence of such a gap, this hypothetical exercise can break this gap into various factors. If they are not currently cultivated, not designated as a protected area, non–forested, and have low population density so that whatever existing interests are displaced can be compensated, areas with high potential could be possible candidates for area expansion. To identify the relevant subsets, we use a number of data sets.[4]

We obtain two main results: First, yield gaps vary widely across regions and are especially large for Africa. In fact, with the exception of South Africa, no country in Sub–Saharan Africa realizes more than 25 percent of potential production. This implies not only a vast potential to increase yields by providing access to technology, infrastructure, markets, and value chains but also, in light of high poverty elasticity of smallholder agriculture (Ligon and Sadoulet, 2008; Ravallion and Chen, 2007), an immense scope to increase poverty by doing so. The absence of economies of scale even at very small farm sizes together with the potential of smallholder agriculture to gainfully employ large amounts of labor (Ali and Deininger, 2013) imply that organic evolution of farm sizes will be the desirable policy and there is no need to shift to larger farms to increase productivity.

Second, there are some countries with land that is not covered by forest, of high value for biodiversity, or already densely populated, that can be suitable for expansion of rainfed agriculture in ways that respect existing rights, generate local benefits, and are environmentally sustainable. As Table 5.4.1 illustrates, a total of 32 countries with more than three million hectares of land each make up more than 90 percent of available land. Of these, 16 are in Africa, eight in Latin America, three in Eastern Europe and Central Asia, and five in the rest of the world. More strikingly, many of the countries with ample amounts of suitable but uncultivated land have limited amounts of land under cultivation. For example, the area of currently uncultivated land suitable for cultivation is more than double what is currently cultivated in 11 countries and more than triple the currently cultivated area in six countries. The seven countries with the largest amount of suitable uncultivated land according to this measure (Sudan, Brazil, Australia, Russia, Argentina, Mozambique, and Democratic Republic of the Congo, in that order) account for 224 million hectares, or more than half of global availability.

5.4.3.2 Establishing a country typology

The above information allows us to establish a typology of countries by plotting potential land availability vs yield gap. Results from doing so in Figure 5.4.2 allow us to distinguish four categories of countries with different endowments and development potential:

Little land for expansion, low yield gap. This type includes Asian countries with high population density, such as China, Vietnam, Malaysia, Korea, and Japan, Western European countries, and some countries in the Middle East with limited land suitable for rainfed production. Agricultural growth

Table 5.4.1 Land use and non–forested, non–protected agriculturally suitable area by region and key countries

| | | | | Non-cropped, non-protected suitable | | | |
| | | | | Forest | Non-forest with pop. density of | | |
	Total area	Forest area	Cultivated area	<25/km²	<25/km²	<10/km²	<5/km²
Sub–Saharan Africa	**2,408,224**	**509,386**	**210,149**	**163,377**	**201,540**	**127,927**	**68,118**
Angola	124,294	57,941	2,930	11,502	9,684	6,625	4,561
Burkina Faso	27,342	2,072	4,817	452	3,713	1,040	256
Cameroon	46,468	23,581	6,832	8,973	4,655	3,205	1,166
Cent. Afr. Rep.	62,021	23,496	1,879	4,358	7,940	6,890	5,573
Chad	127,057	2,280	7,707	680	14,816	10,531	7,061
Congo	34,068	23,132	512	12,351	3,476	3,185	2,661
D.R. Congo	232,810	147,864	14,739	75,760	22,498	14,757	8,412
Ethiopia	112,829	8,039	13,906	534	4,726	1,385	376
Gabon	26,269	21,563	438	6,469	954	927	839
Kenya	58,511	3,284	4,658	655	4,615	2,041	935
Madagascar	58,749	12,657	3,511	2,380	16,244	11,265	6,572
Mali	125,254	3,312	8,338	582	3,908	776	28
Mozambique	78,373	24,447	5,714	8,247	16,256	9,160	4,428
South Africa	121,204	8,840	15,178	918	3,555	1,754	649
Sudan	249,872	9,909	16,311	3,881	46,025	36,400	18,547
Tanzania	93,786	29,388	9,244	4,010	8,659	4,600	1,234
Zambia	75,143	30,708	4,598	13,311	13,020	8,367	3,083
Latin America & Caribbean	**2,032,437**	**933,990**	**162,289**	**290,631**	**123,342**	**91,576**	**64,320**
Argentina	277,400	33,626	28,154	16,228	29,500	23,835	16,856
Bolivia	108,532	54,325	2,850	21,051	8,317	7,761	6,985
Brazil	847,097	485,406	62,293	130,848	45,472	27,654	15,247
Colombia	113,112	64,543	7,339	31,313	4,971	3,776	2,838
Ecuador	25,152	11,631	3,384	3,663	638	415	313

(continued)

Table 5.4.1 Continued

	Total area	Forest area	Cultivated area	Non-cropped, non-protected suitable			
				Forest	Non-forest with pop. density of		
				<25/km²	<25/km²	<10/km²	<5/km²
Guyana	20,845	17,737	464	8,501	210	189	156
Mexico	194,218	64,447	25,845	7,206	4,360	2,857	1,719
Paraguay	39,904	19,112	5,419	10,269	7,269	6,035	5,133
Peru	128,972	68,312	3,799	39,951	496	476	438
Uruguay	17,772	1,323	2,030	731	9,269	8,681	7,340
Venezuela	90,531	48,345	3,912	6,167	8,966	7,725	5,891
E. Europe/C. Asia	2,469,520	885,527	251,811	140,026	52,387	29,965	18,210
Belarus	20,784	7,784	6,019	4,853	3,691	868	204
Russian Fed.	1,684,767	807,895	119,985	128,966	38,434	24,923	15,358
Ukraine	59,608	9,265	32,988	2,594	3,442	394	74
East and South Asia	1,932,941	493,762	445,048	46,250	14,341	9,496	5,933
China	935,611	167,202	136,945	10,514	2,176	1,383	843
Indonesia	183,897	95,700	32,920	24,778	10,486	7,291	4,666
Malaysia	32,243	21,171	7,184	4,597	186	119	50
Middle East/N Africa	1,166,118	18,339	74,189	209	3,043	843	236
Rest of World	3,318,962	863,221	358,876	134,700	50,971	45,687	41,102
Australia	765,074	88,086	45,688	17,045	26,167	25,894	25,593
Canada	969,331	308,065	50,272	30,100	8,684	8,289	7,598
Papua N.G.	44,926	29,387	636	9,746	3,771	3,193	1,917
United States	930,303	298,723	174,515	74,350	8,756	6,818	5,058
World total	13,333,053	3,706,457	1,503,354	775,211	445,858	305,711	198,064

Note: "Suitable" means that at least 60 percent of possible yield can be attained for any of the 5 rainfed crops considered here (wheat, oil palm, sugarcane, soybean, maize). Countries are included if they have a total of at least 3 Mn ha of forested or non-forested suitable area for areas with population density <25/km². Suitable ha per cultivated ha area based on non-protected, non-forest suitable area where the population density of the grid cell is <25/km², <10/km², or <5/km².

Source: Deininger et al. (2011a).

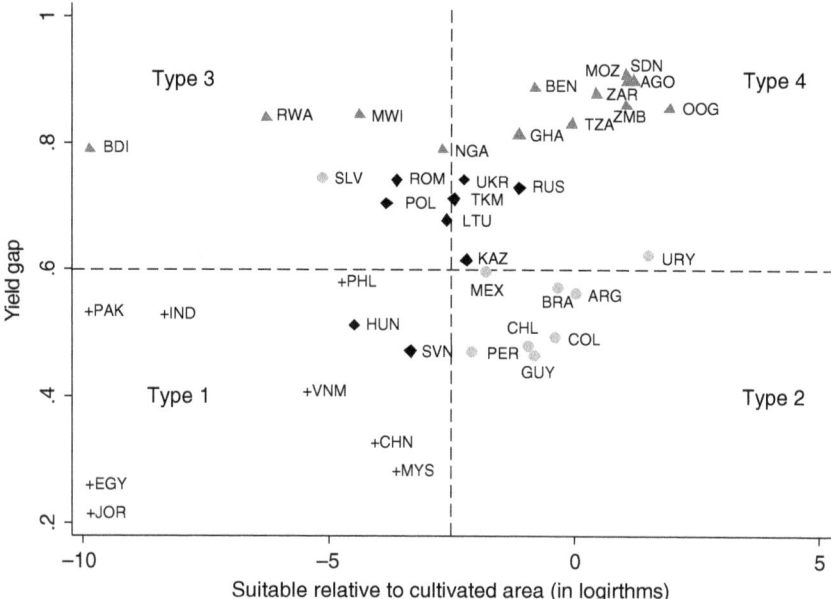

Figure 5.4.2   Potential land availability vs potential for increasing yields
Note: Dashed lines indicate average yield gap and 50th percentile for relative suitability.

was and will be led by highly productive smallholders. To meet expanding demand for horticultural and livestock products, private investors are
likely to provide capital, technology, and market access through contractual
arrangements even more than in the past. With economic growth, land consolidation – largely by entrepreneurial farmers leasing or buying plots from
neighbors – will gradually increase farm sizes. This, as well as increased land
use for nonfarm industries, urban expansion, and infrastructure, requires
well–functioning land markets and institutions.

Suitable land available, low yield gap. Countries in this group have reasonably
well–defined property rights, infrastructure access, and access to technology,
often due to past investment in infrastructure, institutions, and human capital. It is in these cases where institutional investors have exploited opportunities for cropland expansion, in some cases leading to tremendous increases
in land prices and where new forms of institutional arrangements (such as
Argentina's farm management companies) emerged. If property rights are
secure, markets function well, and areas with high social or environmental
value are protected effectively (possibly using payments for environmental
services), the public sector's role is mainly regulatory. But if land rights are
insecure or ill–defined, large–scale land acquisition may threaten forests or
lead to conflict with existing land users. A desire to avoid these negative

outcomes has prompted some countries, such as Brazil, to launch large–scale programs to regularize land and tighten environmental regulation.

Little land available, high yield gap. This category includes the majority of developing countries with limited land and water availability. Large numbers of smallholders may be locked into poverty because the area currently cultivated remains far below the yield potential. Strategic options depend on the size and evolution of the non–agricultural sector. If the sector is small, higher agricultural productivity will be the only viable mechanism for rapid poverty reduction. This process will require public investment in technology, infrastructure, and market development to raise smallholder productivity, following the example of the Green Revolution in Asia. If incomes and employment in the nonagricultural sector grow rapidly, land markets work reasonably well, and population growth is low, there may be scope for land consolidation and an associated move to larger operational units with appropriate technology.

Suitable land available, high yield gap. This category includes sparsely populated countries in Africa (DR Congo, Sudan, Tanzania, Mozambique, and Zambia) with large tracts of land suitable for rainfed cultivation, but also large smallholder populations that only achieve a fraction of their potential productivity. In virtually all African countries where demand for land acquisition has recently increased dramatically, the level of productivity achieved by existing smallholder cultivators is less than 25 percent of potential. Capital–intensive activities with low labor absorption, such as annual crops using fully mechanized production, will be appropriate only if population density is low, the likelihood of in–migration is limited, and the nonagricultural sector can absorb expected growth of the labor force in the medium term. If institutions are available to deal with the associated risks, outside investment can help foster local development. The challenge for such countries is to establish mechanisms to attract capable investors, rather than speculators, to increase productivity, and have benefits accrue to local populations. Rather than relying on ad hoc investor initiatives, provision of basic public services such as infrastructure and technology for areas and crops that fit with the country's comparative advantage may be an option.

5.4.4   Analyzing the size and determinants of the land rush

While experts agree that global land demand reached historic heights following the 2007/8 commodity price spike, data at country and project level remains extraordinarily weak, partly due to lack of a clear methodology. We draw on different sources to illustrate this point and the implications for cross–country analysis and argue that a regular effort building on country inventories – complemented by in–depth evaluation of innovative approaches and detailed case study of failures – will be needed to guide decision–makers at various levels. Uni– and bilateral regressions for land demand (in terms of number of projects) at country level suggest that, in addition to agro–ecological potential, weak land governance is strongly associated with higher levels of investor demand.

5.4.4.1 The challenges of obtaining data on actual land transfers

If "large" land acquisitions constitute an event significant enough to warrant mention in the local press or other media, globally consistent identification of informal expressions of demand is relatively easy and, if one is willing to abstract from issues of illiteracy, press freedom, language, and relative newsworthiness of such events in different settings, may even be done by searching the internet.[5] By comparison, generating meaningful and comparable data on actual implementation is much harder as it requires tracing implementation progress at project level, ideally in a way that is verified with governments or investors. While their precise nature will vary with countries' legal and regulatory requirements, any large land deal will involve three or four main steps, namely: (i) an informal expression of interest that is not legally binding; (ii) design and background studies (soil tests, engineering designs, assessments of social and environmental impact, draft business plans), and negotiations on contract terms up to signature; (iii) investment up to the point where full capacity is reached; and (iv) operation at full scale (possibly different from the originally envisaged one). Regular updating of project–level data to reflect investments' progress from plan to implementation including the extent to which key parameters of business plans are adhered to, and the type and quantity of local benefits, could provide valuable information to, among others: (i) help identify types of investments most likely to be successful in certain settings; (ii) allow investors to develop reputation; and (iii) point out contractual arrangements well suited to different environments. Ideally, such information on actual large–scale land acquisition should thus come from national registries' or investment promotion agencies' records, with some cross–verification by investors. Unfortunately, an overall lack of transparency and weak country–level institutions imply that such data are not yet available; in fact, collecting them on a consistent basis will require significant effort.

Given these difficulties, the claim to report data on actual land transfers that were verified on the ground allowed the "land matrix" (Anseeuw et al., 2012) to attract considerable attention. Closer analysis points, however, toward enormous margins of error and methodological weaknesses that raise serious questions about the suitability of these data for meaningful analysis of actual land deals.[6] These doubts also lead to question the results of studies that rely primarily on these data (Rulli et al., 2013).[7] Thus, while the "land matrix" may provide data on demand for land acquisitions, any claims beyond this seem far–fetched.

Country inventories, often from regional level, and field verification, thus seem to be the only reliable source on actual transfers. Table 5.4.2 provides

Table 5.4.2   Extent of large land acquisitions in selected countries, 2004–2009

Country	Projects	Area (1,000 ha)	Median size (ha)	Domestic share area
Ethiopia	406	1,190	700	49
Liberia	17	1,602	59,374	7
Mozambique	405	2,670	2,225	53
Sudan	132	3,965	7,980	78

Source: Country inventories from Deininger et al. (2011).

evidence from such inventories in a few countries, suggesting that transfers (under various forms) in 2004 to 2009 amounted to 4 million hectares in Sudan, 2.7 million in Mozambique, 1.2 million in Ethiopia, and 1.6 million – mainly renegotiation of existing agreements – in Liberia. They also suggest that, in all of these countries except Liberia, domestic investors accounted for half or more of the area involved in these investments. These figures are broadly consistent with a study of investments based on information by key investors that puts the amount of land transferred across Sub–Saharan Africa at some 15 mn. ha (Schoneveld, 2011).

5.4.4.2   Country–level determinants of investors' land demand

In the absence of reliable data on actual deals, we estimate determinants of investor demand as evidenced by media reports in the immediate aftermath of the food and fuel crisis (that is, October 1, 2008 to August 31, 2009) at country level using both uni– and bilateral estimates. Independent variables include data on physical, cultural, and geopolitical proximity; investor countries' dependence on food imports and target countries' potential for increased agricultural production, standard investment climate measures as proxy for the quality of the legal and regulatory environment, and an index of land governance based on data published by the French Development Agency (de Crombrugghe et al., 2009). This index is interpreted as an indicator of overall tenure security of local users, with low values of the index describing countries with high levels of tenure insecurity.[8]

How good land governance will affect a country's attractiveness for agricultural investment is an empirical issue that is largely related to the balance between quick extraction and long–term investment. Security of property rights will be a key determinant of long–term investment decisions as investors will not tie up major resources in a countries where weak or unclear rights may lead to conflict or expropriation (Schnitzer, 1999) once investments are sunk. On the other hand, approval may be quicker and extractive exploitation easier where property rights and the state's capacity to enforce them are weak. Some investors are quite clear about their ability to enforce property rights through private militias, despite the problematic historical precedents.

For the unilateral case, results from regressing the number of expressions of interest in large–scale land deals in a destination country on the independent variables discussed earlier point towards few regularities (Arezki et al., 2011) as illustrated in Table 5.4.3. Potentially cultivable area outside of forests or the value of potential output on such area (but not in forests) are highly significant throughout, pointing toward land availability as a key motivation for such deals. A 10 percent increase of potential area or output value would increase the number of projects by between 5.1 percent and 7.1 percent. In contrast to the literature on foreign direct investment, indicators of good governance, such as investor protection and the rule of law, are insignificant. An economically meaningful and robust negative association also emerges between investor interest and land tenure security.[9] Thus, instead of being contingent on strong protection of rights, demand for land acquisition is more pronounced in countries with a weak protection of land rights. Weak land governance may attract investors because it may allow them to either fast–track proposals or to defend properties without relying on the state although historically, such arrangements have often had unfavorable consequences.

Poisson regressions for bilateral investor/host relationships in Table 5.4.4 allow a richer categorization of the phenomenon by considering investor and host country characteristics separately and adding bilateral variables. While they confirm some of the conclusions from the unilateral approach, they provide some new insights. On the demand side, the amount of food imports per inhabitant and population size are key determinants of interest for land acquisition, suggesting that countries with large populations that depend on trade for food consumption are more likely to engage in investment projects involving the large–scale acquisition of land. A desire to acquire land thus may increasingly complement more traditional means of dealing with imbalances in food supply through markets and storage. Distance is a significant predictor of interest in acquiring land as in most gravity models, together with a past colonial relationship, although the significance of the latter vanishes when considering projects with actual production.

Host country characteristics that include attractiveness for investors include having large amounts of high potential agricultural (but not forest) land and potential output. A 10 percent increase of potentially cultivable land in a host country would, *ceteris paribus*, increase the number of projects in that country by almost 5 percent. Interestingly, the coefficient on host countries' quality of land governance, in particular the extent of local rights recognition, is highly significant and negative. This result could, of course, be due to the fact that this is a new phenomenon, transparency is lacking, and investors as well as governments still lack experience. This can provide some justification for concerns about "land grabs" voiced by civil society as well as calls for a more proactive international response.[10]

Table 5.4.3 Probability that a country is targeted by investors

	All projects			Projects with some production only		
Potentially cultivable area non-forest	0.4946*** [0.121]			0.6876*** [0.156]		
Potentially cultivable area Forest	-0.0205 [0.070]			-0.0083 [0.094]		
Max. possible output value non-forest area		0.5122*** [0.139]	0.5086*** [0.140]		0.6199*** [0.165]	0.6148*** [0.166]
Max. possible output value forest area		-0.0523 [0.064]	-0.0658 [0.064]		-0.0606 [0.079]	-0.0734 [0.080]
Yield gap	0.6033 [0.416]	-0.2444 [0.710]	-0.0245 [0.696]	0.1057 [0.517]	-0.3172 [1.003]	-0.0872 [1.017]
Land governance		-0.1735** [0.078]	-0.1779** [0.081]		-0.1422 [0.108]	-0.1456 [0.109]
Weak investor protection			-0.0022 [0.003]			-0.0023 [0.003]
No. of observations	137	107	105	137	107	105
Pseudo R²	0.325	0.290	0.292	0.346	0.230	0.229

Notes: All variables are in logs. Robust standard errors in brackets. ***, **, and * denote significance at 1%, 5%, and 10% level. Constant included but not reported.

Source: Based on Arezki et al. (2011).

Table 5.4.4 Poisson regressions for the number of projects in bilateral investment relations

	No. of projects			No. of operating projects		
Bilateral variables						
Distance	-0.5900***	-0.6002***	-0.6165***	-0.7253***	-0.7243***	-0.7066***
	[0.061]	[0.060]	[0.060]	[0.097]	[0.094]	[0.094]
Colonial relationship	1.1699***	1.1558***	1.0550***	0.8934*	0.8914*	0.8718
	[0.263]	[0.265]	[0.221]	[0.530]	[0.513]	[0.578]
Investor country variables						
Net food imports per inhabitant	3.3056***	3.3913***	3.3203***	1.9477*	2.2305**	2.1871**
	[0.368]	[0.354]	[0.373]	[1.080]	[0.926]	[0.953]
Population	0.7817***	0.7771***	0.7634***	0.7522***	0.7379***	0.7285***
	[0.048]	[0.047]	[0.049]	[0.083]	[0.083]	[0.085]
Host country variables						
Food exports	0.0320	0.0345	0.0974***	0.0705	0.0783	0.1318**
	[0.032]	[0.031]	[0.037]	[0.061]	[0.059]	[0.065]
Suitable non–forest land	0.4664***			0.7015***		
	[0.074]			[0.149]		
Suitable forest land	0.0320			0.0154		
	[0.043]			[0.092]		
Max. possible output value non–forest area		0.5162***	0.4830***		0.7000***	0.6124***
		[0.072]	[0.089]		[0.126]	[0.149]
Max. possible output value forest area		0.0280	-0.0114		-0.0251	-0.0415
		[0.041]	[0.043]		[0.072]	[0.077]
Yield gap	0.9486**	1.3042***	0.4959	0.5036	1.1073	0.4565
	[0.376]	[0.404]	[0.519]	[0.681]	[0.754]	[1.002]
Land governance index			-0.2082***			-0.1930**
			[0.049]			[0.095]
No. of observations	25,704	26,838	20,223	25,704	26,838	20,223
Pseudo R²	0.269	0.265	0.261	0.254	0.231	0.217

Notes: Variable in logs. Robust standard errors in brackets ***denotes significance at the 1% level, **at the 5% level, and *at the 10% level. Constant included but not reported.

Source: Based on Arezki et al. (2011).

5.4.5   Policy implications

To reduce the risks associated with increased land demand and increase the likelihood of investments focusing on areas where they can generate maximum social benefit, governments need to adapt. All countries, including those without large amounts of uncultivated land for expansion, are likely to gain from efforts to improve land governance (Deininger et al., 2011b) as a response to higher implicit land values. In countries with land of interest to investors, this may need to be combined with ways to promote investment in line with their comparative advantage, including: (i) targeting investment to specific clusters; (ii) rigorous *ex ante* screening of proposals; (iii) agile mechanisms for dispute resolution and arbitration; and (iv) increased transparency to allow responsible players to distinguish themselves and enable all stakeholders to learn from experience, emulate success in many dimensions, and quickly abandon or restructure unsuccessful ventures before they become focal points for rent seeking.

5.4.5.1   Dealing with higher implicit land demand

Improved land governance is needed in at least four areas, namely to: (i) recognize and map existing rights; (ii) eliminate the scope for using eminent domain to acquire land for transfer to private parties; (iii) establish and sustain property registries to document landownership and facilitate voluntary transfers of land at low cost; and (iv) tax land or profits to fund local public goods and enhance the scope for economic activity and set in motion a virtuous cycle of investment.

Recognition of existing rights. Even if it has been occupied by local communities for a long time, much land in Africa is legally considered state land that can be transferred to investors without first going through a time–consuming process of ascertaining or compensating existing use rights. While supporters of such arrangements have argued that this can help protect ill–informed landholders from "predatory" investors and that the urgency of attracting investment makes it impossible to wait until land rights are determined and mapped. At the same time, the need to deal with informal occupants on land that was granted as supposedly unoccupied state land has emerged as an issue leading to abandonment of high–profile investments. Failure to resolve this issue early may thus merely postpone problems and, in addition, reduce transparency, competition, and the perception of fairness.

Recent examples show that, if legal provisions are in place, rights to large areas of land can be adjudicated quickly, cost effectively, and in a way that includes land use planning, thus identifying areas that could be made available to outsiders. Starting in the 1990s Mexico, with technology that was much less advanced than what is available today, mapped and adjudicated rights to close to 100 million ha (an area larger than Spain and France combined) in less than a decade. The program improved governance greatly by having more than 18,000 communities (*ejidos*) establish internal by–laws, providing a basis for representation and interaction with the outside world, separation of powers, and the establishment of internal controls, with support from central institutions. Contrary to initial fears, this did not prompt a wave of land sales but allowed farmers to enter into contracts or joint ventures with outsiders and thus increase productivity. A key mechanism was to make migration easier, augmenting local welfare via remittances (Valsecchi, 2010) and allowing more able farmers to expand their area (de Janvry et al., 2012). More recently, Rwanda demarcated the entire country (more than ten million parcels) in a participatory process.

Identifying state land. In many countries, legal provisions require land intended to be transferred to investors to be first expropriated or converted into state land. As acquisition and divestiture of state land provide key governance challenges, this creates a serious risk of bad governance. It also means that even communities interested in transferring land to an investor or establish joint ventures will not be able to do so without involving (and often "facilitating") local bureaucrats. Good practice suggests that expropriation should be a last resort to prevent moral hazard and holdout problems by private owners, but that transfers among private parties should be based on agreements between the parties. Legislation that requires expropriation as a precondition for transfers to investors or that gives wide latitude to expropriate for transfer to private interests should be amended to give a clear rationale (for example, in terms of environmental externalities) for declaring areas as state land, follow this up with an inventory that unambiguously demarcates such lands on the ground, and transparent mechanisms for divestiture of land that does not meet these criteria with preference given to actual users.

Ensuring tenure security and allowing voluntary land transfers at low cost. To provide investment incentives and facilitate the movement of land to its best use, it is critical that current and comprehensive information on assignment of property rights is broadly accessible, cost–effective, and verified on the ground. In addition to private land, coverage should include state and community land and documentation should allow low–cost registration of any transfers among private parties and include relevant contractual details. High stamp duties, which in many instances act as a strong disincentive to the transfer of land to better uses or users, should be lowered or replaced with a regime of land taxation (which would provide incentives to bring land into use) or, if administratively feasible, profit taxation.

5.4.5.2   Improving design and implementation of investments

Countries that have been successful in attracting land–based investment were characterized by: (i) a clear vision of how such investment would help to fit with their comparative advantage to promote development; (ii) an active role of the state in providing a regulatory framework and complementary public goods (roads, technology) to attract private investment in areas/regions where it could have impact; and (iii) a highly transparent and technically rigorous process to vet proposed investments, to learn from failure, to quickly dissolve bankrupt ventures, and to disseminate and build on successful approaches. To do so, they need to know what resources are at their disposal, how they can best add value to them.

Clustering and provision of complementary infrastructure. As the value of land that is not currently in use is largely determined by transport cost, targeting investment to areas with potential for complementary efforts (for example, in mining) to pay for the needed infrastructure can be a promising strategy. Land–related agricultural investment is sensitive to infrastructure access – including roads, markets, and technology – so the ad hoc and spatially dispersed approach to large–scale land–intensive investment that many countries have followed thus far is likely to bring limited benefits. Instead, areas with agricultural potential along existing or planned transport corridors can be a natural focal point toward which investment may be channeled. Efforts to fill in infrastructure, plan land use, and systematically document existing rights should initially be focused on such areas to reduce information cost and contribute to the emergence of more transparent and competitive markets. Such clustering could also generate technology and marketing infrastructure that could help integrate smallholders into value chains.

Resource assessment. Countries with large amounts of land of potential interest to investors will need to properly understand the resources at their disposal, the most appropriate ways to add value to these, and ways in which this can contribute to growth and equity on a broader scale. Assessing agro–ecological potential at the local level could help to determine economic values of land available and identify streams of benefits as well as ways to encourage investments by the public or the private sector in an incentive–compatible way. Having a realistic understanding of potential land values and ways to bring land to the market gradually will be important to avoid "fire sales" that give away a key asset well below opportunity cost and thus discourage efficient land use. Higher fees and taxes on land or revenue may be a better way to local revenues if local governments are allowed to retain a share of the tax revenues they collect if technical basis (for example, cadastres) is available, and clear valuation principles allow the avoidance of arbitrariness.[11]

Screening of investment proposals. Local communities in many of the areas of interest to investors may lack the ability to assess the technical and economic viability of investments, identify key challenges associated with them, effectively negotiate complicated contracts, or enforce compliance with such contracts even if judicial infrastructure were accessible. Without ways to rigorously screen proposals for technical viability, this may result in ill–considered investments causing irreversible damage before closing down, bringing disappointment all around. A number of countries found such assistance to bring high returns. In Mexico, communities' ability to draw on technical assistance and independent vetting of all contracts by the *Procuraduria Agraria* significantly improved outcomes. Similarly, in Peru, a public auction process, together with the independent professional vetting of proposals, helped attract investors by reducing red tape, and improved outcomes and local benefits. The institutions involved seem to function best if there is genuine and significant private sector input.

Dispute resolution and arbitration. Many of the investments under discussion venture into novel territory in terms of technology and the organization of production and are conducted in an environment where rights are often vague and fluid. It would thus be surprising if their implementation did not involve some conflicts. Any delays from such disputes can be very costly and potentially compromise the economic viability of an entire project. Avenues for quick and authoritative dispute resolution or bodies for arbitration that are recognized by both parties can thus be a key point affecting location decisions by investors. Having an agreed authority to arbitrate in case of conflict is one option that has been used effectively in other contexts. Similarly, criteria for failure of an investment should be clearly defined, along with ways to liquidate existing assets quickly.

Transparency. Although greater transparency key parameters such as contracts terms, number of jobs generated, total investment, resources transferred to local people, and value added to the local economy can be beneficial in many ways, many of the investments in this space have been shrouded in secrecy. A more open mode of engagement can: (i) generate knowledge and allow emulating success in an area where information is often lacking; (ii) allow investors to distinguish themselves as responsible by following accepted safeguards or performance standards; and (iii) reduce (reputational) risks of investing in specific countries or commodities, ideally in a way that will make it easier for investors to raise funds or reduce their cost of capital. Greater transparency could put risks into sharper relief, thus helping to identify areas where tighter performance standards (up–front or during implementation) can yield benefits, while at the same time identifying minimum conditions in terms of public sector involvement and land governance without which such investment is unlikely to be successful.

Notes

1. Even in cases such as the United States during the late 19th century, high land inequality at county the level reduced taxes and thus investments in public education (Vollrath, 2009).
2. In the late 1980s, the FSU had annual grain deficits of about 34 million t, compared to annual more than 50 million tons of grain and seven million tons of oilseeds exports in the 2005–10 period.

3. Note that all of these simulations focus on potential for rainfed cultivation. Inclusion of a hydrological and irrigation investment, while possible in principle, would be much more complex and may, in particular, involve issues of riparian rights and water pricing.

4. Data used include the GLC2000 land cover, the IFPRI Agricultural Extent database, the FAO 2000 Global Forest Resources Assessment to identify land use, the 2009 World Database of Protected Areas to identify protected areas, and LANDSCAN 2003 data on population density to identify areas with less than 5, 10, or 25 persons per square kilometer, for example some 100, 50, or 20 hectares per household. Also, as market access will affect transport cost, we classify areas based on whether they are within six hours of an urban center with a population of at least 50,000 based on the World Bank's Global Mobility Database.

5. The NGO GRAIN has followed this approach with some success. Use of this method to make inferences on actual land deals (Alomar and Cousquer, 2012) is much more problematic as journalists are normally not aware of legal nuances and thus may erroneously report a transfer as "sealed" even though all that was signed was an exploration license. Tracking of investments using the same method is obviously near–impossible.

6. Key issues include: (i) weak documentation and inconsistent coverage (79 per cent of observations lack information on the year when a deal was concluded or interest expressed; (ii) lack of consistent rules for the "verification" process; and (iii) the fact that data on the website are updated on a continuing basis without keeping a record of previous versions so that replicability is limited. Cross–checks in individual countries point to wide margins of error; for example in Tanzania more than 95 percent of the two million ha of "verified" deals included in the matrix (as compared to six million ha of unverified ones) proved to be incorrect after it had given rise to press reports that the Government had "sold off" two million ha to foreigners. For a list of other inconsistencies and questionable sources, see http://farmlandgrab.org/post/view/20405.

7. A quick analysis of the data in table S1 of Rulli et al. (2013) reveals that of the total volume of 49.7 mn. ha of "grabbed" land reported in this paper, 35 mn. have the matrix and 14.7 mn. the GRAIN website as at least one of their sources and only 239,000 ha are only reported in sources that are independent from these two.

8. The main variables contributing to the first axis of the principal component analysis are listed below (contributions under brackets): "land tenure security" (16 percent), "public policies addressing land rights" (15 percent), "land ownership rights security" (14 percent), "diversity of tenure situations" (11 percent), "recognition by the State of the diversity of tenure situations" (10 percent), "scarcity of land–related conflicts" (10 percent), "traditional collective use and ownership" (9 percent), "significance of land use policies" (6 percent). This first axis captures 40 percent of variance.

9. Everything else constant, a one standard deviation drop in the land governance index – equivalent to the difference between Brazil and Angola – would be predicted to increase the number of investment projects by 33 percent.

10. The "Voluntary Guidelines" (Food and Agricultural Organization of the UN 2012) as well as the "Principles for responsible agricultural investment" (http://unctad.org/en/Pages/DIAE/G–20/PRAI.aspx) aim to respond to this. There are also obvious parallels to mining and extractive industries that could provide lessons on how to fashion a multi–stakeholder process to improve transparency.

11. Historically, use of land taxes has been effective in discouraging speculation and rent seeking in New Zealand, helping to break up a structure that had been dominated by large farms (Deininger and Byerlee, 2012).

References

Ali, D. A. and Deininger, K. (2013) "Is There a Farm Size–Productivity Relationship in African Agriculture? Evidence from Rwanda," Policy Research Working Paper (Washington, DC: World Bank).

Alomar, R. and Cousquer, D. (2012) "A Global Land Purchase Monitor," paper presented at the Annual Bank Conference on Land and Poverty, Washington, DC.

Anseeuw, W., Bache, W., Bru, T., Giger, M., Lay, J., Messerli, P., and Nolte, K. (2012) "Transnational Land Deals for Agriculture in the Global South: Analytical Report Based on the Land matrix Database" (Bern, Montpellier, Hamburg: CDE, CIRAD, CIGA, Bern University, ILC).

Arezki, R., Deininger, K., and Selod, H. (2011) "What Drives the Global Land Rush," IMF Working Paper WP/11/251 (Washington, DC: International Monetary Fund).

Banerjee, A. and Iyer, L. (2005) "History, Institutions, and Economic Performance: The Legacy of Colonial Land Tenure Systems in India," *American Economic Review*, vol. 95, no. 4, pp. 1190–1213.

Barr, C., Dermawan, A., Purnomo, H., and Komarudin, H. (2010) "Financial Governance and Indonesia's Reforestation Fund During the Soeharto and post-Soeharto Periods 1989–2009," CIFOR Occasional Paper 52 (Bogor: Center for International Forestry Research).

Binswanger, H.P., Deininger, K., and Feder, G. (1995) "Power, Distortions, Revolt and Reform in Agricultural Land Relations," *Handbook of Development Economics 3B*, pp. 2659–2772.

Borras, S.M. and Franco, J.C. (2012) "Global Land Grabbing and Trajectories of Agrarian Change: A Preliminary Analysis," *Journal of Agrarian Change*, vol. 12, no. 1, pp. 34–59.

Butler, R.A. and Laurance, W.F. (2009) "Is Oil Palm the Next Emerging Threat to the Amazon?," *Tropical Conservation Science*, vol. 2, no. 1, pp. 1–10.

Byerlee, D., Lissitsa, A. and Savanti, P. (2012) "Corporate Models of Broadacre Crop Farming: International Experience from Argentina and Ukraine," *Farm Policy Journal*, vol. 9, no. 2, pp. 13–25.

Collier, P. and Dercon, S. (2009) "African Agriculture in 50 Years: Smallholders in a Rapidly Changing World." Paper presented at the Expert meeting on How to Feed the World in 2050 (Rome: Food and Agriculture Organization of the United Nations).

Collier, P. and Venables, A.J. (2011) "Land Deals in Africa: Pioneers and Speculators," Discussion Paper 8644 (London: Centre for Economic Policy Research).

de Janvry, A. (1981) *The Agrarian Question and Reformism in Latin America* (Baltimore: Johns Hopkins University Press).

de Janvry, A., Emerick, K., Gonzalez–Navarro, M,.and Sadoulet, E. (2012) "Certified to Migrate: Property Rights and Migration in Rural Mexico," Working Paper (Berkeley, CA: University of California).

DeCrombrugghe, D., Farla, K., DeNeubourg, C., Ould Aoudia, J., and Szirmai, A. (2009) Presentation of the institutional profiles database 2009 (IPD 2009) III. Technical Report Working Paper, Agence Francaise de Developpement.

Deininger, K. and Byerlee, D. (2012) "The Rise of Large Farms in Land Abundant Countries: Do They Have a Future?," *World Development*, vol. 40, no. 4, pp. 701–14.

Deininger, K., Byerlee, D., Lindsay, J., Norton, A., Selod, H., and Stickler M. (2011a) *Rising Global Interest in Farmland: Can it Yield Sustainable and Equitable Benefits?* (Washington, DC: World Bank).

Deininger, K. and Nizalov, D. (2013) "Structural Change in Ukrainian Agriculture 2001–2010," Policy Research Working Paper (Washington, DC: World Bank).

Deininger, K., Selod, H., and Burns (2011b) *Improving Governance of Land and Associated Natural Resources: the Land Governance Assessment Framework* (Washington, DC: World Bank).

Drache, H.M. (1964) "The Day of the Bonanza; a History of Bonanza Farming in the Red River Valley of the North." (Fargo, ND: Institute for Regional Studies).

Fargione, J., Hill, J., Tilman, D., Polasky, S., and Hawthorne, P. (2008) "Land Clearing and the Biofuel Carbon debt," *Science*, vol. 319, no. 5867, pp. 1235–1238.

Fischer, G., v. Velthuizen, H., Shah, M., and Nachtergaele, F. (2002) *Global Agro-ecological Assessment for Agriculture in the 21st Century: Methodology and Results* (Laxenburg and Rome: IIASA and FAO).

Food and Agricultural Organization of the UN (2012) *Voluntary Guidelines on the Responsible Governance of Tenure of Land, Fisheries and Forests in the Context of National Food Security* (Rome: FAO).

Government of Sudan (2009) "Study on the Sustainable Development of Semi-mechanized Rainfed Farming" (Khartoum: Ministry of Agriculture and Forestry).

Grandin, G. (2009) *Fordlandia: The Rise and Fall of Henry Ford's Forgotten Jungle City* (New York: Metropolitan Books).

Iyer, L. (2010) "Direct Versus Indirect Colonial Rule in India: Long-Term Consequences," *Review of Economics and Statistics*, vol. 92, no. 4, pp. 693–713.

Johnson, D.H. (2003) *The Root Causes of Sudan's Civil War* (Bloomington, IN: Indiana University Press).

Koh, L.P. and Wilcove, D.S. (2008) "Is Oil Palm Agriculture Really Destroying Tropical Biodiversity?," *Conservation Letters*, vol. 1, no. 1, pp. 60–64.

Lane, C. and Pretty, J.N. (1991) "Displaced Pastoralists and Transferred Wheat Technology in Tanzania," IIED Gatekeeper Series no 20 (London: International Institute for Environment and Development).

Liefert, W.M., Serova, E., and Liefert, O. (2010) "The Growing Importance of the Former USSR Countries in World Agricultural Markets," *Agricultural Economics*, vol. 21, no. 1, pp. 65–71.

Ligon, E. and Sadoulet, E. (2008) "Estimating the Effects of Aggregate Agricultural Growth on the Distribution of Expenditures.". (Washington, DC: World Bank).

Martinelli, L.A., Garrett, R., Ferraz, S. and Naylor, R. (2011) "Sugar and Ethanol Production as a Rural Development Strategy in Brazil: Evidence from the State of São Paulo," *Agricultural Systems*, vol. 104, no. 5, pp. 419–428.

McCauley, M. (1976) *Kruschev and the Development of Soviet Agriculture: The Virgin Land Porgramme 1953–1964* (London: Macmillan).

Nepstad, D.C., Soares–Filho, B.S., Merry, F., Lima, A., Almeida, O.T., Stickler, C.M., and Lubowski, R. (2009) "The End of Deforestation in the Brazilian Amazon," *Science*, vol. 326, no. 8, pp. 1350–1351.

Pacheco, P. and Poccard Chapuis, R. (2009) "Cattle Ranching Development in the Brazilian Amazon: Emerging Trends from Increasing Integration with Markets" (Bogor: Center for International Forestry Research).

Pantuliano, S. (2007) "The Land Question: Sudan's Peace Nemesis," Humanitarian Policy Group Working Paper (London: Overseas Development Institute).

Pearce, F. (2012) *The Landgrabbers: The New Fight Over Who Owns the Earth* (London: Transworld Publishers).

Petrick, M., Wandel, J., and Karsten, K. (2013) "Rediscovering the Virgin Lands: Agricultural Investment and Rural Livelihoods in an Eurasian Frontier Area," *World Development*, vol. 43, no. 3, pp. 164–179.

Poulton, C., Tyler, G., Hazell, P., Dorward, A., Kydd, J., and Stockbridge, M. (2008) "All–Africa Review of Experiences with Commercial Agriculture: Lesson from Success and Failure." Background paper for the Competitive Commercial Agriculture in Sub–Saharan Africa (CCAA) Study (Washington, DC: World Bank).

Rajan, R. and Ramcharan, R. (2011) "Land and Credit: A Study of the Political Economy of Banking in the United States in the Early 20th Century," *The Journal of Finance*, vol. 66, no. 6, pp. 1895–1931.

Ravallion, M. and Chen, S.H. (2007) "China's (Uneven) Progress Against Poverty," *Journal of Development Economics*, vol. 82, no. 1, pp. 1–42.

Rogers, P. (2008) "The 'Failure' of the Peak Downs Scheme," *Australian Journal of Politics and History*, vol. 10, no. 1, pp. 81–115.

Rogers, P.J. (2004) "Saskatoon on the Savanna: Discursive Dependency, Canadian–guided Agricultural Development and the Hanang Wheat Complex." Paper presented at the 45th Annual International Studies Association Conference, Montreal.

Rulli, M.C., Saviori, A., and D'Odorico, P. (2013) "Global Land and Water Grabbing," *Proceedings of the National Academy of Sciences of the United States of America*, vol. 110, no. 3, pp. 892–897.

Schnitzer, M. (1999) "Expropriation and Control Rights: A Dynamic Model of Foreign Direct Investment," *International Journal of Industrial Organization*, vol. 17, no. 8, pp. 1113–1137.

Schoneveld, G.C. (2011) "The Anatomy of Large–scale Farmland Acquisitions in Sub–Saharan Africa," Working Paper 85 (Bogor: Center for International Forestry Research).

Tyler, G. (2011) "Investments in Agribusiness: A retrospective view of a Development Bank's Investments in Agribusiness in Africa and East Asia" (Washington, DC: World Bank).

Valsecchi, M. (2010) "Land Certification and International Migration: Evidence from Mexico," Working Papers in Economics no. 440 (Gothenburg: University of Gothenburg).

Vollrath, D. (2009) "The Dual Economy in Long–run Development," *Journal of Economic Growth*, vol. 14, no. 4, pp. 287–312.

Wood, D. (2003) "The Tragedy of the Cocoa Pod: Rent Seeking, Land and Ethnic Conflict in Ivory Coast," *Journal of Modern African Studies*, vol. 41, no. 4, pp. 641–655.

World Bank (2009) "Awakening Africa's Sleeping Giant: Prospects for Competitive Commercial Agriculture in the Guinea Savannah Zone and Beyond" (Washington, DC: World Bank).

5.5
Trade Facilitation and African Industrialization in the New Global Order: An Agenda for Action for Textile and Apparel Industry

Dominique Njinkeu, Julie Lohi, and Calvin Z. Djiofack
World Bank

Introduction

Industrialization has driven the economic development of developed and emerging countries (UNIDO, 2009). In recent years the production of manufactured goods has been broken down into tasks by plants located in many countries, most of these increasingly in developing countries. Contrary to past trends, when industrialization required a comprehensive pool of production characteristics, a particular location simply needs to specialize in a small set of tasks that can be competitively undertaken along specific supply chains. This trend offers hope for Africa's reindustrialization; a particular country could focus on the level of industrial agglomeration that would enable its firms reach a threshold above which it can lower the costs of production for manufactured exports and fully exploit its comparative advantage. In Africa, countries are too small for this to materialize unless viewed in the regional context that could nurture such agglomeration such as to facilitate a smooth integration in the world trading system. Against this backdrop, promoting a sound trade facilitation[1] environment is crucial to guarantee essential transport and logistics infrastructures allowing firms to exploit economies of scale related to regional integration and connect efficiently to other segments of the industrial value chain.

The ability of African countries to tap into the modern export sector successfully has been limited, and at best remained fragile (Keane, 2010). Efforts to diversify exports, and harness potential knowledge spillovers to tap into the modern export sector and benefit from latecomer opportunities have not been wholly successful. Because global trade has become so fragmented, African countries' ability to capture and secure market niches in emerging and newly industrialized countries will require a different approach to market access regimes under which they trade internationally. For example, industrial policy could entail government subsidizing

412

the costs of production in order to level the playing field for firms (Collier and Venables, 2007) through the provision of good-quality and extensive infrastructure, especially when clustered in geographically defined export zones.

This paper argues that an outward-looking regional integration approach that is properly implemented is needed to support Africa's reindustrialization. There is a need to take into account design and implementation deficiencies that have prevented past schemes from stimulating enough trade and development. To that effect complementary actions, particularly in trade facilitation and modern telecommunications, can foster opportunities offered by trade in tasks that are highly transport-intensive. Likewise the provision of public goods that facilitate cross-border trade is essential. For the purposes of illustration we use the case of textile and apparels (T&A). The rest of the paper is organized in three sections. Section 5.5.1 reviews how light manufacturing,[2] including the textile and apparel (T&A) industries, have been important in the economic transformation of different countries and argue that this should form a part of Africa's road to industrialization. Section 5.5.2 presents the set of complementary actions for boosting competitiveness and lower associated transaction costs; this section also provides an empirical examination to confirm the necessity of trade facilitation. Section 5.5.3 shows how and the extent to which a coherent bilateral and multilateral trade regime matters in supporting the emergence of African light manufacturing such as provided under AGOA.[3]

The main conclusion derived from the empirical exercise is that trade facilitation by improving transport infrastructures, logistics, and the efficiency of customs operations is a crucial conduit for fostering regional integration and boosting African trade. All dimensions of the logistics performance index (LPI) (which reflect trade facilitation) have positive and statistically significant impacts on trade: a one unit improvement in LPI score would lead to 16 percent increase in trade in general; efficient trade facilitation facilities offset the negative impacts of tariffs on exports; reducing tariffs on export goods has a magnifying effect in countries with relatively efficient trade facilitation. A one unit improvement in LPI score offsets the negative impacts of exports tariffs by 1 percent. In other words, improving LPI by one percent would reduce the impacts of tariffs by 0.01 percent. Our econometric results also show that trade facilitation can amplify the impacts of preferential trade agreements (PTAs) on developing countries' trade, with even better results under generous PTAs. For instance, AGOA has been beneficial to SSA trade compared to the European Union preferential market access to the ACP[4] group and the Everything but Arms (EBA),[5] doubling SSA's trade; a one unit improvement in the LPI score in the presence of AGOA would increase trade by an additional 22 percent in SSA. Combining trade facilitation with generous preferential trade schemes and tariffs reductions in exporting countries is an effective policy toolkit for fostering regional integration and nurturing the emergence of competitive production value chains and African industrialization.

5.5.1 Textile and apparel as trigger for industrial revolution

A labor-intensive process such as under light manufacturing[6] has led to economic transformation in many countries. The generation of jobs in light manufacturing has been an important tool in empowering, increasing productivity, and improving living standards. These characteristics of light manufacturing were at the center of economic development in Asia and in Latin America. The income earned and the knowledge acquired through light manufacturing allowed workers to engage in private entrepreneurship, innovate, and refine production methods, thereby nurturing sustainable economic expansion. China and India are among the fastest-growing economies and one key determinant of such performance has been increased exports obtained through high-productivity growth in the light manufacturing segments of their market (Wacziarg and Welch, 2008; Gilbert, 2011).

Both India and China used their abundant low-cost labor through targeted policies to develop light manufacturing, including in textile and apparel (T&A). As light manufactures fueled exports and increased revenues, countries gradually moved to more sophisticated industries. For instance, the shares of manufactures in China's total exports rose from 78 percent in 1990–94, to 86 percent in 1995–99, 90 percent in 2000–04, and finally 93 percent in the period 2005–10. Not only was the share of manufactures in total export increasing over time, but high-technology manufactures were progressively replacing light manufactures. The share of high-technology manufactures increased from 7 percent in the early 1990s to 28 percent between 2005 and 2010, with the difference being seen in the decline in the country's light manufacturing sector. India followed a similar scenario with the shares of light manufacturing progressively declining over time with simultaneous increases in high-technology manufactures (see Table 5.5.1).

Other emerging countries prioritized light manufacturing industries in order to engineer their economic transformation and reduce poverty in a sustainable manner. The shift from non-remunerated (farming or other types of self-employment) to remunerated jobs (jobs offered in light manufacturing with salaries matching the labor skills) leads to a reduction in poverty levels (WDR, 2013: Box 2.2); the income generated by light manufacturing allows citizens to cover their basic needs and escape poverty. Furthermore, it stimulated exports through the growth in outputs. The shares of light manufacturing in total exports (see Table 5.5.1) of countries such as Cambodia, Vietnam, and Bangladesh have dramatically increased over the past two decades. Although light manufacturing, through its process of jobs creation, can help lift people out of poverty and engineer exports, the sustainability and the success of light manufacturing to foster economic transformation (that is, increase people's productivity by adopting more sophisticated production technology) requires the presence of an overall conducive policy environment (WDR, 2013). For example, the increasing production capacities and the export expansion of Asian countries could be attributed to policies that attracted foreign investment and reduced transaction costs as part of a comprehensive program f trade facilitation (World Bank, 2010). For instance, by establishing a "green channel" for apparels at the customs, creating industrial zones for T&A processing near ports, and by providing automatic and free access to foreign exchanges and reducing the costs of letters of credits, Vietnam's T&A industries managed to achieve export revenues of US$8 billion in 2011 with about 1 million jobs in the sector. In China, for instance, in order to promote the textile and apparel industries, the government created high-speed railways, paved roads, and made available trucks to connect cotton farms and ginning, spinning, and fabric factories. The government reduced the cost of energy for the industry (US$c 5–7/ kWh) and promoted the textile cluster. The availability of such transport and logistics infrastructures and other facilities reduced transactions costs and nurtured the growth of Chinese cotton production (which reached 7.6 million tons in 2008), as well as the textile and apparel production in the country (see ACTIF News Letter, 2009).

In contrast, African performances have lagged significantly behind those of other regions. The share of manufactures in African export has been on average 31 percent between 1995 and 2010 compared with 84 percent, 55 percent, 75 percent, and 51 percent respectively for East Asia and the Pacific, Latin America and the Caribbean, South Asia and all low incomes (see Table 5.5.1). Manufacturing in general remains underdeveloped and has made a relatively small contribution to African GDP. Where successes could be identified in Africa, these have not been sustained over a period long enough to stimulate production and trade that could adequately engineer structural transformation. One of the few successes in African enterprises has been Ethiopia's cutflowers export to the European Union, a sector that employs about 50,000 workers (see Dinh et al., 2011) because of the combination OF preferential access to export markets with local business-friendly environments.

However, the progress that had been achieved seemed to have gone into reverse in the face of increasing competition from Chinese textiles following the ending of the Multi-fiber Arrangement (MFA) in 2005. The exports of African light manufactures have been declining overtime. Figure 5.5.1 and 5.5.2 show that the share of manufactures in African countries' total merchandise exports has been declining over time while their shares of agricultural raw materials in total exports are increasing, suggesting that Africa may have been deindustrializing, with associated job losses. African countries (see Figures 5.5.1 and 5.5.2[7]), have had high and volatile exports

Table 5.5.1 Average shares of manufactures in GDP and export for regions and selected countries

Regions and Countries	Manufactures VA (% of Total GDP)				Manufactures export (% of Merchandise Exports)			
	1990–1994	1995–1999	2000–2004	2005–2010	1990–1994	1995–1999	2000–2004	2005–2010
SSA (all income levels)	16.6	15.4	14.2	13.1	.	29.0	32.8	30.2
Ethiopia	3.8	5.1	5.6	4.5	0.7	8.6	10.5	8.4
Tanzania	8.3	8.3	9.0	9.0	.	15.6	16.7	22.6
Zambia	29.8	12.6	11.6	10.2	4.6	11.9	12.9	7.2
Lesotho	16.2	18.3	20.0	17.8	.	.	90.0	79.1
Nigeria	.	.	3.3	2.7	0.7	1.9	1.9	3.9
Madagascar	10.1	10.4	13.0	14.3	16.3	28.7	40.3	52.9
Mauritius	23.6	23.5	22.4	19.2	67.7	71.3	73.9	60.8
EAP (all income levels)	25.3	23.8	22.2	21.7	81.8	85.2	85.6	81.5
EAP (developing only)	30.2	30.6	30.8	30.7	67.4	76.9	80.3	78.6
South Asia	15.6	15.9	15.2	15.9	74.5	77.6	78.4	68.8
Bangladesh	14.1	15.6	15.7	17.5	81.7	87.9	91.5	90.3
China	33.1	32.8	32.1	32.2	77.8	85.9	89.7	92.9
Indonesia	21.9	25.5	28.4	26.8	45.7	48.8	54.1	41.9
India	15.6	16.0	15.0	15.4	73.2	75.1	75.7	65.8
Pakistan	17.0	15.9	15.8	18.5	80.3	84.2	85.0	77.8
Vietnam	14.2	16.3	19.9	20.6	.	44.4	48.6	56.1
OECD	.	19.1	17.4	16.0	77.4	80.2	79.2	75.2
LAC (all incomes level)	21.5	18.9	18.8	17.9	47.2	56.0	56.9	52.4
All Low income	11.3	11.5	11.9	13.0	.	49.2	51.5	54.0

[1]Note that Light manufacturing reported is the difference between 100 percent manufactures and the share of High Tech. Manufactures
Source: WDI, 2012

of agricultural raw materials over the last two decades while their level of exports of light manufactures remained low. In contrast, the Asian countries experienced a significant and smooth decline in their raw material exports with higher rates of light manufactures exports. African poor performances are explained to a great extent by the deterioration of its competitiveness as a result of, among other factors, infrastructure problems such as inadequate power and water supplies, and an inefficient transportation and trade logistics network (USAID, 2012).

High-Technology Export (% of Manufactured Export)				Light Manufacturures[1] (% of Manufactured Exports)			
1990–1994	1995–1999	2000–2004	2005–2010	1990–1994	1995–1999	2000–2004	2005–2010
.	6.3	3.6	5.1	.	93.7	96.4	94.9
.	0.3	3.4	2.2	.	99.7	96.6	97.8
.	3.2	1.1	1.9	.	96.8	98.9	98.1
2.5	6.9	0.4	1.8	97.5	93.1	99.6	98.2
.	.	0.3	0.2	.	.	99.7	99.8
.	3.8	0.7	2.6	.	96.2	99.3	97.4
4.3	5.2	0.7	1.1	95.7	94.8	99.3	98.9
0.6	0.9	2.9	7.3	99.4	99.1	97.1	92.7
22.6	28.5	31.1	27.9	77.4	71.5	68.9	72.1
18.4	26.7	31.8	29.6	81.6	73.3	68.2	70.4
3.1	4.6	4.9	6.2	96.9	95.4	95.1	93.8
0.2	0.0	0.2	0.6	99.8	100.0	99.8	99.4
7.3	13.7	24.2	28.1	92.7	86.3	75.8	71.9
3.6	9.7	15.7	12.7	96.4	90.3	84.3	87.3
4.3	6.1	6.3	6.9	95.7	93.9	93.7	93.1
0.1	0.1	0.7	1.6	99.9	99.9	99.3	98.4
.	0.1	7.1	6.3	.	99.9	92.9	93.7
19.1	21.1	22.1	17.9	80.9	78.9	77.9	82.1
6.4	10.7	14.4	11.3	93.6	89.3	85.6	88.7
.	2.5	2.8	3.0	.	97.5	97.2	97.0

The performance of African T&A industries better illustrates[8] the dismal performance of Africa's light manufacturing in general. For example, for all of its potential (the abundant land and low-cost labor) to produce high-quality cotton, the performance of Ethiopia's T&A industry is dismal in comparison with that of Vietnam. In 2011, for instance, Ethiopia's export revenue from textiles was US$8 million and just 9,000 workers were employed in the sector, compared with US$8 billion textile revenue in 2011 and about 1 million jobs for Vietnam (see Dinh et al., 2011). As in

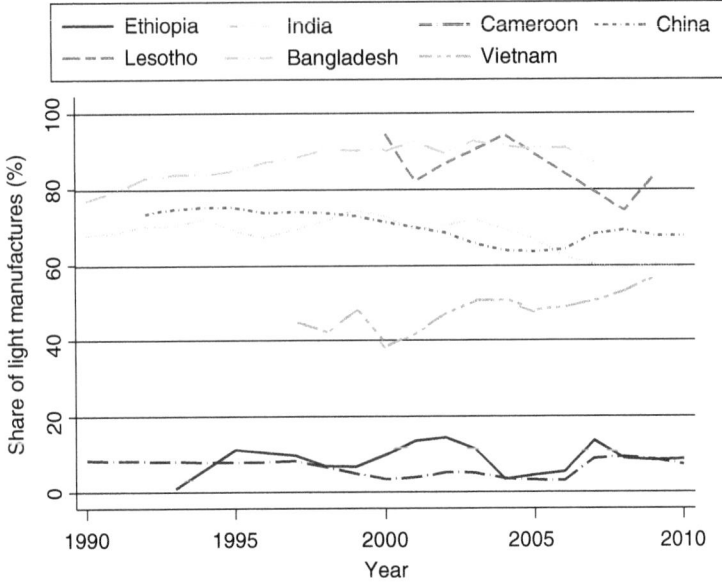

Figure 5.5.1 Share of light manufactures in merchandises exports

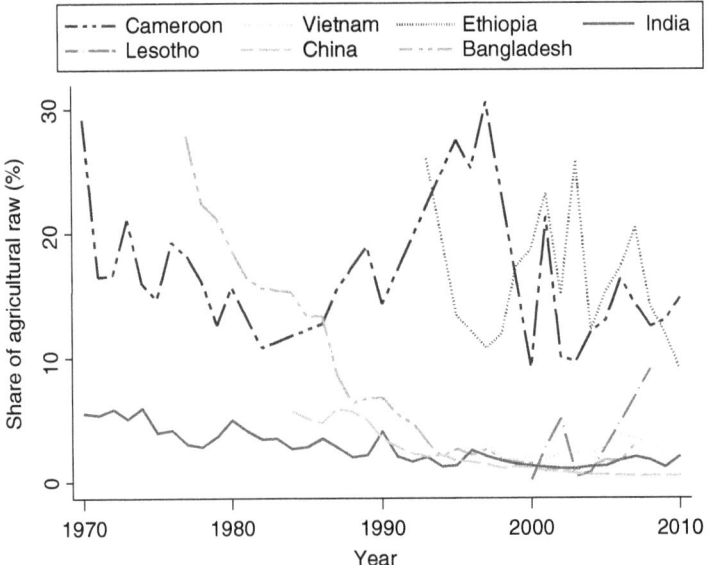

Figure 5.5.2 Share of agricultural raw material in merchandise exports

other regions, textiles and apparels in Africa are the final stage products of a long and labor-intensive production chain. The chain[9] starts with cotton growing in farms and proceeds through different stages of processing before fabrics and apparels are issued in factories and then sold to consumers in different markets. Whether the different production segments of the chain are located in the same country or in different countries, these segments need to be efficiently connected, through transport infrastructures and trade policies; emphasizing the importance of trade facilitation to facilitate efficient productivity. The fabrics and apparel production are classified as light manufacturing according to the Standard Industries Classification (SIC) and the production steps are similar across the cotton-to-textile and apparel chains in different regions. However, the success of the T&A industries as light manufacturing which fueled economic transformation has been very divergent across regions. While other regions, in particular Asia, have been considerably successful in achieving higher T&A production and export capacities, the productivity and export of these industries remain low in Africa (see Figures 5.5.3 and 5.5.4). As of 2008, the whole African textile production was estimated at US$200 million – or 0.05 percent of the total global value. This lower production could be reversed with adequate improvement in trade facilitation. For instance, China alone was able to produce 7.6 million tons of cotton in 2008 (representing 33 percent of world output) by improving infrastructures and

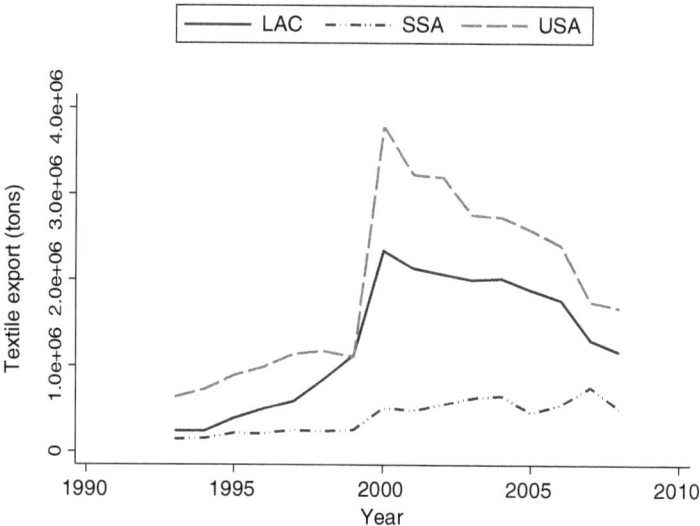

Figure 5.5.3 Textile exports of SSA, LAC, and USA (tons)

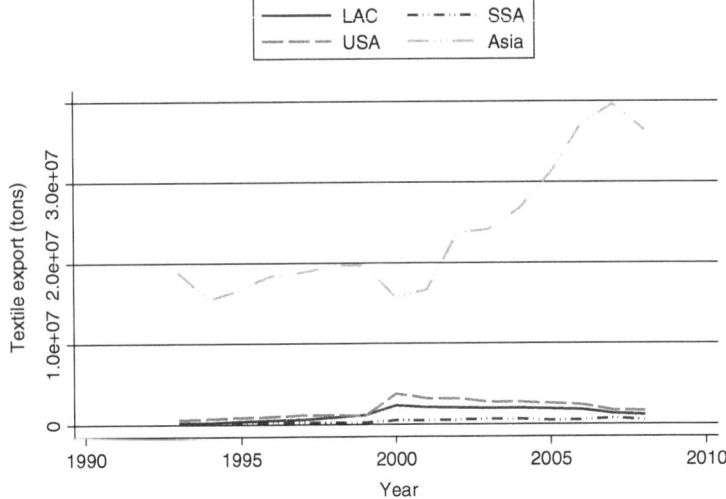

Figure 5.5.4   Textile exports Asia vs. SSA, LAC, USA (tons)

adopting policies that stimulated cotton production (ACTIF, News Letter 2009; ITC Report 2011).

The production cycle[10] highlights more clearly the importance of trade facilitation and the trade regimes. The success of the T&A industries located at the end of the chain is dependent on two major factors. The first determinant is whether production costs throughout the segments of the chain are efficient in such a way that the textile industries can compete internationally. This determinant reflects the quality of trade facilitation through efficient infrastructures and logistics to connect production segments at lower cost. The second determinant is whether there are adequate markets for final products. This determinant suggests the necessity of both regional integration[11] to enlarge the markets available for firms and also a supportive international trade regimes. In this context, the emergence of African light manufacturing requires efficient trade facilitation with particular attention to aspects that foster the region's connectivity within itself such as to bolster vibrant supply chains across its countries. In the next section we use both, qualitative and empirical analysis to assess the role of trade facilitation in enhancing regional production value chain and industrialization in Africa.

5.5.2   Trade costs and African textile and apparel industries

We use a gravity model to assess whether and the extent to which African manufacturing trade performance has been hampered by poor trade facilitation.

5.5.2.1 Trade costs and trade performance: literature review

Trade researchers, policymakers, the private sector, and civil society have reached a consensus that firms will fully benefit from access to export markets opportunities only when they can also offer competitive products (for example, Ndulu et al., 2007; Helble, Mann, and Wilson, 2011; Stiglitz and Charlton, 2012; Hoekman and Njinkeu, 2007). The efficiency of African domestic production should therefore assume center stage in the overall strategy to bolster light manufacturing and economic transformation. The improvement of trade facilitation is key to bolstering manufacturing competitiveness in Africa with more than 40 percent of the population living in landlocked countries (Ndulu et al., 2007).[12] The availability of adequate power and water supplies as well as the availability of efficient transport and trade logistics are essential not only to reduce the production cost of existing firms, but also to attract new foreign direct investment (FDI) in the capital-intensive textile industry (see USITC, 2009).

The importance of lower transport costs in fostering international trade flows has been extensively documented (see Limao and Venables, 2001; Abe and Wilson, 2009). Indeed, transport costs shape trade patterns (Behar and Venables, 2010). The lack of quantity and quality transport infrastructure and the associated higher costs of transaction both impede trade; Limao and Venables (2001) find that improving a country's infrastructure from the 75th percentile to the median leads to an increase of trade volume by 28 percent. Moreover, they show that the trade of landlocked countries is highly dependent on the quality of infrastructure in the transit countries to which they are linked. Behar, Manners, and Nelson (2009) find that for an average-sized developing country, a one standard deviation improvement in logistics is associated with approximately a 46 percent increase in the country's exports. Wilson, Mann, and Otsuki (2005) find a positive correlation between export, import, and the sophistication of all components of trade facilitation. Using the Enabling Trade Index (ETI), countries with better performing logistics tend to export more textile and apparel (T&A) (see Figures 5.5.5 and 5.5.6). Similarly, countries recording lower exports cost by container are likely to perform better in terms of exports (see Figure 5.5.7). Furthermore, the key in boosting export in a sustainable way is to focus on the whole value chain from production to efficient distribution and conservation methods (see WEF, 2012). Innovations in production that preserves resources accompanied by investment in research, storage, and logistics to reshape the production value chain are the foundation on which sustainable growth must be designed.

5.5.2.2 The state of trade facilitation and logistics in Africa

Trade facilitation and logistics involves the extent to which infrastructures and logistics available in a country are efficient in facilitating the movement

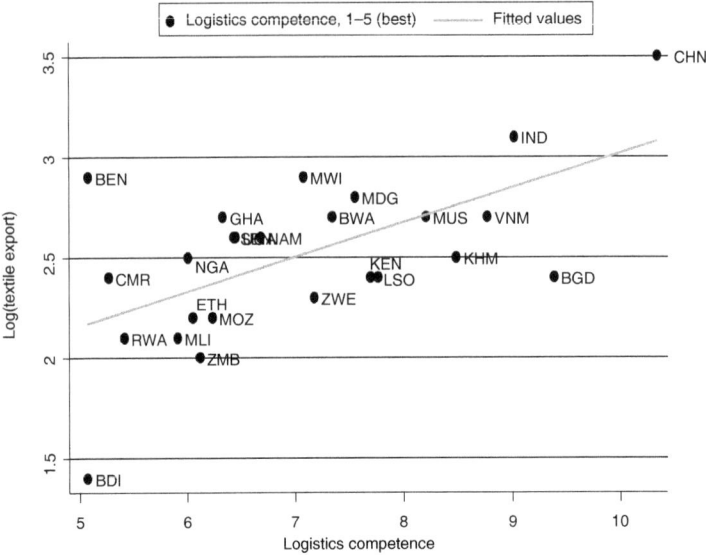

Figure 5.5.5 Correlation between logistics performance and exports

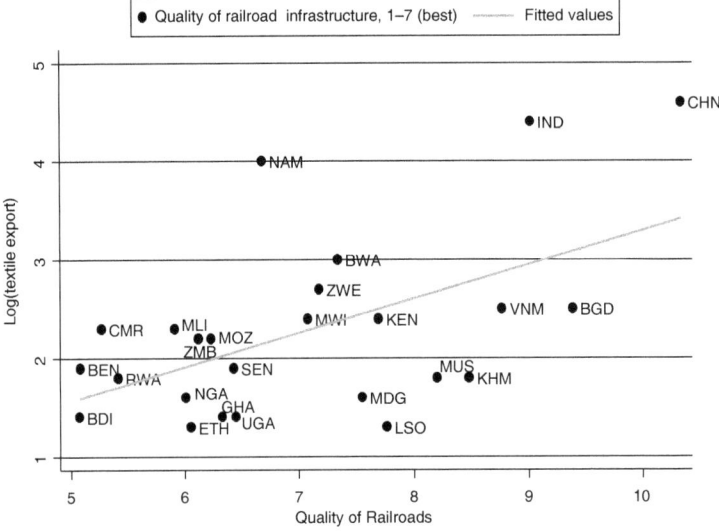

Figure 5.5.6 Correlation between railroads quality and exports

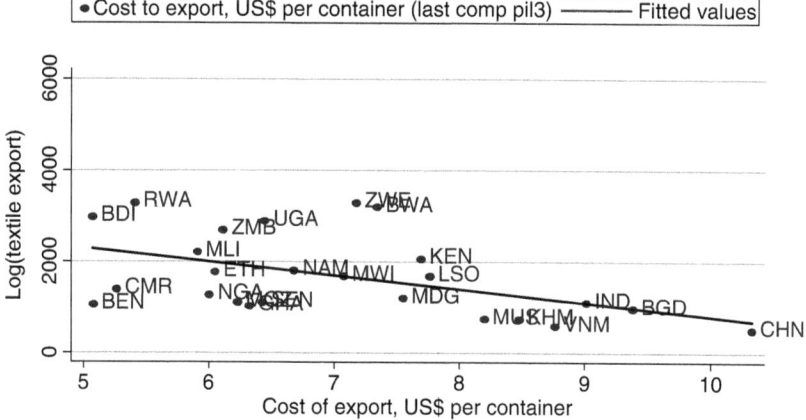

Figure 5.5.7 Correlation between cost of exports per container and exports

of goods and people both within the country and across its borders. The main constraints include: the high costs of engaging in trade, poorly performing gateway ports, poor transport infrastructures and logistics, and weak regulatory capacities. African trade facilitation performances lag behind those of its main competitors for FDI and market share in developed nations (see Tables 5.5.2 and 5.5.3). The regional averages and country-level data show that logistics – as well as the efficiency of the customs clearance process – are weaker in Africa than they are in other regions (see Tables 5.5.2 and 5.5.3). The inefficiency and weakness of trade facilitation facilities is a significant impediment to Africa's industrialization as confirmed by the Global Trade Enabling Report (GTER): "The cost of trading is a more important obstacle to trade development than trade policies" (see GTER, 2012: xvi); with the main problems being the high transaction costs associated with inefficient trade facilitation. Africa can tap into its low-skill-low-wage labor to grow high-quality cotton fibers and produce energy-intensive textile cycles with its large potential of renewal energy resources to plug into the world value chain, provided infrastructure problems are addressed (see GTER, 2012: 38).

5.5.2.3 The empirical investigation: methodology

The empirical analysis uses a gravity model analysis to explain bilateral trade flows as a function of level of development, size of the economy, geographical distance, cultural affinity, trade policies, and other fundamentals as in equation 1.[13]

$$\log(M_t^{ij}) = \alpha_0 + \alpha_1 \log(Y_t^i) + \alpha_2 \log(Y_t^j) + \alpha_3 \log(Pop_t^i) + \alpha_4 \log(Pop_t^j) + \alpha_5 \, contig^{ij}$$
$$+ \alpha_6 \log(dist^{ij}) + \alpha_7 \, comlang\_off^{ij} + \alpha_8 \, col^{ij} + \alpha_9 \, SSA^j + \varepsilon_t^{ij} \qquad (1)$$

Table 5.5.2   Regional Logistics Performance Index

Regions	Logistics Performance Index[1]			
	All Incomes		Developing Only	
	Years		Years	
	2007	2010	2007	2010
East Asia & Pacific	2.88	2.94	2.37	2.46
Europe & Central Asia	2.97	3.03	2.26	2.38
Latin America & Caribbean	2.38	2.45	2.38	2.45
Middle East & North Africa	2.56	2.74	2.21	2.36
South Asia	2.07	2.13	2.07	2.13
Sub-Saharan Africa	2.11	2.05	2.11	2.05

[1]Logistics Performance Index: Quality of trade and Transport-related Infrastructure (1 = low to 5 = high).
Source: World Bank Group, World Development Indicator Database.

Table 5.5.3 Logistics performance and efficiency of customs clearance process: selected African and Asian countries

Countries	Efficiency of Customs Clearence Process[1]		Logistics performance index: Overall[2]	
	Years		Years	
	2007	2010	2007	2010
Benin	1.8	2.38	2.45	2.79
Ghana	2	2.35	2.16	2.47
Zambia	2.08	2.17	2.37	2.28
Burkina Faso	2.13	2.22	2.24	2.23
Ethiopia	2.14	2.13	2.33	2.41
Uganda	2.21	2.84	2.49	2.82
Madagascar	2.24	2.35	2.24	2.66
Lesotho	2.4	.	2.3	.
India	2.69	2.7	3.07	3.12
Vietnam	2.89	2.68	2.89	2.96
China	2.99	3.16	3.32	3.49

Source: World Development Indicators.
[1]Efficiency of customs clearance process (1 = low to 5 = high).
[2]Logistics performance index: Overall (1 = low to 5 = high).

Where; "M^{ij}" is a measure of openness (here we use export flows at constant prices of country j to country i at year t), Y^i and Y^j are respectively the real GDPs of country *i* and country *j*. $dist^{ij}$ is the geographical distance between country *i* and *j*. Pop is the population, a series of dummy controls including: *contig*^{ij} a dummy variable that takes a value one if *i* and *j* share a same border or takes the value zero otherwise. *comlang_off[ij]* a dummy variable that takes the value one if *i* and *j* share the same official language or zero otherwise. *col[ij]* a dummy variable which takes the value one if *i* and *j* share a colonial link. All variables are in logarithms term except for the dummy variables contiguity dummy[14] ε is the error term.

5.5.2.3.1 Data used

The data used in this estimation include many variables from various reliable sources over the period from 2005 to 2012 for 156 countries depending on data availability. The import value from country *i* to country *j* denoted "M^{ij}" is from the WITS database. The GDPs of each country in the trade pair (Y^i) and (Y^j), their populations are from the World Development Indicators database (WDI). The standard variables of the gravity model (distance, common official language, colonial links, and contiguity) are sourced from CEPII.

The extents of infrastructure and logistics competence in the countries are sourced from the Logistics Performance Index (LPI). Each LPI component is computed in a special way using various factors such as they all carry special information about trade patterns (see the LPI website[15] for computation methods). LPI includes six main components. Our approach consisted of testing each of them one at a time to capture the particular information content in them, and how the improvement of any component of the LPI will affect the trade of the exporting country. Note also that the data on the LPI are provided for 2007, 2010, and 2012. However, the years of the LPI data release do not correspond to the survey period. For instance, the data provided in 2012 are the results of the surveys conducted in 2010 and 2011 (see the LPI website). We make the matching by using the data of the following year of data availability in the survey years. For example, the level of each LPI component in 2007 is used for the two preceding years (2005 and 2006), while the data of 2010 is used for 2008 and 2009. Nevertheless, the LPI data could not be extrapolated for years before 2005. Since we are interested in the extent to which trade facilitation of developing countries affects their rates of export, we use the LPI of the exporting country (that is country *j*). Other variables, such as the NTMs, could not be included due to lack of data.

5.5.2.3.2 Econometric estimation and results

Main econometric issues

The first important issue is related to time-invariant variables and their implications for the choice of econometrical approach. Given that our regression is applied to panel data, the adoption of a fixed-effect approach would have been the most appropriate in order to address the heterogeneity problem, while addressing the bias of endogeneity related to omitted variables (see Wooldridge, 2002). However, fixed-effect estimation was not appropriate in this case because many of the gravity variables (distance, common official language, colonial links, and contiguity) are time invariant. We adopted therefore, the Hausman–Taylor's panel approach, incorporating time-invariant variables (see, Hsiao, 2003).[16] Another important issue is the treatment of trade data and potential natural resource bias. We excluded oil flow from total trade. Furthermore, to capture the impact of logistics performances on manufactures, we considered an alternative model using only the textile and trade flows. Equation 1 is applied to the sample including all developing countries.[17] After estimating the reduced form of the gravity equation which shows the basic factors of trade patterns, we augment the gravity equation with the components of the logistic performance index (LPI[18]) to assess the magnitude of the impact of these factors on developing countries' trade in general (equation 2 in the annex). Moreover, we test the impact of different polities (international preferential trade agreements, sub-regional customs unions, tariffs) and their multiplicative effects with the LPI score.

Impact of the logistics performances index on total trade

The empirical results support the importance of trade facilitation in enhancing countries' export. In general, improving the LPI score by one unit increases developing countries' export on average by 16 percent. In the elasticity term, a one percent increase in the LPI score raises the country's export by 0.16 percent. Each component of the logistics performance index (LPI) has a positive and statistically significant impact on export. All components of the LPI are about equally important in boosting trade. One unit improvement in the efficiency of customs operations, infrastructure, international shipment, logistics competence, tracking-tracing shipment, and the timeliness of the shipment is associated with 18 percent, 17 percent, 16 percent, 16 percent, 16 percent, and 14 percent increase in the country's export, respectively (see Table 5.5.4 on the next page).

These findings are consistent with the trade literature on the importance of trade facilitation in enhancing trade flows, although with some caveats. While our results rely on the World Bank LPI as a trade facilitation indicator, previous studies instead used the transport costs as an indicator of trade cost. For instance, Martínez-Zarzoso et al. (2008) used sectoral data obtained from interviews with Spanish exporters and logistics operators to show that a one percent increase in infrastructure in the destination country leads to a 17 percent decrease in transport costs of the agro-industry products; and that a one percent decrease in transport cost in turn is associated with a 3.93 percent increase in export. Although these findings reveal the importance of transport costs for trade, they do not establish a direct correlation between infrastructure and export. Moreover, these results steam from sectoral data as opposed to total trade data.[19]

Impact of the trade facilitation on Africa's trade performances

The inclusion of a Sub-Saharan African (SSA) dummy in the gravity model allows us to capture to what extent Africa's trade performance is

Table 5.5.4 Gravity model applied on total exports (except oil) for developing countries

VARIABLES	Log(M^{ij})	Log(M^{ij})	Log(M^{ij})	Log(M^{ij})	Log(M^{ij})	Log(M^{ij})	Log(M^{ij})	Log(M^{ij})
log(Y^i)	0.524***	0.562***	0.560***	0.560***	0.563***	0.560***	0.562***	0.563***
	(0.0117)	(0.0116)	(0.0116)	(0.0116)	(0.0116)	(0.0116)	(0.0116)	(0.0116)
log(Y^j)	0.204***	0.239***	0.236***	0.237***	0.240***	0.237***	0.238***	0.240***
	(0.0105)	(0.0105)	(0.0105)	(0.0105)	(0.0105)	(0.0105)	(0.0105)	(0.0105)
log(Pop^i)	0.666***	0.586***	0.591***	0.590***	0.586***	0.589***	0.586***	0.585***
	(0.0216)	(0.0216)	(0.0216)	(0.0216)	(0.0216)	(0.0216)	(0.0216)	(0.0216)
log(Pop^j)	0.868***	0.773***	0.779***	0.778***	0.771***	0.776***	0.773***	0.770***
	(0.0220)	(0.0220)	(0.0220)	(0.0220)	(0.0220)	(0.0220)	(0.0220)	(0.0220)
log(dist^{ij})	-1.152***	-1.170***	-1.170***	-1.170***	-1.168***	-1.170***	-1.170***	-1.170***
	(0.0437)	(0.0434)	(0.0434)	(0.0434)	(0.0434)	(0.0434)	(0.0434)	(0.0434)
contig^{ij}	1.819***	1.855***	1.854***	1.855***	1.860***	1.852***	1.854***	1.854***
	(0.216)	(0.214)	(0.214)	(0.214)	(0.214)	(0.214)	(0.214)	(0.214)
comlang_off^{ij}	1.164***	1.140***	1.139***	1.139***	1.143***	1.141***	1.141***	1.141***
	(0.0881)	(0.0875)	(0.0876)	(0.0876)	(0.0875)	(0.0875)	(0.0875)	(0.0875)
col^{ij}	0.657	0.788*	0.782*	0.784*	0.783*	0.785*	0.791*	0.792*
	(0.433)	(0.430)	(0.430)	(0.430)	(0.430)	(0.430)	(0.430)	(0.430)
SSA_dummy	-1.933***	-1.906***	-1.909***	-1.901***	-1.905***	-1.909***	-1.907***	-1.905***
	(0.0649)	(0.0645)	(0.0645)	(0.0645)	(0.0645)	(0.0645)	(0.0645)	(0.0645)

(continued)

Table 5.5.4 Continued

VARIABLES	Log(M^{ij})	Log(M^{ij})	Log(M^{ij})	Log(M^{ij})	Log(M^{ij})	Log(M^{ij})	Log(M^{ij})
LPI_score^j	0.164*** (0.00501)						
Customs^j		0.176*** (0.00547)					
Infrastructure^j			0.173*** (0.00545)				
IS^j				0.163*** (0.00497)			
LC^j					0.165*** (0.00516)		
TT^j						0.161*** (0.00493)	
Timeliness^j							0.137*** (0.00417)
Constant	−17.48*** (0.585)	−16.64*** (0.582)	−16.67*** (0.582)	−16.65*** (0.582)	−16.68*** (0.582)	−16.65*** (0.582)	−16.62*** (0.582)
Observations	65,545	65,545	65,545	65,545	65,545	65,545	65,545
# of Groups	12,747	12,747	12,747	12,747	12,747	12,747	12,747
R_Square	0.4	0.4	0.4	0.4	0.4	0.4	0.4

Note: IS = international shipment; LC = Logistics Competence; TT = tracking-tracing the shipment.
Y^i, Y^j are respectively the real GDPs of country i and j. M^{ij} is the real import value of country i from j.
col = colonial link; comlang-off = common official language; contig = contiguity; pop = population.
The heteroscedastic standard errors in brackets.
*** p < 0.01, ** p < 0.05, * p < 0.1.

different from that of other developing countries. As expected, the results reveal that SSA countries undertake about half the level of trade of other developing countries (see Table 5.5.4). In order to determine the role of trade facilitation in explaining this performance gap between Africa and other developing countries, we compared the coefficients of SSA dummies determined in two different models. A gravity model including the logistic performance index on one hand, and on the other a gravity model excluding this indicator. The results point to a reduction, albeit slight, in the magnitude of the SSA dummy when the LPI is introduced. This indicates that the improvement of trade facilitation in SSA would positively impact its trade performances.

Impact of the logistics performances index on Africa's exports of textile and apparel

To assess the performance of textile exports, we run the gravity model this time using textile trade flows, instead of total trade, as the dependent variable. All the right-hand side variables remain the same on the model as applied before. As expected, African performance in exporting textile is poor compared to other developing countries. The dummy variable capturing Africa's specific effect is negative and significantly different from zero. Its magnitude, −1.9, meaning that Africa's textile export is as much lower as its total trade as shown in Table 5.5.4 above. However, Africa's textile export improves under AGOA. The introduction of AGOA in the model reduces in absolute value the magnitude of the extent to which Africa exports textile less than other countries (from −1.9 to −1.6) (see Table 5.5.5). This suggests that even if Africa is performing poorly in textile sector relative to other regions, AGOA has a positive impact on this sector. Moreover, it is remarkable that a better trade facilitation would have enhanced AGOA's impact on African textile and apparel sector.

In order to determine the impact of the trade facilitation on African textile exports, we generated a variable "LPI_AGOA" by multiplying the AGOA dummy by the LPI score. "LPI_AGOA" gives the multiplicative effect of the LPI on AGOA. The coefficient of the "LPI_AGOA" is .28 and significantly different from zero in the model estimate (Table 5.5.5, end column). Thus, a one unit improvement in LPI trade facilitation will increase Africa's textile export under AGOA by an additional 28 percent. In other words, improving trade facilitation by one percent in the presence of AGOA will increase textile exports from Africa by 0.28 percent; suggesting that trade facilitation explains an important part of the African performance gap in the area of textile exports. Thus, a poor trade facilitation environment impedes African trade in general and the textile sector in particular than the rest of the economic on average. This finding is not surprising, as it largely reflects the new reality of textile industry characterized by fragmented production chains that required quality logistics and communications network.

Table 5.5.5   Gravity model applied on textile exports only for developing countries

VARIABLES	Log(M^{ij})	Log(M^{ij})	Log(M^{ij})	Log(M^{ij})
log(Y^i)	0.684***	0.700***	0.700***	0.700***
	(0.0130)	(0.0125)	(0.0125)	(0.0125)
log(Y^j)	0.132***	0.141***	0.141***	0.141***
	(0.0122)	(0.0118)	(0.0118)	(0.0118)
log(Pop^i)	0.173***	0.185***	0.189***	0.186***
	(0.0240)	(0.0231)	(0.0232)	(0.0231)
log(Pop^j)	0.947***	0.918***	0.917***	0.918***
	(0.0236)	(0.0228)	(0.0228)	(0.0228)
log(dist^{ij})	−1.066***	−1.091***	−1.087***	−1.090***
	(0.0467)	(0.0450)	(0.0450)	(0.0450)
contig^{ij}	1.700***	1.685***	1.682***	1.683***
	(0.208)	(0.200)	(0.200)	(0.200)
comlang off^{ij}	0.371***	0.896***	0.906***	0.899***
	(0.0941)	(0.0927)	(0.0927)	(0.0926)
col^{ij}	0.869**	0.611*	0.604	0.608*
	(0.383)	(0.369)	(0.369)	(0.369)
SSA_dummy		−1.995***	−1.657***	−1.152***
		(0.0727)	(0.0766)	(0.355)
AGOA_dummy			1.183***	
			(0.351)	
LPI_AGOA				0.280***
				(0.0889)
Constant	−17.43***	−17.09***	−17.19***	−17.13***
	(0.608)	(0.586)	(0.587)	(0.586)
Observations	44,669	44,669	44,669	44,669
# of groups	10,286	10,286	10,286	10,286
R-square	0.5	0.5	0.5	0.5

Note: M^{ij} is the real value of textile import from j to i;
Y^i, Y^j are respectively the real GDPs of country i and j;
col = colonial link; comlang-off = common official language; contig = contiguity; pop = population.
The heteroscedastic standard errors in brackets.
*** $p < 0.01$, ** $p < 0.05$, * $p < 0.1$.

5.5.3   Trade facilitation and the efficiency of trade policies

Above the need for domestic reform agenda, trade openness and compliance[20] to multilateral rules that govern international trade have historically been central to economics transformation. Using the data on 113 countries from 1950 to 2009, Wacziarg and Welch (2008) found that, on average, the growth rate of countries across the world improved by 2.1 percent after trade liberalization. In China and India, the post-liberalization growth improvement is even higher, at 2.7 percentage points above the world average; making them the fastest-growing countries. In Africa, decades of multilateral trade liberalization, preferential trade market access, and regional integration initiatives failed to produce substantial results in terms of trade and growth. This section examines to what extent this failure can be associated with the poor trade facilitation environment. More specifically, we analyze to what extent trade policies implemented in a country with quality trade facilitation would have a better outcome in fostering textile exports.

5.5.3.1 Trade facilitation is key for regional integration success in fostering industrialization

Sub-Saharan Africa is fragmented into small geographic areas while countries' geographical sizes and population are important factors for their development and industrialization as market sizes matter for the achievement of economies of scale.[21] Specialization in production was traditionally driven by factor endowment and/or technology differences (Heckscher, 1919; Ohlin, 1933). However, economic activities have converged following economies of scale which led to large intra-industry trade, even in the case of similarities in endowments and technologies (Grubel and Lloyd, 1975). Economies of scale are an important factor in specialization and the spatial dimension of the economies of scale is a crucial determinant for firm's location decision. Two key factors, namely market size and the share of fixed cost in the total cost that drive firms' abilities, are necessary in order to exploit economies of scale, and undertake mass production. The extent of domestic market and regional market opportunities is the first key factor in firms' location decisions and this factor has made Asian emerging countries more attractive to foreign investments[22] (see Global Enabling Trade Report, 2012).

Economies of scale that lead to gains in competitiveness are a necessity for African firms.[23] Poor-quality infrastructure has been identified as an important impediment preventing African firms from fully exploiting economies of scale associated with regional integration initiatives (see UNECA and UA, 2012, p. 23). Our econometric results in Table 5.5.6 shows that being part of a trade integration initiative in Africa is a positive factor in bolstering trade performance, as the coefficient on the regional integration dummy turns out to be positive and statistically significant.

To assess the sensitivity of regional integration to trade facilitation, we introduced into our gravity model a multiplicative variable, multiplying the African regional integration dummy "WithinSSA_dummy" by the trade facilitation indicator (LPI score)- "LPI_WithinSSA_dummy." We also tested the sensitivity of regional integration to each of the LPI components[24] (see Table 5.5.6). Results show that the trade facilitation would boost regional trade performances and enhance textile exports. Each component of the LPI has a positive and statistically significant impact on regional integration in Africa (Table 5.5.6). Therefore, African countries should prioritize trade facilitation in the agenda of regional integration and industrialization.

Table 5.5.6 Regional integration and trade facilitation to boost African textile exports

VARIABLES	Log(M^{ij})	Log(M^{ij})	Log(M^{ij})	Log(M^{ij})	Log(M^{ij})	Log(M^{ij})	Log(M^{ij})	Log(M^{ij})
log(Y^j)	0.745***	0.746***	0.746***	0.746***	0.747***	0.746***	0.746***	0.746***
	(0.0242)	(0.0242)	(0.0242)	(0.0242)	(0.0242)	(0.0242)	(0.0242)	(0.0242)
log(Y^i)	0.0992***	0.100***	0.100***	0.100***	0.100***	0.100***	0.100***	0.100***
	(0.0211)	(0.0211)	(0.0211)	(0.0211)	(0.0211)	(0.0211)	(0.0211)	(0.0211)
log(Pop^j)	0.127***	0.123***	0.123***	0.123***	0.122***	0.123***	0.123***	0.124***
	(0.0440)	(0.0440)	(0.0440)	(0.0440)	(0.0440)	(0.0440)	(0.0440)	(0.0440)
log(Pop^j)	0.268***	0.263***	0.263***	0.264***	0.263***	0.264***	0.264***	0.264***
	(0.0476)	(0.0476)	(0.0476)	(0.0476)	(0.0476)	(0.0476)	(0.0476)	(0.0476)
log(dist^{ij})	-1.178***	-1.177***	-1.176***	-1.177***	-1.177***	-1.177***	-1.176***	-1.177***
	(0.104)	(0.104)	(0.104)	(0.104)	(0.1C4)	(0.104)	(0.104)	(0.104)
contig^{ij}	1.148***	1.155***	1.158***	1.155***	1.156***	1.153***	1.155***	1.152***
	(0.350)	(0.349)	(0.349)	(0.349)	(0.349)	(0.349)	(0.349)	(0.349)
comlang_off^{ij}	0.615***	0.618***	0.618***	0.617***	0.618***	0.618***	0.618***	0.617***
	(0.140)	(0.140)	(0.140)	(0.140)	(0.140)	(0.140)	(0.140)	(0.140)
col^{ij}	-1.052	-1.048	-1.049	-1.048	-1.048	-1.049	-1.048	-1.048
	(0.774)	(0.774)	(0.774)	(0.774)	(0.774)	(0.774)	(0.774)	(0.773)
WithinSSA_dummy	1.664***	1.486***	1.472***	1.485***	1.469***	1.496***	1.497***	1.513***
	(0.284)	(0.292)	(0.292)	(0.292)	(0.292)	(0.292)	(0.292)	(0.292)

433

	(1) LPI	(2) Infra	(3) CUST	(4) IS	(5) LC	(6) TT	(7) TMLNS
LPI_WithinSSA_dummy	0.134*** (0.0517)						
Infra_WithinSSA_dummy		0.164*** (0.0581)					
CUST_WithinSSA_dummy			0.15*** (0.0561)				
IS_WithinSSA_dummy				0.144*** (0.0504)			
LC_WithinSSA_dummy					0.131** (0.0527)		
TT_WithinSSA_dummy						0.124** (0.0509)	
TMLNS_WithinSSA_dummy							0.0956** (0.0430)
Constant	−7.113*** (1.381)	−7.058*** (1.381)	−7.059*** (1.381)	−7.049*** (1.381)	−7.063*** (1.380)	−7.064*** (1.381)	−7.065*** (1.380)
Observations	10,309	10,309	10,309	10,309	10,309	10,309	10,309
# of Groups	2,935	2,935	2,935	2,935	2,935	2,935	2,935
R-Square	0.36	0.36	0.36	0.36	0.36	0.36	0.36

Note: Cust = customs; IS = international shipment; LC = Logistics Competence; TT = tracking-tracing the shipment; tmlns = timeliness; Infra = Infrastructure; Y^i, Y^j are respectively the real GDPs of country i and j. M^{ij} is the real value of textile import from j to i. col = colonial link; comlang-off = common official language; contig = contiguity; pop = population. The heteroscedastic standard errors in brackets.
*** p < 0.01, ** p < 0.05, * p < 0.1.

5.5.3.2   Trade facilitation is important for the success of preferential systems in Africa

Preferential trade schemes – trade arrangements between groups of countries or two countries – are crucial to the process of African industrialization because they enlarge the extent of market to firms while reducing the access costs as a result of the special arrangements. With yhe aim of stimulating sustainable industrialization, preference schemes should enable African firms to progressively secure a strong position in international markets. African countries trade internationally under several preferential trade schemes, with the most important being AGOA, the ACP–EU Cotonou Agreement, the special LDC preference, and the European Generalized System of Preference (GSP) comprising the standard GSP, the special incentive arrangement (GSP+), and the "Everything But Arms" (EBA) agreement. The common feature of all these preferential arrangement remains the extent of the market and the reduced tariff rates that they offer to eligible countries. Despite the dismal level of industrialization that can be attributed to these schemes there are successes when some basic conditions prevail as the case of AGOA illustrates.

AGOA was initiated in 2000 to provide eligible African countries with preferential access (under the generalized preferential system – GPS) to US markets. Export of Africa's textile products more than doubled from its 1998–2000 level. Investment in new manufacturing of textile and garments in the Southern African region (SACU[25] countries) became more attractive under AGOA. The region's textile and garments export increased sharply between 2000 and 2004, moving from 306,516 tons in 2000 to 467,180 tons in 2004, before falling in 2005 to 253,371 tons (see Table 5.5.7). The total textile products export of SSA in 2000 (509,644 tons) was almost twice that the level of 1999 (255,938 tons) – before the implementation of AGOA. SSA's textile products export continued to grow until 2004, reaching

Table 5.5.7   Increase in Africa's textile exports under AGOA (measures in tons)

Year	SSA	Percentage Change in SSA Export
1995	215147	.
1998	238568	11
2000	509644	114
2002	550978	8
2004	657397	19
2005	457105	–30
2006	548009	20

Source: Authors' Calculation using UN COMTRADE Database- 2 digit SITC.
Note: Textile products included are the Code 59, 60, 61, 62, and 63 of the HS.

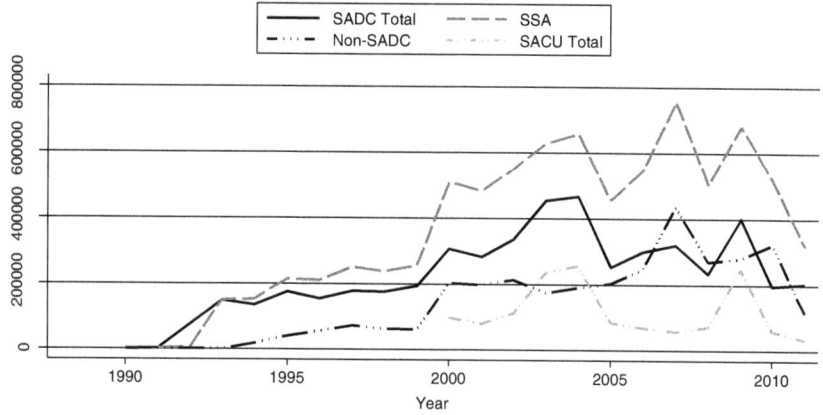

Figure 5.5.8 Sub-regional textile exports under AGOA

657,397 tons. This export boom was accompanied by job creation. AGOA[26] generated in eligible countries more than 150,000 jobs in the T&A sector ("The Whitaker Group"[27]). Although AGOA has been a big push for African export, improving trade facilitation would have magnified its effects (Table 5.5.11 in Appendix 2).[28]

What is the impact of trade facilitation on preferential trade schemes?

We first created a dummy capturing the two most important preferential trade agreements in Africa: AGOA and the ACP–EU Cotonou Agreement. That variable takes 1 when a country is part of at least one of these schemes, and zero otherwise. The preferential dummy is tested relying on a model of textile exports flows from developing countries. Results are not significant, suggesting that preferential trade agreement has not effect on African textile trade.

We also tested the multiplicative dummy multiplying the LPI by the regional agreement dummy. Once again, the results are not significant. However, when we consider preferential agreement separately, the effect of AGOA turns out to be positive. Furthermore, the impacts of the multiplicative effect of LPI on AGOA are positive and significant (see Table 5.5.11 in Appendix 2). Although AGOA doubled SSA trade (see Table 5.5.11), results show that the multiplicative effect of the LPI on AGOA is an additional 22 percent of trade. Which means a one unit improvement of African LPI in the presence of AGOA will provide an additional 22 percent increase in the countries' export. Tables 5.5.10 and 5.5.11 in Appendix 2 also show that the improvement in the LPI scores would offset the negative impacts of tariffs (tariffs of origin and destination) on African exports (see the positive and statistically significant coefficients of *the LPI_tariff_wa_imp and LPI_tariff_wa_exp*).

Conclusion

This paper argues that improvements in the trade facilitation environment would be a crucial driving force for African industrialization. Trade facilitation is also key to optimizing the outcome of trade policies initiated either at national, regional, or multilateral levels. The empirical findings in this paper confirm the importance of trade facilitation for African industrialization regional integration and African industrialization depend to a great degree on the extent to which countries take complementary actions to improve the regional infrastructures and logistics, and increase the efficiency of their customs' operation and other trade facilitation facilities. Supportive market access is also important.

Annex: The Model

The model controls for some trade factors such as the distance between the pair countries ($dist^{ij}$), whether the two countries share a border ($contiguity^{ij}$), whether the countries share a common official language ($comlang\_off^{ij}$). These trade factor dummies are extracted from the Mayer and Zignago (2011).[29] The data also includes the weighted average tariffs of both, importing and exporter country retrieved from WITS database. In order to access the effects of various preferential arrangements (PTA), we created the dummy variables for the PTA of our interest (AGOA, ACP, and EBA). Since AGOA is a PTA between the United States (US) and African countries, the AGOA dummy takes the value one if the exporter is an African AGOA beneficiary and the importer is the USA, or the dummy takes the value zero otherwise. The ACP and EBA are both between the eligible developing countries and the European Union. The ACP dummy as well as the EBA dummy takes the value one if the exporter is ACP/ EBA eligible country and the importer is a European Union country. We also generated sub-regional customs union dummies for WAEMU,[30] CEMAC,[31] SADC,[32] SACU,[33] EAC,[34] ECOWAS,[35] ASEAN,[36] and CELAC[37] to see how each of these unions (Free Trade Agreements -FTAs) trade among themselves relative to other groups. Each FTA dummy takes the value one if both, the importer and the exporter are member of the FTA. To assess the multiplicative effects of LPI on other policies (that is how trade facilitation can impact trade under PTAs, FTAs, and tariffs effects), we further generated the LPI_PTA, LPI_FTA, and LPI_tariffs variables. These variables are obtained by multiplying the LPI score by the PTA, FTA or tariffs. The estimation results on each policy and its multiplicative effects with LPI are given in distinct tables (see Tables 5.5.4, 5.5.8, 5.5.9, and 5.5.10). A sample including SSA countries only is also estimated using the same variables and methodology to emphasize how trade facilitation is particularly important for SSA region in its industrialization goal.

The reduced and augmented forms of the gravity equation are constructed as follow:

$$
\begin{aligned}
\log(M_t^{ij}) = {} & \alpha_0 + \alpha_1 \log(Y_t^i) + \alpha_2 \log(Y_t^j) + \alpha_3 \log(Pop_t^i) + \alpha_4 \log(Pop_t^j) \\
& + \alpha_5 contig^{ij} + \alpha_6 \log(dist^{ij}) + \alpha_7 comlang\_off^{ij} + \alpha_8 col^{ij} + \alpha_9 SSA^j + \varepsilon_t^{ij} \quad (1)
\end{aligned}
$$

$$
\begin{aligned}
\log(M_t^{ij}) = {} & \alpha_0 + \alpha_1 \log(Y_t^i) + \alpha_2 \log(Y_t^j) + \alpha_3 \log(pop_t^i) + \alpha_4 \log(pop_t^j) \\
& + \alpha_5 contig^{ij} + \alpha_6 \log(dist^{ij}) + \alpha_7 comlang\_off^{ij} + \alpha_8 col^{ij} + \alpha_9 SSA^j \\
& + \alpha_{10} LPI_{comp}^j + \varepsilon_t^{ij} \quad\quad\quad\quad\quad\quad\quad\quad\quad\quad\quad\quad\quad\quad\quad (2)
\end{aligned}
$$

$$
\begin{aligned}
\log(M_t^{ij}) = {} & \alpha_0 + \alpha_1 \log(Y_t^i) + \alpha_2 \log(Y_t^j) + \alpha_3 \log(pop_t^i) + \alpha_4 \log(pop_t^j) \\
& + \alpha_5 contig^{ij} + \alpha_6 \log(dist^{ij}) + \alpha_7 comlang\_off^{ij} + \alpha_8 col^{ij} \\
& + \alpha_9 PTA\_dummy_t^{ij} + \alpha_{10} LPI\_PTA\_dummy_t^{ij} + \alpha_{11}\varepsilon_t^{ij} \quad\quad\quad (3)
\end{aligned}
$$

$$
\begin{aligned}
\log(M_t^{ij}) = {} & \alpha_0 + \alpha_1 \log(Y_t^i) + \alpha_2 \log(Y_t^j) + \alpha_3 \log(pop_t^i) + \alpha_4 \log(pop_t^j) \\
& + \alpha_5 contig^{ij} + \alpha_6 \log(dist^{ij}) + \alpha_7 comlang\_off^{ij} + \alpha_8 col^{ij} \\
& + \alpha_9 FTA\_dummy_t^{ij} + \alpha_{10} LPI\_FTA\_dummy_t^{ij} + \alpha_{11}\varepsilon_t^{ij} \quad\quad\quad (4)
\end{aligned}
$$

$$
\begin{aligned}
\log(M_t^{ij}) = {} & \alpha_0 + \alpha_1 \log(Y_t^i) + \alpha_2 \log(Y_t^j) + \alpha_3 \log(pop_t^i) + \alpha_4 \log(pop_t^j) \\
& + \alpha_5 contig^{ij} + \alpha_6 \log(dist^{ij}) + \alpha_7 comlang\_off^{ij} + \alpha_8 col^{ij} \\
& + \alpha_9 Tariff\_WA_t^i + \alpha_{10} LPI\_tariff\_WA_t^i + \alpha_{11} Tariff\_WA_t^j \\
& + \alpha_{12} LPI\_Tariff\_WA_t^j + \alpha_{11}\varepsilon_t^{ij} \quad\quad\quad\quad\quad\quad\quad\quad\quad\quad\quad\quad (5)
\end{aligned}
$$

Where M_t^{ij} represents the real import value of country i from country j at time t. Y^i and Y^j are respectively the real GDPs of country i and country j. Pop^i is the population of country i while Pop^j is the population of country j. Log represents the natural log of the respective values. $dist^{ij}$ is the geographical distance between country i and j; $contig^{ij}$ is the dummy variable that takes a value one if i and j share a same border or takes the value zero otherwise. $comlang\_off^{ij}$ is a dummy variable that takes the value one if i and j share the same official language or zero otherwise. col^{ij} is also a dummy variable which takes the value one if i and j share a colonial link. PTA reflects the preferential trade agreements (AGOA, ACP, and EBA); FTA represents the various customs unions (WAEMU, CEMAC, SADC, SACU, EAC, ECOWAS, ASEAN, and CELAC). $Tariff\_WA$ is the tariff weighted average.

Appendix 1: Cotton-to-Textile Chain and other figures

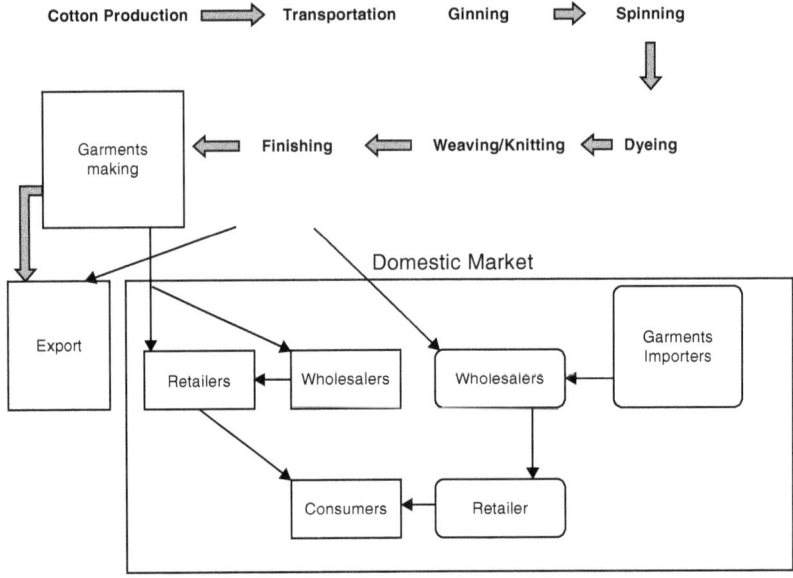

Figure 5.5.9   Scheme of cotton-to-clothing supply chain
Source: Author's design using COMESA's Regional Strategy for Cotton-to-Clothing Value Chain.

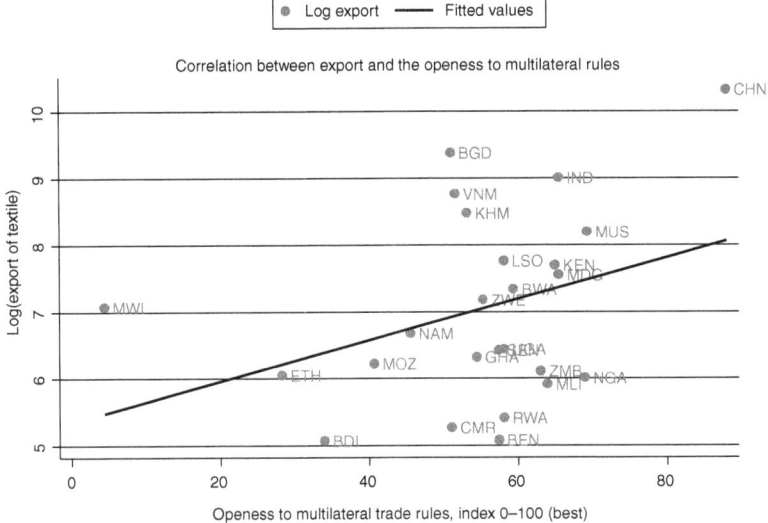

Figure 5.5.10   Correlation between exports and the openness to multilateral rules

Box 5.5.1   Trade Facilitation (TF)

Trade Facilitation can be defined as trade reforms designed to improve infrastructures related to transport and logistics, reduce border thickness to ease cross border trade and the liberalization of foreign exchange markets. Trade facilitation allows countries to produce competitive goods and service by reducing transaction and trade costs. However, trade facilitation is a complex terminology that encompasses various factors. Based on the World Bank's cross-cutting approach to trade facilitation, the major factors that constitute the bottlenecks to trade facilitation include:

- Infrastructure investment
- Customs modernization and border crossing environment
- Streamlining of documentary requirements and information flows
- Automation and EDI
- Ports efficiency
- Logistics and transport services: regulation and competitiveness
- Transit and multimode transport
- Transport security

Given the crucial role of trade facilitation in developing countries' integration in world trade and the great importance that the World Bank attach to it, the Bank has made available a comprehensive index toolkit called "logistics performance index (LPI)" measuring different aspects of trade facilitation.

- For more information on trade facilitation, see http://web.worldbank. org/WBSITE/EXTERNAL/TOPICS/TRADE/0,,contentMDK:20550369~me nuPK:261317~pagePK:148956~piPK:216618~theSitePK:239071,00.html
- For more information about the logistics performance index see http://data.worldbank.org/data-catalog/logistics-performance-index

Box 5.5.2   Light Manufacturing

Light manufactures can be roughly defined as the process of applying manual labor or machineries to assembly raw materials and obtain a new product. Or light manufactures are early stage products after procession through a division of labor. In general, the participation in light manufacturing does not require workers high labor skills. Given its intensive labor and limited skill requirements, the importance of light manufacturing in engineering economic development lies in its ability to generate many remunerated jobs for all. Based on the World Bank's approach to light manufacturing as a development tool, light manufacturing covers various sectors including: textile and apparel, leather goods production, metal products, agribusiness, and wood products.

For more details about light manufacturing, see for example light manufacturing in Africa by World Bank 2010 at http://siteresources.worldbank.org/DEC/Resources/LightManufacturingInAfrica-FullReport.pdf

Appendix 2: Result Tables of the Gravity Equation Estimation

Table 5.5.8   The Impacts of preferential trade agreements on developing countries' trade

VARIABLES	Log(Mⁱʲ)	Log(Mⁱʲ)	Log(Mⁱʲ)	Log(Mⁱʲ)	Log(Mⁱʲ)	Log(Mⁱʲ)
log(Yⁱ)	0.515***	0.515***	0.515***	0.515***	0.516***	0.516***
	(0.0120)	(0.0120)	(0.0120)	(0.0120)	(0.0120)	(0.0120)
log(Yʲ)	0.186***	0.186***	0.188***	0.188***	0.190***	0.190***
	(0.0108)	(0.0108)	(0.0108)	(0.0108)	(0.0108)	(0.0108)
log(Popⁱ)	0.656***	0.656***	0.635***	0.634***	0.628***	0.627***
	(0.0223)	(0.0223)	(0.0224)	(0.0224)	(0.0223)	(0.0223)
log(Popʲ)	0.880***	0.880***	0.866***	0.865***	0.873***	0.871***
	(0.0227)	(0.0227)	(0.0227)	(0.0227)	(0.0226)	(0.0226)
log(distⁱʲ)	−1.092***	−1.092***	−1.089***	−1.089***	−1.106***	−1.106***
	(0.0452)	(0.0452)	(0.0450)	(0.0450)	(0.0449)	(0.0449)
contigⁱʲ	1.949***	1.949***	1.887***	1.887***	1.841***	1.841***
	(0.223)	(0.223)	(0.223)	(0.223)	(0.222)	(0.222)
comlang_offⁱʲ	0.706***	0.706***	0.653***	0.652***	0.612***	0.611***
	(0.0899)	(0.0899)	(0.0898)	(0.0898)	(0.0895)	(0.0895)
colⁱʲ	0.942**	0.942**	1.272***	1.273***	1.294***	1.296***
	(0.448)	(0.448)	(0.449)	(0.449)	(0.446)	(0.446)
agoadummy	1.183***	1.133***				
	(0.351)	(0.378)				
LPI_AGOA		0.0331				
		(0.0926)				
acp_eu_dummy			−1.071***	−1.097***		
			(0.118)	(0.121)		
LPI_ACP				0.0179		
				(0.0178)		
eba_eu_dummy					−1.741***	−1.792***
					(0.129)	(0.132)
LPI_EBA						0.0354*
						(0.0205)
Constant	−17.90***	−17.90***	−17.30***	−17.29***	−17.19***	−17.18***
	(0.606)	(0.606)	(0.608)	(0.608)	(0.604)	(0.604)
Observations	65,545	65,545	65,545	65,545	65,545	65,545
# of Groups	12,747	12,747	12,747	12,747	12,747	12,747
R-Square	0.4	0.4	0.4	0.4	0.4	0.4

Note: Yⁱ, Yʲ are respectively the real GDPs of country *i* and *j*. Mⁱʲ is the real import value of country i from j. Col = colonial link; comlang-off = common official language;
contig = contiguity; pop = population.
The heteroscedastic standard errors in brackets.
*** p < 0.01, ** p < 0.05, * p < 0.1.

Defragmenting African Trade Policies

While the preferential trade schemes offer market opportunities for African firms, the eligibility conditions, and some of their features need to be reviewed as they tend to deteriorate the regional integration objectives. In many cases, not only all countries are not eligible, but import into countries of the same regional integration scheme face different tariff rate structures. For instance, the EBA applies only to least developed countries (LDCs). Imports of all products (except arms) from LDCs enter duty free to the European Union territories under the EBA. Thus, depending on whether they are classified as LDCs or non-LDCs some African countries benefit from a completely duty free access to the European markets under the EBA while others do not enjoy such duty free access. Such fragmentation of countries can explain why preferential trade arrangements like the EBA or ACP have negative impacts on developing countries' trade as shown in the empirical results (see Table 5.5.8 in Appendix 2). To enable non-LDCs products to enter duty free into its markets, the EU has proposed that African countries or group of countries enter into Economic Partnership Agreement (EPA) through which European firms will enjoy greater access to African markets. However, such increased access by European firm on African markets would undermine the investment decision of local firms and thus, retard their emergence and African industrialization.

Based on the latest press release[38] of the European commission, 33 African countries are eligible for the EBA. These countries are: Angola, Burkina Faso, Burundi, Benin, Chad, Congo (Democratic Republic of), Central African (Republic), Djibouti, Eritrea, Ethiopia, Gambia, Guinea, Equatorial Guinea, Guinea-Bissau, Comoros Islands, Liberia, Lesotho, Madagascar, Mali, Mauritania, Malawi, Mozambique, Niger, Rwanda, Sudan, Sierra Leone, Senegal, Somalia, Sao Tome and Principe, Togo, Tanzania, Uganda, Zambia. Thus, not all African countries are eligible. The selection of countries for EBA eligibility is cause of serious concern for African traders. For instance, Cameroon, Côte D'Ivoire and Kenya are the economic hubs for their respective sub-regions and they are not beneficiaries of the EBA. If a decision to create a cotton-to-textile value chain within the West African Economic and Monetary Union (WAEMU) for example was made, Côte D'Ivoire would play a major role. However, the participation of Côte D'Ivoire in such production chain would jeopardize the export of the final product to EU duty free under the EBA as Côte D'Ivoire is not a beneficiary. While the creation of a regional value chain in cotton-to-textile would improve regional productivity of textile and regional integration, the selectivity of the EBA ultimately blocks such initiative.

In addition, applied tariff rates on different goods vary across the origin countries on the European Union markets. While the standard GSP offers different rates of tariff to the eligible countries to access EU markets, the

Table 5.5.9 Trade within subregional customs unions and their sensitivity to the LPI

VARIABLES	Log(M^{ij})	Log(M^{ij})	Log(M^{ij})	Log(M^{ij})	Log(M^{ij})	Log(M^{ij})	Log(M^{ij})
log(Y^i)	0.515***	0.515***	0.515***	0.515***	0.516***	0.517***	0.515***
	(0.0121)	(0.0121)	(0.0121)	(0.0121)	(0.0120)	(0.0120)	(0.0120)
log(Y^j)	0.186***	0.186***	0.186***	0.186***	0.188***	0.189***	0.186***
	(0.0108)	(0.0108)	(0.0108)	(0.0108)	(0.0108)	(0.0108)	(0.0108)
log(Pop^i)	0.660***	0.660***	0.661***	0.661***	0.659***	0.657***	0.660***
	(0.0223)	(0.0223)	(0.0224)	(0.0224)	(0.0223)	(0.0223)	(0.0223)
log(Pop^j)	0.880***	0.880***	0.881***	0.881***	0.878***	0.876***	0.880***
	(0.0227)	(0.0227)	(0.0227)	(0.0227)	(0.0227)	(0.0227)	(0.0227)
log(dist^{ij})	−1.086***	−1.086***	−1.088***	−1.088***	−1.081***	−1.081***	−1.089***
	(0.0453)	(0.0453)	(0.0452)	(0.0452)	(0.0453)	(0.0453)	(0.0452)
contig^{ij}	1.916***	1.916***	1.921***	1.920***	1.886***	1.887***	1.940***
	(0.225)	(0.225)	(0.226)	(0.226)	(0.224)	(0.224)	(0.224)
comlang_off^{ij}	0.708***	0.707***	0.713***	0.713***	0.704***	0.705***	0.716***
	(0.0903)	(0.0903)	(0.0901)	(0.0901)	(0.0900)	(0.0900)	(0.0899)
col^{ij}	0.943**	0.943**	0.938**	0.938**	0.963**	0.965**	0.921**
	(0.449)	(0.449)	(0.449)	(0.449)	(0.449)	(0.449)	(0.449)
waemu_dummy	0.594	0.524					
	(0.542)	(0.561)					
LPI_waemu		0.0417					
		(0.0847)					
cemac_dummy			0.602	0.367			
			(0.803)	(0.815)			
LPI_cemac				0.265*			
				(0.155)			
sadc_dummy					0.983***	0.574	
					(0.369)	(0.376)	
LPI_sadc						0.331***	
						(0.0562)	
sacu_dummy							0.682
							(1.589)
LPI_sacu							
eac_dumy							
LPI_eac							
ecowas_dummy							
LPI_ecowas							
asean_dummy							
LPI_asean							
celac_dummy							
LPI_celac							
Constant	−18.01***	−18.01***	−18.01***	−18.01***	−18.09***	−18.07***	−18.01***
	(0.606)	(0.606)	(0.606)	(0.606)	(0.606)	(0.606)	(0.606)
Observations	65,545	65,545	65,545	65,545	65,545	65,545	65,545
# of Groups	12,747	12,747	12,747	12,747	12,747	12,747	12,747
R.Square	0.4	0.4	0.4	0.4	0.4	0.4	0.4

Note: IS = international shipment; LC = Logistics Competence; TT = tracking-tracing the shipment.
Y^i, Y^j are respectively the real GDPs of country *i* and *j*. M^{ij} is the real import value of country *i* from *j*.
col = colonial link; comlang-off = common official language; contig = contiguity; pop = population.
The heteroscedastic standard errors in brackets.
*** p<0.01, ** p<0.05, * p<0.1

Log(Mⁱʲ)	Log(Mⁱʲ)	Log(Mⁱʲ)	Log(Mⁱʲ)	Log(Mⁱʲ)	Log(Mⁱʲ)	Log(Mⁱʲ)	Log(Mⁱʲ)	Log(Mⁱʲ)
0.515***	0.515***	0.515***	0.516***	0.517***	0.512***	0.512***	0.521***	0.524***
(0.0120)	(0.0121)	(0.0121)	(0.0120)	(0.0120)	(0.0121)	(0.0121)	(0.0119)	(0.0119)
0.186***	0.187***	0.187***	0.187***	0.187***	0.183***	0.183***	0.189***	0.191***
(0.0108)	(0.0108)	(0.0108)	(0.0108)	(0.0108)	(0.0108)	(0.0108)	(0.0107)	(0.0107)
0.660***	0.660***	0.660***	0.660***	0.659***	0.659***	0.658***	0.660***	0.655***
(0.0223)	(0.0223)	(0.0223)	(0.0223)	(0.0223)	(0.0223)	(0.0223)	(0.0221)	(0.0221)
0.880***	0.880***	0.880***	0.880***	0.879***	0.879***	0.879***	0.889***	0.884***
(0.0227)	(0.0227)	(0.0227)	(0.0227)	(0.0227)	(0.0227)	(0.0227)	(0.0225)	(0.0225)
−1.089***	−1.091***	−1.091***	−1.110***	−1.110***	−1.068***	−1.068***	−0.983***	−0.985***
(0.0452)	(0.0452)	(0.0452)	(0.0458)	(0.0458)	(0.0454)	(0.0454)	(0.0453)	(0.0452)
1.940***	1.972***	1.971***	1.973***	1.975***	1.907***	1.907***	1.909***	1.902***
(0.224)	(0.226)	(0.226)	(0.224)	(0.224)	(0.223)	(0.223)	(0.221)	(0.221)
0.716***	0.719***	0.718***	0.712***	0.712***	0.735***	0.735***	0.421***	0.418***
(0.0899)	(0.0899)	(0.0899)	(0.0899)	(0.0899)	(0.0899)	(0.0899)	(0.0910)	(0.0908)
0.921**	0.922**	0.923**	0.905**	0.907**	0.957**	0.957**	1.145***	1.154***
(0.449)	(0.449)	(0.449)	(0.449)	(0.449)	(0.448)	(0.448)	(0.444)	(0.444)
0.599								
(1.622)								
0.0672								
(0.262)								
	−0.686	−1.069						
	(0.796)	(0.810)						
		0.301**						
		(0.120)						
			−1.053***	−1.433***				
			(0.378)	(0.392)				
				0.230***				
				(0.0629)				
					2.551***	2.341***		
					(0.539)	(0.554)		
						0.118*		
						(0.0707)		
							2.732***	2.437***
							(0.174)	(0.177)
								0.187***
								(0.0234)
−18.01***	−18.00***	−17.99***	−17.84***	−17.83***	−17.99***	−17.98***	−19.35***	−19.29***
(0.606)	(0.606)	(0.606)	(0.608)	(0.608)	(0.605)	(0.605)	(0.606)	(0.605)
65,545	65,545	65,545	65,545	65,545	65,545	65,545	65,545	65,545
12,747	12,747	12,747	12,747	12,747	12,747	12,747	12,747	12,747
0.4	0.4	0.4	0.4	0.4	0.4	0.4	0.4	0.4

Table 5.5.10 The impacts of tariffs on developing countries' trade

VARIABLES	Log(M^{ij})	Log(M^{ij})	Log(M^{ij})	Log(M^{ij})
log(Y^i)	0.573***	0.592***	0.575***	0.589***
	(0.0129)	(0.0129)	(0.0129)	(0.0129)
log(Y^j)	0.246***	0.252***	0.264***	0.267***
	(0.0117)	(0.0117)	(0.0118)	(0.0117)
log(Pop^i)	0.537***	0.494***	0.543***	0.510***
	(0.0239)	(0.0239)	(0.0239)	(0.0238)
log(Pop^j)	0.798***	0.750***	0.763***	0.725***
	(0.0249)	(0.0249)	(0.0251)	(0.0251)
log($dist^{ij}$)	−1.123***	−1.121***	−1.122***	−1.120***
	(0.0481)	(0.0478)	(0.0480)	(0.0477)
contig^{ij}	1.835***	1.868***	1.745***	1.774***
	(0.232)	(0.231)	(0.231)	(0.230)
comlang off^{ij}	0.849***	0.819***	0.908***	0.878***
	(0.0953)	(0.0948)	(0.0952)	(0.0946)
col^{ij}	1.074**	1.166**	0.995**	1.073**
	(0.467)	(0.464)	(0.462)	(0.459)
tariff_wa_imp	−0.0593***	−0.0510***		
	(0.00450)	(0.00449)		
LPI_tariffwaimp		0.0138***		
		(0.000686)		
tariff_wa_exp			−0.0854***	−0.0784***
			(0.00451)	(0.00452)
LPI_tariffwaexp			0.0107***	
			(0.000661)	
Constant	−16.93***	−16.36***	−16.69***	−16.21***
	(0.648)	(0.645)	(0.649)	(0.646)
Observations	39,582	39,582	37,697	37,697
# of Groups	11,322	11,322	11,128	11,128
R-Square	0.4	0.4	0.4	0.4

Note: tariffwaexp is tariff weighted average of exporter and tariffwaimp is tariff weighted average importer.
Standard errors in parentheses.
*** $p < 0.01$, ** $p < 0.05$, * $p < 0.1$.

Table 5.5.11 Trade policies with Africa and their sensitivity to the LPI

VARIABLES	Log(Mⁱʲ)	Log(Mⁱʲ)	Log(Mⁱʲ)	Log(Mⁱʲ)	Log(Mⁱʲ)	Log(Mⁱʲ)	Log(Mⁱʲ)	Log(Mⁱʲ)	Log(Mⁱʲ)	Log(Mⁱʲ)
log(Yⁱ)	0.537***	0.537***	0.537***	0.537***	0.537***	0.537***	0.576***	0.589***	0.578***	0.588***
	(0.0194)	(0.0194)	(0.0195)	(0.0195)	(0.0195)	(0.0195)	(0.0212)	(0.0212)	(0.0213)	(0.0212)
log(Yʲ)	0.118***	0.118***	0.117***	0.118***	0.117***	0.117***	0.150***	0.153***	0.166***	0.168***
	(0.0170)	(0.0170)	(0.0171)	(0.0171)	(0.0170)	(0.0171)	(0.0189)	(0.0189)	(0.0190)	(0.0190)
log(Popⁱ)	0.694***	0.694***	0.724***	0.723***	0.689***	0.689***	0.629***	0.599***	0.639***	0.618***
	(0.0361)	(0.0361)	(0.0371)	(0.0371)	(0.0366)	(0.0366)	(0.0392)	(0.0392)	(0.0393)	(0.0392)
log(Popʲ)	0.574***	0.574***	0.577***	0.575***	0.575***	0.575***	0.557***	0.522***	0.454***	0.428***
	(0.0362)	(0.0362)	(0.0364)	(0.0365)	(0.0363)	(0.0364)	(0.0428)	(0.0429)	(0.0442)	(0.0442)
log(distⁱʲ)	-1.294***	-1.294***	-1.275***	-1.275***	-1.281***	-1.281***	-1.383***	-1.380***	-1.389***	-1.397***
	(0.0824)	(0.0824)	(0.0828)	(0.0828)	(0.0826)	(0.0827)	(0.0905)	(0.0902)	(0.0904)	(0.0901)
contigⁱʲ	2.201***	2.201***	2.225***	2.226***	2.148***	2.148***	2.043***	2.060***	1.974***	1.984***
	(0.327)	(0.327)	(0.329)	(0.329)	(0.329)	(0.329)	(0.340)	(0.339)	(0.338)	(0.337)
comlang_offiⁱʲ	0.646***	0.646***	0.716***	0.715***	0.592***	0.592***	0.753***	0.739***	0.748***	0.731***
	(0.121)	(0.121)	(0.124)	(0.124)	(0.123)	(0.123)	(0.131)	(0.131)	(0.131)	(0.131)
colⁱʲ	-0.113	-0.113	-0.344	-0.341	0.159	0.158	9.34e-05	0.0275	-0.101	-0.0622
	(0.788)	(0.788)	(0.803)	(0.803)	(0.795)	(0.796)	(0.828)	(0.825)	(0.819)	(0.816)
agoa_dummy	2.072***	2.056***								
	(0.389)	(0.426)								
LPI_AGOA		0.217**								
		(0.0962)								
acp_eu_dummy			0.167	0.132						
			(0.136)	(0.140)						
LPI_ACP				0.0233						
				(0.0220)						
eba_eu_dummy					-0.598***	-0.591***				
					(0.152)	(0.157)				

(continued)

446

Table 5.5.11 Continued

VARIABLES	Log(M^{ij})	Log(M^{ij})	Log(M^{ij})	Log(M^{ij})	Log(M^{ij})	Log(M^{ij})	Log(M^{ij})	Log(M^{ij})	Log(M^{ij})	Log(M^{ij})
LPI_EBA						-0.00490 (0.0270)				
tariff_wa_imp							-0.0265*** (0.00855)	-0.0259*** (0.00852)		
LPI_tariff_wa_imp								0.0119*** (0.00125)		
tariff_wa_exp									-0.0742*** (0.00904)	-0.0733*** (0.00902)
LPI_tariffwaexp										0.00850*** (0.00118)
Constant	-11.92*** (1.104)	-11.92*** (1.104)	-12.64*** (1.119)	-12.61*** (1.120)	-11.84*** (1.114)	-11.84*** (1.115)	-11.46*** (1.242)	-11.03*** (1.238)	-9.799*** (1.258)	-9.388*** (1.255)
Observations	21,531	21,531	21,531	21,531	21,531	21,531	13,120	13,120	12,504	12,504
# of Groups	4,361	4,361	4,361	4,361	4,361	4,361	3,765	3,765	3,694	3,694
R-Square	0.4	0.4	0.4	0.4	0.4	0.4	0.4	0.4	0.4	0.4

Note: "tariffwaexp" is tariff weighted average of exporter and "tariffwaimp" is tariff weighted average of the importer.
Standard errors in parentheses.
*** p < 0.01, ** p < 0.05, * p < 0.1.

GSP+ provides additional tariff reduction to *"vulnerable developing countries"* to assist them in implementing international conventions for sustainable development and good governance. As shown in Tables 5.5.10 and 5.5.11, tariffs on goods in the destination countries have negative and statistically significant impacts on export. One unit increase in destination tariffs decrease developing countries' export by about 10 percent. Although significant efforts have been made in reducing tariffs, developed nations could enhance African exports towards their markets by further removing most of the existing tariff lines and making rates uniform across developing countries. For instance, for the GSP, countries like Mauritius, Zimbabwe and Seychelles will no longer benefit from the GSP scheme; making these countries subject to higher tariffs rates relative to others. Such differentiation among African countries contributes to the regional disintegration. Overall the multiplicity of conditions attached to these schemes increases transactions cost, causes confusion for trade policy formulation and implementation which could explain failure to foster the region's industrialization.

The EPA would require the beneficiary countries/regions to partially open their markets to European products. While there could be circumstances under which such arrangement would benefit the African non-LDC, the LDCs would not have anything beyond what they already have under the EBA. The negotiations have stalled because of disagreement over the price for these poorest countries of the group to enter into such arrangement. One option pursued by the European has been to deepen their development cooperation only with countries that enter into these arrangements, with the level of development budget in the European Development Fund (EDF) not significantly increased to the level that these African countries find satisfactory. A uniform treatment of African countries is necessary to foster regional integration and industrialization in Africa (see Njinkeu, 2004). Not only the fragmentation by trade policies jeopardizes regional integration and industrialization in Africa, also the multiplicity of the rules of origins (RoO) underlying the trade regimes increase production costs of preferred producer and reduce their comparative advantage relative to their competitors. In the next sub-section we advocate for a uniform RoO across preferential trade agreements for Africa.

Rules of Origin Matter for African Industrialization

We stress in this paper that African reindustrialization requires African firms to offer competitive product, whereas competitive production depends on the extent of transaction costs these firms face and the extent of market available to them. In this sense, any policy that tends to increase production costs to African firms undermines the region's industrialization objectives. While the weakness of trade facilitation tremendously increase production costs, the rules of origins (RoO) that underline preferential trade agreements can have costs increasing effects on African firms as we detailed below. The rules of origin are regulations (in the form of changes in tariff classification, value content, technical requirements etc.) imposed to preferred producers under preferential trade agreements (PTAs). The primary objective of the RoOs is to avoid trade deflection. The intention is to avoid extending the preferences to out-of-block producers so that the benefits of the preferences to the eligible producers are not eroded. To ensure such objective, each preference regime governs specific inputs requirements by the RoO, making the RoO integral parts of each PTA. Given the importance of PTAs for developing countries in general and Africans in particular, the biggest concern about the RoO is the variation in the inputs requirements by RoO across PTAs and destination countries. For instance, over 500 product-specific rules of origin exist across the European Union (Cadot and Melo, 2007). AGOA and EBA for example have the same preferential access, but they differ in the RoO that govern them. According to Brenton and Özden (2005) and ARIA IV, on average, each developing country belongs to six non-reciprocal preferential trade scheme. This implies that producers in a given eligible country are subject to different inputs requirements to produce the same goods for different destinations. Thus, these producers are forced to divert their scarce resources in order to meet different RoOs.

The benefits of African countries from the PTAs could be wiped away by the various RoOs (Carrère and de Melo, 2006). Cadot and Melo (2007) use preference utilization rate and unit value to assess the effects of RoOs on preferred producers and show that RoO are unnecessarily costly to preferred producers, they reduce the benefits associated to the PTAs, and neutralize the development friendly objectives of the PTAs. In the context of Africa, the impacts of AGOA on African trade would have been higher if it offered flexible input sourcing for all African countries for example (see USITC, 2008; Mattoo et al., 2002; Walmsley and Rivera, 2004). Consolidating the RoOs under the PTAs would give incentives for value addition by facilitating the production process for preferred producers. A uniform RoO for all PTAs would help eligible countries achieve economies of scale and industrialization by concentrating their resources. In the next sub-section we focus on the importance of consolidated uniform trade regimes for Africa.

Consolidated Uniform Trade Regimes

The international trade schemes are equally important for African industrialization as we emphasize throughout the paper. However, for these trade schemes to effectively bolster African trade for its development, they need to be consolidated and coherent among themselves. The example of the African textile industry under AGOA and the end of the Multi-Fiber-Agreement (MFA) support the argument that international trade schemes need to be consolidated. For uncompetitive African textile and apparel industries, there is incoherence between AGOA and the agreement on textile and clothing (ATC). This incoherence steams from the fact that while

AGOA promotes African textile and apparel products on US markets, the ATC by liberalizing the textile and apparel market for all countries (including Asian, and Latin American and Caribbean), exposes infant African T&A exporters to fierce competition and thereby undermines the promotion of African fabrics. Indeed, the end of the MFA caused export declines and jobs losses for the African textiles and apparel industries in the face of high competition from Asians on the international clothing and apparel markets. While the AGOA aims to promote African T&A products by allowing their free entry to the United States, these industries have been least prepared to compete against their well-established counterparts from Asia before liberalizing the global textile and clothing markets. The result of liberalizing the T&A market without prior measures has been devastating for the African T&A industries.

Since 2005, the T&A businesses shifted from Africa to Asia (especially to Bangladesh to a large extent and to Cambodia). The first reason for this shift is the limitations in the production capacities in African countries (cotton shortage, restriction on input sources to export to the US with AGOA benefits (AGOA's RoO), infrastructures and logistic issues, etc.). The second reason is the end of the MFA by which the textile firms could now directly export from Asia to the United States duty and quota free. Clearly, the combination of the domestic problems, the restriction of a bilateral scheme-AGOA, and the multilateral regime contributed in diverting the textile business from Africa. With the relatively better[39] production conditions in Asia, the duty free and quota free put Asian countries in a huge comparative advantage as compared to the infant African T&A industries. The preference margins of Africans are therefore reduced as they face high competition. Both, the production environment in Africa and the increase in comparative advantages in Asia through DFQF have made Africa less attractive to foreign investors in the T&A business, destroying the development of its industries.

The incoherence between the ATC and the AGOA provision is more highlighted through the shift of US's textile and apparel imports from Africa to Asia. Such shift has slowed the T&A activities in Africa, leading to jobs losses[40] which contradict the AGOA initiatives. The United States have increased their textile imports from Asia since the end of the MFA. Since 2005, the U.S.'s imports of apparels have increased by 47 percent and 18 percent respectively from Bangladesh and from Cambodia at the cost of textile export drop from Africa (see ACT report 2009). According to the comments submitted to the WTO by the African Coalition for Trade, Inc. (ACT), the intensive textile imports of the U.S. from the Asian countries after the expiration of the MFA led to a drop of 47 percent (by volume) and 41 percent (by value) of Africans' AGOA textile export to U.S. (see Figure 5.5.11 below). Liberalizing the market without taking adequate measures to protect the AGOA incentives made African countries lose their margin of preference in destination markets while this is an important factor of African countries'

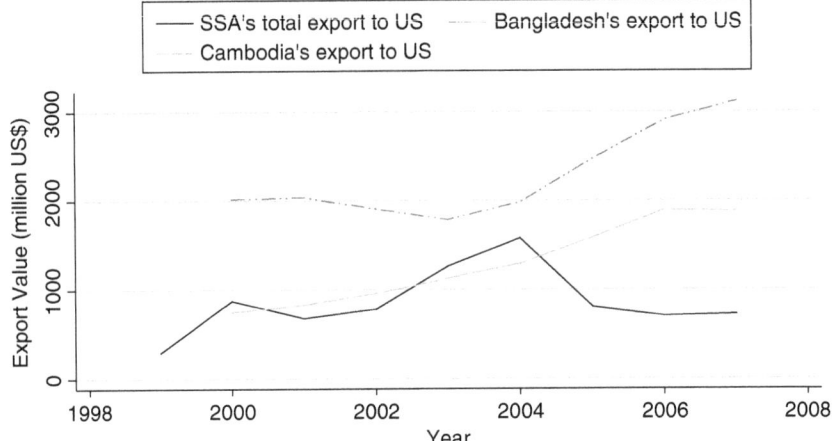

Figure 5.5.11   SSA's textile exports to USA vs. Bangladesh and Cambodia before and during the ATC

T&A exports. Measures need to be taken to consolidate trade rules under which African countries operate in order to preserve their competitiveness. In the context of international trade rules, we discuss in the next sub-section the relevance of subsidies rules in preserving African competitiveness.

Notes

1. We explain the term trade facilitation in Box 5.5.1 of Appendix 1.
2. We explain the term light manufacturing in Box 5.5.2 of Appendix 1.
3. African Growth Opportunity Act.
4. Trade agreement between the European Union and African Caribbean and Pacific countries.
5. Everything But Arms- a trade agreement between least developed countries (LDCs) and the European Union.
6. Light manufactures can be roughly defined as the process of applying manual labor or machineries to assembly raw materials and obtain a new product. Or light manufactures are early stage products after procession through a division of labor. In general, light manufacturing do not intensively require high skilled labor.
7. Figures obtained using the World Bank's World Development Indicators (WDI) database
8. Figures 5.5.3 and 5.5.4 show how scant is Africa's textile and apparel export compared to that of other regions.
9. See the cotton-to-clothing production chain in Appendix 1.
10. See cotton-to-clothing scheme in Appendix 1.

11. As discussed below, regional integration requires trade facilitation between African countries.

12. The importance of lower transport costs in fostering international trade flows has been extensively documented (see Limao and Venables, 2001; Abe and Wilson, 2009), with the major determinants of transport costs being the quality of road, rail infrastructures, the efficiency of transport logistics, and the type of transport mode (air, maritime or overland).

13. The results for the estimations are shown in the box table. The coefficients for the various independent variables have the expected sign and are all significant and robust across specifications. In particular, the coefficient for the size of the economies, proxy by their GDP, ranges between 0.7 and 1. This means that for two countries trading with each other, an increase of one percent in the GDP of either the exporting or the importing country increases trade by about one percent. The coefficient for the distance between capital cities ranges between minus 1.8 and minus 2. Thus one can expect that, everything else the same, countries whose capitals are at larger distances from each other will trade less; a one percent larger distance can result in almost a two percent fall in bilateral trade. The other variables have similar straightforward interpretations.

14. Z represents dummy variables which include: (1) exporting country is landlocked; (2) two trade partners have had a colonial relationship; (3) two countries share the same official language, (4) two countries are bordering, and finally (5) there is contiguity (that is, one state is next to another in space; for example South Africa and Lesotho) between import and export countries. Data on geographic variables come from CEPII (http://www.cepii.fr/distance/). Data on income and population come from World Bank Indicators. Available at http://data.world-bank.org/data-catalog/logistics-performance-index.

16. There is a new method called "the fixed effect vector decomposition (FEVD)" to accommodate time-invariant variables that is increasingly used. However, there is no consensus that this method, proposed by Plümper and Troeger (2004), is the most efficient. In order to check the robustness of our results, alternatives estimate will be provided in annex including: simple OLS, fixed effects, and random effects.

17. Developing countries for which data is available for the variables and years of our interest.

18. The LPI covers key factors of trade facilitation.

19. The logistic performance index (LPI) we use captures infrastructures and institutional factors that affect transport costs. The increase in the LPI score reflects improvements in different policies that affect transport costs to different extent, but LPI is not equal to transport costs.

20. The Enabling Trade Index (ETI) shows countries that are opened to multilateral rules export more than others (see second Figure in the Appendix 1).

21. Although Africa has large and growing population, the size of each of its countries represents a scant share of the world population and put together the thick borders makes the market too small.

22. Thus, the sizes of China and India have played determinant roles in attracting foreign investments. China and India are the world's most populated countries. Their populations together represent 37 percent of the world population with Asia being be most populated continent on the earth (US Censure Bureau, 2012). Brazil was the fifth most populated country in the world as of April 2012. Yet, Africa needs to industrialize in a global trading environment different from the one under which other countries' economies emerged. Other countries industrialized in a global trading environment that allowed for protectionist. For instance, the most

spectacular economic feat of the 20th century- the Asian miracle happened under increasing tariffs. The earlier industrializations such as the British industrialization between 1770 and 1830 occurred in a protectionist world. The current liberalized world means African need to compete to industrialize (Njinkeu and Soludo, 2005).

23. The combination of cost-efficient production and larger markets will allow African firms to offer competitive products by exploiting their comparative advantages (see Hoekman and Njinkeu, 2007).

24. The LPI components are: infrastructure, customs, logistics competence, international shipment, tracing and tracking, and timeliness of shipment.

25. The Southern African Customs Union (SACU) covers Botswana, Namibia, Lesotho, Swaziland, and South Africa.

26. AGOA has also boost footwear export to the US, especially from South Africa.

27. Investigation 332–477, USITC Publication 3989 of April 2008.

28. It is important to underline that not all international preferential schemes have been beneficial to Africa like AGOA as revealed in the empirical exercise (Table 5.5.8 in Appendix 2); leading to the argument that international trade schemes need to be redesigned to foster African re-industrialization.

29. The data on trade control variables can be found at http://www.cepii.com/anglaisgraph/bdd/distances.htm.

30. West African Economic and Monetary Union.

31. Economic Community of Central African States.

32. Southern African Development Community.

33. Southern African Customs Union.

34. East African Community.

35. Economic Community of West African States.

36. Association of Southeast Asian Nations.

37. Community of Latin American and Caribbean States.

38. http://trade.ec.europa.eu/doclib/press/index.cfm?id=840.

39. See Logistics Performance Index and Doing Business index.

40. Mutume (2011) estimated the total jobs lost in African T&A industries as a result of the DFQF at a total of 250,000 continent wide since 2005. The case of Lesotho is a good illustration the impacts of the DFQF on exports and jobs in the African T&A industries. Under the MFA, Lesotho's manufacturing sector was highly dependent on the textile and garment industries and it accounted for more than 75 percent of the country's export revenues and jobs. Lesotho's T&A employed more than 56,000 workers and most of the textile firms were owned by Asians (mainly Chinese and Taiwanese) who had hard time exporting directly their textile from Asia to the U.S. under the MFA. With the end of the MFA, most of Lesotho's textile firms relocated back to Asia causing 6,600 jobs lost. In addition, the surviving firms face demands drop causing additional jobs lost (Mutume, 2011). As shown in Figures 5.5.1 and 5.5.2, Lesotho's export in manufacturing dropped sharply from late 2004 and lasted up to 2006.

References

Abe, Kazutomo, and Wilson, John (2009), "Weathering the Storm: Investing in Port Infrastructure to Lower Trade Costs in East Asia," World Bank Policy Research Working Paper 4911 (Washington, DC: World Bank).

ACTIF News Letter, (2009) http://www.cottonafrica.com/documents/ACTIF Newsletter November 2009.pdf.

African Coalition for Trade, Inc. (ACT) (2009) "ACT Comments on to House Committee on Ways and Means Trade Subcommittee: Preference Reform Must Not Be Allowed to Destroy AGOA." Available online at http://acttrade.org/.

Aranoff, Shara, Pearson, Daniel, Okun, Deanna, Lane Charlotte, Williamson Irving, and Pinkert, Dean (2008) *United States International Trade Commission, year in Review, Fiscal Year 2008*, USITC Publication 4093 (Washington, DC: USITC).

ARIA IV (Assessing Regional Integration in Africa) (2010) *Enhancing Intra-African Trade* (Addis Ababa, Ethiopia: United Nation Economic Commission for Africa (UNECA)).

Behar, Alberto and Venables, Anthony (2010) "Transport Costs and International Trade," in André de Palma, Robin Lindsey, Emile Quinet and Roger Vickerman (eds), *Handbook of Transport Economics* (Cheltenham: Edward Elgar). Available online at http://works.bepress.com/alberto_behar/17.

Behar, Alberto, Manners, Phil, and Nelson, Benjamin, (2009) "Exports and Logistics," Oxford Department of Economics Discussion Paper 439.

Brenton, Paul and Özden, Çağlar (2005) "Trade Preferences for Apparel and the Role of Rules of Origin: The Case of Africa," mimeo (Washington, DC: World Bank).

Cadot, Olivier and Melo, Jaime (2007) "Why OECD Countries Should Reform the Rules of Origin," UNIL (University of Lausanne), 2007.

Collier, Paul and Venables, Anthony (2007) "Rethinking Trade Preferences: How Africa Can Diversify its Exports," *World Economy Journal*, vol. 30, no. 8, pp. 1326–1345.

Dinh, Hinh, Palmade, Vincent, Chandra, Vandana, and Cossa, Frances, (2011), "Light Manufacturing in Africa: Targeted Policies to Enhance Private Investments and Create Jobs", World Bank, 2012

Gilbert, J. (2011), "International Trade, Growth and Structural Changes in Employment in Developing Asia," Paper presented at the Conference on International Collaborative Initiative on Trade and Employment, ADB, Manila, April 18–19.

Grubel, Helbert and Lloyd, Pete, (1975) *Intra-industry Trade: the Theory and Measurement of International Trade in Differentiated Products* (London: Macmillan).

Heckscher, Eli (1919) "The Effects of Foreign trade on the Distribution of Income," *Ekonomisk Tidskrift*, pp. 497–512.

Helble, Matthiew, Mann, Catherine, and Wilson, John (2011) "Aid for Trade Facilitation," *Review of World Economics*, vol. 148, issue 2, pp 357–376.

Hoekman, Bernard and Njinkeu, Dominique (2007) "Aid for Trade and Export Competitiveness: New Opportunities for Africa," Framework paper for the AERC Project on Supply Response. Available online atwww.aercafrica.org.

Hsiao, Cheng (2003) Analysis of Panel Data (Cambridge: Cambridge University Press).

International Trade Center (ITC) Report, (2011) "WTO Business Briefing, 2011: Regional Integration and African Textile Industry V." Available online at http://www.intracen.org/BB-2011-03-07-Regional-Integration-and-the-African-Textile-Industry/.

Keane, Jodie, (2010) "Rethinking Trade Preferences: "How Can Trade in Tasks Be the Potential Lifeline for Sub-Saharan Africa?," (Oxford: Centre for the Study of African Economies (CSAE) Conference 2011 and London: Overseas Development Institute (ODI)).

Lawrence, Robert, Hanouz, Margareta, and Doherty, Sean (2012) "The Global Enabling Trade Report, 2012: Reducing Supply Chain Barriers," World Economic Forum.

Limão, Nuno and Venables, Anthony (2001), "Infrastructure, Geographical Disadvantage, Transport Costs and Trade," *World Bank Economic Review*, vol. 15, no. 3, pp. 451–479.

Martinez-Zarzoso, Inmaculada, Perez-Garcia, Eva Maria, Suarez-Burguet, Celestino (2008) "Do Transport Costs Have a Differential Effect on Trade at the Sectoral Level?," *Applied Economics*, vol. 40, no. 24, pp. 3145–3157.

Mattoo, Aaditya, Roy, Devesh and Subramanian, Arvind (2002) "The African Growth and Opportunity Act and Its Rules of Origin: Generosity Undermined?," World Bank Policy Research Working Paper no. 2908 (Washington, DC; World Bank).

Mutume, Gumisai (2011) "Loss of Textile Markets Costs African Jobs: Diversification, Efficiency Hold Key for Economic Recovery," *Africa Renewal*, April 2006, p. 18. Available online at http://www.un.org/africarenewal/magazine/april-2006/loss-textile-market-costs-african-jobs.

Ndulu, Benno, Chakraborty, Lopamudra, Lijane, Lebohang, Ramachandran, Vijaya, and Wolgin, Jerome (2007), *Challenges of African Growth: Opportunities, Constraints and Strategic Directions* (Washington, DC: World Bank.

Njinkeu, Dominique and Soludo, Charles (2005), "Industrializing Africa Using WTO Framework, Chapter 5." Available online at http://www.aercafrica.org/documents/Chapter%205.pdf.

Njinkeu, Dominique (2004) "Uniform Treatment of Africa in the WTO," *World Trade Review*, vol. 3, pp. 433–440.

Ohlin, Bertil (1933) Interregional and International Trade (Cambridge, MA: Harvard University Press).

Plumper, Thomas and Troeger, Vera (2004) "The Estimation of Time-Invariant Variables in Panel Analysis with Unit Fixed Effects," Konstanz University, mimeo.

Stiglitz, Joseph and Charlton, Andrew, (2012) "Right to Trade," a Report for the Commonwealth Secretariat on Aid for Trade (London: Commonwealth Secretariat).

United Nation Economic Committee for Africa (UNECA) and African Union (UA) (2012) "Economic Report on Africa: Unleashing Africa's Potential as a Pole of Global Growth." Available online at http://reliefweb.int/sites/reliefweb.int/files/resources/ERA2012_ENG_FIN.pdf.

United Nations Industrial Development Organization (UNIDO) (2009), "Breaking In and Moving Up: New Industrial Challenges for the Bottom Billion and the Middle-Income Countries," Industrial Development Report, 2009, Available at http://www.unido.org/fileadmin/user_media/Publications/IDR/2009/IDR_2009_print.PDF

UNIDO ID No. 438 (Vienna: UNIDO).

United States Census Bureau (2012) "World Demographic." Available online at www.USCB.org.

Wacziarg, Romain and Welch, Karen (2008) "Trade Liberalization and Growth: New Evidence," *World Bank Economic Review*, vol. 22, no. 2, pp. 187–231.

Walmsley, Terrie and Rivera, Sandra (2004) "The Impact of ROO on Africa's Textiles and Clothing Trade under AGOA," Center for Global Trade Analysis, the 7th Annual Conference on Global Economic Analysis.

Wilson, John, Mann, Catherine, and Otsuki, Tsunehiro, (2005) "Assessing the Benefits of Trade Facilitation: A Global Perspective," *The World Economy*, vol. 28, no. 6, pp. 841–871.

Wooldridge, Jeffrey (2002) *Econometric Analysis of Cross Section and Panel Data* (Cambridge, MA: MIT Press).

World Bank (2010) "Yes Africa Can: Stories from a Dynamic Continent." Available online at www.worldbank.org/countries/Africa.

World Development Report (WDR) (2013) "Jobs and Living Standards."

World Economic Forum, The Global Competitiveness Report, (2011–2012) at http://www3.weforum.org/docs/WEF_GCR_Report_2011-12.pdf

World Economic Forum (2012) "The Great Transformation: Shaping New Models," annual meeting, Davos-Klosters, Switzerland, January 25–9.

Part VI
Country Experiences and Perspectives

6.1

Industrial Structural Change, Growth Patterns, and Industrial Policy

Ludovico Alcorta, Nobuya Haraguchi, and Gorazd Rezonja
UNIDO

6.1.1 Introduction

Economic growth and development are intrinsically linked to changes in the structure of economic activity. Diversification away from agriculture into manufacturing and, eventually, services (intersectoral structural change), triggers a process of sustained growth. As the share of the total workforce in the primary sector declines in favor of the manufacturing (secondary) and service (tertiary) sectors, the intersectoral process of resource allocation results in systemic changes in the composition of domestic demand, generating a continuous rise in the level of skills, productivity and wages, and, as a consequence, increasing consumer purchasing power.

Shifts also take place across and within manufacturing industries. Domestic and international competition as well as innovation force a country's manufacturing sector to change continuously. Shifts take place in the form of diversification away from labor-intensive industries, such as textiles and apparel, to industries that have high levels of skill, capital, and technology intensity, such as the production of advanced machinery, automobiles, or chemicals (inter-industry structural change). These inter-industry shifts involve the reallocation of investments and resources from one industry to another and the emergence of new industries. Manufacturing structural change also entails shifts in the form of expansion and upgrading within existing industries (intra-industry structural change). Equally, intra-industry shifts involve industrial deepening that results in the creation of more forward and backward linkages within industries, and complementarities between different sectors and industries within a country or region.

Promoting structural change requires both market forces and governments to play a role. While implementing the diversification and upgrading of production structures is predominantly driven by the private sector and market forces, governments can assist entrepreneurs to overcome information, coordination, and externalities problems and help them to explore new and strategic upgrading and diversification opportunities. Industrial policy can support structural change by anticipating trends and patterns, by facilitating it through removing obstacles and by supporting emerging activities. Anticipating the development patterns of the manufacturing sector can help understand when a given manufacturing industry is likely to contribute most to the country's economic development and when to shift to services. If policymakers are aware of which industries would promote or inhibit development at different levels of income and given certain country characteristics, they could pursue a path of industrialization consistent with their country-specific features by investing in those industries that are most likely to succeed.

This chapter will examine the relationship between growth patterns and the changing composition of manufacturing (inter-industry structural change) in large countries (countries with a population above 12.5 million). In particular, it will examine the issues of whether and to what extent output, employment and productivity growth exhibit the same trend for individual industries as incomes expand and manufacturing progressively shifts toward more capital- and technology-intensive industries. Following this introduction, the paper will discuss the relationship between structural change and development. The next two sections will describe the research design and present its main findings. Section 6.1.5 will then examine the implications for industrial policy, in particular methods to identify possible entry and exit points in emerging industries and to benchmark industries with growth potential. Hence, the chapter will also contribute to the Growth Identification and Facilitation approach developed by (Lin and Monga, 2010) and other similar approaches such as the Growth Diagnostics (Hausmann et al., 2005). The chapter will end up with some conclusions and possible research extensions.

6.1.2   Structural change and economic growth

The development literature approaches the concept of structural change from both a positive and a normative perspective. For Syrquin (2007) structural change is any long-term change in the composition of an aggregate. These may include shifts from agricultural to industrial production, from low- to high-skill and/or capital-intensity manufacturing, from low to high levels of human capital production, from consumption patterns based on food and basic necessities to broader consumption patterns including a wide array of manufacturing goods and services, and from largely rural populations to highly urbanized populations with a significant proportion living in large cities. Ocampo (2005), Ocampo and Vos (2008), and UNDESA (2006), for their part, define structural change as the ability of an economy to constantly generate new dynamic activities characterized by higher productivity and increasing returns to scale.

Economic growth and structural change are closely interconnected. In Kuznets's (1966) view, sustained economic growth cannot happen without structural changes while Lin (2012: 3) points out that "all countries that remain poor have failed to achieve structural transformation, that is, they have been unable to diversify away from agriculture and the production of traditional goods into manufacturing and other modern activities." McMillan and Rodrik (2011) and Lin (2011) point out that both the direction and speed of structural change constitute important drivers of the rate of growth. If the direction of structural change is misguided, or if its pace is too slow, an economy will stagnate.

In terms of direction, economic history shows that between the second half of the 18th century and the first half of the 20th century few countries were able to achieve sustained growth rates without a substantive manufacturing industry (Gerschenkron, 1962; Maddison, 1982, 2001, 2007). The rapid growth rates of China during the last 25 years are associated with a growing share of manufacturing in GDP and a large manufacturing sector (Memedovic and Iapadre, 2010a). Econometric evidence from 131 developing countries in the period 2000–05 suggests that economic growth is correlated with manufacturing value-added growth (UNIDO, 2009). A more sophisticated analysis for 89 developed and developing countries in 1950–2005 found that the share of manufacturing is positively related to economic growth and this effect is more pronounced for the poorer countries, confirming the "manufacturing as an engine of growth hypothesis" (Szirmai and Verspagen, 2010). These authors also found, on the basis of a modified version of Hausmann/Rodrik "growth accelerations" (an increase in the growth rate of at least 2 percent sustained over eight years), that the growth impact of manufacturing is particularly pronounced during periods of growth acceleration. These findings are in line with those reported by Rodrik (2006), which indicate that growth accelerations are closely associated with rapid increases in the share of manufactures in total exports or associated with an increase in the share of manufacturing employment in total employment.

Szirmai (2013) provides a good summary of the arguments behind the role of manufacturing in the process. Manufacturing has higher productivity and higher productivity growth than other sectors and, compared to agriculture, capital accumulation can be more easily realized in spatially concentrated manufacturing than in spatially dispersed agriculture. Hence, capital intensity is higher in manufacturing than in other sectors.[1] Manufacturing also offers special opportunities for economies of scale as well as for both embodied and disembodied technological progress, which are less available in agriculture or services (although there is some evidence that agriculture in advanced economies may be catching up). The locus of technological advancement and innovation is the manufacturing sector, from where new technologies diffuse to other economic sectors. Indeed, around two-thirds of total R&D expenditure is in manufacturing. Manufacturing has stronger forward and backward linkages (within and outside) and spillover effects than other sectors and benefits from Engel's Law of consumer behaviour – that is, as income rises expenditure in agriculture declines in favor of expenditure in manufacturing.

While the case for structural change in favor of manufacturing has been made forcefully, there has been much less discussion of structural change within manufacturing. Figure 6.1.1 shows the extent of inter-industrial structural change for large countries (those with a population above 12.5 million) at different levels of GDP per capita (industries ranked increasingly by their manufacturing value added (MVA) share when real GDP per capita reaches US$40,000). Industries such as textiles, tobacco, and wood products, which tend to account for a larger share of MVA at low levels of GDP per capita, reduce their share as GDP per capita increases. By contrast, industries like machinery and equipment, electrical machinery and apparatus, and motor vehicles with a relatively low share of MVA at low levels of GDP per capita, increase their share significantly as GDP per capita increases. Two industries, food and beverages and chemicals, with high shares at low GDP per capita levels keep their shares or reduce them only slightly as GDP per capita increases.

Imbs and Wacziarg (2003), however, suggests that the same rationale that is made for manufacturing as a whole can be applied to structural change within manufacturing. In their influential paper they identify strong evidence suggesting that economies first diversify their productive activities and only at a relatively late stage in their development process do they begin to specialize again, following a U-shaped pattern.[2] The authors point out that this pattern holds not only hold for the structural transformation from agriculture to manufacturing but also, more importantly, for diversifying into new activities within manufacturing industry. Higher productivity and productivity growth rates can be achieved by shifting from lower to higher capital-, skill-. and knowledge-intensive industries, and larger economies of scale can be reaped in the more automated and integrated industries. The potential for more advanced technological progress and for linkages and spillovers increases as the composition of manufacturing production shifts toward more advanced industries and electronic products, which have the highest income elasticity of demand.[3]

The speed of structural change is also an important factor for economic growth. Rapid shifts of economic activity from lower- to higher-productivity sectors will require resources to be reallocated smoothly, new technologies to emerge uninterrupted and skills to be renewed constantly. Optimal production scales will have to be reached promptly and learning processes should not take inordinate amounts of time so that capital accumulation can be sustained. Backward and forward linkages will need to be forged seamlessly and spillovers seized swiftly in order to create strong domestic multiplier effects. Labor absorption will need to proceed apace in order to provide the required demand while unremitting product innovation will have to follow to keep up with market expansion. The more virtuous the combination of these factors, the higher the rate of growth.

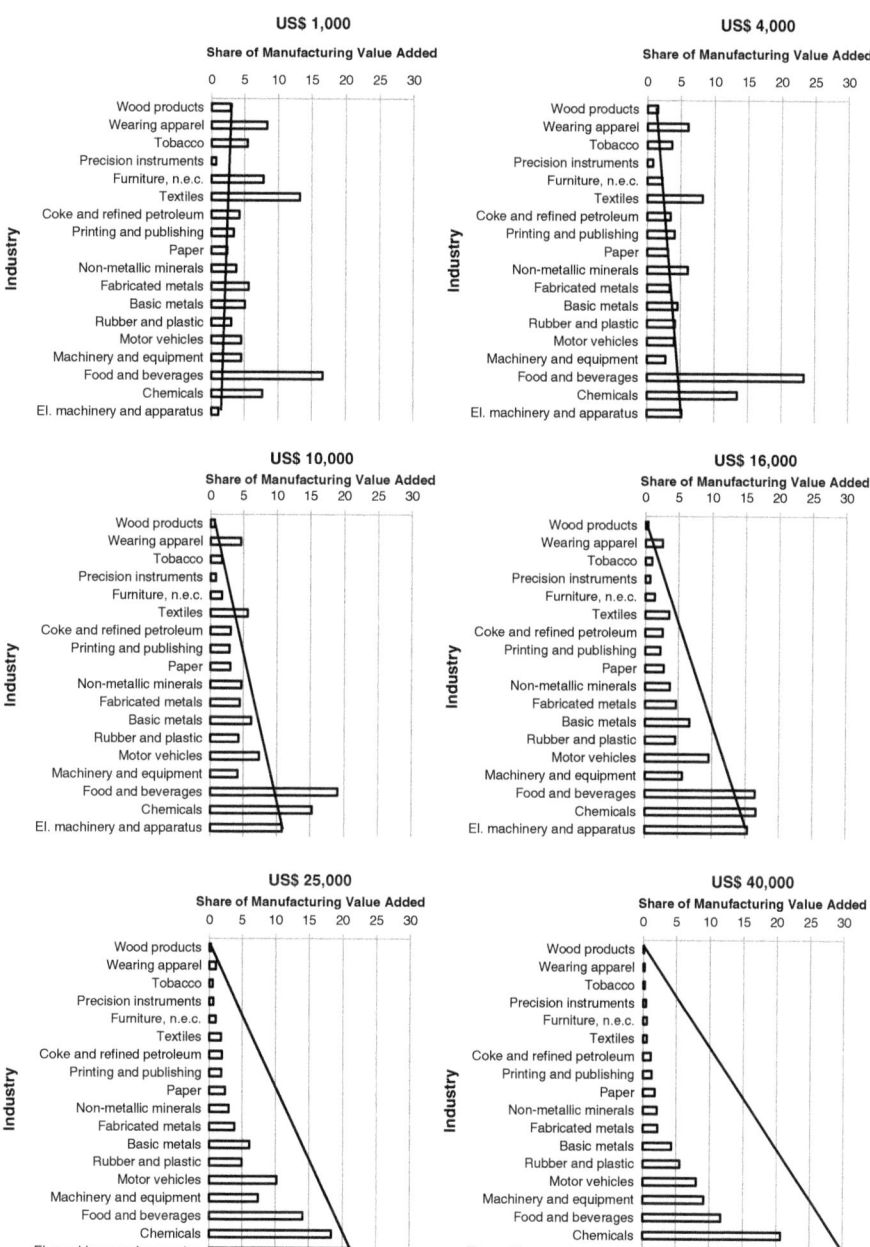

Figure 6.1.1 Structural change within manufacturing at different levels of real GDP per capita (2005 US$ PPP adjusted), large countries
Source: Elaborated on the basis of UNIDO INDSTAT2 (2012).

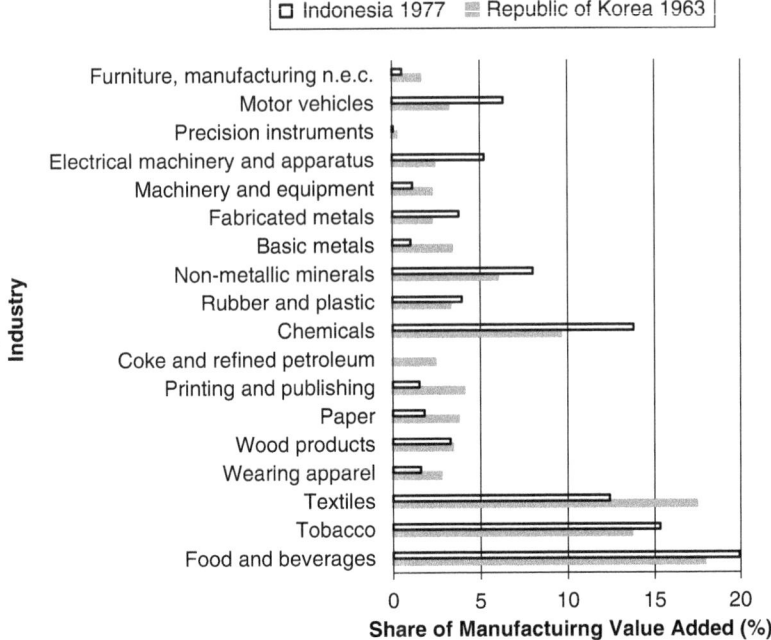

Figure 6.1.2 Share of MVA by industry in the Republic of Korea and Indonesia at US$2,000 GDP per capita (2005 US$ PPP adjusted)
Source: Elaborated on the basis of UNIDO INDSTAT2 (2012).

Figure 6.1.2 compares the structure of the manufacturing sector in the Republic of Korea and in Indonesia at the point when both countries had reached a similar level of development (US$2,000 GDP per capita), namely in 1963 and 1977, respectively. The figures indicate that both countries had comparable production structures, with resource-based and labor-intensive products (such as food and beverages, tobacco, textiles, and wood products) accounting for more than 50 percent of MVA in both countries. Actually, the overall structure of manufacturing in Indonesia was already developing a strong presence in medium- and high-tech industries unlike the Republic of Korea.

Figure 6.1.3 compares MVA in both the Republic of Korea and Indonesia when their income levels reached approximately US$5,200 GDP per capita, in 1977 in the Republic of Korea (that is, within 14 years) and in 2007 for Indonesia (that is, within 30 years). The extent of structural change was higher in the case of the Republic of Korea than in Indonesia, where the economy remained largely unchanged.

The changing pattern of production in the Republic of Korea shows a decline in resource-based low-tech industries and an expansion of

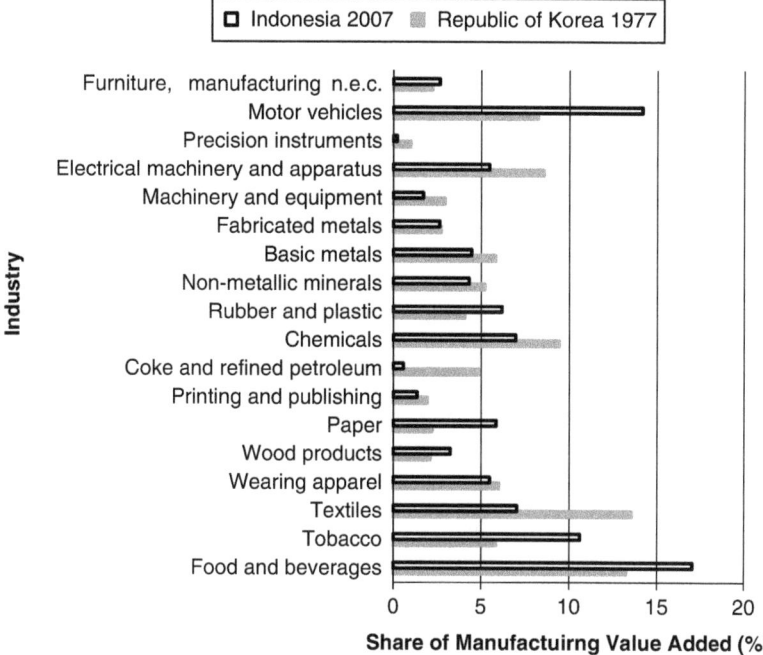

Figure 6.1.3 Share of MVA by industry in the Republic of Korea and Indonesia at US$5,200 GDP per capita (2005 US$ PPP adjusted)
Source: Elaborated on the basis of UNIDO INDSTAT2 (2012).

medium- and high-tech industries. Accordingly, the food and beverages, tobacco, textiles, and wood industries in the Republic of Korea declined by five, eight, four, and one percentage points, respectively, while more high-skill- and capital-intensive industries, such as electrical machinery and apparatus and motor vehicles, grew by six and five percentage points, respectively. In contrast, the pace of structural change was slower in Indonesia: the share of resource-based and low-tech industries and of medium- and high-tech industries has remained basically unchanged despite some important shifts within these classes (the motor vehicle industry has done exceptionally well among high-tech industries).

This variation in the direction and pace of structural transformation is associated with differing GDP per capita growth rates: in the Republic of Korea, real GDP per capita grew at an annual average rate of 7 percent in the period 1963–77, but in Indonesia it increased only by a more modest 3 percent per year between 1977 and 2007. In other words, although both countries started off with similar production structures at the same GDP per capita level, the Republic of Korea was able to successfully transform its structures of production to become one of the fastest-growing manufacturing economy in the world. In Indonesia, by contrast, no profound structural change took place, that is, the composition of industry did not change significantly, resulting in a much slower growth of the country's economy.[4]

A central issue in understanding industrial structural change processes is whether (and the extent to which) the output, productivity, and employment growth patterns exhibited by individual industries change as the composition of manufacturing shifts in the process of economic development. Industrial structural change involves such complex interactions between variables, agents, mechanisms, and objectives that it is unclear whether expected outcomes will ensue. Individual countries face different sets of institutional, technological, managerial, and governance capabilities that may help or hinder the direction and pace of structural transformation. And, there may be new industrial and technological revolutions that may radically change the parameters of performance and operation of manufacturing.

6.1.3   Approach and data

The approach this paper takes as its point of departure is the empirical work initiated by Chenery (1960) and later continued by Chenery and Taylor (1968) and Chenery and Syrquin (1975, 1989) and Chenery et al. (1986). This work aimed at identifying patterns of structural change and development based on cross-sectional and time-series econometric analysis. Over the years, as a result of improvements in econometric techniques, availability of data and methodological approaches, these authors were able to identify and assess the impact of several factors that affect structural change. In particular, their contribution focused on the impact of factors related to the level of income; of factors such as market size or natural resources over which the government has little or no control; of the country's individual history, its political and social objectives; and, of government policies. Unfortunately a full picture of structural transformation in manufacturing worldwide eluded them due to data unavailability at the sectoral level and over long periods of time.

The estimation function for this study builds on the work quoted above. For example, Chenery and Taylor (1968) had already included a quadratic term for income as the decline in elasticities with rising income became apparent. Later on, authors settled with a more general equation allowing a non-linear effect for the population and including dummy variables for identifying period effects (Chenery and Syrquin, 1975). In this study it is assumed that in the long term industries undergo three development stages – pre-take-off, growth, and decline. Industries which can sustain growth over a long period of time may have a more linear development trajectory, while other industries, which experience growth from a very early stage of development and decline at a later stage, may indicate a more quadratic pattern. Hence, we include square and cubic terms of GDP per capita in the equation in order for the results to denote all possible patterns of manufacturing development, depending on the statistical significance of these GDP per capita terms.[5] To control for the effect of unobserved country-specific conditions, we apply the fixed effect estimation procedure. The following equations are used in each manufacturing industry.

$$\ln RVA^i_{ct} = \alpha_1 + \alpha_2 * \ln RGDP_{ct} + \alpha_3 * \ln RGDP^2_{ct} + \alpha_4 * \ln RGDP^3_{ct} + \alpha_c + e^i_{ct} \quad (1)$$

$$\ln EMP^i_{ct} = \alpha_1 + \alpha_2 * \ln RGDP_{ct} + \alpha_3 * \ln RGDP^2_{ct} + \alpha_4 * \ln RGDP^3_{ct} + \alpha_c + e^i_{ct} \quad (2)$$

$$\ln LP^i_{ct} = \alpha_1 + \alpha_2 * \ln RGDP_{ct} + \alpha_3 * \ln RGDP^2_{ct} + \alpha_4 * \ln RGDP^3_{ct} + \alpha_c + e^i_{ct} \quad (3)$$

where:
  – *RVA* indicates real value added per capita
  – *EMP* represents real employment–population ratio
  – *LP* means labor productivity
  – *RGDP* stands for real GDP per capita
  – $RGDP^2$ denotes real GDP per capita square
  – $RGDP^3$ signifies real GDP per capita cubic
  – α_c is country fixed effect
  – e^i_{ct} refers to unexplained residual.

Both dependent and explanatory variables are expressed in logarithmic terms to measure the elasticity of each variable.

The regression uses UNIDO Industrial Statistics for manufacturing industries at the two-digit level of the International Standard Industrial Classification (ISIC), revision 3. The database covers the years 1963–2008 and provides information for nine variables, of which value added and employment were used. There are 23 industrial categories in total. However, as countries often report industries 18 and 19, 29 and 30, 31 and 32, and 34 and 35 together, we combined each pair into one industry category to have a consistent dataset across countries. Furthermore, we dropped industry 37, recycling, as it has only been reported by a very limited number of countries. This left a total of 18 industries to be analyzed, which included: food and beverages (ISIC code: 15), tobacco (16), textiles (17), wearing apparel (18), wood products (20), paper (21), printing and publishing (22), coke and refined petroleum (23), chemical (24), rubber and plastic (25), non-metallic minerals (26), basic metals (27), fabricated metals (28) machinery and equipment (29), electrical machinery and apparatus (31), precision instruments (33), motor vehicles (34), and furniture and n.e.c (36). Population data were obtained from the World Bank's WDI.

One of the challenges posed by the data was to construct a deflator, since price-adjusted data are not available for manufacturing value added (MVA) in a large number of countries, in particular for developing countries. To do so we use the Index of Industrial Production (IIP), revision 3, which is available at the two-digit level of the ISIC and has been widely used since the mid-1980s. To obtain a longer time series, the IIP ISIC revision 3 was combined with the IIP ISIC revision 2, which goes back to the early 1960s, allowing a series of IIPs covering the years 1963 to 2008 for 70 countries. To expand the coverage of the IIP the inflation structure based on the same year's IIP of another country located in the same region and at a relatively similar development stage was applied to countries with no data. This method allowed to include an additional 50 countries without an IIP in our estimations. Overall 120 countries were included in the analysis (see also Haraguchi and Rezonja, 2012).

To classify countries into groups of different sizes, we apply thresholds dividing them into small, medium and large countries, and examine at which threshold level the maximum number of manufacturing industries is obtained, whose development patterns statistically differ from one another in terms of value added per capita. This is achieved by applying the Wald test. Based on the test results, we found thresholds of 3 million and 12.5 million to divide countries into small, medium and large countries.

To ensure countries within each group share a common pattern, there was an examination of the statistical significance of both the individual country intercepts and also the slopes of the explanatory variables used in the equations to estimate the value added per capita. Individual country intercepts are significantly different across most of the countries and industries; therefore, it can be inferred that countries differ in terms of initial conditions. Individual slopes are statistically insignificant for the majority of countries across all industries, which indicates that countries in the same size group do not differ significantly rom each other in terms of patterns of development. Since the three size groups of countries arising from the aforementioned approach need to be dealt with separately, this study will be the first of a series, with this one focusing on large countries.[6]

A further step was to group industries according to the level of GDP per capita at which they achieved the highest MVA share. Insofar as the structure of industry changes as incomes rise, it should be expected that some industries start losing weight at the gain of others, past certain levels of income. In order to create the classification, the share of value added in total MVA for the 18 industries subject to the study were regressed against GDP per capita and their value-added shares plotted against all levels of per capita GDP, from US$1,000 to US$40,000. This allowed to identify the share at which each industry peaked. Table 6.1.1 shows the share at which industries peak and the corresponding GDP per capita. As can be appreciated, some industries cluster at or below US$3,000 GDP per capita. These will be termed "early industries" since they peak at low levels of GDP per capita or early on in the development process. A second group of industries cluster at middle

Table 6.1.1   Industries' peak share

Manufacturing industries	Highest share in MVA (%)	Reached at ($US GDP per capita)
Food and beverages	23.8	3,000
Tobacco	5.4	1,000
Textiles	13.2	1,000
Wearing apparel	8.3	1,000
Wood products	2.9	1,000
Paper	3.1	6,000
Printing and publishing	4.4	2,000
Coke and refined petroleum	4.2	1,000
Chemicals	20.7	40,000
Rubber and plastic	5.5	40,000
Non-metallic minerals	6.2	3,000
Basic metals	6.7	16,000
Fabricated metals	4.7	14,000
Machinery and equipment	9.1	40,000
Electrical machinery and apparatus	30.3	40,000
Precision instruments	0.8	5,000
Motor vehicles	10.2	23,000
Furniture, n.e.c.	7.8	1,000

Source: Elaborated on the basis of UNIDO INDSTAT2 (2012).

levels of GDP per capita, between US$5,000 and US$16,000, and are dubbed "middle industries." Basic Metals and Fabricated Metals also have a "peak" at US$1,000 GDP per capita but were classified as middle industries on account of the later "peak" (see also section 6.1.4.3.2). Finally, "late industries" have their higher shares in MVA at or above US$23,000 GDP per capita.

6.1.4   Results and findings

6.1.4.1   Size matters

Early on in the structural change tradition it was believed that country size had an overarching influence on economic structural change (Chenery and Taylor, 1968; Perkins and Syrquin, 1989). Thus, instead of including population in the equation as an additional explanatory variable, many studies resorted to divide countries into size groups, applying a given population size as a threshold. The problem related to this approach in past studies was that this threshold was often arbitrarily used without determining whether such groups statistically differed in terms of their development patterns.

The procedure described in the previous section applied statistical tests to distinguish threshold values. The results suggested that medium-sized countries with a population between three million to 12.5 million have different development patterns than small-sized countries with a population of less than three million for 13 out of 18 manufacturing industries. The development patterns of all industries in large-sized countries with a population of over 12.5 million differ from those in medium-sized countries. These results would seem to confirm the widely held view that country size matters.

Figure 6.1.4 illustrates some of these differences in the food and beverage industry. Value added per capita in large countries grows faster than GDP per capita up to the US$15,000 mark and continues to grow, although at a comparatively lower rate, at higher income levels. Value added per capita growth in middle income countries is faster than GDP until around US$5,000 GDP per capita, when it starts decelerating, and the industry begins contracting at around US$40,000 GDP per capita. In small countries value added per capita growth would seem to increasingly trail behind real GDP per capita growth.

6.1.4.2   Shifting shares

In examining the graphs depicting the change in MVA share of early, middle and late industries in large countries (Figure 6.1.5), it is noticeable that the weight of early industries declines sharply after their peak. From jointly representing – excluding food and beverages – a combined share of 49 percent of MVA when GDP per capita is US$1,000, their combined share is halved by the time GDP per capita reaches US$10,000. Some industries, such as furniture, wood products, tobacco, and textiles, lose half of their top share in MVA before GDP per capita reaches US$8,000, a relatively short lifespan. Other early industries, such as wearing apparel, printing and publishing, coke and refined petroleum, and non-metallic minerals, exhibit more robustness as they gradually assume a greater importance than other early industries, manage to keep their momentum longer and only lose half of their top share in MVA at levels of GDP per capita between US$11,000 and US$22,000. Beyond this latter level, however, the combined share of all early industries, excluding food and beverages, drops relentlessly, from 12 percent of MVA to just 6 percent when GDP per capita reaches US$40,000.

The food and beverages industry merits a separate account. Having registered its larger share in MVA at US$3,000 GDP per capita, and afterward experiencing the continued decline common to other early industries, the food and beverages industry shows remarkable strength, as it manages to sustain its presence for much longer, losing half of their top share in MVA only at US$39,000 GDP per capita. Furthermore, the graph and accompanying calculations would seem to suggest that the industry's share in MVA faces a floor of around 10 percent in large countries. Both of these findings highlight the food and beverages industry's sustainability and its role as a cornerstone in industrial growth.

The shares of middle industries in MVA follow a much smoother pattern as they gradually expand and, later, decrease. From a top combined share in

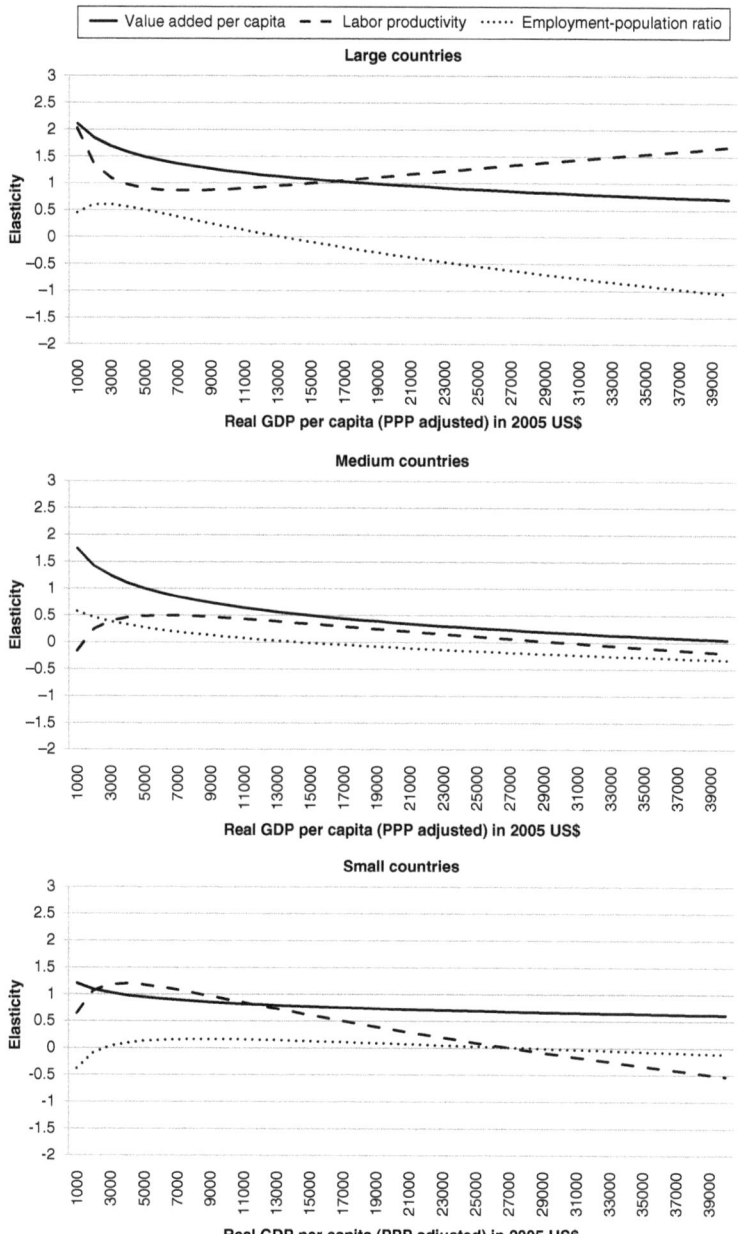

Figure 6.1.4 Value added, labor productivity and employment growth patterns in the food and beverage industry

Source: Elaborated on the basis of UNIDO INDSTAT2 (2012).

470

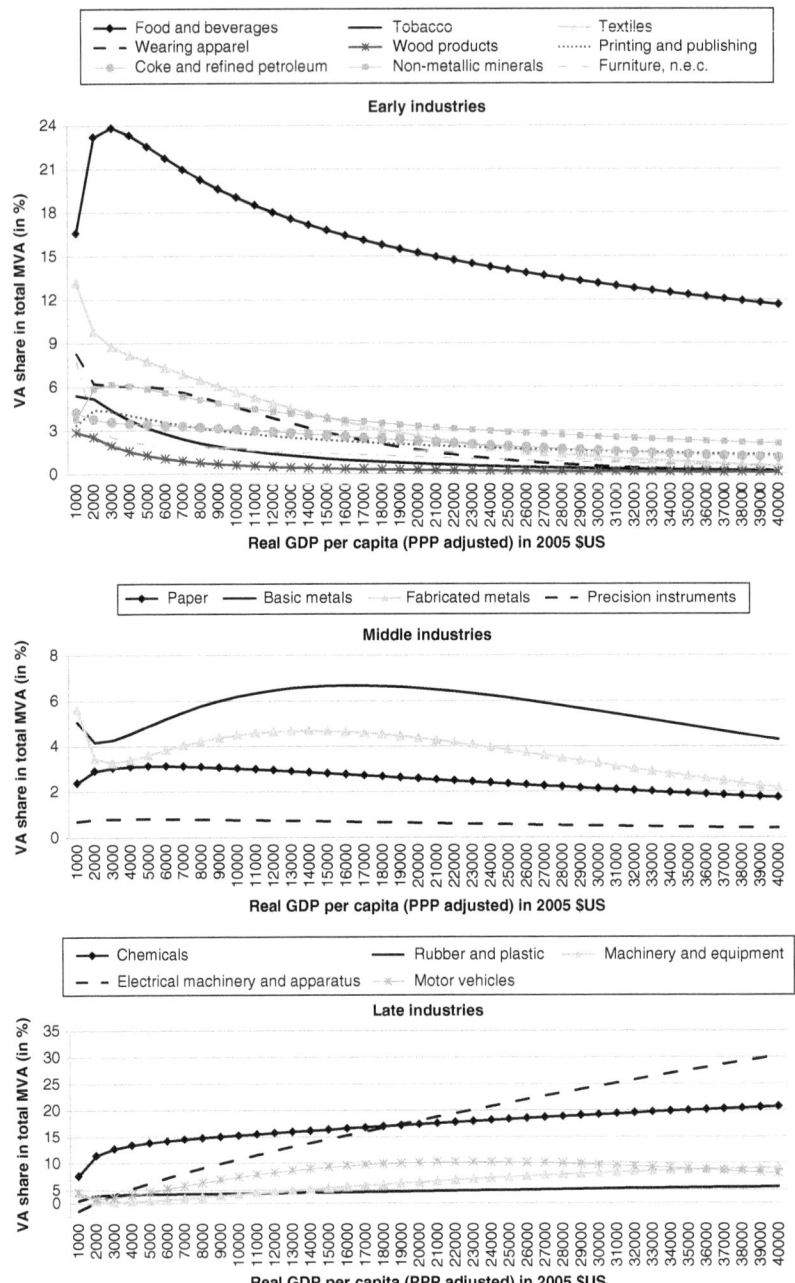

Figure 6.1.5 Change in share of MVA by level of per capita GDP: early, middle and late industries

Source: Elaborated on the basis of UNIDO INDSTAT2 (2012).

MVA of close to 15 percent when GDP per capita stands at US$14,000, these industries slowly lose their weight but still account for a share in MVA of just below 9 percent at US$40,000 GDP per capita. Individually, for almost all per capita GDP levels, these industries retain at least half of their highest share in MVA, pointing to their stability and "long life." The basic metals and fabricated metals industries exhibit a singular pattern, as they actually score two peaks, the first one at US$1,000 per capita GDP. After a sharp decline in weight between US$1,000 and US$2,000 GDP per capita, they show remarkable resilience and achieve a second "peak" at US$16,000 and US$14,000, respectively, suggesting a strong supporting role in the development of both, the early industries and the more dynamic, late manufacturing industries.

The industries classified as late industries are by far the most dynamic – in terms of increasing their share of MVA – continually expanding from a combined share of 20 percent at US$1,000 GDP per capita to over 73 percent at US$40,000. Individually, most of them were still increasing their share in MVA at US$40,000 GDP per capita; only the motor vehicles industry reached a peak earlier (at US$23,000), although it is possible that other industries in this group might see a limit to their share growth.

Summing up, early industries perform a critical role in the take-off of industry and the first stage of structural transformation, moving from primary agricultural activities into manufacturing. However, they are short-lived. Already at around US$5,000 GDP per capita they are no longer the largest group, excluding food and beverages, and by US$10,000 GDP per capita they have lost half of their share in MVA. Inter-industry structural change has already kicked in and shifts within manufacturing are taking place to both middle and late industries. Late industries become the most dynamic industries and double their share in MVA to around 42 percent by the US$10,000 GDP per capita mark.

Structural transformation is consolidated by US$23,0000 as late industries increase their share in MVA by 50 percent. The demise of early industries is completed as they halve again their share in MVA at the same level of GDP per capita. Middle industries share in MVA remains relatively stable throughout.

6.1.4.3 Growth patterns[7]

What is the relationship between growth patterns in value added, labor productivity and employment in large countries as the weight of manufacturing shifts? Does employment growth drive value added growth or is it labor productivity growth? Do the same drivers remain as structural change and economic development take place?

6.1.4.3.1 Early industries

In early industries increases in value added per capita arise through different combinations of both the labor productivity and employment growth rates.

In the first place, in some industries the increases in production take place clearly on account of the steady growth of labor productivity, that is accompanied by a nearly equivalent decline in the employment growth rate. This pattern is evident in the food and beverages industry, usually the largest manufacturing industry up to US$15,000 of GDP per capita, but also in the non-metallic minerals and the printing and publishing industries. The difference between these industries lies in the speed of the process, as the non-metallic mineral industry experiences both a faster productivity growth rate and a faster decline of the employment growth rate while the printing and publishing industry shows a smoother track in both (see top row in Figure 6.1.6).

In a second set of industries, the initial increases in production attributable to fast growth in labor productivity cannot be sustained beyond a certain level of GDP per capita, as the steady decline in the employment growth rate largely offsets any gains. In the case of the textile industry, labor productivity growth is fast but not sufficient to compensate for the steep decline in employment growth. After an initial growth spurt, value added per capita growth rate in the industry starts lagging behind at around US$8,000 of GDP per capita and becomes negative at US$18,000. The tobacco industry exhibits a similar pattern, and although it starts falling behind GDP growth at a figure as low as US$4,000 of GDP per capita, owing to the early mechanization that is possible in this industry, the gains in labor productivity that ensue help sustain increases in production up to US$16,000 GDP per capita. The coke and refined petroleum industry differs in magnitude and timing but shows the same trend as the two industries in this group (see second row in Figure 6.1.6). In the end the very high labor productivity growth rate becomes insufficient to offset the losses brought about by the fall in the employment growth rate and value added per capita starts to fall, albeit at the high level of US$34,000 GDP per capita.

A third group of industries records large increases in production initially, on account of a high employment growth rate, but again they are unsustainable once the employment growth rate enters a sharp decline. This is the case of the wearing apparel industry, which after high value added per capita growth at an early stage of a country's development (from US$1,000 to US$8,000 GDP per capita), starts to contract as early as at US$14,000 GDP per capita, because of the collapse in employment growth and despite a gradual increase in the rate of labor productivity growth. The wearing apparel industry's growth rate, therefore, depends largely on labor's cost competitiveness, as the wearing apparel industry does not seem to render much room for the substitution of labor for capital. The furniture and n.e.c. industries exhibit a somewhat similar pattern, that is, falling output on account of persistent falls in the employment growth rate and despite late labor productivity gains, albeit at a much more moderate pace and therefore reaching negative rates of output growth at US$29,000 GDP per capita (see bottom row in Figure 6.1.6). The wood products industry shares some commonalities with

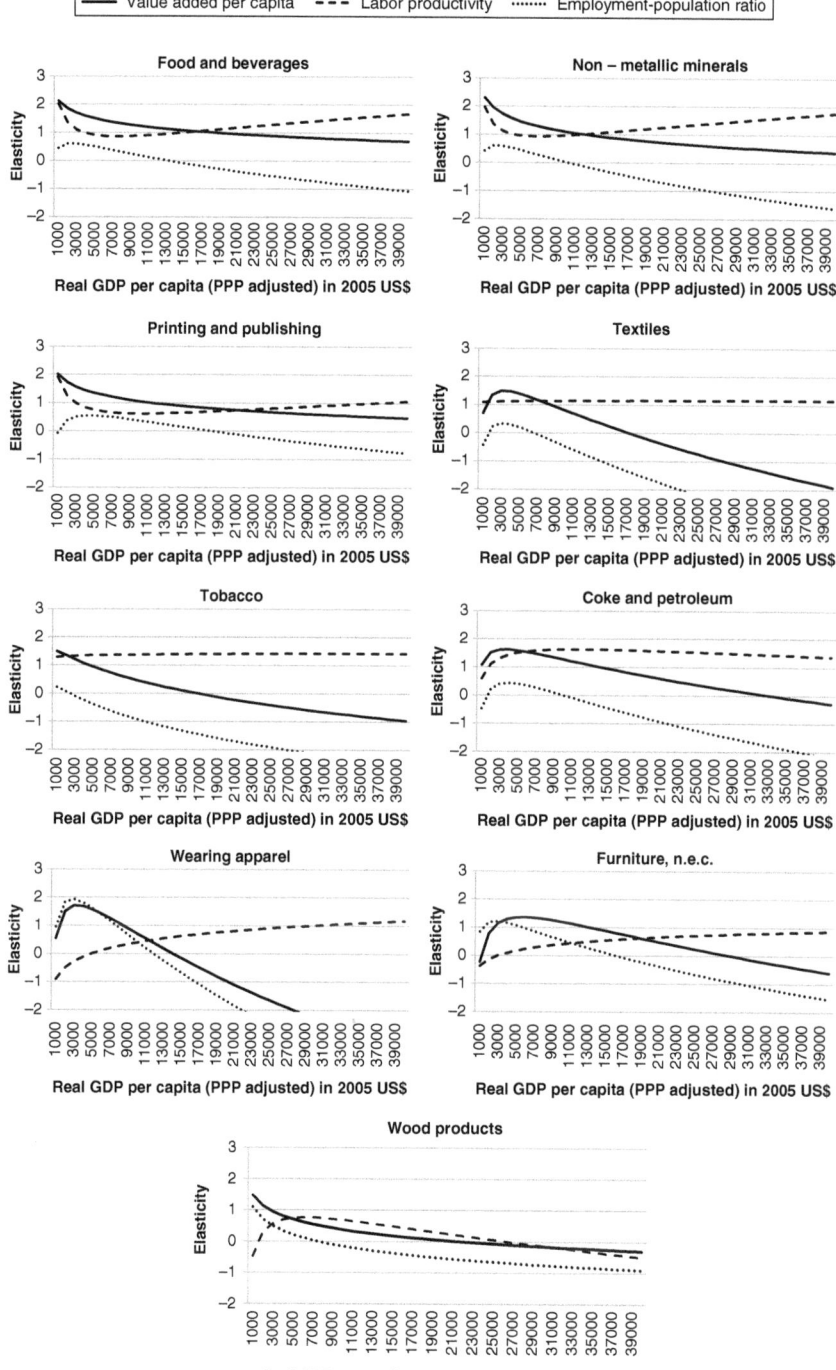

Legend (top): Value added per capita — Labor productivity - - - Employment-population ratio ....

Figure 6.1.6 Early industries: growth of value added per capita, labor productivity and employment population ratio by industry

Source: Elaborated on the basis of UNIDO INDSTAT2 (2012).

the previous two and is therefore included in this group, although there is very modest growth in the early stages and output growth starts lagging behind GDP at US$3,000 GDP per capita. A second difference is that labor productivity growth decelerates as GDP per capita increases, which combines with poor employment growth. However, the pace of decline of labor productivity and employment growth is so slow that output is still able to grow until GDP per capita reaches US$20,000.

When examining these early industries in the light of the structural change that is taking place in manufacturing, using US$10,000 and US$23,000 GDP per capita as reference "breaking points," some interesting findings come to the fore. By the first "hurdle" of US$10,000 GDP per capita, most early industries are either already shedding jobs or are about to start doing so as by now they have lost half their share in MVA. This marks the end of labor-intensive manufacturing. Only three industries (wearing apparel, paper and publishing, and the furniture and n.e.c. industries) still register employment growth at this level of GDP per capita. The remaining industries are busy substituting headcount for improved labor productivity, investing in new technologies and automation, in order to sustain growth – or avoid collapse.

By the second "hurdle" of US$23,000 GDP per capita, five early industries (food and beverages, printing and publishing, coke and refined petroleum, non-metallic minerals, and furniture and n.e.c. industries) still manage to expand output, exclusively on account of the gains in labor productivity enabled by technological upgrading. Initial technological efforts to keep the industries going, are in no way sufficient to arrest the inexorable decline in wearing and apparel, textiles, wood, and tobacco industries. In the long run, only food and beverages, printing and publishing and non-metallic minerals continue to expand.

6.1.4.3.2   Middle industries

The four middle industries exhibit fairly similar relationships between the growth of their value added per capita, labor productivity, and employment ratios; the differences between them, if any, are mostly of timing and degree. They all have a long period of fast expansion of output, from relatively low levels of income up to around US$18,000 GDP per capita (paper: US$18,000; basic metals: US$20,000; fabricated metals: US$18,000; precision instruments: US$17,000), and they all keep growing, although at a lower rate than per capita GDP, until very high levels of income have been reached (see Figure 6.1.7). The paper and the basic metals industries record very high labor productivity growth rates which largely offset the decline of the employment growth rate and helps sustain the growth of value added in both industries up to US$40,000 GDP per capita.

The strong growth of output in the fabricated metals industry arises equally from initially high productivity growth rates and from a moderate expansion of employment. However, as both productivity and employment

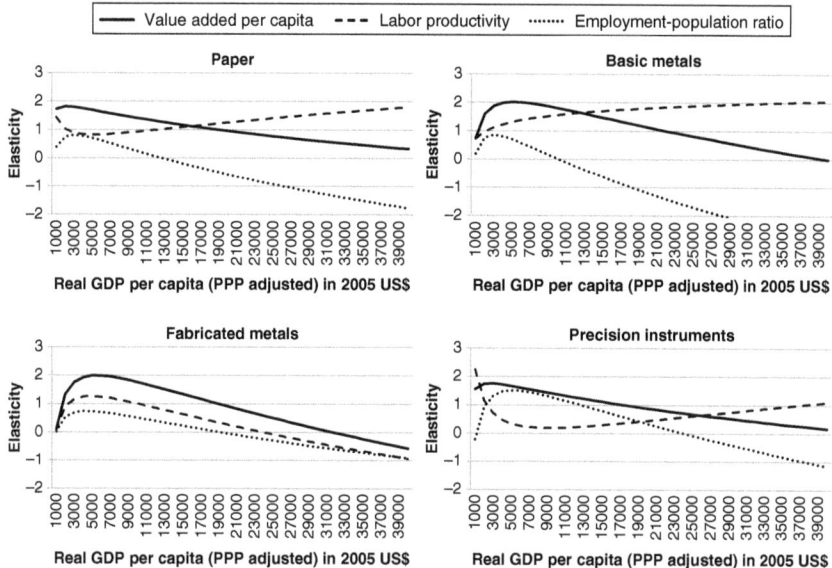

Figure 6.1.7 Middle industries: growth of value added per capita, labor productivity and employment population ratio by industry
Source: Elaborated on the basis of UNIDO INSTAT2 (2012).

have a slowly declining growth rate, the growth of value added per capita is sustained until US$31,000 GDP per capita, a very similar pattern to that observed in the wood products industry.

Despite its relatively small size, the precision instruments industry is a contributor to GDP growth until US$16,000 GDP per capita, thanks, to a large extent, to its employment generation capacity. At middle levels of income, labor productivity starts to take off, substituting for employment growth as the driver and manages to sustain output growth up until US$40,000 GDP per capita.

Given the supporting role middle industries play in the process of industrialization as input providers, it would be interesting to establish how they perform in the presence of structural change. At US$10,000 GDP per capita, the paper and basic metals industries are on the verge of starting to cut jobs. From then on, gains in output per capita in these industries are exclusively accounted for by gains in productivity. By contrast, both the fabricated metal and the precision industries are still generating employment at this level of GDP per capita and contributing to the fast growth in value added per capita. Whereas the former industry also exhibits a healthy rate of productivity gains, the latter is just about to embark in a major technological effort to redress a shortcoming in this area.

At US$23,000 GDP per capita, the growth of value added per capita in both the paper and basic metals industries starts to lag behind GDP per capita growth, which is attributable to the continued loss in employment. In the fabricated metals industry both labor productivity and employment growth becomes negative pre-announcing the eventual decline in output whereas in the precision instruments industry it is only employment that starts falling, as the earlier technological efforts start bearing fruits and prolong the life of the industry. All in all, except for Fabricated metals, middle industries keep output going by increasing the capital intensity and high-tech content of their processes.

6.1.4.3.3   Late industries

These are extraordinarily fast-growing industries that expand their value added per capita at a faster rate than the rest of the economy at all GDP per capita levels and continue to grow when most of the other industries have started to fade away. They owe their dynamism to an unrivaled capacity to sustain a fast growth rate of labor productivity through innovation and technological development, which, in the case of the chemicals and, particularly, the electrical machinery and apparatus industries, by far offsets the contraction in employment that accompanies such technological upgrading.

While labor productivity growth in the machinery and equipment industry is also firm and on the rise at all GDP per capita levels, its impact on the growth of value added per capita is eroded by drastic reductions in employment that set in around US$18,000 GDP per capita. This is in clear contrast with the initial development of this industry, when employment growth is a great contributor to value added per capita growth.

The rubber and plastics industry, despite its comparatively less dynamic labor productivity growth in this group, faces a mild decline in employment growth, which allows the attainment of robust output growth rates. Interestingly enough, this industry scores the highest income level for employment generation: employment is still growing, albeit minimally, at US$28,000 GDP per capita.

The value added of the motor vehicle industry expands faster than the overall economy up to US$26,000 GDP per capita, but because the industry is characterized by heavy automation and the possibility of large scale economies, the amount of labor displaced substantially exceeds the gains in productivity. As a result, the growth in value added per capita quickly falls behind that of GDP per capita and by US$40,000 it is close to become negative.

As to the drivers of growth in manufacturing in the process of structural change, in the case of late industries, it is clear that output growth arises overwhelmingly from productivity gains derived from product and process innovations, increasing returns to scale and growing capital intensity, and

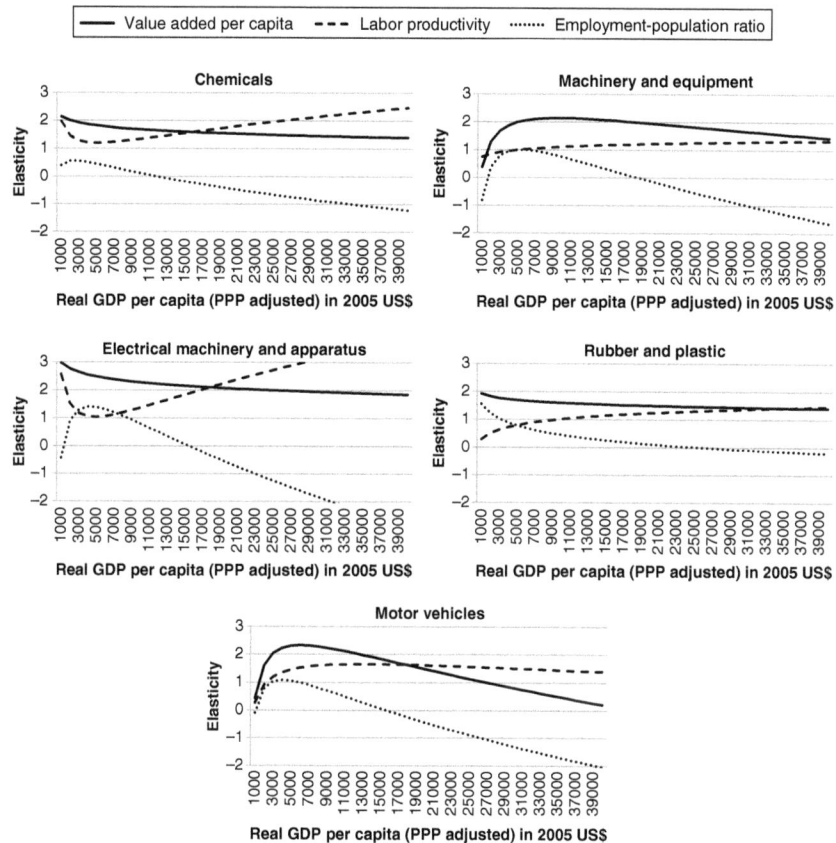

Figure 6.1.8 Late industries: growth of value added per capita, labor productivity and employment population ratio by industry
Source: Elaborated on the basis of UNIDO INDSTAT2 (2012).

improvements in skills and human capital. At low levels of GDP per capita output growth is also coming from moderate gains in employment, depending on the particular industry. The US$10,000 GDP per capita landmark at which these late industries double their weight in MVA bring about no change in the drivers of growth for most of them. The only major event at this point is the fall in employment in the chemical industry. By the second landmark of structural change, at US$23,000 GDP per capita, the situation is different: falls in employment have been registered in all other industries from GDP per capita levels of US$15,000 upwards, the last to turn to job shedding was the rubber and plastics industry. For all industries, however, labor productivity remains a strong pull factor of output growth.

6.1.5   Implications for industrial policy

The last few years have seen a revival of industrial policy as developed country governments attempt to revive the global economy and spur economic growth through financial support for the industrial sector and domestic demand stimulus packages. Industrial policies are meant to play a key role in inducing industrial transformation, diversification and upgrading toward more resilient and competitive industries. A key role for industrial policy is to anticipate and promote structural change, often through facilitating it by removing obstacles and correcting for market failures, other times by building the technological capabilities that will eventually allow new industries to emerge (Chang, 2010; Lall, 1992; Lauridsen, 2010; Lin, 2012; Szirmai et al., 2013; Syrquin, 2007).

Anticipating where to diversify and what to upgrade requires practical approaches to identify sectoral growth. One such approach, called Growth Diagnostics, was developed by Hausmann et al. (2005). Essentially this approach focuses on the binding constraints to growth faced by individual economies, according to their specific circumstances, opportunities, and constraints. Based on economic theory, the authors propose a decision tree that begins by asking two questions: Are the costs of financing domestic investment high? Are the private returns to domestic investment low? The approach then moves down the decision tree with a number of policy questions such as if it is a case of poor finance, are the problems with domestic financial markets or external ones? Or, if the problem is one of low returns, is that due to the insufficient supply of factors of production or poor access to appropriate technologies? The approach does not focus on specific sectoral constraints despite the questions raised can be also asked at the sectoral level.

A more recent approach and specifically developed for the identification of industries at the sectoral level is Lin and Monga's (2010; see also te Velde, 2011). The approach is based on what the authors argue are "latent comparative advantages," that is comparative advantages that exist due to the resource endowment of an economy but that are yet to be detected and exploited by the private sector. Lin and Monga's (2010) approach includes six steps that comprise the identification and selection of firms, the detection of constraints to technological upgrading or entry, the potential for attracting foreign direct investment, attempts at self-discovery by the private sector, the use of special economic zones or industrial parks, and tax, financial, or foreign exchange support for firms entering industries identified through this process. In particular, during the first step "the government in a developing country can identify the list of tradable goods and services that have been produced for about 20 years in dynamically growing countries with similar endowment structures and a per capita income that is about 100 percent higher than their own."

The approach and findings presented in the previous pages can contribute to the identification of new sectors for investment and gaps in industrial structure vis-à-vis countries of similar characteristics. Although there is still some way to go in terms of tradability and endowments, issues that will be addressed in the concluding section of the paper, this "Industrial Structure and Patterns of Growth" approach can provide a dynamic and comparative account of the evolution of industry at different levels of GDP per capita and help explore the issue of which industries are growing rapidly and for how long.[8] It has the added advantage that it can help to examine the questions of whether it is capital (working though labor productivity) or labor that is potentially driving that growth and hence can help select industries that may be more in tune with a particular country's resource endowment, or, at least, provide an indicator of what resources need to be developed.

In order to examine how the "Industrial Structure and Patterns of Growth" approach may help to identify both entry and exit points into different industries in large countries let's consider value added per capita elasticities first. Figure 6.1.9 shows the fastest- and slowest-growing early, middle and late industries. Food and beverages, paper and electrical machinery and apparatus are respectively the fastest growing and are represented by the continuous line. Furniture and n.e.c, fabricated metals and machinery and equipment are respectively the slowest growing and are represented by the dotted line.

In the case of Egypt, with a GDP per capita of US$5,700 in 2007, it pays off to enter the food and beverages industry as the industry will continue growing more rapidly than GDP until GDP per capita reaches US$14,000 and indeed, although the industry growth slows down below GDP thereafter, it may be worth for Egypt to stay in the food and beverages industry as it remains growing at all GDP per capita levels. It also pays off Egypt to enter the furniture and n.e.c. industry as its growth is above GDP per capita growth until US$13,000 although by US$28,000 GDP per capita exiting the industry may be what is needed since beyond that point GDP per capita would be dragged down. In middle industries Egypt may want to enter the paper industry as it grows until US$18,000 GDP per capita faster than GDP growth and remains growing at all levels of income. It may be equally worth it to enter the fabricated metals industry until around US$31,000 GDP per capita, the point at which the industry reduces output per capita. In late industries, it pays Egypt to enter the "fast-" and "slow-" growing electrical machinery and apparatus and machinery and equipment as their growth rate will remain above that of GDP for all levels of GDP per capita.

For South Africa, at a GDP per capita of US$10,400 in 2007, there is little room left to profit from the food and beverages industry although somewhat more from the furniture and n.e.c industry before growth turns negative. In middle industries, South Africa still stands to gain from entering the paper and fabricated metal products industries, although, as in the case of Egypt, the country will have to consider leaving at around US$31,000 GDP

480

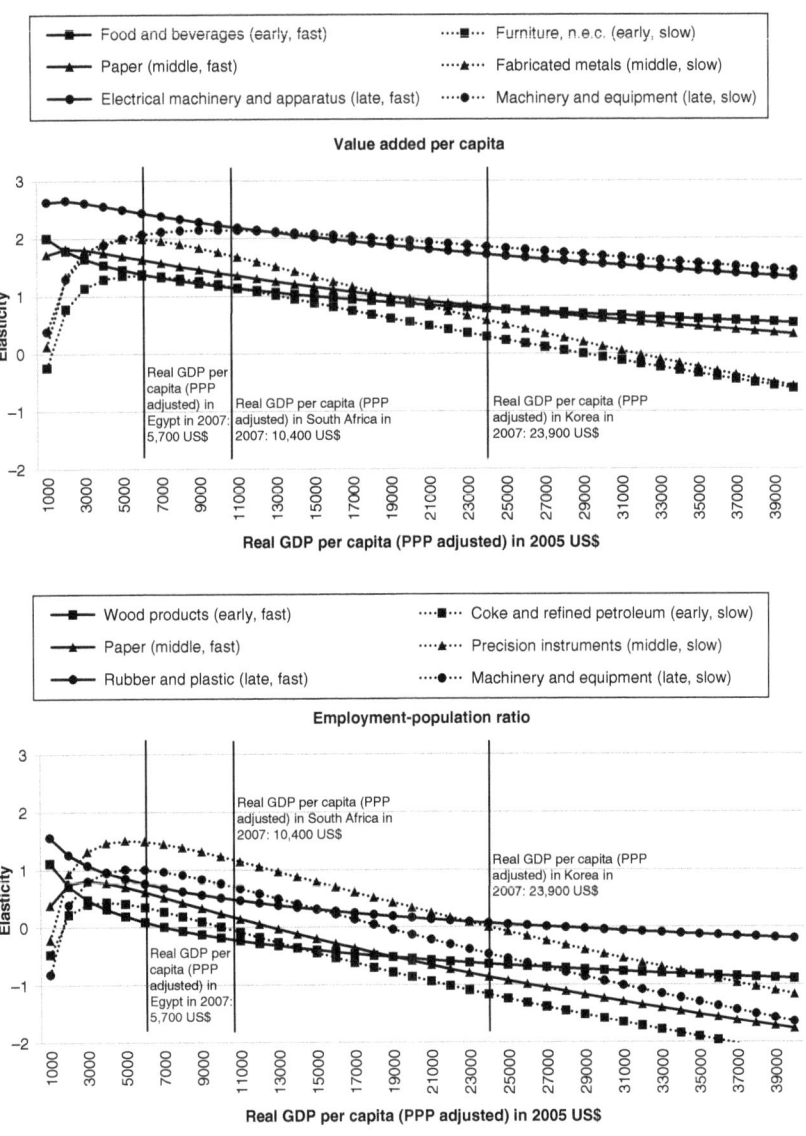

Figure 6.1.9 Fast- and slow-growing early, middle and late industries
Source: Elaborated on the basis of UNIDO INDSTAT2 (2012).

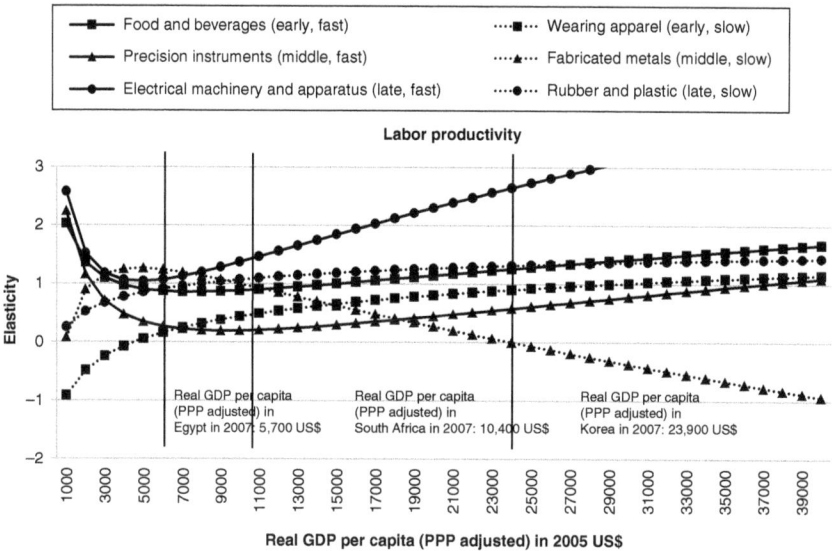

Figure 6.1.9 Continued

per capita. In late industries, South Africa stands to make gains of entering the electrical machinery and apparatus and machinery and equipment.

The Republic of Korea, at a GDP per capita of US23,900 in 2007, faces a much narrower and clearer range of choices. The country will benefit mostly by entering high productivity late industries that are still growing faster than GDP at this level of GDP per capita, entering any of the other industries will mean slower growth than GDP per capita growth or negative growth.

The "Industrial Structure and Patterns of Growth" approach has the advantage that policymakers can take value-added growth, labor productivity growth and employment growth as objectives in themselves and make entry and exit decisions on the strategic premium put into any one of these objectives. In the middle industries, for example, Egypt may consider entering the precision instruments rather than the paper industry. Even though the paper industry has a faster value-added per capita growth rate than precision instruments, the employment population ratio in the latter grows faster than the overall economy between US$2,000 and US$12,000 GDP per capita, and the industry continues generating employment up to US$23,000 GDP per capita. Other countries may be willing to expand investment in physical capital and promote industries with a high labor productivity ratio. While on grounds of value added per capita growth South Africa may have some doubts about entering the food and beverages industry, the potential for labor productivity growth is such that the country may really have little choice but to enter the industry.

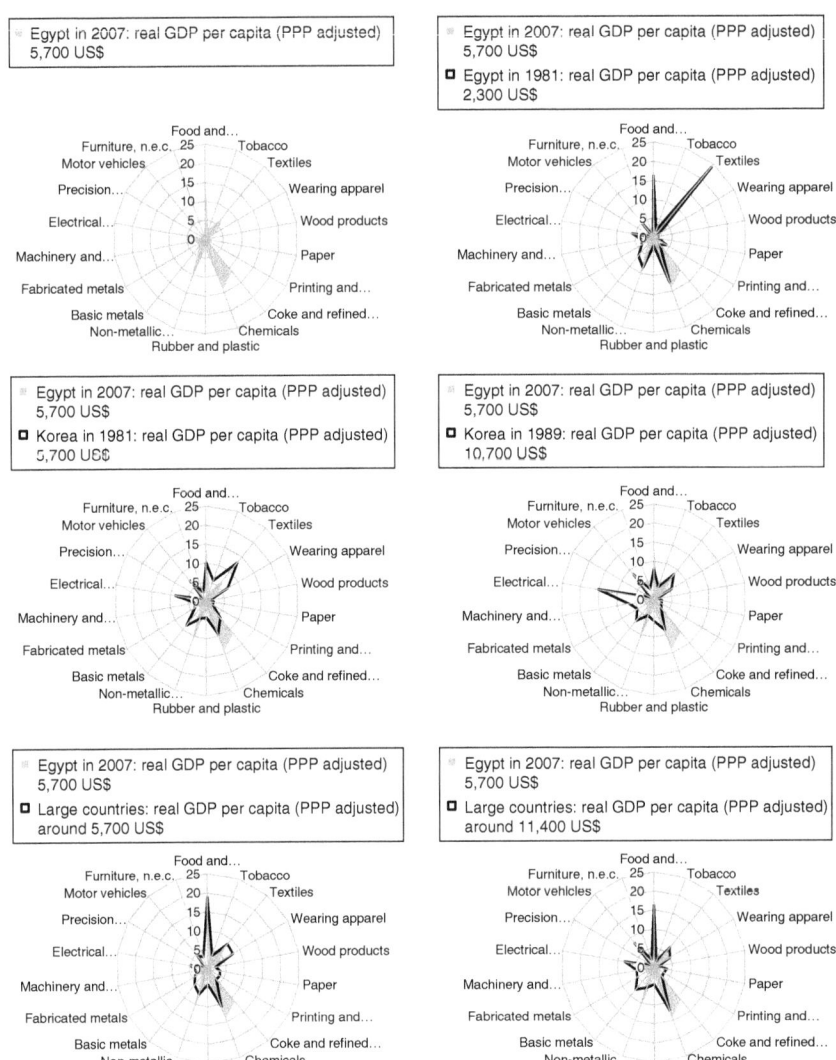

Figure 6.1.10   Share of MVA by industry for Egypt, Republic of Korea and large countries
Source: Elaborated on the basis of UNIDO INDSTAT2 (2012).

It is worth noting that the "Industrial Structure and Patterns of Growth" method should be seen not as a substitute for the Growth Diagnostics or Growth Identification and Facilitation methodologies but rather as a complement to them. No single approach can provide all the necessary information to make a proper decision as to which sectors in which to invest. Rather sectoral choices will be the result of a combination of methodologies and theoretical perspectives; an in-depth examination of the characteristics, conditions, and capabilities available in a particular country; the feasibility of the proposed solutions; and the degree of exploration and information exchange that takes place between relevant stakeholders, including the private sector. In the end, sector identification will be a judgment call by the government based on the best information and analysis available at the time.

One final point regarding the "Industrial Structure and Patterns of Growth" approach. One additional advantage of the method is that it allows for different types of comparisons across countries, levels of GDP per capita and groupings. Figure 6.1.10 shows the industrial structure (share of MVA) of Egypt, the Republic of Korea and large countries, the grouping to which both countries belong. Egypt's industrial structure when GDP per capita is US$5,700 in 2007 is compared with that of 1981, when the country had half the GDP per capita. Comparisons are also performed with the Republic of Korea and the average for large countries at the same and around double the GDP per capita.

While benchmarking can lead to misleading results when the comparators differ significantly and tell us very little of the underlying processes, the approach allows us to compare countries on the same level of income and identify possible performance gaps that can be subjected to further investigation. As was seen in section 6.1.2, where there was a comparison of Republic of Korea and Indonesia, it is also possible to estimate the nature of the effort in terms of growth rate or the number of years required to achieve a desired industrial structure. Labor productivity comparisons may also provide some idea of the technological effort that may be required in the catching-up process. On the whole, this benchmarking approach, if accompanied by further research and understanding of the underlying relations and in the context of a number of complementary methodologies, can help to identify problem areas and provide useful additional insights into the identification of yet to emerge industrial sectors.

6.1.6 Conclusions

The evidence suggested that while some industries can and will initially grow on the basis of adding labor resources more rapidly, it is only those industries that improve productivity substantially that will survive in the long run. Though the paper identified three patterns of growth, one based on increasing labor utilization, a second focusing on both expanding labor use while improving technology and a third one prioritizing technological change and innovation, it was the latter, that continually raised the degree of efficiency in the use of the resources, which is what is behind the industries that have come to dominate the industrial landscape. From early industries, food and beverages, non-metallic minerals, and publishing and printing; from middle industries, basic metals, paper and precision instruments; and all late industries followed this pattern. By US$40,000 GDP per capita these industries account for around 90 percent of all MVA.

In terms of the relationship between growth patterns and structural change, one major conclusion is that US$10,000 GDP per capita is a major turning point in the structure of industry since what at that point used to be labor-intensive industries experience a major erosion of their labor cost advantage and begin to shed labor. The reduction of labor also begins biting the paper and basic metals industries among the middle industries and the chemical industry, among the late industries. Indeed, we have dubbed this the "end of labor-intensive manufacturing." By contrast, structural change beyond the US$23,000 GDP per capita level involves the consolidation of industries that have continuously pursued technological upgrading, innovation, and scale and capital intensity advantages.

The analysis performed also has the potential to address one of the key dimensions of industrial policymaking, namely, the identification of potential growth sectors. Entry points to different industries can be established by connecting the GDP per capita of a country at any point in time and with the growth patterns of individual industries also expressed in terms of GDP per capita. Multiple objectives can be introduced into the methodology and trade-offs between them should be evaluated. Exit points can also be identified as industry growth patterns turn negative. The combination of the values and trends in different forms also allows the benchmarking of industries across countries. The entry and exit and benchmarking methodologies are not substitutes for other available approaches but rather a complement to them as it is argued that a proper evaluation and identification of new industrial sectors requires informed judgment, rather than magical recipes.

The work presented here is in its very preliminary stages. There are a significant number of extensions that could be made with the data already available in UNIDO's industrial statistics. There is potential for expanding the number of variables to include capital–labor ratios, wages, average firm size, and, eventually, total factor productivity (TFP). There is the potential to divide the sample by population density and natural resource endowments or to include control variables in existing regressions taking account of population density and natural resource endowments and other similar factors. The number of industries could be increased to 150–180 by working on more disaggregated ISIC levels. Going beyond available industrial statistics, new variables could be added – such as energy and water intensity as well as other production inputs. Linkages could be explored by connecting to input–output tables. And, finally, the approach could be applied to trade data and/or a combination of industrial and trade data.

Appendix 1: Regression Results

A1.1. Value added per capita regressions

		lrgdpl_pwt63_ln	lrgdpl_pwt63_sq	lrgdpl_pwt63_cu	_cons	N	r2
15	Food and beverages	4.73***	-0.19***	-0.05**	-22.47***	874	0.70
16	Tobacco	-5.21	1.02		4.42	780	0.41
17	Textiles	-34.44***	4.43***	-0.18***	87.45***	916	0.44
18	Wearing apparel	-52.58***	6.70***	-0.28***	134.84***	851	0.40
20	Wood products	4.79***	-0.24***		-22.25***	869	0.26
21	Paper	-8.26*	1.32**	-0.06***	12.36	855	0.71
22	Printing and publishing	4.92***	-0.21***		-24.42***	807	0.48
23	Coke and refined petroleum	-20.47***	2.70***	-0.11***	48.67***	731	0.53
24	Chemicals	3.52***	-0.10***		-19.18***	873	0.70
25	Rubber and plastic	2.89***	-0.07**		-17.19***	876	0.58
26	Non-metallic minerals	5.89***	-0.26***		-28.62***	890	0.62
27	Basic metals	-32.78***	4.07***	-0.16***	84.40***	751	0.74
28	Fabricated metals	-45.88***	5.56***	-0.22***	122.60***	835	0.61
29	Machinery and equipment	-26.85***	3.16***	-0.11***	72.30***	796	0.46
31	Electrical machinery and apparatus	5.04***	-0.15***		-29.29***	824	0.69
33	Precision instruments	-11.35	1.66*	-0.07**	20.19	690	0.53
34	Motor vehicles	-42.51***	5.15***	-0.20***	112.69***	785	0.61
36	Furniture, n.e.c.	-37.84***	4.53***	-0.17***	103.20***	796	0.40

=* p<0.10
** p<0.05
*** p<0.01"

A1.2. Labor productivity

		lrgdpl_pwt63_ln	lrgdpl_pwt63_sq	lrgdpl_pwt63_cu	_cons	N	r2
15	Food and beverages	23.77***	-2.57***	0.10***	-65.82***	758	0.60
16	Tobacco	1.00	0.02	0.00		667	0.52
17	Textiles	0.95*	0.01	-0.25		796	0.50
18	Wearing apparel	-4.77***	0.28***	28.96***		737	0.07
20	Wood products	-27.22***	3.20***	-0.12***	84.02***	753	0.17
21	Paper	17.69***	-1.98***	0.08***	-45.42***	734	0.45
22	Printing and publishing	21.15***	-2.22**	0.08**	-58.97***	683	0.25
23	Coke and refined petroleum	-13.30*	1.59*	-0.06*	43.37*	636	0.47
24	Chemicals	22.80***	-2.54***	0.10***	-61.76***	770	0.66
25	Rubber and plastic	-1.93***	0.16***	13.80***		761	0.43
26	Non-metallic minerals	22.49***	-2.43***	0.09***	-62.22***	770	0.54
27	Basic metals	-1.76***	0.18***	11.07***		659	0.60
28	Fabricated metals	-33.68***	4.12***	-0.16***	97.05***	741	0.40
29	Machinery and equipment	-0.36	0.08*	6.21*		678	0.29
31	Electrical machinery and apparatus	45.60***	-5.26***	0.21***	-125.55***	708	0.47
33	Precision instruments	34.93***	-3.81***	0.14***	-97.59***	608	0.12
34	Motor vehicles	-17.34**	2.00**	-0.07**	54.95**	692	0.44
36	Furniture, n.e.c.	-2.73***	0.17***	19.98***		699	0.04

=* p<0.10
** p<0.05
*** p<0.01"

A1.3. Employment-population ratio

		lrgdpl_pwt63_ln	lrgdpl_pwt63_sq	lrgdpl_pwt63_cu	_cons	N	r2
15	Food and beverages	−12.27***	1.65***	−0.07***	22.76***	1274	0.25
16	Tobacco	−7.52*	1.17**	−0.06***	7.48	1242	0.30
17	Textiles	−37.63***	4.71***	−0.20***	93.46***	1317	0.36
18	Wearing apparel	−56.59***	7.37***	−0.31***	132.29***	1318	0.46
20	Wood products	4.82***	−0.27***	−28.54***		1305	0.09
21	Paper	−22.90***	2.97***	−0.12***	48.76***	1301	0.24
22	Printing and publishing	−18.99***	2.32***	−0.09***	42.83***	1288	0.13
23	Coke and refined petroleum	−32.88***	4.03***	−0.16***	79.64***	1186	0.10
24	Chemicals	−13.13***	1.76***	−0.08***	24.32***	1301	0.23
25	Rubber and plastic	4.87***	−0.24***	−31.24***		1307	0.44
26	Non-metallic minerals	−15.84***	2.12***	−0.09***	30.93***	1313	0.21
27	Basic metals	−35.01***	4.49***	−0.19***	81.60***	1283	0.22
28	Fabricated metals	−22.64***	2.79***	−0.11***	52.30***	1302	0.17
29	Machinery and equipment	−46.96***	5.59***	−0.22***	121.65***	1256	0.19
31	Electrical machinery and apparatus	−58.60***	7.17***	−0.29***	148.60***	1267	0.34
33	Precision instruments	−45.16***	5.46***	−0.21***	111.20***	1207	0.28
34	Motor vehicles	−40.18***	4.96***	−0.20***	98.50***	1286	0.25
36	Furniture, n.e.c.	−22.35***	2.98***	−0.13***	44.67***	1300	0.27

=* p<0.10
** p<0.05
*** p<0.01"

Appendix 2: List of Large Countries*

Algeria	Mozambique
Argentina	Nepal
Australia	Netherlands
Bangladesh	Nigeria
Canada	Pakistan
China	Peru
Colombia	Philippines
Egypt	Poland
Ethiopia	Romania
France	Russian F
Germany	Saudi Arabia
Ghana	South Africa
India	Spain
Indonesia	Sri Lanka
Iran	Sudan
Iraq	Tanzania
Italy	Thailand
Japan	Turkey
Kazakhstan	Uganda
Kenya	Ukraine
Korea, R	United Kingdom
Malaysia	United States
Mexico	Venezuela
Morocco	Vietnam

Note:
*Not all countries have been used in all regressions.

Notes

1. Rodrik (2011) adds that, unlike the case of the economy as a whole, countries' manufacturing sector reveals unconditional convergence. The further a country is behind the technological frontier in a manufacturing industry, the faster the growth of the industry's labor productivity will be.
2. Recent research by Kaulich (2012) with a longer time database suggests an L-rather than U-shaped patterns, meaning that countries do not respecialize or do not respecialize very much after reaching their maximum diversification point.
3. Some services may also exhibit high income elasticity of demand. However, the demand for some of these services, as in the case of software or computer games, is complementary to the demand electronic goods.
4. This example is drawn from UNIDO (2012).
5. A quadratic formulation had already been tried in Haraguchi and Rezonja (2010a, b).
6. For a comparison between small and large countries, including population size, see Haraguchi and Rezonja (2011).
7. Regression results are included in Appendix 1.

8. Already some export performance constant market share analysis began to be performed (Memedovic and Iapadre, 2010b).

References

Chang, Ha-Joon (2010) "Hamlet without the Prince of Denmark: How Development Has Disappeared from Today's 'Development' Discourse," in S. Khan and J. Christiansen (eds), *Towards New Developmentalism: Market as Means rather than Master* (London: Routledge).

Chenery, H.B. (1960) "Patterns of Industrial Growth," *The American Economic Review*, vol. 50, no. 4, pp. 624–654.

Chenery, H.B. and Taylor, L. (1968) "Development Patterns: Among Countries and Over Time," *The Review of Economics and Statistics*, vol. 50, no. 4, pp. 391–416.

Chenery, H. B., Robinson, S. and Syrquin, M. (eds.)(1986) *Industrialization and Growth: A Comparative Study* (New York: Oxford University Press).

Chenery, H.B. and Syrquin, M. (1989) "Patterns of Development, 1950 to 1983," World Bank Discussion Paper WDP41 (Washington, DC: World Bank).Chenery, H.B. and Syrquin, M. (1975) *Patterns of Development 1950–1970* (London: Oxford University Press).

Gerschenkron, A. (1962) *Economic Backwardness in Historical Perspective* (Cambridge, MA: Harvard University Press).

Haraguchi, N. and Rezonja, G. (2012) "Unravelling Manufacturing Development: The Role of Comparative Advantage, Productivity Growth and Country-specific Conditions," UNIDO Development Policy, Statistics and Research Branch Working Paper 16/2011 (Vienna: UNIDO).

Haraguchi, N. and Rezonja, G. (2011) "Emerging Patterns of Manufacturing Structural Change," UNIDO Development Policy and Strategic Research Branch Working Paper 04/2010 (Vienna: UNIDO).

Haraguchi, N. and Rezonja, G. (2010a) "In Search of General Patterns of Manufacturing Development," UNIDO Development Policy and Strategic Research Branch Working Paper 02/2010 (Vienna: UNIDO).

Haraguchi, N. and Rezonja, G. (2010b) "Patterns of Manufacturing Development Revisited," UNIDO Research and Statistics Branch Working Paper 22/2009 (Vienna: UNIDO).

Hausmann, R., Rodrik, D. and A. Velasco (2005) *Growth Diagnostics* (Cambridge, MA: Harvard University Center for International Development. Available online at www.hks.harvard.edu/fs/rhausma/new/growthdiag.pdf.

Imbs, J., and Wacziarg, R. (2003) "Stages of Diversification," *American Economic Review*, vol. 93, no. 1, pp. 63–86.

Kaulich, F. (2012) "Diversification vs. Specialization as Alternative Strategies for Economic Development: Can We Settle a Debate by Looking at the Empirical Evidence?,", UNIDO Working Paper 3/2012 (Vienna: UNIDO).

Kuznets, S. (1966) *Modern Economic Growth: Rate, Structure, and Spread* (New Haven and London: Yale University Press).

Lall, Sanjaya (1992) "Technological Capabilities and Industrialization," *World Development*, vol. 20, no. 2, pp. 165–186.

Lauridsen, L.S. (2010) "Strategic Industrial Policy and Latecomer Development: The What, the Why and the How," *Forum for Development Studies*, vol. 37, no. 1, pp. 7–32.

Lin, J. (2012) *New Structural Economics: A Framework for Rethinking Development and Policy* (Washington, DC: World Bank).

Lin, J. (2011) "From Flying Geese to Leading Dragons: New Opportunities and Strategies for Structural Transformation in Developing Countries," Policy Research Working Paper Series 5702 (Washington, DC: World Bank).

Lin, J. and C. Monga (2010) "Growth Identification and Facilitation: The Role of the State in the Dynamics of Structural Change," World Bank Policy Research Working Paper 5313 (Washington, DC: World Bank).

Maddison, A. (2007) *Contours of the World Economy* (Oxford: Oxford University Press).

Maddison, A. (2001) *The World Economy: A Millennial Perspective* (Paris: OECD).

Maddison, A. (1982) *Phases of Capitalist Development* (Oxford: Oxford University Press).

McMillan, M. and Rodrik, D. (2011) "Globalization, Structural Change, and Productivity Growth," mimeo. Accessed from http://www.hks.harvard.edu/fs/drodrik/Research%20papers/Globalization,%20Structural%20Change,%20and%20Productivity%20Growth.pdf.

Memedovic, O. and Iapadre, L. (2010a) "Structural Change in the World Economy: Main Features and Trends," UNIDO Research and Statistics Branch, Working Paper 24/20009 (Vienna: UNIDO).

Memedovic, O. and L. Iapadre, L. (2010b) "Industrial Development and the Dynamics of International Specialization Patterns," UNIDO Research and Statistics Branch, Working Paper 23/2009 (Vienna: UNIDO).

Ocampo J.A. (2005) "The Quest for Dynamic Efficiency: Structural Dynamics and Economic Growth in Developing Countries," in J.A. Ocampo (ed.), *Beyond Reforms: Structural Dynamics and Macroeconomic Vulnerability* (Santiago: Economic Commission for Latin America and the Caribbean and Stanford University Press).

Ocampo, J.A. and Vos, R. (2008) "Structural Change and Economic Growth," in J.A. Ocampo and R. Vos (eds), *Uneven Economic Development* (London: Zed Books).

Perkins, D. and Syrquin, M. (1989) "Large Countries: The Influence of Size," in H. Chenery and T.N. Srinivasan (eds), *Handbook of Development Economics*, vol. II (Phiiadelphia: Elsevier Science Publishers).

Rodrik, D. (2011) "The Future of Economic Convergence", NBER Working Paper Series, No. 17400, National Bureau of Economic Research.

Rodrik, D. (2006) "Industrial Development: Stylized Facts and Policies," Harvard University, draft.

Syrquin, M. (2007) "Structural Change and Development," in A.K. Dutt and J. Ros (eds), *International Handbook of Development Economics* (Cheltenham: Edward Elgar).

Szirmai, A. (2013) "Manufacturing and Economic Development," in A. Szirmai, W. Naudé, and L. Alcorta (eds), *Pathways to Industrialization in the Twenty-First Century: New Challenges and Emerging Paradigms* (Oxford: Oxford University Press).

Szirmai, A., Naudé, W., and Alcorta, L. (2013) "Introduction and Overview: The Past, Present and Future of Industrialization," in Szirmai, A., Naudé, W. and L. Alcorta (eds), *Pathways to Industrialization in the Twenty-First Century: New Challenges and Emerging Paradigms* (Oxford: Oxford University Press).

Szirmai, A. and B. Verspagen (2010) "Is Manufacturing Still an Engine of Growth in Developing Countries?", paper prepared for the 31st General Conference of the International Association for Research in Income and Wealth, St Gallen, Switzerland, August 22–8.

te Velde, D.W. (2011) "Introduction to the DPR Debate: Growth Identification and Facilitation: The Role of the State in the Dynamics of Structural Change," *Development Policy Review*, vol. 29, no. 3, pp. 259–310.

United Nations Department of Economic and Social Affairs (UNDESA) (2006) *World Economic and Social Survey 2006: Diverging Growth and Development* (New York: United Nations Department of Economic and Social Affairs).

UNIDO (2012) "Climbing the Stairway of Development: Structural Change is the Driver of Economic Growth," UNIDO Policy Brief Issue 2 (Vienna: UNIDO).

UNIDO (2009) *Industrial Development Report 2009. Breaking In and Moving Up: New Industrial Challenges for the Bottom Billion and the Middle-Income Countries* (Vienna: UNIDO).

UNIDO INDSTAT2 (2012) *Industrial Statistics Database* (Vienna).

6.2

Industrial Policy and Economic Transformation in Africa: Strategies for Development and a Research Agenda[1]

Yaw Ansu
African Center for Economic Transformation

Introduction: industrial policy – what is it?

Discussion of industrial policy tends to generate much controversy and passion, a key reason for this being the lack of a clear and generally accepted definition of the term. In this paper, we use industrial policy to refer to any set of policies pursued by a government with the explicit goal of promoting the expansion, technological upgrading, or international competitiveness of a targeted set of economic activities. Targeting is key. The implementation of policies that improve the general environment for all economic activities (for example, a stable macroeconomic environment, a friendly private sector environment, promotion of education in general... and so on), while highly desirable and, in most cases, necessary for the successful promotion of targeted activities, are not by themselves, in our view, sufficient to constitute the existence of an industrial policy regime.

We note that the definition is not restricted to industrial products, despite reference to industry in the term "industry policy." For example, under our definition, the implementation of policies targeted at expanding or upgrading the production and exports of a particular set of agricultural products or of service activities qualifies as industrial policy, just as targeting a set of manufacturing products would.[2]

While industrial policy as defined here could be pursued in any type of economy, our interest in this paper is on economies in Sub-Saharan Africa (SSA) that seek to promote economic transformation. By economic transformation, we mean a process that leads to the narrowing of the gap between SSA countries and the industrialized countries in the following key variables: technological capabilities, productivity, economic diversity, competitiveness in exports, incomes per capita, and the share of the labor force having formal employment. These variables appear to us to be the most important

492

features in distinguishing the industrialized, developed, and modern economies from the primary commodity- and extractives-producing poor countries of SSA.

Under certain conditions an activist role for the state in promoting economic transformation – that is, industrial policy – can be justified by both economic theory and development experience.[3] Central to economic transformation is learning about and introducing new economic activities, technologies, and processes, and also breaking into new markets. These involve information asymmetries and externalities, coordination challenges, and production technologies with increasing returns. These are areas where the market often fails, and where therefore there could be scope for state involvement. In addition, in order to provide public infrastructure and skills at the quality levels that would make a country internationally competitive, the state in view of tight fiscal constraints would initially have to be very selective in its investments in thee areas; hence the rationale for industrial parks (and also partly for special economic zones or export processing zones—SEZs/EPZs) and specialized technical training programs funded by the state. However, there are serious challenges to implementing industrial policy, as we make clear in the discussion that follows.

The plan of the paper is as follows: Section 6.2.1 provides an overview of the evolution of economic development policy in SSA over the forty-year period from 1970 to 2010, focusing on the state-led import-substitution approach (1970 to early 1980s) and the approach pursued under the "Structural Adjustment Programs" (SAPs; mid-1980s to early 2000s). Section 6.2.2 reviews performance on economic transformation in SSA over the 40-year period, comparing the import-substitution and SAP subperiods, and also comparing trends in the region to those in successfully transforming countries in East Asia and Latin America. It shows that whether one looks at the period of import-substitution or the period of SAPs, there has been very little progress on economic transformation. In Section 6.2.3, we outline a framework for the kind of industrial policy that we think countries in SSA that seek to proactively transform their economies could consider. We present some emerging examples of the approach in selected SSA countries. Section 6.2.4 discusses important challenges that the approach entails. Section 6.2.5 briefly outlines a research program that could inform policy under the industrial policy approach proposed. Section 6.2.6 concludes.

6.2.1 Overview of SSA's development policy experience

6.2.1.1 State-led import substitution

After independence in the 1960s, many African countries pursued import substitution as a development strategy. This was industrial policy in as much as it targeted a particular set of products – imported manufactured products, often simple consumer goods. However, in many countries import substitution was embedded in a broader strategy of state-led economic development. Under this broader strategy, the state aspired to control the "commanding heights" of the economy, which in the nascent industrial settings of the countries included the import-substituting factories that were being promoted. Thus governments either went into production themselves through state-owned enterprises or controlled the entry of entrepreneurs and heavily regulated the operations of private firms.

Despite initial successes in expanding the manufacturing sector, on the whole the results of the industrial policy pursued within the context of the state-led import substitution strategy subsequently proved to be quite disappointing. The main causes are now familiar: Most of the state enterprises were poorly run and lacked the incentives and budget discipline required to make efficiency and market competitiveness top priority. Innovation was stifled due to the generally hostile attitude to the private sector and also to the fact that often it was more profitable for enterprising businessmen and businesswomen to devote their efforts to chasing rents induced by government controls than to developing their firms to be efficient and competitive. Added to these were poor macroeconomic management and increasing balance of payments difficulties. The latter stemmed from the indirect discouragement of exports by the import-substitution trade and exchange rate policy stance, the high import intensity of the capital and intermediate inputs required by the import-substituting factories, and periodic export revenue shocks due to the extreme dependence on commodity exports. By the end of the 1970s and the beginning of the 1980s, severe balance-of-payments problems had made the state-led import substitution strategy difficult to sustain in almost all the SSA countries involved, and country after country turned to the International Monetary Fund (IMF) and the World Bank for help.

6.2.1.2   Structural Adjustment Programs (SAPs)

Help from the IMF and the World Bank often came in the form of countries agreeing to a macroeconomic stabilization program with the IMF and a program of structural reforms with the World Bank. These programs, often jointly referred to as "Structural Adjustment Programs (SAPs)" typically had the following elements: fiscal adjustment (to reduce fiscal deficits); exchange rate devaluations; trade (particularly import) liberalization; privatization of state-owned enterprises; and active discouragement of government involvement in production or support for any particular set of economic activities or actors.

With initial success in the macro-stabilization programs and in response to a growing outcry against perceived adverse social impacts, the programs began to increasingly also focus on social expenditures. Poverty Reduction Strategy Papers (PRSPs) prepared by governments in consultation with civil society, but in reality financed and directed by donors, particularly the

World Bank and the IMF, became the main vehicles for articulating development strategy. The strategy in these papers was essentially the earlier
emphasis on macro-stabilization and market liberalization enhanced with
increased emphasis on social expenditures and on strengthening market
institutions along the lines of Anglo-American models.

Despite the general thrust of the SAPs, there were instances of support to
productive sectors. There were programs to support traditional export sectors, such as providing better producer price incentives, improved roads, and
other support to farmers producing traditional export commodities. There
were also some programs to provide incentives to non-traditional exports,
including assistance to potential exporters to explore foreign market prospects
and matching grants to exporters. Financial assistance was also given for the
construction and operation of Export Processing Zones in some countries.
However, providing direct support to expand and upgrade production and
exports of particular products, particularly manufacturing and non-traditional
exports, was generally not a focus of the SAPs.

As in the case of the import-substitution strategy, the results of the SAPs
were also disappointing. After about thirty years of structural adjustment programs, many important results have been achieved, including the resumption
of per capita GDP growth and reduction of poverty in several countries starting from the mid-1990s. But the structures of economies have not adjusted
in ways that make them more globally competitive in the production and
export of higher-technology goods and services, and a large share of the
labor force in many countries is engaged in the informal sector. Furthermore,
despite the expectation, the economies did not become prosperous enough
to be able to service the loans that the external partners of SAP provided to
finance the programs, and substantial parts of the debts have had to be written off. The next section provides an in-depth review of the performance of
economic transformation in SSA over the forty-year period from 1970 to 2010
and compares it to that of a group of successful countries from East Asia and
Latin America.

6.2.2   Performance on economic transformation in SSA

We illustrate some of the points made in the earlier section on economic
performance, focusing on the key variables in our definition of economic
transformation – that is, GDP per capita, economic diversification, technological levels, export competitiveness, and the share of labor force in formal
employment. We review trends in: (a) SSA as a whole; (b) a set of 15 SSA
countries; and (c) a set of eight comparator countries. For all three groups,
we use simple instead of weighted averages. Data for the figures are presented in Table 6.2.1 for five-year intervals.

The 15 countries are those on which the African Center for Economic
Transformation (ACET) is conducting case studies on economic transformation.

Often referred to as "ACET-15" in this paper, they are: Senegal, Burkina Faso, Ghana, and Nigeria in West Africa; Ethiopia, Kenya, Uganda, Tanzania, and Rwanda in East Africa; Cameroon in Central Africa; and Zambia, Botswana, South Africa, Mozambique, and Mauritius in Southern Africa. They constitute (in 2010): 70 percent of the population; 76 percent of GDP; 85 percent of manufacturing value added; 65 percent of agricultural value added; and 80 percent of exports. All the geographical subregions are represented (although some more than others), and so are the major official languages of English, French, and Portuguese. Countries in conflict or recently emerging from conflict are not included, since in those countries reconstruction is a more pressing issue than economic transformation.

The comparator countries are: South Korea, Singapore, Malaysia, Thailand, Indonesia, Vietnam, Chile and Brazil. The success that South Korea and Singapore have had in transforming their economies is well known; and that each country in its own way used industrial policy to drive its transformation process is undeniable.[4] The other East Asian countries have also attained some success at economic transformation using some of the industrial policy elements that had been used earlier by South Korea and Singapore (and by others such as Japan and Taiwan, China). These other East Asian countries have the additional attraction that their levels of per capita income were close to those of several of the ACET-15 countries 30 to 40 years ago. The Latin American countries of Chile and Brazil have also attained success at economic transformation using their own versions of industrial policy.[5]

6.2.2.1 GDP per capita growth and poverty

Figure 6.2.1a shows performance on GDP growth per capita from 1970 to 2010. Note the high growth rates in the comparator countries relative to the African countries. For the African countries, the trend shows a "V"-shaped pattern; falling from 1970 to 1995 and rising after that. In fact, the economies contracted in the 1980s, as per capita growth rates turned negative. Figure 6.2.1b presents the growth experience from a different perspective; for each group, it shows the level of GDP per capita relative to the level in 1970. While in the comparator countries per capita GDP in 2010 was four and half times (i.e. 450 percent of) the level in 1970, in the ACET-15, the increase was less than double, and in SSA as a whole, it was less than 50 percent. However, note the slow but steady increase in Africa since 1995. Nevertheless, the increase has been even faster in the comparator countries. Reflecting the pick-up in GDP per capita growth rates in the mid-1990s, headcount poverty levels, though still high, fell from almost 60 percent in 1990 for SSA to around 43 percent in 2005.

6.2.2.2 Employment

Well-remunerated employment is the most effective way for economic growth or transformation to improve peoples' lives. Also, if an economy is

Table 6.2.1 Economic transformation indicators (SSA, ACET-15 & COMP)

ATI Indicator	Country Groupings	Year								
		1970	1975	1980	1985	1990	1995	2000	2005	2010
GDP per capita growth (annual %)	SSA	.	1.94	0.83	−0.16	0.47	−0.76	1.96	2.00	2.42
	ACET15		2.31	1.67	−0.68	1.56	−0.22	2.23	3.11	3.41
	Comp	.	4.20	5.71	1.96	.	5.81	1.91	3.48	3.54
5-yr Moving average (Growth Rates of World Exports Shares)	SSA	−2.05	−1.26	−2.67	2.75	−7.21	3.32	1.30	4.82	.
	ACET15	−0.95	1.26	−3.64	3.84	−7.83	3.36	0.35	4.12	.
	Comp	−0.47	12.01	6.25	−1.74	7.59	9.10	0.44	2.42	.
% of Top 5 (%)	SSA			86.03	82.67	78.22	79.40	78.17	76.29	74.62
	ACET15			79.54	82.14	66.11	75.90	72.25	68.84	70.40
	Comp			63.09	53.57	43.38	39.67	43.04	42.07	43.11
% of Med & High Tech cd'ty Exports	SSA			3.15	4.48	8.31	7.36	5.76	7.99	8.56
	ACET15			4.42	2.29	8.10	5.40	5.43	8.72	8.00
	Comp			14.04	17.19	27.36	37.27	39.11	37.11	33.61
Gross fixed capital formation (% of GDP)	SSA	16.39	20.29	22.41	18.05	19.06	20.07	18.42	20.65	23.16
	ACET15	18.96	19.56	17.72	15.05	19.41	19.22	20.14	21.72	23.72
	Comp	22.15	25.84	26.38	25.49	29.54	30.65	23.22	23.45	25.18
Manufacturing, value added (% of GDP)	SSA	10.17	10.83	10.03	10.85	11.88	10.68	10.68	10.23	10.07
	ACET15	12.39	13.64	12.69	13.42	14.56	12.21	12.39	11.26	10.33
	Comp	18.77	19.83	23.09	21.20	21.50	22.47	24.91	24.80	22.25
% of Med & High Tech Manufactures (%)	SSA	14.84	16.93	17.27	18.16	16.94	18.64	17.55	14.88	.
	ACET15	19.19	20.20	22.32	18.95	20.42	20.54	19.09	15.71	.
	Comp	32.72	36.17	39.86	46.44	46.14	52.64	47.14	57.79	.
MVA per Manufacturing Worker (current US$)	SSA	2848	5705	10610	6211	100.5	10494	9119	9364	.
	ACET15	3047	6578	11152	7905	9693	10647	10720	14014	.
	Comp	3564	5976	13973	14709	190.7	35004	25418	52029	.

(continued)

Table 6.2.1 Continued

Indicator										
Manuf & Serv. Exports (% Total Exports of G&S)	SSA	.	18.16	26.22	34.93	34.59	35.46	44.12	40.82	42.48
	ACET15	.	19.62	23.43	17.77	44.87	46.14	44.12	44.26	41.88
	Comp	.	32.69	37.78	38.18	54.88	63.16	64.28	62.17	56.98
Manuf Exports (%of total Exports)	SSA	.	7.02	5.23	6.42	11.27	9.46	18.05	17.24	14.28
	ACET15	.	9.33	7.20	3.50	19.44	16.70	18.86	18.48	17.82
	Comp	.	17.40	23.31	25.82	40.15	48.17	50.17	48.43	42.28
Comm. Services Exports (% of Total Exports of G&S)	SSA	14.34	14.10	16.35	18.60	19.76	22.93	25.86	22.27	23.15
	ACET15	14.34	14.28	14.68	17.04	20.62	24.06	25.71	24.23	24.06
	Comp	.	15.29	14.47	12.36	14.74	14.99	14.11	13.74	13.93
Cereal Yield (kg per hectare)	SSA	917.7	995.1	1006	1174	1138	1144	1333	1331	1552
	ACET15	954.1	1080	1116	1386	1325	1360	1776	1851	2240
	Comp	2109	2176	2405	2780	2987	3222	3339	3946	4462
EXPY (GDP, PPP 2005 Int. US$)	SSA	.	.	1902	995.7	1883	3003	5305	5607	3690
	ACET15	.	.	1848	937.8	2431	3462	6425	7263	7291
	Comp	.	.	3734	6561	8132	8253	10506	11369	8618
Gross Domestic Savings (% of GDP)	SSA	13.81	10.27	8.56	8.15	8.14	7.55	8.98	9.68	13.23
	ACET15	16.33	13.97	10.74	13.91	12.13	12.01	12.46	13.47	14.16
	Comp	19.84	23.22	27.79	28.37	28.44	31.23	31.96	33.38	33.39
Ratio of formal employment to labor force (%)	SSA	.	.	.	.	.	27.00	27.37	27.37	.
	ACET15	.	.	.	.	.	19.65	29.74	29.74	.
	Comp	.	.	.	.	.	53.26	54.72	54.72	.
Poverty headcount ratio at $1.25 a day (PPP) (% of population)	SSA	.	.	76.06	51.02	59.39	57.51	48.49	43.44	60.70
	ACET15	.	.	66.22	54.30	53.86	50.60	55.64	43.91	65.58
	Comp	.	.	25.71	21.60	24.80	18.84	13.22	8.59	18.06

Sources:

GDP per capita growth (annual %)?: World Bank national accounts data, and OECD National Accounts data files. Via World Bank Development Indicators database.

Manufacturing, value added (% of GDP): World Bank national accounts data, and OECD National Accounts data files via World Bank Development Indicators database (Based on International Standard Industrial Classification (ISIC), revision 3.).

% of Med & High Tech Manufactures (%): ACET Staff Calulations from UNIDO INDSTAT2, Rev 3 Digit 2.

MVA per Manufacturing Worker (current US$): UNIDO INDSTAT2, Rev 3 Digit 2, World Bank national accounts data, and OECD National Accounts data files.

5-yr Moving Avg. (Difference in Growth rates of exports…): World Bank national accounts data, and OECD National Accounts data files. Via World Bank Development Indicators database.

Manuf & Serv. Exports (% Total Exports of G&S): World Bank Development Indicators, International Monetary Fund, Balance of Payments Statistics Year book and data files, World Bank staff estimates from the Comtrade database maintained by the United Nations Statistics Division; World Trade Organization. World Bank national accounts data, and OECD National Accounts data files.

Manuf Exports (% of total Exports): ACET Calculation from World Trade Organization. & World Bank staff estimates from the Comtrade database maintained by the United Nations Statistics Division.

Comm. Services Exports (% of Total Exports of G&S): International Monetary Fund, Balance of Payments Statistics Yearbook and data files.

Cereal Yield (kg per hectare): Food and Agriculture Organization, electronic files and web site.

% of Top 5 Exports: ACET Staff Calculations from UN ComTrade. Rev 2 Digit 3.

% of Med & High Tech cd'ty Exports: ACET Staff Calulations from UN ComTrade. Rev 2 Digit 3.

EXPY (GDP, PPP 2005 Int. US$): ACET Staff Calulations from UN ComTrade. Rev 2 Digit 3, World development Indicators.

Gross fixed capital formation (% of GDP): World Bank national accounts data, and OECD National Accounts data files.

Gross Domestic Savings (% of GDP): World Bank national accounts data, and OECD National Accounts data files.

Ratio of formal employment to labor force (%): International Labour Organization, using World Bank population estimates; International Labour Organization, Key Indicators of the Labour Market database.

Poverty headcount ratio at $1.25 a day (PPP) (% of population): ACET staff calculations using data from World Bank, Development Research Group (Please see PovcalNet (http://iresearch.worldbank.org/PovcalNet/index.htm). For any country the poverty rate for the year shown is the average of any poverty rates available for the 5 yrs leading to that year.

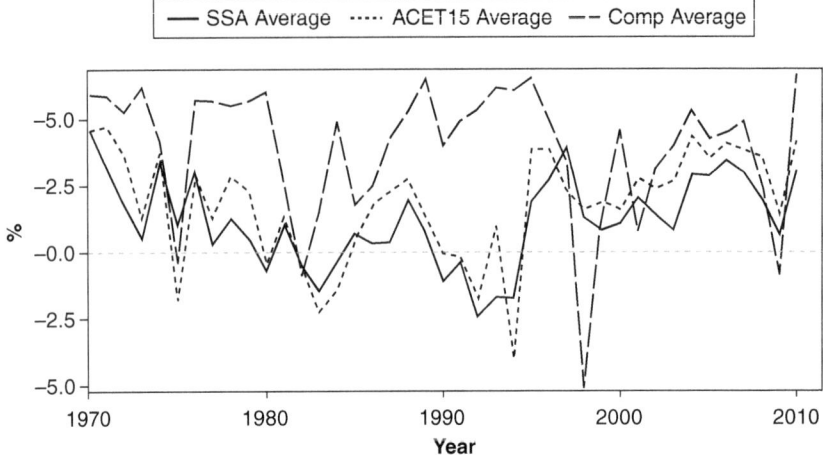

Figure 6.2.1a Annual GDP per capita growth
Data Source: World Bank Development Indicators

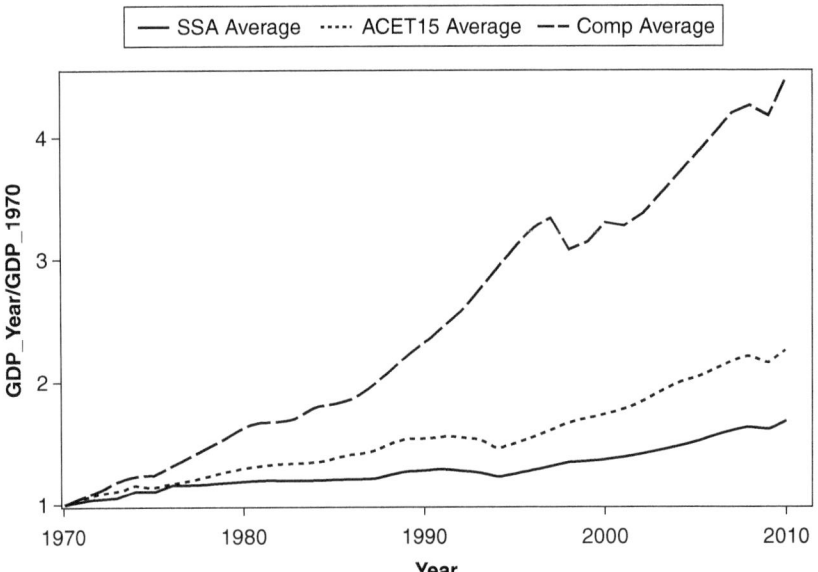

Figure 6.2.1b Index of GDP per capita (Constant 2000 US$) (1970=1)
Data Source: World Bank Development Indicators.

transforming, then we expect to see an increasing share of the labor force in formal employment as the shares of industry, including manufacturing, and high-value services in GDP expand. So the ratio of formal employment to the labor force, which is the product of the share of formal employment in total employment and the rate of employment, is a good measure to track the employment impact of economic transformation.[6] It takes account of the need to increase overall employment as well as to formalize or modernize it. Unfortunately, many African countries do not have credible data on employment. Labor surveys are few and far between. Reported low unemployment rates belie the actual situation on the ground, which is much worse. A large number of the people classified as employed are engaged in low productivity agriculture or services; are severely underemployed and barely eking out a living. The problem is particularly serious among the youth, a significant number of who have been educated at considerable national expense, but who cannot find jobs for which they have trained for or to which they aspire. Quite apart from the economic waste and human tragedy that this situation represents, it also poses a serious threat to political and social stability, as the recent uprisings in a number of Arab countries partly demonstrate.

In view of the difficulties with data, we estimate the share of employment in the labor force by the product of the employment rate and one minus the percent of "vulnerable employment" as measured by the ILO.[7] It is not possible to have a consistent annual or even fove-year series on the measure for most SSA countries. In Mauritius and South Africa, two SSA countries that produce data on a regular basis, it is around 70 percent. For the rest of the ACET-15, data are sparse but the share is often not higher than 25 percent. In Zambia, the share fell from 31 percent in 1990 to 16 percent in 2005.[8] In contrast, the share of formal employment in the labor force is over 50 percent in the comparator countries.

6.2.2.3 Investment, domestic savings, and the sustainability of growth

Part of the recovery in GDP growth in Africa results from rising levels of investment beginning in the mid-1980s, which reverses the investment collapse of a decade earlier (Figure 6.2.2a). For both SSA and the ACET-15 countries, the average ratio of investment (that is, gross fixed capital formation) to GDP has been around 24 percent over the past five years. However, this elevated rate, while welcome, is still well below the rates of around 30 percent that the East Asian Tiger economies maintained in the periods of their transformation drive (and the comparator countries maintained in the 1990s – Figure 6.2.2a). High investment rates are needed not only for expanding existing production capacity, but also, more importantly for introducing new machinery, which is often a very important channel for technological upgrading, the introduction of new economic activities, and for productivity increases. High investment rates are therefore an important aspect of the transformation process and African countries still have more work to do on this front.

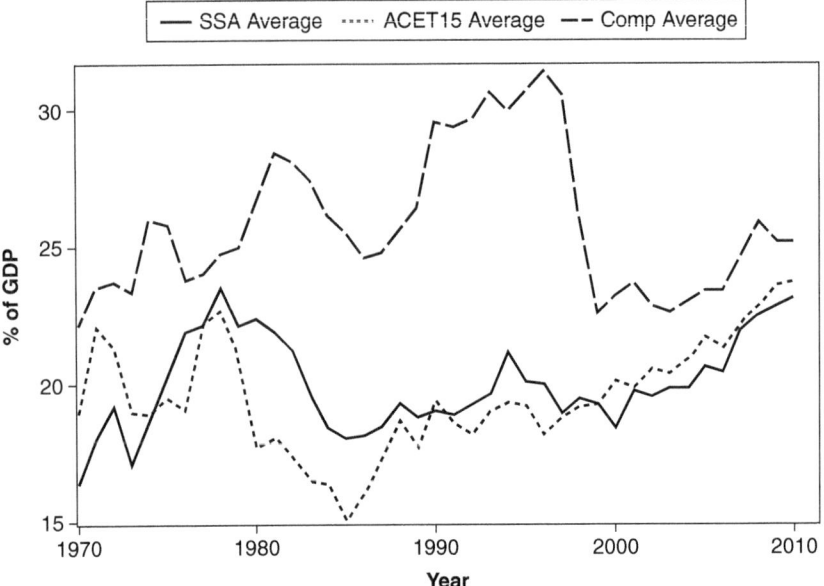

Figure 6.2.2a Investment-Gross Fixed Capital Formation
Source: World Bank Development Indicators.

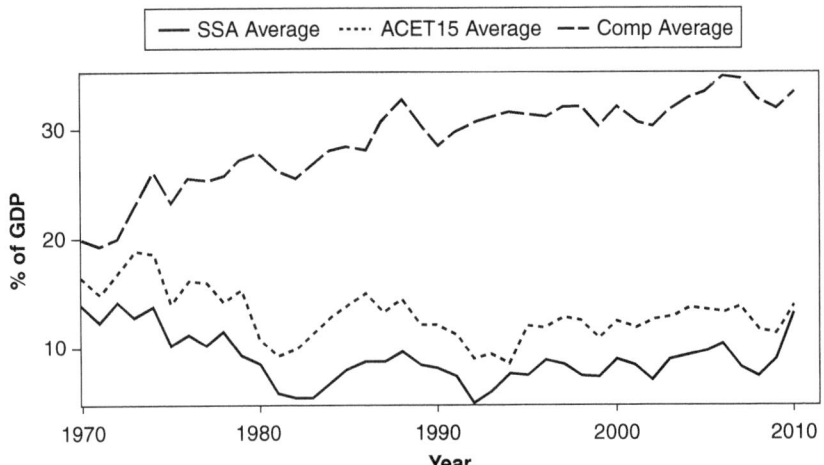

Figure 6.2.2b Domestic Savings-Gross Domestic Savings
Source: World Bank Development Indicators.

Significant parts of the rising investment in Africa have been financed by external aid as domestic savings are low – around 14 percent for ACET-15 and 13 percent for SSA in 2010 (Figure 6.2.2b).[9] To ensure that investment rates rise and are sustained over a considerable number of years, domestic savings need to rise (before possibly falling at very high levels of per capita incomes).

6.2.2.4   Diversification of production and exports

The range of products and services that a country produces matters. Ultimately, an essential part of economic development is acquiring the capability to produce a widening array of goods and services and then having the option to choose which ones to specialize in based on international relative price signals. This has been the experience of economically developed countries. They have gone through a phase of increasing the diversity of production before specializing later to better take advantage of market opportunities.[10] In this sense, specialization is a conscious market-based decision to focus on a subset of a wide array of economic activities that a country is technically capable of engaging in rather than a situation forced upon a country because it lacks technological capacity, and the best it can do is to try to rely on its relative natural endowments as is the case among African countries now.[11] In other words, *desirable specialization is one that results from choice rather than from lack of options*. The only effective way to acquire the capability for new economic activities is through learning-by-doing. African countries therefore need to purposively seek to learn to produce new goods and services. In particular, they need to expand their economies from ones based mainly on primary and extractives production to ones that also increasingly include manufactures and high value services.

The average share of manufacturing value added in GDP in SSA was 10 percent in 2010, hardly any change from the 1970s (Figure 6.2.3a).[12] For the ACET-15, the share has actually fallen from around 13 percent in the 1970s and 1980s to a little over 10 percent in 2010. For our comparator countries, the share rose from under 19 percent in 1970 to almost 25 percent in the mid-2000s before falling to 22 percent in 2010. Indeed, it appears that countries in SSA are moving straight from agriculture being the largest economic sector to services playing that role without passing through the intermediate phase of industrialization and an expanding manufacturing sector, the process that has characterized the economic transformation experiences of almost all successful countries. Furthermore, a large part of the service sector in many of the countries consists of low-technology and low-value activities. This trend is of great concern, since historically manufacturing has been the main source of technological learning and advancement on how to produce the material things we need and on how to shape our environment. This is still true even in our current knowledge economy, since for example a large part of the value of computer software derives from its impact on manufacturing technology and processes.

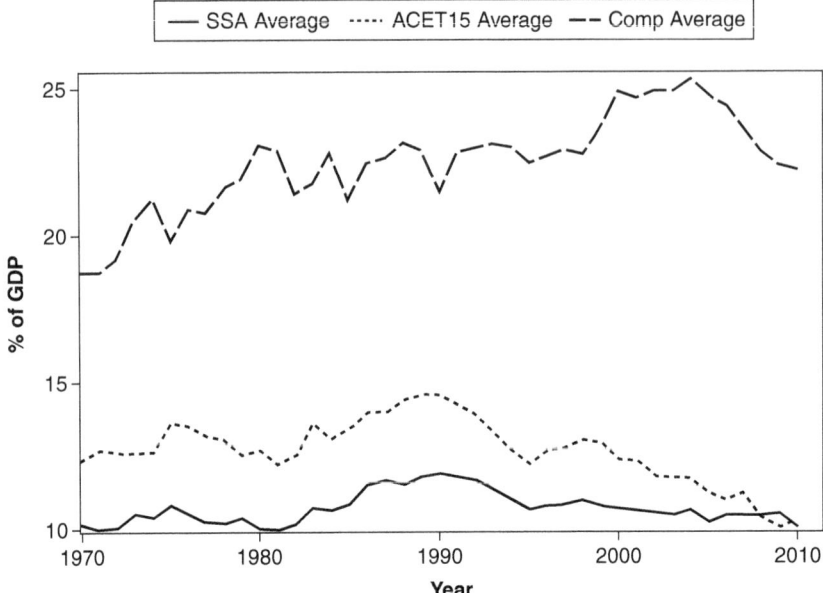

Figure 6.2.3a   Share of manufacturing value added in GDP
Source: World Bank Development Indicators.

The above points about the importance of diversity and of manufacturing in production apply equally to exports.[13] In addition, a diverse exports base is particularly important for minimizing volatility in foreign exchange earnings, which for small open developing economies, as in SSA, is critically important for assuring access to critical intermediate and capital inputs as well as technology. Unfortunately, for many African countries, the export base is very narrow, consisting of a small number of mainly primary products, which have remained more or less the same over the forty-year period. Figure 6.2.3b shows trends in export concentration using the share of the top five export commodities in total commodity exports.[14] We see that although export concentration has fallen over time in Africa, it is still rather high. The top five export commodities make up about 70 percent of exports in SSA compared to the comparator countries where they constitute about 54 percent.

We also think that it is important for African countries to broaden their export baskets from primary commodities to include manufacturing and high-value service exports. Figure 6.2.3c shows the share of manufacturing and services in total exports as a second measure of export diversification. While SSA is below the comparators, it seems to have experienced a steady rise since the mid-1990s. Much of the growth has come from services instead of manufactures (Table 6.2.1).

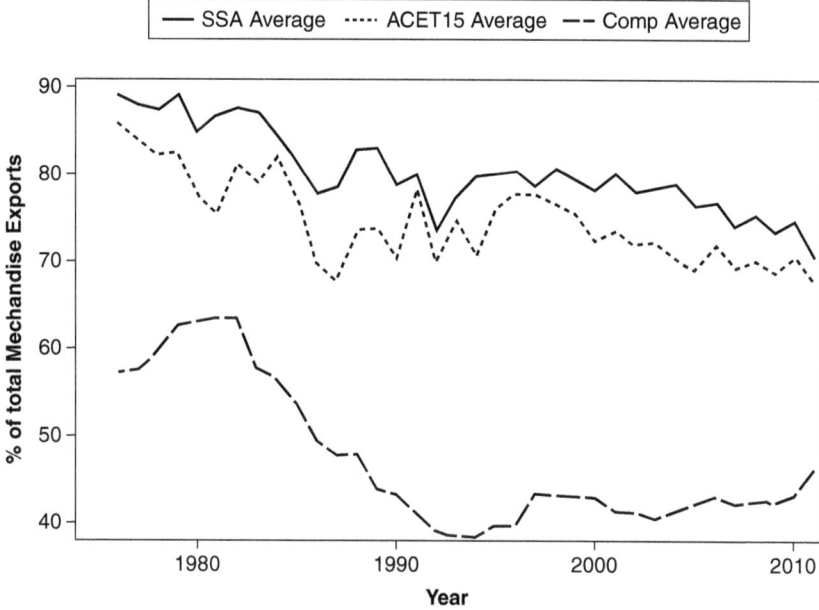

Figure 6.2.3b Concentration of exports-percentage of Top5 exports
Source: UN ComTrade Rev 3 Digit 2.

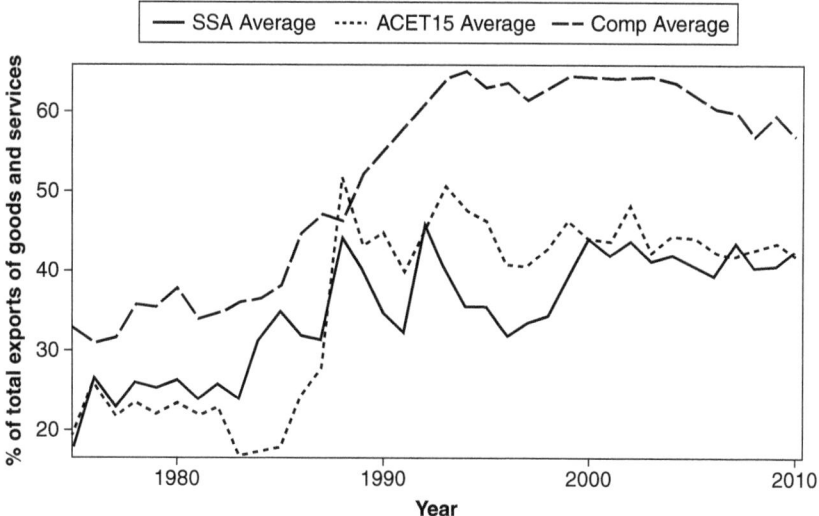

Figure 6.2.3c Manufactures plus services exports
Source: World Bank Development Indicators

6.2.2.5   Technology

Just having a large manufacturing sector is by itself not enough. The sector has to advance its technological level (and in productivity) over time. The share of medium- and high-technology manufactures in production using the Lall decomposition applied to ISIC data (Rev 3; digit level 2) remained around 15 percent in SSA over the 40-year period from 1970 to 2010.[15] Meanwhile, the share in the comparator countries rose from 33 to almost 58 percent (Table 6.2.1). For commodity exports (SITC Rev2, digit level 3), we find that the share of medium- and high-technology exports from SSA (and ACET-15) rose from around 4 percent in 1980 to a low 9 percent in 2010, while the share in the comparator countries rose from around 14 percent to 34 percent over the same period (Table 6.2.1). Both in production and exports the levels of technology in SSA are much lower than those in the comparator countries. More importantly, while the comparator countries have experienced a rising level of technology in the production of manufactures, in SSA the situation has been one of stagnation.

6.2.2.6   Productivity

We use trends in manufacturing value added (MVA) per worker as an indicator of productivity in manufacturing. In 1970, the MVA per worker (in current US dollars) in SSA was US$2,848 compared with US$3,564 in the comparator countries (Table 6.2.1). The ratio of comparator countries to SSA was therefore 1.25. By 2010, the ratio had jumped to 5.6 (that is, US$5,2029 to US$ 9364). This means the productivity gap in manufacturing between the comparator countries and SSA in 2010 was more that four times what it had been in 1970.

We use cereal yields (kilograms per hectare) to indicate productivity in agriculture. In 1970, yields in SSA were about 44 percent of those in the comparator countries; by 2010, they had fallen to 35 percent. This reflects slower growth in SSA (annual average of 1.5 percent over the forty-year period from 1970 to 2010) compared to the comparator countries (average annual rate of 2.0 percent). The ACET-15 experienced a higher growth in yields (average annual rate of 2.4), raising their average yield level from 954 kg per hectare in 1970 to 2240 kg per hectare in 2010 (Table 6.2.1).[17]

6.2.2.7   Competitiveness in exports markets

Figure 6.2.4 shows trends in the growth of the world market shares for exports of goods and services for the three country groups.[18] The measure is simple and intuitive. If a country's share is rising, which is the same as the country's exports of goods and services growing faster than the world average, then it is becoming more competitive in export markets; if the share is falling, then it is becoming less competitive.[19] The figure shows that

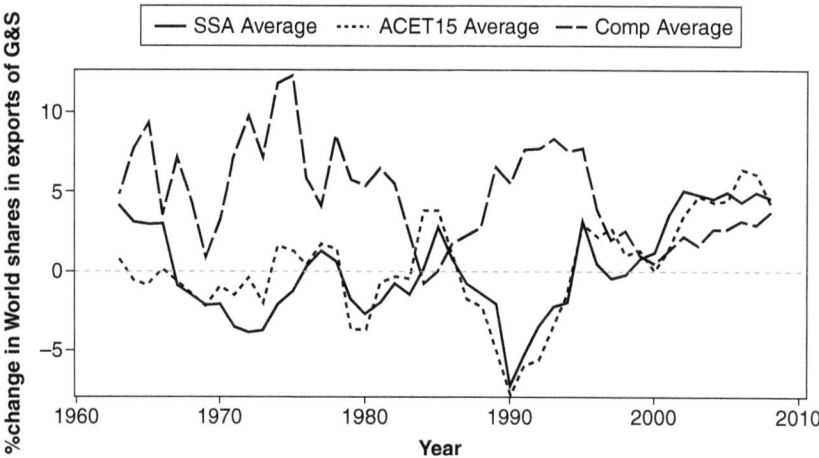

Figure 6.2.4   Growth rate of world exports share 5-years moving average
Source: World Bank Development Indicators.

in general the African countries have been less competitive relative to the
world average (that is, lying below zero on the graph) while the comparator
countries have been more competitive relative to the world average (that is,
lying above zero). Note the deterioration in competitiveness for the African
countries (particularly for the ACET-15) around 1980, a development that
contributed to many countries in SSA seeking balance of payments support
from the IMF and the World Bank in the form of SAPs, and also around
1990. The trends in SSA countries tend to largely reflect global commodity
prices, given the structure of exports from those countries.[20]

6.2.2.8   Has industrial policy failed or succeeded in Sub-Saharan Africa?

It is difficult to answer this question. We do know from the review above
that both of the broad development strategies pursued by countries in SSA
since the 1960s have generally failed to achieve economic transformation.
The import-substitution strategy was more explicit about targeting economic activities so in that sense it can be said to have incorporated an
industrial policy regime. However, it is not clear whether the failure was
due to the targeting of activities or to the deficiencies of the state-led and
private sector-hostile (and in many countries the socialist) strategy in
which it was embedded. The SAPs were more encouraging of the private
sector, but generally perceived government as the problem; government
was standing in the way of good economic performance, and the solution
was therefore to limit its involvement in the economy. The role of

government was to provide a good macroeconomic environment, to deliver public goods and social services, and then to keep out of the way of the private sector, which thus unleashed would generate growth and exports. The SAPs were therefore in principle against industrial policy. Instead of targeting production and export activities, they focused on a growing array of targets on macroeconomic variables, institutional reforms, and social sector expenditures. Ultimately, despite the name, the SAP programs failed to lead to significant positive structural adjustment of the economies that pursued them.

What explains the failures? Quite apart from specific policy mistakes, we think the key to the failure of the state-led import-substitution strategy in SSA, and the industrial policy practiced under it, was that it was not sufficiently supportive of the private sector. In fact the state often regarded the private sector with suspicion and sought to supplant it or restrict its activities. Similarly, a large part of the failure of the SAPs derived from the fact that they generally perceived state–private sector relations through the prism of conflict and sought to "roll back" the state from economic activities and to protect the private sector from the "predatory state". The idea of the government and the private sector acting as strategic partners to promote structural change and economic transformation was not one that was favorably entertained.

In contrast to the experiences of SSA, a number of countries in other parts of the world have been able to successfully transform their economies by targeting and increasing their capabilities in particular production activities and exports; that is, by pursuing industrial policy. In these countries, the state and the private sector have generally tended to collaborate as strategic partners, rather than as antagonists as implied by either the state-led import-substitution strategy or the SAPs. In view of this and of the failures in SSA, we think it is time for SSA countries to begin a search for pragmatic new approaches. This search should entail learning from the past experiences in the region as well as from those of the successful countries outside SSA and then fashioning approaches that are adapted to individual country situations.

6.2.3 The emerging balance: toward a Market-supporting industrial policy

In the past decade a number of African countries have begun to be more assertive in setting their own development visions. The PRSPs sponsored by donors are being complemented or replaced by country-developed medium- and long-term development plans, or strategic vision documents that aim to promote growth and structural transformation in addition to reducing poverty. These plans or strategy documents attempt to strike a balance between the statist approach of the import-substitution era and the laissez-faire approach of the SAPs. Often inspired by the recent successful experiences of East and South-East Asian countries, these plans are built on the premise that the private sector is the driver of economic activities, but they envisage a more activist state that goes beyond the provision of macroeconomic stability and traditional public goods and social services to actively support the private sector and promote selected new economic activities. The new activities could be either the introduction of completely new products and services, the introduction of new and improved ways of carrying out existing activities, or the expansion into new markets.

We provide below a framework to enable us to track and assess the emerging industrial policy regimes in Africa. The framework derives from our definition of industrial policy above together with the condition that industrial policy must be supportive of the market and the private sector. It also reflects the experiences in SSA as well as in the countries, particularly in East Asia, that have been successful in transforming their economies. In addition, the framework benefits from a number of works in the literature.[21] The elements are listed below:

- Existence of a coherent national medium-term (that is, one to five years) or long-term (more than five years) economic plan aimed at economic transformation;
- A set of targeted economic activities (not necessarily restricted to industrial products) nested within the economic plan;
- A conducive environment for private business, including
  ○ A stable macroeconomic environment
  ○ Competitive trade and exchange rate policies
  ○ Friendly regulatory environment; and
  ○ Efficient provision of public goods, particularly infrastructure and education
- A strategic partnership between the state and the private sector, with mechanisms for ongoing joint deliberations that enable the private sector to be active contributors to the:
  ○ Content of the medium- or long-term economic transformation plan;
  ○ Targeting of economic activities; and the
  ○ Design of the package of policies and incentives to be deployed to promote the targeted activities. The incentives should include, and indeed often should start from, removal of impediments placed on the targeted activities by existing government policies or processes.
- Performance control – setting standards for the targeted activities and monitoring them, entailing use of clear criteria for:
  ○ Gaining access to the promotional package of incentives and support;
  ○ Results required in order for a beneficiary to have continued access to the incentives and support;
  ○ When a beneficiary should exit or graduate from the incentives or support program;

o Monitoring, reviewing and providing timely statistics and publications on the programs; and
o Modification or cancellation of programs that fail to meet the set objectives.
• Strengthening of state capacity, or at least creation of centers of excellence within government, to plan, coordinate, execute, and monitor key economic transformation strategies and initiatives; to effectively interface with the private sector; and to produce quality and timely economic statistics.

Clearly, no country in Sub-Saharan Africa, with the possible exception of Mauritius, meets all the requirements of this framework. However, the framework provides a useful guide to the design, implementation, and tracking of the emerging industrial policy regimes in SSA. Given the framework, the specific instruments of industrial policy will depend on the context and the activities to be targeted. They would also depend on what is permissible under prevailing international trade obligations of the country, particularly those under the World Trade Organization (WTO). As an illustration of the possible use of the framework, we provide below a very preliminary assessment of the emerging industrial policy regimes in five SSA countries.

6.2.3.1   Toward a market-supporting industrial policy – case studies of selected African countries

Given the strong disapproval of government intervention in production by Africa's external financiers and policy mentors during the SAP era, for a long time not many governments in the region would advertise that they were practicing or aspiring to industrial policy even when their actions sometimes indicated otherwise. However, this is beginning to change. A number of countries now have plans and strategy documents that advertise their intent to practice industrial policy and some of their practices point in that direction albeit generally in a rather uncoordinated manner. We provide overviews for five countries (that is, Ghana, Nigeria, Ethiopia, Kenya, and Rwanda) using the framework above and drawing from material in the transformation case studies commissioned by ACET.

6.2.3.2   Ghana[22]
6.2.3.2.1   National plan and targeted activities
Ghana has in many respects been an early adopter of and a poster-child for the two development strategy extremes of state-led import-substitution and structural adjustment programs. It is now trying to move to the middle. In the mid-2000s, in addition to producing PRSPs, which it called Growth and Poverty Reduction Strategy Papers (GPRSPs) because of the government's interest in emphasizing growth in addition to the poverty reduction focus

of the donors, it also started work on a Seven-year Development Plan. This was aborted when the government changed in 2009 and replaced with a "Ghana Shared Growth and Development Agenda" (GSGDA, 2010–13). In addition, there have been Private Sector Development Strategy Papers (2005 and 2010); a National Trade Policy document (2005); and a Ghana Industrial Policy paper (2011).

The Industrial Policy paper states that it is derived from the development planning frameworks contained in the GSGDA. The key objectives are: (1) to expand productive employment in the manufacturing sector; (2) to expand technological capacity in the manufacturing sector; (3) to promote agro-based industrial development; and (4) to promote spatial distribution of industries in order to achieve reduction in poverty and income inequalities.[23] The policy seeks to "... alter the industrial structure by developing a competitive manufacturing sector (and other sectors that add value to manufactures) over the medium term, whilst pursuing economy-wide factor productivity growth over the long term."

The Industrial Policy aims at structural transformation. However, the policy does not go much beyond a listing of general economy-wide or sector constraints and expressing government's intention to address them. An "Industrial Sector Support Programme" (ISSP 2011–15) is supposed to be the implementation arm of the Policy, but it is basically a long list of projects that are expected to be financed mostly by donors. There are no targets for outputs, exports, technology upgrading and no indication of how the structure of the economy would change as a result of implementing the program.

6.2.3.2.2 *Business environment and public–private collaboration*

The orientation of Ghana's industrial policy is clearly market-supporting. In fact, according to the paper, "Ultimately, the success of the Industrial Policy will be measured by the extent to which it empowers the private sector..."[24] The private sector environment is actually much improved in recent years (as is borne out, for example, by the "Doing Business" rankings of the World Bank). The relationship between the various governments since the early 2000s and the private sector has been cordial, and a major private sector program was launched in 2011. However, a formalized ongoing collaboration between the state and private sector in designing and implementing industrial policy and economic transformation is yet to take hold. Despite the improvement in the environment for the private sector, major impediments still exist, particularly corruption, which slow down the pace and increases the cost of doing business by the private sector.

6.2.3.2.3 *Promotional package for targeted activities and performance control*

Two areas where there have been noticeable progress with respect to targeting and promotion are cocoa production and processing. Here the government set clear targets and supported the private sector to pursue them. By providing subsidized inputs and raising the share of the foreign price of cocoa paid to the farmer, successive governments in Ghana have been able to increase production from around 400,000 tons in the early 2000s to their target of 1 million tons by 2012. The fact that the exchange rate was market-based and hence realistic also helped in translating the raised share of the foreign price into remunerative domestic prices. For processing, the government set a target of 50 percent by 2012, from about 25 percent of domestic production in 2005. Through facilities provided by the Special Economic Zone (The Tema Free Zone) and associated incentives, major international cocoa processors (for example, Cargill, ADM and Barry Callebaut) and small joint-ventures between Ghanaians and foreign partners have located in Ghana to undertake first-stage grinding of cocoa. By 2012, the share processed domestically had risen to around 30 percent, but this represented around only 60 percent of installed capacity. If the plants were operating at full capacity, processing would be close to the target of 50 percent. The government would therefore need to engage the firms and work with them to find solutions to the problems restricting capacity utilization.

6.2.3.2.4 *State capacity*

State capacity in Ghana is generally weak. The main reason for this is not the lack of competent Ghanaians or poor remuneration. In large part, it is due to a partisan political environment that produces a large turnover of senior staff and technocrats whenever governments change, as they do in Ghana. This undermines professionalism, continuity, long-term planning orientation, learning and innovation in the public service. A surprising weakness in Ghana is the lack of timely and quality economic statistics. Although the authorities talk of transforming the economy and increasing employment, there are no comprehensive current data on the production sectors or on employment. The latest data on manufacturing are for 2003, and there are no labor force surveys to provide reliable data on employment.[25]

An important challenge is the lack of effective coordination and management of strategic planning and public finance between the National Development Planning Commission (NDPC) and the Ministry of Finance and Economic Planning, two key state institutions charged with these functions. For example, it does not appear that the type of coordination within government necessary to make implementation of government strategic economic plans (for example, the GSGDA, the Industrial Policy paper, and so on) a central focus of government economic management actually exists. Many of the objectives set in previous plans have never been achieved due in part to lack of continuity in the planning process, the pressure to attend to short term social and economic needs, and in particular the lack of strong institutional mechanism to coordinate and manage medium and long term strategic planning. Recognizing this fundamental weakness, the Government of Ghana (GoG) has been keen on strengthening its planning processes and institutions, and as part of a recent constitutional review process included an assessment of the NDPC to strengthen its constitutional role.

6.2.3.3   Nigeria[26]

6.2.3.3.1   National plan and targeted activities

Nigeria came out with the National Economic Empowerment and Development Strategy (NEEDS) in 2004 after initially dragging its feet on producing the World Bank/IMF-sponsored Poverty Reduction Strategy Paper (PRSP) because of the belief in the country that the earlier Structural Adjustment Programs had not been helpful. Though hewing closely to the Bank/Fund approach on macroeconomics, it had some departures on sectoral policies. In 2009, Nigeria produced the Nigeria Vision 20:2020. A number of economic activities are targeted under the Vision for promotion. These are: chemicals and pharmaceuticals based on the country's oil and gas resources; food and beverage products (including rice, processed cocoa, sesame oil, frozen shrimps and prawns, cashews, and fruit juice); textiles and garments; and leather products and footwear. Overall, the strategy aims to raise the share of manufacturing in GDP from 4 percent to 25 percent by 2020, and the share of non-oil exports from under 6 percent to 40 percent.

6.2.3.3.2   Business environment and public–private collaboration

Nigeria has a vibrant and entrepreneurial private sector, but it is has been held back by a poor and erratic policy environment, corruption, rent seeking, very poor provision of infrastructure, particularly power, and poor business ethics among sections of the private sector itself. On the policy front, there has been significant progress since the early 2000s. Reforms and liberalization has led to a buoyant telecommunications, ICT, and banking sectors that are in fact expanding outside Nigeria into other African countries. However, the manufacturing sector continues to languish.

The state has set up a number of institutions to help promote economic transformation. They include: the Bank for Industry (BOI), the Bank for Agriculture (BOA), the Small and Medium Enterprises Development Agency (SMEDA), and the National Information Technology Development Agency (NITDA). In addition, the Export Promotion Council has been strengthened. However, there does not appear to be formalized and effective institutions for state-private sector collaboration on promoting economic transformation.

6.2.3.3.3   Promotional package for targeted sectors and performance control

Nigeria is developing a number of Special Economic and Free Trade Zones to provide special incentives to manufacturing exports. These include those at Omne, Maigatari, and Lekki. In addition to the special incentives, these zones could provide relief on the poor access to reliable power supply, perhaps the biggest problem facing manufacturing industry in Nigeria. Nigeria is fortunate in having manufacturing clusters that have grown-up organically. One is the Otigba Computer Village (OCV) near Lagos that assembles computers and other ICT hardware. The Lagos State Government is in consultation with the cluster entrepreneurs to develop a public-private partnership arrangement aimed at relocating the cluster to a new location with adequate and modern ICT infrastructure support that will help transform the cluster into an innovation hub that would be internationally competitive.[27] Other important clusters are the one at Nnewi that supplies automobile spare parts to Nigeria (about 80 percent of domestic supply) and other neighboring countries, and the one at Aba producing footwear and leather goods. It is not clear to what extent these clusters are receiving special help from the Federal or State governments. An instrument that Nigeria, given its large domestic market, is controversially using is import bans, to promote import-substitution of consumer items such as packaged fruit juices, and even rice.

6.2.3.3.4   State capacity

In recent years macroeconomic management has witnessed significant improvements with the institution of the "Economic Management Team." Started in the early 2000s, the team includes the: Minister for Finance; Minister for Economic Planning, Director of the Budget Office, the Governor of the Central Bank, and the Economic Advisor to the President. Recently, the head of the team, the Minister for Finance, appears also to have been empowered to act as the "Coordinating Minister" in the government. The achievements under this structure include: the introduction of the Fiscal Responsibility Act (FRA); the preparation of and discussion of a Fiscal Strategy Paper by the Federal Executive Council before the annual budget is prepared; and a more disciplined adherence to the Medium-Term Expenditure Framework tool. All of these have helped improve fiscal management, but the institutional structure and capacity for planning and implementation of economic transformation are not strong.

The National Planning Commission (NPC) appears to have the technical structures under it to enable it to carry out its mandate. It has under it, the Nigerian Institute of Social and Economic Research (NISER) responsible for research into social and economic issues related to economic transformation, the National Bureau of Statistics (NBS), the Centre for Management Development (CMD), which is responsible for capacity building, setting standards, and regulating training activities in Nigeria. However, the NPC has no central role in budgeting, which is carried out by the Budget Office, a parastatal under the Ministry of Finance and also with direct access to the President. Its influence in translating plans and transformation studies into funded programs is therefore limited. This apparently also affects its ability to collect economic statistics, as basic fiscal data on Nigeria appear not to be available to the public.

6.2.3.4   Ethiopia[28]

6.2.3.4.1   National plan and targeted activities

Ethiopia has launched a five-year "Growth and Transformation Plan" (GTP; 2010/2011–2014/2015) that aims to double the size of the economy by the end of the plan period. The plan includes clear targets for a number of products, including: exports of flowers, coffee, meat, and vegetables in agriculture, and exports of sugar, textiles and garments, leather and leather products in agro-based manufacturing. It also targets the pharmaceutical and medical supplies industry, and metal and engineering industry. For pharmaceuticals and medical supplies, the target by the end of the plan period is to raise the share of local production to 50 percent from its current level of less than 15 percent. For basic metal and engineering, the plan aims to raise capacity utilization of the sector to 95 percent, improve per capita metal consumption to 34.72 kg from its current 12 kg, and eventually meet the demand for components and parts of key manufacturing sectors such as leather, textile, cement, agro-processing and so on from local production.

6.2.3.4.2   The business environment and public–private collaboration

The private sector in Ethiopia is weak. This is partly due to inherent weaknesses in the sector itself and also to the approach of government that tends to be oriented more toward control. The indigenous private sector is marked by contractual risks, particularly by widespread credit defaults. FDI has been low, although it has been picking up in recent years. Discussions with the Chamber of Commerce and Sectoral Associations carried out for the Ethiopian case study indicate that the private sector view is that the GTP does not give adequate attention to private sector development and does not clearly outline the sector's role. Members of the sector are, however, appreciative of the results of the government's Business Process Reengineering, which has reduced red tape in government offices.

6.2.3.4.3   Promotional package for targeted activities and performance control

In addition to a general push to increase infrastructure for production, Ethiopia uses a number of instruments to support the activities targeted for promotion. Chief among them are increased access to credit and land. These were instrumental in the success of the Ethiopian flower industry. Industrial parks, tax holidays, and duty-free importation of machinery and equipment are also used, particularly to attract FDI. For small and medium-sized enterprises, training and government procurement (for example, office furniture for government organizations) are also provided as assistance instruments.

It is not clear whether the government has well-designed and implemented performance monitoring and control mechanisms. However, some of the measures used to enforce performance appear to be having unintended negative effects. Examples include: coffee exporters claiming that over-ambitious export targets cause them to export at a loss, which has led some of them to mix export grade coffee with beans of lower grade, thereby causing the country to lose some export markets. Another concern comes from tannery operators who are apprehensive about the government banning the export of process leather in order to force them to sell to domestic shoe manufacturers, an activity that the government is trying to promote.

6.2.3.4.4   State capacity

The Ministry of Finance and Economic Development (MOFED) leads in planning and coordinating the transformation process. Another important institution is the Central Statistical Agency (CSA), which the government is in the process of strengthening to enable it to play a more effective role in providing timely and quality data for the planning and monitoring of the economic transformation process. Though disciplined, the Ethiopian civil service is weak. The government recognizes this and is implementing a program to raise capacity in the service. The Ethiopian Development Research Institute (EDRI), an independent think-tank but with strong links to the government, provides analytical capabilities on economic transformation issues.

6.2.3.5   Kenya[29]

6.2.3.5.1   National plan and targeted activities

In 2008, the Kenyan governemnt produced "Vision 2030" to guide its economic, social, and political progress up to the year 2030. The economic part of the vision was to make Kenya a middle-income country by the year 2030. GDP growth was to be raised to around 10 percent a year over the period. The Vision targeted the following areas: (1) tourism – expanding revenues four-fold; (2) increasing value in agriculture; (3) better and more inclusive wholesale and retail trade, including raising sales in formal channels from around 5 percent to 30 percent by 2012 by attracting large retailers; (4) increased manufacturing for the regional market; (5) ICT and Business Process Offshoring (BPO) – making Kenya one of the top three BPO centers in Africa and creating around 7,500 jobs; and (6) financial services – creating a globally competitive sector that generates high levels of savings to help finance Kenya's investment needs. The Vision is translated into implementation through the five-year rolling Medium-Term Plan (MTP). Despite the post-election violence in early 2008, the first MTP (2008–13) seems to be on course. One of its key elements, on the political front, has been the introduction of a new constitution that among other things aims to strengthen the governance environment for economic management.

6.2.3.5.2 *The business environment and public–private collaboration*

Although the private sector environment could be improved (that is, as per Doing Business and Global Competitiveness rankings), Kenya has always had a strong private sector. Increasingly, the private sector is being brought in by government to collaborate in formulating transformation strategies and in addressing implementation issues. Vision 2030 was spearheaded by the National Economic and Social Council (NESC), which includes the private sector. It is chaired by the President of the country, and the Prime Minister serves as the alternate chair. The management team of the NESC is drawn from both the public and private sectors. There is also a Prime Minister's Forum, where the Prime Minister meets with the private sector to discuss their concerns. There are also sector-based associations such the Kenya Flower Council through which dialogue takes place with the government on matters affecting specific sectors. Finally, the government also consults the private sector during preparation of the budget.

6.2.3.5.3 *Promotional package for targeted activities and performance control*

The government has put a lot of emphasis on promoting its ICT and BPO vision. This vision seeks in part to leverage on the emerging software industry based on mobile phone applications ushered in by the M-Pesa mobile phone-based banking system. The government has made considerable investments in ICT infrastructure to increase internet bandwidth, and is developing a "techno-city" called Konza, which is about 60 kilometers outside the capital Nairobi and is anticipated to become the largest such city in Africa. It is expected to have business and science parks and a university. The government aims to attract at least five major leading IT suppliers and at least ten large multinationals in BPO to the city, which is dubbed "Africa's silicon savannah." In a related development, in August 2012 IBM announced its intention to set up, in partnership with the government, its first research lab in Africa (one of only 12 in the world) in Kenya (near Nairobi). However, the incentive framework appears to be still in need of improvement. For example, in early September 2012, Craft Silicon, a software development company based in Kenya, announced its decision to relocate to Singapore because of high taxes in Kenya.[30]

6.2.3.5.4 *State capacity*

Regarding state capacity, efforts have been made to put in place an elaborate performance management system for the entire public service, where all ministries, state corporations, and local authorities are ranked annually on performance. Government capacity to analyze transformation issues is augmented by the Kenyan Institute of Policy Research and Analysis (KIPPRA), a government-affiliated think-tank.

6.2.3.6   Rwanda[31]

6.2.3.6.1   National plan and targeted activities

Rwanda's Vision 2020 plan puts a strategic focus on manufacturing export growth in the medium term. The Rwanda Development Board (RDB), inspired by Singapore's Economic Development Board, has been established as a one-stop center for attracting FDI and increasing jobs. Following analysis, the RDB has selected six clusters to focus on. They are: (1) mining services; (2) niche tourism; (3) ICT and business process outsourcing; (3) silk textiles; (4) fruits and vegetable processing; and (5) dairy manufacturing. Rwanda aims to take advantage of ICT to establish the country as a regional hub that provides high-value services. To this end, in addition to new investments in a railway line, an airport and an airline, the country is constructing a convention center, and it has also established partnerships with international centers of excellence in ICT, including the Carnegie-Mellon University in the USA.

Rwanda is also implementing a Strategic Plan for Agricultural Transformation (SPAT) which includes a land reform policy aimed at increasing agricultural land productivity and replacing subsistence farming with a fully monetized and commercial agriculture by 2020. However, there are questions about the likely impact of this commercialization push on poor risk-averse farming households.

6.2.3.6.2   The business environment and public–private collaboration

Vision 2020 stresses government commitment to facilitating the emergence of a strong and modern private sector to drive growth, competitiveness, economic diversification, and export promotion. In 2010, Rwanda was named in the Doing Business Report as the world's top reformer, rising in the "ease of doing business" rankings from number 143 in 2009 to number 67 in 2010. In 2011, it was number 58 out of 183 countries. However, there does not appear to be strong institutionalized mechanisms for public–private collaboration in policy formulation or implementation.

6.2.3.6.3   Promotional package for targeted activities and performance control

The key strategic thrusts of Rwanda's Vision 2020 appear to be state-led (for example, the infrastructure investments and the ICT development), although FDI and PPP projects are also being promoted. However, the government also plays an active role in identifying and removing constraints to the private sector and providing support. Examples include support to

SMEs by reducing the cost of complying with taxation, facilitating access to existing funds, and working with business development services to facilitate SME access to market information and skilled labor.

6.2.3.6.4 *State capacity*

Human and institutional capacity is weak, but the government appears to be disciplined and well coordinated. The government organizes an annual Leadership Retreat where priorities for achieving private sector-led growth are identified. The retreat involves the President and heads of government ministries and state enterprises.

6.2.4 Challenges to the emerging approach to industrial policy

The emerging trend toward industrial policy in several SSA countries, while more private-sector-friendly than the earlier approach under the import-substitution strategy, nonetheless entails a more active role of the state in the economy than envisaged under the SAPs. This poses three important questions: (a) Will the state be taking on roles that are best left to the private sector?; (b) Does the state have the capacity to take on additional roles in the economy when it is still struggling to adequately fulfill its traditional roles of providing public goods and social services?; and (c) Will the increased role of the state in the economy lead to increased corruption? We think these questions are important and legitimate and should inform the design of programs under the approach. However, we also think their importance tend to be exaggerated by the opponents of industrial policy, and that they are in fact not unique to that approach.

At the core of the emerging industrial policy approach is a partnership between the state and the private sector; a strategic partnership in which the state, in consultation with the private sector, sets the overall direction for economic transformation, and the private sector, actively supported by the state, leads in implementation. The state supports the private sector not only by providing the traditional public goods, social services, and a good general policy environment, but also by providing specific support, including assistance in confronting specific market failures and also removing government imposed distortions, so as to encourage and facilitate the private sector to undertake transformational projects identified through consultations. It is in this sense that an effective mechanism for ongoing substantive deliberations between the state and private sector is key. The deliberation mechanism provides a process by which the relative roles of the state and the private sector in promoting transformation are defined in a pragmatic and on an ongoing basis to reflect the country's situation and relevant factors in the global economy. There is no need to lay down a rigid division of roles a-priori based on theory or ideology.[32] The challenge then is to have deliberative mechanisms that actually serve as forums for substantive discussions that inform transformation strategy and policy instead of forums that are used for public relations by the state of for lobbying by the private sector. Several SSA countries have some forms of state–private sector consultation mechanisms, but many are not effective. There is work to be done in this area.

State capacity is indeed weak in many countries in SSA. This applies in particular to the capacity to generate the data and analyses necessary for planning and for monitoring implementation of plans. It is therefore fair to question the wisdom of states taking on more activist roles even where the need for such roles can be established. There can be three responses to the question. First, it is not clear that state capacity in the South East Asian countries in the 1960s and 1970s when they embarked on their activist transformation drives was that much higher than what currently exist in several SSA countries (for example, Senegal, Ghana, Nigeria, Kenya, and South Africa). Second, it is debatable whether the heavy focus on institutional reforms and delivery of social services that SSA countries are urged to undertake under the SAPs and good governance agenda are any less demanding of state capacity than what it would require to provide targeted facilitation to the private sector in order to promote economic transformation.[33] Perhaps a refocusing of the existing state capacity to support the pursuit of economic transformation would help. Third, in several SSA countries human capacity for administration and management may not be weak even if they are within the state. What is needed are ways for qualified nationals (both within and outside the countries) to be attracted to and retained in public service. This requires more than better pay. Equally as important are: (a) an environment in the public service that encourages professionalism and open discussion based on data and analysis; and (b) an environment that is open to all qualified nationals to serve in public service, and where job tenure in senior professional positions is not dependent on changes in government administrations.[34] So while we recognize weak state capacity as a challenge that must be addressed, we do not think the active pursuit of economic transformation therefore has to wait. The two should be pursued together. However, attempts to strengthen capacity by increasing supply without addressing the issues regarding the working environment for professionals in public service are not likely to succeed.

Greater involvement of the state in the economy is likely to increase the opportunities for public officials to extract rents. However, if the push to proactively support the private sector succeeds, there would be more opportunities for people to be rich by being in the private sector, so the relative attractiveness of holding state positions for extracting rents would diminish. Furthermore, progress on economic transformation will provide increased resources to the state to improve the pay of its officials, thereby reducing to some extent the motivation for state officials to extract rents. On the other hand, in a stagnant economy with few profitable opportunities in the private sector, government becomes the main source of economic advancement, and where public pay is low, there will be high levels of corruption whether or not the state plays an activist role in the economy. It could also be argued that where there is no strong commitment to national goals such as economic transformation to motivate political leaders and state officials, personal gain assumes prominence as the motivator in the state apparatus.

What has happened in many SSA countries over the past thirty years reflects the points made above. The activist and import-substituting state was rolled back, and governments in many countries took a back seat to donors and foreign experts who set the economic agenda. With the SAPs (despite their pro-private sector orientation) not actively promoting programs to create profitable opportunities for the indigenous private sector in modern economic activities, government service and contracts, contracts for donor projects, and employment in donor agencies and in donor-sponsored non-governmental organizations (NGOs) have become among the main money-making pursuits. It will be very difficult for one to make the case that corruption in SSA countries is lower now than it was during the era of state activism in the economy.

Similarly, globally it is unclear if one can make the case that countries with more active state involvement in the economy are necessarily more corrupt than those with less state involvement. Can anyone really say that Singapore, where the state was active in promoting economic transformation, is more corrupt than Hong Kong, where the state was more hands-off? Corruption is definitely a menace that needs to be tackled aggressively, but the causes and the solutions do not necessarily correlate with the degree of government activism in promoting economic transformation.

6.2.5 Research program on industrial policy and economic transformation

The foregoing discussion has established that SSA has underperformed relative to other developing countries, specifically the comparator countries, with respect to a number of areas: (a) economic diversification; (b) technology; (c) productivity; (d) export competitiveness; and (e) the creation of formal employment. While performance on per capita GDP growth in SSA has been high in the past decade relative to the historical record, it is unlikely to be sustained if the countries in the region do not address their deficiencies in the five areas reviewed in this paper. Research therefore has to be focused on these areas. It will have to be very practical in nature; the theoretical issues have been well trodden, and more of it is not likely to be helpful to policymakers in SSA. What is needed is an analysis of issues pertaining to the five areas above in specific SSA country contexts, bringing to bear relevant experiences from elsewhere. The list of such issues include:

- Strengthening state capacity – what is the minimum feasible set of necessary reforms and actions in a particular country to enable the state to: (a) provide effective leadership in the formulation of coherent, ambitious, but feasible medium-term economic transformation plans; (b) provide coordination and monitoring of the implementation of such plans; (c) to select, appraise, and monitor implementation of public sector projects efficiently; and (d) to reduce opportunities for corruption and other hold-up behavior by the state that adversely affect private sector operations even as the state proclaims it is seeking to proactively promote private sector activities?
- Strengthening the institutional mechanisms for state–private sector deliberations and collaboration on economic transformation.
- Raising the rate of domestic savings – going beyond financial sector liberalization to improvements in fiscal policy and also in financial institutions and instruments.
- Skills development, including: (a) a strategy to improve scientific and technical education at the secondary and tertiary levels over the medium to long term; and (b) a short-term strategy of skills development targeted at the requirements of the country' economic transformation plan.
- Studies on potential diversification opportunities: Studies on products (and subsectors) to explore potential pathways for increasing international competitiveness and thereby increasing export diversification and the range of efficient import substitution. Each such study would take into consideration: global demand trends, the global value chain, the key factors that contribute to success in dynamic exporting countries, and the domestic supply, policy and institutional constraints affecting the product in the country.
- Technology acquisition studies: (a) prioritization of the technologies that national efforts should be focused on, consistent with the country's economic transformation strategy; (b) identification of cost-effective ways to assist the private sector to acquire technology from abroad; and (c) how to develop a targeted domestic technology development effort.
- Export promotion: Identification of the policies, instruments, and institutions that a particular country could use, which are consistent with the international trade regime (particularly the WTO); and how to design them.
- Role of regional trade and integration.
- FDI policies: How a particular country attracts the types of FDI that lead, beyond exports and employment, to technology spillovers and linkages to the domestically-owned firms, and the complementary policies and measures (for example, skills development) that facilitates this objective.

The list above is broad, but by no means exhaustive. However, it follows from the review carried out in this paper. It also motivates the research program being carried out at my institution, the African Center for Economic Transformation (ACET), whose principal objective is to promote economic transformation in Africa through research and advisory work.

6.2.6 Conclusion

This paper has reviewed the performance of SSA countries on economic transformation over a forty-year period from 1970 to 2010. In addition to GDP per capita growth, the paper defined economic transformation to include progress on: diversification, technology, productivity, export competitiveness, and the share of formal employment in the labor force. Although several countries in SSA have performed well in the past decade and half on GDP per capita growth, from the point of view of economic transformation, there has not been much progress, particularly when compared to a group of developing countries in East Asia and Latin America. This lack of progress is observed both during the period of state-led import-substitution development strategy of the 1970s and also the period of structural adjustment programs from the 1980s to the early 2000s. We have argued that there is now a need to search for different approaches.

Despite their different orientations, the two main development strategies implemented in SSA in the past tended to view relations between the state and the private sector largely through the prism of conflict. The state-led import-substitution strategy sought to control or to supplant the private sector, while the structural adjustment programs sought to "roll back" the state in order to promote the private sector. The experiences of the successful East Asian countries suggest that an approach under which the state and the private sector operate as strategic partners can produce better results on economic transformation. Under that approach, the state targeted specific new activities for the country to enter into or existing activities to be upgraded and expanded. Such targeting was often done in close consultation with the private sector. The private sector firms led in implementation of the activities, but the state provided the support necessary to help them succeed. Such support was monitored to ensure results. We have labeled the approach "market-supporting industrial policy," and shown that a number of countries in SSA are beginning to experiment with elements of it. However, the approach has risks and challenges. These include: the danger of the state getting involved in activities best left to the private sector; the overstretching of states that already have weak capacity, the possibility of increased corruption, and the lack of timely and quality data and analyses for good economic management. We have argued for the need to monitor the new industrial policy attempts in SSA and to produce data and analyses to help reduce the risks and challenges, and have briefly outlined a research agenda that could inform policy under the approach.

If SSA countries desire that their economic performance over the course of the next 40 years be dramatically better than that of the last 40, then the "market-supporting industrial policy" discussed in this paper merits careful consideration.

Notes

1. Assistance from Mr. Kwaku Damoah of ACET on data is gratefully acknowledged.
2. In terms of the distinction that is often made between "horizontal" and "vertical" industrial policies, our definition is closer to the latter. While recognizing the insights that the distinction brings in highlighting possible distortions of policy interventions, we do not think it should be the central focus of discussion. To us the aim of industrial policy is to change economic structure by introducing new products or economic activities or upgrading their technology. So the nature of policies is purely dictated by what is required operationally for the targeted products or activities to succeed, given fiscal and capacity constraints. The insights of the "horizontal"/"vertical" distinction can, however, help inform the choice among a particular set of feasible policies for promoting the targeted products or activities.
3. For theory see, for example, Greenwald and Stiglitz (2012) and Rodrik (2007). For development experience, see, for example, (Johnson (1982)), Evans (1995), Wade (1990), World Bank (1993), Chang (2002, 2006), Lim (2011) and Lin and Monga (2011).
4. For Korea, see Amsden (1989); Kim, Linsu (2003); Rhee, Ross-Larson, and Pursell (2010); Lim (2011), and Kim (2011). For Singapore see Chang (1998); For East Asia, see Lall (1997 and 2003), Suehiro (2008), Weiss (2005), and World Bank (1993).
5. On Chile, the examples of Fundacion Chile and the Chilean Development Corporation (CORFO) are cases in point. See Agosin (1997). On Brazil, the examples of the development of Embraer Airplane and the giant Development Bank, BNDES, (bigger than the World Bank) come to mind.
6. FE/TL=(FE/TE) * (TE/TL), where: FE is formal employment; TL is the total labor force; and TE is total employment. The first term on the right is the share of formal employment in total employment and the second term is the total employment rate.
7. ILO, KILM (Key Indicators of the Labour Market), various issues.
8. The estimate for Kenya was 33 percent in 1999, but that is the only year for which data is available to construct the estimate.
9. Private foreign investments have also been low, although beginning to rise in a number of countries.
10. Imbs and Wacziarg (2003) show that countries diversify their production base (that is, decrease specialization) as they develop, up to around US$9,000 per capita. Then they begin to respecialize. So a plot of the level of production specialization (vertical axis) against per capita income (horizontal axis) shows a "U" relationship. Alternatively, a plot of diversification shows an inverted "U" relationship.

11. The classical (Ricardian) theory that implies a country should focus on its relative comparative advantage has nothing to say about the possibility of a country learning to improve its relative comparative advantage over time. And the more common (Heckscher–Ohlin–Samuelson) relative factor proportions theory of comparative advantage assumes each country is equally capable technologically of engaging in any economic activity, which clearly is not the case for African countries vis-à-vis the developed industrial countries.

12. Although there are more sophisticated ways of measuring production diversity, for example as in the "product-space" approach of Hidalgo, Klinger, Barabasi, and Hausmann (2007), we focus on the share of MVA in GDP due to data constraints and a desire to focus on simple measures that policymakers can easily understand.

13. For instance, see Greenwald and Stiglitz (2006) and Hausmann, Huang, and Rodrik (2007).

14. Again, a more sophisticated measure such as the Herfindahl Index could be used, but we think the simple measure is more readily grasped by policymakers and is more likely to focus discussion on increasing the number of export products.

15. Lall (2000); UNIDO (2009). Several African countries are deficient in reporting a consistent series of manufacturing production data. The low digit level is therefore necessitated by data availability.

16. MVA/Wage bill = MVA/(# of workers'*average wage) = (MVA/#of workers)/(average wage).

17. We use these simple measures to measure productivity, instead of the more sophisticated Total Factor Productivity (TFP) measure because of lack of consistent and comparable cross-country data.

18. The measure is calculated as the growth rate of the country group's exports of goods and services minus the growth rate of the world's exports of goods and services. We then take a five-year moving average to smoothen the annual fluctuations. We use the percentage change in the shares rather than the shares themselves to eliminate possible bias due to country economic size.

19. The measure is susceptible to bias from price movements. For example, if the price of oil exports goes up, a country like Nigeria with about 90 percent of its exports being oil is likely to experience an export growth rate that is higher than that of total world exports. For SSA and ACET-15, this is likely to happen during commodity price booms or busts. A possible way to reduce the bias would be to use world market shares of individual products – for example, say the average of the shares of the top five exports. But since for SSA countries the top five exports tend to be mostly primary exports, increasing world market shares would not necessarily be desirable from the point of view of economic transformation. Besides, there is some advantage to a country for exporting products that experience sustained rise in prices.

20. The export "sophistication" measure of Lall, Weiss, and Zhang (2006) and Hausmann, Huang, and Rodrik (2007) could also be used in a sense to show trends in export competitiveness. This measure is essentially the per capita income equivalent of a country's export basket. Hausmann, Huang, and Rodrik call their version EXPY. A country has a high EXPY if its export basket includes a high share of products also exported by high-income countries. In that sense, the country's export basket could be said to be "sophisticated," since the country appears to be competing with higher-income, and therefore usually more developed, countries. We use the simpler measure in the text instead of EXPY because we think it has more direct policy implications for export competitiveness, but

we report the EXPY values in Table 6.2.1. (Note that a country whose exports basket is dominated by a product that tends to be exported by high income countries, would necessarily have a high EXPY even if the product is unsophisticated. This is the case with Nigeria. About 90 percent of its exports come from crude oil, and oil-exporting countries tend to be high income.)

21. The framework also benefits from Rodrik (2007), Page (2011), Johnson (1982), Komiya, Okuno, and Suzumura (1988), Evans (1995), Amsden (1989), Jones and Sakong (1980), Wade (1990), Chang (1998), World Bank (1993), Kohli (2004), and Suehiro (2008).
22. The material here is mainly from "Ghana Economic Transformation Case Study," a case study commissioned by ACET.
23. Republic of Ghana, "Ghana Industrial Policy" (p. 4).
24. Ibid.
25. A main source for data on the labor force has in recent years been estimates based on the results from the donor-financed Living Standards Measurement Surveys.
26. Material here is taken mainly from "African Transformation Report: Nigeria Case Study on Economic Transformation," a study commissioned by ACET.
27. African Transformation Report: Nigerian Case Study on Economic Transformation (p. 67).
28. The material here is taken mostly from "Country Case Studies on Structural Transformation: the Case of Ethiopia," a study commissioned by ACET.
29. The material here is taken mostly from "Economic Transformation in Kenya" (2012), a case study commissioned by ACET and conducted by the Kenya Institute for Public Policy Research and Analysis (KIPPRA).
30. "SCI & Tech" of Kenya, September 3, 2012. Accessed at http://www.standardmedia.co.ke/?articleID=2000065325&story_title=Big-blow-for-Kenya-as-software-firm-relocates-to-Singapore.
31. The material on Rwanda is taken mostly from "Rwanda Case Study on Economic Transformation," commissioned by ACET and conducted by Institute of Policy Analysis and Research (IPAR)—Rwanda.
32. On the role of state-private sector deliberation councils, see, for example, Johnson (1982), Komiya, R. et al (1988), Evans (1995), Okazaki (2001), and Rhee et al. (2010).
33. Khan (2012); Meles (2012).
34. Results of a pilot study conducted on behalf of ACET by the Center for Democratic Development (CDD) in 2011.

References

African Center for Economic Transformation (ACET) publications:

Ghana (2011) "Driving Transformation through the Capable State," Pilot Study, Ghana (conducted on behalf of ACET by the Center for Democratic Governance).

Ethiopia (2012) "Country Case Studies on Structural Transformation: the case of Ethiopia," mimeo.

Ghana (2012) "Ghana Economic Transformation Case Study," mimeo.

Kenya (2012) "Economic Transformation in Kenya," mimeo.

Nigeria (2012) "African Transformation Report: Nigeria Case Study on Economic Transformation," mimeo.

Rwanda (2012) "Rwanda Case Study on Economic Transformation," draft paper.

Agosin, Manuel (1997) "Export Performance in Chile: Lessons for Africa," World Institute of Development Economics Research (WIDER), Working Papers No. 144.

Amsden, Alice H. (1989) *Asia's Next Giant: South Korea and Late Industrialization* (New York: Oxford University Press).

Chang, C.B. (ed.) (1998) *Heart Work: Stories of How EDB Steered the Singapore Economy from 1961 into the 21st Century* (Singapore: Singapore Economic Development Board and EDB Society).

Chang, H.-J. (2002). *Kicking Away the Ladder: Development Strategy in Historical Perspective* (London: Anthem Press).

Chang, H.-J. (2006). *The East Asian Development Experience: The Miracle, the Crisis and the Future* (Penang: Third World Press).

Evans, P. (1995) *Embedded Autonomy: States and Industrial Transformation* (Princeton, NJ: Princeton University Press).

Greenwald, B. and Stiglitz, J.E. (2006) "Helping Infant Economies Grow: Foundations of Trade Policies for Developing Countries". American Economic Review, vol. 90, no. 2, pp. 141–146.

Greenwald, B. and Stiglitz, J.E. (2013) "Industrial Policies, the Creation of a Learning Society, and Economic Development," in this volume.

Hausmann, R., Hwang, J., and Rodrik, D. (2007) "What You Export Matters," *Journal of Economic Growth*, vol. 12, pp. 1–25.

Hidalgo, C.A., Klinger, B., Barabasi, A.-L., and Hausmann, R. (2007) "The Product Space Conditions the Development of Nations," *Science*, vol. 317, pp. 482–487.

International Labour Organization (ILO) "Key Indicators of Labour Markets (KILM)" (various issues) (Geneva: ILO).

Imbs, Jean and Wacziarg, Romain (2003) "Stages of Diversification," *American Economic Review*, vol. 93, no. 1, pp. 63–86.

Johnson, Chalmers (1982). *MITI and the Japanese Miracle: The Growth of Industrial Policy, 1925–1975* (Stanford, CA: Stanford University Press).

Jones, Leroy P. and Sakong, Il (1980) *Government, Business, and Entrepreneurship in Economic Development: The Korean Case* (Cambridge, MA: Harvard University Press).

Khan, Mushtaq, H. (2012) "Governance and Growth Challenges in Africa," in A. Noman, Botchwey, H. Stein, and J. Stiglitz (eds), *Good Growth and Governance in Africa* (New York: Oxford University Press).

Kim, Chung-yum (2011) *From Despair to Hope: Economic Policy-Making in Korea, 1945–79* (Seoul: Korea Development Institute).

Kim, Linsu (2003) "The Dynamics of Technology Development: Lessons from the Korean Experience," In Sanjaya Lall and Shujiro Urata (eds), *Competitiveness, FDI and Technological Activity in East Asia* (Cheltenham: World Bank Institute/Edward Elgar).

Kohli, Atul (2004) *State-Directed Development: Political Power and Industrialization in the Global Periphery* (Cambridge: Cambridge University Press).

Komiya, R., Okuno, M., and Suzumura, K. (eds) (1988) *Industrial Policy of Japan* (New York: Academic Press, Inc.).

Lall, Sanjaya (1997). "Selective Policies for Export Promotion: Lessons from the Asian Tigers," UNU World Institute for Development Economics Research (UNU/WIDER) Research for Action 43.

Lall, Sanjaya (2000) "The Technological Structure and Performance of Developing Country Manufactured Exports, 1985–98," *Oxford Development Studies*, vol. 28, no. 3, pp. 337–369.

Lall, Sanjaya (2003) "Foreign Direct Investment, Technology Development and Competitiveness: Issues and Evidence," in Sanjaya Lall and Shujiro Urata (eds), *Competitiveness, FDI and Technological Activity in East Asia* (Cheltenham: World Bank Institute/Edward Elgar).

Lall, S., Weiss, J., and Zhang, J. (2006) "The "Sophistication" of Exports: A New Trade Measure," *World Development*, vol. 34, no. 2, pp. 222–237.

Lim, Wonhyuk (2011) "Joint Discovery and Upgrading of Comparative Advantage: Lessons from Korea's Development Experience," in Shahrokh Fardoust, Yongbeom Kim, and Claudia Sepulveda (eds), *Postcrisis Growth and Development: A Development Agenda for the G-20* (Washington, DC: The World Bank), pp. 173–226.

Lin, Justin Y. and Celestin Monga (2011) "DPR Debate: Growth Identification and Facilitation: The Role of the State in the Dynamics of the Structural Change," *Development Policy Review*, vol. 29, no. 3).

Meles, Zenawi (2012). "States and Markets: Neoliberal Limitations and the Case for Developmental State," in A. Noman, K. Botchwey, H. Stein, and J. Stiglitz (eds), *Good Growth and Governance in Africa* (Oxford: Oxford University Press)

Okazaki, Tetsuji (2001) "The Government–Firm Relationship in Postwar Japan: The Success and Failure of Bureau Pluralism," in Joseph E. Stiglitz and Shahid Yusuf (eds), *Rethinking the East Asian Miracle* (Oxford: World Bank and Oxford University Press).

Page, John (2011). "Can Africa Industrialize?". Paper Presented at the Africa Economic Research Consortium (AERC) Bi-Annual Plenary Meeting, Nairobi, Kenya May 29 2011.

Republic of Ghana (2011), *Ghana Industrial Policy* (Accra, Ghana: Government of Ghana (Ministry of Trade and Industry)).

Rhee, Yung Whee, Bruce Ross-Larson, Gary Purcell (2010). *How Korea Did It*, 2nd edition (Seoul: World Bank/Random House, Korea)

Rodrik, Dani (2007) "Industrial Policy for the Twenty-First Century," in *One Economics, Many Recipes: Globalization, Institutions, and Economic Growth* (Princeton, NJ: Princeton University Press).

Suehiro, Akira (2008) *Catch-Up Industrialization: The Trajectory and Prospects of East Asian Economies* (translated by Tom Gill) (Honolulu: University of Hawaii Press).

UNIDO (2009). *Industrial Development Report, 2009*. United Nations Industrial Development Organization (Vienna: UNIDO).

Wade, Robert (1990) *Governing the Market: Economic Theory and the Role of Government in East Asian Industrialization* (Princeton, NJ: Princeton University Press).

Weiss, John (2005) "Export Growth and industrial Policy: Lessons from the East Asian Miracle Experience," Asian Development Bank (ADB) Discussion Paper No. 26.

World Bank (1993) *The East Asian Miracle: Economic Growth and Public Policy* (Oxford: Oxford University Press).

6.3

The Premature Deindustrialization of South Africa

Jean Imbs
Paris School of Economics

6.3.1 Introduction

Manufacturing activities are on the wane in Sub-Saharan Africa. With the relocation of many industries into Asia, the trend is widespread across the world economy. The USA and most of the European Union are also deindustrializing, but at higher levels of per capita GDP than Africa. Their economies tend to move into services. In contrast, the deindustrialization of Sub-Saharan Africa is often associated with the rising importance of extractive activities in its economy, exported to emerging Asia. Thus, contrary to the developed world, Sub-Saharan Africa is not moving away from industries and into services. Rather it is moving back into extractive activities, to take advantage, so the argument goes, from temporarily sky-high commodity prices. Such a trend has far-ranging consequences for the region's aggregate activity, which then depends on commodity prices. It also raises the question of the long-run desirability of structural change there.

This paper verifies the empirical support for such an argument in South African data. The richest economy in the region has also the best data coverage. Though it is impossible to ascertain for lack of the relevant data, South Africa may give a preview of the path that will be followed (or perhaps that is being followed) elsewhere in Sub-Saharan Africa. Data suggest the South African economy was diversifying throughout most of the 1970s, 1980s, and 1990s. In the opening years of the 2000s, South Africa displayed a reversal in this trend, a respecialization of the economy back to 1970 levels. The reversal happened in 2003, when per capita GDP was slightly above US$6,200 evaluated at PPP exchange rates in 2005. This is much lower than usual, thus giving credence to the notion that South African deindustrialization was indeed premature.

Interestingly, the bulk of this respecialization corresponds to an increase in the average share of *services* in the South African economy, at the expense of manufactures. Deindustrialization (that is, the respecialization of the economy away from manufactures) continues to appear in 2003 if mining or manufacturing sectors are omitted. But there is no respecialization when services are omitted. In other words, South Africa respecializes because the share of services trends upwards from the early 2000s, while at the same time the shares of manufacturing *and of mining* drop. Thus the pattern of structural change in South Africa is largely similar to what other developed economies have gone through: deindustrialization happens to the benefit of services. It just happened much sooner in South Africa, but not because extractive activities took over the economy.

Why did South Africa experience such an accelerated sequence of otherwise customary changes in the structure of its production? This paper shows the country's specialization into services was homogeneous across its constituent regions. The share of services – and especially of financial services – increased in all South African provinces, to the detriment of manufactures. As a result, the production of services became geographically spread out across the country, and different regions increasingly resembled each other in terms of their production patterns. Thus, the respecialization of the country reflected a homogeneous move into (financial) services across all of its regions.

The paper conjectures this pattern is a reflection of the international openness of South Africa. As South African external trade boomed in the 2000s, it became possible for all of its constituent regions to produce according to the country's overall comparative advantage. The country specialized, and deindustrialized as a whole, as each of its constituent regions moved into services. Imports served to meet the local consumption needs that were not produced domestically. Of course, a natural corollary to this argument is that South African diversification into manufactures between 1970 and 2000 was associated with regional heterogeneity. The country diversified as its constituent regions specialized in different (manufacturing) activities. This presumably was made possible by local market access, with regions specializing in different sectors as they increasingly traded with each other. For South Africa, regional data on sectoral production are missing or unreliable prior to 1996. Thus, it is impossible to ascertain whether the earlier diversification of South Africa reflected such local divergence. But the respecialization the country has experienced since 2003 is especially prevalent in traded sectors. This is suggestive that trade, both local and global, contributes to accounting for South African structural change.

If such is the case, South African deindustrialization is not necessarily evil per se. It is the reflection of a perennial pattern in economic development, rather than an opportunistic shift into extractive activities. The transition to services happened earlier, and faster than elsewhere. It is tempting to associate this accelerated pattern with the sudden large spike in trade openness the country experienced in the early 2000s. It happened at levels of per capita GDP that are substantially lower than is customary, and at lower levels of local integration. Access to local markets was limited when South Africa opened, and manufacturing sectors (especially small manufactures) were not as developed then as they could have become had local markets integrated further. Inasmuch as this deindustrialization reflects market integration, there is no reason to deem it as fundamentally inefficient. Of course, as with any trade-induced structural change, questions of social protection and retraining are of the essence.

The rest of the paper is structured as follows. Section 6.3.2 characterizes the pattern of structural change in South Africa since 1970, using output data at the level of two- and three-digit sectors. Section 6.3.3 introduces geographic data to show the specialization of South Africa was homogeneous across its constituent regions. The importance of financial services is also emphasized. Section 6.3.4 concludes.

6.3.2   The deindustrialization of South Africa into services

This section characterizes structural change in South Africa. Structural change is understood as the time pattern of the allocation of resources across sectors. Following a large literature, this paper documents the specialization of the economy using a concentration index, the Herfindahl.[1] Let Y_{st} denote real production in sector s at time t. The Herfindahl index H_t is defined as:

$$H_t = \sum_{s=1}^{N} \left(\frac{Y_{st}}{\sum_{s=1}^{N} Y_{st}} \right)^2$$

H_t takes high values when the economy is specialized, that is, when the majority of output is produced in a few sectors, and the distribution of sector-level output is skewed. Structural change happens as H_t displays time trends, which is the focus of this paper, rather than the actual level of the Herfindahl.[2]

Herfindahl indexes are computed using data on real production at the sector level. The data are collected by Statistics South Africa, and report real output for 46 sectors between 1970 and 2011. Aggregation level varies between two and four digits, depending on sectors. The full list is reported in Appendix A.

Figure 6.3.1 reports the value of H_t over the full sample. Except for a short spike in the late 1970s, the bulk of the 1970–2011 period is characterized by South Africa diversifying. This trend is customary for developing and emerging economies, which display on average highly specialized initial patterns of production. Across countries, a systematic first stage of development consists in diversifying away from such high specialization, which is typically focused on primary activities.[3]

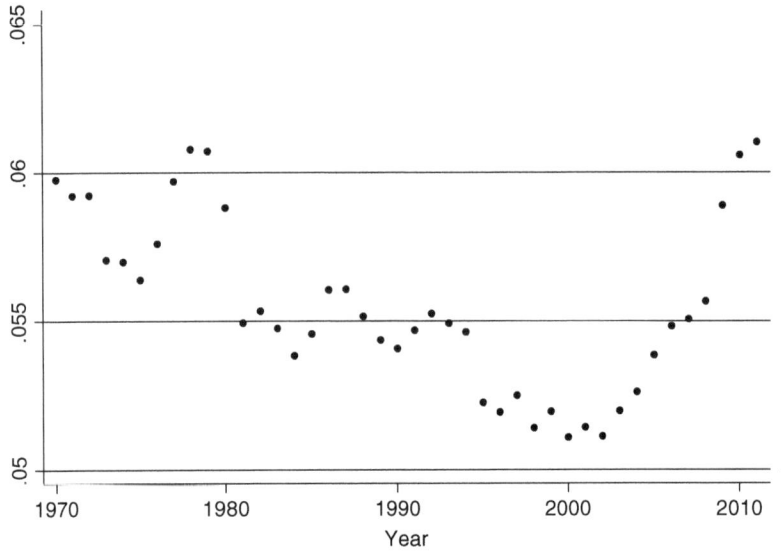

Figure 6.3.1   Sectoral Specialization (Herfindahl all sectors)

Interestingly, the downward trend in H_t reverts in the early 2000s, and the country specializes back to levels not seen since the early 1970s at a spectacular rate. Such a reversal is also customary in the data: Imbs and Wacziarg (2003) showed that a long period of diversification is followed by respecialization at later stages of development. What is striking in South Africa is the suddenness and severity of the reversal, which undoes 30 years of diversification in the course of fewer than ten years. This specificity is absent even from respecializing developed countries, which typically display a mild upward trend in their Herfindahl index.

Furthermore, respecialization in South Africa happens at much lower levels of per capita GDP than in the average country. In a sample of 63 countries, Imbs and Wacziarg (2003) show that respecialization happens on average at the level of per capita GDP reached by Ireland in 1992. In 2005 PPP dollars, this means US$18,719, according to the latest version of the Penn World Tables. Compare this with US$6,246 in South Africa in 2003, the year of the reversal, almost exactly a third of the average level in international data.

Thus, South Africa represents a confirmation of a pattern found elsewhere in developing economies. But it is also a striking exception, for the pace at which structural change happened there is unique. This begs the question of the driving forces for such abrupt respecialization in 2003. A natural, parsimonious first pass at this question consists in recomputing Herfindahl indexes for subsamples of sectors, excluding some subcategories.

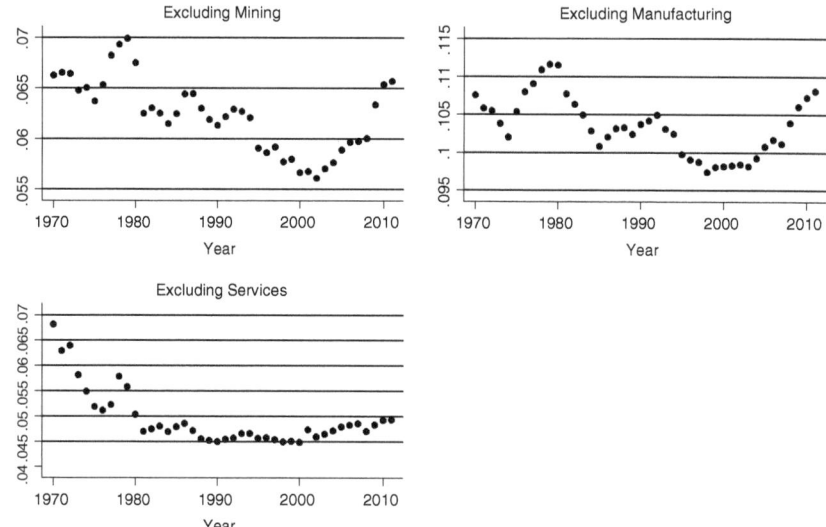

Figure 6.3.2 Sector specialization (Herfindahl)
Source: Stats SA. 6 sectors.

The subsample that ceases to display a sudden reversal in 2003 must have excluded the category of sectors that were responsible.

Figure 6.3.2 reports the results of this experiment. The three panels continue to report the values of H_t between 1970 and 2011, but for three different samples of sectors. The first panel excludes mining sectors (121, 122, and 123 in Appendix A). The second one excludes manufactures (2101 to 2193 in Appendix A), and the third one excludes services (sectors 311 to 343 in Appendix A). Remarkably, the first two panels of Figure 6.3.2 display a virtually identical shape as Figure 6.3.1 did: an overall downward trend, with a spike in the late 1970s, and a sudden reversal upwards from the early 2000s. Put differently, neither Mining nor Manufacturing sectors can have caused the re-specialization of South Africa in 2003, since it survives their omission from the data.

The same is not true of Services. The third panel of Figure 6.3.2 displays a monotonic downward trend over the period, without much of a respecialization in the 2000s. Omitting services from the sectoral output data of South Africa yields a picture that is much more similar to an average emerging economy: starting from a highly specialized distribution, the allocation of output across sectors becomes increasingly diversified over time. The reversal does not happen in sample. That must mean the reason why South Africa respecialized in 2003 in Figure 6.3.1 is the increasing prevalence of Services in the aggregate economy. South Africa respecialized early on, and it did so into Services – not into extractive activities.

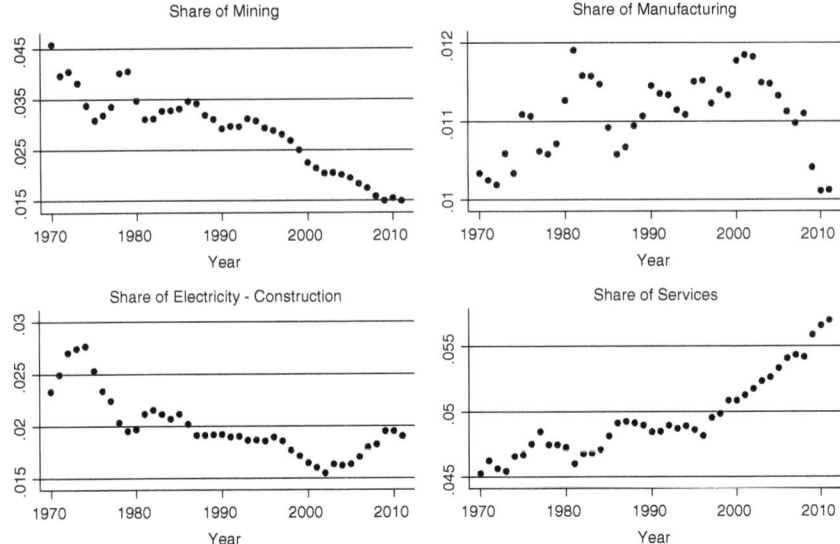

Figure 6.3.3   Average sector shares
NB: Average are computed for each of 46 sectors at same level of aggregation as specialization.

Figure 6.3.3 illustrates the point directly. Each of the four panels report the raw dynamics of the *average* output shares used in computing Herfindahl indexes:

$$\frac{Y_{st}}{\sum_{s=1}^{N} Y_{st}}$$

with shares computed for each of the four main sector categories: mining, manufacturing, electricity and construction, and services. Importantly, these shares are computed at the same level of aggregation as the Herfindahl indexes: they do not represent the total share of each subcategory. Rather, they represent the average size of each sector in each of the subcategory. This is what is needed for the purpose of understanding the dynamics of Herfindahl indexes, that is, structural change.

Strikingly the average share of each mining sector falls over the sample. This result runs exactly contrary to some common wisdom often applied to Sub-Saharan Africa: at least in the South African case, the economy is not specializing into mining sectors.

The second panel of Figure 6.3.3 confirms South Africa is deindustrializing. After three decades of a mildly positive trend, the average share of manufacturing sectors has collapsed since the early 2000s. Indeed, this collapse correlates almost perfectly with the respecialization pattern observed in Figure 6.3.1. This result reinforces the notion that the respecialization observed in Herfindahl indexes effectively reflects de-industrialization.

But what sectors are replacing manufactures? As already mentioned, they are not mining activities, nor indeed electricity production or construction, whose shares fall throughout the sample. Rather, as illustrated in the fourth panel of Figure 6.3.3, it is in services that the South African economy is respecializing. The upward trend in the share of services has been uninterrupted since the 1970s. There is no sudden spike in 2003. It is therefore the joint collapse in manufactures and the somewhat accelerated specialization in services that can explain the results in Figures 6.3.1 and 6.3.2. South Africa deindustrialized from 2003, so that the trend increase in the share of services translated into a sudden increase in the concentration of services. Mining sectors contribute very little, if at all, to this phenomenon. What enabled such sudden move away from manufactures and into services? The next section formulates a conjecture.

6.3.3 The regions of South Africa

This section investigates the geographic distribution of the deindustrialization of South Africa. Are manufactures being replaced by services in all of the country's regions? Or is the phenomenon caused by a few large changes, perhaps centered on the industrial hubs of the country? If the former is true, chances are the forces at play are largely external to South Africa.

To address the question, this section uses information about sector-level activity by South African region. The objective is to capture the geographic concentration of economic activity across the nine regions that constitute South Africa. This requires information about the allocation of sector-level activity at the regional level. Such data are exceedingly difficult to obtain in a systematic manner. A homogeneous, reliable source exists in census data, which collect the distribution of employment at sector level, and by region. But population census data have at least three limitations: (i) they are collected at low frequencies; (ii) sectors are observed at the one-digit level at best; and (iii) they report employment rather than production data. In fact, waves of census are unavailable for most of Sub-Saharan Africa, which is the main reason why this paper focuses on South Africa.

Census waves are available for South Africa in the years 1996, 2001, and 2007. Such coverage is limited, but sufficient to give an indication of the geographic component of the "Great Specialization" that happened from 2003. Appendix B lists the ten one-digit sectors with employment data from Census. These data are first used to recompute the specialization index H_t to verify South Africa is also specializing in these data.

They are then used to compute two measures of the geographic concentration of economic activity. Define N_{srt} real employment in sector s, region r, and at time t. Let A_t denote a measure of geographic agglomeration over time, defined as:

$$A_t = \sum_{s=1}^{N} \frac{N_{srt}}{\sum_{s=1}^{N} N_{srt}} \sum_{r=1}^{R} \left(\frac{N_{srt}}{\sum_{r=1}^{R} N_{srt}} \right)^2$$

A_t represents a weighted average of each sector's geographic concentration, captured by a Herifndahl index that is analogous to H_t. A_t takes high values when a sector that is large in the aggregate economy tends to be highly agglomerated geographically, that is, produced in few regions only.

Following Krugman (1991), introduce D_t a measure of the dissimilarity in the production patterns of the regions that constitute a country. Define

$$D_t = \sum_{s=1}^{N} \frac{2}{R(R-1)} \sum_{r<r'}^{R} \left| \frac{N_{srt}}{\sum_{r=1}^{R} N_{srt}} - \frac{N_{sr't}}{\sum_{r=1}^{R} N_{sr't}} \right|$$

D_t represents the average of bilateral differences in sector employment shares, across the universe of (distinct) pairs of regions that constitute a country. For instance, for South Africa, a total of nine regions means D_t

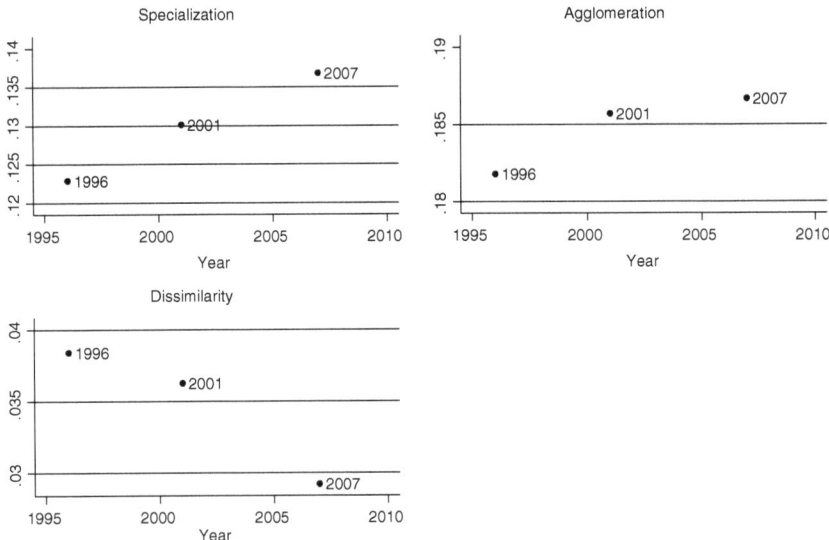

Figure 6.3.4   Three measures (all sectors)
Source: Census Data from IPUMS. Ten 1-digit sectors.

is computed on 36 pairs, for each sector. D_t takes high values when the distribution of employment tends to be different across the regions that constitute South Africa.[4]

Figure 6.3.4 plots the three indexes, H_t, A_t, and D_t for the three years with Census data. As was the case with output data, South Africa specializes throughout the period, with H_t taking increasing values. Interestingly, D_t displays a marked downward trend: the regions of South Africa display an increasingly similar production pattern. It is tempting to conclude this happens as the country as a whole specializes in a narrowing range of sectors, as that would be consistent with the dynamics of H_t. But that would also imply that the geographic agglomeration of economic activity should fall, i.e. a downward trend in A_t. Yet Figure 6.3.4 suggests the opposite: A_t displays a mildly increasing trend over the period, although it is virtually flat between 2001 and 2007.

The conjunction of these facts suggests the dynamics of A_t are driven by a subsample of sectors only. If they were not, A_t and D_t should display similar trends. Figure 6.3.5 splits the sample according to the traded-ness of each sector. Traded sectors are assumed to include: (i) Agriculture, Hunting, etc.; (ii) Manufacturing; (iii) Mining; and (iv) Finance and Business Services. As the traded-ness of that last category is less straightforward than the three others, the lower panel of Figure 6.3.5 presents evidence when Financial services are categorized as non-traded goods as well.

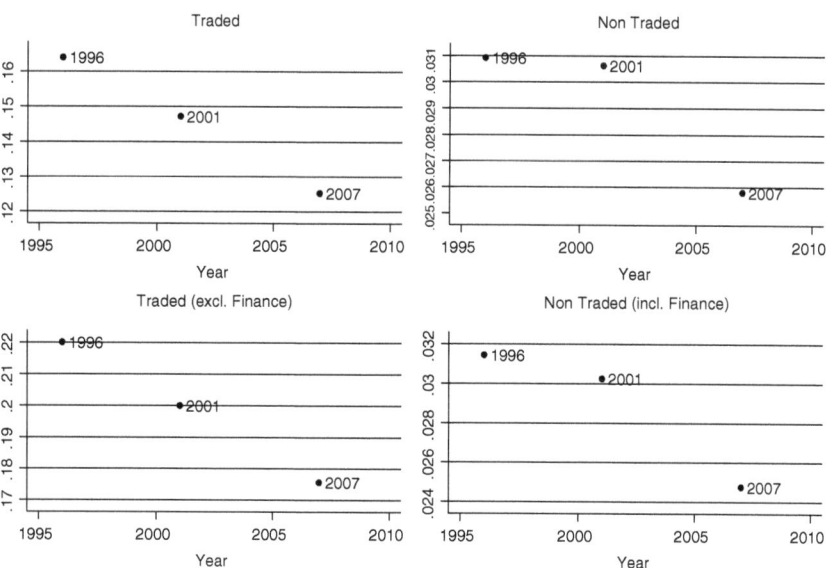

Figure 6.3.5   Agglomeration(Sub-Samples)
Source: Census Data from IPUMS. Ten 1-digit sectors.

The upper panel of Figure 6.3.5 illustrates the importance of traded-ness for the dynamics of A_t. Traded goods are clearly de-agglomerating over the period, whereas the opposite is true amongst non-traded goods. Put differently, traded goods are increasingly produced in all regions of South Africa, which is consistent with the downward trend in D_t. The lower panel of Figure 6.3.5 illustrates the importance of financial services: if they are excluded from traded sectors, there is no evidence of de-agglomeration any more. Regional data in South Africa is suggestive of the increasing prevalence of services, and especially financial services, in the production of the country's regions. Financial services are spreading across the country's nine regions, just as they appear to be deindustrializing.

It is tempting to interpret both trends as the result of the same phenomenon. As South Africa opens to international trade, manufacturing sectors delocalize, and services (rather than extractive sectors) take over. This is not unlike the conventional dynamics of structural change that many developed countries have experienced over the last decade. The specificity of South Africa lies in the speed and suddenness of the change, which makes it especially difficult for the labor market to accommodate.

6.3.4   Conclusion

South Africa has been deindustrializing. The share of manufacturing output had been rising since 1970, but the trend suddenly reversed in 2003. Interestingly, this sudden reversal is not due to the rising prominence of extractive activities. Rather, the country has specialized increasingly in services. Thus, structural change in South Africa is not qualitatively different from the conventional stages of diversification most developing economies go through. But it happened at unusual speed. This paper argues the reversal is related to international trade: the emergence of services (and especially financial services) happened homogeneously across the country's nine regions. This is consistent with the country specializing in its comparative advantage relative to its main trade partners. Thus, the de-industrialization that South Africa experienced is not necessarily inefficient, although given the speed with which it unraveled, it has undoubtedly come with substantive social costs.

Appendix A: The 46 Sectors from Statistics South Africa

11: Agriculture, forestry and fishing [1]

121: Coal mining [21]
122: Gold and uranium ore mining [23]
123: Other mining [22/24/25/29]
2101: Food [301–304]
2102: Beverages [305]

2103: Tobacco [306]
2111: Textiles [311–312]
2112: Wearing apparel [313–315]
2113: Leather and leather products [316]
2114: Footwear [317]
2121: Wood and wood products [321–322]
2122: Paper and paper products [323]
2123: Printing, publishing and recorded media [324–326]
2131: Coke and refined petroleum products [331–333]
2132: Basic chemicals [334]
2133: Other chemicals and man-made fibers [335–336]
2134: Rubber products [337]
2135: Plastic products [338]
2141: Glass and glass products [341]
2142: Non-metallic minerals [342]
2151: Basic iron and steel [351]
2152: Basic non-ferrous metals [352]
2153: Metal products excluding machinery [353–355]
2154: Machinery and equipment [356–359]
2160: Electrical machinery and apparatus [361–366]
2171: Television, radio and communication equipment [371–373]
2172: Professional and scientific equipment [374–376]
2181: Motor vehicles, parts and accessories [381–383]
2182: Other transport equipment [384–387]
2191: Furniture [391]
2193: Other manufacturing [392–393]
221: Electricity, gas and steam [41]
222: Water supply [42]
231: Building construction [51]
232: Civil engineering and other construction [52–53]
311: Wholesale and retail trade [61–63]
312: Catering and accommodation services [64]
321: Transport and storage [71–74]
322: Communication [75]
331: Finance and insurance [81–82]
332: Business services [83–88]
3411: Medical, dental and veterinary services [93]
3412: Excluding medical, dental and veterinary services [94–96]
342: Other producers [98]
343: General government services [99]

Appendix B: The 10 Sectors from Census Data

1. Agriculture, Hunting, etc.
2. Construction
3. Finance and business services
4. Manufacturing
5. Mining

6. Other Services
7. Public Administration
8. Public services
9. Retail, Hotels
10. Transport and telecommunications

Notes

1. See Imbs and Wacziarg (2003).
2. The level of the Herfindahl index is directly affected by the number of sectors used to compute it. The paper computes concentration indexes over a variety of different sub-samples, with a view to identifying which sectors are relevant in explaining structural change. The analysis is therefore conducted on trends in Herfindahl, because that is independent on the number of sectors considered.
3. See Imbs and Wacziarg (2003).
4. For details, see Imbs, Montenegro and Wacziarg (2012).

References

Imbs, Jean and Wacziarg, Romain (2003) "Stages of Diversification," *American Economic Review*, vol. 93, no. 1, pp. 63–86.
Imbs, Jean, Montenegro, Claudio, and Wacziarg, Romain (2012) "Economic Integration and Structural Change," mimeo.
Krugman, Paul (1991) *Geography and Trade* (Cambridge, MA: MIT Press).

6.4

How Ethiopia Can Foster a Light Manufacturing Sector[1]

Vandana Chandra
The World Bank

6.4.1 Introduction

Like other low-income countries, Ethiopia aspires to catch up and become a middle-income country. It covets a modern economy which can produce more than coffee and sesame seeds and offer its 85 million citizens better livelihoods. And this is no fantasy. Economic diversification from agriculture to manufacturing and services has happened elsewhere[2] and not too long ago. This paper tries to understand what the Ethiopian government will have to do to bring it about.

Economic history indicates that to achieve economic prosperity all of today's high income countries charted a course of structural transformation. The Industrial Revolution in the 18th century spurred the transformation of predominantly agrarian economies into industrial ones (Kuznets, 1966, Chenery (1979), Abramowitz (1983), Syrquin (1988), Lin (2009, 2010 and 2011)). The evolution of the industrial economies ensued as the share of employment declined in agriculture and increased in industry. As technological progress spurred, labor-intensive production processes were replaced by more capital intensive ones (Kuznets, 1966). It took the western countries almost 300 years to industrialize, Japan 100 years, the East Asian countries about 40 years, and China less than 30 years (Lin, 2012). At varying speeds, industrialization is occurring in several Asian developing countries. Most developing countries in Sub-Saharan Africa have yet to start industrializing in a serious way. Some, like Ethiopia, are impatient to forge ahead and are keen to know what it will take. This paper is about why and how Ethiopia can transform itself from a predominant coffee exporter into an industrial country by first starting to produces more of its own food, and manufacture simple products for its domestic and export markets. This stage of light manufacturing is only the first stage of industrialization and is expected to lead the way to heavy industry and eventually, a service economy, much like today's high income countries.

This paper draws generously from the recently published *Light Manufacturing in Africa – Targeted Policies to Enhance Private Investment and Create Jobs* published with co-authors Hinh Dinh, Vincent Palmade and Frances Cossar (2012). Section 6.4.2 discusses the Ethiopian reality. Section 6.4.3 briefly discusses the approach and tools used to discuss the issues in this paper. Is there indeed a case for industrialization in Sub-Saharan Africa? What the gurus say is discussed in Section 6.4.4. In section 6.4.5, I evaluate whether Ethiopia has the potential for a competitive light manufacturing sector. The constraints to developing a light manufacturing sector in Ethiopia are noted in Section 6.4.6. Is industry-specificity important is discussed in Section 6.4.7. The last section concludes.

6.4.2 The Ethiopian reality

As late as 1980, Ethiopia shared several fundamental economic characteristics with at least six low-income countries, including Vietnam and China. All were poor, predominantly agricultural economies that exported mostly agricultural commodities and minerals, and imported nearly all manufactured goods they consumed. Today, Vietnam is more than 200 percent and China more than 600 percent richer than Ethiopia (Figure 6.4.1). Bangladesh, the poorest country in the set of seven shown in Figure 6.4.1, is about 60 percent more prosperous than Ethiopia. With the exception of Ethiopia, the other six labor-abundant countries started industrializing by first developing their light manufacturing industries.

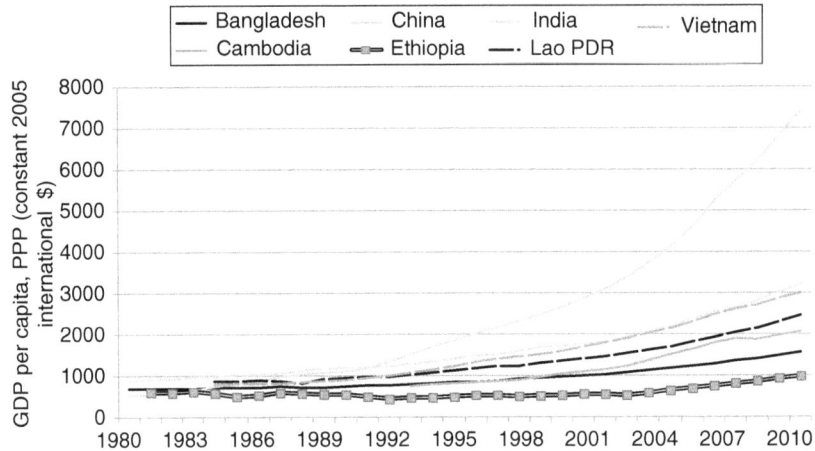

Figure 6.4.1 In 1980, China, Vietnam and Bangladesh were as poor as Ethiopia
Source: WDI 2011

The closest parallel to Ethiopia is to be found in Vietnam, East Asia's star performer. With a population of 88 million, Vietnam is almost as large as Ethiopia (85 million), exports coffee, has a large agricultural sector and, albeit shrinking, still has a prominent state presence in its economy.

There are several explanations for why Ethiopia has not yet begun to industrialize. One explanation is that even though Ethiopia's economy grew at almost 6 percent per annum in the last decade, it was growth without structural transformation. The dominance of agriculture ensued. Between 1980 and 2010, the share of agriculture in the economies of the 6 comparators declined and that of manufacturing increased to over 15 percent (Table 6.4.1). In comparison, in Ethiopia agriculture still accounts for about 47 percent and manufacturing only 4 percent of the economy. The share of manufacturing in the economy has declined from 5 to 4 percent in 30 years. It seems improbable that structural transformation will happen on its own especially when investment in manufacturing is decreasing. Overall, private investment in the economy declined from 12 percent in the 1980s to 7 percent in the last decade. Economic growth in the past decade was fuelled by consumption but it is well known that a consumption-driven development model is unlikely to steer Ethiopia to a middle income status.

A second and more popular explanation for why Ethiopia has not industrialized is the unfriendly business environment facing domestic or foreign firms at a time when most developing countries are offering lucrative incentives to lure foreign investors. On almost every Logistics Performance and Doing Business indicators list, in comparison to Vietnam and China, the Ethiopian economy records a significantly lower rank. Some of the constraints related with the regulatory environment covering customs, permits, and time taken to process the paperwork could be eliminated with greater political will and capacity building in government.

Table 6.4.1 To be a modern economy, Ethiopia must industrialize

	Share of Agriculture in GDP		Share of Manufacturing in GDP	
	First 3 years after 1980*	2008–2010	First 3 years after 1980*	2008–2010
Bangladesh	31	19	14	17
China	32	10	37	33
Ethiopia	60	47	5	4
India	34	17	15	16
Cambodia	48	35	9*	18
Lao PDR	61	33	10	20
Vietnam	40	21	14	20

Source: World Development Indicators, 2012. Due to missing data in 1980-85, statistics available for the first 3 years is used.

But infrastructure constraints that require high fixed investment cannot be improved country-wide to meet the minimum investment climate standards needed to attract investors any time soon.

Historically, coffee and sesame seeds have comprised 60 percent of Ethiopian exports. As a result, government's temptation to nurture manufacturing by leveraging protectionist policies and subsidies is enormous, not least because the external trading environment is intimidating for small Ethiopian exporters who must contend with fiercely competitive counterparts from the more industrialized developing countries. Government's commitment to manufacturing industries has taken the form of a tax on the exports of hides and skins with the expectation of developing a leather goods sector. Yet, in spite of a natural comparative advantage in sheepskin, leather products do not feature in even the top 10 products of Ethiopia exports. A 10 percent tariff on imports of wheat has failed to develop a competitive wheat flour-milling industry; similarly a ban on exports of cotton has not led to the emergence of a competitive cotton textiles industry.[3] For skeptics, such policy stances make a persuasive case for retracting experiments in industry-selectivity and staying with the agenda to alleviate industry-neutral, economy-wide constraints to facilitate a light manufacturing sector. To those more anxious to jumpstart the manufacturing sector, such polices would increase the dominance of coffee exports. There are no easy options.

6.4.3   Approach, tools, and data

A prerequisite for a sustainable and large light manufacturing sector is its global competitiveness regardless of whether it produces for the domestic or the export market. In the initial stages of development, new or nascent industries may have to learn to compete with imports in the domestic market before competing with foreign products in foreign markets. In some industries, Ethiopian firms may not be able to export but may be competitive in the domestic market. This is likely to be the case when the costs of transporting inputs and final products are too high.

Economists use a variety of instruments to analyze the competitiveness of a country's products in the global market. The conventional trade-theoretic "revealed comparative advantage" lens is useful as it could indicate whether Ethiopia is competitive in the global market. However, it does not indicate "what" Ethiopia needs to do to sharpen its competitive edge. Firm surveys can be useful for estimating industry-level firm productivity but are less useful for isolating input cost margins that firms need to reduce to compete.

Value chain analysis (VCA) at the sub-industry level is useful in identifying cost margins that Ethiopian firms need to reduce to compete with global competitors. It is equally useful in explaining "how" the Ethiopian policymakers can facilitate private firms in this process. A set of six comparative value chain (VC) studies[4] were conducted to understand what it will take for Ethiopia to scale up its light manufactured exports sector. Six products were selected to represent five sub-industries: apparel (polo shirts), leather products (leather loafer), wood furniture (wood chair), light metal products (crown corks), agroindustry – wheat milling (wheat flour) and dairy (processed milk). Each industry was evaluated on the basis of its competitiveness with respect to China, the global benchmark and leading exporter of light manufactures. Vietnam was used as a comparator, given its similarities with Ethiopia in size, economic history, institutions and less-skilled labor pool.

The relative performance of Ethiopia, Vietnam, and China in each sub-industry was recorded in terms of productivity and costs to identify some of the main factors contributing to low productivity and high costs. The advantage of this approach relative to the firm survey analysis is that it highlights specific factors such as additional costs associated with policy-related distortions as well as industry-specific natural factors. This is extremely valuable in documenting, for example, how many additional cents per pair of shoes Ethiopian shoemakers incur because of a specific tariff on imported leather. Similarly, the VC tool is useful in recording the additional costs per pair of shoes shoemakers incur because of Ethiopia's landlocked location. The VCA makes it possible to assign real costs related with government and market failure and present policy makers the option to help improve the competitiveness of a specific light industry's exports by removing policy-created distortions. In short, the VC studies:

- Benchmark the competitiveness (productivity and costs) of Ethiopian producers against Asian competitors China and Vietnam.
- Review the detailed breakdown of costs and productivity for each product and identify the main reasons for the productivity and cost gaps.
- Identify the most important and common constraints for each product and across the sample of products.

6.4.4 Is there a case for industrial policy in Sub-Saharan Africa?

Is there a case for sector-specific industrial policy? There is no apparent reason why countries in Sub-Saharan Africa should not industrialize. In a study of firm surveys from 89 countries Harrison, Lin, and Xu (2013) reject the common perception that African manufacturing firms are not globally competitive and cannot be competitive in manufactured products. They find that "formal manufacturing firms in Africa do not perform much worse than those in other countries at similar income levels but they do exhibit structural problems: similar sales growth and higher labor growth, but slightly lower productivity and much lower export intensity and investment rates."

There is copious literature both for and against the case for industrial policy. On each side passions run high. The proponents usually contend that industrial policy is necessary to offset market, information, and coordination failures and harness spillover effects. The opponents dissent by noting that the markets are far more efficient, especially when governments leave them alone and do not distort them. Invariably, the lack of rigorous empirical support is hailed as the reason why the case for industrial policy ought to be dismissed. Comprehensive discussions and reviews of industrial policy can be found among others in Harrison and Rodríguez-Clare (2010), Cimoli, Dosi, and Stiglitz (2009), Hausmann and Rodrik (2006) and Pack and Saggi (2006) and are not discussed here.

The industrial policy literature directly pertinent to the Ethiopian case is slim and, in some ways, in the parlance of Hausmann and Rodrik (2006), is indeed a "predicament." The justification for industrial policy in Ethiopia rests on a very specific argument. The Ethiopian economy features numerous constraints. Government's actions to address them seem like a patch work – lower a tariff here, build a road there – but the investment climate remains far from the "ideal" required by the pundits who believe in the magic of the markets. Since the government cannot fix all the constraints at once, the smart approach is to identify the key constraints that affect the overall cost competitiveness of each light manufacturing industry and fix the most critical ones first.

This brand of industrial policy is about industry-specificity. The reason for selectivity is not that government is better at identifying potentially competitive industries but that it cannot afford to attend to all. Its capacity and resources to address economy-wide constraints such as infrastructure and power are severely limited. To guard against the risk of backing the wrong industries, it would be prudent for the government to leverage Ethiopia's comparative advantage in less-skilled labor-intensive industries; select light manufacturing industries instead of heavy industries that are capital intensive and require higher skill levels (glass, chemicals, hydrocarbons, metals, machinery, construction, and so on); encourage competition and ensure that the industries are powered by private firms. Light manufacturing industries also create more jobs for less-skilled labor, which Ethiopia desperately needs for its large pool of labor currently employed in poorly paying agricultural jobs.

The value chain analyses (VCA) for Ethiopia's light manufacturing industries point to the presence of large Marshallian externalities, especially in input industries. If there are market failures and externalities associated with the size of a particular industry, it is appropriate for a government to foster the industry in the interest of enabling the economy to produce a larger variety of products, upgrade its industrial sector, and grow faster. While the authors find no empirical support for protectionist trade policies, they justify "soft" industrial policy to help an industry in which the country has a latent comparative advantage to scale up (Harrison and Rodríguez-Clare (2010).

Several light manufacturing industries in Ethiopia justify industry-specific "soft" industrial policies. An example from the leather industry illustrates how the Ethiopian government can indeed catalyze this industry. Leather products manufacturing is not scaling up. Large tanning firms are hesitant to enter the industry for lack of a sufficient large stock of high-quality wet blue. There is a market failure in the production of high-quality skins and hides by small farmers because of the lack of veterinary services. The VCA shows that without the development of the upstream leather supply chain that facilitates large scale production of inputs, Ethiopia's leather industry is unlikely to become competitive. In more developed countries, the demand for wet blue has fostered upstream linkages to cattle ranching, dairy, and meat processing industries, all of which are cost competitive when they enjoy economies of scale. Clearly, there is both market and government failure in the leather products industry. Market failures require government to facilitate small farmers' access to veterinary services. Doing so would be an example of industry-specific targeting.

The absence of a vibrant cotton apparel export industry and wheat milling industry for the domestic market post-protectionist policy regimes are classic examples of well-intentioned targeting that failed. The country has a latent comparative advantage in both. The VCA shows that these industries are unlikely to take off unless Ethiopian policymakers target them with appropriate instruments to remove the binding constraints. Low yields and poor quality characterize wheat production in Ethiopia. Why targeted intervention to correct the industry-wide coordination failure through the facilitation of better seed and farming technologies is efficient because without it, Ethiopia's wheat milling industry cannot compete with imported wheat. This situation is consistent with the case for "soft" industrial policy as diversification in agriculture and wheat milling is linked to productivity. "... if there is a market failure reducing the level of diversification below the optimal one (as in Hausmann and Rodrik, 2003), then a policy of encouraging discovery and diversification would indeed be welfare enhancing" (Harrison and Rodríguez-Clare, 2010).

How can governments identify industries that are appropriate for their country? Lin (2010) and Lin and Monga (2010) have argued that industries that are appropriate for a country must reflect its latent comparative advantage. Abandoning comparative advantage can lead governments to identify industries incorrectly. In the case of soft and hard infrastructure, which requires large financial investments and is invariably country and industry specific, misidentification can result in a waste of fiscal resources. Misidentification can also nurture uncompetitive firms that require permanent government support, such as heavy protection through import substitution and subsidies such as those given to state-owned enterprises. Worse, "comparative advantage defying" policies lead to governance problems and the risk of elite capture (Chandra, Lin and Wang, 2013; Lin, 2010).

6.4.5   A selective approach to light manufacturing

Ethiopia is more fortunate than many other Sub-Saharan African countries. It has several ingredients that would serve it well in a selective approach to developing a light manufacturing sector: the demand for its exports is almost infinite; it has one of Africa's largest labor pools of relatively less skilled workers and productivity levels that are comparable to those of its competitors in some light manufacturing industries; and it is well endowed with several key inputs. With appropriate policies that can facilitate the supply of the remaining inputs, Ethiopia should be able to jumpstart the process of transformation of its agricultural economy into an industrial one.

6.4.5.1   Sufficient market demand

To the opponents of industrial policy, nothing is more worrisome than industrial policy-favored firms that have no buyers for their products. Fortunately, with a population of over 85 million, Ethiopian firms have potential access to a large domestic market and several neighboring markets such as Kenya, Eritrea, and Sudan which offer a growing demand for manufactures. Ethiopian producers also have access to the global market which has almost infinite demand for light manufactures exported by a small, open economy if the products that its firms produce are globally competitive in price and quality.

Ethiopian producers can exploit the size of the domestic market to offset the transport cost penalty imposed by Ethiopia's landlockedness. As in the case of other small exporters, foreign demand for Ethiopian light manufactures would be infinite if it were to become globally competitive.

For first-time producers, entry into the global markets is not easy. In comparison to most other Sub-Saharan African countries, Ethiopia's domestic market is large enough to serve as the learning ground for its fledgling light manufacturing industries until they achieve the global standards needed for export. If they can compete with foreign products in the domestic market, the large size of the latter can also prove useful for Ethiopian producers interested in manufacturing import replacements. Currently, the share of imports in the Ethiopian economy is between 30–40 percent (Figure 6.4.2). In countries that are far from large markets, transport costs play an important role in determining the export feasibility of a product. In landlocked Ethiopia, the distance-to-market disadvantage is magnified as many manufacturing firms also require imported inputs.

Currently, Ethiopia is a net importer of all light manufactures except leather products (Table 6.4.2). For each dollar of leather imports, it currently exports $6 of leather products. Relative to domestic demand, in all other industries Ethiopia's exports are near negligible. The contrast is particularly stark with Vietnam as Ethiopia shares several common factors with it. These include low labor costs, similar size of the labor force and local demand.

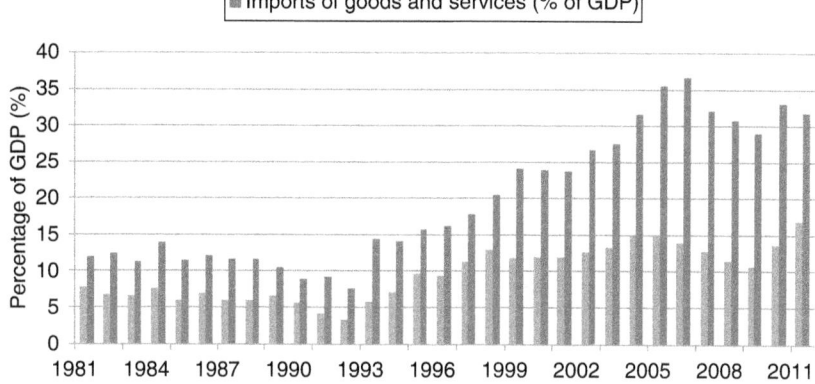

Figure 6.4.2 Trade is dominated by imports in Ethiopia, 1980–2011
Source: World Development Indicators 2012.

Table 6.4.2 Excess local demand for light manufactures in Ethiopia

	Ratio of exports to imports		
	China	Vietnam	Ethiopia
Apparel - clothing	60.83	13.64	0.14
Leather upper footwear	19	359	6
Wood products and wood furniture	3	6	0.1
Processed metal products	4	0.5	0.003
Wheat or Meslin Flour	15	0.6	0.0002

Source: Global Development Solutions, LLC.

In the last ten years, economic growth rates of about 7–8 percent per annum in Ethiopia have created a substantial demand for new construction which has in turn boosted the demand for wood products. In addition, due to the rapid pace of urbanization, the demand for contemporary furniture as opposed to traditional furniture has been rising in recent years. Currently, the demand for modern furniture designs from young urban consumers is fulfilled largely by imports, mostly from China.

6.4.5.2 Low-wage labor

With the vantage of Africa's second-largest labor pool that affords it a low-wage advantage, Ethiopia is well suited for a variety of labor-intensive light manufacturing industries. In practically every industry, Ethiopian wages are significantly lower than either Vietnamese or Chinese wage levels (Table 6.4.3).

Table 6.4.3 Ethiopia's labor cost advantage over China and Vietnam

Product	Labor type	China	Vietnam	Ethiopia
Polo shirts	Skilled	$311 – $370	$119 – $181	$37 – $185
Dairy milk	Skilled	$177 – $206	-	$30 – $63
Wood chairs	Skilled	$383 – $442	$181 – $259	$81 – $119
Crown cork	Skilled	$265 – $369	$168 – $233	$181
Leather loafers	Skilled	$296 – $562	$119 – $140	$41 – $96
Milled wheat	Skilled	$398 – $442	$181 – $363	$89 – $141
Average	Skilled	$305 – $399	$154 – $235	$77 – $131
Polo shirts	Unskilled	$237 – $296	$78 – $130	$26 – $48
Dairy milk	Unskilled	$118 – $133	$31 – $78	$13 – $41
Wood chairs	Unskilled	$206 – $251	$85 – $135	$37 – $52
Crown cork	Unskilled	$192 – $265	$117 – $142	$89 na
Leather loafers	Unskilled	$237 – $488	$78 – $93	$16 – $33
Milled wheat	Unskilled	$192 – $236	$78 – $207	$26 – $52
Average wage range	Unskilled	$197 – $278	$78 – $131	$35 – $53

Source: Global Development Solutions, LLC.

In comparison to Vietnam and China, which are leading exporters of many light manufactures, Ethiopia has a strong wage-cost advantage in both unskilled *and* skilled labor. In the apparel, leather, wood furniture, metal products and agro-industries, on average, Ethiopian wages for unskilled labor are 50 percent of Vietnamese wages and about 25 percent of the corresponding Chinese wages. For skilled labor, the Ethiopian wage is about 40 percent of the Vietnamese wage and about 20 percent of the corresponding Chinese wages.

Generally, an abundance of unskilled workers does not automatically translate into an abundance of skilled workers and this also applies in the case of Ethiopia. However, the types of light manufacturing industries being discussed here do not require highly skilled labor. In most cases, a few weeks of basic pre-employment training and more learning-by-doing or on the job training is sufficient as evident from the Chinese model where it takes about four weeks of training to prepare unskilled workers for the apparel production chains on the factory floor.

The advantage of low wages vanishes rapidly if labor productivity levels are low. Fortunately, in several industries Ethiopia enjoys low wages and labor productivity levels that are comparable to those of China and Vietnam (Table 6.4.4). In the apparel industry, Ethiopia's most productive firms can match Chinese productivity levels. In the production of wooden chairs and crown corks, Ethiopian productivity levels are substantially below Chinese and Vietnamese levels. Labor productivity can be enhanced with modern technologies of production, factory floor re-organization, and more training. All of these practices themselves need modern managerial skills which are in short supply in Ethiopia.

Table 6.4.4 Ethiopia can compete: labor productivity in leather and garments

Labor productivity	China	Vietnam	Ethiopia	Tanzania
Polo shirts (pieces/ employee/day)	18–35	8–14	7–19	5–20
Leather loafer (pieces/ employee/day)	3–7	1–6	1–7	4–6
Wood chair (pieces/ employee/day)	3–6	1–3	0.2–0.4	0.3–0.7
Crown corks (pieces/ employee/day) x 1000	13–25	25–27	10	
Wheat processing (Tons/ employee/day)	0.2–0.4	0.6–8.6	0.6–1.9	1–22
Dairy farming (Litres/ employee/day)	23–51	2–4	18–71	10–100

Source: Global Development Solutions (2011).

6.4.5.3 Several key inputs are available locally

Ethiopia's climate, soil, and other agronomic conditions give it a natural comparative advantage in a large variety of fine-quality animal skins and hides. Currently, most raw materials are exported raw and in small quantities (Table 6.4.5). With scaling up, they could support a leather footwear exports industry. Some of this is already happening on a small scale, but the potential is huge.

Ethiopia's inputs sectors are poorly organized. Scaling up seems to be the key constraint across most industries. In spite of a natural comparative advantage in cotton, a well-organized value chain from the cultivation of cotton to the production of fabrics and garments has yet to emerge and transform into a large-scale export industry. The story of the agro-processing industries is similar.

The most telling example of the absence of an export sector in spite of the locally available inputs is Ethiopia's wood furniture and other wood products industry. In addition to hardwood, Ethiopia has forests with red and white pines although it is not yet clear whether it has a natural comparative advantage in wood. Currently, Ethiopia imports almost all the wood furniture it consumes and exports a variety of low value-added or unprocessed coniferous woods. Wood products comprise a small-scale industry that produces traditional furniture but this is not what is required by either global consumers or even Ethiopian urban consumers. In recent years, the increase in urban incomes has led to a rapidly growing demand and clear preferences for contemporary furniture. Private efforts to begin production for the domestic market are yet to unfold. It seems unlikely that the industry will be able to export.

Ethiopia has to import metals for its metal products industry.

Table 6.4.5   Ethiopia exports many domestic inputs and raw materials

SITC code	Exports in 2008–10 (average)	('000s of USD)
	Cotton	
2632	Cotton linters	255
2633	Cotton waste, not carded or combed	247
2634	Cotton, carded or combed	242
	Animal industry	
12	Sheep and goats, live	120191
2111	Bovine and equine hides, raw	522
2112	Calf skins, raw	506
2114	Goat and kid skins, raw	497
2116	Sheep and lamb skin with the wool on, raw	491
2117	Sheep and lamb skin without the wool, raw	489
2119	Hides and skins, nes; waste and used leather	476
2687	Sheep/lambs' wool, other animal hair, carded/combed	189
6112	Composition leather, in slabs, sheets or rolls	17
6113	Calf leather	17
	Forestry related industry	
2471	Sawlogs and veneer logs of coniferous species	301
2472	Sawlogs and veneer logs of non-coniferous species	297
2482	Wood of coniferous species, sawn, planed, grooved	280
2483	Wood, non-coniferous species, sawn, planed, grooved	279
6341	Wood sawn,veneer sheets max 5 mm in thickness	12
6342	Plywood consisting solely of sheets of wood	11
6343	Improved wood and reconstituted wood	11
6344	Wood-based panels, nes	11
6349	Wood, simply shaped, nes	11
6351	Wood packing cases, boxes, cases, crates, etc, complete	11
	Agricultural crops	
411	Durum wheat, unmilled	4255
412	Other wheat and meslin, unmilled	3803
488	Malt extract; cereals preparations with less 50% of cocoa	1683
440	Maize, unmilled	2926
451	Rye, unmilled	2920
452	Oats, unmilled	2425
459	Buckwheat, millet, etc, and other cereals, unmilled, nes	2047

Source: COMTRADE SITC2 – 4 digit.

6.4.6   Why industry-specificity is critical for Ethiopia's light manufacturing

The preceding section raises an important question. If Ethiopia has a comparative wage-cost advantage, productivity levels that are comparable in at least one or two industries, some locally produced inputs with a high volume/weight to value ratio that help to offset some of the transports costs generated by its landlocked nature, and a large local demand for light manufactures, then why is Ethiopia's light manufacturing export sector so small? And why has Ethiopia not been able to expand its global market position in, for example, the leather products industry in which it has a significant cost advantage? Why has the light manufacturing sector not attracted investors?

Compared to most developing countries that experienced a decline, during 2008–11, the Ethiopian economy grew at an impressive rate of 8 – 9 percent. Yet, structural change in favor of manufacturing has been stubbornly slow to emerge in the Ethiopian economy. During 2009–11, the share of manufacturing in the economy dropped from 5 to 3.8 percent. It is unlikely that government's attempts to improve the investment climate alone will steer the economy any closer to an industrial economy.[5]

Any study of economic diversification that avoids focusing on manufacturing as a step toward industrialization would overlook the enormous untapped opportunities that can be exploited by leveraging Ethiopia's natural wealth to jumpstart its light manufacturing sector.

The comparative VCA study indicates that there are several factors that constrain the light manufacturing sector but as few apply across the board to most or all industries, any assessment of a standard investment climate misses them. More importantly, they are industry-specific and size-specific, that is, they apply more to small firms. And, even within an industry, some are more important than others – that is, all constraints do not have to be resolved for the industry to become globally competitive. Some of the constraints are policy-induced and can be resolved without any fiscal costs, others are an outcome of market failure and need corrective interventions. Since the reforms and interventions are industry-specific, they are, by definition, industrial policies.

A closer examination of these industry-specific constraints shows that they erode the competitiveness and scaling up of Ethiopia's light manufacturing industries. Competition is low or absent in input markets, especially where Ethiopia's natural wealth can be transformed into industrial inputs for its light manufacturing industries. Other obstacles include a paucity of industrial and agricultural land; poor connectivity to the port in Djibouti; finance, particularly for smaller firms; and entrepreneurial capital.

6.4.7 Why generic solutions are insufficient

While a labor cost advantage is an important factor in achieving global competitiveness, it is insufficient because the latter is determined by a country's *overall* cost advantage over competitors, and the ability to scale up production by alleviating supply-side constraints and exporting products that meet the minimum quality standards. With the aid of examples, this section shows that supply-side constraints – inputs, trade logistics and technological sophistication – and lack of competition are the critical constraints to scaling up the export sector in Ethiopia, even when wages are low, and skills are not a constraint. A critical finding is that these constraints do not apply to every industry, nor are they equally important when they do. Resolving one or two critical ones seems sufficient to restore the industry's global competitiveness.

Table 6.4.6 provides a summary of the various supply-side constraints that, relative to China, offset Ethiopia's labor cost advantage and raise its overall costs. Compared to China, with the exception of leather and garments, Ethiopia has a significant cost disadvantage in all industries. In comparison, compared to Chinese production costs, the penalty for lower labor productivity is 10 percent, for higher input costs 17 percent, and for poor trade logistics another 10 percent. Broadly, Ethiopia has a cost disadvantage of approximately 30 percent across the five industries.

Cost differentials vary across Ethiopian industries and are industry-specific, suggesting that improvements in some areas may be sufficient to raise competitiveness to global standards not unreasonably assumed to be set by China. As an example, trade logistics penalizes the extremely time-sensitive apparel market by reducing the f.o.b. price associated with late delivery to the port, but in the wood furniture industry, it raises the cost of hauling, storing, and processing imported wood from the port in Djibouti and the local forests to the factories of Addis Ababa by 87 percent (Table 6.4.6). While it may be possible for policymakers to fix the trade logistics problem for the apparel industry, the same interventions are unlikely to work for the furniture industry. These details are important for resource- and capacity-constrained policymakers interested in reducing the cost-related disadvantages Ethiopia's that face light manufacturing industries.

Overall, compared to China, Ethiopia's total cost of production is 28 percent lower in the leather and only 5 percent higher in the garments industries, but in some industries – such as wood furniture – the differential is as large as 125 percent. In the leather products industry, Ethiopian wages afford producers a 16 percent advantage over Chinese wage costs,

Table 6.4.6   Ethiopian costs as a share of China's cost of production (%)

	Apparel	Leather	Wood	Metal	Agri/wheat	Average
Wages	−8	−37	−17	−10	−10	−16
Labor productivity	3	2	40	5	−1	10
Inputs costs	4	2	87	14	28	17
Trade Logistics costs	6	5	15	6	18	10
Total Cost of production	5	−28	125	15	35	30

Note: *(−) denotes Ethiopia's cost advantage.
Source: Global Development Solutions (2011).

but Ethiopian productivity imposes a 10 percent cost penalty. On average, higher inputs costs offset Ethiopia's labor cost advantage over China. If a few of the constraints that add to the cost disadvantage the most are released, it is possible that global competiveness can be achieved.

6.4.7.1 Labor productivity, technology, and technical efficiency

On average, compared to China, lower labor productivity adds about 10 percent to the overall costs of production in Ethiopia's light manufacturing industries, the highest is about 40 percent in the wood furniture industry (Table 6.4.6). While the margins are much smaller in other light manufacturing industries, any gains in labor productivity can be valuable in raising Ethiopian producers' labor cost advantage. One of the main reasons for lower labor productivity is that Ethiopian workers do not use cutting-edge technology, even in simple machines such as sewing machines, or carpentry tools or agricultural implements. Older machines and factory equipment breaks down frequently and holds up assembly line operations. The machines used to sew or cut fabrics to produce polo shirts are, on average, between four and 14 years old compared to Chinese ones that are only between 1 and 2.5 years old. Similarly, the machines used to produce leather loafers are between 5 and 10 years old compared to China where they are between 3 and 5 years old. In the wood furniture industry, some of the oldest machines are 25 years old and in the flour milling industry 63 years old. The newer equipment used by Vietnamese and Chinese producers raises productivity by reducing the costs of maintenance and repair, withstands multiple shifts, and facilitates precision cutting and sewing operations that reduce waste and time costs. It also raises the technical efficiency of production in Ethiopia's competitors.

In comparison to China, the proportion of waste during production is also significantly higher in the garment, leather, wood furniture, and metal products industries in Ethiopia. As an example, in the leather shoes industry, the leather-to-shoe cutting waste is as high as 30 percent in some Ethiopian firms compared with 10 percent in a comparable Chinese firm where workers use newer and better templates. In addition to older machines, poor labor skills, particularly poor manual skills, and the low levels of technical skills employed by workers to effectively utilize tools and equipment also contribute to low productivity. Low technical efficiency rates in Ethiopian factories can be blamed partly on high labor absenteeism, labor turnover and lower motivation.

6.4.7.2 Trade logistics

Relative to China, on average, poor trade logistics increases production costs in Ethiopia's light manufacturing industries by about 10 percent. The highest costs are in furniture (15 percent) and food processing (18 percent). Even if trade logistics were improved to eliminate Ethiopia's cost disadvantage in these two industries, it would be insufficient to raise their competitiveness.

Located 800 kilometers away from the port of Djibouti, Ethiopian firms must meet the same just-in-time delivery deadlines as Vietnamese or Chinese firms located on the coast. The locational disadvantage affects Ethiopian exporters in two ways: they incur higher inland transportation costs and, equally importantly, they incur longer travel times which cut into their production schedules between the time they receive orders to the time they deliver the product to buyers in time sensitive markets.

Four main factors compound the cost of trade logistics. Every twenty-foot container hauled between Djibouti and Addis Ababa costs the Ethiopian exporter about $1,000 compared with only $230 for a Vietnamese and $120 for a Chinese exporter (Table 6.4.7). The terminal handling fee paid by an Ethiopian exporter for the same container is about 300 percent higher than a Vietnamese counterpart and 600 percent higher than a Chinese counterpart. The margins for customs clearance and letters of credit and document preparation are similarly high. Collectively, all four factors add about $2440 to the cost of hauling a twenty-foot container from the port to the factory costs in Ethiopia compared with only $600 in Vietnam and $520 in China.

6.4.7.3 Inputs costs and land markets

For   Ethiopia's furniture, metal products and agro-processing industries to become viable, input cost-related disadvantages need to be eliminated (Table 6.4.8).

In the furniture industry, for example, elimination of the 87 percent cost disadvantage is related to the price of domestically sourced lumber that costs nearly 100 percent more than in China and more than 380 percent than in Vietnam. Similarly, in the agro-processing industry, a reduction in the input price of wheat is necessary to achieve cost competitiveness. Currently, it is more than 65 percent higher than in China and 39 percent higher than in Vietnam. In the metal industry, this may be difficult to achieve as Ethiopia must depend upon imported tin.

Table 6.4.7   Comparison of trade logistics costs (US dollars) per 20 foot container

	Inland Transportation	Port and Terminal Handling	Customs Clearance	Preparation of Documents and Letters of Credit	Total
Ethiopia	1000	500	340	600	2440
Vietnam	230	160	100	110	600
China	120	80	70	250	520

Source: World Bank, *Doing Business 2011*.

Table 6.4.8 Comparison of input prices in Ethiopia, China and Vietnam (US dollars)

	Ethiopia	Vietnam	China
Pine lumber (m^3)	667	176	344
Tin free steel (ton)	1,414	1,371	1,101
Wheat (ton)	330	237	199
Milk	32	22	24
Non-wood inputs for chairs	0.52	0.2	0.1
Adhesives			
Varnish and finishing oils	1.11	0.84	0.25
Other inputs	2.59	0.44	0.16
Total Adhesives	4.22	1.48	0.51

Source: Global Development Solutions, LLC.

6.4.7.4 Inability to scale up is the crux

Government regulations and an efficient land market for commercial agriculture constrain the supply of basic agricultural inputs at competitive costs and in sufficient quantities in the garments, leather, furniture and food processing industries in Ethiopia. The scaling up of cotton cultivation for the production of local textiles is constrained by land. The production of large-scale quality leather is constrained by small-scale cattle breeding for skins and hides because herders do not have access to commercial ranches. Cereal and dairy farming are not practiced on a large scale because farmers do not have access to large plots of land. Government ownership of land makes land purchases lengthy and risky and discourages large investors. For small farmers, access to finance for the purchase of large plots of land is limited because cattle and land, which are their only assets, are not acceptable to banks as collateral. And regulations to facilitate land use for commercial forests to develop a local wood-producing sector to, support Ethiopia's furniture industry are missing.

6.4.8 When constraints are industry-specific, they need industry-specific solutions

6.4.8.1 Apparel exports are constrained most by trade logistics

Ethiopia's export and employment potential in the apparel industry is severely underutilized, as is clear from a quick comparison with Vietnam which is one of the leading exporters of apparel. In 2009, Ethiopia's apparel exports were about US$8 million compared to US$8 billion for Vietnam and its apparel industry employed only 9,000 workers compared to 1 million in Vietnam. To jumpstart the industry requires eliminating its cost disadvantage over China and scaling up exports.

The detailed VCA of polo shirts shows that *poor trade logistics*:

- impose a 13 percent cost penalty on the free-on-board (FOB) price of polo shirts in Ethiopia compared with China's (this includes the cost penalty associated with having to import most inputs);
- lead to longer and more uncertain delivery times (75 days from order to delivery, compared with 30 for China and 45 for Vietnam), a big part of the reason for the 40 percent price discount that global buyers impose on Ethiopian polo shirts. Due to the frequent failure to meet just-in-time orders deadlines, large buyers in the U.S. and Europe are unwilling to place orders with Ethiopian exporters. Ethiopian producers are unable to benefit from special trading privileges afforded to them by duty-free access to the European Union (EU) and U.S. markets (African Growth and Opportunity Act).
- Poor trade logistics also raise the price of imported inputs for firms. Imported inputs add 4 percent to the total costs of garment production but importing them adds an additional 15 *day delivery cost*/penalty over China.

Poor trade logistics in Ethiopia can be attributed to two factors: high handling and financing costs and the physical distance from production centers to the Djibouti port. The high handling costs are related to delays due to inefficient paperwork and foreign exchange-related transactions in the National Bank of Ethiopia, delays at customs and the port. Financing costs are associated with higher fees (than are in place in China and Vietnam) paid by exporters for letters of credit, customs and port fees, and financial transactions costs. Transportation costs are higher because the costs of shipping inland are higher in Ethiopia, mostly because of the lack of competition in the trucking industry and the absence of railways. Evidently, it costs 60 percent more to ship to the United States from Djibouti than from China.

In comparison to China and Vietnam, the cost of inputs in Ethiopia's apparel industry is high mostly because the large scale of production in these countries has made it possible to produce textiles from locally grown or imported cotton. In comparison, in spite of a large cotton sector, imported inputs – fabric, collars, thread and buttons – for the apparel industry account for more than 70 percent of the production costs and add 4 percent to the total costs of garment production. Vietnam and other low-wage East Asian garment exporters benefit from their proximity to China which is the region's supplier of apparel inputs.

Evidently, Ethiopia has a natural comparative advantage in cotton production, but its farming industry is not organized on a commercial scale. The VCA study estimates that if Ethiopia could develop a competitive cotton value chain, it would be able to narrow its cost differential over China by 4 percent but in order for this to happen, it needs a large investor who can establish an efficient textile industry that sources domestically grown and spun cotton.

To compete globally, Ethiopia's apparel industry will also need to over-come some invisible constraints associated with entrepreneurial or mana-gerial capital embedded in: (i) managerial skills that boost factory floor organization and raise productivity; (ii) have information about the latest designs and industry trends, and cater to rapidly changing global demand from fashion-conscious buyers, access to buyers and sellers;[6] and (iii) invest in the latest technologies and worker training to raise labor productivity and reduce costs. East Asian firms in the apparel industry raise the productivity levels of less-skilled workers with proper incentives and a few weeks of on the job training.

Smaller apparel manufacturing firms in Ethiopia are particularly disadvan-taged because of: a lack of access to industrial land equipped with utilities and access to markets that raises transport costs, finance, market informa-tion, and old technologies.

6.4.8.1.1 *Possible solutions*

China and Vietnam have achieved global competitiveness in the garment sector by developing world-class trade logistics, including export industrial zones located next to efficient ports. Given that higher transport costs are result of market failure, government needs to take corrective action. Access to a state-of-the-art container port (Djibouti), with a favorable geographic posi-tion is key to resolving the multiple trade logistics-related problems. It seems that connecting the 800-kilometer stretch between Addis Ababa and Djibouti port, a multimodal transport arrangement combining trucking, rail, air, and shipping would improve connectivity and increase competition. In the short term, rehabilitating the railroads from Addis Ababa to Djibouti, and introduc-ing competition in trucking, would further reduce transportation costs and delays. This could occur through partnerships with private (including foreign) firms that bring both the capital and the managerial skills necessary for these types of projects. An important ingredient of this intervention would have to be policies that eliminate customs costs and delays.

In addition, the development of a plug-and-play industrial park in Addis Ababa (and a feasibility study to build one closer to Djibouti) would sig-nificantly reduce the transport costs of inputs and exports. In the initial stage of the development of their apparel export industries, both China and Vietnam leveraged industrial zones next to world-class ports. By making available access to industrial land for large and small, foreign, and domestic producers, the Ethiopian government would be leveling the playing field for firms of all sizes. Access to industrial land that smaller firms can rent would reduce their need for fixed investment capital and provide them with the same access to markets and the port as larger firms. In China, the govern-ment has facilitated producers' access to industrial land, standardized fac-tory shells, and workers' housing, as well as training facilities and one-stop shops for business regulations – all in one industrial park.

The Ethiopian government could also implement other measures in the short term to reduce the costs of inputs for the apparel industry. Currently, tariffs of between 10 to 35 percent are imposed on apparel inputs to encourage value addition through the domestic production of textiles for the apparel export industry. In the absence of a large-scale and quality textile industry, this measure simply adds to the cost disadvantage of producers and exporters. Exporters are restricted from selling material waste to the smaller firms who produce for the domestic market, penalizing both types of firms. It is equally important that the government address the issues that have led to a market failure in the emergence of a domestic cotton to textile to apparel supply chain in spite of Ethiopia's favorable climatic and soil conditions for cotton production. Current policies that ban exports of cotton to subsidize textile production are not working because of quality and cost factors, and the small scale of apparel production. Farmers get low prices for cotton, and have no incentive to improve quality. Distorted land markets exclude commercial-scale cultivation of cotton for the large-scale production of textiles. Clearly, to establish a competitive apparel industry, piecemeal reform and interventions are unlikely to work.

6.4.8.2   Leather product exports are constrained most by the supply of quality leather

Ethiopia's leather industry is globally competitive but supply-side factors constrain it from scaling up. The industry is composed of small firms that employ about 8000 workers compared to Vietnam's industry that generates 600,000 jobs. Ethiopia exports only US$8 million of leather products annually compared to US$ 2.3 billion that Vietnam exports. The untapped growth and job potential in this industry in Ethiopia is significant.

Ethiopia's elevation above sea level, climatic, and soil conditions produce some of the world's best sheep skins. In the leather shoes industry, the unit cost of sheepskin used for export-quality leather to make a pair of loafers is US$1.00 per square foot in Ethiopia compared with approximately US$2.36 per square foot in China. Because of a low unit price of inputs (sheepskin) and labor costs, Ethiopian producers produce leather loafers at a unit production cost of US$2.65 per pair for the local market and US$8.66 per pair for the export market. In China, a similar loafer is produced at a cost of between US$9.39 per pair for the local market to US$16.17 per pair for scaling up the export market. The potential for Ethiopian leather exports is enormous.

In spite of highly competitive unit costs, Ethiopian leather shoe producers are unable to scale up exports to the EU and US markets because of a poorly developed value chain that cannot support vast quantities of quality leather. Contrary to the conventional wisdom that a large wage cost advantage over its Asian competitors is sufficient, the performance of the leather industry demonstrates that for scaling up exports, the number of pieces of output a worker is able to turn out per day is an equally important factor for a firm's expansion.

As in the case of the apparel industry, in the leather products industry too, relative to similarly sized Chinese and Vietnamese firms, Ethiopian firms are unable to produce at the same scale. Evidently, this is not attributable to their smaller size. The experience of Chinese producers suggests that that large volume production does not necessarily need large-scale production facilities. Scaling up requires keeping overhead costs low and increasing equipment, labor utilization rates, factory floor or assembly line efficiency that increases profits. The VCA of Ethiopia's leather products industry shows that Ethiopian firms have rates of high labor absenteeism and poor capacity utilization rates which constrain scaling up (Table 6.4.9).

Cognizant of Ethiopia's natural comparative advantage in sheepskin and the potential for a large-scale leather products industry, the Ethiopian government has taken discrete measures to support the export industry through a high export tariff to encourage leather processing and to create a disincentive to export unfinished (pickle and wet blue) leather. Unfortunately, this policy has unintended consequences that have exacerbated the problem.

The most binding constraint to scaling up leather product exports is the shortage of quality processed leather.[7] The reasons reflect why, even with the best of intentions, the combination of market and government failure have distorted and stifled the domestic production of quality skins and starved producers of import leather as a substitute.

The shortage of quality domestic processed leather has several causes. Poor disease control of ectoparasites that eat into animal skins is one important reason why quality Ethiopian leather is available in only small pieces of skin that are spoilt by blemishes. Even though farmers are willing to pay for timely veterinary services, the paucity of the latter results in widespread disease and is an unambiguous sign of market failure.

The livestock industry comprises small farmers who own few animals that they sell when they are cash-strapped. As a result, the market for the supply of skins is informal and small scale. Ethiopia's tanneries are few, operate with outdated technologies, and cannot produce sufficient quantities of quality leather. The government imposes high taxes on exports of skins and semi-processed

Table 6.4.9 Ethiopia: Technical efficiency of leather shoe production

	China	Vietnam	Ethiopia
Annual output of shoe per stitch Pairs/Machine	1820–4800	2165–4839	171–1008
Labor absenteeism	1%	2%	3%–12%
Capacity Utilization	60%–98%	90%	60%–87%

Source: *Global Development Solutions, LLC.*

skins which further dampen the incentives for animal farmers and tanneries to increase supply. Even worse, effective bans on imports of quality leather further starve leather product firms of the raw materials they need to scale up.

Other constraints to scaling up leather product exports are less important. Poor trade logistics impose less of a penalty, especially because there are no costs and delays due to imported inputs. Ethiopia's wage cost advantage in the leather industry is large although the workers need modern equipment and training to produce world class designs and quality.

Though less important than in the apparel industry, high-quality entre-preneurial and managerial skills are in short supply in Ethiopia and are evident in the lower f.o.b. price for leather shoe manufacturers in Ethiopia relative to exporters from China. In an attempt to improve managerial skills the government has established the Leather Institute in Ethiopia with tech-nical assistance from India. Incentives to foreign investors are beginning to attract some firms interested in entering the Italian market. These are posi-tive signs of the industry's export potential. As in the case of the apparel sector, smaller Ethiopian entrepreneurs are constrained by finance, access to new technologies, industrial land and skills.

6.4.8.2.1   Possible solutions

The potential of the leather products export industry is enormous and the government should adopt a comprehensive approach to help it to scale up. This implies unleashing firms' potential to scale up current production as well as invest in the factors necessary to expand and accelerate exports in the medium term. Immediate results could ensue from relaxing the con-straints that limit the supply of quality leather. These include lifting the ban on leather imports and exports. The former will immediately increase supply and permit existing producers to scale up exports of leather shoes. Allowing exports of leather will incentivize existing tanneries to produce more leather though, in the short term, some of it may be exported. However, for a sus-tained scaling up of exports of quality leather shoes, lifting trade restric-tions will be insufficient. Both measures should increase supply.

To take full advantage of its natural endowment of fine sheepskins, a comprehensive strategy that ensures quantity and quality at every step of the value chain is a requisite. Interventions to correct market failures such as the absence of veterinary services even when there is a large demand are necessary. There is a need for the public provision of vaccines to treat cattle disease and ensure that existing cattle farmers, however small, can produce better-quality and larger skins from the same number of cattle heads. This will be far from sufficient for scaling up. Cattle farming needs to be promoted on a commercial scale which implies attracting large farmers by relaxing restrictions on the sale/rental of pasture land. The value chain would generate greater value if it were coordinated with the development of dairy and meat-processing industries that would, in addition to the leather industry, also take Ethiopia a step closer to manufacturing in a true transformation of agriculture to industry.

According to a 2008 US Agency for International Development (USAID) study, with four treatments a year for each animal at a total cost of US$0.10, the infestation rate of ectoparasites could be reduced from 90 to 5 percent. The total cost for such a program to cover the whole country would be less than US$10 million a year which is a small amount in comparison to the potential benefit of scaling up the leather industry as well as fostering new industries such as dairy and meat processing. This approach requires large-scale agricultural land reform but could be a win–win solution for poor Ethiopian cattle farmers, and the emergence of larger and quality leather, dairy and meat-processing industries.

Albeit on a limited scale, government is facilitating technical assistance to Ethiopian shoe producers through the Indian Footwear Design and Development Institute to improve entrepreneurial skills, footwear design, factory floor efficiency, footwear quality and faster production techniques. Such assistance is also needed for smaller producers to help them to integrate with the export industry. The development of plug-and-play industrial parks recommended for jumpstarting the garments industry will help to foster a large and sustainable leather export industry in Ethiopia.

Scaling up leather product exports is unsustainable without a strong base of managerial capital. In the longer term, Ethiopia will need to foster or attract managerial capital that has embedded in it intangible assets such as links to foreign buyers, information about industry trends and fashions, and modern technologies necessary to keep an industry globally competitive. The recent entry of a large-scale Chinese investor exporting leather shoes is evidence that managerial capital embedded with intangible assets is almost a prerequisite for scaling up Ethiopia's leather product exports industry in the short term.

6.4.8.3   Wood products industry is constrained by lumber and technical skills

The demand for wood products, especially furniture, is high and growing rapidly in the high-income American and European markets. Vietnam successfully tapped into these markets. Evidently, in 2009, Vietnamese wood product exports to OECD were growing at 18–20 percent per year and exceeded US$ 2.4 billion. In Ethiopia, over the past few years, the economy has grown at about 8–9 percent a year and boosted demand in the construction materials and furniture industries. There is also substantial potential for import replacement. Currently, the local industry employs more than 40,000 workers mostly in small, low productivity informal firms producing low quality products.

Ethiopia has 125 percent overall cost disadvantage in the wood products industry relative to China (Table 6.4.6). The latter is a pertinent benchmark because the Ethiopian markets are prolific with Chinese imports, mostly of contemporary design, which young urban Ethiopians prefer. Price and quality competitive locally produced furniture is conspicuous by its absence.

Several factors pose a natural disadvantage for Ethiopia's wood products export industry. The greatest is its landlocked location and costly trade logistics for a low value to high weight input such as lumber. The price of lumber and adhesives increase the cost of Ethiopian wood products by 87 percent. The cost of a cubic meter of lumber is US$667 in Ethiopia compared with US$176 in Vietnam and US$344 in China. The cost of adhesives is US$4.22 in Ethiopia compared with US$1.22 in Vietnam and US$0.51 in China. Since lumber accounts for more than 70 percent of the cost of simple wood products such as wooden chairs and doors, Ethiopian furniture makers are unable to compete with imported furniture. An export or even domestic industry dependent on imported lumbar is infeasible.

Labor productivity is very low in both large and small firms. For example, workers produce 4.5 chairs a day in China, 1.9 in Vietnam, and only 0.3 in Ethiopia (Table 6.4.4). Clearly, Ethiopia's low labor costs advantage does not apply to the wood products industry. This is mostly because the industry comprises of mostly small, informally trained carpenters with weak technical skills reflected in poor craftsmanship, and an absence of managerial capital.

6.4.8.3.1   *Possible solutions*

Input costs are at the core of Ethiopia's wood products industry. Given Ethiopia's natural wealth of bamboo forests, currently believed to be the largest endowment in Africa, it is possible to develop a viable domestic wood products industry if it uses domestic lumbar short term.

The absence of land for commercial forestry is currently a binding constraint. To scale up, the government needs to allow an efficient market for wood by facilitating access to land and financing for sustainable private wood plantations of fast-growing species on degraded land close to the main urban centers. Such a policy should increase and improve wood quality and reduce its cost via economies of scale and lower transportation costs if it is not overtaxed. The government would need to regulate the market to prevent excessive logging. Evidently, China, Vietnam, and Tanzania all have successful wood plantations. Ethiopia should be able to grow them too.

Policies that help to expand the domestic supply of lumber to scale up the domestic industry would benefit directly the large number of small or micro firms currently in business. However, given that these firms have limited or no access to the critical inputs such as finance, industrial land, and access to markets, entry into plug-and-play industrial parks would be a large step toward jumpstarting Ethiopia's wood products industry.

6.4.8.4   Agribusiness: reforming key agricultural inputs and outputs

In spite of the natural conditions for a productive agricultural sector, a poorly organized seed production and distribution system, delays in the certification of imported seeds and the absence of commercial-scale wheat farming have stymied the development of a competitive wheat-producing sector and a flour milling industry. Similarly, the small size of cattle farms with only about ten animals compared to more than several hundred on farms in China and Vietnam, poor cattle-breeding practices and veterinary services, and a fixed price system that is a disincentive to producers have stalled the emergence of a large-scale and competitive dairy industry in Ethiopia. In spite of its potential, Ethiopia is currently an importer of milk. In 2009, Ethiopia imported US$368 million of cereals and millions of Ethiopians continue to depend on emergency food aid.

A ton of wheat costs US$330 in Ethiopia compared to only US$199 in China. However, the milling costs per ton of wheat are only US$29 in Ethiopia compared to US$55 in China and US$89 in Vietnam. As a consequence, in Ethiopia a ton of wheat flour costs US$407 compared with US$274 in China and US$325 in Vietnam. And a liter of raw milk costs US$0.37 in Ethiopia but US$0.22 in Vietnam.

6.4.8.4.1 *Possible solutions*

As in the case of apparel, leather, and wood manufacturing industries, the solutions to creating a viable wheat flour or milk industry rest in a well-organized agricultural sector that produces wheat or milk, at globally competitive prices. Policies for land reforms that facilitate the commercial production of wheat and milk would not be sufficient as the small Ethiopian producers or farmers do not have access to finance to purchase or rent land. For them, policies that enable the use of land and cattle as collateral for loans, thus fostering increase in productivity and scale should be designed. New investors could also be encouraged to bring good practices that can benefit all sectors.

6.4.8.5 Metal Products are constrained by the high cost of imported steel

Ethiopia's competitiveness in metal products is constrained by poor skills and high input costs. Imported steel costs 30 percent more than in China and is subject to import tariffs. However, even if the import tariffs were eliminated, in the absence of the domestic availability of steel, the metal products industry would not be competitive in Ethiopia. Currently, steel costs US$1,414 per ton in Ethiopia compared to US$1,101 in China (Table 6.4.8). Similarly, the cost of steel per 1,000 crown corks (bottle caps) is US$5.61 in Ethiopia as against US$4.50 in China and US$3.82 in Vietnam.

6.4.9 Conclusion

In focusing on what the Ethiopian government can do to jumpstart light manufacturing and move a step closer to the goal of middle-income status, this paper points to some unconventional measures that could be broadly referred to as a brand of "industrial policy." There are several markers of this brand. One is sector-specificity, motivated by the fact that due to resource and capacity constraints, the government cannot resolve all constraints at once to achieve its goal. It makes sense to limit its policy interventions to areas where they can make the biggest impact. This implies, selecting a set of industries and within each industry, carefully prioritizing the areas of intervention. The identification of industries is guided by Ethiopia's natural comparative advantage in less-skilled labor. Two, within each industry, there are a variety of constraints associated with high inputs costs, access to land, finance, trade logistics, labor productivity, and managerial and worker skills. These affect overall cost competitiveness. Careful analysis shows that resolving a few leading constraints is usually sufficient to achieve cost competitiveness, as shown by the case of the leather products and apparel industries. Selectivity in government interventions makes the task manageable. Three, the key challenge is to scale up the supply of inputs and final products. For this, competition in all stages of production is essential. The role of government is to resolve market failures, redress government failures, and facilitate private firms. The interventions involve a combination of "soft" industrial policies when Marshallian externalities are present and standard interventions. Four, the benefits of industrial policy should also spill over to smaller producers by interventions that level the playing field between large and small, domestic and foreign firms.

The precise interventions identified through the VCA are related with scaling up through a series of measures: (i) a reduction in input costs. In four out of five industries, these entail the backward integration of the value chain, that is, from farm to firm; (ii) land reform in rural areas to foster farm-to-firm linkages, and the availability of industrial land for plug-and-play industrial parks for both large and small firms; (iii) improvement in trade logistics to reduce the costs and time delays of transporting goods; (iv) worker training to improve productivity; and (v) attracting foreign investors to boost the accumulation of managerial capital to bring global best practice to Ethiopian industry. There is no bias toward any particular firm size. All proposed policies are intended to reach out to large and small firms.

Evidently, China and Vietnam also followed selective strategies. They ensured a scaling up of inputs, established world-class trade logistics and plug-and-play industrial parks.

Notes

1. The findings, interpretations, and conclusions expressed in this publication are those of the author(s) and should not be attributed in any manner to The World Bank, its Board of Executive Directors, or the governments they represent.

2. In the early stages of economic development, there is a negative relationship between concentration in agriculture and/mineral resources and income per capita until the $10,000 (2000 constant US dollars) mark after which the relationship turns positive as countries with higher income levels typically specialize in goods' exports and the share of services in their overall exports also rises (Imbs and Wacziarg, 2003). At a product level, we find a close relationship between low and medium tech manufactured products and GDP per capita. In a related context, Hesse (2007) and Lederman and Maloney (2007) also find a positive relationship between diversification and GDP per capita.

3. All tariff related statistics are from "The Value Chain and Feasibility Analysis; Domestic Resource Cost Analysis," *Global Development Solutions* (2011).

4. Global Development Solutions (2011).

5. The Ethiopian government is committed to achieving continued growth within a stable macroeconomic framework, in the context of the new five-year development plan (Ministry of Finance and Economic Development 2010). The strategic pillars for the plan include sustaining rapid economic growth through investment in agriculture and infrastructure, the promotion of industrialization, enhancement of social development, and strengthening of governance and the role of youth and women.

6. Quantitative surveys of Ethiopian apparel producers show that smaller entrepreneurs in Ethiopia have less access to skills and information than their Asian counterparts (Fafchamps and Quinn, 2011).

7. Low wages and high labor intensity offset any trade logistics related production cost disadvantage. Unlike the apparel industry, the leather products industry is not too sensitive to just-in-time delivery delays.

References

Chandra, Vandana, Justin Yifu Lin and Yan Wang (2013) "Leading Dragon Phenomenon: New Opportunities for Catch-up in Low-Income Countries," *Asian Development Review*, vol. 30, no. 1, pp. 1–32.

Chenery, Hollis (1980) "Interactions between Industrialization and Exports," *American Economic Review*, vol. 70, no. 2, pp. 281–287.

Cimoli, Mario, Dosi, Giovanni, and Stiglitz, **Joseph E. (2009)** *Industrial Policy and Development: the Political Economy of Capabilities Accumulation* (Oxford: Oxford University Press).

Dinh, Hinh T., Palmade, Vincent, Chandra, Vandana, and Cossar, Frances (2012) *Light Manufacturing in Africa: Targeted Policies to Enhance Private Investment and Create Jobs* (Washington, DC: World Bank).

Fafchamps, Marcel, and Quinn, Simon (2011) "Results of Sample Surveys of Firms," in Hinh Dinh and George R.G. Clarke (eds), *Performance of Formal Manufacturing Firms in Africa – An Empirical Analysis* (Washington, DC: The World Bank).

Global Development Solutions (2011) "The Value Chain and Feasibility Analysis; Domestic Resource Cost Analysis," Background paper (*Light Manufacturing in Africa Study*) (Washington, DC: The World Bank). Available online as Volume II at http://worldbank.org/africamanufacturing.

Harrison, Ann, and Rodríguez-Clare, Andres (2010) "Trade, Foreign Investment, and Industrial Policy for Developing Countries," in Dani Rodrik and Mark Rosenzweig (eds), *Handbook of Development Economics*, vol. 5 (Amsterdam: North-Holland), pp. 4039–4214.

Harrison, Ann E., Lin, Justin Y., and Xu, L. C. (2013) *Explaining Africa's (Dis)advantage* (Cambridge, MA: National Bureau of Economic Research).

Hausmann, R. and Rodrik, D. (2006) "Doomed to Choose: Industrial Policy as Predicament," John F. Kennedy School of Government, Harvard University.

Hesse, Heiko. (2008) *Export Diversification and Economic Growth* (Washington, DC: Commission on Growth and Development).

Imbs, J., and Wacziarg, R. (2003) "Stages of Diversification," *American Economic Review*, vol. 93, no. 1, pp. 63–86.

Kuznets, Simon (1966) *Modern Economic Growth: Rate, Structure, and Spread* (New Haven, CT: Yale University Press).

Lederman, Daniel, and Maloney, William F. (2007) *Natural Resources: Neither Curse Nor Destiny* (Palo Alto, CA: Stanford Economics and Finance, an imprint of Stanford University Press).

Lin, Justin Yifu (2009) "DPR Debate: Should Industrial Policy in Developing Countries Conform to Comparative Advantage or Defy it? A Debate between Justin Lin and Ha-Joon Chang," *Development Policy Review*, vol. 27, no. 5, pp. 483–502.

Lin, Justin Yifu (2010) "New Structural Economics: A Framework for Rethinking Development," Policy Research Working Paper 5197 (Washington, DC: World Bank).

Lin, Justin Yifu (2011) "From Flying Geese to Leading Dragons: New Opportunities and Strategies for Structural Transformation in Developing Countries," Policy Research Working Paper 5702 (Washington, DC: World Bank).

Lin, Justin Yifu and Monga, Celestin (2010) Growth Identification And Facilitation: The Role of The State In The Dynamics of Structural Change. Washington, D.C.: The World Bank. Accessed at http://proxy.library.carleton.ca/login?url=http://elibrary.worldbank.org/content/workingpaper/10.1596/1813-9450-5313.

Pack, Howard, and Saggi, Kamal (2006) *The Case for Industrial Policy: a Critical Survey*, Development Research Group, Trade Team (Washington, DC: World Bank).

Syrquin, Moshe (1988) "Patterns of Structural Change," in Hollis Chenery and T. N. Srinivasan (eds), *Handbook of Development Economics*, vol. 1 (Amsterdam: Elsevier Science).

World Development Indicators 2012 (Washington, DC: The World Bank).

6.5

Industrialization: The Mauritian Model

Streevarsen Pillay Narrainen[1]
Ministry of Finance, Mauritius

6.5.1 Introduction

"Today, both our countries are hailed as economic miracles, perhaps because conventional wisdom had doomed us to failure after independence". S.R. Nathan, President of the Republic of Singapore.[2]

On March 12 1968, when Mauritius became an independent nation, it was no more than another third world economy taking its destiny in its own hands. All the development indicators were despondently off the acceptable norms. The country, facing a demographic explosion and high and rising unemployment, depended almost entirely on a one-crop sugar economy. The ratios of population to doctors, lawyers, and other professionals were extremely high. So was the infant mortality rate. Life expectancy was low. More than 50 percent of houses were vulnerable to damage by cyclone. The literacy rate was low, reflecting poor enrolment in secondary schools. Public infrastructure was dilapidated even by third world standards. For some analysts the constraints to industrialization and growth were simply too overwhelming. A few years before independence, James Meade et al. (1961) thought there was little scope for industrialization because of the lack of skills. Four years after independence, V.S. Naipaul (1972) added to such pessimism when he described Mauritius as an 'overcrowded barracoon' where 'problems defy solutions' and as a country plagued by despair.

In the early years following independence the challenges were indeed tough. An exceptional surge in the price of sugar in 1974/75 raised the hope of more prosperous years ahead. But the price of sugar fell again, and the oil-price hike of 1973 took a heavy toll on the economy, paving the way to a 10.1 percent contraction in 1980, when the second oil price shock struck. The exchange rate was significantly overvalued. Inflation was high and volatile. Unemployment kept on rising, official reserves were depleting, budget and current account deficits became unsustainably high and the terms of trade were rapidly deteriorating. It looked like the Mauritian model was cracking at the seams, that a severe crisis was unfolding and that the country would be stuck in the low-income trap for decades to come. However, the opposite happened. Mauritius pulled itself out of that predicament and went on to become, within a relatively short span of time, an upper middle-income economy. The much-feared demographic explosion was brought under control allowing per capita income to increase from US$200 to the current level of US$9,000.

Between 1968 and 2000, real GDP expanded at an annual average rate of 5.3 percent and exports in value terms went up by around a hundred times. The unemployment rate fell significantly, to a low of 2.7 percent in 1991 after reaching a peak of 20.9 percent in 1982. Inflation was brought under control. The debt service ratio dropped from a peak of 26 percent in 1983 to below 4 percent currently. The official reserves that had collapsed to barely three weeks of import cover by 1980 were significantly replenished and now stand at close to five months of imports.

Going into the new millennium the country's economic landscape had changed beyond recognition as a result of successful industrialization and diversification policies. Along with economic progress came noticeable improvements in the indicators of development. The Gini coefficient declined from around .50 in the 1970s to .38. Latest data show an adult literacy rate of 88 percent, and gross enrolment ratios of around 96 percent in pre-primary schools, 100 percent in primary schools, 75 percent in secondary schools, and 37 percent in tertiary institutions. Infant mortality per 10,000 births fell from 58 in 1968 to 14.4 in 2010. Life expectancy at birth has risen to 73 years. Almost all housing units have access to tap water and electricity and more than 80 percent are cyclone resistant. Some 85 percent of families own their houses, one of the highest owner-occupancy rates in the world. Less than one percent of the population live in absolute poverty as measured by one US dollar a day and less than two percent as defined by US$2 a day.[3]

The perennial diversification thrust that cuts across all industrialization strategies since independence has also been a great success. Mauritius has been transformed into a well-diversified economy with more than ten different sectors contributing to growth.

Those who saw no end to the predicaments of Mauritius were proven wrong. Paul Mathieu and Patrick Imam (2008) refer to the economic performance of Mauritius as a growth miracle.

6.5.2   Explaining the Mauritian miracle

Why is the Mauritian growth experience heralded as a miracle? Perhaps the best answer to this question is the one given by the President of the Republic of Singapore in the citation introducing this paper. It would have been difficult, even for the most foresighted development economists, to predict the achievements of Mauritius if they stayed within the orbits of prevailing orthodoxy in their analysis. It is equally difficult, even with hindsight, to capture fully all the underpinnings of the Mauritian industrialization experience if we base our analysis solely on the postulates of theories of economic development. As Subramaniam and Roy (2001) and Frankel (2012) put it, there are more to the Mauritian model than can be captured by econometric and other empirical methods.

This paper attempts to provide greater insights into the underpinnings of the Mauritian industrialization miracle by looking beyond the conventional wisdom of development economics. It does so on the presumption that there must be at least one feature of the model that is unique to Mauritius and that accounts for its success where some countries with a similar and even better start have either failed or achieved much less. When development models are referred to as a Mauritian, Singaporean, Japanese, or other model, it is usually because each one is distinct in some ways or in one way at least.

Figure 6.5.1 identifies and organizes twelve main attributes of the Mauritian model into a hard core, a soft core and three distinct industrialization strategies.

The hard core explains the uniqueness of the Mauritian Model. At independence, Mauritius started off with a legacy of strong institutions that suited its development ambitions, an ethnic mix which could prove either to be lethal or something of an asset, an already well-structured private sector, and a class of indigenous entrepreneurs. Together they account for the distinctiveness of the model, giving legitimacy to the appellation "Mauritian Model" and are considered as having been crucial to the development achievements

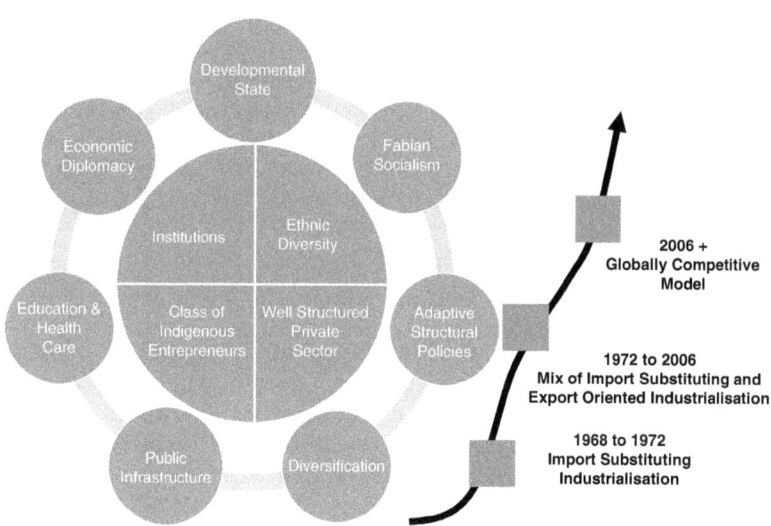

Figure 6.5.1   The Mauritian Model

of the past four decades. *Ex post*, few development economists, if any, would deny that this legacy constituted a rare combination of favorable preconditions for growth although this was much less clear *ex ante*. However, they were not sufficient.

The soft core comprises eight features that, together with the legacy at the hard core, have fashioned the Mauritian model. They are considered as part of the soft core because they are in no way unique or specific, though critical to its development. These are: a developmental state, Fabian socialism, adaptive structural policies, a perennial diversification thrust, timely expansion of public infrastructure aimed at crowding in private investment and improving domestic and international connectivity, right education and health care policies to build human capital, and economic diplomacy.

To these legacies and policy approaches at the hard and soft cores, Mauritius has, since independence, embedded three main industrialization strategies. They are an inward-looking import-substituting industrialization (ISI) that can be dated to between 1968 and 1972; a heterodox mix of ISI and export-oriented industrialization (EOI) between 1972 and 2006 and a globally competitive paradigm from 2006 on.

Together, the legacy at the hard core, the elements at the soft core, and the industrialization strategies make up the Mauritian model.

6.5.3   The components of the hard core

6.5.3.1   Institutions

In seeking to explain the failed predictions of James Meade et al., Subramaniam and Roy (2001) focus on three determinants of long-run growth performance: institutions, initial conditions and openness. They conclude that "To some considerable extent, strong domestic institutions have contributed substantially to the Mauritian success, and are a good candidate for underlying explanations of the Mauritian miracle." They also conclude that "In standard cross-country growth regression models, Mauritius is an outlier, implying that conventional determinants do not fully capture the country's performance."

Matthew Lange (2003) also supports the critical role of institutions in the development of Mauritius. He argues that

> ... a prolonged period of labour riots beginning in the late 1930s and the more interventionist policy of the British government after World War II combined to initiate a "critical-juncture period" that increased relations between state and societal actors. This increased embeddedness made possible state–society synergy, which promoted broad-based development by engaging and strengthening both state institutions and societal associations, thereby endowing Mauritius with the institutions necessary for broad-based development after colonial independence as well.[4]

The British also contributed significantly to the creation of strong democratic institutions based on power sharing. This helped to maintain political balance so that the focus could be on economic and social development. As the British were not interested in settling in Mauritius, they played the role of honest broker and arbitrated between the Franco-Mauritian planters/magnates and the rest of the population. As honest brokers the British could impose on the white sugar magnates that they would have to give up political power. However, in this role, the British were also able to manage the demands of the majority by saying that universal franchise would be attained but gradually (from 1948 to 1963). Moreover, the British insisted that there would not be a winner takes all political result. After every election, a coalition was put together which taught compromise and pragmatism and tempered some of the stronger ideological currents that might have pushed ruinous economic solutions. This set the stage for creating a social balance that was crucial to keeping at bay ethnic tensions with economic power remaining with the Franco-Mauritians whilst political power shifted to the rest of the population. Strong democratic institutions based on power sharing contributed significantly to maintaining this balance so that the focus could be on economic and social development.

However, there were hiccups along the way. Race riots in 1967 on the eve of independence cast a shadow that could have led to the deterioration seen in many other ethnically diverse countries. Instead, the riots brought the realization that in a small island with no escape hatches, tolerance was the only viable option. Efforts by civil society to bridge ethnic divides were joined by religious leaders who preached coexistence and mutual respect. A significant number of political leaders also made concerted efforts to promote unity in diversity.

But the institutional legacy, no matter how prominent its role in the development of Mauritius, cannot by itself explain the uniqueness and effectiveness of the Mauritian model. Subramanian and Roy (2011) recognize that their econometric results, even after accounting for the role of institutions leave out a sizable unexplained component to Mauritian growth. The 11 other determinants that make up the hard and soft cores at Figure 6.5.1 can be strong candidates to explain more fully the Mauritian Model.

6.5.3.2 An appropriate ethnic mix

Mauritius has developed as a multi-ethnic society that comprises people of Indian, Chinese, European (mainly French), and African origins. This ethnic diversity has had multiple benefits to the development of the country. The Indians, who were brought in as indentured laborers, played a predominant role in agriculture, principally as workers on the sugar estates. Some Indians also came to Mauritius as traders. The French owned the sugar estates. The Chinese played a prominent role in trade and commerce. A large number of the Africans who were brought to Mauritius as slaves to work in the sugarcane fields left agriculture when slavery was abolished and went into various other economic activities, including as artisans and craftsmen.

James Meade et al. (1961) thought that ethnic diversity and fragmentation would lead to social unrest and act as a curse on development under the pressure of population growth. Today, with the benefits of hindsight, we know for sure that he was wrong. However, in judging his concerns we should recall that similar pressures partly explain the tragedies in Burundi and Rwanda, also countries characterized by high and rising population density (Diamond, 2005). In the case of Mauritius, ethnic diversity instead became an important asset for development, perhaps because unlike other places with ethnic conflict, ALL the ethnic groups came from outside the country.

Subramanian and Roy (2001) think that one possible candidate to explain the significant unexplained component of their econometric results appears to be the ethnic diversity of the country. They identify important benefits from the ethnic diversity, namely creative positive externalities from the diaspora with important linkages to the rest of the world. According to them, this forced the need for economic balance that preserved the cash cow, namely the sugar sector. It forced the need for participatory political institutions that are important in maintaining stability, law and order, the rule of law, and mediating conflict. Moreover, because no one was native to Mauritius, all ethnic groups saw links to the rest of the world as positive, encouraging the country to be open, and linked to far-off markets for both its consumption and its main production.

Jeffrey Frankel is the latest advocate of the beneficial role of ethnic diversity:

> A case in point is the high level of ethnic diversity in Mauritius, which in many places would make for dysfunctional politics. Here, however, it brings cosmopolitan benefits. The institutions manage to balance the ethnic groups; none is excluded from the system. It is intriguing that the three African countries with the highest governance rankings (Mauritius, Seychelles and Cape Verde) are all islands that had no indigenous population. It helps that everyone came from somewhere else.[5]

6.5.3.3 A well-structured private sector and a class of indigenous entrepreneurs

A well-structured and dynamic private sector was an important lever to getting the economy out of the quagmire in the early years following independence. It was fully capable of fulfilling its various functions in the economy, which were to create jobs, expand entrepreneurial activities, enable technology transfer, build human capital, and meet the needs of the population for goods and services. There were already a number of key private institutions that were more than a hundred years old. Such initial conditions were crucial to ensuring that industrialization could take place not at the expense of, but in addition to a consolidation and diversification of the agricultural sector. Having an agricultural sector that brought in foreign currencies was a tremendous plus for a country that needed to import capital equipment to develop its manufacturing sector.

The sugar sector was ready to liberate labor resources without undermining its own growth.[6] Moreover, as a country with surplus rather than subsistence agriculture, the sugar magnates had accumulated financial resources that needed to be channeled into other activities. As the scope for investment in the agricultural sector was limited, the obvious alternative was to turn to manufacturing.

The private sector was led by a class of indigenous entrepreneurs who had the skills, the right attitude to risk, and a significant and growing amount of investible funds. They needed to diversify their investments both in and outside agriculture. Thus Mauritius was able to start off with a shared vision between the private sector and government both on the need for diversifying the economy and on the roadmap to getting there. This allowed for the gradual unfolding of an exemplary framework for public/private sector dialogue that culminated in a broader and well-structured partnership with all societal actors, and which turned out to be crucial to the developmental role of the state.

6.5.4   The developmental state and Fabian Socialism

The state has played an indisputably positive role in the country's development. At the very outset, the political leadership entrenched the importance of a "developmental state."[7] While the intensity of involvement of a developmental state can range from hard authoritarianism to democratic capitalism, Mauritius chose democratic socialism with a strong commitment to instituting, maintaining, and strengthening the welfare state. Sir Seewoosagur Ramgoolam, the leader of the Labour Party, who led the country to independence, was well imbued with the tenets of Fabian Socialism. He believed in the principles of democratic socialism via gradualist and reformist means. The developmental approach was thus placed at the center left, around which, over the years, the ideals of the major political parties have come to gravitate. This explains the significant overlapping of the ideals of the major political parties in Mauritius. Generally, the population expects all governments to operate at the center left. Fabian socialism has thus survived all changes in government and never lost its hold, even when the process of economic liberalization, inspired by Reaganism and Thatcherism, was taking roots in the early 1990s.

Thus, the state has led the industrialization process. It set out the regulatory framework to govern the economy, provided collective goods, invested to fill in gaps in the financial sector, offered fiscal and other incentives to encourage private investments in priority sectors, and ensured that long-term national interests dominated over the short termism of the corporate class. Since independence, around 120 public sector statutory bodies (parastatals, state-owned enterprises, and trusts) have been set up to promote development policies and industrialization. Among the most prominent examples are Air Mauritius to build connectivity and support the development of the tourism and export industries, the Development Bank of Mauritius to support industrialization (including the Export Processing Zone), the Mauritius Cooperative Bank and the Mauritius Housing Corporation to bridge gaps in the financial sector, and the State Trading Corporation to provide goods that the corporate class would only import with high margins.

The state also took the lead in key industries, such as the tourism sector itself and ICT/BPO, sometimes investing directly to prime the pump but, more generally, by investing in the basic infrastructure and creating the right environment for private investment. From the mid-1970s to the mid-1980s, the state devoted a growing share of the national budget to physical infrastructure to facilitate private investment and attract more foreign investment.

The Fabian ideas of social justice have underpinned the welfare system and distribution policies of the developmental state that in turn have been crucial to social coherence and political stability in a democratic context. In particular, education and healthcare policies bear the imprints of political leadership influenced by the ideals of Fabian socialism. Subsidies on flour and rice, price controls, universal old age pensions, free education and health care, free public transport for students and the elderly, subsidized houses for the very low-income families, subsidized housing loans, to name but a few, have been maintained even in years of severe crisis and austerity. The population counts on the government to promote social harmony in diversity, to ensure social equity, foster employment creation and improve the standard of living of those at lower income levels.

6.5.5   Adaptive structural policies

A crucial feature of the Mauritian Model is its flexibility. This is particularly important to a small open economy with an export-oriented growth strategy. The developmental state has constantly evolved since independence to adapt to the changing international panorama, that include events such as trade liberalization, the dismantling of trade preferences, globalization, the new regionalism and the wave of neo-liberalism that swept the world in the late 1980s and the 1990s.

While government evolved into more of a facilitator, it nonetheless maintained a hold on the trajectory of economic development. Some of the policies to liberalize the economy include a cut in the maximum income tax rate from 75 to 35 percent in 1984 for corporations and in 1985 for individuals. In 2006, the maximum income tax rate was again cut drastically to a flat 15 percent, but this time accompanied by the abolition of all tax incentive schemes which numbered 21 in total. Thus, Mauritius became one of the lowest tax jurisdictions in the world with also one of the simplest tax return systems. In the early 1990s, the interest rate was liberalized, as was the capital account of the balance of payments with the abolition of foreign exchange control. Export taxes were also abolished and import duties on inputs were totally phased out, as part of a plan to make of Mauritius a duty-free island.

The rebalancing of the world economy and the current euro crisis are the newest challenges to which Mauritius, which is very euro-centric, is having to adapt. It depends on Europe for some 65 percent of its exports and tourist arrivals. This is compelling the country to align its industrialization policy with the global economic rebalancing, putting more emphasis on producing for markets in India, China, Russia, Brazil, and Africa.

6.5.5.1 A realistic diversification policy

The successful diversification of the Mauritian economy was both a result of and a contributor to the miracle. Reducing reliance on sugar exports was a theme around which there has always been broad political consensus and private sector commitment. Mauritius has gone through three distinct phases of economic diversification.

In the early years of independence the focus was on identifying areas where new activities could be developed. Analysing trends in other countries that had diversified, the government provided incentives to encourage a broadening of activities in agriculture, and investment in manufacturing and tourism. The financial sector was also growing as it expanded its financing activities to support the various sectors that were driving GDP growth. These industries, commonly referred to as the four pillars of the economy until the 1990s, have been the stage where the economic miracle has played out.

Within a relatively short span of time Mauritius transformed itself into one of the biggest producers of woolen knitwear, a holiday destination that attracts hundreds of thousands of high-end visitors every year and a financial services sector aspiring to become the region's financial hub.

In the 1990s Mauritius started the second wave of diversification with the offshore center, which is now the Global Business Centre, a Freeport, and an ICT/BPO sector. The four traditional pillars of the economy were also being broadened with plans to produce energy from sugarcane, diversify the tourism product, move into high-end textile production and internationalize the financial services sector.

Mauritius entered the new millennium by embarking on a third wave of diversification. This includes the seafood hub, real estate, luxury villas for high net-worth foreigners, renewable energy, a knowledge centre of excellence, health center of excellence, and a creative industry. As a result of diversification efforts, the contribution of the four traditional pillars to GDP now add up to only 22 percent. The latest grand endeavor in diversification was announced in the Government Programme 2012. This proposed the development of Mauritius into an Ocean State. The aim is to promote the economic exploitation of its Marine Exclusive Economic Zone which spans some 2.3 million square kilometers and which is some more than one thousand times bigger than the country's land area.

Thus the developmental state still leads the diversification drive but more as a facilitator. The state has always charted the course and even set the ball rolling in many areas, and most of the time private investments have followed.

6.5.6   Education and healthcare

Who can gainsay that commitment to education has been an indubitable critical success factor in the country's development? It is conventional wisdom that there is a high positive correlation between the level of education and development. At independence there was already a marked commitment by the government, religious organizations and the private sector to education. The majority of parents made the education of their children as one of their top priorities.

The history of educational facilities in Mauritius can be said to go as far back as 1791 with the setting up of the "College National", also known as the "College Colonial," in Port Louis. However, most of the efforts started in 1944, when far-reaching reforms were made in the educational system and which culminated in a rapid expansion in primary and secondary schools. Since independence, new dimensions have been added to education. The whole system has been gradually democratized by extending free access to secondary and tertiary education, as well as giving free transportation facilities to all students.

Giving free access to education when per capita income was still dismally low and poverty widespread was crucial to enhancing social justice. It also contributed significantly to eliminate a gender bias in education and in the entire development process. It was part of the social compact reflecting power sharing whereby government got to use surplus from the sugar sector to invest in social welfare.

Like education, healthcare has always been considered as a cornerstone of development and an integral part of the Mauritian development philosophy. For most of its history, Mauritius has provided free and universal health care to all Mauritians as well as non-Mauritian residents and tourists. Medicines are also provided free to patients at the public hospitals. This strong emphasis on public health care, including the eradication of malaria, has underpinned a rapidly improving life expectancy.

Investment in education and healthcare has always been considered as crucial to human capital and an important engine of growth. And this conviction and commitment continue to pay a hefty dividend in terms of development.

6.5.7   Economic diplomacy

Economic diplomacy has always been a forte of the developmental state, in particular to consolidate the sugar industry and develop the textile sector. Like most commodity-exporting economies, Mauritius was exposed to price and demand fluctuations on the international market for sugar. This vulnerability was successfully abated through economic diplomacy that led to a sugar protocol that, for over four decades, practically eliminated the risk from low world sugar prices and guaranteed the sales of a given quantity of sugar.

Mauritius also benefited from preferential access to the European markets for textiles through the Multi Fibre Arrangement (MFA). Paradoxically, with the MFA, Mauritius seized opportunities from an attempt of western countries to protect their markets from textiles imports. Even though Mauritius was not globally competitive in textile production, it acted on opportunities from the MFA which shifted textile manufacturing to higher-cost producers. For a number of years the textile industry was the main driver of growth and one of the makers of the miracle. Economic diplomacy had a vital role in minimizing adverse impact from the dismantling of the MFA on the economy. The government has also lobbied strongly for the Africa Growth and Opportunity Act. Through economic diplomacy it bought time to allow both the sugar and textile industries to hone their competitiveness so that they can operate in a free trade environment. In fact, economic diplomacy has played an undeniable role in preventing these two industries from collapsing under the pressures of trade liberalization and globalization.

But economic diplomacy transcended trade preferences. Regional integration policies and creating and strengthening bilateral relations with friendly countries were and still are important components of the diplomatic efforts. As the country seeks to be a bridge between Africa and Asia efforts are underway to expand relations with African countries, including those in the West (Gabon, Ghana and Nigeria) whilst deepening relations with India and China.

6.5.8   The three industrialization strategies pursued since independence

The model in Figure 6.5.1 illustrates the three industrialization strategies that have been implemented since independence: (i) inward-looking import substitution; (ii) an unorthodox mix of highly protected import-substituting and liberal export-oriented growth, from the early 1970s to 2006, with a gradual move toward economic liberalization; and (iii) a globally competitive thrust from 2006 onward, which brought a complete end to any inward-looking tendencies while also stripping the export-oriented strategy of its dependence on trade preferences.

6.5.8.1   Following prevailing orthodoxy: import-substituting industrialization

In common with most other newly decolonized countries, Mauritius became a battlefield for the ideologies of Marxism and democratic capitalism which were competing for world dominance. The growth models were of four main types: Rostovian, neoclassical, structural, and Marxist and there was no "one size fits all" solution for the underdeveloped economies. However, one common theme that cuts across the various development models, implicit in some and explicit in others, was that underdeveloped economies could only achieve higher standards of living by industrializing. The prevailing orthodoxy was for underdeveloped countries to implement import-substituting industrialization (ISI) strategies, through higher tariffs on imported goods and exchange control.

Like many other countries, Mauritius experimented with an ISI strategy in the early years of independence that focused on consumption goods, while at the same consolidating its agricultural sector. The ISI path was not only a matter of conventional wisdom but seemed to be the only viable option since the constraints on manufactured exports looked overwhelming. Mauritius did not have the technology, know-how, and capital base to diversify its exports. World trade was highly protectionist and particularly hostile to manufactured products from underdeveloped countries

But the ISI strategy in Mauritius was flawed. Without economies of scale most new industries required a very high level of protection from imports to survive. Most of them were producing below the critical mass and at high unit cost. The welfare cost of ISI turned out to be conspicuously high, with protective tariffs in some cases being set at 715 percent. Mauritius was among the countries with the highest effective rates of tariff protection. The government was inexorably pressed to create jobs for the vast pool of unemployed, yet the ISI strategy could not make any significant contribution to reducing the high unemployment rate which continued to rise.

6.5.8.2   The heterodox mix: the first turning point

The close partnership between private and public sectors facilitated a fundamental shift. Mauritius Inc. recognized the limitations of the ISI strategy soon enough and realized the risk of relying on such an auto-centric development model. It was quickly realized that only an outward-looking growth strategy would reduce that risk. Partly due to segments of the population having links to Africa, Asia and Europe, policymakers were encouraged to be more outward-looking. There was a combination of strategy options to open up the economy, including the development of the tourism industry. It had the advantage of being a labor-intensive service industry that could also bring in foreign currencies to finance the imports of the capital goods needed to industrialize. A second option was to join in the regional integration efforts that were being pursued in those days (now referred to as the first wave of regionalism) by underdeveloped countries to broaden their markets, benefit from economies of scale resulting from specialization, and widen the scope for cross-border investment. A third option was export-oriented industrialization (EOI) along the same lines as the East Asian economies. The success of the outward-looking strategies of these countries was a source of encouragement for Mauritius.

Mauritius chose to adopt all three options – EOI, tourism development, and regional integration in addition to the ISI. This was the first turning point for the Mauritian economy and it entered a second phase of its development with a heterodox mix of inward- and outward-looking strategies. It continued until the 1990s to maintain a high average effective rate of protection to shield domestic-oriented manufacturing from more competitive imports. This unorthodox mix turned out to be a winning formula that transformed the country from a mono-crop to a well-diversified export-oriented economy. The traditional society gave way to modern sectors.

6.5.8.3 The globally competitive paradigm: the second turning point

The mix-strategy of ISI and EOI growth maintained its ascendancy until the year 2006 when fundamental and far-reaching reforms were implemented to adapt to the pressures of globalization and trade liberalization in a world of accelerating change. With rapid technological innovation, shorter product life cycles and the emergence of new economic powers it became increasingly hard for government to identify future growth areas. Government would need to offer a globally attractive platform for producing goods and services for the world and give greater freedom to the market to pick areas of comparative advantage. Moreover, comparative advantage could be expected to be ever more dynamic and to shift in relatively short cycles.

This gave a totally new thrust to the development policies, focusing on global competitiveness and openness of the country not only to trade and foreign capital but also to ideas, technology, and expertise. The development strategy which relied on high levels of trade protection for its local manufacturing and on trade preferences for its sugar and textile exports became obsolete. It was incapable of delivering growth and prosperity in the new world economic order.

The government considered that repairing and adapting the ISI–EOI model would not have been enough. It had to be cast aside in favor of a completely new paradigm. This was accomplished in the 2006/2007 Budget and marked the second major turning point in the development of Mauritius. The new development thrust started off with cross-cutting, bold and fundamental reforms to: (i) secure a world-class doing business environment; (ii) open up the economy further to foreign capital, talents, expertise, and ideas; (iii) consolidate the economic structure and step up the perennial endeavour to diversify and build new economic pillars; (iv) strengthen macroeconomic fundamentals, in particular, consolidating public finances and reengineering tax policy; (v) ensure more flexibility, fluidity, and security on the labor market; and (vi) empower workers, entrepreneurs, the young, men, and women to succeed in the transition to global competitiveness.

The new strategy has passed the tests of external shocks. Soon after it was implemented, food and petroleum prices surged globally, and this was followed by the global financial turmoil, the worldwide great recession, the euro crisis which erupted in 2010, and the political upheaval in North Africa. In spite of being hit by this continuous series of external shocks, the new strategy delivered positive growth and high levels of FDI. Once again, Mauritius was on the right development track.

These three growth strategies are major constituents of the Mauritian development course. They were not unique in any way except perhaps for the unorthodox mix of high protection for manufacturing for the domestic market and very liberal policies for the export sector.

Going forward and drawing inspiration from the early demonstration of success from the globally competitive model, Mauritius has now set its sights on becoming a high-income economy by 2022.

6.5.9 Conclusion

The Mauritius success story is about how a small island resource-poor economy can still build comparative advantages by industrializing and benefiting from trade with the rest of the world. There are a number of factors besides natural resources that, if weaved in judiciously, can lead to successful development. The model in this paper highlights a number of them. It could have taken the country much more time to be where it is now, had it not been for priority public investment in human capital through education and health care. Considering the experiences of some other countries, one can also imagine that without strong institutions and an unflinching respect for human rights in a democratic context, the story of Mauritius could have been unpleasantly different. Mauritius is also an example of the never-ending job of a reformer. The shift from an ISI to an EOI strategy was rapid and appropriate. And the mix ISI–EOI strategy has constantly adapted to the changing global environment. The shift to the globally competitive paradigm, with more than forty reforms at one go, ranging across various aspects of economic management and fiscal policy, was timely. The success of Mauritius also lends strong support to the need for a developmental state, dirigiste but not necessarily authoritarian, to chart the growth course and ensure social equity, especially in a small economy where the distribution of productive assets is extremely skewed and where market failures can be conspicuously significant. It was the state that has set the mode of economic, social, and political development. Yet it must be emphasized that Mauritius has always taken the middle-of-the-road approach, applying the dirigiste approach of the Asian countries without, however, eschewing western liberalism – another heterodox mix. It is an example of how the interests of society can be reconciled with that of the individual. Thus the Mauritius success story cannot be attributed to any one factor in particular. The answer lies at the intersection of a number of features as expounded in this model.

Notes

1. I am grateful to Ali Michael Mansoor, Financial Secretary, Government of Mauritius for very positive and instructive comments on the paper and to my other colleague Dominique Theodore for assisting with the research. However, the views expressed in this paper are mine only and not necessarily those of the Ministry of Finance.
2. S. R. Nathan, President of the Republic of Singapore in his address to the National Assembly in Mauritius in June 2011.
3. Based on a survey carried out by the Central Statistical Office (now Statistics Mauritius) in 2008.
4. Lange (2003: 372–407).
5. Frankel (2012: 2).
6. The number of workers employed per 100,000 tons of sugar declined from 10,300 in 1970 to 3,500 in 2010.
7. The first person to seriously conceptualise the development state was Chalmers Johnson (1982).

References

Amédée, Darga, "The Mauritius Success Story: Why is this Island Nation an African Political and Economic Success?," in Moeletsi Mbeki (eds) *Advocates for Change: How to Overcome Africa's Challenges* (Johannesburg: Picador Africa).

Burton, Benedict (1965) *Mauritius: Problems of a Plural Society* (New York: Frederick A. Praeger).

Diamond, Jared (2005) *Collapse: How Societies Choose to Fail or Succeed* (London: Penguin Books).

Frankel, Jeffrey (2012) "Mauritius: African Success Story," Center For International Development', Working Paper no. 234 (Cambridge. MA: Harvard University).

Johnson, Chalmers (1982) *MITI and the Japanese Miracle* (Stanford, CA: Stanford University Press).

Lange, Matthew (2003) "Embedding the Colonial State: A Comparative-Historical Analysis of State Building and Broad-Based Development in Mauritius," *Social Science History*, vol. 27, no. 3, pp 397–423.

Meade, J.E. et al. (1961) *The Economic and Social Structure of Mauritius* (London: Methuen).

Lall, Sanjaya and Wignaraja, Ganeshan (1998) *Mauritius Dynamising Export Competitiveness*, Economic Paper 33 (London: Commonwealth Secretariat).

Mathieu, Paul and Imam, Patrick (2008) "Mauritius: Paving the Way for a Second 'Growth Miracle,'", *IMF Survey Magazine: Countries and Regions*, July 23.

Naipaul, V.S. (1972) *The Overcrowded Barracoon* (New York: Random House).

Subramanian, Arvind and Roy, Devesh (2001) "Who Can Explain The Mauritian Miracle: Meade, Romer, Sachs, or Rodrik?," IMF Working Paper WP/01/116 (New York: IMF).

6.6

Sharing of Singapore's Industrial Policy Insights

Thia Jang Ping
Civil Service College, Singapore

Unusually for a global city, Singapore has consistently maintained a sizeable share of manufacturing at around 20–25 per cent of GDP. This is a level below that of China and Korea, on a par with Germany and Switzerland, and certainly above the USA and the UK.

Land, labour and energy costs in Singapore rank amongst the world's highest. Land, in particular, is a scarce resource in Singapore that other larger economies have in greater abundance. Hence, the fact that manufacturing exists in Singapore is not the result of a completely free market. Policymakers have to work hard behind the scenes to create the supportive conditions – industrial policy if you will – to allow for the manufacturing sector to continue thriving in Singapore. In this short article, I will share some policy insights on Singapore's industrial policy, and draw some possible learning points for South Africa.

6.6.1   Focus on capabilities and value chains

The world's production network is highly fragmented, and increasingly specialized. A single final product will have many intermediates sourced from multiple locations, and a product sometimes shift through many countries before its completion and final sales. Economists have only belatedly studied and modeled "Vertical Specialization," "Off-shoring," and "Trade in tasks." It is important for policymakers to recognise this, take stock of the resources in a country including human capital, and decide which parts of the value chain, in which industry, the country has a realistic chance to excel in.

Here is an example of an industry that one would probably not associate with Singapore. Singapore companies have a 70 percent global market share in jack-up oil rigs, and a 50 percent market share in semi-submersible rigs, though Singapore does not have any oil or gas resources. The firms in this industry were in fact shipbuilders, which turned their marine engineering capabilities into the manufacture of offshore rigs when there was an increase in the demand for energy. In fact, Singapore companies do not produce the entire rigs, but focus on integrating the many different machines and systems into a single platform. They occupy a small, but profitable part of the value chain.

It is probably more accurate to characterize trade as an exchange of capabilities or factors, more so than goods. Industrial strategy should recognise that harnessing the capabilities of a country is, on balance, more important than picking specific goods to produce. Often the type of workforce a country has will determine the set of capabilities, and this leads me to the next point.

6.6.2   Deal with externalities

Having made the decision on which industry and parts of the value chain to focus efforts on, the developmental process is then not so much about picking winners but about creating the right kind of environment for those parts of the value chains to exist and thrive. In Singapore's experience, this involves the preparation of infrastructure, promoting local and inward investments, and also providing the necessary tax incentives. To give a specific example, once the decision was made to enter into the petrochemicals industry in the 1990s, infrastructural investments were made in land reclamation for an offshore island to house these petrochemical plants. The Economic Development Board (EDB), Singapore's investment promotion organization, immediately started the process of attracting firms to come to Singapore. The necessary incentives were also put in place, often involving tax breaks for key companies to locate in Singapore.

Education is seldom seen as an externality, but is in fact probably the critical one over the long term. In a free market, companies often do not invest in the training of workers, because workers are mobile across firms and skills are rarely specific to any single firm. It is left to the policymakers to solve this externality. Over the long term, the key is to ensure that the educational system continues to grow a workforce that has the capabilities to support the high-value industries. The reality is that industrial strategy is closely linked to the capabilities of the workforce. In the late 1990s, Singapore decided to push into the biomedical sciences industry in a major way. In the initial years, Singapore did not have the necessary indigenous manpower to sustain this industry. Therefore foreign workers were attracted to Singapore to kick-start the sector. However, the education policy was quickly tweaked to prepare Singaporeans for participation in the new industry. This included expanding university and vocational training places and providing generous scholarships for students to study in the field. It is through many years of policy focus that more Singaporean expertise is developed, and with more jobs in the sector going to Singaporeans.

6.6.3   Recognize the value of clusters

The third important point about industrial strategy is to recognise the so-called economic geography effects. Firms within an industry are often more productive located together. This could be due to the reduction of transport cost, labour market externality, knowledge spillover, and so on. The exact nature of agglomeration productivities may not be the same in each industry, but common across various threads is the productivity enhancement when firms locate together. The policy implication is to pick and grow clusters to ensure that these economies are reaped. Due to external economies, it is sometimes necessary to provide the first-mover investors with tax holidays. Economists generally agree that a small incentive to the first few catalytic investors can be welfare improving. Once these investors are anchored, it becomes progressively easier to attract the other firms due to agglomeration economies. However, Singapore is also mindful of concentration risks. An economy concentrated in too few clusters might not be resilient against shocks. Hence, Singapore's manufacturing strategy is organized around a few key clusters including electronics, biomedical sciences, petrochemicals, and transport engineering. In each of these clusters, there is also a specific part of the value chain on which Singapore is focused.

The unique challenge facing South Africa is that it is not located in a region of thick merchandise trade. Unlike Singapore, it is not located near other centers of manufacturing, or major shipping routes. For manufacturing companies to make the effort to anchor parts of its value chain in South Africa will be more challenging than for Singapore. Perhaps the way to go is to find natural industries that make use of the resources of Africa – not necessarily just mineral resources, but also agriculture resources, and cluster a few industries around them.

6.6.4   Free trade

If not managed well, industrial strategy often carries with it considerable downsides. Firstly, industrial policy that tilts the playing field to promote certain sectors and not others may create distortions. As far as possible, policy actions should be limited to correcting market failures, which should be articulated from the onset.

To mitigate against "picking winners," industrial policy should be applied as "evenly" as possible. For example, Singapore provides tax incentives or grants to certain industries, but these are applied in a nationality-blind basis. The best firms that satisfy a range of criteria have access to these incentives. There are no special provisions for domestically owned companies or national champions, for example. Secondly, Singapore has always had a free trade DNA. There are no custom duties, except for some specific items like cars and other sin goods. Free trade is an important disciplining device, and arguably a key complementary component to industrial policy. Free trade exposes industries to intense competition and puts firms to the test in the international marketplace. A tax incentive or grant introduced to certain industry may sometimes create some unintended consequences. Firms may use the advantage in one sector to move into other areas that are not always part of their core capabilities. Large conglomerates, spanning many unrelated sectors, are often a feature in Asia. This is possibly the by-product of industrial policy. Economists have found that exposure to trade can improve national productivity by driving out less productive firms, and also limiting the extent to which firms can veer away from their core competencies.

It may come as surprising to some that I make a distinction here between trade policies (tariffs, export subsidies and so on) and industrial policy levers (grants, tax incentives). Often, trade policy carries a larger distortion because it impacts the consumption sector as well as the production sector. Singapore's experience is that free trade acts as a good policy complement to industrial policy because it disciplines the later, and mitigates against potential downsides.

6.6.5 Managing resources

Africa is blessed with abundant mineral resources. While this offers a good source of extractive income, it probably makes the industrialization process more challenging. The basic economic transmission – the "Dutch Disease" – is intuitive and well known. The trade surplus coming from resource extraction will create upward real exchange rate pressures that render manufacturing uncompetitive.

Singapore may also have a policy insight in this respect. Though Singapore does not have natural resources, it is a global city, attracts global capital and talent, and has a high population density, all of which contribute to a high land price, which becomes a form of resource rent. There are several institutional mechanisms Singapore has developed over the years to help manage this. Firstly, specific land parcels are set aside in the zoning process to cater only to industries, thereby allowing industrialists to pay on average a lower land price than commercial users. Secondly, land sales proceeds are constitutionally required to be transferred into the national reserves, which the government cannot use to fund current expenditure. This instils fiscal discipline, and limits the crowding-out expansion of government expenditure. Thirdly, the reserves are then invested, some in overseas assets, which is an avenue for capital to be recycled away from the domestic economy. Though a real exchange rate appreciation is inevitable over the longer term, these institutional mechanisms help manage the rate of increase in a way that the manufacturing sector can continue upgrading and thriving in Singapore. Norway's management of oil revenue is also another model worthy of study.

The question facing Africa's policymakers is how to manage the resource windfall, to ensure that they are properly invested for future generations, and also to ensure the resources do not end up hurting the real economy. The solutions are often there, and perhaps obvious, but the difficulty is really having the real political will to implement them.

6.6.6 Conclusion

Industrial policy has always been controversial within academia as well as policy making circles. Singapore's own experience is that industrial policy can work, but it must be accompanied by a strong educational sector, free trade, and good institutions to limit the potential downsides.

Index

Lightning Source UK Ltd.
Milton Keynes UK
UKHW020731181221
395730UK00003B/52